THE ILLUSTRATED ENCYCLOPEDIA
of GLASS

edition 2

Mark Pickvet

Schiffer Publishing Ltd

4880 Lower Valley Road Atglen, Pennsylvania 19310

Other Schiffer Books By the Author:
The Encyclopedia of Glass, 0-7643-1199-9, $19.95
Shot Glasses, 0-7643-2079-3, $39.95

Library of Congress Control Number: 2011942466

Designed by Justin Watkinson Cover by Bruce Waters
Type set in Adobe Caslon Pro/Humanist 521

ISBN: 978-0-7643-3925-7
Printed in China

Acknowledgments

Naturally, a project of this magnitude is never completed alone. There are many, many people who helped along the way and I sincerely hope that I do not forget anyone: Robin Rainwater; Kate, Louis, Fairy, and Leota Pickvet; Tim and Cathy Rex; Ward Lindsay; Robert Davidson; Robert and Susan Darnold; Rick Patterson; Paul Traviglia; Dr. Fred Svoboda; Dr. Arthur Harshman; Dr. David Churchman; Dr. Howard Holter; Dr. Mark Luca; Susan Kelly; Alane Laws-Barker; Joy McFadden; Gail Grabow; Bonnie Van Sickle; Donna Williams; Jack Adamson; Gary Crossen; Joan Mogensen; Herbert Smith; David Hill; James Smith; George Nichols; Julie Barnett; Johanna Billings; Lori Whetzel; John and Karen Halsey; Sheryl Laub; Carol O'Laughlin; Nadine Wallenstein; Carol Buntrock; Brad and Vera Decker; Gordon Ferguson; Tammy and Forrest Kimble; John Lander; Carl Mann; Joan Lynn; Kathy Simon; Rita Erickson; Mary Blake; Larry Dearman; Ruth Bagel; Larry Mitchell; Connie DeAngleo; Brian Hill; Joseph Bourque; Don Kime; Virginia Scott; Wilma Thurston; Karen Skinner, Tom McGlauchlin; Adrienne Esco; Eunice Booker; Mary Sharp; Ellen Hem; Larry Branstad; Marie Heath; Kathy Harris; Marie McGee; Judy Maxwell; Barbara Hobbs; Harold Mayes; Pat McNeil; Judy Givens; Norman Madalin; Sandy Redmond; Jo Anne Andrews; Pam Sullivan; Bob Gingerich; Linda Walker; Melissa Boarman; Janet Davis; Michael Della Vecchia; Loraine DeWitt; and Richard Godwin.

Librarians and personnel from the following libraries: Bellaire Public Library; Boston Public Library; Carnegie Institute; Chrysler Museum Library; Corning Museum of Glass Library; Detroit Public Library; Fenton Art Glass Company Library; Flint Public Library; Franklin Institute; Harvard Widener Library; Historical Society of Pennsylvania; Jeannette Public Library; the Library of Congress; Martins Ferry Public Library; Milwaukee Public Library; Muncie Public Library; New York Public Library Annex; Ohio County Library in Wheeling, West Virginia; Toledo-Lucas County Library; Toledo Museum of Art Library; Wheaton Village Library; and the University of Michigan.

Museum and company personal: Christine Mack, the Allen Memorial Art Museum; C. J. Arnsbarger, the Anchor Hocking Corporation; Anndora Morginson, The Art Institute of Chicago; David Reese, the Barlett-Collins Company; Barbara Anderson, the Bergstorm-Mahler Museum; William Blenko Jr., Richard Blenko, and Virginia Womack, the Blenko Glass Company; Bernard C. Boyd, Susan Boyd, and Luke Boyd, the Boyd Art Glass Company; Roger Dodsworth, the Broadfield House Glass Museum; Kimberly Cady, the Cabell County Library, Huntington, West Virginia; Ann Lloyd and Sarah Nichols, Carnegie Museum of Art; Donna Sawyer, Rosemary Dumais, Gary Baker, and Peter Dubeau, the Chrysler Museum; Jane Shadel Spillman, Jill Thomas-Clark, Gail Bardhan, Rosalind Young, and Virginia Wright, the Corning Museum of Glass; Darlene Antonellis-LaCroix, the Currier Gallery of Art; Frank Thrower and Sophia Dewhurst, Dartington Crystal; William Gates, East Liverpool Museum of Ceramics; Frank Fenton, the Fenton Art Glass Company; David Dalzell (former president), the Fostoria Glass Company; Kaisa Koivisto, the Finnish Glass Museum; Cathleen Latendresse, the Henry Ford Museum; Jack Wilkie, The Franklin Mint; Lisa Gibson, the Gibson Glass Company; Jim Hill, Greentown Glass Museum; Arthur Harshman, the Indiana Glass Company; Reva Ashcraft, Jefferson County Historical Association, Steubenville, Ohio; Ulrica Hydman-Vallien, Bertil Vallien, Kjell Engman, Gunnel Sahlin, and Goran Warff at Hosta-Boda; Julia Lee Cook, the Libbey Glass Company; Carrie Brankovich, the Lotton Art Glass Company; Erika Hoglund and Mats Jonasson, Maleras Glassworks; Josef Marcolin and Pamela Nicola, Murano Glass; Susanne Frantz and Lucie Hofmanova, Museum of Decorative Arts, Prague; Cherry Goldner and Katherine McCracken, the National Heisey Glass Museum; Philip F. Hopfe, the New England Crystal Company; Mia Karisson, the Nybro Glass Company; Donna Baron of Old Sturbridge Village; Maj Britt, Orrefores; Erica Smith and Frances Haggart, Perthshire Paperweights; Peter Moore, Pilgrim Glass Corporation; Kirk Nelson, The Sandwich Glass Museum; Paula Belanger of the Showcase Antique Center; Gunnel Holmer, the Smalands Museum, Sweden; Sheila Machlis Alexander, Smithsonian Institute; Maria Ayckbourna, Swarovski Crystal; Mary O'Reilly and Michelle Power, Tipperary Crystal; Sandra Knudsen, Toledo Museum of Art; the Havenmeyer collection, University of Michigan Museum of Art; Viviana Terkuc, Venini Art Glass; Don Ritz, (the former) Viking Glass Company; William Hosley and Linda Roth, the Wadsworth Athenum; Ellen Marts, Beverly Narbut, and Gay Taylor, The Wheaton Village Museum; and Redmond O'Donahough, Ruth Coughlan, Sean Flynn, Tom Gleeson, Pat Brophy, Karen Power, John Stenson, and Pat Boyce, Waterford Crystal.

Finally, a special thanks also to the people at Schiffer Publishing.

Introduction

Welcome to the second edition of *The Encyclopedia of Glass*. This printing is easily 35-40% larger than the first edition for two primary reasons. One, I have been fortunate enough to travel to Europe to tie up some loose ends, as well as gather more concrete information. The first edition weighed a little heavier with American firms while this one includes a good deal of additional information on those based in Europe. Second, over the past few years, I have received a good deal of correspondence and emails from various collectors and people related to the glass business (i.e. companies, historians, researchers, and even museums). I do appreciate these people pointing out some any errors that appeared in the book, the most frequent was listing the New Jersey based Mikasa Crystal firm under "Japanese Glass." That, along with a few other minor inconsistencies, has hopefully been cleaned up for this edition.

Dating companies still remains one of the most challenging aspects, as local libraries and company documents do not necessarily tell the whole story. Most individual glass-makers generally worked as apprentices for others, until they fully learned their skills, before setting off on their own, sometimes establishing a shop in a barn, attic, basement, or small glass house with a single furnace. They might work there for a number of years prior to establishing or filing an official company name. If they didn't make it on their own, they could always join up with another established firm.

Immigrants like many cut glass engravers from Germany/Bohemia in the nineteenth century often stayed with a friend for a year or two prior to settling on their own. They would work in a factory during the day and then engrave glass on their own time; when they had saved enough money, they would then send for their wife and children. Others moved from factory to factory when one venture failed or simply to make more money. Those who gained reputations for high quality work were often in demand and recruited by others.

Glass pioneers in America, like Deming Jarves or Benjamin Bakewell, would establish many separate companies, which, in turn, would go through numerous name changes, even though common factories would continue to employ the same workers and produce the same products. I have found companies that established names in the early 1900s only to find catalog and/or trade information on them in the 1890s! Even well-known firms like the Fenton Glass Company officially established their business in Martins Ferry, Ohio, in 1905 — only to move the following year to Williamstown, West Virginia. In this case, I go with the company founding date of 1905. Naturally, glass production didn't begin until 1906. Another problem are firms with the same exact name — I have run across at least ten firms bearing the "American" or "Union" Glass Company name.

Another insurmountable task is trying to track the hundreds of short-lived companies that simply didn't make it. This is true in America from Colonial times up to the mid-to-late nineteenth century as in Europe for many centuries. Early Americans lacked the capital and many of the skills necessary to manufacture glass. What was needed aside from financial backing for equipment were knowledgeable foreign workers, the proper ingredients, good formulas, and a ready market for finished products. Even when all of these were present, there was the challenge of producing usable/quality goods while keeping the business operating long enough to achieve long-standing profit margins. Countless other difficulties came along — wars, economic depressions, and even transportation problems — that resulted in shipping that was too difficult and costly. Needless to say, hundreds of companies went bankrupt and shut down after only a few short years in operation.

Glass-making in European countries in the past was just as volatile as the New World. The most difficult area is that old Bohemian region that encompasses Austria, southern Germany, and the modern Czech Republic/Slovak region. After World War II, many companies became part of nationalized conglomerates; however, the trend over the past couple of decades was for many individuals to break off again as independents. Some went on to form new firms and factories while others remained with the original company.

What I have attempted to do is to proceed with company sources first — patents, founding dates, property deeds, closing/bankruptcy filings, old journals, wills, death certificates, tax records, old maps, and newspapers — in order to date them. In some cases, death certificates were not filed, a common practice prior to the twentieth century. Birth records are even more difficult since many immigrants came to America with little in the way of official records. Those in Europe are nearly impossible to obtain since two World wars wiped out a good deal of order data. Note also that journals in America were not published until about 1874 while trade directories of glass firms were not published until the early twentieth century.

When none of these sources worked, museums and local libraries were used next. Many archives have been depleted of material; sometimes microfilmed and discarded afterward. Over time, libraries and archivists are replaced too, with materials constantly shifting places and sometimes forgotten.

Original trade catalogs, old journals, and the like are getting more difficult to find, especially those where decent photo copies can be made.

When those sources were lacking, I then attempted to use what I consider very good secondary resources: noted researchers, historians, authors, and museum personnel, especially those in Europe. With every new book published, researchers dig up new facts and challenge past information. Some of my favorites include George Avila, Fred Bickenhauser, Estelle Sinclair Farrar, Carl Fauster, Gene Florence, William Heacock, Lowell Innes, Ruth Webb Lee, George and Helen McKearin, James Measell, J. Michael Pearson, Albert Christian Revi, Lawrence Selman, Jane Schadel Spillman, Martha Louise Swan, Robert and Deborah Truitt, Hazel Marie Weatherman, Kenneth Wilson, and a few select others. Though some are now deceased, I have been able to correspond with many in order to check facts and data. Others, I am simply grateful for much of their pioneering research skills and the accuracy of their published works. Using many of their sources and contacts has been beneficial in verifying information.

If there is a major dispute in dating, but only by a few years, then I will say something like "the company closed in the early 1870s." Some factories simply lapsed due to lack of operating capital, floods, fires, labor disputes, and owners who simply died. Prior to the 1880s, most local maps actually showed the names of property owners; unfortunately, this practice was discontinued. Large populated glass-making towns like Pittsburgh changed and re-used the names of streets. Glass-making companies too might list their headquarters as a small sales office or storage warehouse rather than that of the factory itself. Even today the glass industry, especially where smaller companies are concerned, is volatile. Companies are still going out of business or perhaps reforming while small studios spring up everywhere.

Glass and glass-making is such a broad subject that a complete definitive guide where nothing can be refuted is literally impossible. Much information has simply been obscured over time and will never be recovered. Once again, I am always searching for the most accurate data, so if you do see a mistake, dispute, or error, please feel free to correct me and, for accuracy, please inform me as to where you obtained your information for verification purposes. I am also always on the lookout for more individual contemporary artists, particularly those who have been recognized with awards, endowments, grants, commissions, and fellowships for their work in glassware. If you know of any, send me their biographies and drop me an e-mail at MPickvet@aol.com.

Aa

{ Aa }

A CANNE — A Venetian term for a filigrana style of glass made by fusing a row of fine, colored canes in order to produce a striped pattern.

AB ARVID BOHLMARKS LAMOFABRIK — Refer to PUKEBERG.

ABC PLATE — A pressed glass plate that contains embossed and/or stippled letters, and at times, times, the complete alphabet that usually surrounds the rim. ABC plates originated in England in the late eighteenth century, and gained popularity in the tenth century as American manufactures made them in some quantity. In addition to lettering, ABC plates may contain other designs (i.e. commemorative events, nursery rhymes, and so forth).

ABELMAN, STUART — A successful and popular American Studio glass artisan of the late twentieth century and early twenty-first centuries. Mr. Abelman received his fine arts degree from Carnegie Mellon University in Pennsylvania. He went on to establish Abelman Art Glass in 1977 and is renowned for his paperweights, vases, and sculptures created in vibrate colors (including iridescent).

Iridescent Jack-in-the-Pulpit style vase.

ABILDGAARD, MARK — Refer to the NORTH STAR GLASS COMPANY.

ABRASION — The technique of grinding shallow decorations in a glass object with the use of a wheel. The decorated areas are usually left unpolished. Glass decorated in this fashion is also known as abraded glassware.

ABTEILUNG KUNSTAGLAS — Refer to VEREINIGTE LAUSITZER GLASSWERKE AG.

ACANTHUS — A common gilded decoration applied to glassware in the form of an acanthus leaf. The decoration may be applied in a series of scrolled leaves as well. Acanthus is a spiked plant native to Southern Europe, Northern Africa, and Eastern Asia (Acanthus Spinosus).

ACID CUT BACK — The process of dipping an object into acid for a controlled amount of time in order to achieve a desired cutting depth. This method is often completed with stencils in order to outline where the acid resistant wax would be applied. The acid solution is then used to cut or melt away the area not protected by the wax.

ACID ETCHING — The process of covering glass with an acid-resistant protective layer, scratching on a design, and then applying hydrofluoric acid to etch the pattern into the glass. Richardson's of Stourbridge, England, registered the first patent for this process in 1857.

Etched candleholders.

ACID POLISHING — The technique of giving cut glass a polished surface by dipping it into a mixture of hydrofluoric mad sulfuric acid.

ACID STAMPING — The process of etching a trademark or signature in glass with acid after it has been annealed. Acid stamps are similar to rubber stamps.

ADAMS AND COMPANY — An American company that was originally founded by John Adams and Mr. Macklin as the "Adams, Macklin & Company" at Pittsburgh, Pennsylvania, in 1851. The name was changed to Adams & Company in 1861 when Macklin left. Adams was a major producer of presses pattern glass as well as an occasional producer of colored opalescent glassware. The firm became part of the U.S. Glass in 1891 as Factory A. Also note that there was another Adams Glass Company that was founded in 1812 at Adams, Massachusetts. This was a short-lived venture that produced some glass panes for windows.

ADAMS, MACKLIN & COMPANY — Refer to ADAMS AND COMPANY.

ADOLFSHUTTE — A Bohemian glass company founded by Josef Meyr in 1815 near Vimperk. The firm produced some glass in typical Bohemian styles. Josef Meyr was instrumental in establishing several Bohemian firms in the early nineteenth century including Kaltenbach, Idathal, and Luisenhutte. He passed then down to his son Jan Meyr (1775-1841), who in turn passed them on to his nephews, Josef Taschek and Wilhelm Kralik. *See also* KRALIK, WILHELM.

ADVERTISING GLASS — A glass vessel displaying information about a manufacturer, company, proprietor, brand, person, establishment, event, and so on.

AEOLIPILE — An ancient Greek word for a globular-shaped container with a narrow neck and mouth. Aeolipiles are also found in Islamic glass.

AETNA CUT GLASS COMPANY — (1) A short-lived American cut glass-making firm that was established at Meriden, Connecticut in 1907 by Alfred & Joseph Pelerin. The firm was out of business by 1909. (2) Another firm of the same name was established in Bridgeton, New Jersey originally as the Acme Cut Glass Company in 1916. *See also* ACME CUT GLASS COMPANY.

AETNA GLASS AND MANUFACTURING COMPANY — A short-lived pressed glass manufacturing established at Bellaire, Ohio in 1879 by R. T. DeVries, C. H. Strahl, and Colonel E. B. Bowie. The firm was a maker of pressed glass tableware, especially goblets, some opalescent glass, and a bit of lighting-related glassware (i.e. lamps and lamp shades). Bowie sold his interest in 1889 and the other partners offered the plant up for sale or lease. In 1891, it was sold to William Sinram, who operated it as the Bellaire Bottle Company (production of the plant was then switched to bottles exclusively). Sinram, along with DeVries, Bowie, Owen Meehan, and George Jennings, founded the Aetna Manufacturing Company with the glass portion of the firm leased to the Bellaire Bottle Company. Nearly all glass-making ceased in 1891; however, the factory was occasionally leased out to other short-lived firms throughout the 1890s (i.e. Lantern Globe Works, the Century Glass Company, and the Novelty Stamping Company).

AFORS GLASBRUK — A Swedish firm founded in Smaland in 1876 by Carl, Oskar, and Alfred Fagerland (all brothers who had formerly worked at Kosta), and Carl Carlsson. The firm was purchased by Ernst and Oscar Johansson in 1916. Ernst's son, Erik, changed his last name to Afors and became the firm's manager in 1919. In 1935, Erik purchased a full half share of Kosta. Afors is noted for decorative cut glass, tableware, and many traditional Scandinavian art styles of glass. The firm remained in family control up until 1975; however, they merged with Kosta and Boda in 1964. In 1970, the new conglomerate all became part of the Afors Group ("Aforsgruppen" in Swedish); currently the largest glass-producing firm in Sweden. The glass-making firm of Johansfors was acquired in 1972, and even Orrefors joined on in 1990. The company is also known today as the Royal Scandinavian Group.

AGATA GLASS — Art Glass characterized by mottled purple or brown finishes as a result of metallic satin coupled with an alcohol solution added on top of the base color. Agata Glass was patented by the New England Glass Company 1887 under the direction of Joseph Locke.

New England Glass Co. Agata pitchers.
Items courtesy of Wheaton Village.

AGATE GLASS — An opaque style of Art Glass produced by mixing metals of many different colors before the object is shaped. The result is a finish that resembles semi-precious stone like agate, chalcedony, jasper (French jaspe), onyx, malachite, and lapis lazuli. *See also CHALCEDONY and MARBLED GLASS.*

AGATINE — A style of Bohemian hyalith glass developed under Count Buquoy that resembles bluish-gray semi-precious stones or agates. The formula for agatine was perfected in 1835 and followed two previous hyalith color creations (black and reddish brown). Agatine was then further decorated with gold enamel and/or trim. *See also BUQUOY or HYALITH GLASS.*

AHLSTROM GROUP — Refer to LITTALIA GLASSWORKS and RIIHIMAKI GLASSWORKS.

AHNE, JOSEF — A noted Bohemian glass artisan of the tenth and early twentieth centuries, Ahne (1830-1909) worked as an apprentice with several glass firms as well as under the glass painter, Emanual Hess. His stepfather, Franz Horn, has also been a glass cutter. Ahne opened his own studio in 1860 and specialized in painting figural compositions on glass based on Italian & German oil paintings of the day. He won an award at the World Exposition held in Vienna in 1873, and a bronze medal in Paris in 1878. The majority of his creations were imported to America. His two sons, Gustav (1861-1925), and Theodor (1863-1907) were also painters and assumed their father's business. When Gustav passed on in 1925, his son Wilhelm sold the business.

AIR LOCKS OR AIR TRAPS — A technique patented by Benjamin Richardson in 1857 whereby embedded air pockets, larger then typical bubbles, are arranged in a decorative pattern within a glass object.

AIR RING — An elongated air inclusion encircling a paperweight near its base, usually just above and below a torsade.

AIR TWIST — An eighteenth century English decorating technique were air bubbles were purposefully injected in the base of an object and then pulled down and twisted into a stem. Air twists are prevalent in the stems of goblets.

AKRO AGATE GLASS COMPANY — An American firm founded in 1911 at Akron, Ohio; then incorporated in Clarksburg, West Virginia, in 1914. They were most famous for manufacturing opaque and swirled colored glass marbles but added other opaque novelty items (i.e. toothpick holders, children's miniature dishes, ashtrays, paperweights, etc.) after they moved operations to West Virginia in 1914. The company closed permanently in 1951 when it was sold off to the Clarksburg Glass Company.

Akro Agate Glass Company Trademark.

ALABASTER GLASS — A translucent ornamental glass first developed in Bohemia in the late nineteenth century, and then later perfected by Fredrick Carder at Steuben in the early 1920s. Alabaster resembles the white color of the mineral after which it is named and is produced by spraying stannous chloride (a form of salt) on a piece before it is reheated. A similar, though less expensive method, was used to create translucent marbles in the 1920s and 1930s.

Steuben Glass Co. Aurene and Alabaster vases.
Courtesy of Wheaton Village.

ALABASTRON — A Greek term for a small perfume or oil bottle. Alabastrons are usually cylindrical or rounded in shape, contain a narrow neck, flattened rim, and two small handles (the word is "Alabastrum" in Latin). They were originally made of the soft stone alabaster (hence the name alabastron); nevertheless, ancient examples were also made of glass.

First century B.C. Eastern Mediterranean Alabastron. *Courtesy of the Corning Museum of Glass.*

ALASKAN — A name given to a Carnival Glass color produced by the Northwood Glass Company. Alaskan consists of glass with a green base color that is then iridized with the common Carnival marigold color.

ALBANY GLASS COMPANY — Albany Glass was first founded in the 1780s in Albany, New York, and lasted until about 1820. They made windows, bottles, and a few other items.

ALBERTINE GLASS — A style of Art Glass produced by the Mt. Washington Glass Company in the late nineteenth century. It is characterized by opaque colors and ornate decoration that was applied primarily to show items such as vases. It is sometimes referred to as "Crown Milano" of which Mt. Washington patented as a trademark name.

Mount Washington Albertine vase. *Photo by Robin Rainwater.*

ALE GLASS — An early seventeenth century English glass with a capacity of 3-5 ounces that is generally short-stemmed, and used for drinking ale or beer. Original designs sport a conical-shaped cup/bowl and may be decorated with hops and/or barley (i.e. enameled, etched, engraved, or gilded). Over time, ale glasses of increased capacity were produced.

ALEMBIC — An inverted bowl, with a condensing tube made of metal or glass, used in the distillation process of alcoholic beverages. Alembic derives from the Arabic word *Al-anbiq*, meaning "the still."

ALEXANDRIAN GLASS — Glass objects produced in the Nile Delta area (in and around the ancient city of Alexandria) from the fourth century B.C. to the fourth century A.D.

ALEXANDRITE GLASS — Art glass produced by Thomas Webb in England in the late nineteenth century. It is characterized by various shadings of blue, pink or red, and yellow achieved through several stages of refiring. Stevens and Williams of England produced similar wares.

ALFORD, C.G. & COMPANY — An American firm founded in 1872 in New York City, Alford operated as a retail watch and jewelry store and sold cut glass as well. Note that although Alford stamped their company name on cut glass products, they did not manufacture them. The firm closed in 1918.

Alford, C. G. & Company Trademark

ALKALI — A soluble salt mixture consisting primarily of potassium carbonate and sodium carbonate, the alkali is an essential ingredient in glass that helps reduce the melting point of silica.

ALLEN CUT GLASS COMPANY — An American film founded in 1905 by William Allen as Johnstown, Pennsylvania. Allen had previously worked for Hoare before cutting glass in his own firm. The company remained in business until 1925.

Reproduction of a 1913 Allen Cut Glass Co. patent.

ALLEY AGATE COMPANY — An American marble-making firm founded by Lawrence E. Alley in 1929 at Paden City, West Virginia. Alley had previously worked for Akro Agate. Aside from marbles, the firm expanded into glass lamp production in the early 1930s — Berry Pink joined with the Alley and the firm's name changed to the Lawrence Glass Novelty Company. The firm moved to Sistersville, West Virginia, in 1932, again to Pennsboro, West Virginia, in 1934, and yet a third move to St. Marys, West Virginia, in 1937. The name was changed again in 1939 to the Alley Glass manufacturing Company. The firm was a major marble supplier to the toy company, Pressman. In 1949, Alley sold out to Berry Pink and Seller Peltier and the name was changed to Marble King. Marbles are still made today under the Marble King name.

ALLEY GLASS MANUFACTURING COMPANY — Refer to the ALLEY AGATE COMPANY.

ALLOA GLASSWORKS — A forest glasshouse established in 1750 in Alloa, Scotland. The firm produced practical glass items such as bottles and drinking vessels.

ALMOND THUMBPRINT — A pattern in pressed glass, it consists of adjacent pointed ovals and resemble thumb-prints.

ALMY & THOMAS — An American company founded in 1903 by Charles H. Almy and G. Edwin Thomas. They purchased the Knickerbocker Cut Glass Company and continued cutting glass until 1918. The Corning Glass Work supplied them with blanks.

Almy & Thomas Trademark

ALOX MANUFACTURING COMPANY — An American marble-making firm founded by John Frier in 1919 AT St. Louis, Missouri. The firm began as a whole sale seller of marbles, but purchased marble-making machines in the late 1930s to produce their own glass marbles. Frier's son Jack operated the firm but production shut down during World War II. It was briefly revived after the war; but production halted soon after; however, the on-hand stock of marbles was sold into the early 1960s.

ALSACE GLASS — A tall glass with foot and stem along with a round shallow bowl specifically designed for serving Alsace wine. Alsace glasses are like tall wine glasses with a more rounded and shallower bowl. The name originates from wine produced in the Alsace-Lorraine region in France.

ALUMINOSILICATE GLASS — A type of heat resistant glass developed by Corning for their "Flameware" brand of Pyrex kitchenware. This formula is more heat resistant then the original borosilicate formula.

ALUMINUM — A somewhat bluish-white light metal that, when combined with sodium (sodium aluminum fluoride, also known as cryolite) and then added to a batch of glass, produces a somewhat opaque white color. Aluminum sodium is rarely used to color glass since it tends to have a destructive effect on clay pots. Aluminum combined with fluorine, are the two primary additives in making modern milk glass.

ALUMINUM OXIDE — AL203 is one of the most abundant metallic oxides and forms the basis of many soils and rocks. It exists in combinations with silica and potash in feldspar, granite, and china clay. In glass-making, it is an important constituent of clays used in making glass lenses.

AMALGAM — A process used in gilding both porcelain and glass. Gold is usually mixed with an alloy of mercury and other metals, and then applied as a decorating technique, usually by hand.

AMBER — A yellowish brown colored glass produced by the addition of iron, carbon, and sulphur. The color resembles fossilized tree sap of the same name. Amber comes in many hues – dark amber is a somewhat deep-reddish blood amber while light amber is sometimes called HONEY AMBER due to its pale color. *See also* HOLLY AMBER.

An 1815-1835 blown glass compote by the Zanesville Glassworks of Ohio. *Item courtesy of the Corning Museum of Glass.*

AMBERETTE — Pressed glassware that was frosted or stained with dark yellow or yellowish-brown colors that resemble Art Glass.

AMBERGRIS — A style of Art Glass created by Victor Durand Jr. that consists of a light amber/yellowish color. Ambergris was mostly a light yellow base color used in much of Durand's art glass. Durand's workers referred to it as OIL GLASS while the color itself has been DURAND and the VINELAND FLINT GLASS MANUFACTURING COMPANY.

AMBERINA — A type of Art Glass produced in American in the late tenth century. It is characterized by transparent glass that is lightly shaded with light amber at the base that gradually shades to a darker ruby red color at the top (Reverse Amberina has the opposite color scheme). Amberina contains acidized gold to produce the red color and is very heat sensitive (known to turn a reddish purple if overheated). While working for the New England Glass Company, Joseph Locke received a patent for Amberina in 1883. New England licensed others such as Hobbs Brockunier and English firms to produce it but sued Mt. Washington who made a similar styled glass. Mt. Washington continued to produce it under the ROSE AMBERINA name. *See also* PLATED AMBERINA.

Mount Washington Ambero compote. *Item courtesy of Wheaton Village.*

Hobbs, Brockunier Amberina dishes. *Items courtesy of Wheaton Village.*

AMELUNG GLASS — High quality glass made in America in the late eighteenth century by German immigrant John Frederick Amelung, who established a short-lived glasshouse in Frederick County, Maryland, in 1785 and another, slightly more successful operation in 1794, the New Bremen Glass Company, also founded in Maryland. Amelung, along with Caspar Wistar and Henry Stiegel, is often credited with being the first glass-maker in America to produce table items (i.e. decanters, tumblers, goblets, etc.) comparable to the quality of European products at the time.

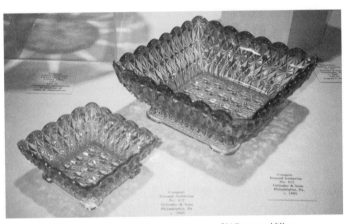

Amberina comports. *Items courtesy of Wheaton Village.*

AMBERO — A style of Art Glass created by the Mount Washington Glass Works in the 1890s. It is crystal with a light yellow (somewhat light amber) tint. The exterior contains a chipped glass surface texture while the interior is smooth and enameled. Multicolored enameled scenes include such things as foliage/floral motifs, forest and/or village scenes, and some nautical themes. Primary items produced in this style include vases, hurricane lams, and lamp shades. The style of glass was continued by Pairpoint, who purchased Mt. Washington in 1894.

A 1790s engraved tumbler by John Frederick Amelung's New Bremen Glass Manufacturing Company in Maryland. *Photo courtesy of the Corning Museum of Glass.*

Mount Washington Ambero lamp. *Item courtesy of Wheaton Village.*

AMEN GLASS — Refer to JACOBITE GLASSWARE.

AMERICAN BRIDGE COMPANY — Refer to the TAREBTYN GLASS & LAMP COMPANY.

AMERICAN ART GLASS & LAMP COMPANY — Refer to the BYESVILLE GLASS & LAMP COMPANY.

AMERICAN CUT GLASS COMPANY — (1) An American firm established in 1897 in Chicago, Illinois, by William Anderson (a previous designer and craftsman for Libbey), the company was moved to Lansing, Michigan, in 1900 and continued to produce cut glass up until World War I. (2) Another cut glass operation bearing the same name was established at Port Jarvis, New York, in 1902 by J. S. O'Connor. It ceased operation in 1903. *See also* O'CONNOR, J.S. *and* ARCADIA CUT GLASS COMPANY.

AMERICAN FERRALINE COMPANY — Refer to the NEW BRIGHTON GLASS COMPANY.

AMERICAN FLINT GLASS WORKS — (1) An American pressed glass- and lamp-making firm founded by Patrick Slane at South Boston, Massachusetts, in 1843. Slane leased a factory that had previously been operated by the SOUTH BOSTON CROWN GLASS COMPANY (a window pane maker that closed in 1827). Burrell joined in 1848. Fire damaged the plant in both 1852 and 1853; however, it was rebuilt both times. The firm operated successfully until closing in 1858. Note that the firm was also known as the SOUTH BOSTON WORKS and advertised occasionally as SLANE & BURRELL. (2) Another firm of the same name was established at Wheeling, Virginia (before West Virginia became a state), in 1850 when David Southwick joined the Andersons (Edward, William, & Franklin). The firm was also known as D. SOUTHWICK & COMPANY and produced pressed, mold-blown, and hand-blown glass in crystal (using flint and lead) and colored glass until 1852. Hobbs, Barnes & Company was the firm's major creditor and foreclosed on them, acquiring all equipment and molds. *See also* ANDERSON & COMPANY, HOBBS, BARNES & COMPANY, EAST WHEELING GLASS WORKS, *and* WHEELING GLASS WORKS.

AMERICAN GLASS — General term for glassware made in America since the sixteenth century. Glass was first made in the New World with the Spaniards who set up a glass house in 1535 in Argentina and another one in 1592 at the town of Cordoba del Tucaman in the Territory of the Rio de la Plata; both were very short-lived operations (broken glass from Europe was remelted and formed into crude objects). The first permanent English settlement was established in North America (Jamestown, Virginia) in 1607. In 1608, Captain Christopher Newport brought eight Polish and Dutch glassmakers who established a glasshouse in 1609. Some crude tableware items (mostly bottles) were made and were included in the first cargo exported from the New World. The operation was short-lived. A second glasshouse was constructed at Jamestown in 1620 by the London company and six Italian workers were imported to work there; the workers primarily made beads and marbles to trade with Native American Indians. This glasshouse lasted only a few short years.

In 1739, a German immigrant named Caspar Wistar built a factory in New Jersey. He hired skilled German glassworkers and became the first commercially successful glass manufacturer in the United States. When he passed on 1752, his son Richard Wistar ran the firm until it closed permanently in 1780. From 1763-1774, another German by the name of Henry W. Stiegel operated a glasshouse in Manheim, Pennsylvania. Stiegel acquired some of the former employees of Wistar's business and hired a few additional experienced foreign workers from both Germany and England. He went bankrupt in 1774, but did manage to create some window and bottle glass. The American Revolution forced his glasshouse to shut down permanently. One year after the revolution, another German immigrant opened a glass factory in America. In 1784, John Frederick Amelung produced a fair amount of hand cut tableware, much of it engraved. Amelung's factory made Benjamin Franklin a pair of bifocals. They too could not operate consistently at a profit and shut down in 1795. The first truly long-lived successful American glass-making firms were established by Deming Jarves and Benjamin Bakewell in the early nineteenth century. Jarves aided in founding the New England Glass Company in 1818 and the Boston & Sandwich Company in 1825. Bakewell established several firms beginning in 1807.

America led the world in the production of hand-pressed glass products after inventing the mechanical pressing machine in the late 1820s (Enoch Robinson, while working for the New England Glass Company, is often credited with inventing it in 1827). The new invention led to the mass production of glassware and was America's greatest contribution to glass-making. Hand pressing revolutionized the industry; it was very fast, efficient, and could be run with less-skilled workers. One other important American invention was the discovery of a cheap lead substitute in 1864 by William Leighton, who was employed by Hobbs, Brocunier and Company at the time. He developed a glass formula that substituted lime for the much more expensive lead. The glass products manufactured with lime still maintained a good degree of clarity. Though the brilliance was not as sharp as lead crystal, the price savings and practicality of it more than made up for the difference in quality. Most companies were forced to switch to lime in order to remain competitive. Numerous American firms produced cut glass during what was known as the Brilliant Period (roughly 1880 to 1915). It was characterized by deep cutting, exceptional brilliance or sparkle. Heavy lead crystal formulas, and very elaborate and ornate designs. In the midst of the Brilliant Period, American artists and firms also followed the Art Nouveau movement began in Europe in the early 1880s. Noted American art glass designers included Louis Comfort Tiffany and Frederick Carder of Steuben; however, there were many others. English immigrant Joseph Locke of the New England Glass Company patented Amberina in 1883, and Agata in 1887. Another English immigrant, Frederick Shirley of the Mount Washington Glass Company, patented Burmese in 1885. Many firms patented their own styles of Peachblow, opal, satin, cameo, custard, cranberry, and other popular styles of Art Glass.

Five American glass firms (Dugan, Fenton, Imperial, Millersburg, and Northwood) sparked the Carnival Glass movement that began around 1905 and lasted until the late 1920s. Carnival Glass was an inexpensive machine-pressed iridescent substitute for more expensive Art Glass. When the fad for this style of glassware ended, manufacturers were left with huge inventories and this remaining stick was sold to fairs, bazaars, and carnivals (hence the name "Carnival Glass") at below wholesale prices to rid themselves of it. Another popular American product is what is referred to as Depression Glass, which was mass-produced, inexpensive, and primarily machine-made pressed glass dinner sets and giftware made in America in the 1920s and 1930s. Depression was made in both clear as well as in many colors. Pink and green were the most prevalent colors. Since the 1960s, Depression Glass has been one of America's most poplar collectible categories in glassware.

A collection of 20th century American Glass items.
Photo by Robin Rainwater.

AMERICAN GLASS COMPANY — Many American glass-making firms, most short-lived, sported the "American Glass Company" name. (1) An American pressed glass-making firm that was originally established as the "American Flint Glass Works" began in 1843 at South Boston, Massachusetts. The firm's name was changed to the American Glass Company in 1854. (2) In 1889, another company bearing the "American" name was founded by W. H. Tallman and John Miller at Anderson, Indiana. The firm produced lamps, novelties, and pressed glass in both crystal and color. Noted glass artisan Jacob Rosenthal worked here prior to joining the Indiana Tumbler & Goblet Company. The firm closed in 1891. (3) Established in 1899 at Indiana, Pennsylvania, another "American Glass Company" purchased the Dugan/Northwood factory and made some pressed wares. They sold out to the Diamond Glass Company in 1913. *See also* AMERICAN FLINT GLASS WORKS.

AMERICAN GLASS WORKS — Many American firms were established under this name, most of them short-lived. (1) One was established at Pittsburgh, Pennsylvania, in the early 1860s. The firm produced window panes for a few short years before going out of business. (2) A couple of early twentieth century American bottle makers also established businesses under the "American Glass Works" name: one in Richmond, Virginia, in 1908; another at Paden City, West Virginia, in 1918.

AMERICAN MARBLE COMPANY — Refer to the STEUBENVILLE GLASS COMPANY.

AMERICAN PATTERN — A prolific cube-like pressed pattern first made by the Fostoria Glass Company in 1915. The design was made mostly in crystal but colors such as amber, blue, green, yellow, and milk glass were also produced. The pattern was in continuous production until Fostoria closed in 1986.

No. 2056 American Pattern

Reproduction of a 1910s Fostoria Glass Company catalog.

AMERICAN PRESSED GLASS COMPANY — An American pressed glass-making firm established at Staunton, Illinois, by William Barris in 1908, the firm operated a few short years as a maker of pressed and blown glass crystal, as well as some limited amount of opalescent glass, before ceasing operations.

AMERICAN RICH CUT GLASS COMPANY — Refer to J. S. O'CONNOR.

AMERICAN SPECIALTY COMPANY — An American glass decorating firm established at Monaca, Pennsylvania, in 1902, the company purchased pressed crystal tableware and decorated the objects with staining. The firm ceased operations during World War I.

AMERICAN WHOLESALE CORPORATION — A trademark occasionally found on cut glass products (also the initials "A.W.C" and the "Baltimore Bargain House"). The firm registered trademarks for cut glass in 1922, but did not produce cut glass of their own; rather, they were a wholesale distributor of products made by other cut glass firms. American Wholesale was also known as the Baltimore Bargain House and operated out of Baltimore, Maryland.

American Wholesale Corporation Trademark.

AMETHYST — A light purple-colored glass produced by the addition of manganese. Some amethyst glass is made so dark that it is referred to as BLACK AMETHYST.

AMETHYST OPALESCENT — Light purple or amethyst colored glassware with a white opalescent edge or background (usually found in iridized Carnival Glass).

AMPHORA — An ancient Greek jar, vase, or urn that is characterized by a large oval body, a narrow cylindrical neck, and two mall curved handles that rise from the top of the oval body almost to the level of the mouth. Most amphoras were made of porcelain and were used in Greek/Roman times to hold wine, oils, and other liquids. They were also occasionally made of glass. Smaller versions were also called AMPHORISKOS by the Greeks. A wide variety of Czechoslovakian-designed glass and porcelain objects in the early-to-mid twentieth century expanded the use of the word amphora to encompass similarly styled vases, jars, and drinking vessels. *See also* URN.

1st-2nd century B.C. Eastern Mediterranean Amphora. *Photo courtesy of the Corning Museum of Glass.*

AMPHORISKO — Refer to AMPHORA.

AMULET — A jeweled inscribed ornament usually worn around the neck as a charm to ward off evil. Glass amulets were made by the ancient Egyptians as early as the fourteenth century B.C.

ANCHOR CAP AND CLOSURE CORPORATION — An American manufacturer established at Long Island City, New York, in the early 1900s; they were a major manufacturer of containers and merged with Hocking in 1937 to form the Anchor-Hocking Glass Corporation.

ANCHOR GLASS COMPANY — An American Glass Company established at Mt. Pleasant, Pennsylvania, in 1906, the firm produced bottles before going bankrupt. In 1909, the factory was acquired by the L. E. Smith Glass Company.

ANCHOR-HOCKING GLASS CORPORATION — A huge American glass manufacturer of containers, tableware, and other items established in 1937 when the Anchor Cap and Closure Corporation merged with the Hocking Glass Company. In 1969, the firm changed its name to the Anchor Hocking Corporation, but still contains many subsidiary names today (Anchor Glass Container Company, Anchor Hocking Company, Anchor Hocking Glass, and Anchor Hocking Consumer Glass Company). The company acquired many other firms along the way, including the Lancaster Glass Company, the Monongah Glass Company, and the Standard Glass Company. The firm operates plants in California, Florida, Georgia, Illinois, Indiana, Minnesota, New Jersey, New York, Oklahoma, and Pennsylvania. Noted collectible Anchor Hocking patterns/designs include "Bubble," "Early American Precut," "Fire King," "Forest Green," "Manhattan" or "Horizontal Ribbed," "Moonstone," "Oyster & Pearl," "Queen Mary" or "Vertical Ribbed," "Royal Ruby," "Sandwich," and "Stars and Stripes."

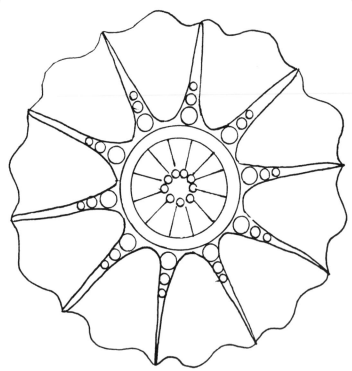

Oyster & Pearl pattern by Anchor. Hocking.
Drawing by Mark Pickvet.

Anchor-Hocking Glass
Corporation Trademark.

ANCIENT GLASS — A general term referring to all glass made from its very development in Mesopotamia/Ancient Egyptian (around 200 B.C.) through the ancient Roman era (5th century A.D.).

ANDERSON & COMPANY — An American pressed glass-making firm established by Edward, William, and Franklin Anderson, and Alfred Evans at Wheeling (prior to West Virginia becoming a state) in 1845, the firm was first known as "Evan and Anderson" until 1847, when a new factory was built (the firm had previously leased a factory previously occupied by the defunct East Wheeling Glass Works). When Evans left in 1849, the name was changed to Anderson & Company. David Southwick joined in 1850 and the name was changed again to the AMERICAN FLINT GLASS WORKS (also known as D. SOUTHWICK & COMPANY). The firm went bankrupt in 1852, and reverted back to their creditors, Hobbs, Barnes & Company.

ANDERSON, DOUG — A noted American Studio Glass artisan who was born in Erie, Pennsylvania, in 1952, Anderson received his Master of Fine Arts degree from the Rochester Institute of Technology and was awarded a Rakow Commission by The Corning Museum of Glass in 1986. Anderson lives in Warsaw, Ohio, and works full-time as an independent glass artist.

ANGUS & GREENER — Refer to HENRY GREENER.

ANIMAL DISHES — Covered glass dishes or glass objects made in the shapes of various animals (roosters, horses, cats, dogs, elephants, etc.), Animal dishes were very popular from about 1890-1910, a little during the Depression era, and from the 1970s on (especially those made of milk glass). Between the Depression and through the 1960s, originals were reproduced in some quantity.

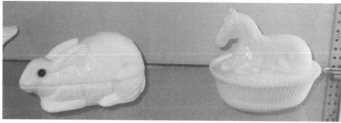

Covered milk glass animal dishes: Atterbury bunny and McKee horse. *Items courtesy of Wheaton Village.*

Reproduction from an 1891 U.S. Glass Company catalog.

Boyd colored covered animal dishes.

ANIMALS — Novelty glass items made in the shape of animal figurines. Around 200 BC, the ancient Egyptians produced glass crocodile figurines, which are the earliest known animal figures made in glass. Animal figurines have been popular since the early twentieth century and have been a favorite of collectors ever since. A huge host of companies produced or continue to make them today in all shapes, sizes, and colors — Baccarat, Boyd, Cambridge, Guernsey, Heisey, Lalique, L.E. Smith, L.G. Wright, New Martinsville, Pisello, St. Clair, Steuben, Swarovski, Tipperary, Viking, Waterford, and Westmoreland.

Boyd colored carousel horses.

ANNAGRUN — An early style of uranium glass developed by Josef Riedel of Germany in the 1830s, Annagrun is characterized by a bright yellow or yellowish-green color made by adding uranium to a batch of glass. Note that Riedel named the glass for his wife Anna and produced it through the 1840s. *See also* RIEDEL FAMILY.

ANNAHUTTE — A German word for a glass hut located in the town of Annathal, several Bohemian glass firms went by this name through the seventeenth and twentieth centuries.

ANNEALING — A process that toughens glass and eliminates stress by heating and gradually cooling over a lengthy time period in an annealing oven or lehr. Slow cooling for many hours prevents fracturing in such objects as paperweights.

ANNEALING CRACK — A crack or fissure that develops in glass from improper cooling or annealing.

ANNIVERSARY PATTERN — A pressed pattern first made by the Jeannette Glass Company from 1947-1949 (later reproduced by them in the 1960s and 1970s), the pattern was applied to a wide variety of tableware and consists of a central circle made up of molded lines that emanate from the center (start at a point and then expand slightly outward), along with a similarly designed wide outer circular band. It was primarily in pink; however, crystal, lightly iridized, and opaque pink pieces were also produced. Anniversary is easily confused with Depression Glass; however, it was made later.

Reproduction from a 1949 Jeannette Glass Company catalog.

ANTIMONY — A silvery-white colored, somewhat crystalline metal element that, when combined with sulphur (antimony sulphide), produces a yellow-colored glass. Large quantities of antimony (without the addition of sulphur) will produce an opaque white color in glass. Antimony was used by both the ancient Egyptians and Romans to color glassware.

ANTIQUE GREEN — A dark somewhat opaque off-green Art Glass style created and named by Steuben in the early twentieth century.

ANTIQUE METHODS — Refer to DRAWN ANTIQUE, FULL ANTIQUE, and SCRIBED ANTIQUE.

Antonin Dul or Antoninodol — A Bohemian/Czechoslovakian glass-making firm founded at the Antonin Duk in 1845 by K. A. Ascherl, the firm produced both crystal and colored ornamental glass in traditional Bohemian styles until merging with Josef Inwald in 1945 to briefly form the Jihlava Glassworks. When all Czechoslovakian firms were nationalized after World War II, it eventually became part of the Bohemian Glassworks National Corporation conglomerate in 1965. The firm regained its independence in 1993 and produces cut glass products today under the Jihlava name. *See also* BOHEMIAN GLASSWORKS NATIONAL CORPORATION.

AOP — An abbreviation for ALL-OVER PATTERN. All-Over Patterns generally cover the entire glass object, but may be limited to the outside only.

APOTHECARY GLASS — Glass vessels used for storing and transporting medicines or the ingredients for them, Apothecary glass dates back to ancient Greek and Roman times and most contain some type of stopper device to prevent the liquids from leaking. *See also* UNGUENTARIUM, MEDICINE BOTTLE, PHARMACY GLASS, *and* VIAL.

APPLE — A common glass ornament or novelty item made in the shape of the rounded red, yellow, or green fruit of its namesake. Some are solid white while others are hollowed in the center. Apples are made in both crystal and color.

APPLIED OR APPLICATION — Attaching molten glass rods to blanks in to form handles, foots, pedestals, and other exterior forms/decorations. Long coils are at times applied to glass objects in concentric circles or in ascending/descending spirals.

Glass apple. *Photo by Robin Rainwater.*

Waterford glass workers in the process of applying a handle.

APPLIQUÉD — A decorating technique featuring hand-applied three-dimensional trim. The trim is applied in a molten state while the object itself is still hot; thus becoming a permanent part of the object. The trim is often worked into fruit or flowering vines.

APRICOT — A deep yellow- or dark amber-colored glass.

AQUA OR AQUAMARINE — A light greenish-blue color in glass like the color of sea water, it is usually made with the addition of copper and chromium oxide in a batch of glass. Frederick Carder, while working at Steuben, patented a style of Art Glass called "Aqua Marine." Like the name applies, it is characterized by a silky iridescent greenish-blue finish.

AQUA OPALESCENT — Aqua or aquamarine colored glass with an opalescent edge. Aqua opalescent is ordinarily found in Carnival Glass.

AQUA REGIA — A mixture of two strong acids that serve to dissolve gold dust in the making of red or ruby red glassware. In more recent times, selenium has replaced gold in producing the color red.

AQUARIUM — A glass enclosed tank or fish bowl in which living aquatic animals and/or plants are kept. Aquariums designed for home use can very from a gallon capacity to over 100 gallons. See *also* FISH BOWL.

ARABESQUE — A style of decoration originating in the Islamic world (early seventh century through the early fifteenth), Arabesque is a pattern of interlaced stems and tendrils that end in leaves. It was later copied during Europe's Renaissance era in a wide variety of scroll, leaf, and stem motifs. Arabesque-like designs are common in both Art Glass styles and pressed glass patterns.

ARC INTERNATIONAL — A subsidiary of the international firm of J. G. Durand Industries, Arc was established in France in 1825 and is presently the world's leader in automated crystal and tableware production. It is commercially present in 160 countries with production facilities in France, America, Spain, and China. Annual sales now eclipse $1 billion euros. Under Arc, the noted glass brands of Arcoroc, Cristal d'Arques, JG Durand, Luminarc, and Salviati are produced. Durand also owns the brand Mikasa Crystal. See *also* DURAND, J.G. INDUSTRIES *and* MIKASA CRYSTAL, INC.

ARCADIA/ARCADIAN CUT GLASS COMPANY — An American cut glass operation founded in 1901 at Newark, New York, by Frank Burgess, John Ferris, Ernest Peirson, Caleb Tylee, and George Tylee, the firm reorganized in 1902 as the American Cut Glass Company and then again in 1903 as the Arcadian Cut Glass Company. Operations were moved to Lestershire, New York, in 1908. The firm produced cut glass up into the World War I era.

ARCH — A rounded or curved design that spans an opening, arches usually expand outward at the bottom and then taper to a point at the top. Interlocking or adjacent rows of arches are a common design applied to pressed glass objects. Arches also come in a wide variety (i.e. rounded, horseshoe, lancet, ovals, trefoil, tudor, pointed, Roman, gothic, etc.).

ARCOROC — A modern brand of crystal glass tableware produced under the Arc International glass conglomerate. See *also* ARC INTERNATIONAL.

ARGAND, AIME — A Swiss immigrant and physicist who was the first to patent an oil lamp with a chimney in America in 1784. The first lamps utilized whale oil as the primary fuel until the widespread use of kerosene around 1850. Argand had also invented the tubular wick burner in 1782 which was more efficient than earlier models since the wick fed oxygen to the flame while the chimney increased the draft. Some of his lamp inventions are known as "Argand Lamps." The invention of the electric light bulb by Thomas Edison in 1879 brought on the decline of oil-burning lamps.

ARGUS — A name for a nineteenth century pressed glass thumbprint pattern or design, Argus differs slightly from full thumbprint since it has a row of stretched ovals (wide horizontally but narrow vertically) between the thumbprint rows. See *also* THUMB-PRINT.

ARGY-ROUSSEAU — Refer to ROUSSEAU, JOSEPH GARBRIEL ARGY.

ARIEL GLASS — A patented style of ornamental glassware created by Vicke Lindstrand and Edwin Ohrstrom in 1927 at the Orrefors Glassbruk in Sweden, Ariel is a style of cased glass with carefully controlled embedded air bubbles that are formed into decorative patterns. Ariel is also, at times, combined with Orrefors' noteworthy Graal technique. Also note hat the name was derived from the spirit in Shakespeare's "Tempest." See *also* GRAAL.

ARISSING — The process of removing sharp edges from glass.

ARMLET — Refer to BANGLE.

ARMORIAL GLASS — A general term used to describe glassware produced throughout Europe through the seventeenth and nineteenth centuries, it consists of functional glass objects (beakers, plates, goblets, flasks, etc.) decorated with coats-of-arms that were usually engraved or enameled.

ARROWHEAD — A cane, usually millefiori, with an upward-pointing three-pronged arrowhead motif. They are also known as a Crow's Foot.

ARSAL OR ARSALE — Refer to D'ARGENTAL and SAINT LOUIS.

ARSENIC — A somewhat grayish-white metal; in its powdered form (oxide of arsenic), it is ordinarily mixed in a small quantity in a batch of lead crystal. Arsenic tends to improve the clarity and brilliance of lead crystal. In larger quantities, it is also used to produce an opaque or semi-opaque form of white opal glass.

ART OR ART NOUVEAU GLASS — Expensive hand-blown glass with unusual effects of color, shape, and design. Art Glass is primarily ornamental and was most popular from the 1880s-1920. Noted makers and pioneers in the Art Nouveau movement included Galle and Rousseau of France; however, the movement quickly spread throughout Europe and in America with Tiffany and Carder. Many countries had their own name for this revolution in glassware; "Sucession" in Vienna, "Jugendstil" in Germany, "Stile Liberty" in Italy, and "Modernismo" in Spain. Still, it was the original French term of "Art Nouveau" that struck. In modern times, Art Glass is a general term for any ornamental glassware.

Fenton Art Glass vases and lamp. *Photo by Robin Rainwater.*

Steuben Art Glass vase.
Photo by Robin Rainwater.

ART DECO GLASS — An Art Deco decorative style in many mediums, it has its origins in the Art Nouveau period, but peaked in the 1920s and 1930s. Glass objects include many that contain fairly straightforward frosted or colored motifs, with or without the typical and somewhat elaborate geometric designs associated with this style. Noted French makers included Marinot and Lalique.

Steuben Art Deco vases.
Courtesy of the Corning Museum of Glass.

ART STUDIO GLASS MOVEMENT — This movement began in March 1962 with Harvey Littleton, a professor of ceramics at the time with the University of Wisconsin. Littleton held a workshop at the Toledo Museum of Art and proved that Art glass could be blown by independent artists in small studios. Out of his new design program at Wisconsin, Littleton inspired many students including Dale Chihuly and a host of independent modern art glass makers.

ARTE VETRARIA MURANESE — Also known as A.V.E.M., the company was founded in 1932 in Murano, Italy, by a group of artisans who had previously worked for Successori Andrea Rioda and Emilio Nason (1891-1959), along with five members of the Ferro family – Antonio, Egidio (1899-1968), Gallano (1896-1984), Ottone, and Ulisse. Noted artisan Giulio Radi (1895-1952) became a partner and artistic director in 1935. The firm continues today producing colored art glass in traditional Venetian styles.

ARYBALLOS — An ancient Greek term for a small rounded container with two handles that is used to hold perfumes or other oiled scents, Aryballos were popular in both ancient Greek and Roman times.

ASH — The powdery residue of matter that remains after burning. In glass-making, ash, or potash, from burning various plant materials is used as a substitute for soda as an alkali source including such chemicals as sodium carbonate ($NaCO_3$), potassium oxide (K_2O), or potassium carbonate (K_2CO_3). At one time, ashes from bones were also used as both a flux and an opacifier in making various shades of opaque white glass (i.e. milk glass, opal, and white opalescent colors). *See also POTASH.*

ASH TRAY — A shallow bowl-like glass receptacle used for holding cigarette butts and tobacco ashes.

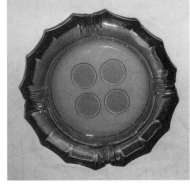

Coin glass ash tray by Fostoria.
Photo by Robin Rainwater.

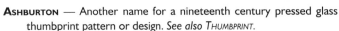

ASHBURTON — Another name for a nineteenth century pressed glass thumbprint pattern or design. *See also THUMBPRINT.*

ASPERSORIUM — A small bowl-like basin with a bail handle used to hold holy water. They were first made of glass in both Spain and Italy (Murano, Venice) in the sixteenth century.

ATKINS, LLOYD — A noted twentieth century American glass designer born in Brooklyn, New York, in 1922, Atkins graduated from Brooklyn's Pratt Institute and served as a designer for Steuben from 1948 to 1984.

ATLANTIC CUT GLASS COMPANY — An American firm established in 1920 at Egg Harbor City, New Jersey, by Henry Theilacker, the firm produced some limited cut glass, but operated primarily as a wholesale/retail distributor of glass made in both Europe and America. It was out of business by World War I.

ATLAS GLASS COMPANY — Refer to the HAZEL GLASS COMPANY and the HAZEL-ATLAS GLASS COMPANY.

ATOMIZER — A small glass receptacle with a narrow neck that contains a small spray nozzle or pump at the very top. Atomizers are used for spraying on perfumes or colognes while the vessel itself is used for holding perfumes or colognes. Most were made to be placed on dressing tables and may have matching powder jars and under trays. Some atomizers may have covers (usually metal) that fit over the spray nozzle. Atomizers are also sometimes called "Perfume Sprinklers." *See also* Cologne Bottle and Perfume Bottle.

Reproduction from an early 20th century S.F. Myers Co. catalog.

No. 276 Cut Glass, Chased Top....$5 63
Capacity 5 oz.
Quadruple Plate.
Meriden Britannia Co.

Steuben Glass Co. Aurene Art Glass vase. *Courtesy of the Corning Museum of Glass.*

ATTERBURY GLASS COMPANY — An American pressed glass-making firm established at Pittsburgh, Pennsylvania, in 1859 as the White House Works, the firm went through several name changes prior to becoming the Atterbury Glass Company in 1893 (i.e. Hale, Atterbury & Company; White House Glass Works; Atterbury, Reddick & Company; Atterbury & Company; and J.S. & T.B. Atterbury). In 1865, the firm was purchased outright by brothers James Seamen Atterbury and Thomas Bakewell Atterbury (grand nephews of noted glass industrialist Benjamin Bakewell) and the name was changed to Atterbury & Company. The final name change occurred in 1893 when the sons of the two founders resumed control. The firm produced a good deal of pressed tableware, bar bottles, lamps, kerosene, globes, and lamp chimneys; much of it in opaque colors including milk glass.

Despite winning an award for their lime glass lamps at America's Centennial Exhibition held in Philadelphia in 1876, the firm ceased operations in 1903.

Atterbury covered milk glass fox dish. *Courtesy of Wheaton Village.*

AURENE — An iridescent ornamental art glass created by FREDERICK CARDER at the STEUBEN GLASS WORKS around 1904, aurene was produced by spraying the surface with a combination of metal oxides and stannous or lead chloride. The two primary colors consisted of gold and cobalt blue. Other aurene-like colors were soon added as well; namely red, green, and brown.

Steuben blue Aurene Art Glass. *Courtesy of Wheaton Village.*

AURORA — (1) A transparent reddish-amber Art Glass style created and named by Pairpoint in the early-to-mid twentieth century. Items produced in this color style included vases and candy jars (with or without covers), creamer and sugar sets, and a few other odd items. Some contain clear bubble connectors and finials. (2) Aurora was also a pattern name given to a style of Depression Glass created by the Hazel Atlas Glass Company in the late 1930s; it was a fairly simple design characterized by adjacent vertical panels that form a circle in each piece.

AUSTRALIAN CRYSTAL GLASS COMPANY LTD. — An Australian firm established in 1914 at Sydney, the company made pressed tableware and a wide variety of iridized Carnival Glass patterns. *See also* CRYSTAL GLASS WORKS.

AUSTRALIAN GLASS MANUFACTURERS COMPANY — Refer to NEW ZEALAND GLASS.

AUSTRIAN GLASS — General term for glassware made in Austria since the early fifteenth century. The first operation was established east of Innsbruck by the German immigrant Wolfgang Vitl in 1534. It was known as the Hall-in-Tyrol. Archduke Ferdinand II established a rival glasshouse at Innsbruck in 1570 with Venetian workers. The firms produced a wide variety of glass items in the German, Bohemian and Venetian styles of the time (window panes, goblets, drinking vessels, ewers, and some colored and engraved wares). During the Art Nouveau period, Austrian makers didn't really join in until a decade or two after the movement's beginning. The primary art glass factories of Austria were Lotz, Lobmeyer, Bakalowits, Adolph Zasche, Graf von Harrach, and Moser & Sons. Austrian's most noteworthy glass firm today is Swarovski.

Austrian Glass: A 1915 Austrian blown glass by Josef Hoffman for Wiener Werkstatte. *Courtesy of the Corning Museum of Glass.*

AVENTURINE — An ancient Egyptian technique of applying small flakes of metal such as gold and copper in colored glass that resemble the mineral aventurine. It was further experimented with by Venetian glass-makers in the fifteenth century and became popular during the Art Nouveau period. Metals such as copper, chrome, and/or iron pyrite flecks (less expensive than true gold) were used to achieve the desired effect. Copper resembles gold (sometimes called "Goldstone"), iron produces red aventurine, and chromic oxide makes green aventurine. Beginning in the mid-twentieth century, Venetian makers produce a good deal of glass with copper flecking. Note that the spelling is sometimes given as "Aventurina." Also, the French term is "Aventure," meaning "chance."

AVERBECK CUT GLASS COMPANY — An American firm established in New York, New York, in 1892, Averbeck ran a jewelry store and a mail-order business featuring cut glass products. The firm employed cutters in a small factory located in Honesdale, Pennsylvania. They ceased operation in 1923.

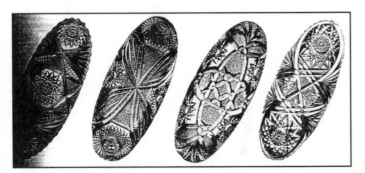

Reproduction of an early 20th century Averbeck catalog.

Averbeck Cut Glass Company Trademark.

AVON COLLECTIBLES — Though not a maker of glass objects, Avon has commissioned hundreds of products as far back as 1886 (the first glass items appeared in the 1920s). Popular pieces at the time (two or three annually) include the abundant ruby red "Cape Cod" pattern (made by the Wheaton Glass Company and discontinued in 1997), the "Hummingbird" crystal pattern (made in France and discontinued in 1994), and even some coin and other glass products once produced by Fostoria.

Fostoria coin glass goblet of George Washington commissioned by Avon. *Photo by Robin Rainwater.*

AWASHIMA GLASS — Refer to JAPANESE GLASS.

AYOTT, ROLAND "RICK" — Born in Nashua, New Hampshire, in 1944, Ayott has gained a reputation as one of America's leading paperweight makers in the late twentieth and early twenty-first centuries. He studied at the Lowell Technological Institute and worked as a scientific glassblower. He currently works as an independent artist in Nashua.

Bb

{ Bb }

BACCARAT — The original company was founded in 1764 in Baccarat, France, as the Verreries Renaut & Cie. It was quickly changed to the Verreries de Baccarat around 1769, and then to Verreries de Sainte-Anne in 1773. Sainte-Anne happened to be the patron saint of the chapel within the glassworks. In 1816, Aime-Gabriel d'Artigues purchased the factory and the name was changed to Verrerie de Voneche Baccarat. In 1823, d'Artigues sold the company to three businessmen. Early on, the company produced practical lead crystal items including tableware and chandeliers. In the 1840s, they began producing art-style paperweights along with tableware, cut glass, and other decorative colored glass. Paperweight production ended around 1860, but was revived in the post-World War II era (both sulphides and colorful millefiori/lampwork designs). The company is still in operation today with a factory, museum, and showroom in Baccarat, France, as well as a second museum and showroom in Paris, France. They are noted for producing some of the finest crystal, colored glass, and paperweights being made in the world today.

Baccarat four-piece Loch Ness Monster. *Photo by Robin Rainwater.*

The Baccarat factory at the city of Baccarat, France.

Baccarat Trademark.

BACHMETOV GLASS — Refer to the BAKHMETIEV GLASS FACTORY.

BACK PAINTING — Refer to REVERSE PAINTING.

BACKSTAMP — An identification mark printed or molded on a piece of glass, the mark may include a company name, logo, item number, etc.

BAGLEY GLASS — An English glass-making firm established at Knottingly in Yorkshire in 1871 as a bottle maker. In 1890, they reorganized as Bagley & Company; in 1912, they added the Crystal Glass Company name as a subsidiary. Under Crystal, they expanded into cut crystal and pressed glass wares. In the 1930s, the firm produced some colored wares in both pastel satin and opaque finishes as well as dome that were iridized. In 1962, Bagley was taken over by Jackson Brothers, also of Knottingly; in turn, Jackson Brothers was absorbed into the Rockware Group in 1968. The Crystal Glass Company and factory closed permanently in 1975.

BAKEWELL, PEARS AND COMPANY — An American company established in Pittsburgh, Pennsylvania, in 1807 by Benjamin Bakewell and Edward Ensell, originally as Bakewell & Ensell. Bakewell, along with Benjamin Page, bought out Ensell in 1809; however, Ensell stayed on as a factory superintendent. The company went through many name changes, including Bakewell & Company; Pittsburgh Flint Glass Manufactury (name of factory); Bakewell's Pittsburgh Glass Work; Bakewell, Payn, and Page Co.; Bakewell, Page & Bakewell; Bakewell, Ensell, and Pears; and Bakewells & Anderson. The name the company was known most as was Bakewell, Pears and Company; this occurred in 1844 after Benjamin, Sr. died. They began producing glass furniture knobs and handles, and were one of the first firms to add a full load of crystal tableware and barware. For Bakewell's early success (when most firms were failing), Deming Jarves referred to Benjamin Bakewell Sr. as "The father of the American Glass Industry." They employed noted French glass cutter Peter Eichbaum, who cut the first crystal chandelier in America for the firm. Other principals who joined the firm included Bakewell's three sons: Thomas (1813), John Palmer (1827), and Benjamin Jr.; Thomas Pears (1816); Thomas' son (and Bakewell's nephew) John Palmer Pears (1830); Alexander Anderson (1832); Benjamin Bakewell Campbell (1854); Bakewell's grandson Benjamin Bakewell III (1859); and the three sons of John Palmer Pears: Thomas Clinton, Benjamin Bakewell, and Harry (1874). The business closed in 1882.

BAKHMETIEV GLASS FACTORY — A glasshouse founded by A. Bakhmetiev in 1763 at Nikol'skoye, Russia, near St. Petersburg, the firm specialized in inexpensive colored objects, such as tableware, and some window glass. A second house was added at Pestravka in the Penza region. In 1884, ownership of the firm was sold to Prince Alexander Dmitriyevich Obolensky, who owned it up until the Russian Revolution in 1917. It then became a state-run operation. Note that the spelling of Bakhmetiev is sometimes given as Bachmetov.

BALDWIN, H. C. CUT GLASS SHOP — A small American cut glass operation founded by Herbert C. Baldwin at Meriden, Connecticut, in 1911, Baldwin moved the company to Wallingford, Connecticut, in 1914 and continued to produce cut glass until closing just after the end of World War I.

BALL BROTHERS GLASS MANUFACTURING COMPANY — An American glass firm founded in 1888 at Muncie, Indiana, they produced blown glass fruit jars and pressed glass necks/lids for the jars. In the early twentieth century, they switched to machine-made jars and later became part of the Ball Corporation in 1969. Ball acquired the French firm St. Gobain and expanded into the production of sheet glass. The firm still makes "Ball Mason" fruit/canning jars today under the Ball-Foster Glass Container Company name in plants throughout the United States: California, Illinois, Indiana, Louisiana, Massachusetts, Missouri, North Carolina, New Jersey, Oklahoma, Pennsylvania, South Carolina, Texas, Washington, and Wisconsin.

Ball Brothers canning jar with pressed glass lid and bail wire. *Photo by Robin Rainwater.*

B

BALL STOPPER — A spherical glass object that rests at the top of glass bottles, jugs, and decanters, its diameter is larger than the mouth of the vessel.

BALTIMORE BARGAIN HOUSE — Refer to the AMERICAN WHOLESALE CORPORATION.

BALTIMORE PEAR — A pressed pattern with a pair of fruits (pears) that make up the basic design. *See also* PEAR.

BALUSTER — A type of English drinking glass or goblet created in the late seventeenth century, the stem is in the shape of a short vertical support with a circular section (baluster-shape).

BANANA BOAT OR DISH — A long flat or shallow dish, with sides that are possibly curved upward and with or without a separate base, used for serving bananas or banana splits. They are sometimes referred to as "Banana Splits" or "Banana Split Dishes."

Reproduction from a 1930 Indiana Glass Company catalog.

FOOTED BANANA SPLIT
Packs 10 doz. to bbl. Weight 125 lbs.
Packs 3 doz. to ctn. Weight 30 lbs.

BAND OR BANDED — A fairly common decorative add-on consisting of a horizontal row or strip that completely encircles an object. Bands can be thick or thin, molded or enameled with various colors, bonded with metals like silver or platinum, gilded or cut, applied around the rim, placed in parallel lines to make up an entire pattern, applied at the top or bottom, curved or zigzag, or combined with other patterns. The bands themselves may be further decorated as well. Items may also contain diagonal bands or vertical bands; however, vertical bands are generally known as ribs. *See also* RIB.

BANGLE — Another name for a ring-shaped bracelet that does not have a clasp. Those made of glass originated in India and are called "Bangli" or "Bangri." Bangles are typically made by rotating a pliable glass ring around an iron rod until the joint disappears. At times, bangles are worn in group units where larger ones that rest further up the arm are also called armlets.

BANK — A whimsical glass object, toy, or souvenir made to hold coins. Like most whimsies, banks were designed to be gifts and some were elaborate one-of-a-kind productions (mostly in the late nineteenth century).

BAR — A single piece of glass made by fusing several rods or canes together; like canes, bars are cut up into small slices and arranged into various patterns for producing inlays in paperweights or for mosaics.

BAR TUMBLER — A glass tumbler, with or without flutes, produced in the United States in various shapes and sizes beginning in the mid-nineteenth century. Bar tumblers were primarily made for use in hotels and saloons.

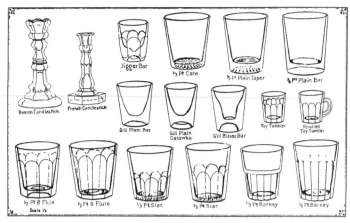

Bar Tumbler. Reproduction from an 1880 McKee Brothers catalog.

BARBARICO VETRO — An ornamental glass design created by Ercole Barovier of Murano's Barovier & Toso in the early 1950s, it is characterized by an all-over pattern of iridescent blue spots within a transparent casing.

BARBER BOTTLE — A colored glass container with a narrow neck and mouth for holding liquids used by barbers (i.e. shaving solutions, tonics, colognes, etc.); barber bottles may or may not have handles, but usually do contain stoppers. They were popular in the late eighteenth and nineteenth centuries.

BARBINI GLASSWORKS — Established by noted Venetian glass-maker Alfredo Barbini in Murano, Italy, in 1950, the company operates today creating Venetian sculptured forms, novelties, figurines, and other knickknacks. Barbini (b. 1912) studied design at the Murano Glass Museum and is noted for developing a technique dubbed "masello," which involves sculpturing a solid block of molten glass without molding or blowing. Barbini's son Flavio later joined the firm as a designer, and his daughter, Oceania, serves as the firm's sale manager.

BARIUM — This silvery-white metallic element is occasionally added to a batch of glass in order to obtain a somewhat silvered or frost-like coloring. When combined with sulphur, barium also aids in producing deep yellows and greens in glass.

BARNES & COMPANY — Refer to HOBBS, BARNES AND COMPANY.

BARNES, FAUPEL & COMPANY — Refer to the BELMONT GLASS COMPANY.

BAROLAC GLASS — A style of glass produced in Czechoslovakia by Inwald Glassworks (Josef Inwald and family) during the 1930s, it is characterized by opalescent color effects, opaque ultramarine and custard colors, and some clear and/or transparent colors. It was made solely for export to England and was occasionally mold-embossed or enameled with flowers, trees, wildlife (typical Bohemian themes), and English scenes. The glass was reproduced in the 1950s and 1960s; however, less expensive finishes and transparent colors only were used in the reproduction.

BAROQUE PATTERN — A popular style and general term of the nineteenth and early twentieth century pattern that consists of molded Baroque styles and designs (i.e. ribs, shells, stars, scrolling, trefoils, guilloches, etc.).

BAROVIER — A noteworthy family name of Murano glass-makers who have been making glass in Venice, Italy, for hundreds of years. Anzolo Barovier aided in the development of the first clear glass, cristallo, in the fifteenth century. In 1878, Antonio Salvati founded a glass firm in Murano that was changed to Artisti Barovier in the late 1890s and then to Vetreria Artistica Barovier in 1919. The latest venture, Ferro-Toso-Barovier, was founded in 1936 when Artemio and Decio Toso merged with Barovier (the firm officially became Barovier & Toso in 1942). The new firm first specialized in producing lighting fixtures such as chandeliers. Beginning in the 1950s, the firm created several unique art designs such as vetro barbarisco (textured patchwork and murrhine surfacework on glass), vetro damasco and vetro diafano (glassware characterized by several broad bands of varying color effects); vetro gemmato (gem-like glass made with a roughened surface that resembles a stone); vetro parabolico (glass made with alternating vertical and horizontal stripes like a checkerboard); vetro pezzato (various colors arranged in a patchwork design); vetro primavera (a cracked translucent form of glass with black banding); vetro ramarro (glass with a mottledgreen surface that resembles the skin of a lizard); vetro rugiadoso (glass whose surface resembles that of fine dew); and vetro sidone (striped opalescent glass in square/rectangular patterns). The firm is still in operation today and even acquired the Bohemian Art Glass (BAG) Company in 1998.

BARRYVILLE CUT GLASS SHOP — Refer to GIBBS, KELLY & COMPANY.

BARTLETT-COLLINS COMPANY — An American pressed glass-making firm originally established as the Pioneer Flint Glass Company in 1903 at Coffeyville, Kansas, by George F. Collins Sr. and R. H. Thomas, the firm was also known as the Cicero Glass Company and the Coffeyville Glass Company. The company produced some fruit jars and lantern globes before reorganizing in 1907 under the Premium Glass Company name. By 1910, the firm had filed for bankruptcy, and Collins was able to purchase it; however, a fire destroyed the plant in 1911. A new plant was built at Sapulpa, Oklahoma, in 1912. H. U. Bartlett joined on as a partner in 1915 and the firm became the Bartlett-Collins Company. They are noted for producing a good deal of machine-made tableware, ashtrays, lamps, kitchenware, jars, and glass decorated with Western themes. A bottle factory was added in 1919 and was named the Liberty Glass Company. Up through the Depression era, they were the only major glass company operating west of the Mississippi River. The firm continues in operation today in Sapulpa, Oklahoma, as a division of the Indiana Glass Company; which in turn is owned by the Lancaster Colony Corporation.

Bartlett-Collins Company Trademark.

BARWARE — A general term for items used in a bar. *See also* TUMBLERS, COCKTAIL SHAKERS, COCKTAIL CUPS, HIGHBALL GLASSES, PITCHERS, TRAYS, SHOT GLASSES, AND OTHER ASSOCIATED BARWAR ITEMS.

Tipperary Crystal Barware.

BASAL RIM — The ring around the bottom of a concave base in a paperweight where it comes in contact with a supporting surface.

BASAL RING — A flange typically found on the base of some English paperweights that results from some inward cutting slightly above the base. Note that the clearance is so small that it is not considered to be a separate foot.

BASDORF GLASS — A style of glass produced in Basdorf, Germany, (near Potsdam) in the second half of the eighteenth century (from about 1750-1783). Two firms produced an opaque style of functional green glass products such as drinking vessels, bowls, and other somewhat crude tableware.

BASE — The bottom part of a glass object (i.e. the underside of a vase or paperweight).

BASE COLOR — The color of the base that often reflects upward in a clear glass object. It is also the color of glass before any coating is applied, usually the color of certain art styles and especially Carnival Glass before any iridization takes place.

BASE-RING — A ring at the bottom of an object that is made by applying a small gathering of glass to form a base; they are also referred to as "Pad-Bases."

BASKET — A latticino ground where such things as fruits and/or flowers are set in. Also, a striped or plain casement of staves resembling a basket. Most baskets sport a semicircular handle.

Fenton Art Glass baskets.

Reproduction from an early 20th century Pitkin & Brooks catalog.

BASKET WEAVE — A common pressed pattern consisting of an all-over design resembling an interlocking checkered pattern of a plaited basket. The design can be found in American Carnival and Depression glass patterns too.

Northwood Carnival Glass basket weave patterned basket. *Photo by Robin Rainwater.*

B

BASTOW GLASS COMPANY — Refer to the COUDERSPORT TILE & ORNAMENTAL GLASS COMPANY.

BATCH — The mixture of raw materials fused together before heating. Primary ingredients include silica, soda or potash, and lead or lime. Ordinarily, 10-20% of a new mixture contains cullet, which is recycled shards or scraps of glass that aid in the fusion process. Note that a batch is sometimes referred to as the "Mix."

BATHGATE GLASS COMPANY — Refer to the WEST LOTHIAN GLASSWORKS.

BATTLEDORE — Refer to PADDLE.

BATTUTO — A Venetian term for striated glass produced by an all-over cutting of the surface usually by a series of short olive or mitre-shaped lines.

BAVARIAN GLASS — Glass articles produced since the seventeenth century in southern Germany, Bavaria is adjacent to Bohemia with the glassware usually more widely known as Bohemian Glass. *See also* BOHEMIAN GLASS.

BAY STATE GLASS COMPANY — An American firm founded in East Cambridge, Massachusetts, in 1849 by Norman Cate and others, the company produced some limited cut and pressed glass tableware before selling out in 1873. Note that in the early 1850s, the firm was also known as Norman S. Cate & Company.

BEAD — A tiny glass object that comes in a wide variety of shapes: spherical, hemispherical, polyhedral, cylindrical or semi-cylindrical, elliptical or semi-elliptical, or most any odd shape. They originated with ancient Egyptians and were continued by the Romans, mostly for trade and for jewelry. Glass beads have been made in large quantities by the Venetians for over 1,000 years and are referred to as "Margarite" or "Conterie."

BEADED EDGE — An edge or rim of an object that contains beading. Note that Westmoreland produced a milk glass pattern of glass that collectors nicknamed "Beaded Edge." The original name of this pattern is Westmoreland's "Pattern #22 Milk Glass." As one would expect, the edge is beaded on Westmoreland's pieces. Further decorated (enameled) patterns include eight different fruits as well as eight different flowers (total of sixteen decorated patterns). A few rare and more valuable pieces were produced with a red edge that Westmoreland referred to as coral red. Westmoreland also made a few pieces in a similar pattern referred to as "108."

BEADING — The process of fusing chips or small relief beads to a glass object in a continuous row.

BEAK — A style of lip or pouring sprout, typically found on pitchers, jugs, and creamers, that extends to a point similar to that of a bird's beak.

BEAKER — A fairly large, wide-mouthed, cylindrical drinking vessel. Beakers do not have handles, but may flare in at the base or top, or both. They also may or may not be footed. A laboratory beaker is a cylindrical glass vessel with a pouring lip. Beakers have been popular in Germany and the Bohemian region for centuries and come in a variety of sizes; some even have covers.

A Bohemian mid-19th century blown, cut, and engraved beaker.
Photo courtesy of the Corning Museum of Glass.

BEAR JAR — A pressed glass vessel that originated in England in the mid-nineteenth century. As the name implies, the jars were in the shape of a bear and were used to hold such things as honey and even bear grease. The design was also produced in America and Russia in the later part of the nineteenth century. Note that they were also referred to as "Bear Pomade Jars."

BEATTY, ALEXANDER J. & SONS — The first firm bearing the Beatty name was founded at Steubenville, Ohio, in 1845 by Joseph Beatty, Sr. Beatty, along with his partner Edward Stillman, purchased the abandoned and bankrupt glass firm of Kilgore & Hanna and named their new firm Beatty & Stillman. The firm produced some pressed and blown wares before selling out to David and Neal Hall in 1846. In 1847, the Halls sold out to a partnership known as Knowles & Taylor, which built a new factory to produce tumblers and goblets, both blown and pressed. In 1852, the firm was acquired by Alexander J. (A. J.) Beatty and was briefly named the Steubenville Flint Glass Works. A new and much larger plant was built in 1862, and the firm's name was changed to A. J. Beatty & Sons. The company moved to Tiffin, Ohio, in 1889 when a new factory was completed. As a major producer of pressed glass, the company became part of the U.S. Glass Company conglomerate as Factory R on January 1, 1892, with the Steubenville plant designated as Factory S. However, no further glass was produced at Factory S and the U.S. sold it in 1895 to the Beatty-Brady Glass Company. In 1916, the company operated as a distinct subsidiary known as the Tiffin Glass Company. *See also* TIFFIN GLASS COMPANY.

BEATTY-BRADY GLASS COMPANY — A pressed glass manufacturer established at Steubenville, Ohio, in 1895. Though the Beatty family had been active for several decades in the glass-making business, in this new venture George Beatty and James C. Brady purchased the factory owned by U.S. Glass; however, no glass was made by them in Steubenville. They purchased an industrial building in 1895 in Dunkirk, Indiana, and pressed glass tableware production began there in 1898. The following year, the firm became part of the National Glass Company. When National dissolved, the factory was purchased and operated by the Indiana Glass Company beginning in 1904. *See also* BEATTY, ALEXANDER J. AND SONS.

BEAUMONT COMPANY — An American firm incorporated in 1916 at Morgantown, West Virginia, by Percy Beaumont, the company began as a pressed glass maker of desk-related items (i.e. inkwells, ink stands, pen trays, small cups, etc.) and lighting fixtures/lamp parts. They expanded into colored tableware during America's Great Depression as well as some art forms later. When Beaumont passed away in 1947, his son Arthur Beaumont assumed control. The firm suffered labor troubles and, when the workers went on strike in 1991, the factory closed permanently. It was demolished in 1998. *See also* BEAUMONT GLASS COMPANY.

BEAUMONT GLASS COMPANY — An American firm established at Martins Ferry, Ohio, in 1895 by Percy Beaumont (brother-in-law of noted glass-maker Harry Northwood). Beaumont leased the factory as a decorating workshop from Northwood in Martins Ferry when Northwood moved his own operations to Ellwood City, Pennsylvania. In 1889, Beaumont became a maker of pressed glass and moved operations to Gafton, West Virginia, in 1902. They also produced a little opalescent glassware until selling out to the Hocking Glass Company in 1905. Beaumont went on to establish the Beaumont Company.

BEAVER FALLS COOPERATIVE GLASS COMPANY — A pressed glass manufacturer established at Beaver Falls, Pennsylvania, in 1879 when a group of labor strikers left McKee, it was originally known as the Co-Operative Flint Glass Company, Ltd. In 1887, it was renamed the Beaver Falls Glass Company. The firm produced novelties and pressed glass tableware, including colored Depression Glass, until closing in 1937.

BEAVER VALLEY GLASS COMPANY — An American pressed glass-making firm founded at Rochester, Pennsylvania, in 1904 by brothers Henry C. and J. Howard Fry, the firm operated as a subsidiary of the H. C. Fry Glass Company. The company went bankrupt in 1925 and the plant was purchased by the decorating firm William A. Meier Glass Company. In 1935, the firm incorporated and went back to using the Beaver Valley name; both William A. Meier and Harry C. Fry (son of Henry C. Fry) were major stockholders. Beaver Valley eventually became a subsidiary under the Hans Meier Specialty Company, a firm that still decorates glass today primarily by machine-applied transfers.

BECK, PHILLIPS & COMPANY — Refer to PHILLIPS & COMPANY.

BECKER & BRISBOIS — An American cut glass operation founded in 1912 at Brooklyn, New York, by Benjamin Becker and Victor Brisbois. The two split in 1919-20. Becker continued to cut glass and turned operations over to his son, Charles Becker, who added an additional cutting shop on Long Island (the firm was out-of-business by the late 1920s). In the meantime, Brisbois produced cut glass lamps and lighting fixtures in Brooklyn until the early 1930s.

BECKER & WILSON — An American cut glass firm founded in 1896 by Charles Becker (a German immigrant) and Joseph Wilson in Brooklyn, New York. In 1903, they moved to Montrose, Pennsylvania, and again in 1908 to New Brunswick, New Jersey. The company produced cut glass tableware until 1914.

BEER BOTTLE — A glass container with a narrow neck and mouth designed to hold beer. Dark amber was the most popular color for beer bottles from the nineteenth to mid-twentieth centuries. Beer bottles usually do not contain handles.

BEER GLASS OR MUG — A large cylindrical drinking vessel that usually has a flat base and a single handle. As the name implies, they are designed for drinking beer and usually contain a minimum of 12 ounces in capacity. Mugs with hinged metal lids are usually referred to as "Steins" or "Tankards."

BEILBY GLASS — A mid-eighteenth century style of hand-enameled English glassware by William and Mary Beilby (son and daughter of William Beilby, a noted gold and silversmith), Beilby Glass products usually contain coats of arms, heraldic motifs, landscape scenes, gardens, and ruins.

BELGIAN GLASS — General term for glass made in the region of modern-day Belgium since as early as the fifth century. In the mid-sixteenth century, Venetian workers settled in Antwerp and Leige, and Belgian products were produced in the popular Venetian styles of the day. *See also* SOUTH NETHERLANDS GLASS, VONECHE, and VAL ST. LAMBERT.

BELGRADE GLASS COMPANY — Refer to the "Valley Glass Company."

BELL OR DINNER BELL — A hollow device with ringer and single top handle used for summoning or signaling when rung (such as to announce dinner time). Glass bells come in a wide variety of shapes, sizes, and colors.

Glass bell made in Zweisel, Germany.

Cut Glass Call Bell.
Fine Buzz Star Cutting.
No. 9587.............................. $3.45

Reproduction from an early 20th century S. F. Myers Company catalog.

BELL & COMPANY — Refer to SWEENEY, MICHAEL, THOMAS, & R.H.

BELLAIRE BOTTLE COMPANY — Refer to the AETNA GLASS & MANUFACTURING COMPANY.

B

BELLAIRE GOBLET COMPANY — An American pressed glass manufacturer established at Bellaire, Ohio, in 1976 by Henry Blackburn, W. A. Gorby, E. G. Morgan, C. H. Over, and John Robinson, the firm moved to Findlay, Ohio, in 1888, and then joined the U.S. Glass Company in 1891 as Factory M. The factory closed permanently in 1892. *See also* FINDLAY GLASS.

BELLAIRE TUMBLER COMPANY — An American pressed glass tumbler producing firm established at Bellaire, Ohio, in 1915, the company installed an automatic press for making ashtrays, small dishes, and tumblers. It closed permanently in 1938.

BELLEVILLE GLASS COMPANY — A short-lived Canadian cut glass firm established at Belleville in 1912, the company produced some cut glass before ceasing operations a few short years later.

BELLOWS BOTTLE OR FLASK — Pressed or free-blown whimsical objects that cologne bottles were often turned into, usually by the addition of applied handles. Bellows bottles and/or flasks were briefly popular in the later nineteenth century.

BELMONT GLASS COMPANY — An American pressed glass-making firm established at Bellaire, Ohio, in 1865 by W. G. Barnard, Henry Faupel, H. Over, and John Robinson, it was also briefly known as "Barnes, Faupel & Company." The company produced pressed glass crystal tableware, and added color in 1855. By 1890, the firm was not operating profitably and the molds were sold to the CRYSTAL GLASS COMPANY (Bridgeport, Ohio) and the CENTRAL GLASS COMPANY (Wheeling, West Virginia). The factory was torn down in 1893, and a new factory was built on the site by the Novelty Stamping Company (a metal stamping firm).

BELMONT TUMBLER COMPANY — An American company established in 1866 at Bellaire, Ohio, they produced blown glass tumblers, bowls, ashtrays, and some Depression items (i.e. the ROSE CAMEO pattern). The firm itself actually closed during the later Depression years (late 1930s) the factory burned to the ground in 1952 and was never rebuilt.

BENT GLASS — Refer to SLUMPING.

BERANEK GLASSWORKS — A glass-making firm founded in the Czech Republic in 1940 by Emanuel Beranek (b. 1899) and his three brothers, the firm is still in operation today producing both crystal and colorful art glass objects including a wide variety of vases.

BERGEN, J. D. COMPANY — Founded in Meriden, Connecticut, by James D. Bergen and Thomas Niland in 1880; Bergen bought out Niland in 1885 and continued as a cut glass operation until 1922. *See also the* NILAND CUT GLASS COMPANY.

Bergen, J. D. Company Trademarks.

BERKEMEYER — A German-styled drinking glass that consists of a fairly large funnel-shaped mouth, a wide hollow stem, and a flared foot; they were popular in the sixteenth and seventeenth centuries and most are often decorated in a wide variety of styles (i.e. engraved, prunts, gilded, etc.). *See also* ROMER.

BERLUZE VASE — A French-styled vase created by Daum around 1900, Berluze vases are characterized by very long necks, ovoid bodies, and applied floral decorations.

BERRY BOWL — A concave glass vessel used for serving fruits and other foods. Note that a berry set is a large bowl with one or more matching smaller bowls.

BERRY SET — A table service consisting of one large bowl accompanied by several matching smaller bowls (usually four or six), the large bowl is generally used for serving fruit or other desserts. *See also* SERVICE.

BEST METAL — The highest quality batch of glass made by a company using the purest ingredients and highest lead content.

BEVEL — Slanted or angle cuts usually beginning at the bottom or sides of a glass object (sometimes referred to as flutes at the bottom) that are ground and polished to an angle other than ninety degrees. Mirrored and other panes of glass are often beveled along the edges to prevent chipping. Bevels also give a prism-like effect since light is refracted around them.

BEVERAGE SERVICE — A pitcher with several matching water goblets or tumblers (four or six glasses are the most common in a set); also note that a beverage service may or may not include a matching tray. *See also* SERVICE.

BICENTENNIAL GLASS — Commemorative glass items produced in 1976 for America's bicentennial celebration. Companies like Fenton produced a wide variety of items, including liberty bells, candy dishes, plates, and tumblers. They all contained patriotic designs like bald eagles, Independence Hall, Valley Forge, the Jefferson Memorial, and so forth. *See also* COMMEMORATIVE GLASSWARE.

BIEDERMEIER STYLE GLASS — Refer to BOHEMIAN GLASS.

BIEMANN, DOMINIK — A noted Bohemian glass engraver, Biemann (1800-1857) once served as an apprentice under Johann Pohl at the Harrachov Glassworks and then trained for several additional years at Karkachov in Silesia. Though he was most noted for engraving private portraits of wealthy clients in glass, including glass medallions, on goblets and beakers, Biemann also engraved landscapes and other typical Bohemian subjects. He worked primarily as an individual artist

Reproduction from an early 20th century Higgins-Seiter catalog.

near Prague and particularly at the summer spa of Franzensbad in western Bohemia (where many of his clients frequented). Note that Biemann's last name can be found on his creations as "Biman," "Bieman," or "Bimann."

BIGAGLIA PIETRO — A nineteenth century Italian glassmaker, while working on the island of Murano in Venice, Italy, produced what is considered the first millefiori paperweight. It was displayed at Vienna, Austria, in 1845. Soon after, an entire golden era of paperweight making followed in France by such noted companies as Baccarat, St. Louis, and Clichy.

An 1845 Italian Millefiori paperweight by Pietro Bigaglia.
Photo by Robin Rainwater.

BIMINI WERKSTATTE — An Austrian firm founded in 1923 at Vienna by Fritz Von Lampl (1892-1955) and brothers Arthur (1891-1981) and Josef Berger (1898-1989), the company began as a producer of furniture and toys and then expanded into glassware in 1926. It was noted for producing very thin, lightweight colored art style goblets, drinking glasses, and lamp work animals and figurines. Much of their work is similar to that of Venetian workers, such as the use of diagonal filigree; however, their products can be distinguished by the extreme thinness of the glass. Products produced by the firm are also known as "Bimini Glass." The firm closed in 1938 at the brink of World War II. Lampl emigrated to England, set up Bimini, Ltd. (also known as "Orplid Glass"), and continued producing glass there into the 1950s.

BININGER BOTTLE — Refer to WHISKEY BOTTLE.

BIRKS — Refer to HOUSE OF BIRKS.

BIRMINGHAM FLINT GLASS COMPANY — Refer to the O'LEARY MULVANEY COMPANY.

BIRMINGHAM GLASS WORKS — An American glass-making firm established at Birmingham, Pennsylvania (Southside Pittsburgh), in 1810, the company produced some limited amounts of blown glass tableware and window panes. It was acquired by Sutton, Wendt & Company, which, in turn, sold out to Whitehead, Ihmsen & Phillips in 1836. *See also WHITEHEAD, IHMSEN & PHILLIPS.*

BISCHOFF, A. F. GLASS COMPANY — An American glass-making firm established by the Bischoff family (headed by Anthony F. Bischoff, his father, and two sons) at Culloden, West Virginia, in 1922 (originally as Bischoff, Sons & Company), the company produced colored

tableware and novelty items. A fire destroyed two plant buildings in 1950; however, they were rebuilt. Anthony F. Bischoff purchased Bernard F. Bischoff's interest in 1959 (when Bernard died) and changed the name to two entities: A. F. Bischoff, Inc. (for colored glass) and the Culloden Lighting Glass Company (for glass-illuminating products). Anthony passed away in 1960 and the business was briefly carried on by his family until they sold out to the Lancaster Colony Corporation in 1963.

BISCUIT JAR — A tall, wide mouthed canister-shaped glass receptacle with cover used for holding biscuits, crackers, or cookies (predecessor of the cookie jar).

C. F. Monroe Wave Crest Biscuit Jar. *Courtesy of Wheaton Village.*

BITNER, S. K. & COMPANY — An American cut glass operation established in 1913 at Philadelphia, Pennsylvania, by S. K. Bitner, the firm produced some limited cut glass until ceasing operations in 1928.

BITTERS BOTTLE — Small bottles used for containing bitters or tonic made in the United States in the mid- and late-nineteenth century. Many so-called bitters were made purposefully with alcohol to avoid being taxed as liquor.

BLACK AMETHYST — An extremely dense, nearly opaque shade of purple made by the addition of manganese. Black amethyst glass is so dark that it cannot be seen when held to light.

BLACK BOTTLE — A dark opaque green or brown English invention in the mid-seventeenth century used for transporting and storing various beverages such as water, beer, wine, rum, and cider.

BLACK GLASS — Dark opaque ebony glass created by the combination of oxide of manganese, cobalt, and oxide of iron added to a batch of glass; true black glass originated in England in the late seventeenth century, but was still usually a very dark brown or green (so dark that it appeared black). Some attribute a Bohemian formula developed around 1817 by Count Georg Von Buquoy at his estate in Silesia as being the first tried black glass. Bohemians referred to it as "Hyalith." *See also HYALITH GLASS.*

Fenton hand-painted black glass basket with applied crystal handle. *Photo by Robin Rainwater.*

B

BLACKMER CUT GLASS COMPANY — Established by Arthur L. Blackmer in New Bedford, Massachusetts, in 1894 and incorporated as A. L. Blackmer in 1902. Blackmer had been a former employee of Mount Washington/Pairpoint. The company produced cut glass products until 1916.

BLAIR GLASS COMPANY — An American firm founded at Washington, Pennsylvania, in 1893 by J. H. Blair, it produced some novelty wares before going bankrupt in 1894. The firm was purchased in 1895 by Novelty Glass Works. *See also* NOVELTY GLASS COMPANY.

BLANK — An uncut piece of glass ordinarily in the shape of a block, bowl, or vase that has been specifically made of heavy, high-quality lead glassware; many glass companies of the nineteenth and early twentieth centuries provided blanks to various cut glass operations that did not produce raw glass of their own.

BLAZE CUT — A decorative pattern in cut glass characterized by a zigzag pattern of parallel groups or vertical or diagonal flute cuts. See also *FRINGE CUT*.

BLEEDING CUP OR GLASS — A small glass cup in which a vacuum is created for drawing blood to the surface of the body by heating (also known as "Cupping"). The term bleeding or cupping glass originated in the Middle Ages when blood-letting was erroneously believed to be essential to the healing process.

Bleeding cups.
Items courtesy of Wheaton Village.

BLEEDING HEART — A pressed glass pattern containing the Bleeding Heart flower as its primary design (variations include scrolling, dots, sandwich-like designs, and cables).

BLENKO GLASS COMPANY — An American firm originally founded in 1922 by English immigrant William John Blenko, along with his son, William H. Blenko, at Milton, West Virginia. The company started out as a maker of stained glass windows and later switched to contemporary art forms. The firm then gained a reputation for one of America's leading producers of mold-blown and free-blown colored tableware and art form-like vases.

A collection of Blenko glass vases and bowls.
Photo by Robin Rainwater.

Reproduction of a 1966 Blenko advertisement.

Blenko Glass Company Trademark.

BLOB — A quantity of molten glass gathered at the end of a pontil or blowpipe and then either worked by the blower or dropped into a mold. A uniform weight of molten glass that is fed into an automatic pressing machine is also known as a "Blob" or "Gob."

BLOBBING — The process by which chips of colored glass are embedded in the thickness of hot blown glass to form an irregular scattering of contrasting colors.

BLOB-TOP BOTTLE — A style of bottle whose name derives from its round, heavy, applied collared lip. The larger, blob-like lip, served to secure the cork stopper, was held in place by a wire that went over the top and around the neck. Blob-Top Bottles were developed in the late eighteenth century and used through most of the nineteenth century.

BLOCK — (1) A piece of wood used to form a gather of glass into a ball prior to blowing, the block is usually hallowed out to form a somewhat semicircular recess. It is then dipped in water to reduce charring and to provide a cushion of steam. (2) A fairly common design in pressed glass consisting of several interlocking or interconnected rows of squares or rectangles. Block is usually combined with other designs to form a unique pattern (i.e. block and bar, block and circle, block and fan, block and honeycomb, block and lattice, block and palm, block and panel, block and pillar, block and rib, block and rosette, block and star, red block or ruby-stained blocks, block and thumbprint, cat's eye and block, crossed block, frosted block, and regal block).

BLOMDAHL, SONJA — A noted American Studio Glass artisan who was born in Waltham, Massachusetts, in 1952, Blomdahl received her Fine Arts degree from the Massachusetts College of Art in 1974 and was awarded a National Endowment for the Arts Fellowship in 1986. Blomdahl lives in Seattle, Washington, and works full-time as an independent glass artisan.

BLOOMINGDALE FLINT GLASS WORKS — An American Company founded in 1819 by John and Richard Fisher and John Gilliland in Manhattan, New York. John Fisher and Gilliland had previously worked for the New England Glass Company. The firm produced some pressed wares until closing in 1840. Gilliland went on to form John L. Gilliland & Company in Brooklyn, New York. Note that the company was also called the New York Glass Works, but was better known for the Bloomingdales section of the city where the plant was located.

BLOWING — The process of blowing air through a metal tube or blowpipe in order to shape the molten glass blob attached to its end. Pieces can at times be re-blown and reshaped several times. Shaping techniques include swinging or rolling, blowing directly into a mold, rolling it on a marver, or shaping it into the desired form with the use of various tools. Glass blowing was invented by the Romans in the first century B.C. *See also FULL ANTIQUE.*

BLOWN 3-MOLD — Glass blown into a pre designed mold made up of two, three, or even more hinged parts. The three-part mold is the most common and leaves two sets of mold lines. This style of glass originated around 1820 in America and was made throughout the nineteenth century.

BLOWPIPE — A hollow metal tube used to gather molten glass from the pot and then blow air through it in order to shape glass, blowpipes are typically made of forged steel and contain a mouthpiece at one end and a metal ring at the other for gathering molten glass. Venetian glassmakers from the Middle Ages referred to the blowpipe as a "bocca."

Blowtorch — Refer to TORCH.

BLUE GLASS — In light blue glass, copper is the metallic coloring agent added to a batch of glass. For a deep dark blue color, refer to COBALT BLUE.

BLUE-GREEN GLASS — Refer to AQUA OR AQUAMARINE.

BLUE OPALESCENT — Blue colored glassware with a white opalescent edge or background (usually found in iridized Carnival Glass).

BLUERINA — Art Glass made in America in the late nineteenth century that is very similar to Amberina, only the colors gradually meld from blue at the base to Amberina at the top. It is sometimes referred to as "Blue Amberina."

BOAT — Glass made to resemble that of a sailing ship or a simple floating vessel, boat-shaped serving dishes come in a variety of styles and some are designated for serving specific foods. Ornamental and more elaborate ships often made within a bottle. *See also BANANA BOAT, GRAVY BOAT, and SHIP-IN-A-BOTTLE.*

BOCCA — The Italian or Venetian term for "blowpipe."

BOCELLAS — An Italian term for the glory hole. *See also GLORY HOLE.*

BODA GLASSWORKS — Founded in 1864 in southern Sweden by R. Wictor Scheutz and Wrik Widlund, who had previously worked with Kosta Glassworks. In the beginning, the firm produced bottles and both blown and pressed tableware. In 1918, it was sold to Arvid Reiner and the firm began producing some limited art glass. From this time forward, Boda is noted for decorative cut glass tableware and many traditional Scandinavian art styles of glass. When Eric Afors purchased the firm in 1946, it was merged with Kosta to form Kosta-Boda. In 1970, the new conglomerate all became part of the Afors Group ("Aforsgruppen" in Swedish), currently the largest glass-producing firm in Sweden. The glass-making firm of Johansfors was acquired in 1972, and even Orrefors joined on in 1990. The company is also known today as the Royal Scandinavian Group.

BODY — The middle or main portion of a glass vessel, the body is separate from the base, handle, cover, spout, or any item including decorations that are applied or attached to it.

BODY GLASS — Glass used to form the material or central portion of round glass marbles; in veneered marbles, the body glass is usually made of scrap glass in order to reduce costs.

BOGARD COMPANY — An American marble-making firm founded in 1971 by Clayton E. Bogard and his sons Jack and Jerry Bogard at Cairo, West Virginia. The Bogards purchased the Heaton Agate Company (established in 1939) and renamed it C. E. Bogard & Sons. The name was changed again in 1983 to "The Bogard Company." The firm ceased marble production in 1987 and sold its machinery to Jabo, Incorporated. *See also HEATON AGATE COMPANY and JABO, INCORPORATED.*

BOHEMIAN ART GLASS (BAG) COMPANY — A modern art glass-making firm founded in the Czech Republic (at Vsetin in East Moravia) in 1992, the company began as an offshoot of the Glass Service, a research and engineering firm. As a consequence, the new glass-making venture is equipped with state-of-the-art equipment (i.e. electric pot furnaces with computer controlled melting and cooling processes, optic molds, etc.) The firm employs many local artisans and was acquired by Barovier & Toso in 1998. Glass is still produced today under the BAG namesake.

BOHEMIAN GLASSWORKS NATIONAL CORPORATION — The original Bohemian Glassworks was founded at Podebrady in southern Austria/Germany (Bohemian region) in 1876. The firm produced lamp chimneys, soda siphons, and ink bottles early on. In 1893, it was acquired by Josef Inwald and lead crystal production began in 1927. In 1965, it was merged into a glass-making conglomerate in the modern Czech Republic with four smaller firms at Podebrady: Dobronin, Antonin Dul, Nizbor, and Josefodol (note that Josefodol was in turn made up of two smaller firms, Sazavou and Svetla). After the merger, the firm became the largest producer of lead crystal products in Czechoslovakia; nevertheless; they did produce some crystal and colored ornamental art styles as well. The corporation became part of Crystalex in 1974; however, the separate factories split up in 1989. *See also BAROLAC GLASS.*

B

BOHEMIAN GLASS — German-made glass produced as early as the late thirteenth century in a region covering southern Germany, Austria, and the Czech Republic. Early on, many glass operations were small-time forest houses (called huts or "Huttes" by Germans). The first products produced were practical items like window panes, drinking vessels, storage jars, beads, and some basic crude tableware. Beginning as early as the late sixteenth century, the Germans revived and refined wheel-engraving and applied it to both crystal and colored glass. Since then, Bohemian-styled glassware has been characterized by ornate

decoration (castles, forest, scenery, wildlife, commemorative battle, hunting scenes, architectural views, etc.), heavy cutting or engraving, and bright colors. From the 1820s to the 1860s (prior to the Art Nouveau movement), stained Bohemian glass that was then wheel cut, engraved, enameled, or gilded (or any combination of them) were some of the finest art objects made in the world. One such style, from about 1820 to 1840, was known as "Biedermeier" (named for two fictional bourgeois characters, Biedermann and Bummelmeier, in the satirical verses of Ludwig Eichrodt); and was targeted especially for middle-class consumers.

Bohemian tumbler.
Photo by Robin Rainwater.

BONBON OR BON BON DISH — A small, usually flat or shallow circular dish, with or without handles (center handle possible), used for serving small finger foods such as nuts, bonbons, or tiny fruits.

Handled Bon Bon, Priscilla.
No. 205, 5 inches, $3.00.

Bon Bon, Priscilla.
No. 235, 6 inches, $5.00.

Reproduction from a late 19th century Mount Washington catalog.

BONE ASH — The powdery white residue of matter that remains after the burning and pulverizing of bones. At one time, ashes from calcined bones were used both as a flux and an opacifier in making various shades of opaque white glass (i.e. milk glass, opal, and white opalescent colors). Modern milk glass usually contains aluminum and fluorine as additives rather than bone ash. See also ASH.

BONHOMME GLASS FACTORY — A glasshouse purchased in Leige, Belgium, by Henri and Leonard Bonhomme in the late 1630s, the firm operated for well over one hundred years, producing crystal tableware and other functional glass products.

BONITA ART GLASS COMPANY — Refer to the BONITA GLASS COMPANY.

BONITA GLASS COMPANY — 1) An American firm founded in 1897 in Cicero, Indiana, by Otto Jaeger, who had previously worked as a glass decorator with several glass firms including Hobbs and Brownier prior to establishing his own firm, Bonita produced pressed glass bar goods, tumblers, vases, and tableware; some in transparent or opaque colors. In 1900, the firm was sold to J. E. Bert, who ran it for two additional years before closing. Note that "Bonita" in Spanish means "Beautiful." Jaeger later recognized the Bonita Art Glass Company at Wheeling,

West Virginia, in 1920. The new venture produced pressed colored Depression Glass, much of which was decorated with banding (gold, platinum, silver, turquoise, etc.). In 1924, the business was moved to Huntington, West Virginia, where it served mostly as a decorating shop prior to closing in 1929. 2) A second unrelated firm to sport the Bonita Glass Company name was established in Huntington, West Virginia, in 1941. This company produced some hand-blown wares, along with machine-etched barware and a few novelty items, before closing in 1962.

BOOKENDS — A matching pair of supports placed at the opposite end of a row of books. Such noted companies as Hesisey, Baccarat, Lalique, and Venetian makers have produced bookends made of glass (usually in the shape of animals, but other designs were made as well).

BOOT GLASS — A glass drinking vessel, with a handle, shaped like a boot. Large examples, some over calf high, originated in Europe in the late seventeenth century. Modern examples are often sold as souvenirs and are quite small (capacity of about three ounces). *See also* SHOE.

Boot Glass. *Drawing by Mark Pickvet.*

BOOZE BOTTLE — A flask made in America in the 1860s in the form of a two-story house by the Whitney Glass Works for Edmund G. Booze. The house usually contained a shingled roof and a chimney that served as a spout.

BORAX — Refer to BOROSILICATE GLASS.

BORDEAUX GLASS — A tall glass, with a foot, stem, and a large round deep bowl, specifically designed for serving Bordeaux wine. Bordeaux glasses are very similar to standard wine glasses, but tend to have a deeper bowl; thus leading to a little more capacity (five or six ounces in lieu of four by standard wine glasses).

BORDEN, GEORGE L. & COMPANY — An American firm founded in 1910 at Groveville, New Jersey, by George L. Borden; in 1912, Borden added a second location for cutting glass in Trenton, New Jersey. Cut glass in Trenton was produced under the name of "Krystal Krafters." Borden produced cut glass tableware in the early 1920s.

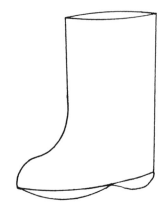

Borden, George L. & Company Trademark.

BORGFELDT, GEORGE & COMPANY — An American wholesale distributor established in New York, New York, in 1881 by George Borgfeldt, the firm did not make any cut glass; however, they did apply their company trademarks to products made by others. The firm sold cut glass up into the World War I era.

Borgfeldt, George & Company Trademark.

BOROSILICATE GLASS — The original or first heat resistant formula for glassware containing boric oxide (B203), it was developed by the Corning Glass Works for more durable railroad lantern lenses as well as for battery cases. In 1915, it was adapted to Pyrex Kitchenware and then to scientific and industrial glass. Note that boric acid (H3B03) is a source of boric oxide. Also note that boric acid itself is usually combined with sodium in a batch of borosilicate glass to form Borax (sodium borate or Na2B407).

BORSELLA — The Italian term for tongs. *See also* TONGS.

BORSKE SKLO OR BORSKE SKLARNEY NATIONAL CORPORATION — A large conglomerate of small Czechoslovakian glass firms in the Novy Bor region that were combined into one large nationalized corporation in 1948. By the late 1920s, there were over three hundred small-glass related firms working in the region. In 1975, the conglomerate became part of Crystalex. There is still a glass design and instructional studio operating today as Crystalex-Kombinat.

BOSTON & SANDWICH GLASS COMPANY — An American company established at Sandwich, Massachusetts, by Deming Jarves in 1825, it was known as the Sandwich Manufacturing Company until 1826. The firm started as a producer of blown glass items, but switched over primarily to pressed, as well as some cut, glassware. Jarves left in 1858 to establish the Cape Cod Glass Company and Sewell Fessenden succeeded him as superintendent. The firm became one of America's most successful operations and produced certain glass in color, including some forms of Art Glass and paperweights. A serious labor strike occurred in 1887 and the plant closed down. In 1888, a small amount of glass was produced by ten previous workers who named their venture the Sandwich Cooperation Glass Company. It failed and, in 1907, the plant was acquired by the Alton Manufacturing Company. A maker of lighting fixtures, Alton closed in 1908 and all buildings were permanently demolished by 1920. Along with Bakewell and New England, Boston & Sandwich was one of first early successful American glass-making firms that remained in business for several decades. The company name is where the title "Sandwich Glass" originates.

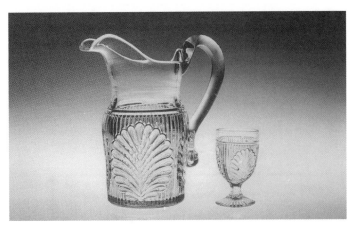

Pressed glass ribbed palm patterned pitcher and tumbler. *Courtesy of the Sandwich Glass Museum.*

BOSTON ANTIQUE GLASS COMPANY — Refer to the SUFFOLK GLASS WORKS.

BOSTON CROWN GLASS WORKS — Refer to the SOUTH BOSTON FLINT GLASS WORKS.

BOSTON PORCELAIN & GLASS COMPANY — Refer to the NEW ENGLAND GLASS COMPANY.

BOSTON SILVER GLASS COMPANY — An American firm established in 1857 by Alonzo Young and John Haines at Cambridge, Massachusetts, in 1868, the company was also known as Young, Haines & Dyer. It produced some pressed glassware and silver-plated wares before closing in 1871.

BOTTLE — A glass container with a narrow neck and mouth, which may or may not have a handle, bottles come in all shapes and sizes and can be made of other materials. *See also* BEER BOTTLE *and* WINE BOTTLE.

Glass Pepsi and 7-Up soda bottles. *Photo by Robin Rainwater.*

BOTTLE CAP — A metal (usually tin or aluminum) seal that is crimped on drinking bottles (i.e. soda or beer) to seal them. First known as metal crown seals, they were developed in 1891. The bottles required a bottle opener to be removed. In the latter twentieth century, twist caps were invented to eliminate the need for a bottle opener (on most modern glass beer bottles), though some caps, mostly on glass soda bottles, still require an opener. *See also* BOTTLE MARBLE, METAL CROWN SEAL, *and* STOPPER.

BOTTLE MARBLE — A small spherical glass object once used (from the 1870s–1920s) as a stopper in the neck of the bottle to hold liquids within (most were used in certain soda bottles).

BOUQUET — An arrangement of natural or stylized flowers within a paperweight, usually with leaves too. Bouquets can either be laid flat (known as "Nosegay") or upright depending upon the designer.

BOUQUET DE MARRIAGE — An arrangement of white canes set among a mass of millefiori pieces within a paperweight that are formed into a mushroom-like design.

BOURNIQUE GLASS COMPANY — An American firm founded by French immigrant Adolphe Bournique (1863-1913) in Kokomo, Indiana, in 1908. Bournique was born in Baccarat, France, in 1863 and moved to Brooklyn, New York, with his family is 1881. He worked for other glass-making firms prior to establishing his own business. Bournique produced opalescent art glass, colored vases, candlesticks, tableware, and lamp shades. His wife continued to operate the firm after his death until selling it in 1926.

BOW LATHE — Refer to LATHE-CUTTING.

B

BOWL — A concave glass vessel, hemispherical in shape, used for holding liquids and other foods (i.e. soup, salad, cereal, berries, and vegetables). The bowl of a wine or stemmed beverage glass is the portion that holds the liquid.

Tipperary cut crystal bowl.

Genuine American Cut Glass Bowl. Combination Hob Star and Engraved Strawberry Pattern. Diameter, 8 inches.
No. 9278..$13.50 Each
See No. 9279 Plates to Match.

Reproduction from a late 19th century Higgins-Seiter catalog.

BOWMAN, GEORGE H. COMPANY — An American wholesale/retail operation established at Cleveland, Ohio, in 1888 by George Bowman, F. T. Engler, R. Peck, and F. F. Pfifferkoon, the firm represented china, glass, and pottery makers; however, they did employ their own glass cutters from 1910 to 1918.

BOX — A glass receptacle that usually contains a cover, which may or may not be hinged, and the overall shape is usually round, oval, or rectangular. Colorfully decorated boxes are usually very small and were popular during the Victorian era. Most were designed to hold small jewelry or powders.

BOYD'S CRYSTAL ART GLASS COMPANY — An American firm established at Cambridge, Ohio, in 1978 by Bernard C. Boyd and his son Bernard F. Boyd. When the elder Boyd passed away in 1988, the firm came under the control of Bernard F. Boyd, along with his wife Sue and their son John. In the beginning, the Boyds purchased the Degenhart factory and acquired fifty of Degenhart's molds. As business expanded, they added their own molds, as well as purchasing others from companies that had gone out of business (Imperial for instance). Boyd is noted for highly collectible miniature Art figurines and animals created in a variety of colors and styles (mostly iridescent and slag).

A 1995 Boyd's advertisement.

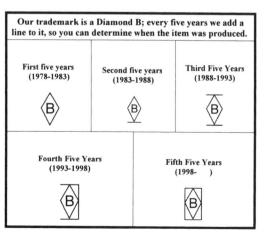

Boyd novelty animal figurines. *Photo by Robin Rainwater.*

Our trademark is a Diamond B; every five years we add a line to it, so you can determine when the item was produced.		
First five years (1978-1983)	**Second five years (1983-1988)**	**Third Five Years (1988-1993)**

Fourth Five Years (1993-1998)	**Fifth Five Years (1998-)**	

Boyd's Crystal Art Glass Company Trademark.

BRACELET — Refer to BANGLE.

BRANDENBURG GLASS — Enameled and engraved Bohemian glassware that originated in Brandenburg, Germany, in the seventeenth century.

BRANDY GLASS — A short rounded glass with a foot and very tiny stem; much shorter but wider as compared to as rounded wine glass.

BREAD AND BUTTER PLATE — A round flat glass article that is usually six inches in diameter.

BREAD PLATE OR TRAY—A flat rectangular or oval platter that was specifically designed for serving breads, rolls, or sandwiches. Most were made of pressed or cut glass in the late nineteenth and early twentieth centuries, some were part of a glass or china set and may contain embossed designs such as commemorative events.

BRIDE'S BASKET — A fancy bowl held within a silver or silver-plated frame. They were popular wedding gifts during the Brilliant Period of Cut Glass after they debuted at the World's Columbian Exposition held in Chicago, Illinois, in 1893.

BRIDGE FLUTING — A cut glass design originating in England in the early nineteenth century, Bridge Fluting is characterized by short, but wide faceted vertical cuts along the upper stems and lower parts of bowls in drinking glasses.

BRILLIANT — The term applied to fine cut glass with a lustrous finish, it was borrowed from gem-cutting whereby multiple cuts and facets produced a sparkling, brilliant finish. There was also a "Brilliant" pattern of pressed glass produced by McKee Brothers in the late nineteenth century. However, pressed glass rarely approaches the striking appearance of high quality cut glass. *See also the BRILLIANT PERIOD.*

BRILLIANT GLASS WORKS — An American company established by Joseph Beatty Sr. at Brilliant, Ohio, in 1880, the firm produced pressed glassware before merging with the Novelty Glass Works in 1889.

BRILLIANT PERIOD — The era of quality American hand-made lead crystal glassware from about 1880 to 1915 (though some estimate its beginning in 1876 when several cut glass manufacturers displayed their wares successfully at the Centennial Exhibition held at Philadelphia, Pennsylvania). The period was characterized by a variety of elaborate patterns fashioned by fine cutting, engraving, and polishing.

BRISBOIS, VICTOR — Refer to BECKER & BRISBOIS.

BRISTOL GLASS — Crystal, colored, and milk glass items produced in several factories in Bristol, England, in the seventeenth and eighteenth centuries. The majority of the products were cut, engraved, gilded, and enameled with a variety of decorations.

Bristol Glass Bristol glass vases. *Photo courtesy of the Wichita Museum.*

BRISTOL-TYPE GLASS — Nineteenth century American and English-made Victorian opaque glassware characterized by hand-enameling, similar to the older style of BRISTOL GLASS.

BRISTOL YELLOW — A bright light gold-hued color of Art Glass created and named by Steuben in the early twentieth century.

BRITISH CAST PLATE GLASS COMPANY — An English firm established in 1773 at Ravenhead, near St. Helens, the firm specialized in making window panes and became part of Pilkington Brothers in 1901. *See also PILKINGTON BROTHERS, LTD.*

BRITISH HEAT-RESISTING GLASS COMPANY — An English firm established at Birmingham in 1934 by a former employee of Chance Brothers, the company moved to Bilston in Staffordshire in 1937. The firm purchased the rights to make Orlak heat-resistant glassware from Chance in 1933 similar to that of Pyrex (note that the firm of James Jobling received an exclusive UK license to produce Pyrex from Corning, New York, in America). The company was sold to United Glass in 1966 and the factory closed a short time thereafter.

BROAD GLASS — A term for a large sheet or pane of glass.

BROKEN-SWIRL RIBBING — Refer to RIB OR RIBBING.

BROOKE GLASS COMPANY — An American firm founded at Wellsburg, West Virginia, in 1891, it produced pressed and blown glass flasks, bottles, fruit jars, and novelty items. The firm sold out to the North Wheeling Glass Company in 1899. *See also SWEENEY, MICHAEL, THOMAS, & R. H.*

BROOKLYN FLINT GLASS WORKS — An American pressed and cut glass firm established in Brooklyn, New York, in the 1820s, the factory was purchased and operated by John L. Gilliland in 1822 and then sold to Amory Houghton Sr. and Jr. in 1864. The Houghtons moved their glass operations to Corning, New York, in 1868 while the Brooklyn plant was purchased by John Hoare. *See also CORNING GLASS WORKS and J. HOARE & COMPANY.*

BRONSON CUT GLASS COMPANY — A short-lived American firm established at Painted Post, New York, in 1910 by three Bronson brothers (Frank, George, and Williard); the firm specialized in cutting inkwells from crystal blanks provided by T. G. Hawkes. It went out of business in 1912.

BRUISE — A small irregular defect in a paperweight that usually occurs during the production process. Most appear just below the surface of the crown. The flaw can at times be removed by grinding or polishing; however, this reduces the size of the paperweight. Some artists and/ or companies will discard those that appear defective while others sell them as seconds (less than perfect or with minor flaws).

BRYCE BROTHERS — A pressed glass manufacturer formed after the break-up of Bryce, Walker and Company in 1882. The firm, which moved to Hammondsville, Pennsylvania, in 1889, specialized in hand-blown stemware and barware and then joined the U.S. Glass Co. in 1891 as Factory B. In 1893, Andrew Bryce and J. McDonald formed a new Bryce Brothers Company at Hammondsville. In 1896, the company moved to Mt. Pleasant, Pennsylvania, where it was incorporated and a new factory was built. The firm continued producing glassware (mostly tumblers, stemware, and barware) until selling out to the Lenox Corporation in 1965. Lenox continues to produce glassware today. *See also LENOX, INC.*

B

BRYCE, HIGBEE AND COMPANY — An American pressed glass manufacturer established at Pittsburgh, Pennsylvania, in 1879 by John Bryce, his son Charles Bryce, A. Doyle, and John Higbee. Due to its location on the southeast side of Pittsburgh, the factory was also called the Homestead Glass Works. A flood destroyed the plant in 1907, and the property was sold off to Carnegie Steel in 1908. Higbee went on to found his own firm, the Higbee Glass Company, in Bridgeville, Pennsylvania, in 1907.

Reproduction from an 1891 advertisement
in *China, Glass, & Lamps*.

BRYCE, MCKEE AND COMPANY — A short-lived pressed glass manufacturer established in Pittsburgh, Pennsylvania, in 1850 by Fred M. McKee (not of the famous McKee glass-making family) and three Bryce brothers – James, Robert D. and John P. Bryce. McKee left in 1854 and William Hartley and Joseph Richards joined in as partners; the new firm became Bryce, Richards & Company. In 1865, Hartley & Richards left to form their own firm, and William Walker joined; the firm then became the Bryce, Walker, and Company. In 1879, John Bryce left and aided in founding the Bryce, Higbee & Company. In 1882, Walker left and the firm reorganized as the Bryce Brothers. *See also* BRYCE BROTHERS.

BRYCE, RICHARDS, AND COMPANY — Refer to BRYCE, MCKEE & COMPANY.

BRYCE, WALKER, AND COMPANY — Refer to BRYCE, MCKEE & COMPANY.

BRYDEN, ROBERT — Bryden joined the Pairpoint Manufacturing Company as a trainee in 1950. He became sales manager in 1952 and was instrumental in moving the firm to East Wareham, Massachusetts, in 1957 in an attempt to save the firm (the old plant in New Bedford was deteriorating to some extent). The firm closed in 1958; however, Bryden moved on to Spain and leased facilities there for making glass until 1970. Glass made at Wareham is sometimes referred to as "Bryden's Pairpoint" or "Pairpoint of Wareham." Glass made in Spain was marked with a paper label that read "Pairpoint – Made in Spain."

BUBBLE — (1) An air- or gas-filled cavity within glass. Intentional bubbles are often created for decorative effects while unintentional ones result from improper fusing of the ingredients. Tiny bubbles are also known as seeds. Stueben produced an Art Glass form that they named "Bubbly" in the 1920s and 1930s: bubbles were created intentionally by rolling molten glass over spiked molds that left marks. A second layer of glass was then applied over it to trap the impressions, thus creating a controlled bubble effect. The Italian term for an air bubble is "Puliga." (2) Anchor Hocking produced a pattern of glass from 1940 to 1965 that they named "Bubble." It is characterized by an all-over pattern of round molded bubble-like circles that protrude outward. It was also made in a variety of colors, including forest green, sapphire blue, royal ruby, pink, plain crystal, and amber. Anchor Hocking's bubble has also been called "Bull's Eye" and "Provincial." *See also* PULEGOSO.

BUCKET — A cylindrically-shaped object with a bail handle, which may or may not taper slightly outward at the top, used for holding or carrying liquids (typically water). Glass buckets were made by the Romans as early as the first century A.D. and the Venetians in the sixteenth century. Water, ice, and measuring buckets were fairly common in nineteenth century cut glass as well as in the 1920s and 1930s colored Depression glass. Large buckets are also used for chilling wine or champagne. *See also* CHAMPAGNE BUCKET *and* WINE BUCKET.

A Cambridge green glass bucket with etched floral design and metal handle.

BUCKEYE GLASS COMPANY — (1) An American pressed glass manufacturer founded by Henry Helling in 1878 at Martins Ferry, Ohio. Along with pressed glass, the firm also produced colored glass lamps and blown stemware up until 1893. The company attempted to continue as a non-union shop in 1894-95; however, labor troubles forced them to shut down. The plant burned in 1896 and was never rebuilt. (2) An American pressed glass manufacturing established at Wheeling, West Virginia, in 1849, the firm moved to Bowling Green, Ohio, in 1887 and became the Buckeye Novelty Glass Company with F. W. Merry as president, C. N. L. Brudeworld as vice-president, and Charles Reed as secretary. In 1889, it reorganized with J. W. Newton as president, Daniel Coyle as general manager, and M. L. Case as treasurer. Aside from pressed glass tableware, the firm also produced lamps and blown glass; it filed for bankruptcy in 1890 and the plant was sold to the Ohio Flint Glass Company in 1891. Fire destroyed the factory in 1895; however, Ohio Flint continued on at their Dunkirk, Indiana plant. (3) A couple of other short-lived glass firms also sported the "Buckeye" name: one in Malta, Ohio (1904); another tumbler-producer located at Shadyside, Ohio, known as the Buckeye Tumbler Company (1909). *See also* OHIO FLINT GLASS COMPANY.

BUCKHANNON CUT GLASS COMPANY — Refer to the VALLEY GLASS COMPANY.

BUCKLE — A common molded design found in pressed glass consisting of an oval, or several interlocking ovals, that resemble belt buckles. The buckles themselves may contain further patterns within them (i.e. squares, diamonds, bands, interlocking designs, etc.), and are sometimes combined with other patterns too, such as the buckle with star, the buckle with diamond band, and the banded buckle.

Pressed glass buckle pattern goblets. *Photo by Robin Rainwater. Items courtesy of the Corning Museum of Glass.*

BUDDY BRAND MARBLES — Refer to the "Ravenswood Novelty Works."

BUFFALO CUT GLASS COMPANY — An American cut glass operation founded in 1902 at Buffalo, New York, by a group of fourteen stockholders. Three of the stockholders (Michael Kallighan, Daniel McGettigan, and Joseph Schmitt) bought the others out and moved operations to Batavia, New York, in 1905. The firm produced cut glass tableware until ceasing operations in 1918.

Reproduction from an early 20th century Buffalo Cut Glass Company catalog.

Buffalo Cut Glass Company Trademark.

BULB — Refer to LIGHT BULB.

BULLET-PROOF GLASS — Thick layers of laminated glass that are ordinarily separated by plastic or vinyl layers. Bullet proof glass is usually over 1-1/2" thick and is used in windows (i.e. bank teller/convenience store windows) as well as a security measure in cars.

BULLICANTE — A technique, originating in Venice, that places air bubbles in a regular pattern within glass (popular in modern paperweights, vases, and other forms of art glass).

BULL'S EYE — A popular decorating technique in pressed glass whereby raised adjacent circles (bull's eyes) were applied around an object. Bull's eyes were usually combined with other patterns such as diamond points, loops, stars, thumbprints, bars, floral designs, and panels. Note that a Bull's Eye pane of glass is one with a pontil mark in the center that is surrounded by concentric ridges.

BUMPER — A term for firing glass. *See also FIRING GLASS.*

BUQUOY — A noble Bohemian family that began producing glass in the early seventeenth century; the first Count Buquoy migrated to Bohemia from the Spanish Netherlands and was a close friend of the Austrian-Hapsburgs. Under Count Georg Von Buquoy (1781-1851), glass artisans developed a formula for what they named HYALITH, a glass that resembled semi-precious stones. The formula was perfected around 1817 and was made in both black and a reddish-brown color. It was further decorated with engraving, along with the application of gold enamel/trim. In 1835, a third bluish-gray color called "Agatine" was added to the hyalith line. *See also BLACK GLASS and HYALITH GLASS.*

Items made from Buquoy Glassworks of Bohemia, 1830s. *Photo courtesy of the Corning Museum of Glass.*

BURETTE — The French name for a specialized sacramental wine cruet used during certain Christian church ceremonies. Burettes typically contain gilding, curved spouts and looped handles.

B

BURGUNDY GLASS — A certain style of wine glass characterized by a large globular bowl and inverted rim. The glasses are ordinarily a bit larger than the standard 4-oz. wine glasses and, as the name implies, were intended for drinking wines produced in Burgundy, France.

BURLEY & TYRRELL COMPANY — A trademark occasionally found on cut glass products, Burley & Tyrrell was established at Chicago, Illinois, as a large wholesaler of crockery, glass, and china around 1870. The firm registered a trademark for cut glass, but did not produce cut glass of their own; rather, they represented products made by other glass firms. The firm was out of business by 1920.

Burley & Tyrrell Company Trademark.

BURMESE GLASS — Art glass objects characterized by various light opaque shadings in pastel colors of pink, yellow, and white produced with the addition of uranium. It was first created by the Mt. Washington Glass Company and patented in 1885. A license was granted to Thomas Webb & Sons of England who also produced glass in this style.

A collection of Burmese Glass.

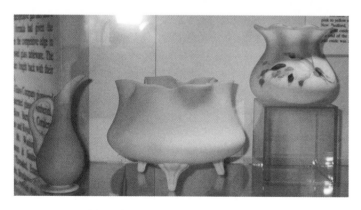

Mount Washington Burmese glass items.
Courtesy of Wheaton Village.

BURNER — The part of a lamp where the fuel-burning device lies. Lamp burners were designed specifically to suit the type of fuel that was used: whale oil, camphene, and kerosene were common fuels. Early nineteenth century lamps had drop burners, which consisted of a cork between two tin plates and one or two tin tubes that held the wick. Some later whale oil burners screwed into a peter or brass collar at the mouth of the font.

BURNING — Refer to STAINING.

BUSH CUT GLASS COMPANY — Refer to the BUSH GLASS COMPANY.

BUSH GLASS COMPANY — An American cut glass operation founded in 1911 at Lansing, Michigan, by Edgar Bush and Harris Thomas, the firm was also known as the Bush Cut Glass Company. Bush had previously managed the Michigan Cut Glass Company prior to establishing his own firm. The company produced cut glass products until 1916, the same year the firm's name was changed to the Lansing Cut Glass Works. Lansing operated as a retail outlet for glass and china until closing in 1921.

BUSHWICK GLASS COMPANY — An American firm founded by William Brookfield in 1879, the company produced insulator, vials, bottles, and other pharmaceutical-related items prior to closing in 1899.

BUTTER DISH — A glass dish that is ordinarily flat or footed, with or without glass dome or rectangular cover, used for serving butter, margarine, or other spreads. Butter dishes were quite small until the widespread introduction and use of those with dome covers in the mid-nineteenth century. Note that a 1/4-pound butter dish is rectangular in shape with a matching under tray (designed to hold a 1/4-pound stick of butter).

4¾ In. Butter Dishes May be used for jelly or preserves.
50R-3611—3 doz in carton, 38 lbs.
Doz .85

6¾ In. Butter Dishes
50R-3613—3 doz in carton, 62 lbs.
Doz .92

Reproduction from a 1930 Butler Brothers catalog.

Jeannette Iris patterned butter dish with dome cover. *Photo by Robin Rainwater.*

BUTTER PAT — A miniature glass plate (round, square, or rectangular) used for serving an individual pat or single portion of butter.

BUTTER PLATE — A small glass plate used for serving individual portions or butter, margarine, or other spreads.

BUTTER TUB — A glass vessel shaped as a small bucket or pail (usually smaller than an ice bucket) with or without a semicircular handle, and used for serving butter balls.

BUTTON — A common molded design found in pressed glass consisting of a series of interlocking rounded or oval button-like objects, the buttons might be plain circles or contain further patterns within them (squares, diamonds, bands, interlocking designs, etc.). Furthermore, the buttons are sometimes combined with other patterns too: daisy and button, button arches, button band, button and star, button block, button panel, paneled star and button, and sunken button.

BUTTON PAPERWEIGHT — A small, miniature, or tiny paperweight the size of a button; most are usually equipped with a clasp or small ring at the bottom for threading, and are around 1/2" in diameter though some of the largest examples might exceed 1 inch.

BUZZ STAR — A cut glass star design with may points that comes in many styles and shapes. Buzz stars are generally cut with 24 or 32 points for symmetry, though those with less points have been cut as well (a 12-point Buzz Star is synonymous with "Pinwheel"). The center portion of the stars (usually round) is also cut into many different geometrical patterns while curving lines emanate from the center into a whirling effect of buzz stars. Note that stars that are molded into pressed glass are made to resemble those of cut glass, but the edges are not nearly as sharp. *See also* HOBSTER and STAR-CUTTING.

BYESVILLE GLASS & LAMP COMPANY — An American pressed glass and lamp making company founded by John Beckett, Charles Brudewold, and Charles Campbell, at Byesville, Ohio, the firm was first filed as the American Art Glass & Lamp Company in 1899. However, the name was changed to Byesville later in the year. The firm filed for bankruptcy in 1904 and was purchased by Charles Schott and P. H. Kelso. Under Schott & Kelso, production was very limited. They in turn sold the factory to the Cambridge Glass Company in 1911. Cambridge operated the plant as a second factory until the plant was permanently closed in 1917.

B

Buzz Star. Reproduction from a 1900 Pitkin & Brooks U.S. patent.

Cc

{ Cc }

CABBAGE ROSE — A pressed glass pattern that contains the Cabbage Rose flower as its primary design (variations include scrolling, dots, Sandwich-like designs, bands ovals, etc.). Note that a similar design was made in Depression Glass by the Federal Glass Company from 1935 to 1939 called the "Sharon Cabbage Rose."

CABLE — A pattern in glass resembling the twisted strands of a rope or cable, glass cables are most often made of opaque white and are used to decorate goblet stems and paperweights. They are also common in pressed glass and may be combined with other designs (grape and cable, cable with ring, swirl cable, cherry and cable, etc.).

CABOCHON — A Roman style of decoration involving small drops or blobs of various colored glass that are in turn arranged in decorative patterns when applied to the exterior of objects. Note that the precious stone known as cabochon, from which this decorating technique derives its name, is generally hemispherical or oval in form and is usually polished, but not cut into facets.

CADDY — A small glass container with a cover used for holding tea or tea bags.

CADMIUM — A bluish-white metal that, when combined with sulfur, produces a rich yellow color when added to a batch of glass. Cadmium is also used with selenium to produce ruby red glassware.

CAGE CUP — A beaker or cup-like object that is decorated by undercutting so that the surface decoration stands free of the body and is supported by struts. The final appearance resembles that of a vessel within a network or cage. Cage cups date to Roman times and can be suspended by ropes or chains, and even serve as hanging lamps.

CAINES & JOHNSON — Refer to PHOENIX GLASS WORKS.

CAINES, THOMAS H. & SONS — Refer to PHOENIX GLASS WORKS.

CAINES, WILLIAM & BROTHER — Refer to PHOENIX GLASS WORKS.

CAIRO NOVELTY COMPANY — An American marble-making firm founded in 1948 at Cario, West Virginia, by Dennis Farley, Oris Hanlon, and John Sandy, a flood destroyed most of the company's buildings in 1950, and the business closed permanently in 1951.

CAITHNESS GLASS, LTD. — Caithness was founded in 1960 by Robin Sinclair and has factories at Wick (the original), Perth, and Oban in the region of Perthshire, Scotland. In its beginning, Caithness produced colored table and ornamental glass. In 1969, the first paperweight was produced and the firm also expanded into novelties as well as some limited crystal tableware. Noted glass artisan Paul Ysart joined Caithness in 1962, and Caithness acquired the Whitefriars name in 1981 after that factory closed. In 1991, Caithness was purchased by Drambuie and then it was acquired by Royal Doulton in 1996. Paperweights, along with other items, are still produced today under the "Caithness" namesake.

A Caithness green paperweight with etched Scottish Highlander cattle.

CAKE PLATE — A large flat or footed glass plate, usually round in shape, used for holding cakes.

Hocking Glass Company's green Cameo Ballerina patterned Depression Glass cake plate. *Photo by Robin Rainwater.*

CAKE SALVER — A larger platter or tray that is usually stemmed and contains a pedestal foot; as the name implies, cake salvers were specifically designed to serve cakes, but they can also be used to serve other foods. Most are circular in shape. *See also* CAKE SAVER *and* SALVER.

Avon Cape Cod patterned ruby red cake salver commissioned for Wheaton Industries. *Photo by Robin Rainwater.*

CAKE SAVER — A larger platter or tray that usually contains a pedestal foot and a larger domed cover. As the name implies, cake savers are designed specifically to preserve the freshness of cakes; however, they can also be used to store other foods as well. Most are circular in shape. *See also* CAKE SALVER.

CALCAR — A term for an oven or furnace in which fruit was originally made and silica (sand) was burned.

CALCEDONIO — Refer to CHALCEDONY.

CALCINING — The process of heating inorganic materials at a high temperature, but less than that necessary for ordinary fusion. The process is necessary at times to prepare the ingredients for a batch of glass (i.e. for removing impurities, pulverizing or grinding).

CALCITE GLASS — A brightly colored cream-white translucent glass that resembles the mineral calcite (calcite is not used in its manufacture; rather calcium sulfate is the key coloring agent). Calcite Glass was first produced by Frederick Carder at the STEUBEN GLASS WORKS in the early twentieth century.

CALCIUM — A silvery white metallic substance that, when combined with phosphorus (calcium phosphate) or sulfur (calcium sulfate), produces an opaque white color when added to a batch of glass. *See also* CALCITE GLASS.

CALICO — Refer to MARBLED GLASS.

CALIFORNIA GLASS INSULATOR COMPANY — An American firm established at Long Beach, California, in 1912 by A. C. Munn, the firm produced pressed glass insulators before going out of business in 1917.

CALIPERS — A metal tong-like tool used to measure a glass object for its diameter as well as symmetry, Calipers are sometimes referred to as "Dividers."

CAMBRIDGE GLASS COMPANY — (1) An attempt was made in 1873 to establish the first Cambridge Glass Company (in Cambridge, Ohio) by a group of eight speculators; however, they did not raise enough capital to get the venture off the ground. As a consequence, a factory was not built and no glass was produced; nevertheless, their charter had not been canceled. (2) A second venture was more successful in 1901 as a separate group of investors, who happened to own the National Glass Company, built a new factory in Cambridge, Ohio. Glass production began in 1902. The company was first managed by Arthur J. Bennett and the firm became a major producer of colored glassware, some opaque styles including milk glass, cut and etched crystal tableware/stemware, and novelties, up until 1958 when the factory closed. The Imperial Glass Company was able to purchase many of the company's molds, as well as the "Cambridge" name; however, glass was no longer made under Cambridge. Popular large tableware patterns made by Cambridge include "Apple Blossom," "Candlelight," "Cascade," "Chantilly," "Decagon," "Everglade," "Gloria," "Martha Washington," "Mount Vernon," "Portia," "Rosalee," "Square," and "Wildflower." In 1981, the vacant factory was refurbished as an antique mall, museum, and small glass-making facility. Also note that some of the Cambridge animal molds were acquired by the Summit Art Glass Company in 1980s while some have been reproduced.

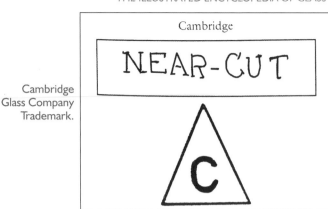

Cambridge Glass Company Trademark.

CAMDEN **C**ITY **C**UT **G**LASS **C**OMPANY — An American cut glass-making firm founded in 1910 at Camden, New Jersey, by Bernard Gerety, Albert Priestly, and Bernard Weiner, the company produced cut glass tableware into the early 1920s. Note that the firm was also known as the Camden Cut Glass Company.

CAMDEN **C**UT **G**LASS **C**OMPANY — Refer to the CAMDEN CITY CUT GLASS COMPANY.

CAME — A slender grooved strip of lead with an H-shaped cross section used to hold panes of glass together (usually in stained glass windows).

CAMEO — (1) A circular or oval (though shapes may vary) decoration in the form of a portrait, emblem, picture, commemorative, or inscription; most are made in low relief and bear the portraits of famous people, replica coins, historical subjects or symbols, or simple decorations as in some pressed glass patterns. (2) The Hocking Glass Company produced a large set of pressed colored (pink, green, yellow, and a little crystal with a platinum band rim) Depression Glass tableware pattern from 1930-1934 that they named "Cameo." It contains a small dancing girl in a cameo frame along with drapery. Because of the design, it is also referred to as "Ballerina" or "Dancing Girl." Note that this design was also reproduced in miniature by Mosser in the 1980s. (3) The Belmont Tumbler Company produced a very small set of Depression green glass tableware (a few bowls, plate, sherbet glass, and tumbler) in 1931 that they named "Rose Cameo." It is similar to Hocking's cameo, only there is a rose present in the cameo shape rather than a dancing girl. *See also* MEDALLION.

Cameo patterned Depression Glass cookie jar from the Hocking Glass Company. *Photo by Robin Rainwater.*

Cobalt blue decanter, tray, and tumbler set with silver deposit.
Items courtesy of Wheaton Village.

New! 6-piece place setting

CAMBRIDGE SQUARE

"designed for present-day living"

Here's the exciting new crystal you've been hearing about — "Cambridge Square," created by famous Cambridge and now available in smart 6-piece place settings, neatly packaged! Selected by the Museum of Modern Art for outstanding design. The perfect gift for *every* gift occasion!

6-piece place setting illustrated: 9½" luncheon plate, 7½" salad plate, coffee cup & saucer, goblet, sherbet.   **$0.00**

Reproduction from a 1950 Cambridge catalog.

Etched-Like Cameo Design

EMERALD GREEN, pressed glass, etched-like cameo design

15-PIECE SET	21-PIECE SET
C-1361—1 set in carton, 10 lbs.	C-1362—1 set in carton, 16 lbs.
Set **$1.10**	Set **$1.50**
Consists of 4 cups, 4 saucers, 4 salad plates, serving plate, sugar bowl and creamer.	Consists of 6 cups, 6 saucers, 6 salad plates, serving plate, sugar bowl and creamer.

Reproduction from a 1932 Butler Brothers catalog.

CAMEO ENCRUSTATION — Another name for sulphide style paperweights. *See also SULPHIDE.*

CAMEO ENGRAVING — An engraving process whereby the background is carved away to leave the primary design in relief. Cameo glass may be produced in more than two layers. Cameo engraved glass originated in Egypt at the beginning of the first millennium. It was most popular by English and French makers during the late nineteenth and early twentieth century Art Nouveau movement. *See also RELIEF CUTTING.*

English cameo engraved glass.
Courtesy of the Corning Museum of Glass.

A collection of English cameo engraved glass. *Photo by Robin Rainwater. Courtesy of the Corning Museum of Glass.*

CAMPBELL, JONES AND COMPANY — An American pressed-glass making firm established in 1865 at Pittsburgh, Pennsylvania, by James Campbell, Jenkin Jones, John Davis, and John Loy. The men had purchased a failed plant that had been built by the Shepherd Company in 1863. In 1879, James Dalzell Jr. served as a foreign agent for the firm in Scotland. Campbell left in 1885, and the firm was reorganized as Jones, Cavitt & Company, Ltd. Jones served as president while A. M. Cavitt became treasurer and Harvey Wilson secretary. The firm primarily made pressed glass wares before a fire destroyed the plant in March 1891. The Thomas Evans Company, a blown glass manufacturer, purchased the property and what was left of the structures in June 1891.

CAMPBELL, THOMAS B. AND COMPANY — An American cut glass firm founded by Thomas B. Campbell in 1905 in Brooklyn, New York; Campbell moved operations to Manhattan in 1913 and continued to produce cut glass products until 1918.

CAMPHENE LAMP — An early nineteenth century oil lamp that used camphene (a cheaper mixture of turpentine and alcohol) as the primary fuel source. Although camphene produced a brighter light, it was highly explosive; so burners had longer wick tubes as opposed to whale oil burners. Caps were often attached to the burners on chains of camphene lamps to snuff out the flame.

CAMPHOR GLASS —A nearly opaque, somewhat cloudy white, pressed glass produced in America in the nineteenth century by treating an object with hydrofluoric acid. *See also FROSTED GLASS.*

CANADIAN GLASS — General term for glassware made in Canada since the early nineteenth century, the first operations were established in 1825 at Mallorytown, Ontario. Glassware produced included blown vessels and containers. Others followed and a wide variety of mostly pressed glass, along with some limited amounts of art and cut glass, were made by Canadian glass companies. Canadian firms tended to follow the trends set by European and American glassmakers throughout the nineteenth and twentieth centuries. *See also DOMINION GLASS COMPANY, GOWANS, KENT AND COMPANY, GUNDY-CLAPPERTON, JEFFERSON GLASS COMPANY, LAKEFIELD CUT GLASS COMPANY, MALLORYTOWN GLASS WORKS, and RODEN BROTHERS.*

Reproduction of an early 20th century Dominion Glass Company catalog.

CANARY YELLOW — A bright yellow-colored glass similar to amber-colored glass (also made with various amounts of iron, carbon, and sulfur). In the early twentieth century, Pairpoint produced an Art Glass style they named "Canaria," which was characterized by a bright yellow hue (like canary) that was further colored with light green tints as in Vaseline glass.

CANDELABRA OR CANDELABRUM — A branched candlestick with two or more sockets that are utilized for holding candles. Most were made in matching pairs. Also note that the candle socket is sometimes referred to as a candle nozzle.

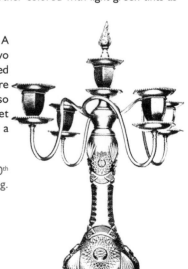

Reproduction from an early 20th century J.D. Bergen catalog.

CANDLE CHANDELIER — A chandelier that uses candles as the primary source of light, they were popular prior to the invention of gas and electric lights. *See also* CHANDELIER.

CANDLE COVER — Refer to SHADE.

CANDLEHOLDER — A small glass tumbler-like vessel designed to hold candles of 2-inch diameter or smaller.

CANDLESTICK — A raised glass object with one socket for holding a single candle. Like Candelabra, candlesticks usually are produced in matching pairs.

Fenton hobnail patterned milk glass candlesticks.
Photo by Robin Rainwater.

CANDLETTE — A small bowl-like glass object with one socket designed for holding a single candle.

CANDLEWICK — A style of glass decoration characterized by crystal drop beading around the edges, feet, handles, stems, stoppers/finials, and other trim areas of objects. Imperial was noted most for a huge lime of tableware in this design that was produced from 1936 to 1982. The name of the pattern derives from American pioneer women since the basic design resembles tufted needlework made centuries earlier.

Reproduction of 1940s Imperial Glass Company advertisement.

IMPERIAL GLASS CORPORATION, BELLAIRE, OHIO

IMPERIAL CANDLEWICK, CUT. No. 108

Reproduction of 1940s Imperial Glass Company advertisement.

CANDY — A name for a scrambled, brightly colored millefiori paperweight, Venetians also created small colorful glass sculptures in the shape of wrapped candy often with twists.

CANDY DISH — An open shallow bowl-like glass receptacle with cover used for serving candy. Candy dishes may or may not be footed.

Candy dishes from the Viking Glass Company. *Photo by Robin Rainwater.*

Venetian glass candy in a Fenton Emerald Crest milk glass candy dish. *Photo by Robin Rainwater.*

CANDY JAR — A tall wide mouthed glass receptacle with cover used for serving candy. Like candy dishes, candy jars may or may not be footed.

Depression green glass crackle-style candy jar. *Photo by Robin Rainwater.*

CANDY STRIPES — Hand-made glass marbles containing spirals or swirls. *See also LUTZ GLASS and MARBLE.*

CANE — (1) A cylindrical piece or stick of glass used either for stems of drinking glasses or in paperweight making, canes are often made up of many colored glass rods, and, when cut up into tiny slices or cross-sectional pieces, florets are used for producing millefiori paperweights. Note that canes may be of a single color or composites of two or more colored canes that have been fused together into a single unit. (2) A cylindrically-shaped walking stick from about three to four feet in length that usually contains a knobbed or curled end for grasping with one's hand. Glass canes are generally made as delicate whimsical objects that are more suited for decoration/display rather than for practical use.

CANNING JAR — A glass vessel, usually rounded or somewhat cylindrically-shaped (though other shapes like squares do exist), used for preserving fruits, vegetables, and meats. Canning jars usually come in standard measurement sizes such as 1/2-pint, pint, quart (the most common), 2-quart, and gallon.

During the latter half of the nineteenth century, it is estimated that hundreds of manufacturers designed nearly 5,000 styles of jars. Originally containing pressed glass necks and lids that were held in place by a wax seal or wire bail, later models supported screw on bands and lids made of zinc and then brass or tin. Canning jars are also commonly referred to as "Fruit" or "Mason" Jars.

Canning Jar with pressed glass lid and bail. *Photo by Robin Rainwater.*

CANTIR OR CANTARO — A style of jug originating in Spain that is characterized by a squat ovoid body, a vertical ring handle at the top for carrying, and two spouts (1 narrow for pouring and 1 wide for filling).

CANTON GLASS COMPANY — An American company established a Canton, Ohio, in 1883 by Joseph Brown, David Barker, and other associates. Glass production began in 1885 when the firm leased the Sippo Valley Glass factory located in Massillon, Ohio. Canton left the same year, moving all equipment to its Canton, Ohio, facility. Brown left in 1888 and was succeeded by Charles Bockius. In 1890, fire destroyed the Canton factory and operations were moved temporarily to a vacant factory previously operated by the Beaver Falls Glass Company in Beaver Falls, Pennsylvania. The firm permanently moved to Marion, Indiana, in 1894 when their new factory was complete. Canton was noted for making pressed glass tableware in crystal and color, clear glass condiment containers, glass skylights, and some novelty items including a few glass coffins that were guaranteed to be air-tight. They joined the National Glass Company in 1899. The factory site was moved once again to Cambridge, Ohio, in 1902-03 as all equipment was removed form the Marion, Indiana, plant. Note that another short-lived Canton Glass Company was founded in Marion, Indiana, in 1902. The firm closed after a few short years of operation and the plant was eventually purchased by the Sinclair Glass Company; the equipment was taken to Sinclair's operation in Hartford City, Indiana.

CAP RING — A mold part in making pressed glass that rests on top of the base mold and surrounds the plunger, a cap ring helps center the plunger in order to control the flow of molten glass into the mold cavity.

CAPE COD GLASS WORKS — Established in 1858 by Deming Jarves and James Lloyd in Boston, Massachusetts, the firm produced pressed wares and art designs such as gold-ruby, PEACH BLOW, and SANDWICH ALABASTER up until Jarves' death in 1869.

CAPE COD PATTERN — A mold-pressed sandwich-style of pattern glass characterized by an all-over pattern of small dots that are present in mold. The dots serve as the background for other designs such as floral patterns, foliage, and scrolling. Many Cape Cod patterns have been produced sine the nineteenth century; including one during America's Great Depression by the Imperial Glass Company, and more recently, a huge ruby red pattern produced by Wheaton for Avon (discontinued in 1997).

A Ruby red Cape Cod patterned bowl; an Avon commission for Wheaton Industries. *Photos by Robin Rainwater.*

CAPEWELL & BROTHERS — Refer to the EXCELSIOR GLASS WORKS.

CAPRI — A large pattern of machine pressed tableware produced by Hazel Ware (Division of Continental Can) in the 1960s, pieces were primarily made in a light coppery blue color that the company referred to as "Azure Blue." Pieces generally contain a straight-edged geometrical base (square, pentagon, hexagon, or octagon); however, since Capri really refers more to the color than a pattern, a wide variety of straight and swirled designs were produced in it. Patterns include ALPINE, COLONIAL, SWIRL COLONIAL, and SEASHELL.

CAPSTAN GLASS COMPANY — Refer to RIPLEY & COMPANY.

CARAFE — A large glass bottle with a stopper used for serving beverages (usually water or wine). Some carafes contained tumblers that rested upside down as stoppers. *See also TUMBLE-UP.*

Reproduction from an early 20th century Higgins-Seiter catalog.

CARAMEL SLAG GLASS — A style of glass characterized by colorful tan and brown swirling or marbleized designs. Note that chocolate-colored glass is sometimes confused with caramel slag; however, the two are made differently as chocolate is not true slag glass. *See also CHOCOLATE GLASS and SLAG GLASS.*

CARBON — A common nonmetallic dark or black-colored element found as a constituent of coal, petroleum, asphalt, limestone, and so on. In its powdered form, carbon is added in a batch of glass to aid in producing colors between light yellow and dark amber. Carbon also occurs naturally as diamonds, graphite, and in most life forms.

CARBORUNDUM — A man-made stone that is second only to diamonds in hardness. It is produced by heating sand and carbon together in an electric resistance furnace. Revolving wheels made of carborundum proved to be superior to iron and regular stone in the glass cutting/engraving process. *See also "Wheel Cutting."*

CARD TRAY — A flat glass object, usually rectangular in shape, with possibly a center handle and two separate sections, used for holding standard-size playing cards.

CARDER, FREDERICK — A famous glass maker, designer, and producer from Stourbridge, England, Carder (1863-1963) studied art glass styles with Galle and served as a designer for Stevens & Williams before migrating to America in 1903. Carder founded the Steuben Glass Company in 1903 and was responsible for most of the factory's production, including the creation of a wide variety of art styles and unique colors up until his retirement in 1933. They include Antique Green, Aurene, Bristol Yellow, Bubbly, Cardinal Red, Celeste Blue, Cerise Ruby, Cluthra, Cyprian, Diatreta, Flemish Blue, Florentine, French Blue, Intarsia, Ivrene, Moonlight, Moresque, Orchid, Plum Jade, Pomona Green, Quartz, Rosa, Rosaline, Rouge Flambe, Tyrian, and Verre-de-Soie.

Various Frederick Carder signatures for the Steuben Glass Works.

CARDINAL RED — An off-colored strawberry red transparent opalescent colored Art Glass style created and named by Steuben in the early twentieth century.

CARLSON, WILLIAM — A noted American Studio Glass artisan born in Dover, Ohio, in 1950, Carlson received his Master of Fine Arts degree from Alfred University and served as Head of the University of Illinois' glass program beginning in 1976. Carlson lives in Urbana, Illinois, where he runs his own small glass studio.

CARNIVAL GLASS — Pressed glassware with a fired-on iridescent finish made primarily in the Untied Sates from 1905-1925 (reproductions were produced later beginning in the 1960s). The finish has been sometimes referred to as resembling oil on water. A few other countries like England and Australia produced some limited Carnival glass. The name was derived from fairs or carnivals since it was often given away as a prize.

Dugan Carnival Glass Question Marks' patterned plate and a Fern patterned pitcher and tumbler. *Photos by Robin Rainwater. Courtesy of the Fenton Art Glass Museum.*

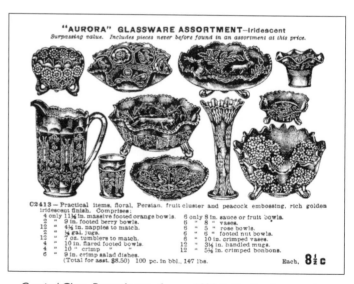

Carnival Glass. Reproduction from a 1920 Butler Brothers catalog.

Fenton Carnival Glass Peacock and Grape patterned plate. *Photo courtesy of the Henry Ford Museum.*

Millersburg Carnival Glass Trout and Fly patterned bowl. *Photo by Robin Rainwater. Courtesy of the Fenton Art Glass Museum.*

CARPET — A condensely arranged set of canes that forms the internal bottom, base, or background of a paperweight, mostly used in millefiori designs.

CARRE, JEAN — A French immigrant who came to England in 1567 during the reign of Queen Elizabeth, Carre managed the Crutched Friars Glass Works and, in 1571, was able to import six men from Antwerp who were skilled in Venetian glass-making techniques. Carre died in 1572; however, Giacomo Verzelini resumed supervision of the workers and successful glass-making in England had its beginnings here.

CARVING — The removal of glass from the surface of an object by means of sharp, precision hand-held tools.

CASCADE GLASS WORKS — Refer to KING, SON & COMPANY.

CASED GLASS — Glass that is blown in multiple layers of separate colors and then decorated by cutting away all parts of these layers. By cutting away the top layer(s), it would expose a contrasting base color, which is almost always transparent. Cased multiple-colored glass was most popular during the nineteenth century Art Nouveau period and is sometimes referred to as PLATED GLASS. *See also* CAMEO ENGRAVING.

A colection of Cased Glass bowls and vases by Val St. Lambert.

CASING — The process of creating cased glass, originally it was produced by applying a layer of clear glass over a contrasting color. After a vessel is cooled and/or annealed, the upper layer is then cut in relief to produce cameo glass.

CASSEROLE DISH — A deep round, oblong, or square dish, with or without cover, handles, or tabs, used to bake as well as serve food.

Covered glass casserole dish. *Photo by Robin Rainwater.*

CAST GLASS — Glass made in simple molds and then surface-ground with polishing wheels fed by abrasives. The ancient Egyptians were producing cast glass around simple sand or clay molds nearly 3,000 years ago. Certain styles of Art Glass are still being cast today around molds made of sand or metal.

CASTER OR CASTOR — (1) A glass bottle or cruet used for holding a condiment; (2) A small object with an indentation that is set under a piece of furniture to protect the floor or carpet surface below. The legs of the furniture fit into the indented or recessed area within the caster. Note that glass casters do not have swivels or wheels for moving like standard centers. *See also* CASTER OR CASTOR BOTTLE.

CASTER OR CASTOR BOTTLE — A glass container with a narrow neck and mouth, which may or may not have a handle, Castor bottles usually have a perforated or squirt top necessary for dispensing spices, salt, or other condiments in wither dry or liquid form (i.e. vinegar, oil, etc.).

CASTOR JAR — A fairly wide-mouthed container of various shapes and sizes that were used to hold a variety of substances, usually foods like pickles, fruits, etc. Jars vary greatly in size and shape and generally do not contain handles or necks, but do ordinarily have covers or lids. Castor jars were popular in the mid-to-late nineteenth century as a table accessory and were often placed in metal holders that may have had a top handle.

CASTOR SET — A set of glass serving objects held on glass or metal trays, these objects might include small pitchers, cruets, bottles, small jars, salt and pepper shakers, and other fairly small serving dishes. Castor sets are also referred to as CONDIMENT SETS.

A Burmese caster set by Mount Washington.
Items courtesy of the Corning Museum of Glass.

CAT EYE — A style of machine-made glass marble made in Japan that was introduced in America in the early 1950s. It is characterized by a central colored vane or small ellipsoid that resembles a cat's contracted pupil, which in turn is set within a transparent sphere.

CATE, NORMAN S. & COMPANY — Refer to the BAY STATE GLASS COMPANY.

CATHEDRAL — A pressed glass pattern consisting of arched panels that are usually decorated by a pressed diamond design within the arches (made to resemble a cathedral window). Diamond bands are usually present too, at the top/bottom of objects in this pattern.

CATHEDRAL GLASS — A single sheet (monochromatic) of transparent colored glass that is usually smooth on both sides, but may be textured on one or both. Slabs of cathedral glass, at least 1" in thickness, are sometimes referred to as DALLES. Two or more cathedral glasses mixed together to create a multicolored sheet are referred to as STREAKY GLASS.

CATSPAW — A surface texture achieved in glass by chilling molten glass on a cool table, the final appearance resembles those of the paw prints of a cat.

CAVAN CRYSTAL — An Irish firm established in 1969 at Cavan, Ireland, the company is most noted as a producer of hand-made crystal stemware, tableware, and novelty items. The firm is still in operation today.

CELERY DISH — A long flat or shallow narrow dish, usually oval in design and used for serving celery, they are also referred to as CELERY TRAYS. A few odd celery dishes have been produced in tall cylindrical shapes (CELERY VASES).

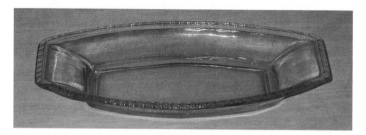

Cambridge Glass celery dish. *Photo by Robin Rainwater.*

No. 23Y. Dixie Celery Tray. 11 in. Each. $6.50

Reproduction from a late 19th century Higgins-Seiter catalog.

CELERY TRAY — Refer to CELERY DISH.

CELERY VASE — A tall glass receptacle resembling a vase used for serving upright stalks or celery. Most were made in the eighteenth and nineteenth centuries in pressed cylindrical form and may or may not be stemmed and footed.

Reproduction from an 1891 U.S. Glass Company catalog.

339 Celery Decorated. №25

CELESTE BLUE — An iridized light shade of blue Art Glass created and named by Steuben in the early twentieth century.

CENEDESE, GINO — A Venetian glass artisan who founded a glass operation in 1945 on the island of Murano, Cenedese (1907-1973) is most noted for his ornamental glass and tableware with a variety of special surface effects, including vetro scavo (a rough gray matte surface finish splashed with a wide variety of color effects). When Cenedese passed away, the firm became known as Cenedese and Figlio, as Gino's son Amelio (b.1946) became active in the firm. Today, the firm employs over one hundred workers and is one of the largest on the island of Murano.

CENTERPIECE — A large circular or oval fancy glass bowl, or other ornate object, used as an adornment in the center of a table. Some contain under plates or stands. Some are used to serve foods such as fruits. See also FRUIT BOWL and ORANGE BOWL.

Baccarat camel centerpiece.

The Central Glass Works

Reproduction from an 1890s Central Glass Company catalog.

CENTRAL CITY GLASS COMPANY — Refer to the HUNTINGTON GLASS COMPANY.

CENTRAL CUT GLASS COMPANY — An American firm established in 1906 at Chicago, Illinois, by Swedish immigrant Herman Roseen and Andrew Swanson. A new factory was built in 1909 at Walkerton, Indiana, and that is where most of the production took place (the company's sales office and original factory remained in Chicago). The firm produced cut glass until a fire destroyed the Walkerton factory in 1918; the plant was not rebuilt. The company remained in business in Chicago, but most cut glass production ended. In 1925, the firm's name was changed to ROSEEN & COLLINS, which produced some engraved glassware until closing permanently in 1932.

CENTRAL GLASS COMPANY — (1) An American pressed glass-making firm established in 1863 at Wheeling, West Virginia, by John Oesterling, Roy Combs, Andrew Baggs, William Elson, Henry James Leasure, Peter Cassell, and John Henderson — all of them former dissatisfied workers of Barnes, Hobbs & Company. The original name of the firm was Oesterling & Hall. In 1864, it was renamed Oesterling & Henderson Company, Oesterling & Company, and the Central Glassworks. In 1867, it was finally reorganized simply as the Central Glass Company. Central was noted most for pressed patterns, especially Art "Coin Glass," and was one of the first company's to develop popular colors of the Depression era. Central became part of the U.S. Glass Company in 1891 as Factory O. The plant was shut down by U.S. Glass in 1893; and then purchased by Nathan Scott and others in 1895. Pressed glass production resumed under the Central name until the factory closed permanently in 1939. Note that because of its location in Wheeling, the firm was also known as the EAST WHEELING GLASS WORKS. In 1939-40, the Imperial Glass Company acquired many of the firm's molds. (2) There was another smaller pressed glass-making firm located in Summitsville, Indiana, that also sported the name CENTRAL GLASS COMPANY. This firm was established in 1892 primarily by Christian Sigelen, William & Ralph Alford, and Robert Thomas and produced pressed glass tableware. It became part of the National Glass Company conglomerate in 1899. National closed the plant in 1901.

Central Glass Company coin glass and novelties.
Courtesy of the Corning Museum of Glass.

CENTRAL GLASS WORKS — The firm was established as a cooperative in 1863 by workmen from the J. H. HOBBS, BROCKUNIER AND COMPANY at Wheeling, West Virginia, (originally as the Oesterling, Henderson and Company). It failed and was reorganized three years later as the Central Glass Company. See also CENTRAL GLASS COMPANY.

CERISE RUBY — A deep cranberry red style of Art Glass created and named by Steuben in the early twentieth century.

CESKY KRISTAL — A Czechoslovakian firm founded in 1891 by C. Stolze & Sohne at Chlum u Trebone, the company initially produced pressed and blown glassware, but closed in 1910 because of financial difficulties. It was reopened in 1919 by Vaclav Hrdina producing traditional Bohemian cut/enameled glassware. Like all Czech firms, it became part of the state in 1948. It was eventually absorbed by the conglomerate Crystalex, but turned independent in 1993. Today it operates as the Sumava Glassworks.

CHADE MONOGRAM GLASS COMPANY — An American firm founded in 1930 at Valparaiso, Indiana, by Charles Gilliland, the company produced some cut and engraved glass into the early 1940s.

CHAIN — Glass threads formed or applied to objects in interconnected links or rings. Chain is a common decorative add-on in pressed glass that has been combined with many other designs, including chain and shield, chain thumbprints, and chain with star.

CHAIR — An object that serves as the master glassblower's work seat or bench; the blower sits and rolls the blow-pipe or pontil back and forth on the flat extended arms of the chair while working the glass with a tool held in his/her other hand. Specialized chairs date back to the Venetians in the early seventeenth century; in the sixteenth century, Venetians simply used boards strapped to the glass-blower's thighs. *See also* GAFFER.

CHALCEDONY — An opaque style of glass resembling the semi-precious stone of the same name, Chalcedony is a type of agate or translucent quartz that is commonly pale blue or gray with a wax-like luster. In Italy, it is spelled as "Calcedonio" and glassware made in this style was first produced on the island or Murano in the late fifteenth century.

CHALICE — A fancy drinking vessel with a large rounded bowl of various sizes and shapes that may or may not be stemmed. Chalices were originally designed for sacramental use in churches. The German term for chalice is "Kelch."

CHALK GLASS — A colorless glass containing powdered chalk as the primary ingredient, it was developed in Bohemia in the late seventeenth century for making think vessels, which in turn, were then engraved or enameled.

CHALLINOR, HOGAN AND COMPANY — An American pressed glass-making firm established by David Challinor and Edward Hogan at Pittsburgh, Pennsylvania, in 1864. Challinor had worked for several firms, including BAKEWELL & PEARS AND DITHRIDGE, before establishing his own. The two partners purchased the Pittsburgh Glass Manufacturing Company. Hogan moved on after two short years and David Taylor purchased his interest. *See also* CHALLINOR, TAYLOR, & COMPANY, LTD.

CHALLINOR, TAYLOR & COMPANY, LTD. — An American firm founded in 1866 by David Challinor and David Taylor at Pittsburgh, Pennsylvania, Challinor, along with Edward Hogan, had purchased the PITTSBURGH GLASS MANUFACTURING COMPANY in 1864. The company moved to Tarentum, Pennsylvania, in 1884 and produced pressed glass, opaque (including milk glass) and colored glass, lamps, novelties, and some slag glass (Challinor received a patent in 1886 for his unique style of slag glass referred to as MOSAIC GLASS). In 1885, the plant itself was known as the STANDARD GLASS WORKS. The firm became part of the U.S. Standard Glass Works in 1891 as Factory C, but the plant was destroyed by fire in 1893. *See also* CHALLINOR, HOGAN AND COMPANY.

Covered milk glass duck dish by Challinor, Taylor & Company. *Courtesy of Wheaton Village.*

CHAMALEON-GLASS — Refer to LITHYALIN.

CHAMPAGNE BUCKET — A large rounded object used for chilling and holding champagne bottles. Ice is usually stored in the bottom and sides for chilling purposes. As with all glass buckets, champagne buckets may or may not have a handle, and typically taper outward at the top. *See also* BUCKET and WINE BUCKET.

Waterford crystal champagne bucket.

CHAMPAGNE GLASS — A tall glass goblet with foot and stem, along with a large round but shallow bowl.

Cut Glass Saucer—
Champagne.
Buzz Star Cutting.
No. 9533........$2.75 Each

Reproduction from an early 20th century S.F. Myers Company catalog.

CHAMPION AGATE COMPANY — An American marble-making firm founded in 1938 at Pennsboro, West Virginia, by Yucca Jones and Ralph Michels. In 1849, it was to Roy and Murphy Michels who continued to operate under the same name. The firm has been producing glass marbles continuously and is still part of the Michels family today.

CHANCE BROTHERS — An English firm founded in 1824 at West Smethwick by Robert Lucas Chance, who had previously served as manager of the Nailsea Glass Works and acquired British Crown Glass Company when he went into business for himself, the firm officially became Chance Brothers when his younger brother William joined it in 1832. Initially, the firm produced improved designs for window panes and was chosen to supply the Crystal Palace Exhibition in London in 1851. They expanded into optical including the production of giant lighthouse lenses. During World War I, they developed a version of heat-resistant glass and patented Orlak heat-resistant ovenware in 1929 (the rights were sold to James Jobling in 1933 for ovenware). The firm was sold to Pilkington Brothers in 1945, but glassware, including tableware, was produced under the Chance name until 1981 when the factory closed.

CHANDELIER — An ornate branched glass lighting fixture ordinarily suspended from a ceiling. Prior to the invention of gas and electric lighting fixtures, candles were used within the chandelier's sockets (sometimes called "Candle Chandeliers"). Other smaller versions of chandeliers with a limited number of sockets (around four or six) were used in the eighteenth and early nineteenth century as free-standing table units or "Table Chandeliers." Note that the word "Chandelier" is French for CANDLESTICK.

CHAPIN GLASS WORKS — An American firm established at Portland, Oregon, in 1981 by Michael Chapin, who completed a stained glass coursework at Mt. Hood Community College and then worked at his instructor's (Michael Pfieffer) studio before establishing his own company. Chapin specialized in decorative Art Glass including commercial applications (leaded stained and beveled glass, etched glass, and fused and slumped glass).

CHARACTER GLASS — A general term for cartoon, comic book characters, movie stars, and others who have been etched, enameled, transferred, or might contain fired-on decals upon glassware. They originated in 1937 when Libbey won a contract with Walt Disney to produce tumblers depicting *Snow White and the Seven Dwarfs*. The movie was a smash hit and eight separate tumblers with a picture of each little character (enameled upon the surface) were filled with cottage cheese and shipped to thousands of dairies across the country. The immense popularity of the "character" tumbler had its beginning here. Other food items included cheese spreads and jams and jellies. Since the 1970s, fast food restaurants, often with the backing of the soft drink industry, promote decorated tumblers far more than any other medium (usually Disney films). Note that their items are sometimes referred to as FAST-FOOD COLLECTIBLES and PROMOTIONAL GLASSWARE. *See also* SWANKY SWIGS.

Welch's jelly character glass tumbler from the Endangered Species Collection. *Photo by Robin Rainwater.*

Character Glass tumblers. *Photo by Robin Rainwater.*

CHARGE — The process of feeding raw materials into a pot or tank furnace.

CHARTREUSE — Yellowish-green colored opaque glass.

CHATTANOOGA GLASS COMPANY — An American firm founded at Chattanooga, Tennessee, in 1887 by R. G. Hutchinson & Associates, the plant was completed the following year and the company produced fruit jars and soda bottles for Coca-Cola. The firm was acquired by the Dorsey Corporation in 1959. Once glass bottles went out of fashion in the soda industry (1970s), Dorsey switched primarily to the production of plastics.

CHEATERS — Small whiskey tumblers with extremely thick glass bottoms and walls that were made to look as if they held more capacity than they actually did.

CHECK — A term for a crack in glass that occurs at a joint (i.e. where the stem connects to the base or bowl in a goblet, at the base of an applied handle or other applied form, and so forth). Checks are usually caused by unequal stress when the temperature difference between the body and the applied form is too great. It is also known as a Heat Check.

CHECKER OR CHECQUER — A paperweight resembling a checker or chess board, its usually flat, square-cut millefiori pieces from canes are scattered or spaced symmetrically by latticino twists of alternating or contrasting colors.

CHECKERBOARD — A common pressed glass pattern consisting of an all-over design of interlocking squares or rectangles. The design can be found in other categories of glass such as America's Carnival Depression glass patterns and cut glass.

CHECKERED DIAMOND — A cut design pattern with several small diamonds inscribed within one large one.

CHEESE AND CRACKER DISH — A serving dish with two levels (2-tiered); one for holding cheese or a cheese ball (usually the upper part), the other for crackers (the lower portion that surrounds the upper part).

Cut Glass Cheese and Cracker Dish. Floral Design.
No. 9316 . . . . $9.00 Each

Reproduced from a late 19th century Higgins-Seiter catalog.

CHEESE DISH — A glass dish, ordinarily flat or footed with a separate glass cover (usually domed-shaped), used for serving cheese. Note that cheese dishes are ordinarily slightly larger than dome-covered butter dishes.

CHERRY — A molded pressed glass pattern containing cherries, accompanied by some vines as its primary design (variations include scrolling, dots, panels, cables, wreaths, etc.), cherries are a popular motif in pressed, Carnival, Depression, and some cut/engraved glass.

CHESS SET — A game that features sixteen pieces for each of two opponents and an accompanying board (each side has eight pawns, two knights, two bishops, two rooks, a queen, and a king). Glass chess sets are often made as whimsical, one-of-a-kind objects; though mass-produced late twentieth century models sport one side with clear pieces, and the other with black or frosted glass pieces. The boards may contain mirrored glass finishes as well.

Glass chess set with crystal and frosted pieces and glass-mirrored board. *Photo by Robin Rainwater.*

CHEVRON — A decorating style in the form of an inverted "V," usually in a repetitive series like a zigzag pattern.

CHICAGO FLINT & LIME GLASS COMPANY — An American firm founded at Chestertown, Indiana, by James Hastings, Charles Murphy, and Louis McCall, the company produced some pressed glass tableware, especially nappies, before ceasing production in 1906.

CHIGGER BITE — A small chip or nick in a piece of glass.

CHIHULY, DALE — Known as America's greatest glass artisan of the latter twentieth century, Chihuly began producing art glass objects in 1964. He studied at the University of Washington, the University of Wisconsin, the Rhode Island School of Design (where he established a glass department and taught until 1983), and at the Venini Glass Factory on the island of Murano in Venice, Italy (1968). He later opened his own studio in Seattle, Washington, and founded the Pilchuk Glass Center at Stanwood, Washington, in 1971. As an artisan, he is noted most for monstrous, multicolored opalescent objects, including huge spheres, massive bowls, chandeliers, and flamboyant seaforms. Chihuly has won a number of awards. Frequent tours, as well as permanent collections, of his creations can be found in museums worldwide, including New York's Modern Museum of Art, the Louvre in Paris, and the Victorian and Albert Museum in London.

Chihuly Art Glass basket group.
Courtesy of the Corning Museum of Glass.

CHILLER — A two-piece unit consisting of a globe shaped bowl and a cone-shaped glass vessel that rests within the bowl. The bowl is usually filled with ice while the cone-shaped insert is filled with alcoholic beverages or foods like caviar that are best served cold or chilled (hence the name "chiller").

CHIMNEY — A cylindrically-shaped glass tube, open at both ends, used to shield the flame of an oil lamp, trap soot, and increase the draft.

CHINESE GLASS — General term for glass products made in China from as early as the fourth century B.C. Glassware in China was often made to resemble the more desirable porcelain. Glass was considered inferior and only an imitation by the Chinese; however, they experimented with opaque glassware including cameo designs in the late seventeenth century. Glass items made in China in some quantity include vases and snuff bottles. Note that Art-styled glass once made for the Imperial Court is referred to as "Kuan Liao." *See also* PEKING GLASS.

A reverse painted Chinese glass rose bowl. *Photo by Robin Rainwater.*

CHINTZ — (1) A style of glass patented by A. Douglas Nash, who developed it while working for Tiffany. It was characterized by colored ribbed, striped, or swirled glass marveled into opaque, opalescent, and transparent glass. The process was expensive and difficult since the separate colors often ran together. (2) From the 1940s–1970s, Fostoria produced an all-over crystal floral pattern that it named "Chintz." It was also known as Fostoria's "#338 Line" and was made in a good deal of tableware and stemware. (3) Consolidated also patented a line of Art Glass in the 1920s that they named "Chintz."

CHOCOLATE GLASS — A variegated opaque glass that shades from dark brown to light tan. It was first developed by Jacob Rosenthal, who worked at the Indiana Tumbler and Goblet Company in the 1890s. Rosenthal combined cryolite with manganese to produce the desired color. It is sometimes referred to erroneously as "Caramel Slag" and was made by others such as Fenton. *See also* CARAMEL SLAG GLASS *and* INDIANA TUMBLER & GOBLET COMPANY.

Chocolate Glass bowl by the Indiana Tumbler & Goblet Company. *Courtesy of Wheaton Village.*

Fenton Chocolate Art Glass. *Photo by Robin Rainwater. Items courtesy of the Fenton Art Glass Museum.*

CHOCOLATE POT — A pear-shaped or cylindrical receptacle, with handle and cover, used for serving hot chocolate. Most contain a long spout that is placed at a right angle to the handle. Most were made of porcelain or silver; however, glass chocolate pots were also made in the nineteenth century.

CHOISY-LE-ROI — Refer to ETLING GLASS.

CHOP PLATE — A large flat glass serving dish, usually round or oval in shape, used for serving food. A chop plate serves the same function as a platter, tray, or salver.

CHOPE — A large French-styled tumbler similar to that of the German humpen. See also HUMPEN.

CHOUFLEUR — A French term for cauliflower, it is a ground in paperweights made up of canes and loosely set with a twist.

CHRISTENSEN AGATE COMPANY — An American marble-making firm founded in 1925 at Payne, Ohio, by H. H. Cupler, Beulah Hartman, W. F. Jones, Owen Roderick, and Robert Ryder. Marble production began in 1927 when a plant was built in Cambridge, Ohio, and ended when the firm went out of business in 1933.

CHRISTENSEN, M. F. GLASS COMPANY — An American marble-making firm founded by Martin F. Christensen at Steubenville, Ohio, in 1905; Christensen received a patent for a marble-making machine in 1905 and went into business for himself by purchasing the factory of the failed Navarre Glass Marble and Specialty Company. Christensen's firm closed in 1917 and he passed away in 1920. Note that Martin F. Christensen had no involvement nor did his family in another Ohio marble-making firm that bears his name. See also CHRISTENSEN AGATE COMPANY.

CHRISTMAS ORNAMENT — A fairly small glass object designed for hanging and displaying on a Christmas tree. Fancy crystal and colored ornaments have been produced by such noted firms as Waterford, Baccarat, Steuben, Orrefors, and Lenox. A good deal of spun glass ornaments have been made by individual artists and are also mass-produced in both China and Taiwan.

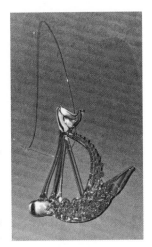

Sailing ship spun glass Christmas ornament. *Photo by Robin Rainwater.*

CHROMIUM — A bluish-white metal that, when oxidized (chromium oxide) and mixed in a batch of glass, produced a yellowish-green color or green color depending on the quantity used. Chromium is also combined with iron to produce a blue color, with copper to make sea-green, and is used in some quantity to produce AVENTURINE GLASS.

CHRYSANTHEMUM — A curved and split star-like design (usually a 20-point star) found in cut glass. The original was designed by the cut glass firm of T. G. Hawkes, who won the Grand International prize for cut glass at the Paris Exposition in 1889. The style was later copied by others such as Libbey.

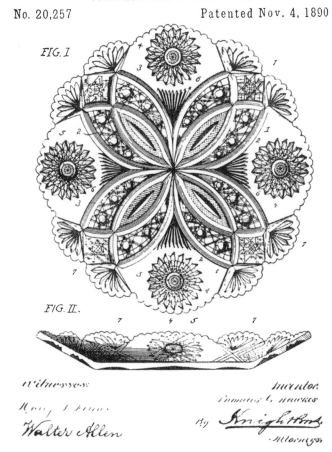

T. G. HAWKES
ORNAMENTATION OF GLASSWARE.

No. 20,257   Patented Nov. 4, 1890

FIG. I

FIG. II.

Reproduction from an 1890 T. G. Hawkes U.S. patent.

CHRYSOPRAS — A style of Art Glass created by the Mount Washington Glass Works in the 1890s, it is characterized by marbleized brown streaking. The style of glass was continued by Pairpoint, who purchased Mt. Washington in 1894.

CHRYSOPRASE — An apple-green color. See also GREEN GLASS.

CHUNKED — Glass that has been heavily damaged usually through cracking, serious chipping, or is just considerably worn.

CICERO GLASS COMPANY — Refer to the BARTLETT-COLLINS GLASS COMPANY.

CIGAR JAR — A large, wide mouthed glass canister, with a cover, used for holding and storing cigars and/or tobacco. See also HUMIDOR.

CIGARETTE BOX — A small covered glass receptacle designed to hold a single standard pack of cigarettes.

CIGARETTE HOLDER — A flat glass dish or ash tray, containing notches, used for holding cigarettes (may or may not have a cover).

CIGARETTE JAR OR URN — A small, wide-mouthed glass canister, with cover, used for holding and storing cigarettes.

CINERARY URN — Refer to URN.

C

CINTRA — A style of art glass developed by Frederick Carder of Steuben in the early 1910s. It was produced by coating a glass object with finely-sifted powdered colored glass, and then further coating the object with a thin layer of crystal embed the fused particles. Most objects were made in vertical strips of two separate alternating colors and may or may not contain controlled bubbling.

CINQUEFOIL — A garland of canes in a paperweight that has five loops.

CIRCLETS — Small circles of millefiori canes in paperweights.

CIRE PERDUE — A French term meaning "Lost Wax," the lost wax process was originally invented for bronze-casting, but was later adapted to glass-making. Under this technique, a model is carved in wax, encased in a mold, and then heated to melt off the wax. The mold is then filled with molten glass. Rene Lalique and Frederick Carder were the most noted glass artisans to utilize this technique.

A 1926 Cire Perdue (lost wax) bowl by Lalique.
Photo courtesy of the Corning Museum of Glass.

CISTERN — A large circular basin or oval receptacle used to hold a quantity of water. Glass cisterns were first made in Venice as early as the sixteenth century.

CITIZENS GLASS COMPANY — Refer to the EVANSVILLE GLASS COMPANY.

CLAMBROTH OR CLAM BROTH — Grayish-colored, semi-transparent glass, in Carnival Glass, clambroth is an iridized pastel color often compared to ginger-ale. The name was derived from the color of the broth produced by boiling clams. Clambroth is also sometimes called "Clam Water" or "White Translucent."

CLAMP — A tool used in place of a pontil to hold a blown glass vessel at its closed end while the open end is being shaped (usually avoids leaving a pontil mark).

CLAPPER — A tool with two wood arms joined at one end by a curved leather hinge. There is usually a small protrusion on one arm designed to fit around the stem of a glass. Clappers are used primarily to form a foot from a blob of molten glass.

CLAPPERTON & SONS — Refer to GUNDY-CLAPPERTON.

CLARET GLASS — A tall glass with foot and stem, along with a large round deep bowl, specifically designed for serving claret (red) wine. Claret glasses are very similar to standard wine glasses, but tend to have a narrower bowl that is flared at the top and a shorter stem.

Cut Glass Claret.
Buzz Star Cutting.
No. 95|35......$2.45 Each

Reproduction from an early twentieth century S. F. Myers Company catalog.

CLARK BROTHERS GLASS MANUFACTURING COMPANY — An American glass firm founded at Blairsville, Pennsylvania, in 1891 by Peter, Charles, and Frank Clark, the glass operation was actually a subsidiary of the Clarks' New Jersey business, the Clark Brothers Lamp, Brass and Copper Company. In 1898, they purchased a plant in Ellwood City, Pennsylvania, that was previously occupied by Northwood and moved glass operations there. The firm produced glass lamp chimneys and some pressed glass tableware before going bankrupt in 1904.

CLARK, T. B. & COMPANY — An American firm established in Honesdale, Pennsylvania, in 1884 by Thomas Byron Clark, the company was first known as Hatch & Clark and then as Clark & Wood before becoming T. B. Clark & Company in 1886. Wood remained on as an employee of Clark. The firm cut high quality lead crystal blanks provided by Dorflinger, and became one of the most successful cut glass companies up until the time they closed in 1930. Clark had also purchased the Maple Leaf Glass Company in the early 1920s; and he and Wood established the Wayne Silver Company (also in Honesdale) in 1895 to produce silver mounting for their glassware.

Reproduction from a 1908 *Good Housekeeping* advertisement.

Clark, T. B. & Company Trademark.

CLASSIC PERIOD — The height of paperweight production in France from the early-to-mid 1840s up until 1860.

CLAW-BEAKER — A glass drinking vessel, usually somewhat conically-shaped (tapers in at the bottom and out at the top), that contains several applied claw-shaped protrusions. Claw-beakers date back to the fifth century in Germany.

CLAY POT — Refer to POT.

CLEAR — Crystal or lightly colored glass that transmits light without appreciable scattering so that the objects lying beyond are clearly visible (as opposed to Translucent and Opaque). Clear glass is also referred to as TRANSPARENT.

CLEAR GROUND — A term used in paperweights and other objects to denote a crystal or clear base and/or background.

CLICHY — A famous French glass-making town (suburb of Paris) that was noted most for paperweight production beginning in the 1840s and lasting into the 1870s. The first Clichy glasshouse opened in 1839 by M. Roiuyer and G. Maes (Rouyer & Maes had founded an operation in 1837 at Pont-de-Sevres, but moved it to Clichy two years later). The factory was sold in 1885 as the popularity for paperweights declined. When the popularity of paperweights rose once again in the latter twentieth century, paperweights production resurfaced in the Clichy area. Note that the highly regarded "Clichy Rose" style of paperweight is one made from a slice of cane to resemble an open rose bloom.

An 1845-1850 Clichy, France, Millefiori vase. *Photo by Robin Rainwater. Item courtesy of the Corning Museum of Glass.*

CLINTON CUT GLASS COMPANY — An American firm established at Aldenville, Pennsylvania, in 1905, the company produced cut glass tableware until selling out to the Elite Cut Glass Company in 1918. *See also* ELITE CUT GLASS COMPANY.

CLOSE CONCENTRIC — A spacing pattern in millefiori paperweights that consists of tightly packed concentric circles of canes.

CLOSE-PACK MILLEFIORI — Millefiori pieces packed as closely together as possible within a paperweight.

CLOSED HANDLES — Refer to TAB HANDLES.

CLOUD GLASS — A style of Art Glass created in 1922 by the English firm of Davidson's Glassworks in Gateshead, it is made by adding a small amount if dark colored glass to a lighter batch of molten colored glass at the last minute, prior to being pressed into a mold. The result is an object that contains a unique pattern of cloud-like streaks. The style was made in a wide variety of geometrical and art-deco designs with various color effects (mostly amber, blue, brown, green, orange, and purple; though rare red and gray versions exist).

CLOVER CUT — Intersecting surface-cut facets in paperweights first made by the New England Glass Company.

CLUSTER — A collection or gathering of similar canes used in making millefiori paperweights.

CLUTHA GLASS — A style of art glass patented in the 1890s by the firm of James Couper & Sons of Glasgow, Scotland, it is characterized by a somewhat greenish color mixed with yellow, brown, black or turquoise, pink and white streaking, specks of aventurine, and controlled embedded bubbling.

CLUTHRA — An Art Glass form developed by Frederick Carder of Steuben in 1920, it is characterized by a cloudy opaque design permeated by various-sized bubbles, some quite large. Offshoots of the basic design were produced by others such as Kimble.

CLYDE GLASS WORKS — An American glass company founded at Clyde, New York, in 1864 by Orrin Southwick and Almon Woods, the firm produced blown glass fruit jars as well as pressed glass necks and lids for the jars. The firm was taken over by Southwick, Reed & Company in 1868 and then, in 1870, by the Consolidated Fruit Jar Company, which ceased operations in 1882.

COACHING GLASS — A small drinking glass developed in England around 1800 that has no foot. They are also referred to as a "Fuddling Glass."

COASTER — A very shallow or flat container used to place other glass objects on (such as tumblers) to protect the surface beneath it (i.e. tabletops, counters, etc.). Coasters originated in the mid-eighteenth century in England and are usually circular in shape.

COBALT BLUE — Cobalt is a silver white metallic element that, when oxidized (cobalt oxide or CoO), turns somewhat into a steel-gray or bluish-black powder. When this powder is added to a batch of glass, it produces the most powerful deep dark blue color. When cobalt is combined with oxides of lead and antimony, it will produce a deep green color.

Baccarat cobalt blue egg and emerald green shell. *Photo by Robin Rainwater.*

C

COCA-COLA — The originator of the soft drink was John Pemberton, a pharmacist from Atlanta, Georgia, who patented a medicine in 1886 to relieve headaches, stomach disorders, and other minor maladies. In 1888, Pemberton sold his interest to Asa G. Chandler, who improved the formula and, by accident, mixed the medicine with carbonated water instead of regular water. The result was a more tastier soft drink. Since the late 1890s, the Coca-Cola name has appeared on a wide variety of collectibles including glassware (i.e. ashtrays, pitchers, tumblers, bottles, plates, trays, coasters, lamps, dispensers, paperweights, etc.).

COCKTAIL GLASS — A tall glass with a foot, stem, and an angled or straight-edged bowl, Cocktail glasses are usually funnel-shaped and only have capacity of about three ounces.

Reproduction from an early 20th century S. F. Myers Co. catalog.

Cocktail.
Cut Glass Cocktail Glass.
Buzz Star Cutting.
No. 9532.......$2.45 Each

COCKTAIL SHAKER — A tall, tumbler-like glass vessel, with cover, used for mixing alcoholic drinks by shaking.

Cocktail shakers.

CODD-STOPPERED BOTTLE — A style of glass bottle invented by Hiram Codd of England (patented in the U.S. in 1873) that used a marble for sealing. The bottle was pinched in the upper neck to hold the marble, which was put in at the time of the bottle's manufacture. The pressure of a carbonated beverage kept the marble pressed against a rubber ring in the neck to complete the seal. Codd-Stoppered bottles were briefly popular in the late nineteenth century.

COFFEYVILLE GLASS COMPANY — Refer to the BARLETT-COLLINS GLASS COMPANY.

COG CANE — A molded millefiori cane in paperweights with a serrated edge.

COG METHOD — A special notation for the identification of Saint Louis paperweights.

COHANSEY GLASS COMPANY — An American firm established at Bridgeton, New Jersey, in 1880, the company produced windows and bottles up until 1899. The firm closed due to labor troubles.

COHN, MICHAEL — A noted American Studio Glass artisan born in Long Beach, California, in 1949, Cohn attended many schools to study glass-making including the University of California; California State University; and the Pilchuk School. He has also won numerous awards including the National Endowment for the Art Fellowship (1977-1978 and 1984-1985). He lives in Emeryville, California, where he works full-time as an independent glass artisan.

COIN GLASS — Originally in the seventeenth through mid-nineteenth centuries, a tumbler or tankard would contain a real coin visibly placed in the foot or stem. Coin glass originated in England and was invented to commemorate noteworthy public events. Late nineteenth and early twentieth century American versions contain glass coin replicas or medallions inscribed or molded within the glass. Both Central Glass Works (nineteenth century) and Fostoria (twentieth century) produced popular coin-styled glass in America.

*Coin glass covered cheese dish from the Central Glass Company.
Photo by Robin Rainwater.*

*An emerald green coin glass ash tray from Fostoria.
Photo by Robin Rainwater.*

COIN SPOT — An art decorating technique consisting of an all-over pattern of coin-like circles that are part of the glass, Coin spot designs are most prevalent in colorful opalescent objects (i.e. cranberry opalescent, blue opalescent, etc.), but may be combined with other decorations such as "Coin Spot & Swirl."

*Cranberry cruet and cranberry coin spot pitcher.
Courtesy of Wheaton Village.*

COLD CUTTING — The process of cutting a block of glass that has not previously been cast or formed into shape.

COLD-WORKED — A general term for any decorating technique (i.e. cutting, enameling, engraving, etching, sandblasting, etc.) applied to glass once it has cooled.

COLLAR — In paperweight making, it is a metal ring used to surround the disc or template in order to help center the design picked up by molten crystal. Collars are also associated with stemware, such as wine glasses. It is the circular portion around the upper part of the stem of a drinking glass or goblet.

COLOGNE BOTTLE — A small glass receptacle, with a narrow neck and stopper, used for holding colognes or perfumes. Most were made to be placed on dressing tables and may have matching powder jars and under trays.

Crystal Glass Cologne Bottle. Floral Cutting. No. 9446..........$2.70

Cut Glass Cologne Bottle. Floral Cutting. 6-oz. Size. No. 9447..........$4.00

Cut Glass Cologne Bottle. Fine Cutting. Height, 6½ inches. No. 9448..........$7.50

Cut Glass Cologne Bottle. Floral Cutting. Comes 4 and 6-oz. Size. No. 9449—4-oz...$3.40 No. 9450—6-oz.... 4.25

Reproduction from a late nineteenth century Higgins-Seiter catalog.

COLONIAL CUT GLASS COMPANY — A short-lived American cut glass operation established at New York, New York, in 1910 by C. B. and J. Warner. The firm produced some cut glass until closing in 1916.

COLOR AGENT — Various powdered elements, primarily metallic oxides, that when mixed in a batch of glass produce a variety of coloring effects.

COLOR BANDING — A decorating technique whereby the trails of colored glass or enamels are encircled (usually horizontally) around an object.

COLOR ETCHING — A Bohemian decorating technique whereby a then-trailing or flashing of colored glass is etched or inscribed into a clear object.

COLOR GROUND — A colored lower surface of the paperweight above which the design is set.

COLOR UNDERLAY — Refer to SOMMERSO.

COLUMBIA GLASS COMPANY — (1) A short-lived American pressed glass manufacturer established at Findlay, Ohio, in 1886 by David Jenkins Jr., William Patterson, and Lucas Minehart, the firm produced pressed glass tableware and became part of the U.S. Glass Company in 1891 as Factory J. U.S. Glass Company closed the plant in 1893. (2) Another company known as the Columbia Cut Glass Company operated for one year in Columbia, Pennsylvania, as a cut glass operation in 1918. See also FINDLAY GLASS.

Reproduction from an 1888 *Crockery & Glass Journal* advertisement.

COLUMN — An enclosed section on a glass object, usually rectangular or horizontal, that contains a single or series of vertically-spaced sections. In turn the sections may contain additional decorations. *See also "Panel."*

COLUMN VASE — A fairly small case made in the shape of a vertical or cylindrical column; Column vases originated in ancient Egypt around the fifteenth century B.C. Most are only about four inches in height or less.

COMBING — A decorating technique where bands of molten or soft colored glass are dragged along the surface of an object at right angles to form a repetitive pattern.

COMET — A cut glass design inspired by Halley's Comet, it consists of a central star surrounded by smaller stars that are interspersed with flowing comet-like tails (adjacent rows of curved cuts).

Comet pattern pressed covered butter dish. *Photo by Robin Rainwater. Item courtesy of the Corning Museum of Glass.*

C

COMMEMORATIVE GLASSWARE — Glass objects decorated usually with mold-embossed, engraved, or enameled designs that commemorate a significant event, famous person, or cause. The Romans were noted for commemorating gladiator events and great battles. Such pieces like tumblers, vases, goblets, and bowls are also referred to as "Presentation Glass." See also HISTORICAL FLASK, SOUVENIR GLASS, and WORLD'S FAIR.

COMPANION PIECE — An object that relates or matches another in order to make a pair, set, or group (i.e. a creamer to go with a sugar, the tumbler with a bottle in a tumble-up, or a serving spoon with a serving dish).

COMPORT OR COMPOTE — A glass serving bowl that may contain a base, stem, or foot(s) used for serving candy, fruits, or nuts. Comports are most commonly referred to as raised candy dishes and may or may not have matching covers. Compotier and Comportier are French terms for this style of serving dish.

Comport or Compote: Fenton emerald crest compote filled with Venetian glass candy. *Photo by Robin Rainwater.*

Reproduction from an early twentieth century Higbee trade catalog.

CONCAVE BEAKER — A Roman-style drinking vessel with sides that curve inward from the rim down to the bottom. Most contain a fairly low base that is about half the diameter of the rim.

CONCENTRIC — A design or style of paperweights consisting of ever-increasing circles radiating out from a central cane or canes. Concentric patterns are usually made in millefiori designs.

CONCENTRIC RINGS — A decorative technique usually molded or applied with enamels in concentric circles. Generally, smaller circles are enclosed by ever-increasing larger circles. Paperweights often contain sliced canes carefully placed in a concentric design.

CONDIMENT SET — Refer to CASTOR SET.

CONDON CUT GLASS COMPANY— Refer to the CONDON GLASS COMPANY.

CONDON GLASS COMPANY — A short-lived American cut glass operation founded in 1916 by James Condon in Toledo, Ohio. Condon had previously worked as a glass cutter for both Libbey and Corona prior to establishing his own firm, but the company was out of business by 1921. Note that the firm was also was known as the Condon Cut Glass Company.

CONE BEAKER — A Roman-style drinking vessel in the form of an inverted cone, most have wide rims that taper down to a small rounded or flattened point at the bottom; hence, cone beakers could only be rested on the rim. Therefore, they had to be drained in one drought or held upright by the drinker, or perhaps by a servant.

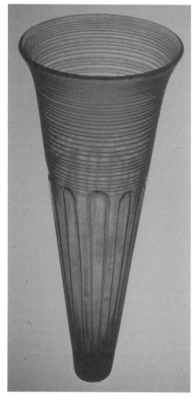

A sixth century A.D. European Cone Beaker. *Photo courtesy of the Corning Museum of Glass.*

CONFECTION TRAY — A flat glass object, usually rectangular in shape, used for holding or serving ice cream products. Confection trays were used mostly in the late nineteenth and early twentieth centuries by ice cream parlors.

CONLOW & DORWORTH — An American cut glass-making operation founded in 1915 at Mt. Holly and Palmyra, New Jersey, by Agustus Conlow and George Dorworth. The two also ran a sales outlet in Philadelphia, Pennsylvania, for their cut glass wares. The firm closed in 1920.

Conlow & Dorworth Trademark.

CONNELLSVILLE FLINT GLASS COMPANY, Ltd. — A short-lived American pressed glass-making firm that was established at Connellsville, Pennsylvania, in 1888. Glass production ended in 1890 and all materials/inventory were auctioned off in 1896.

CONRADSMINDE GLASSWORKS — A Danish glass operation founded in 1834 near Aalborg in Jutland, the firm made practical crystal tableware as well as tinted cobalt blue products. The firm closed permanently in 1857.

CONSOLE BOWL — A large concave, hemispherical shaped glass vessel used as a centerpiece or for serving large items. Console bowls are sometimes accompanied by a pair of matching candlesticks.

CONSOLE SET — A set of tableware usually consisting of three pieces: a pair of candlesticks and center or console bowl.

CONSOLIDATED LAMP & GLASS COMPANY — This American firm established in 1893 after the merger of the Wallace and McAfee Company (a glass lamp maker located in Pittsburgh, Pennsylvania) and the Fostoria Shade and Lamp Company of Fostoria, Ohio. Primary founders included F. G. Wallace, J. B. Graham, Joseph Walter, Hugh McAfee, and Charles Dean. In 1895, the Fostoria plant burned and the company built a new factory at Coraopolis, Pennsylvania. By the early twentieth century, Consolidated became the largest lamp, globe, and shade manufacturer in America. The company was noted most for creating many colored Art Glass Lamps, along with several lines of colored Art Glass ("Catalonian," "Chintz," "Florentine," "Martele," "Ruba Rombic," and "Santa Maria"). Consolidated was sold to the Dietz Brothers in 1962; after a fire destroyed most of the plant in 1963, the firm closed permanently in 1964.

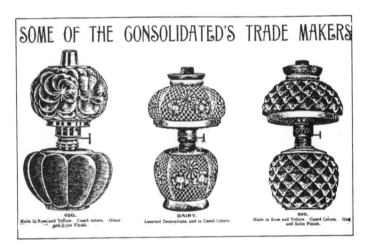

Reproduction from a 1902 Consolidated advertisement.

CONSTITUTION FLINT GLASS WORKS — A short-lived American cut glass operation established in 1867 at Brooklyn, New York, the firm produced cut glass perfume bottles including some in color. In 1876, the firm was acquired by the LaBastie Works, which continued to produce perfume bottles until 1886.

CONTEMPORARY GLASS — Glass made since the early to mid-1970s by independent artisans in small studios, including paperweights, one-of-a-kind sculptures, and artistic expressions. *See also* ART GLASS STUDIO MOVEMENT *and* STUDIO GLASS.

CONTINUOUS FURNACE — An enclosed structure for the production and application of heat. In a continuous furnace, the molten glass level remains the same over the life of the furnace. The introduction of a batch of glass into the furnace displaces existing glass and forces it out of the furnace (down below into a hearth for forming into objects). Some large industrial furnaces work continuously for years without being shut down. *See also* FURNACE.

COOKIE BASE — A thick shaped pad or base (like that of a cookie) that forms the base in fruit motif paperweights made by the NEW ENGLAND GLASS COMPANY.

COOKIE JAR — A tall, wide mouthed, canister-shaped, glass receptacle (larger than a candy jar), with a cover but without foots or stems, used for holding cookies. Biscuits jars were the predecessors of cookie jars.

CO-OPERATIVE FLINT GLASS COMPANY — An American pressed glass manufacturer established at Beaver Falls, Pennsylvania, in 1879, the company had purchased an existing glass plant that had been built in the late 1860s. The firm was also known as the Beaver Falls

No. 557
8 Oz. Footed Tumbler

Cooperative Glass Company until a permanent name change in 1889. The firm produced tumblers, stemware, and other items primarily for hotels, restaurants, and ice cream shops/fountains along with some unique novelty items (animal figurines, animal containers, gazing balls, bird baths with seed cups, cake covers, pipe rests, furniture knobs, and sample bottles). They also expanded into colored Depression glass tableware; however, most glass production ended in 1934 while the firm itself ceased operations completely in 1937. *See also* BEAVER FALLS COOPERATIVE GLASS COMPANY.

CAKE COVER

No. 570 — Dog.

Reproduction from a 1920 Co-Operative advertisement.

COOPERATIVE GLASS & ELECTRIC COMPANY — Refer to the HASKINS-JACOBS GLASS COMPANY.

COPIER, ANDRIES DIRK — The most noteworthy Dutch glass designer of the twentieth century, Copier began working for LEERDAM GLASSWORKS in 1914 and became the director of Leerdam's Unica Art Studio in 1923. He is noted for producing single-piece ornamental art objects and unique tableware.

COPPER — A somewhat reddish-tan metallic element that, when oxidized (copper oxide) and added to a batch of glass, produces a light blue color (sometimes referred to as peacock blue). If the oxide is increased, the color changes to a bluish-almost emerald green. When copper is combined in a reducing atmosphere with carbon dioxide, and then slowly cooled, it produces a somewhat coppery-red or deep crimson color. Copper and tin oxides are also combined to produce a turquoise blue color.

COPPER WHEEL ENGRAVING — Process of hand-engraving by holding a glass object (like a paperweight) to a revolving copper wheel that instantly cuts through the exterior surface. In paperweights, copper wheels are generally used for exterior decorating only.

A Copper wheel engraver at Waterford.

CORAL — Various shadings of yellow to red layers applied to glass objects with opaque-colored bases, the final result resembles that of marine coral.

CORALENE GLASS — Art glass that was first made in nineteenth century Europe and then in America, it is characterized by enamel and colored or opaque glass drops/beads applied to raised branches that resemble marine coral. The name itself was given to glassware produced by the Mt. Washington Glass Company. Beginning in the late twentieth century, a cheaper substitute has been produced by gluing on decorations that easily scrape off (originals are applied or fused directly to the surface of glass).

Mount Washington Coralene bowl. *Courtesy of Wheaton Village.*

CORD — A decorative add-on consisting of a band or rope, or series of bands and ropes, that may circle around an object or be applied horizontally, vertically, diagonally, or in various curved designs. Cords are common in pressed glass and often combined with other decorations to form patterns, i.e. cord and tassel, cord drapery, and reticulated cord.

CORDIAL GLASS — A miniature wine glass with a foot, stem, and tiny bowl of small capacity. Most have a capacity of between 1 and 1-1/2 ounces.

CORE — An object or mold-like portion that shapes the interior of a hallow casting. Ancient Egyptians created core molds of mud and straw and then covered them with spun glass trailings. Once the glass cooled, the core was them removed.

CORE-FORMING — The process of glass-making by spinning glass around a core. Once the object has cooled, the core was then removed.

A 14th –15th century B.C. Ancient Egyptian core-formed bottle. *Photo courtesy of the Corning Museum of Glass.*

CORK GLASS COMPANY — The general name for glassware produced by three separate factories in Cork, Ireland, beginning in the late eighteenth century (c. 1783) and ending in 1841. Objects produced included cut crystal tableware and other practical items.

CORNING GLASS WORKS — An American glass factory established in Corning, New York, in 1868 as the Corning Flint Glass Works by Amory Houghton Sr. and his son, Amory Houghton Jr. The firm went bankrupt in 1870, but obtained new financing in 1871. Amory Houghton Jr. stayed on as manager and the name was changed in 1975 to the Corning Glass Works. The company gained a reputation (especially at the Centennial Exposition held in Philadelphia in 1876) as a quality maker of cut crystal as well as a producer of lead crystal blanks purchased by other firms/cutters. The company's most notable purchase was that of Steuben in the 1930s. The firm produced a good deal of tableware and invented ovenproof glass they named "Pyrex." The company continues to operate today as Corning, Inc. (final name change in 1989) in many states: Kentucky, North Carolina, New York, Ohio, Pennsylvania, Virginia, and West Virginia. *See also* PYREX.

CORNUCOPIA — A receptacle in the shape of a horned vase, most have scalloped rims and were either utilized as vases, wall pockets, or simply ornaments. Cornucopia also refers to a pressed glass pattern with a cornucopia design applied from a mold.

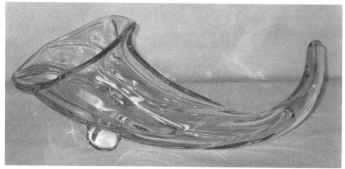

Cornucopia vase. *Photo by Robin Rainwater.*

CORONA CUT GLASS COMPANY — An American cut glass-making firm founded in 1906 at Toledo, Ohio, by James Condon and Samuel Heinzelman (both former employees of Libbey). The firm was incorporated in 1911 and was joined by Harry Kelly and Robert Loosely. Condon left in 1916 to form his own firm. Corona produced cut glass wares before closing in 1920. *See also* CONDON GLASS COMPANY.

Corona Cut Glass
Company Trademark.

CORREIA ART GLASS — An American firm founded in 1973 by Steven V. Correia in Santa Monica, California. Correia earned a Masters of Fine Arts from the University of Hawaii, where he worked in both glass sculpture and ceramics. The company's contemporary Art products (paperweights, vases, lamps, etc.) can already be found in the major art museums featuring glass in America (i.e. the Smithsonian, Corning Museum of Glass, Metropolitan Museum of Art, etc.). The firm continues in operation today by members of the Correia family.

53. *Cats from Correia Art Glass*—The black silhouettes of cats in distinctly feline poses preen on the surface of a frosted crystal globe. Available with a ruby or purple center. Signed. Dia. 3 1/4". (SC884) $110

54. *Tropic from Correia Art Glass*—The black silhouettes of fish and seahorses swim on the surface of a frosted weight with an aqua center. Signed. Dia. 3 1/8". (SC891) $110

55. *Iridescent Gold Hearts from Correia Art Glass*—Shimmering hearts float on a frosted crystal dome. Signed. Dia. 3 1/8". (SC887) $90

Reproduction from a 1994 Correia advertisement.

CORROSO — A Venetian term for glass with an irregular mottled surface produced by acid-etching the exterior.

COSMETIC BOTTLE — A clear colored glass container with a narrow neck and mouth used to hold a variety of cosmetic-type liquids (i.e. hair restorer, hair dye, creams, rosewater, etc.). Cosmetic bottles may or may not have handles, but usually do contain stoppers. They were popular in the late eighteenth and nineteenth centuries and a good deal contain papers labels.

COSMOS — A name for a pressed milk glass made in America in a wide variety of patterns in the early eighteenth century.

COUDERSPORT TILE & ORNAMENTAL GLASS COMPANY — An American firm founded at East Coudersport, Pennsylvania, in 1900 by brothers Joseph and E. Fitzroy Webb. The company produced glass tiles and limited amounts of milk glass, opaque and transparent colored glass, slag glass, and pressed tableware up until the factory burned to the ground in 1904. Note that the firm filed several other company names

too: Bastow Glass Company, Coudersport Tile & Glass Company, Joseph Webb Glass Works, Joseph Webb Decorative Glass Company, and the Webb Patent Tile Company.

COUPER, JAMES & SONS — Refer to WEST LOTHIAN GLASSWORKS.

COVER — An unattached top for closing the mouth of a jar, vase, dish, pot, bowl, or other open vessel, Covers may be flat or domed and contain finials and handles. Note that they are distinguished from lids that ordinarily contain hinges.

COVERED ANIMAL DISH — Refer to ANIMAL DISH.

CRACKER JAR — A tall wide-mouthed canister-shaped glass receptacle, with a cover, used for holding crackers. Originally, they were referred to as biscuit jars.

CRACKING OFF — The process of removing an object from the pontil. Cooled by scoring, the pipe is then gently tapped and the object falls into a sand tray or V-shaped holder held by an assistant.

CRACKLE GLASS — A style of glassware that has a rough irregular surface resembling cracked ice (sometimes referred to as ICE GLASS); it is made by the technique of crackling. It is also given the spelling "Craquelle" or "Craquele."

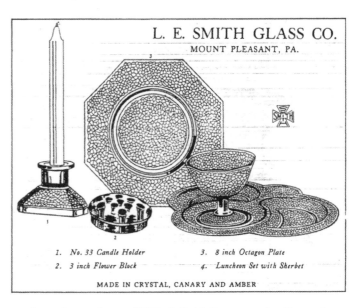

Reproduction from a 1928 L. E. Smith Company advertisement.

Durand art glass crackle vases. *Items courtesy of Wheaton Village.*

CRACKLING — A decorating technique applied to glassware by plunging a hot object into cold water to induce radical, random fissures (cracks) and then reforming the piece within a mold after reheating.

CRAIG & O'HARA — Refer to the PITTSBURGH GLASS WORKS.

CRANBERRY GLASS — First developed in England in the nineteenth century, cranberry glass is characterized by a light red tint (the color of cranberries) produced by the addition of gold dust that is dissolved in two acids (aqua regia). Originally it was a cheaper substitute for ruby red but now the name is applied to any glass made of the cranberry color.

CREAM SOUP BOWL — A concave glass vessel, hemispherical in shape and usually with two small or tab handles, used for serving soup or other foods.

CREAMER — A small glass cup-like vessel, ordinarily with handle and spout,

used for serving cream (with coffee and tea, usually paired wit a sugar dish). Creamers were once referred to by the English as "Cream Boats."

Avon Cape Cod pattern ruby red creamer; commission of Wheaton Industries.
Photo by Robin Rainwater.

CREMAX — An opaque lightly beige-colored glass first produced and named by the MacBeth-Evans Glass Company in the early twentieth century.

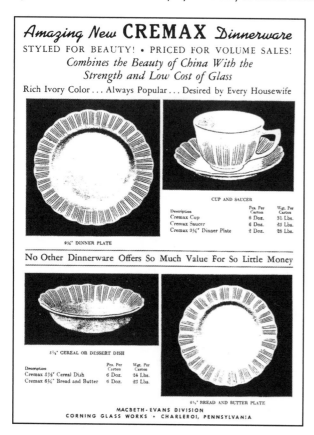

Amazing New **CREMAX** *Dinnerware*
STYLED FOR BEAUTY! • PRICED FOR VOLUME SALES!
Combines the Beauty of China With the Strength and Low Cost of Glass
Rich Ivory Color... Always Popular... Desired by Every Housewife

CUP AND SAUCER

Description	Pcs. Per Carton	Wgt. Per Carton
Cremax Cup	6 Doz.	31 Lbs.
Cremax Saucer	6 Doz.	25 Lbs.
Cremax 9¼" Dinner Plate	2 Doz.	28 Lbs.

9¼" DINNER PLATE

No Other Dinnerware Offers So Much Value For So Little Money

5¼" CEREAL OR DESSERT DISH

Description	Pcs. Per Carton	Wgt. Per Carton
Cremax 5¾" Cereal Dish	6 Doz.	24 Lbs.
Cremax 6¾" Bread and Butter	6 Doz.	23 Lbs.

6¾" BREAD AND BUTTER PLATE

MACBETH-EVANS DIVISION
CORNING GLASS WORKS • CHARLEROI, PENNSYLVANIA

Reproduction from a 1939 MacBeth-Evans Company advertisement.

CRESCENT CUT GLASS COMPANY — An American firm founded in 1900 at Newark, New Jersey, the company produced limited amounts of cut glass up into the early 1920s.

CRESCENT FLINT GLASS WORKS — A short-lived American firm founded at Pittsburgh, Pennsylvania, in the late 1860s, the company produced some pressed glass tableware; blown, cut and engraved wares; and some kerosene and gas lamp shades. The firm was out of business by 1873. Note that company was also known as Semple, Reynolds & Company.

CRESCENT GLASS COMPANY — An American firm established at Wellsburg, West Virginia, in 1908 by Henry Rithner and Ellery Worthen. Rithner had previously worked for both the Consolidated Lamp & Glass Company and the Fostoria Glass Company. The company purchased a plant previously occupied by the Riverside Glass Company and moved operations there after a fire destroyed the Crescent plant in 1911. The firm made blown glass tumblers, headlights (red taillights for Ford), signal lenses, lantern globes (some in color), pressed wares, lamp parts, and other pressed items. They also purchased the Lobmiller Decorating Company in 1911 and operated it as a subsidiary. When Worthen passed away in 1920, his interest was purchased by the Rithner family. The company is still in operation today under Henry Rithner III and they produce lamp parts, novelty items, signal globes, and votive glass.

CRESCENT GLASS WORKS — Refer to the MACBETH-EVANS GLASS COMPANY.

CREST — A name given to several Fenton Glass products containing a base color (most often milk glass) and a colored or crystal trim. *Aqua Crest* includes a greenish-blue or aqua trim while *Blue Crest* contains a darker blue trim; *Emerald Crest* obviously has an emerald green trim while the *Silver Crest* contains a crystal trim; the *Peach Crest* also contains a clear glass trim along with an exterior of milk glass and a pink interior; *Snow Crest* is forest green or rose or ruby red or amber glass with a milk white trim; *Rose Crest* contains a pink trim while *Silver Rose* is opaque pink glass with a clear glass trim; *Ruby Crest* contains a ruby red trim while the *Gold Crest* contains an amber trim; *Silver Jamestown* contains a milk glass exterior, a transparent light blue interior and a crystal trim while *Silver Turquoise* is light blue opaque glass with a crystal trim; *Black Crest* contains a black trim while the *Flame Crest* contains an orangish-red trim.

Fenton Emerald Crest vases.
Photo by Robin Rainwater.

Fenton opalescent diamond lace patterned Emerald Crest epergne.

CRESTING — A decorative ornament that projects outward from the edge of certain glass objects like the rims of drinking vessels or the handles of serving pitchers.

CRIMP — A metal tool inserted into molten glass to form three-dimensional designs in paperweights; Millville is noted most for creating rose and lily designs in this fashion.

CRIMPED CANE — A vertically ribbed or corrugated style cane used in paperweight making.

CRIMPING — A method of decorating the rims of objects common in such items as bowls and vases. A hand tool is utilized to manipulate molten glass to form a ribbon-like design around the rim.

CRISTAL D'ARGUES — A modern brand of crystal glass tableware produced under the Arc International glass conglomerate. *See also "Arc International."*

CRISTALES DE MEXICO — A Mexican glass company founded in the early twentieth century at Nuevo Leon, the firm produced tableware and some iridized Carnival glassware in the 1920s and 1930s. The company's products usually contain an "M" within a "C" mark on the underside.

Cristales de Mexico Trademark.

CRISTALLO — A nearly colorless highly esteemed soda glass invented by Venetian glassmakers in the mid-to-late fifteenth century. Angelo Barovier is credited with much of its development and perfection. Originally, the barilla plant was burned to make the ash necessary for the production of glass; the result was the first clear glass that was similar in appearance to rock crystal.

CRIZZLING — A deteriorated condition resulting from alkaline elements in the glass that react to moisture. The consequence is the formation of droplets or tears of alkaline moisture on the surface that, in turn, induce hair-like internal cracks. Crizzling is also known as weeping, sweating, or sick glass (also spelled "Crissling," "Crisseling," or "Crisselling").

CROSETTI, J. C. — Refer to the JEANNETTE TOY & NOVELTY COMPANY and STOUGH, TURNEY H. COMPANY.

CROSS-HATCHING — A glass cutting technique whereby parallel lines are cut vertically, horizontally, and sometimes diagonally to intersect in a crisscross pattern (sometimes found on the exterior of cut glass paperweights). *See also* HATCHING.

CROWN — A dome style of paperweight consisting of alternating twisted colored (one or more colors) ribbons that radiate from a central cane. The ribbons typically flow symmetrically from the base to the dome filling most if not all of the internal space of the paperweight. St. Louis is noted for producing crown paperweights.

CROWN CRYSTAL GLASS — A New Zealand firm established at Christchurch in 1950, the company produced both pressed and blown glass tableware until closing in 1987. Note that when the firm closed, employees went on to the HOKI TIKA GLASSWORKS and NEW ZEALAND GLASS.

CROWN MILANO — Refer to ALBERTINE.

CROWN WEIGHT — A style of paperweight made with filigree canes arranged vertically along the sides and then drawn together at the top. Originally, the canes used were white in color; however, single color or multicolored canes are also used.

CROW'S FOOT — Refer to ARROW CANE.

CRUCIBLE — A pot used for melting glass. Crucibles originated in ancient times and were originally constructed of fired pottery materials.

CRUET — A small glass bottle, jug-shaped vessel, or decanter, with a stopper, designed for use at the table. Cruets generally were invented to hold a condiment such as oil, vinegar, or salad dressing. At times, sets of two or more cruets were fitted into stands made of metal that included a center carrying handle.

Reproduction from a late 19th century T. G. Hawkes advertisement.

Hawkes Cut Glass.

No piece is genuine without this trade-mark.

Hobbs, Brockunier Peachblow cruet.
Courtesy of Wheaton Village.

CRYOLITE — Refer to ALUMINUM.

CRYSTAL — The general term for colorless glass containing a high lead content. Lead or Half-Lead Crystal contains a minimum of 24% lead content while Full-Lead Crystal contains a minimum of 30% lead content. Crystal is actually derived from the Greek word meaning "Clear-ice."

Crystal knife rest.
Photo by Robin Rainwater.

CRYSTAL ART GLASS COMPANY — Refer to the DEGENHART CRYSTAL ART GLASS COMPANY.

CRYSTAL CUT GLASS COMPANY — An American cut glass operation established at Honesdale, Pennsylvania, in 1913, the firm operated a few short years under Dr. Pierson B. Peterson until closing in 1918.

Crystal Cut Glass Company: Trademark.

CRYSTAL GLASS COMPANY — (1) A pressed glass manufacturer established at Pittsburgh, Pennsylvania, in 1869 by Daniel, William, and M. James Bennett, the firm produced some pressed wares before going out of business in 1873. The factory was temporarily leased to King, Son & Company in 1884 when fire destroyed the King plant. The plant was razed in 1890. (2) An American pressed-glass making firm established at Pittsburgh, Pennsylvania, in 1879, the firm moved to Bridgeport, Ohio, in 1882 where it burned to the ground in 1884. The firm produced some limited amounts of clear pressed glass tableware. Under J. N. Vance, Edward Muhleman, and Addison Thompson, the firm reorganized in 1888 and purchased a plant previously owned by the LaBelle Glass Company in Bridgeport, Ohio. Pressed glass production resumed and the firm eventually joined the National Glass Company in 1899. It reorganized again in 1905; however, glass production halted in 1908. Despite several reorganization attempts, the plant remained idle and finally burned to the ground in 1914. Note that the plant here was also known as the New Crystal Glass Works. (3) An American firm founded by S. L. Boughton in 1888 at Bowling Green, Ohio, the company produced some limited amounts of bottles and pressed glass tableware before ceasing operations in 1892. (4) An American glass company founded at Los Angeles, California, in 1921, the firm produced some blown and pressed tableware before closing permanently in 1929. (5) There were many other short-lived firms known as the Crystal Glass Company: one in Baltimore, Maryland, that produced window panes (1873); another in Pittsburgh, Pennsylvania, that produced lamp chimneys (1869); one in Bellaire, Ohio, that made window panes (1882); and one in Morgantown, West Virginia, that produced blown glass tableware and tumblers (1911). The Morgantown company was also known as the Crystal Tumbler Company and was established by George W. Fry. See also KING, SON & COMPANY and ECONOMY TUMBLER COMPANY.

CRYSTAL GLASS COMPANY, LTD. — Refer to BAGLEY GLASS.

CRYSTAL GLASS WORKS — An Australian company founded in Sydney in 1914, they were noted for Carnival and other glass production. The firm was also known as the AUSTRALIAN CRYSTAL GLASS COMPANY.

CRYSTAL MINIATURE — Small figurines and novelty items made of faceted (cut like gemstones) crystal that were first made by the Austrian firm of Swarovski in 1976. Some do contain colored accents such as facial features. Many firms followed Swarovski in the making of faceted crystal miniatures soon after. See also SWAROVSKI SILVER CRYSTAL.

A collection of crystal miniatures. *Photo by Robin Rainwater.*

CRYSTAL PALACE — A famous structure built in Hyde Park, London, in 1851 to house the Great Exhibition (much like a World's Fair), the building was iron-framed and contained 300,000 panes of glass. It was later moved to Sydenham where it burned to the ground in 1936.

1851 Crystal Palace Exhibition.
Photo courtesy of the Corning Museum of Glass.

CRYSTAL TUMBLER COMPANY — Refer to the CRYSTAL GLASS COMPANY and the ECONOMY TUMBLER COMPANY.

CRYSTALEX — Founded in 1974, this firm became the largest of the National Corporations in the Czech Republic after all glass corporations in Czechoslovakia became part of the state in 1948. Under Crystalex, multiple factories previously under Sklarney Bohemia (also known as the Bohemia Glassworks), the Crystalex Branch Corporation at Novy Bor, Karlovarske Sklo, Morsvske Sklarney, and Cesky Kristal; all became part of this new conglomerate. Since then, many factories became independent again; today, there are only six left under Crytalex: Kombinat, Zahn Glassworks, Cesky Kristal, Kvetna Glassworks, Karolinka Glassworks, and Vrbno Glassworks. Still, the firm produces a good deal of tableware and ornamental glassware of which two-thirds is exported.

CRYSTOLENE CUT GLASS COMPANY — A short-lived American cut glass operation established in 1918 by Hugo Engelke and Louis Stanner in Brooklyn, New York, it produced cut glass products before going out of business in 1921.

CUBE OR CUBIST — A three-dimensional mold-pressed pattern consisting of a series of interlocking or all-over pattern of small squares or rectangles; the squares/rectangles resemble cubes since they are faceted to stick out from the flat surface. Cube patterns were first produced in the nineteenth century and were sometimes combined with other designs (i.e. cube with fan, daisy and cube, etc.). Fostoria was noted for producing a huge variety of pieces in this style with their "American" pattern while Jeannette produced similar colored glass during America's Great Depression ("Cube" or "Cubist" pattern).

Reproduction from a 1930 Jeannette Glass Company advertisement.

Cube-patterned plate. *Photo by Robin Rainwater.*

CULLET — Chards or scraps of glass that are remelted and added to a new batch of glass to aid in the fusion process. Aside from the benefits of recycling, cullet usually melts faster and may make up 20-30% of a typical batch of glass.

CULLODEN LIGHTING GLASS COMPANY — Refer to the A. F. BISCHOFF GLASS COMPANY.

CUMBERLAND GLASS COMPANY — (1) A short-lived American pressed glass manufacturer established at Cumberland, Maryland, in 1882 by Joseph and Anton Zihlam, the firm produced some pressed glass tableware and blown tumblers prior to becoming part of the National Glass Company in 1900 (joined as the Cumberland Glass Works). National stopped making glass at the plant in 1904. In 1909, it was acquired by the Wellington Glass Company, a maker of glass lamp chimneys. (2) Another company known as the Cumberland Glass Company was founded in 1909 at Fairmont, West Virginia. The firm produced blown glass tumblers a few short years before going out of business.

CUNEO FURNACES — A West Coast art studio founded by Steven Maslach in California in 1971, the firm was one of the first contemporary glass companies to be established in Western America and is noted most for producing collectible glass hearts and cast and blown glass accessories.

CUNNINGHAM & COMPANY — An American window glass and bottle-making firm founded at Pittsburgh, Pennsylvania, in 1849 as B. Cunningham & Company, the firm was also called the Pittsburgh City Glass Works. It was established by members of the Cunningham family along with George Duncan; after Duncan left in 1857, Dominick Ihmsen joined

and the firm's name was changed to Cunningham & Ihmsen. The company expanded into both blown and pressed glass tableware. In 1875, the brothers Robert & Wilson Cunningham, along with Wilson's son Dominick, bought out Ihmsen's interest and the name changed back to Cunningham & Company. Dominick became sole owner in 1886 and the name was changed once again to D. O. Cunningham & Company; however, the firm closed two years later.

CUNNINGHAM & IHMSEN — Refer to CUNNINGHAM & COMPANY.

CUP — An open, somewhat bowl-shaped or cylindrical vessel, usually with a handle, used for drinking liquids such as coffee, tea, or punch. Note that as a measure of volume, a cup is equal to eight ounces. *See also* MEASURING CUP.

Reproduction from a late 19th century Higgins-Seiter catalog.

Cut Glass Lemonade or Punch Cup. Illustration One-Half Size. No. 9252......................$1.75 Each

CUP PLATE — A flat or shallow concave glass vessel, usually round in shape (occasionally square or oval), used as an under dish or plate for handle-less cups and saucers. Used primarily in the nineteenth century, handle-less cups included deep saucers; in turn, the saucers were used to hold hot liquids from which they were sipped. This necessitated the need for another plate to rest under the cup; hence, the "cup plate."

CUPPING GLASS — Refer to BLEEDING GLASS.

CURLING, R. B. & SONS — An American pressed glass manufacturer established at Pittsburgh, Pennsylvania, in 1827 as Curling, Price & Company, founders included Robert B. Curling and William Price. In 1828, Price withdrew and Curling's sons, William and Alfred, joined (name changed to R. B. Curling & Company). In 1834, the name was changed again to R. B. Curling & Sons; however, a separate corporate name – the Fort Pitt Glass Works – was also established by the firm. In 1835, the firm was known as Curling & Robertson, or Curling, Robertson & Company, when Morgan Robertson joined the firm as a partner. The firm produced some limited pressed wares before selling out to Edward Dithridge Sr. in 1860. *See also* DITHRIDGE & COMPANY.

CURRIER & IVES — A mid-nineteenth century pressed glass design that was supposedly inspired by a Currier & Ives art print. The pattern is similar to Daisy & Button, but contains plain buttons that are more convex.

CURTAIN — A pressed glass pattern that derives its name from the horizontal curtain-like folds in the design.

CURTAIN TIE-BACK — A small glass ornament affixed to a wall bracket for tying back and holding a curtain in place.

CUSHION — A paperweight made in the form of a rounded pincushion.

CUSPIDOR — A fancy glass vessel or receptacle used for containing saliva. *See also* SPITTOON.

CUSTARD CUP — A smaller than ordinary cup, with or without a handle, used for serving desserts in small portions, such as pudding, custard, and jell-o.

Reproduction from an 1893 U.S. Glass Company catalog.

Custard Cup.

CUSTARD GLASS — A yellowish-colored or yellow cream-colored opaque glass (the color of custard) first developed with English and Bohemian makers in the 1870s and 1880s. American makers soon followed with their own custard formulas. It was first referred to as ivory and the color was originally produced by the addition of uranium salts and sulphur compounds. The color itself can vary from a "drab" of yellow, almost like a pale milk glass, to a bright or light lemon yellow. Generally, the more uranium added, the brighter the yellow color. *See also* IVRENA VERDE.

A Heisey custard glass vase.

CUT GLASS — Heavy flint or lead crystal glass cut with geometric patterns into the glass with grinding wheels and abrasives. The design is further smoothed and polished. Cutting originated as far back as the 8th century B.C. with stone wheels while modern cutting techniques originated in Germany in the sixteenth century (i.e. copper and diamond-edge cutting wheels). Cutting was introduced in the United States in the late 18th century. In paperweights, cutting is generally applied to the exterior only. *See also* BRILLIANT PERIOD.

EVERYBODY'S MAGAZINE

Cut Glass: Reproduction from an early 20th century *Higgins-Seiter Magazine* advertisement.

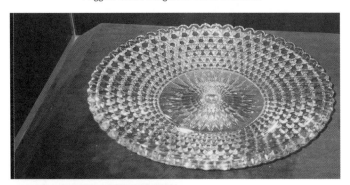

A cut glass snowflake patterned dish by Nehemiah Packwood and a hobnail cut glass platter by T. G. Hawkes.

CUT GLASS CORPORATION OF AMERICA — Refer to the QUAKER CITY CUT GLASS COMPANY.

CUT VELVET — Colored Art Glass consisting of two fused, mold-blown layers that leaves the outer surface design raised in relief. In most cases, a pastel color was applied over a white casing, and then cut to expose portions of the casing. The finish had a satiny velvet texture (hence the name). Cut velvet styles were popular from about 1870 to the end of the nineteenth century.

CYLINDER — (1) A three-dimensional figure consisting of equal circles for the bottom and top (uniform diameter) and a height that can vary from short and square to tall and narrow. In glass, cylindrically-shaped objects are generally made into jars, tumblers, and vases. In laboratory glass, a graduated cylinder is tall and narrow and contains measuring lines. Graduated cylinders usually have a separate base made of another material (i.e. plastic) in order to stand upright. (2) Window glass can be made by inflating a large gather of glass and then swinging it until it forms a cylinder. The ends of the cylinder are removed by shears and then are cut lengthwise, reheated, and then allowed to slump into a flat sheet or pane of glass.

CYPRIAN GLASS — A style of bluish-green Art Glass developed by Frederick Carder of Steuben around 1915. It is characterized by a celeste-blue coloring techniques (similar to aqua marine) applied around the rim of glass objects.

CYPRIOTE GLASS — A style of Art Glass developed by Arthur Nash while working for Tiffany. It is characterized by a rough pitted surface created by rolling a heated object on a marver spread with finely-powdered glass.

A Tiffany Cypriote vase. *Photo by Robin Rainwater. Item courtesy of the Corning Museum of Glass.*

CZECHOSLOVAKIAN GLASS — Glassware produced in the former Bohemian region beginning in 1918, when Czechoslovakia was officially recognized as a separate country. Before breaking up in 1992, a good deal of glass was made by several firms in a wide variety of styles including traditional Bohemian motifs: Mary Gregory glass (especially with bronzed accents), colored Art Glass (especially orange), Carnival colors, engraved crystal, and glassware that is sometimes referred to as "Peasant Glass." All firms in Czechoslovakia became nationalized concerns at the end of World War II; nevertheless, many individual makers stayed on as managers and directors. Since January 1, 1993, glass is still being made in this region, but is usually marked "Czech Republic." At that date, the country split into the Czech Republic and the Slovak Republic. *See also* PEASANT GLASS.

Czechoslovakian Glass: Trademarks.

C

Dd

{ Dd }

DAGNIA FAMILY — An Italian family of glassmakers who are credited with establishing the first English glass operation at Bristol around 1651. Around 1630, Sir Robert Mansell was able to arrange for their passing from Italy to England, and glass operations actually began soon after in L'Altare. As the family became well established, three brothers (Edward, John, and Onesiphorous Dagnia) branched off and established another glasshouse at Newcastle-upon-Tyne in 1648. Much of the glass made by the Dagnias was practical (i.e. windows, bottles, etc.); however, they branched into lead crystal tableware after Ravenscroft's discovery. John Williams of Stourbridge married into the family and the Dagnia-Williams Glassworks was established in 1725; the firm produced cut crystal products through much of the eighteenth century. *See also GEORGE RAVENSCROFT and ENGLISH GLASS.*

DAHLIA — A pressed glass pattern that contains the Dahlia flower as its primary design (variations include scrolling, dots, sandwich-like designs, cables, etc.). Dahlia designs are found in cut/engraved glass as well.

DAILEY, DAN — A noted American Studio Glass artisan born in Philadelphia, Pennsylvania, in 1947, Daily received his Masters of Fine Arts degree from the Rhode Island School of Design and was awarded numerous fellowships and endowments for his work. He is also a noted studio art glass instructor and has served in a teaching capacity at the Rhode Island School of Design, Massachusetts College of Art (where he founded the glass program), Pilchuk Glass Center, Haystack Mountain School of Crafts, and the Center for Advanced Visual Studies at the Massachusetts Institute of Technology. Daily also works as an independent glass artisan in Amesbury, Massachusetts.

DAIRY BOWL — A low concave glass vessel, hemispherical in shape, used for separating cream. Some have pouring lips.

DAISY — A floral design in glassware that resembles the circular head of a daisy; daisies can be found commonly in both cut and pressed glass and are usually combined with other decorations (i.e. daisy and button, daisy and bluebell, daisy whorl, daisy in diamond, daisy in square, daisy medallion, paneled daisy, daisy and cube, stippled daisy, and so on). More elaborate full-flowered daisies can also be found in a wide variety of Art Glass styles.

An Amberina daisy and button patterned compote.
Photo by Robin Rainwater.

DAISY-IN-HEXAGON — A cut design pattern featuring a flower (a daisy) inscribed within a hexagon.

DAISY-IN-SQUARE — A cut or pressed design pattern featuring a flower (a daisy) inscribed within a square.

DALLES — Refer to CATHEDRAL GLASS.

DALLES DE VERRE — Refer to STAINED GLASS.

DALZELL, GILMORE AND LEIGHTON GLASS COMPANY — An American pressed glass manufacturer established at Brilliant, Ohio, in 1883 originally as Dalzell Brothers and Gilmore (also known as the Dalzell Glass Company). The principals included brothers Andrew, James, and William A. B. Dalzell and E. D. Gilmore. James Dalzell had previously worked for Adams while Gilmore was a banker from Pittsburgh. The firm began at an idle plant that had once been operated by the Brilliant Glass Company. In 1884, the firm moved to Wellsburg, West Virginia, where a new factory was built; in 1888, it moved to Findlay, Ohio, where another factory was constructed. George Leighton joined the firm in 1888 and the name was changed to the Dalzell, Gilmore and Leighton Glass Company. The company produced pressed glass tableware, bottles, novelty items, and onyx glass until becoming part of the National Glass Company in 1899. National closed the plant in 1902 and the buildings were sold for salvage. *See also FINDLAY GLASS and FINDLAY ONYX.*

Reproduction from an 1891
Pottery and Glassware Reporter advertisement.

DALZELL-VIKING — Refer to the "Viking Glass Company."

DANISH GLASS — Glass made in Denmark from as early as the sixteenth century. The first operation opened in Jutland to produce windows and practical containers. Many other factories sprang up in the nineteenth century and produced mostly functional tableware. *See also* KASTRUP & HOLMEGAARDS.

DANNEHOFFER & BROTHERS — Refer to the WILLIAMSBURGH FLINT GLASS WORKS.

D'ARGENTAL — A mark or signature of the French firm of St. Louis that was applied to a wide range of cameo glass produced by them in the late nineteenth century. The factory was located in the Alsace-Lorraine region (eastern France) that was once part of western Germany. Pieces were also marked "Arsale," "Arsal," or "St. Louis-Munzthal." Note that "D'Argental" is simply the French name for the German "Munzthal."

DARNER — A glass needle with large eye for use in darning. Glass darners are sometimes whimsical creations and served as gifts in the latter nineteenth century. Larger versions are sometimes referred to as "Sock Darners."

Glass sock darners. *Courtesy of Wheaton Village.*

D'ARTIGUES, AIME-GABRIEL — D'Artigues (1778-1848) was one of France's noteworthy owners of some of that country's most famous glassworks. He directed St. Louis from 1791–1795, he purchased Voneche in 1802, and acquired Baccarat in 1816. Eventually he sold his interests but managed to keep France's glass industry alive during difficult periods in history.

DARTINGTON CRYSTAL — An English firm established at Tortington in North Devon in 1966 under the direction of Swedish immigrant Eskil Vilhelmsson, who recruited sixteen skilled Swedish glass blowers along with a few local apprentices. The firm specializes in producing hand-made crystal goblets, tableware, and some novelty items. In 1982, Wedgwood purchased a 50% stake in Dartington; who in turn sold it to the Rockware Group in 1989. Rockware was taken over in 1991 by BTR; however, Dartington returned to private ownership in 1994. Today, the firm is one of England's leading manufacturers of plain crystal (especially stemware and vases), exporting products to more than fifty countries worldwide, and employing over three hundred people.

Reverse cut ice sculpture of a thistle.

DATE OR DATE CANE — A small internal millefiori cane that has a date inserted into it. *See also* SIGNATURE.

DAUM — A French glass company (Verrerie Sainte-Catherine) was purchased by Jean Daum (1825-1885) in 1875 in the town of Nancy, France. "Daum," "Nancy Daum," "Daum Frers," "Crisalleries de Nancy," and "Daum & Cie" are all names associated with glass produced by this company. Daum began as a producer of many styles of Art Nouveau glass, particularly opaque and pate-de-verre styles. When Jean died, the company was inherited by his sons, Jean-Louis Auguste (1853-1909) and Jean-Antonin (1864-1930). From there, it was passed down to their grandsons Paul and Henri Daum. The Daum factory, as well as the glass school in Nancy, France, continues to operate today. The glass produced in this region is usually referred to as DAUM GLASS and still consists of many opaque art sculptural forms and some clear crystal.

The Daum showroom in Nancy, France, and a Daum glass sculpture.

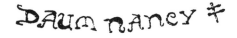

Trademarks.

DAVIDSON, GEORGE & COMPANY, LTD. — An English pressed glass-making firm established in 1867 by George Davidson (1822-1891) in the Newcastle area (Team Valley, Low Fell in Gateshead). Davidson had previously worked as a butcher and had little in the way of experience in glass. The firm began as a maker of oil lamp chimneys and was first known as the Team Flint Glass Works. They expanded soon after into pressed glass and, in the 1880s, they further expanded into opaque colored glassware (mostly white and blue), along with some marbleized and a line called "Pearline" (blue and yellow glass with a white opalescent edge). The yellow in Pearline was made with uranium salts to give it a vaseline-like appearance. When the elder Davidson passed away, his son Thomas Davidson (1860-1937) assumed control. In 1922, Davidson's invented cloud glass, a style produced by adding a small amount of a darker color to a lighter batch of colored glass just prior to being filled in a mold (produced cloud-like streaking). The firm also produced cut/engraved glass and iridescent Carnival Glass up into the early 1950s. Note that the firm is also known as "Davidsons of Gateshead." The firm was taken over by Abrahams, an electroplating company. Glassware was made until the factory closed in 1987.

Davidson, George & Company, Ltd.: Trademark.

DAVIDSONS OF GATESHEAD — Refer to DAVIDSON, GEORGE & COMPANY, LTD.

DAVIES GLASS AND MANUFACTURING COMPANY — A short-lived American firm established at Martins Ferry, Ohio, in 1921, the company produced some limited pressed glass products until ceasing operation in 1925.

DAY TANK — A glass furnace that is designed to operate on a 24-hour schedule; in the beginning, a batch is added to the furnace at a steady rate until the chamber is full. Once all of the molten glass is removed for production (usually in one day), the furnace is filled once again (usually at night) and the process continues the next day. Day tanks usually have small ports around the sides for gathering glass for use in pressing.

DE VEZ — A mark found on glassware produced by the French art glass firm of VERRERIES CRISTALLERIES DE ST. DENIS ET PANTIN REUNIES. The firm was created when Legras merged with Pantin in 1920. De Vez is actually a pseudonym for the firm's art director, De Varreux. See also LEGRAS and PANTIN.

De Vez: Trademark.

DE VILBISS COMPANY — A decorating firm established around 1900 in Toledo, Ohio, the company primarily decorated perfume bottles and atomizers in many Art Glass styles until they closed in the late 1930s.

MADE De Vilbiss IN U.S.A.

De Vilbiss Company: Trademark.

DECAL — A picture, design, or label from specially prepared paper that is transferred to glass, usually by heating.

DECANTER — An ornamental or fancy glass bottle, with a cover or stopper and with or without handles, used for serving wine or other alcoholic beverages. Decanters originated in the mid-seventeenth century in England and were known as decanter jugs or decanter bottles.

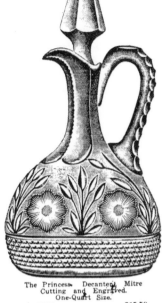

Reproduction from a late 19th century Higgins-Seiter catalog.

The Princess Decanter, Mitre Cutting and Engraved. One-Quart Size.
No. 9526.................$15.50

A cut glass red decanter from J. Hoare. *Courtesy of Wheaton Village.*

DECANTER RINGS — Protrusions around the neck of most early (seventeenth-eighteenth centuries) decanters produced by England and Ireland. The rings usually numbered from one to four, came in a variety of shapes (rounded, square, triangular, etc.), and were used to afford a better grip on the decanter.

DECEPTIVE GLASS — A drinking vessel, usually stemmed, with a bowl that has unusually thick sides and a thick base, so as to contain a lesser quantity than the size of the glass would visually suggest. Smaller tumblers were made in this fashion as well. See also "Cheaters."

DECORATIVE PAPERWEIGHT — General name for an inexpensive paperweight produced in some quantity as opposed to a potentially more valuable limited edition. Most are unsigned, but may contain a paper seal.

DECOLORIZING AGENT — An element or mineral used to counteract the murky green or brown color resulting from tiny iron particles present in sand. Oxides of manganese, nickel, and cobalt used in small quantities are the most prevalent forms of neutralizers.

D

DEGENHART CRYSTAL ART GLASS FACTORY — An American firm established in Cambridge, Ohio, in 1947 by John and Elizabeth Degenhart, the company was also known as the Crystal Art Glass Company. John Degenhart had previously worked for the Cambridge Glass Company prior to establishing his own firm. Early on, the company specialized in making paperweights and then expanded into miniature colored art novelty items. The company closed in 1978 after the death of Elizabeth (John had passed away in 1964). Beginning in 1972, most products can be found with a mold mark that consists of a "D" or a "D" within a heart. Some of the company molds were retired; however, Zack Boyd, an employee of Degenhart, purchased many and founded the Boyd Art Glass Company in 1978. *See also* BOYD ART GLASS COMPANY.

DEGUE — A mark found on glassware produced by the French art glass firm of VERRERIES CRISTALLERIES DE ST. DENIS ET PANTIN REUNIES. The firm was created when Legras merged with Pantin in 1920. Degue was the name of one of the firm's glass artisans. *See also* LEGRAS *and* PANTIN.

Degue: Trademark.

DEIDRICK GLASS COMPANY — An American cut glass operation established at Monaca, Pennsylvania, just prior to world War I. The company produced cut glass tableware into the early 1920s (sold and marked under the name "Silvart").

SILVART

Deidrick Glass Company: Trademark.

DELATTE — Glass created and signed by French maker Andre de Latte of Nancy, France, beginning in the early 1920s. His art forms consist mostly of opaque and cameo engraved vases and lighting fixtures.

DeLatte: Trademark.

DELFT WARE — A style of Art Glass created by the Mount Washington Glass Works in the late 1880s. It is a translucent white opal glass that was both free and mold-blown, and then further decorated with light colored scenery of sailboats, canals, and windmills. The style of glass was continued by Pairpoint, who purchased Mt. Washington in 1894.

DELL GLASS COMPANY — A short-lived glass manufacturer that operated in Millville, New Jersey, in the 1930s. The firm produced some colored machine pressed tableware before going out of business (i.e. the Depression "tulip" pattern).

DELPHITE — A lightly colored pale blue opaque glass, it is sometimes referred to as "Blue Milk Glass."

DEMA — The British Thomas Houston (BTH) Company, a maker of electric lamps and valves, opened a glass factory in 1923 at Chesterfield, Derbyshire. In 1948, BTH merged with General Electric (GE) to produce light bulbs. Factory production was soon expanded to include the machine production of tumblers, mugs, and stemware. Eventually, Dema, along with Webb's Crystal and Edinburgh Crystal, became part of Crown House Ltd. in 1971. Crown House was in turn taken over by Coloroll; however, Coloroll went bankrupt in 1990. A new company, Dema Ltd., was founded and continues to produce light bulbs, lamps, and scientific glassware today.

DEMER BROTHERS COMPANY — An American cut glass operation founded in 1911 at Hallstead, Pennsylvania, by six Demer brothers: Frank, Fred, Henry, Jacob, Joseph, and Phillip. The firm produced cut glass tableware until just after the end of World War I.

DEMITASSE — Matching cups and saucers that are much smaller (1/2 size or less) than their ordinary counterparts; note that Demitasse cups and saucers are still slightly larger than those found in children's miniature tea sets.

DENALI CRYSTAL — A modern American Art Glass firm established by Peter Temple at Santa Fe, New Mexico, in 1983 as "Peter A. Temple – A Glass Center," the name was changed to Denali Crystal in 1986 (Denali is an American Indian word for "the shining one") and the studio moved in 1987 to Albion, California. Desmond Hatfield also joined on in 1989. The firm specializes in paperweights (crystal and color) that are faceted with both straight and elaborately curved cuts; the end results are prism-like effects.

DENNIS GLASSWORKS — An English glass operation founded near Stourbridge, England, by the Webb family in 1855. Early on, the company produced art glass and continues to operate today as part of the DEMA GLASS, LTD. *See also* WEBB, THOMAS & SONS.

DEPRESSION GLASS — Mass-produced, inexpensive, and primarily machine-made pressed glass dinner sets and giftware made in America in the 1920s and 1930s, Depression Glass was made in both clear and color. Pink and green were the most prevalent colors. Since the 1960s, Depression Glass has been one of America's most popular collectible categories in glassware.

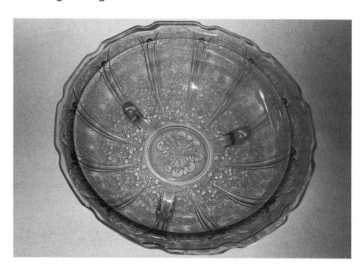

A cherry blossom patterned Depression Glass bowl from the Jeannette Glass Company. *Photo by Robin Rainwater.*

Colored Depression Glass tumblers. *Photo by Robin Rainwater.*

DESPREZ, BARTHELEMY — Desprez (1773-1819) was a French sculptor who introduced the process of making sulphides, which are ceramic reliefs of medals, busts, or portraits of famous people. Later, they were incrusted within clear glass paperweights. *See also* SULPHIDES.

DESSERT GLASS — A medium to fairly large glass receptacle originating in Europe in the early eighteenth century. The vessel was used to serve sweetmeats and fruits. Dessert glasses were eventually replaced by "Sweetmeat Glasses" and "Fruit Bowls."

DEVIL'S FIRE — A flame-like swirling paperweight motif used by Millville.

DEVITRIFICATION — A deteriorated condition of glass in which crystals have formed within the glass due to technical faults in the manufacturing process. Devitrification usually occurs if the temperature of a batch is too high and/or if the cooling process is rushed too quickly or slowed significantly.

DEWDROP — An all-over pattern of small beads or drops commonly found in mold-pressed glassware. Dewdrops resemble small hobnails and are often combined with other designs to create distinct patterns (i.e. dewdrop and flowers, dewdrop in points, dewdrop with star, jewel with dewdrop, lacey dewdrop, loop with dewdrop, dewdrops with flowers, paneled dewdrop, and striped dewdrop).

Line Drawing by Mark Pickvet.

DIAGONAL BAND — A decorative feature consisting of an angled or cross strip that is applied to an object in a slanted fashion (usually from top to bottom). Diagonal bands are common in pressed glass and are often combined with other features to create distinct patterns (i.e. clear diagonal band, diagonal band with fan, etc.). *See also* BAND.

DIAMETER — The most commonly used physical measurement to denote the size of such glass objects as bowls, plates, and paperweights.

DIAMOND AIR TRAP — A design in glass first patented by the W. H. B. & J. Richardson Company of Wordsley, England, in 1857; trapped air bubbles in the shape of diamonds were achieved by blowing glass into a mold with small indentations, and then covering the designed object with a second layer of glass (the second or outer layer covers the diamond-shaped indentations that were created in the mold).

DIAMOND ART GLASS COMPANY — Refer to the DIGBY CUT GLASS COMPANY.

DIAMOND CUT GLASS COMPANY — Refer to the DIGBY CUT GLASS COMPANY.

DIAMOND CUT GLASS WORKS — An American firm founded in 1910 on Manhattan Island, New York, by Lawrence & Minnie Cohn, the company produced limited cut glass prior to closing in 1918.

Diamond Cut Glass Works: Trademark.

DIAMOND-DAISY — A cut-glass design pattern featuring daisies inscribed within diamonds or squares.

DIAMOND GLASS COMPANY — Refer to the DUGAN GLASS COMPANY.

DIAMOND GLASS COMPANY, LTD. — A Canadian company that operated in both Trenton and Montreal from 1890-1902, the firm was noted for many pressed glass designs, tableware, and lamps; along with some blown and cut glass products. The firm was also known as the Lamont Glass Company.

DIAMOND GLASSWARE CORPORATION — Refer to the DUGAN GLASS COMPANY.

DIAMOND-MOLDED — A pressed pattern design developed in America in the mid-nineteenth century. The inner iron molds varied and usually contained small circular or oval diamonds that formed an overall pattern, a checkered pattern, or perhaps a few rows for vertical fluting. Several distinct pressed patterns contain many diamond variations (i.e. diamond and sunburst, diamond band, diamond block with fan, diamond swirl, diamond mirror, diamond point, diamond point with panels, diamond prisms, diamond quilted, diamond thumbprint, diamond lace, diamond bar, diamond horseshoe, diamond lattice, and diamond medallion).

A pressed glass diamond-molded patterned decanter.

DIAMOND POINT — A cut glass design pattern featuring faceted diamonds intersecting at a common point. For pressed diamond designs, see also DIAMOND-MOLDED above.

DIAMOND POINT ENGRAVING — Hand cutting or machine cutting of glass with a diamond point tool (note that hardened metal by heat treating to a sharp point has since replaced the more expensive diamonds for machine cutting). Engraving in paperweights generally takes place on the exterior only.

DIAMOND-QUILTED — A cut or pressed pattern consisting of angular diamonds that formed an overall pattern, much like a checkered or patchwork quilt design. Diamonds are sometimes referred to as "Lozenges" in cut glass.

DIATRETA GLASS — Art glass made by applying tiny pieces of ornamental glass in patterns to other larger glass objects. This process was first developed by Frederick Carder in the early 1900s and was made to simulate Roman Glass in this style. *See also* VASA DIATRETA.

A 1953 Diatreta vase by Frederick Carder. *Courtesy of Wheaton Village.*

DICHROIC GLASS — A modern creation in glass that reflects different colors (two or more) within the full color spectrum, somewhat like a prism, depending upon the angle of light that falls on it. Such additions as uranium (low grade) or copper oxide, or even colloidal gold causes this effect. *See also* DICHROMATIC GLASS.

D

DICHROMATIC GLASS — Glass that reflects different colors, like a prism, depending on the angle of light that falls upon it. One or more additions of uranium or copper oxide, neodymium or praseodymium (rare examples of lead or uranium ore), or perhaps colloidal gold causes this dual or multi-color effect. Most examples have a somewhat lavender hue under incandescent light and a bluish hue under fluorescent light. The term is sometimes referred to as "Dichroic," which ordinarily refers to an object showing two transparent colors.

DIDERS & McGEE — Refer to the McGEE-DIETERS GLASS COMPANY.

DIE-PATTERNED PAPERWEIGHT — A type of souvenir or advertising paperweight made by placing powdered glass (usually colored) that is picked up on a molten gather of clear glass within the pattern grooves of a metal mold.

DIETERS-McKEE — Refer to the McGEE-DIETERS GLASS COMPANY.

DIGBY CUT GLASS COMPANY — An American cut glass operation founded in 1919 at Seattle, Washington, by John Digby and Paul Kowarsh, the firm was reorganized as the Diamond Cut Glass Company in 1920 and remained in business until 1924. The firm was also known as the DIAMOND ART GLASS COMPANY.

DILUVIUM — A style of iridized Bohemian-colored glass produced by Josef Rindskopf during the Art Nouveau period, the glass was marbleized in appearance and further cut and/or engraved in high relief. See also JOSEF RINDSKOPF.

DINNER PLATE — A flat glass object, usually round in shape and about eight and eleven inches in diameter, used for serving the late afternoon or evening dinner meal.

DIP MOLD — A one-piece mold with an open top used for embossing or imprinting decorations and lettering. Dip molds are most often used for creating such things as ribs, spirals, and diamond effects in all-over patterns.

DIPSTICK — Refer to GATHERING IRON.

DISK PITCHER — A wide mouthed glass vessel with spout, pouring lip, and handle, used for pouring or serving liquids. Disk pitchers get their name for their unique circulars shape (like a disk). See also MILK PITCHER, PITCHER, and WATER PITCHER.

DISNEYANA — The name given to collectibles related to the creations of Walt Disney and his successors. Disney began as a maker of animated cartoons and introduced "Steamboat Willie," a Mickey Mouse cartoon, in 1928. Walt, along with his brother Roy, began licensing the reproduction of Disney characters on a wide variety of products including glassware. Some of the first glass products produced was a set of eight tumblers featuring Snow White and the Seven Dwarfs. The tumblers were produced by Libbey in 1937. Since then, other Disney glass collectibles include bells, mugs, figurines, and many limited edition hand-sculptured crystal items. See also CHARACTER GLASS.

DISPENSER — A large glass container or bottle with a spigot originally used for obtaining cold water from the refrigerator. Dispensers were readily adapted for a wide variety of pharmaceutical usage as well as for dispensing juices and soft drinks.

DITHRIDGE & COMPANY — An American firm founded by Edward Dithridge Sr. and David Challinor at Pittsburgh, Pennsylvania, in 1860. Dithridge purchased the Fort Pitts Glass Works (part of R.B. Curling & Sons) for which he worked in the 1850s. Challinor moved on to other ventures in 1864. Dithridge's son, George, joined in 1867 and the firm was briefly known as "Dithridge & Son." When the elder Dithridge died in 1873, George and Dithridge's other son, Edward Dithridge Jr., continued operations until reorganizing and moving to a new location (Martins Ferry, Ohio) in 1881. See also DITHRIDGE FLINT GLASS COMPANY.

DITHRIDGE FLINT GLASS COMPANY — An American firm founded by brothers George Dithridge and Edward D. Dithridge Jr. in 1881 at Martins Ferry, Ohio, the business was moved to New Brighton, Pennsylvania, in 1887 (name changed to Dithridge & Sons) and continued to produce cut and engraved glass as well as blanks for other companies. As a subsidiary, Dithridge also ran the Dithridge Chimney Company, which produced glass lamp parts. In the latter 1880s, the firm produced some crystal and milk glass tableware novelty items. The factory shut down permanently in 1901 and was then acquired by the Pittsburgh Lamp and Brass Company.

FLORAL CRYSTAL

Dithridge Flint Glass Company: Trademark.

DIVIDERS — Refer to CALIPERS.

DIXON, FRANCIS AND COMPANY — An English firm founded in 1842 when Francis Dixon (1819-1915), along with his brother-in-law John Merson, purchased a bottle-making factory at Thatto Heath near St. Helens. They built a new factory in 1850 near Ravenhead Colliery (note that glassware, mostly bottles and some tableware made by them, is also known as "Ravenhead Glass"). Merson left in 1854 and, in 1859, after Dixon inherited the estate of his uncle, Thomas Nuttall, the name was changed to Nuttall & Company. The factory was sold to the Pilkington Brothers in 1872; however, Dixon built a new glassworks at Ravenhead. Dixon retired in 1900 and was succeeded by his son, Frederick Richard Dixon-Nuttall (1853-1929), who in turn was succeeded by his son, William Francis Dixon Nuttall (1885-1981). In 1913, Nuttal merged with five other local glass manufacturers (Alexander, Brefflit, Candlish, Shaw, and Moore & Nettleford) to form United Glass Bottle (UGB) Manufacturers Ltd. See also UNITED GLASS BOTTLE MANUFACTURERS LIMITED.

DOLOMITE — A mineral ($CaCO_3$ or $MgCO_3$) often used as a source of calcium oxide in glass production.

DOLPHIN — (1) A late nineteenth century pressed glass pattern that contains molded dolphins on the circular base of various tableware pieces. (2) A covered dish in the shape of a dolphin made by the Indiana Tumbler & Goblet Company in 1899, the cover sports a fish finial. Similar dishes were made by various companies later as well (many Carnival glass dolphin dishes were also produced). (3) A general term for the thick curled handles or decorative features on objects such as beakers, bottles, candlesticks, vases, jars, and other products; that are made to resemble dolphins. The term "Double Dolphin" is sometimes used to describe a matching pair.

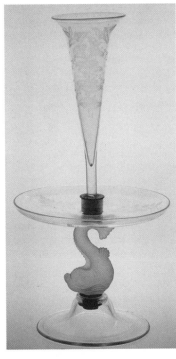

An 1870s Boston & Sandwich etched/engraved epergne with dolphin stand. *Photo courtesy of the Sandwich Glass Museum.*

DOME — The curved form of a glass above the internal design that makes the overall shape of the paperweight. *See also* CROWN.

DOME COVER — A type of top or cover that is circular and domed in shape and fits on a collar or ridge of a vessel. They are ordinarily found on many butter and cheese dishes. Some are double-domed with a small domed finial resting upon a larger one.

Dome Cover: A decorated custard domed cover butter dish from the Jefferson Glass Company. *Courtesy of Wheaton Village.*

DOMINION GLASS COMPANY — A Canadian company that operated from 1886-1898 (separate from the modern company of the same name) in Montreal, they were noted for producing pressed wares and lamps. It was purchased by the Jefferson Glass Company, of Toronto, which continued to produce lamps.

Reproduction from an early twentieth century Dominion catalog.

Dominion Glass Company Trademarks.

DOMINO TRAY — A serving dish with a built-in center container for cream that is in turn surrounded by a flat or slightly curved surface area specifically designed for holding sugar cubes.

DOOR KNOB — A handle, usually round in shape, used for releasing the latch of a door; glass door knobs were popular during the Victorian era and were either clear cut crystal or were made in color. Some examples have been found with millefiori designs.

DOOR PLATE — A rectangular piece that rests in the panel of a door that serves to protect the door from marring. Glass door panels are usually secured by external framing (wood or metal) with fasteners such as screws or nails.

DOORSTOP — A very large or heavy glass object, like an oversized paperweight, used to prop open doors and prevent them from closing.

DOOR STOPPER — A solid heavy object, with a flat bottom, designed to rest on the ground in order to hold doors open. Glass door stoppers are usually rounded or ovoid in shape and may resemble paperweights, only they are much larger and typically weigh several pounds.

DORFLINGER GLASS WORKS — The original factory was established in White Mills, Pennsylvania, in 1846 by German immigrant Christian Dorflinger (1825-1915), who purchased the Long Island Flint Glass Works in Brooklyn, New York, in 1852, and officially founded the Dorflinger Glass Works later in 1865 in White Mills. Dorflinger was noted as a major supplier of lead crystal blanks utilized by other factories and cutters. Cut crystal made by Dorflinger was sold in the finest department stores and graced the tables of Presidents Lincoln, Grant, Harrison, and Wilson; along with many crowned heads of Europe. The elder Dorflinger passed away in 1915; his death, combined with World War I, led to the demise of the firm in 1921. *See also* WHITE MILLS GLASSWORKS.

Trademark.

Reproduction from an 1888 Dorflinger U.S. Patent.

DOUBLE BOTTLE — A bottle that has two separate internal compartments, each with its own separate mouth and spout.

DOUBLE CRUET — Two glass bottles (cruets) fused together into one larger capacity bottle and used for serving condiments. Although it is one object, there are still two separate necks, mouths, stoppers, and inner compartments. They originated in the late sixteenth century in Europe and were originally used to hold oil and vinegar separately.

DOUBLE OVERLAY — A paperweight encased with a thin layer of opaque glass (usually white) and then layered again with another color. The outer layer is then usually cut with windows or some other design (i.e. floral) so that the inner layer serves as a background or frame for what design is cut above it.

DOUBLE ROLL METHOD — Sheet glass formed when molten glass is passed between a pair of rotating metal rolls.

DOUBLE WALL GLASS — A Bohemian style of glass consisting of a decoration that is applied between two panels or walls of glass (Germans referred to it as "Doppelwaldglas"). In turn, the outer wall was often engraved or enameled as well. The most noteworthy example of a double wall glass is made with gold enamel and/or gold leaf. *See also ZWISCHENGOLDGLAS.*

DOUBLE WINE GLASS — A wine or stemmed glass with a bowl at each end of the stem. The glass rests on the rim of one bowl while the other remains upright for filling and/or drinking. One bowl (red wine) is usually lager than the other (white wine). Some are in the shape of a figural woman, so that when the vessel rests on the larger bowl, the object resembles a woman carrying a basket.

DOVE FLASK — A small glass container made in the shape of a dove, with a narrow neck and mouth and a stopper or cover, used for holding perfume. Dove flasks originated with the ancient Romans where elongated tails served as spouts. Colorful European examples were produced in the eighteenth century.

DOYLE AND COMPANY — An American pressed glass manufacturer established at Pittsburgh, Pennsylvania, in 1866 by Wiliam Doyle, Joseph Doyle, William Beck, and other associates. A fire destroyed the plant in 1878, but it was rebuilt. In 1881, they established a subsidiary known as Doyle Sons & Company with Joseph Doyle as president and Henry Doyle (who produced glass chimneys for lamps at a separate plant in Phillipsburg, Pennsylvania). The lamp parts were also manufactured under the Phillipsburg Glass Works name. The firm was purchased by the Phoenix Glass Company of Phillipsburg, New Jersey, in 1890 and then became part of the U.S. Glass Company in 1891 as Factory P. U.S. Glass continued to produce pressed glass at the original plant until 1931.

DRAGON GLASS — A style of goblet made in both Germany and the Netherlands in the late sixteenth and early seventeenth centuries. The stem of the goblet consists of threads that are twisted into the shape or form of a dragon. Note that the Germans refer to it as "Drachenglas"

DRAHONOVSKY, JOSEF — A noted Czechoslovakian sculptor and art professor, at age thirteen Drahonovsky (1877-1938) studied stone cutting at the Industrial Art School in Turbov and then went on to study with Dorflinger in Vienna at age seventeen. Two years later, he returned to Prague, where he entered the Academy of Applied Arts. He eventually became both an artist and instructor at the Academy, creating sculptured artwork in clay, marble, plaster, metal, and glass. He also produced elaborate hand-engraved glass in typical Bohemian styles in both crystal and multi-layered colors.

DRAKE, GEORGE CUT GLASS COMPANY — An American cut glass-making firm established at Corning, New York, in 1900 by George Washington Drake (1870-1910), the business closed in 1910 when Drake passed away.

Trademarks.

DRAM GLASS — Small English or Irish glasses made of metal used for drinking a single measure of strong liquor (most were made between 1750 and 1850 and imported to the United States). Dram glasses were predecessors of shot glasses.

DRAPE OR DRAPERY — A decorative add-on design found in pressed glass consisting of flowing fan-like projections that resemble curtains or drapes. This design is usually combined with others to form distinct patterns (i.e. cord drapery, draped fan, draped garland, draped jewel, draped window, heavy drape, Lincoln drape, ribbed drape, etc.). Glass sheets with multiple folds are also referred to as "Drapery" since they resemble the folds of hanging drapes.

Drape, drapery.
Drawing by Mark Pickvet.

DRAWN ANTIQUE — Glass similar to that of full antique, only it is made by the vertical draw method rather than by blowing. If textural striations are desired, then they are mechanically applied in this method as opposed to those that are hand-applied in full antique. *See also FULL ANTIQUE and VERTICAL DRAW METHOD.*

DREISBACH, FRITZ — A noted American Studio Glass artisan born in Cleveland, Ohio, in 1941, Dreisbach received a Master of Fine Arts degree from the University of Wisconsin in 1967. He soon became a noted studio art glass instructor and has served in a teaching capacity at Kent State University, the Rhode Island School of Design, Ohio University, the Toledo Museum of Art, the Chicago Art Institute, and the Pilchuk Glass Center. He resides in Seattle, Washington, where he also works as an independent glass artisan.

DRESSER SET — A set of glass bath or bedroom objects held on a matching tray. These objects might include a combination or ring stands, perfume or cologne bottles; powder bowls or jars; and tiny boxes for gloves, hair or hat pins, and jewelry.

Depression glass dresser set. *Photo by Robin Rainwater.*

Cut Glass Dresser Set. Floral Engraving. Set
Consists of 9¾-inch Tray, 3¾-inch Puff
Jar and Hair Receiver, Cologne and
Salve Jars.
No. 9430—Complete................. $22.50

Reproduction from an early twentieth century
S.F. Myers Co. catalog.

DRESSING — Ornamental glass objects that make up certain parts of a chandelier. These might include the drops, snakes, arms, pinnacles, icicles, prisms, and candle holders or multiple piece candelabrum.

DRINKING BOWL — A large concave glass vessel, hemispherical in shape, used for sharing liquids communally. Drinking bowls were popular during the early Middle Ages (5th though the 11th centuries).

DRINKING GLASS — A very general term for most any hollow glass vessel designed for the consumption of liquids. *See also GOBLET, STEMWARE, TUMBLER, and WINE GLASS.*

DROP — A smooth, faceted, or decorative glass ornament suspended from lighting fixtures such as chandeliers, girandoles, candlesticks, and candelabrum.

DUBLIN GLASS — Glass products made in Dublin, Ireland, in the late eighteenth through the mid-nineteenth centuries. The goods consisted of quality lead crystal tableware, as well as new wheel cutting and engraving techniques, prevalent with the Irish during this period. Nearly all Dublin products produced during this time are marked "CM & Co." for Charles Mulvaney & Company, the principal and most prolific glasshouse that resided in the city (1785-1835).

DUFFNER & KIMBERLY — An American firm founded in New York, New York, in 1906, the company produced Art Glass lamps and leaded glass shades until 1911. The firm was briefly carried on as the Kimberly Company, but ended in the World War I era.

Reproduction from a 1907
Duffner & Kimberly advertisement.

Trademark.

DUGAN GLASS COMPANY — (1) An American firm established at Indiana, Pennsylvania, in 1904 by G. C. Dickie, Thomas E. Dugan, John Elkin, W. G. Minnemyer, Edward G. Minnemeyer Jr., D. B. Taylor, and H. Wallace Thomas. The company purchased the old Northwood plant from National Glass and produced a good deal of pressed glass, of which most was iridized Carnival Glass. Dugan had been the superintendent of the plant under National and his brother, Al Dugan, became the new factory manager. After Thomas Dugan resigned in 1913 (briefly going on to work for Duncan & Miller), the business became the Diamond Glass Company with Elkin as president. The firm reincorporated as the Diamond Glassware Corporation and continued in operation until it was destroyed by fire in 1931. Aside from Carnival glass, Diamond created some colored Depression glass, such as the "Victory" pattern. (2) After his brief stint at Duncan & Miller, Thomas Dugan, along with his brother Al Dugan, founded a new corporation in 1914 under the Dugan Glass Company name in Lonaconing, Maryland. The firm produced pressed glass tableware, bar goods, decorated goods, and lime blown tumblers. Thomas Dugan resigned in 1915 and the firm became the Lonaconing Glass Company. The new entity specialized in blown glass tableware (mostly tumblers) and produced some cut glass as well. Fire destroyed the plant in

1916 and it was rebuilt in 1917; however, the plant closed because of a natural gas shortage during World War I. In 1920, the plant reopened under the name Utility Glass Company, which leased the plant briefly to the Potomac Glass Company. An explosion resulting in a fire destroyed the plant in 1932 and it was not rebuilt.

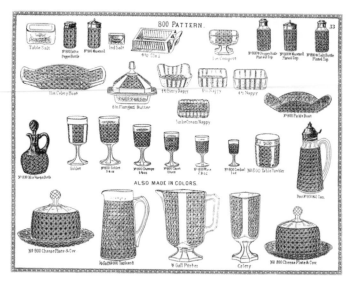

Reproduction from an 1890 Duncan catalog.

A Carnival Glass grape and cable patterned beverage set from the Dugan Glass Company. *Photo by Robin Rainwater.*

Trademark.

DUMMER, GEORGE & COMPANY — Refer to the JERSEY CITY GLASS COMPANY.

DUMMER, P. C. & COMPANY — Refer to the JERSEY CITY GLASS COMPANY.

DUNBAR GLASS COMPANY — An American firm founded at Dunbar, West Virginia, in 1913 as the Dunbar Flint Glass Corporation, the company began as a manufacturer of crystal lamp chimneys and changed its name to Dunbar Glass Company around 1930. The company also produced some blown and machine-pressed tableware, including both iridescent and Depression colored glassware, before closing in 1953.

DUNCAN, GEORGE & SONS — George Duncan and Daniel Ripley established the American pressed glass firm of Ripley & Co. in 1865-66 at Pittsburgh, Pennsylvania. Duncan's sons, George Jr., Harry B., and James E., along with his son-in-law Augustus Heisey, were also active in the company. Duncan and Ripley split in 1874 and went on to form their own companies. George Duncan & Sons was founded in Pittsburgh in 1874 and produced pressed glass items. The firm's name was briefly changed to Duncan & Heisey (for James E. Duncan and Augustus Heisey) around 1887 before becoming part of the U.S. Glass Company in 1891 as Factory D. The plant burned in 1892 ending the affiliation with U.S. Glass. A new plant was built in Washington, Pennsylvania, and the new firm was organized as the Duncan & Miller Glass Company.

DUNCAN & MILLER GLASS COMPANY — An American firm established in 1892 by James E. and George Duncan Jr., along with John Ernest Miller, at Washington, Pennsylvania, it was incorporated in 1900 consisting of officers/owners James E. Duncan, Anna Duncan, Andrew Duncan, Harry Duncan, and John Ernest Miller. The company produced pressed wares and novelty items through the Depression era. The firm closed in 1955 (fire destroyed the actual factory in 1956). The molds equipment, and factory machinery were all purchased by the U.S. Glass Company located in Tiffin, Ohio. Patterns produced by the company include "Canterbury," "Caribbean," "Early American Sandwich," "First Love," "Tear Drop," and "Terrace."

DURAND ART GLASS COMPANY — An American firm established at Vineland, New Jersey, by French immigrant Victor Durand Jr. in 1924. The company produced several Art Glass styles up to Durand's death in an automobile accident in 1931. Durand was actually born in 1870 in Baccarat, France, and apprenticed at the Baccarat Glassworks, where several generations of his family had worked. His father (Victor Durand Sr.) migrated to America in 1882 to join Wheaton Glass and then Whitall-Tatum & Company, both in New Jersey. Durand joined his father there in 1884 at the age of fourteen; and then the two went on to lease the Vineland Glass Company in Vineland, New Jersey, in 1897 after working for several glass-making firms. *See also* VINELAND FLINT GLASS MANUFACTURING COMPANY.

Iridescent Art Glass vases from the Durand Art Glass Company. *Photo courtesy of Wheaton Village.*

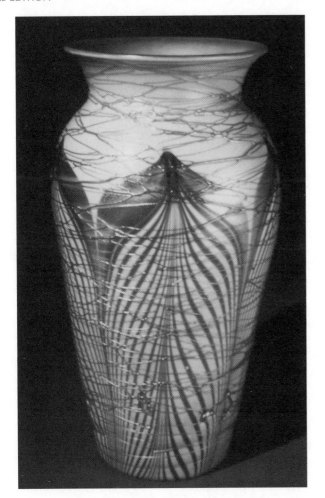

Durand Art Glass vase. *Photo by Robin Rainwater.*

Trademark.

DURAND, J. G. INDUSTRIES — The parent company of many subsidiaries that includes Arc International. Under Arc, the noted glass brands of Arcoroc, Cristal d'Arques, J. G. Durand, Luminarc, and Salviati are produced. In 2001, Durand also acquired Mikasa, which operates as a stand-alone subsidiary. With these combined brands, Durand is now the world's largest glass and crystal manufacturer. *See also "Arc International"* and MIKASA CRYSTAL, INC.

DUROBOR — A Belgian firm founded at Soignies in 1928, the company purchased automated machinery from America's Libbey-Owens and was the first to produce machine-made tumblers in Europe. In 1935, the firm changed its name to Dur-o-bor from "Dur-au-bord," meaning "hard at the rim." The company specialized in making very durable drinking vessels with a flame-finished bead-like rim that was more resistant to chipping. In 1960, Owens-Illinois obtained a 99% share of the firm and the dashes were removed from the name (simply "Durobor"). In 1990, the firm was sold to Sadetam, a Belgian holding company. The firm continues as one of Europe's largest producers of crystal tumblers and mugs, particularly for the bar and restaurant market.

DUTCH GLASS — Refer to "Netherlands Glass" and the "Royal Dutch Glass Works."

DYAT'KOV CRYSTAL WORKS — Refer to the MAL'TSEV GLASSWORKS and SOVIET GLASS.

DYOTTVILLE GLASS WORKS — English immigrant Thomas Dyott (1771-1861) acquired an interest in the Philadelphia & Kensington Glass Works in America in the early 1800s and then was able to purchase the firm outright in 1831. Under his direction, the company produced a good deal of bottles and historical flasks depicting famous people (like presidents of the United States). Dyott went bankrupt in 1838 and the factory was taken over for awhile by his brother Michael Dyott. The firm changed hands several times before closing in the 1920s.

D

Ee

{ Ee }

EAGLE CUT GLASS COMPANY — An American cut glass operation founded at Minneapolis, Minnesota, in 1908 by A. W. Benson, August Eckman, and Knute Eckman, the firm produced some cut glass tableware into the World War I era.

EAGLE GLASS AND MANUFACTURING COMPANY — An American firm established at Wellsburg, West Virginia, in 1894 by four Paull brothers (H. W., James, Joseph, and S. O.), the company produced pressed glass, lamps, globes, shades, jars, pharmaceutical bottles, and some opaque/milk glass novelty items. The firm ceased making glass items in 1924 (the word "Glass" was dropped from the company name); however, they did remain in business as a metal fabricator (i.e. gas cans and oil containers).

Reproduction from an 1899 Eagle advertisement.

EAGLE GLASS WORKS — A short-lived American firm established by J. H. (Harvey) Leighton in Keota, Iowa, in 1879, the company closed the following year; however, it did produce some pressed glass tableware that is also known as "Keota Glass." Note that Leighton was the nephew of William Leighton Sr., who was famous for inventing the soda lime formula as a substitute for lead crystal while working for Hobbs, Brockunier.

EARLY AMERICAN PATTERN GLASS — General term for glass made in America from the Colonial times up to the late nineteenth century. It includes cut, engraved, pressed, blown, blown-molded, lacy, and general patterned glass made by such firms as Boston & Sandwich, New England, South Jersey, Stiegel, and a host of pressed glass manufacturers throughout the early-to-mid nineteenth century. Glass produced during this time is sometimes referred to as the "Early American Period" of glass-making.

EARLY AMERICAN PRESCUT — A huge line of pressed glass made and named by the Anchor Hocking Company in 1960 through the mid-1970s, it is similar in style to older pressed glass and contains alternating rows of 10-point stars with fan-like leaves.

EAST LIVERPOOL GLASS MANUFACTURING COMPANY, LTD. — An American firm founded by George Fry and Fred Hendrick in 1882 at East Liverpool, Ohio, the company produced blown and pressed glass tableware and limited engravings of crystal. The firm was also known as the East Liverpool Glass Works, the East Liverpool Cooperative Glass works, and the Liverpool Manufacturing Company. It filed for bankruptcy in 1883 and ceased operations. The plant was sold in 1888 to Novelty Glass Works, which was established by George Irwin and Frank Kubler. They changed the name shortly after to Specialty Glass Works. See also SPECIALTY GLASS WORKS.

EAST RIVER FLINT GLASS WORKS — Refer to the LAFAYETTE FLINT GLASS WORKS.

EAST WHEELING GLASS WORKS — (1) An American pressed glass-making firm established at Wheeling, West Virginia (prior to West Virginia becoming a state), in 1837 by Francis Plunkett and H. M. Miller. Note that Plunkett and Miller established a second venture in the same city that same year. Operations were moved to South Wheeling and renamed the South Wheeling Glass Works in 1840. The firm produced lead cut/engraved crystal and colored tableware before going bankrupt in 1841. The idle factory in East Wheeling was leased for a couple of years by Edward, William, and Franklin Anderson, who built a new factory in South Wheeling and renamed the company Wheeling Glass Works. (2) The Central Glass Company has also been referred to as East Wheeling. See also PLUNKETT & MILLER, WHEELING GLASS WORKS, ANDERSON & COMPANY, AMERICAN FLINT GLASS WORK, and CENTRAL GLASS COMPANY.

EBENEZER CUT GLASS COMPANY — An American firm founded in 1915 by Louis, Frances, and Earl Erckert at Ebenezer, New York, the firm served as a decorator by engraving crystal. The factory burned to the ground in 1957 and was not rebuilt.

EBONY GLASS — Another name for black-colored or very dark black opaque glass. See also BLACK GLASS.

ECKHARDT, EDRIS — A noted twentieth century American glass artisan and instructor, Eckhardt was born in Cleveland, Ohio, in 1910. After receiving her Fine Arts degree from the Cleveland Art Institute, she headed the ceramics and sculpture division of the Federal Art Project in Cleveland (1935-1962). She spent her career as an art/studio glass instructor having taught at the Cleveland Institute of Art, Western Reserve University, the University of California, Cleveland College, and Notre Dame College. Awards for her glass-making include the Guggenhiem (1956, 1959) and a Louis Comfort Tiffany Foundation Fellowship (1956).

ECLIPSE TUMBLER COMPANY — Refer to the FINDLAY CUT GLASS COMPANY.

ECONOMY GLASS COMPANY — Refer to the ECONOMY TUMBLER COMPANY and MORGAN GLASS WORKS.

ECONOMY TUMBLER COMPANY — An American firm established in Morgantown, West Virginia, in 1903 by George W. Fry and Frank P. Corbin, the company had purchased the Morgantown Glass Works and renamed it the Economy Tumbler Company. Fry had also run a brief cut glass operation when he purchased the Thompson Glass Company factory in 1900 at Uniontown, Pennsylvania. Fry ran the Uniontown plant as the George W. Fry Glass Company before moving all equipment to Economy. Fry left in 1909 and went on to establish the Crystal Tumbler Company (a short-lived blown tumbler producing firm, also established at Morgantown,) in 1911. When the company introduced colored wares in 1924, the name was changed to the "Economy Glass Company"; however, products throughout the company's history are still referred to as "Morgantown Glass." In fact, the firm reverted back to the "Morgantown Glass Works" name in 1939. The business closed permanently in 1972. *See also* THOMPSON GLASS COMPANY, LTD. *and* MORGANTOWN GLASS WORKS.

EDA GLASSWORKS — A Swedish glass company established in the Varmland region in 1833 as the Emterud Glasswork, the factory burned soon after opening and was rebuilt in 1843; at that time, the name was changed to Eda. Early on, the firm produced functional items such as window panes, flasks, and bottles. Gradually, they added pressed and mold-blown tableware as well as some cut glass products. During the 1920s, they produced some Carnival Glass and art glass styles when Edvard Stromberg (1872-1946, previous manager of Kosta) was hired. Stromberg's wife Gerda (1879-1969) was also hired as a designer; however, the Strombergs left in 1933 to form their own firm, Strombergshyttan. The factory changed ownership several times until closing in 1953.

EDELWEISS CANE — A white star-shaped millefiori cane in paperweights that surrounds a core of bundled yellow rods. The end result resembles that of the Swiss national flower, the Edelweiss.

EDENHALL — Refer to the T. G. HAWKES & COMPANY.

EDGE — The thin straight-line surface where two plane faces meet or the narrow band along the rim of a plate, vase, bowl, or similar object. Edges may be even or uneven, ruffled, rounded, flattened, roped, contain teeth (sawtooth), and further colored or decorated.

EDINBURGH CRYSTAL GLASS COMPANY — A glass operation originally founded in Leith, Scotland (near Edinburgh), in 1884 as the Edinburgh and Leith Flint Glass Company, in its beginning the company produced hand-cut crystal wares and imported some of these products to America. In 1919, the firm was acquired by Webb's Crystal Glass Company, which continued to use the Edinburgh name. In 1951, they acquired the firm of John Walsh Walsh and produced some scientific and industrial-related glassware. In 1964, they became part of Dema Glass, Ltd. and operations were later moved to Penicuik (a small town also located near Edinburgh) in 1974. The company is noted in the twentieth century to the present for the production of crystal tableware. Products are still made today under the "Edinburgh Crystal" namesake.

EDWARDS, STEPHEN DALE — A noted American Studio Glass artisan who was born in Fort Worth, Texas in 1948, Edwards received his Master of Fine Arts degree from the University of Iowa. He is also a noted studio art glass instructor and has served in a teaching capacity at the Pilchuk Glass School, the Pratt Fine Arts Center, and the Miasa Bunka Center in Nagano, Japan. Edwards lives and works as an independent glass artisan in Kirkland, Washington.

EGERMANN, FRIEDRICH — A noted Bohemian glass artisan of the late eighteenth and nineteenth centuries, Egermann (1777-1864) worked as an apprentice with several glass firms including Anton Kothgasser and his uncle, Antonin Kittle. He studied under porcelain painters as well and began purchasing clear and plain milk glass from other firms in which he matted and decorated with semi-opaque enamels. Egermann soon gained a reputation for superior craftsmanship and is noted for inventing numerous unique color stains and enamels, especially a complicated form of red glazing that involved three separate firings and lithyalin, an oily free-flowing swirled enameled technique. He rented a large house as a showroom to display his creations in Haida in 1820. His firm eventually expanded to include two hundred full-time decorators and, as a consequence, became one of the largest producers of Bohemian-styled enameled glass in the nineteenth century. *See also* BOHEMIAN GLASS *and* LITHYALIN.

A cut and decorated glass beaker of Francis I and Caroline Augusta (emperor and empress of Austria) by F. Egermann, 1831. *Photo courtesy of the Museum of Decorative Arts, Prague.*

EGG — An ornamental ovoid glass object made to resemble an egg. Eggs originally served as hand-coolers and may or may not be formed with their own stand in one solid piece (those without stands generally come with a stand that may be made of glass, metal, or plastic).

Hand-painted Fenton glass eggs. *Photo by Robin Rainwater.*

EGG CUP OR HOLDER — A small cup-like vessel without a handle that has room enough for holding a single egg. Egg cups are generally stemmed and somewhat ovoid in shape. Occasionally, double egg holders have been made (separate holders for two eggs).

EGG PLATE — A flat thick plate with oval indentations for serving boiled or deviled eggs.

EGGINGTON, O. F. COMPANY — An American cut glass operation established at Corning, New York, in 1896 by Oliver Eggington (1822-1900). A former foreman of T. G. Hawkes, Eggington purchased blanks from the Corning Glass Works and, when he died in 1900, his son Walter E. Eggington resumed control. The firm operated as a cut glass business, but went bankrupt in 1918 (though there have been some reports that glass may still have been produced under the Eggington name as late as 1920).

Reproduction of a 1903 Eggington U.S. patent.

Eggington, O. F.
Company Trademark.

EGLOMISE — A French decorating style that consists of applying gold and/or silver leaf to a glass object and then further engraving it by fine needlepoint. The practice actually originated with the ancient Egyptians and Romans; and was further carried on by Venetian and Bohemian glass decorators. The French term is named for Jean Baptiste Glomy, an eighteenth century French artist, writer, and art dealer, who decorated a good deal of glassware in this fashion. Note that since objects are no longer fired after the engraving, the design has a tendency to wear off if applied to the front; therefore, most items decorated in this fashion were completed on the reverse outer surface and may further have been protected by a foil, varnish, or a thin coating of glass.

EGYPTIAN GLASS — Glass objects made in ancient Egypt from about the fifteenth century B.C. up until Roman times. Glass-making originated in Mesopotamia around 2,000 B.C. and soon spread to Egypt. Most Egyptian items consisted of core-formed vessels, which is the process of glass-making by spinning glass around a core. *See also* CORE *and* CORE-FORMING.

13th-14th century B.C. Egyptian glass flakes and amphoras.
Items *courtesy of the Corning Museum of Glass.*

EICHBAUM, PETER — After the fall of the Bastille during the French Revolution, Eichbaum immigrated to America with the help of Benjamin Franklin in 1796. He had descended from a family of glass cutters in Westphalia and helped found the St. Louis glass village in honor of King Louis XVI. Eichbaum cut glass on his own, briefly headed the Pittsburgh Glass Works, and cut glass for Bakewell, Pears, & Company, including America's first cut glass chandelier. Eichbaum is also noted for introducing the German "Kugel," a round, concave cutting technique (referred to as "Bullseye" in America glass cutting); and the concave, hexagonal diamond cutting motif (which he referred to as the "St. Louis Neck").

EICHBAUM, WENDT & COMPANY — Refer to the PITTSBURGH GLASS WORK.

EIFF VON, WILHELM — One of the most noteworthy glass engravers of the twentieth century, the German-born Eiff (1890-1943) trained under Lalique and is most known for engraving miniature portraits and other figures in relief. He also served as a glass engraving instructor in Stuttgart, Germany, and even invented a new flexible engraving tool in the 1930s.

EINTRACHTHUTTE — Refer to the MSTISOV GLASSWORKS.

EISELT, RUDOLF — A Czechoslovakian glassmaker who established a refinery at Novy Bor in 1925; the firm produced engraved and enameled glass in typical Bohemian Style up until World War II.

EISCH, VALENTIN — A German glass-making firm founded at Frauenau in Bavaria in 1946 by Valentin Eisch (1901-1983) and his wife Therese Eisch (1909-1994). It originally served as an engraving workshop until a furnace was added in 1952. A new factory was built in 1957 and the company produced decorated cut/engraved glass tableware. When Valentin retired in 1963, his three sons – Erwin (b. 1927), Erich (b. 1928), and Alfons (b. 1930) – took over. Today the firm is run by Ebehard Eisch (b.1965), Erich's son. Over 150 workers are employed, making etched, engraved, cut, and some abstract art styles.

EISLE & COMPANY — Refer to the NIAGARA CUT GLASS COMPANY.

EKENAS — A Swedish glass-making firm founded in the Varmland region by R. Stahl and Hjalmar Stahl in 1917. Both were previously employed by Orrefors. In 1922, the firm was sold to Sven Westberg, who ran it until his death in 1962. The firm produced machine-made container glass, scientific glass, tableware, and some Swedish art glass. After Westberg's death, the firm was managed by Claes Tell and his son until closing permanently in 1976.

ELECTRIC — An effect attributed to some Carnival Glass. The iridescence applied is so bright that it resembles neon or electric light.

ELEONORAHUTTE — A Bohemian glass company founded by Jan Meyr in 1834 near Vimperk, the firm produced glass in typical Bohemian style before being sold to W. Kralik & Son in 1881.

ELITE CUT GLASS COMPANY — An American firm established at Aldenville, Pennsylvania, in 1918, Elite was formed when the founders purchased a cut glass operation previously known as the Clinton Cut Glass Company. Elite continued to produce cut glass tableware until closing in 1924. *See also "Clinton Cut Glass Company."*

ELLIOT, JOHN & COMPANY — An English firm that established the Kensington Glass Works in Philadelphia, Pennsylvania, in 1772, the company produced some lead cut crystal tableware before ceasing operations in 1804.

ELLWOOD CITY GLASS COMPANY — An American firm established at Ellwood City, Pennsylvania, in 1905 by Charles Runyon and associates, the company purchased the plant that had previously been occupied by Clark Brothers Glass Company. In 1909, Runyon moved operations to Rochester, Pennsylvania, when he purchased a plant formerly owned and occupied by the Rochester Tumbler Company. The firm produced pressed glass tableware up until just after World War I. In 1918, it was sold to General Electric, which operated it as the Rochester Bulb Corporation (a division of General Electric).

ELME — A Swedish firm founded in 1917 in the Varmland region, initially it was to produce lenses for lighthouses and signals; however, operations were switched over to pressed and blown glass tableware. The firm went bankrupt in 1921, but reopened in 1923. In 1925, Sten Kjellgren purchased it and soon after hired noted painter/designer, Edvin Ollers (1888-1959), who had previously worked for Kosta. Under Ollers, noted designs included etching, engraving, and enameling with raised scrolling, stylized leaves, matte grounds, and other forms of Swedish art glass was produced. The firm was sold in 1935, again in 1940, and then purchased by the Borgarp family in 1962. Due to constant financial struggles, the factory closed permanently in 1970.

ELMIRA CUT GLASS COMPANY — A small American cut glass operation established at Elmira, New York, in 1899 by John Ferris, the firm purchased blanks made by Corning, and was sold to the J. Hoare & Company in 1913. Cut glass was produced at the shop up until the firm shut down in 1917. Ferris also operated the Ferris Glass Company. Note that the firm was also known as the Elmira Glass Cutting Company. *See also FERRIS GLASS COMPANY.*

ELMIRA GLASS CUTTING COMPANY — Refer to the ELMIRA CUT GLASS COMPANY.

ELMIRA WINDOW GLASS WORKS — An American firm established at Elmira, New York, in 1896, the company primarily produced glass window panes along with some whimsical items (glass walking canes and paperweights).

ELSON GLASS COMPANY — An American pressed glass-making firm established at Martins Ferry, Ohio, in 1882 by William Elson, William Robinson, and M. Sheets, the company produced both clear and colored pressed glass tableware, along with a small amount of cut glass. They purchased some molds from the defunct BELMONT GLASS COMPANY in 1890. The firm reorganized in 1893 as the West Virginia Glass Company with William Robinson, H. E. Waddell, and Percy Beaumont as principal owners. The plant closed in 1895 and was reorganized again in 1896 as the WEST VIRGINIA GLASS & MANUFACTURING COMPANY. Production resumed a short while in 1898 before the firm joined up with the NATIONAL GLASS COMPANY in 1899. The plant itself was shut down in 1903, and then leased briefly to the Fenton

Brothers in 1905. Fenton stayed until building its own factory in 1906 in Williamstown, West Virginia. When Fenton left, the HASKINS GLASS COMPANY purchased the plant to make lighting glassware.

EMBOSSING — Mold-brown or pressed glassware where the design is applied directly upon the object from the mold. Embossed patterns are usually somewhat in relief.

EMERALD GREEN — A deep, powerful green color usually made with chromium and iron (the color of the gemstone emerald). Steuben produced a very rich, vivid emerald green style of Art Glass in the early twentieth century that they simply referred to as "Green #5."

EMPIRE CUT GLASS COMPANY — An American cut glass operation established in New York City in 1895 by Harry Hollis; in 1902, Hollis sold the company to his employees and they operated it briefly as a cooperative. In 1904, they sold it to H. C. Fry, who moved operations to Flemington, New Jersey. Fry sold it in 1908 to the Flemington Cut Glass Company. *See also FLEMINGTON CUT GLASS COMPANY.*

Empire Cut Glass Company: Trademarks.

EMPIRE GLASS COMPANY — (1) An American glass decorating company founded at Zelienople, Pennsylvania, in 1899, the firm produced some pressed wares, but primarily worked as a glass decoration firm. Operations ceased in 1903. (2) Refer to the JEANNETTE SHADE & NOVELTY COMPANY, which also operated under the "Empire" name.

EMPIRE STATE FLINT GLASS WORKS — An American firm founded in 1857 at Brooklyn, New York, by Francis Thill, the company produced blown and cut glass, including some in color. The name was changed to Thill and Company in 1866, and then to F. THILL SONS & COMPANY in the early 1890s when Francis Sr.'s son – Francis Jr. and Harry – joined. The company went out of business in the mid-to-late 1890s.

EMPRESS GLASS COMPANY — A short-lived American glass-making firm established at Grafton, West Virginia, in 1905 by G. H. A. Kunst and George Whitescarver, the firm produced a limited amount of cut, pressed, and blown glass tableware before ceasing operation in 1910.

EMTRUD GLASSWORKS — Refer to EDA GLASSWORKS.

ENAMELING — A liquid medium similar to paint applied to glassware and then permanently fused on the object by heating.

An enameled German Zweisel green glass bell. *Photo by Robin Rainwater.*

ENCASED OVERLAY — A single or double overlay design further encased in clear glass. Paperweights are generally made in this style.

ENCLOSED ORNAMENTATION — The interior decoration enclosed within glassware. Enclosed ornamentation usually refers to the interior portion of such objects as paperweights, doorstops, eggs, and other solid objects with inner designs.

ENCRUSTED CAMEO — An English term for sulphide paperweight. *See also* SULPHIDE.

END-OF-DAY — A somewhat haphazard paperweight, usually millefiori in design, made from whatever colored canes are left by glassmakers at the end of their workday. *See also* SCRAMBLE.

ENGLISH GLASS — General term for glassware made in England from the late sixteenth century. The first operations were established by Jean Carre and Giacomo Verzelini, who made glass similar to that of the Venetians. Sir Robert Manell is also credited with pioneering the glass industry in England, where he recruited an Italian family (the DAGNIAS) to set up operations on L'Altare, England, in 1630. In 1676, George Ravenscroft developed the first durable lead crystal formula, which revolutionized the glass industry. As result, Ravenscroft became the first commercially successful glassmaker in England and lead crystal became the world standard for high quality clear glass. English makers followed other trends in glass-making and were significant producers of Bohemian-styled or "Bristol" glass (crystal, colored, and milk glass items produced in several factories in Bristol in the seventeenth and eighteenth centuries); "Victorian" glass (named for Queen Victoria and produced from about the 1820s through the 1940s, it is characterized by bright colors, opalescence, opaqueness, Art Glass, and unusual designs and shapes); pressed and cut glass in the nineteenth century; and Art Nouveau styles of the French, most notably those by Thomas Webb & Sons. *See also* CARRE, JEAN, DAGNIA FAMILY, RAVENSCROFT, GEORGE, BRISTOL GLASS, VICTORIAN GLASS, *and* WEBB, THOMAS & SONS.

English cameo vase by
Thomas Webb & Sons.
Courtesy of the Chrysler Museum.

ENGRAVING — An elaborate cut decoration of glass applied by holding a glass object against the edge of a revolving wheel. The wheels are ordinarily made of stone, copper, or other materials while the tips of the wheels are often made of diamonds or other very sharp metal alloys.

Engraved blue
glass tumbler.
*Photo by Robin
Rainwater.*

Engraved Austrian beaker.
Photo courtesy of the Corning Museum of Glass.

ENSELL & PLUNKETT — In 1830, the American partnership of Ensell & Plunkett, a Pittsburgh firm, leased the Virginia Green Glass Works from Charles Knox & Redick at Wheeling (prior to West Virginia becoming a state). The two continued to produce bottles and window panes at the factory until 1833 (they did not renew their lease). Ensell & Plunkett established a new firm at North Wheeling that briefly produced some bottles and flasks.

ENTERPRISE CUT GLASS COMPANY — (1) An American firm founded by George E. Gaylord in 1905 at Elmira Heights, New York, Gaylord had previously worked for both T. B. Clark and the Quaker City Cut Glass Company before establishing his own firm. Enterprise actually obtained a good deal of their blanks for cutting from Belgium; others they purchased from Union Glass Works. Like so many others, the advent of World War I cut off supplies and they went out of business in 1917. (2) Another light engraving operation known as Enterprise Cut Glass Company operated in the early 1920s in Hammonton, New Jersey. It was purchased by John Rothfus in 1926, and continued to decorate glass by engraving until 1949.

ENTERPRISE GLASS COMPANY — A short-lived American firm established at Sandusky, Ohio, in 1903 by D. E. Carle, James Merry, and associates, the company produced some window glass, bottles, and pressed tableware before closing in 1904. Note that there were a few other glass companies that sported the Enterprise name: at Ravenna, Ohio, that produced some blown and pressed glass wares (1878); at Beaver Falls, Pennsylvania, that produced prescription lenses (1894); and at Wheeling, West Virginia, that made pressed tableware (Enterprise Specialty Company, 1907). *See also* ENTERPRISE CUT GLASS COMPANY.

EPERGNE — The French term for a large table centerpiece that includes a sizeable bowl containing or is surrounded by several matching smaller dishes. Matching dishes might entail cruets, salt dips (sometimes on branched arms), trumpet-styled floral inserts, candle nozzles, or small bowls or plates.

Fenton Silver Crest milk glass epergne. Photo by Robin Rainwater. Courtesy of Wheaton Village.

ERICKSON GLASSWORKS — An American firm established at Bremen, Ohio, by Swedish immigrants Carl and Steven Erickson in 1943. The brothers produced mold-blown glass products distinguished by heavy casing, controlled bubbles, and a heavy ball for a base. The company ceased operations in 1961.

ERSKINE GLASS & MANUFACTURING COMPANY — An American firm founded in 1919 at Steubenville, Ohio, by John and W. S. Erskine, Robert Cain, J. G. Simpson, and D. S. Swaney, the company produced pressed glass lamp shades, lamp parts, and novelty items up until the plant was sold in 1980.

ESTONIAN GLASS — Glassware produced in Estonia beginning in the eighteenth and nineteenth centuries. Estonia was ceded to Russia by Sweden in 1721 and the first Estonian glass company was established in the 1730s (Pirsalche Glase Fabrik). Most glass produced consisted of functional items such as window panes, bottles, mirrors, and some limited tableware.

ETCHING — Refer to ACID ETCHING.

ETLING GLASS — A French firm founded by Edmond Etling in 1920 at Paris; Etling commissioned numerous artists in metals (like bronze), ceramics, and glass to sell in his shop. Most glass sold by Etling was made at a small glass studio at Choisy-le-Roi, a suburb of Paris, and is marked "Etling France." Etling sold glass vases and nude figurines designed by Georges Beal, Genevieve Granger, Lucille Sevin, and Hungarian sculptor Geza Hiecz. Most were made in opalescent and frosted colors. Etling closed during World War II; however, reproductions in clear and frosted crystal were produced by the Sevres Glass Company in the 1970s.

EVANS & ANDERSON — Refer to the WHEELING GLASS WORKS.

EVANS & COMPANY — Refer to the MACBETH-EVANS GLASS COMPANY.

EVANS, SELL & COMPANY — Refer to the MACBETH-EVANS GLASS COMPANY.

EVANSVILLE GLASS COMPANY — An American firm founded at Evansville, Indiana, in 1903 by Jacob Rosenthal and William Barris, the company produced some blown and pressed tableware before going bankrupt in 1907. In 1908, the plant, stock, and contents were purchased by Alexander Hutchinson, F. W. Reitz, Gilbert Walker, Frank Zipp, and John Zutt. It was reorganized as the Citizens Glass Company; however, production never resumed as the purchasers were sued by the former stockholders.

EWER — A round glass jug-like object, with or without a foot, that usually contains a long handle and spout. They are sometimes described as a vase that pours. The French refer to them as "Aiguiere."

An Egyptian ewer with stopper, 1970s. Photo by Robin Rainwater. Item courtesy of the Corning Museum of Glass.

EXCELSIOR GLASS WORKS — (1) An American pressed glass manufacturer founded at Camden, New Jersey, in 1841 by John and James Capewell and John Bamford. After Bamford left in 1843, the firm became CAPEWELL & BROTHERS and produced some pressed tableware before closing during the economic depression of 1857. (2) An American pressed glass manufacturer established in Wheeling, West Virginia, in 1849, the factory was purchased by John Hobbs in 1863 while the company became part of the BUCKEYE GLASS COMPANY. Buckeye moved operations to Martins Ferry, Ohio, in 1879. The Martins Ferry factory burned to the ground in 1894 and was not rebuilt. (3) A couple of other plants bore the "Excelsior" name: one was a short-lived maker of window glass, established at Pittsburgh, Pennsylvania, in 1856; another was owned by Sweeney. *See also* SWEENEY, MICHAEL, THOMAS & R. H.

EXCELSIOR PATTERN — A fairly common mid-nineteenth century pressed glass pattern consisting of large arched loops on the bottom with inverted loops above. Larger pieces made with this design may have a layer of sizable circles between the two rows of loops.

EXPANDED GLASS — Glass objects, after being shaped in a mold, that are further enlarged by blowing. Most were then decorated after the expansion process.

EXTRINSIC DECORATION — A general term for applying decorations to glass objects after they have been shaped and cooled (annealed). Common decorating techniques include etching, engraving, cutting, and enameling.

EYE — A term used to describe the round center of the grate (the hottest part of the furnace) in a circular glass furnace.

EYGABROAT-RYON COMPANY, INC. — An American cut glass operation founded in 1898 by Fred Eygabroat and W. H. Ryon at Lawrenceville, Pennsylvania. An additional cutting shop was added in Corning, New York. In 1906, Ryon bought out Eygabroat's share and the name was changed to the Ryon Cut Glass Company. The firm went bankrupt in 1913.

E

Ff

{ Ff }

FABERGE — A firm of jewelers and goldsmiths that was founded at St. Petersburg, Russia, in 1842 by Gustav Faberge; his son, Peter Carl Faberge, became the head jeweler of the Russian Imperial Court from about 1870 to 1914. The firm is noted most for producing exquisite porcelain eggs, jewelry, and other valuable items including some modern art forms of glass today (i.e. colored glass eggs with gilding).

FABLE GLASSWARE — Glassware that was once decorated (enameled and/or painted) with animals and figures from "Aesop's Fables" and "Grimm's Fairy Tales." Most are found on large German tumblers produced in the 16th and 17th centuries. See also HUMPEN.

FACETED GLASS — Glass objects decorated by grinding several small flat surfaces at different angles. Faceting or beveling is commonly found on the stems of drinking glasses and modern crystal miniatures like Swarovski and in the making of windows or printies for paperweights. See also SWAROVSKI.

FACON DE VENISE — Refer to VENETIAN GLASS.

FACTORY MARK — An inscription or imprint on glassware that indicates the place it was made. Typically, the mark is etched, engraved, or impressed on the bottom of a glass object.

FAIRMONT GLASS COMPANY — A short-lived pressed glass manufacturer established at Fairmont, Maryland, in 1898 by J. B. Crane, J. M. Hartley, and Z. G. Morgan. The firm produced pressed glass and blown glass tumblers before joining the NATIONAL GLASS COMPANY conglomerate in 1899. Later, after National broke up, the factory was leased to the MONONGAH GLASS COMPANY in 1912; Monongah ended up purchasing it in 1916. Also note that there were several other firms sporting the Fairmont name: a maker of fruit/canning jars at Fairmont, West Virginia (FAIRMONT BOTTLE & FRUIT JAR COMPANY, 1892); a maker of blown tumblers (FAIRMONT GLASS COMPANY, 1892); a window pane maker at Indianapolis, Indiana (FAIRMONT GLASS WORKS, 1911); and a bottle factory at Fairmont, West Virginia (FAIRMONT BOTTLE COMPANY, 1907).

FAIRVIEW GLASS WORKS — An American firm established by Jesse Wheat and John Price when they purchased a half interest in the Virginia Green Glass Works in 1833 at Wheeling, the company was sold a year later to the Ritchies and George Wilson. See also VIRGINIA GREEN GLASS WORKS and RITCHIE.

FAIRY LAMP — A style of lamp originating in England in the 1840s; they are small candle burning night lamps that were used in halls, nurseries, children's rooms, in dim corridors of homes, and even as food warmers since most contain a vent hole in the top. Some are two-piece (candle cup and shade) while others contain three pieces (candle cup, shade, and saucer).

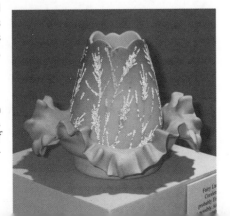

A Mount Washington fairy glass lamp. *Courtesy of Wheaton Village.*

FAKE — A glass object that has been purposefully made or altered to resemble an older, more valuable piece and then sold as a forgery. See also REPRODUCTION.

FALCON GLASSWORKS — The first Falcon Glassworks was founded in the Southwark region of London, England, in 1693. The firm operated for nearly one hundred years as a maker of practical glass items (i.e. windows and bottles) before closing. A second glass operation to bear the same Falcon name opened in the 1750s in London and lasted until the 1830s. The firm was purchased by the Pellatt family in the early 1800s and they produced some sulphides, which they were referred to as "Cameo Incrustations."

FALMOUTH GLASS COMPANY — An American pressed glass company established at Falmouth, Massachusetts, in 1849 by Jabez Swift and associates, it was known during the first year as the United States Glass Company, but sold out to a new firm in 1850 (it then became known as the Falmouth Glass Company). The firm produced pressed glass tableware until closing in 1854. Note that this firm had no relationship with the United States Glass Company conglomerate established in 1891. See also UNITED STATES GLASS COMPANY.

FAN CUT — A series of mitered grooves cut in a scallop-like shape made to resemble an open fan. This style is popular in cut glass and is often found along the rims of bowls, goblets, and other objects. It is also combined with the strawberry diamond cut pattern to produce the Strawberry Diamond and Fan Cut design. The original cut design has been copied in mold-pressed glass as well; however, pressed glass rarely is as sharp or precise as hand-cut glass. Both cut and pressed fans are often combined with other designs to produce such patterns as fan and star, fan band, fan with diamond, fan with flute, leaf and fan, palm leaf fan, and fan and feather.

FAN VASE — A style of vase having a narrow bowl with parallel sides made to resemble a triangular fan.

A Fenton Silver Crest fan vase. *Photo by Robin Rainwater.*

FAST-FOOD GLASSWARE — Refer to CHARACTER GLASS.

FAVRILE — An American Art Nouveau style of glass created by Louis Comfort Tiffany, who received a patent for it in 1892. The original pieces are often referred to as "Tiffany Favrile" and are characterized by a lustrous iridescent finish in a variety of colors (blue-green and/or gold were the most prevalent) that were further decorated with applied or embedded designs. Favrile was one of the leading designs in the Art Nouveau period as others sought to copy or create similar color effects.

Tiffany gold Favrile vases. *Courtesy of Wheaton Village.*

Collection of Favrile Art Glass vases.
Photo courtesy of the Corning Museum of Glass.

FAZZOLETTO — A style of vase originally designed by Fulvio Bianconi for the Venetian firm of Venini in 1949, it is in the shape of a handkerchief and was widely copied in the 1950s by others.

A 1950 Fazzoletto vase by Fulvio Bianconi. *(Note: This photo also contains an Italian Reticello goblet – see Reticulated Glass.) Courtesy of the Corning Museum of Glass.*

FEATHERED DECORATION — A decoration style developed by the ancient Egyptians. Under this technique, zigzag patterns of glass trailings were formed into feather-like structures and then applied to core-formed vessel. In modern times, feathering styles have been revived in Art Glass and can also be found in both cut and pressed glass. In cut glass, small miter cuts were made to produce feather-like designs. In pressed glass, feathers exist as a single molded design or in combination with others (i.e. feather duster, feather swirl, princess feather, etc.).

FEDERAL GLASS COMPANY — An American company established at Colombia, Ohio, in 1900 by brothers Robert and George Beatty, John Kuntz Jr., and James and W. C. Bracken. They began as a cut glass operation and then added machine-pressed wares in 1906. In 1916, the firm received a patent for a gob feeder (patented as the "Tucker-Reeves-Beatty" machine), that fed uniform globs of glass into an automatic glass pressing machine. They switched entirely to automation during the Depression era, producing both clear and colored tableware, jars, and tumblers. In 1958, the firm became a subsidiary of the Federal Paper Board Company, and continued producing glass up until 1980. Popular Federal patterns/designs include "Colonial Fluted" or "Rope," "Columbia," "Diana," "Georgian" or "Lovebirds," "Golden Glory," "Heritage," "Madrid," "Mayfair," "Normandie" or "Bouquet & Lattice," "Park Avenue," "Parrot," or "Sylvan," "Patrician" or "Spoke," "Raindrops," or "Optic Design," "Rosemary" or "Dutch Rose," "Sharon," or "Cabbage Rose," "Star," "Thumbprint" or "Pear Optic," and "Yorktown."

Federal Glass Company's Georgian Lovebirds patterned Depression Glass saucer. *Photo by Robin Rainwater.*

Trademark.

FELDSPAR — Feldspar is an abundant mineral made of aluminum, potassium, and silicon oxides. It is commonly used for vitreous enamels, pottery, and glass.

FENICIO — A Venetian decorating technique whereby fine threads of molten glass are pulled at intervals to create a festooned pattern.

FENTON ART GLASS COMPANY — Established at Martins Ferry, Ohio, in 1905 by brothers Frank Leslie Fenton (1880-1948) and John W. Fenton (1869-1934) under the Fenton Brothers name, the firm briefly leased the old West Virginia Glass Company plant as a decorating shop prior to building and moving to their own factory at Williamstown, West Virginia, in 1906 (factory was actually completed and up and running in 1907). Another brother, Charles Fenton, joined in 1906, and noted chemist Jacob Rosenthal (1855-1933) served as factory manager until 1929. In 1908, a fourth Fenton brother, James Fenton, joined; however, John left to establish the Millersburg Glass Company. Fenton was a major producer of carnival, opalescent, and other pressed and molded glassware. Fenton still operates today in Williamstown, producing hand-decorated glassware including lamps, baskets, and a wide variety of Art Glass and novelty items. The firm is still owned and operated by members of the Fenton family. Popular Fenton patterns/designs include "Crest" and "Hobnail" milk glass, "Old Virginia" milk/opaque glass, "Lincoln Inn" Depression Glass, and opalescent "Coin Dot" styles.

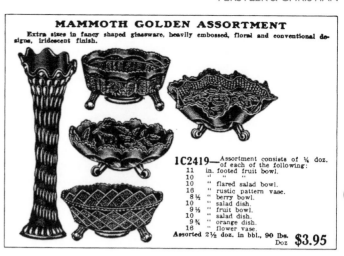

Reproduction from a 1925 Butler Brothers catalog.

Trademarks.

Fenton Carnival Glass plaid patterned platter.
Items *courtesy of the Fenton Art Glass Museum*.

FERN BOWL OR FERNERY — A glass container with a liner, with or without feet, designed specifically for holding ferns or other plants.

FERN GLASS — Glass objects decorated with etched or engraved ferns or similar leaf patterns.

FERNERY — A somewhat wide glass vase used to hold floral arrangements including flower blooms and ferns. Larger ferneries may consist of an entire glass case where ferns are grown in some quantity.

FERRIS GLASS COMPANY — An American firm established in 1910 at Corning, New York, by John Ferris. Fire destroyed much of the equipment in 1913, and the firm closed shortly afterward. Ferris was also active in other firms, including the Arcadia Cut Glass Company and the Elmira Cut Glass Company.

FERSTLER & CHRISTIAN — A short-lived American cut glass operation founded in 1912 in Brooklyn, New York, by Christopher Ferstler and M. D. Christian, the firm was out of business by 1919.

FESTOON — A swag-like design found in marbled or marbrie paperweights. This design is in the shape of garlands, which vary widely in terms of floral designs, foliage, fruit, ribbons, and drapery.

FIBER GLASS — A thin thread or filament drawn from molten or sun glass used primarily in insulation compounds. *See also GLASS FIBER.*

FIERY OPAL — Refer to OPAL GLASS.

FIGUEROA CUT GLASS COMPANY — An American cut glass-making firm founded in 1914 at Hammonton, New Jersey, by John Rothfus (1884-1944) and Charles Strunk. Rothfus had previously worked for the Skinner Glass Company, as well as in two partnerships: one with Miskey & Reynolds; another with Henry Nicolai. Figueroa produced cut glass tableware until closing in 1926. Rothfus continued in the glass business by purchasing the Enterprise Cut Glass Company in 1926. *See also MISKEY-REYNOLDS-ROTHFUS COMPANY, ROTHFUS-NICOLAI COMPANY, and ENTERPRISE CUT GLASS COMPANY.*

FIGURE OR FIGURINE — A small individually etched or molded glass statue (or figure), figurines may consist of one or more human-like figures as well as animals.

FIGURE CANDLESTICK — A candlestick with its stem or shaft in the shape of a figure. The figure, which may be in the form of a person or animal, rests on the base and supports the candle nozzle.

FIGURED ENGRAVING — A finely cut design made by revolving wheels to resemble a famous person, mythological figure, or other elaborate design. Engraved figures appear on glassware originating in Roman times. During the Art Nouveau period, most were created in colorful multicolored cameo styles.

FILAMENT STEM — A style of stem in stemware that was popular in the early twentieth century. In producing a filament stem, a core of glass (usually colored) is poured in a mold for the article stem. Crystal glass is then forced into the same stem mold, which in turn pushes the colored core back and out of the mold through the center of the hot crystal. The result is an inner colored stem (the filament) encased in crystal.

FILIGRANA — A general term for blown glass made with white or sometimes colored canes. *See also FILIGREE and LATTICINO.*

FILIGREE — A technique developed in Venice that utilizes glass threads or fine canes twisted around a clear cane to produce finely threaded patterns. In paperweights, they are often twisted together in small bundles similar to that of muslin. The Venetian term is "Filigrana" or "Vetro Filigrana" meaning "Thread-Grained." *See also LATTICINO and MEZZA FILIGRANA.*

A 3rd century B.C. Egyptian glass figurine.
Photo courtesy of the Corning Museum of Glass.

A 17th century Venetian filigree candleholder.
Photo courtesy of the Corning Museum of Glass.

FINDLAY CUT GLASS COMPANY — An American firm originally established as the Eclipse Tumbler Company in 1912 at Lansing, Michigan, by John Randall and F. G. L. Warner, in 1913 it was moved to Findlay, Ohio, and the name was changed to the Findlay Cut Glass Company. The firm produced cut glass tableware, specializing in tumblers. In 1915, a separate entity was filed, the Warner Cut Glass Company, in order to handle Findlay's sales; however, it was dissolved in 1916. Findlay went out of business in 1918.

FINDLAY FLINT GLASS COMPANY — A short-lived pressed glass manufacturer established at Findlay, Ohio, in 1888 by J. Q. Ashburn, Elijah Dunn, William Ely, Charles Klein, and William McNaughton, the firm produced limited amounts of barware, goblets, tumblers, lamps, and pressed tableware. A fire destroyed the factory in 1891; it was not rebuilt. See also FINDLAY GLASS.

FINDLAY GLASS — A general name for pressed tableware and other glass products produced in and around the town of Findlay, Ohio, in the late nineteenth and early twentieth centuries. Firms included the BELLAIRE GOBLET COMPANY; COLUMBIA GLASS COMPANY; DALZELL, GILMORE AND LEIGHTON COMPANY; FINDLAY FLINT GLASS COMPANY; and MODEL FLINT GLASS COMPANY. One style of so-called Findlay Glass was characterized by varying shades of brown that some refer to it as "Syrup Brown." It was first made by Dalzell, Gilmore, and Leighton, a firm that also patented "Findlay Onyx." See also FINDLAY ONYX, as well as the individual companies listed.

FINDLAY ONYX — In the late nineteenth century (patented in 1889), the firm of Dalzell, Gilmore, Leighton, and Co. of Findlay, Ohio, was noted for producing a specific styles of Onyx Glass by adding several metals in the batch. The result was a lustrous silver color with white streaking. Other colors were blended in like cream, cinnamon, and light rose or cranberry to create the onyx-like effect. See also FLORADINE.

FINE CUT — A term that really refers to overall pressed glass designs, which are imitative of true cut glass, but it has been applied also to many pressed patterns such as fine cut and block and fine cut and panel.

FINGER BOWL — A small concave glass vessel, usually circular and shallow in shape, used for rinsing fingers at the table. Finger bowls are usually the smallest of bowls with a capacity of only a few ounces. They are also used to serve finger foods as well.

FINIAL — A crowning ornament or decorative knob found most often on the stem of stemware and at the top of glass covers. Finials come in a wide variety of forms (i.e. animals, figures, flowers, fruits, geometrical shapes, etc.) and often double as handles for grasping objects.

FINISHED GLASS — A general term ordinarily used in Art Glass to indicate that an object has been completed.

FINISHING — A final step in the production of glass that may involve grinding, cutting, polishing, manipulating an object for the last time into its final shape: crimping an edge, forming a lip on a jug, straightening a foot or stem, or simply cleaning it for packing. A person who performs one of these tasks is sometimes referred to as a "Finisher."

FINNISH GLASS — General term for glassware made in Finland since the late seventeenth century. The first firms were established by Swedish glassmakers who made practical items such as windows and tableware. Although similar to modern Swedish art styles, a distinct form of Finnish Art Glass surfaced in the late 1920s with the opening of such firms as Riihimaki, Iittala, and Notsjo.

FIRE-KING — Kitchenware, dinnerware, and ovenware first produced by the Hocking Glass Company in 1937. A good deal was produced in the 1940s on up when Hocking merged with Anchor. Fire-King comes in clear and opaque varieties that are often decorated. Like Pyrex, it was specifically designed with borosilicates, which in turn allow a good degree of heat resistance for oven use.

Reproduction from a 1947 Anchor Hocking advertisement.

Trademarks.

FIRE POLISHING — Reheating a finished piece of glass at the glory hole in order to remove tool marks (more commonly replaced with acid polishing).

FIRED-ON — Finishing colors that are baked on or fused by heating onto the outer surface of glass objects.

FIRED-ON IRIDESCENCE — A finish applied to glass by adding metallic salts after which the glass is refired. Many art styles (like Tiffany's FAVRILE) and nearly all CARNIVAL GLASS finishes were created this way.

FIREGLOW — An art style of glass that originated with the Boston & Sandwich Glass Company in the mid-nineteenth century, the wares were produced with a reddish-brown/reddish-tan color to resemble the glow of a fire.

F

FIRING GLASS — A small glass vessel made specifically with a heavy base, thick wasted sides, and possibly a stem that could withstand considerable abuse. The resulting noise of several being slammed at once was comparable to that of a "musket firing" (hence the name "firing glass"). Some were made of metal and most were produced in the late eighteenth and early nineteenth centuries in both Europe and America.

FISCHMANN S. AND SONS — Refer to the MSTISOV GLASSWORKS.

FISH BOWL — A large glass bowl in which freshwater fish (most commonly goldfish) or other aquatic creatures like snails are kept. Fish bowls tend to be a gallon or two in capacity and are generally much smaller than aquariums. Glassmakers began making them in the nineteenth century and some came with a matching glass pedestal stand. *See also AQUARIUM.*

FISH SCALE — A pressed glass pattern containing vertical bands of curves or half-ovals resembling the scales of fish.

FISHERMEN NET FLOATS — Refer to FLOATS.

FLACCUS BROTHERS COMPANY — An American company originally known as E. C. Flaccus and George Flaccus & Sons. It was founded at Wheeling, West Virginia, in 1876 by George C. Flaccus and his sons, George A. and William C. Flaccus, as a food/condiment business (i.e. makers of catsup, mustard, vinegar, preserves, and mincemeat). The name was changed to Flaccus Brothers in 1879 when George C. Flaccus retired. Also in 1879, George C. Flaccus' nephew, Charles L. Flaccus, purchased a glass factory in Tarentum, Pennsylvania, that was formerly owned by Lippencott & Company. George A. Flaccus designed milk glass containers for his food products, and commissioned other glassmakers, including his cousin Charles L. Flaccus, to make them. Another son of George C. Flaccus, Edward C., was also active in the family business. Edward C. Flaccus split off in 1898 to form his own packing and canning firm known as the E. C. Flaccus Company (this name appears on some milk glass food containers). All Flaccus-related firms were out of business by 1929.

FLACCUS, C. L. COMPANY — Refer to the FLACCUS BROTHERS COMPANY.

FLACCUS, E. C. COMPANY — Refer to the FLACCUS BROTHERS COMPANY.

FLACON — Another name for a small perfume or smelling bottle with a stopper. *See also COLOGNE BOTTLE or PERFUME BOTTLE.*

FLAGON — A pouring vessel, usually with a handle and spout, used to hold and serve liquids. Flagons were developed in the first century A.D. by the Romans and were the predecessors of decanters and pouring tankards. Later examples might, at times, contain screw caps or hinged metal lids.

FLAMBEAU — A style of Art Glass created by Pairpoint in the 1920s primarily for the holiday (Christmas) season, it is a red opaque color often compared to that of a bright red tomato. Some contain a silver overlay and/or black accents (i.e. feet and stems of goblets). Note that it is also spelled as "Flambo."

FLAMEWORKING — The technique of shaping objects when they are hot (heated by a gas-fueled torch) from rods or tubes of glass. Up until the early twentieth century, oil or paraffin lamps were used with foot-operated bellow to increase the temperature. Flameworking is used to produce elaborate and finely detailed glass sculptures as well as paperweights.

FLASHED-ON IRIDESCENCE — A bright, colorful, finish applied to glass by dipping hot glass into a solution of metallic salts, flashing is most often performed with a thin layer of colored or opaque glass over the surface of clear glass.

FLASHED GLASS OR FLASHING — A very thin applied exterior coating of a different color from that of the base color (thinner that a casing or an overlay). Flashing is usually completed by dipping a gather of hot glass of one color into a pot or crucible that contains a different color in such a manner as to cause only a thin layer to adhere.

FLASK — A glass container, with a narrow neck and mouth and a stopper or cover, used for carrying alcoholic beverages in modest quantities. Most are fairly small or pocket-sized and have a capacity of up to eight ounces. *See also HISTORICAL FLASK.*

Reproduction from an early 20th century S. F. Myers Company catalog.

No. FLASK.
2816 4 Inches High....**$5 95**
Cut Glass, Sterling Silver
Top.

A liquor flask with half Brass mold featuring an 1824-25 picture of Maiquis de Lafayette. *Item courtesy of the Corning Museum of Glass.*

FLAT DIAMOND CUTTING — A variation of the basic diamond cutting whereby an uncut area between the crisscrossed diagonal grooves is left to form a flat area rather than the standard pointed diamond design.

FLAT GLASS — Refer to PLATE GLASS.

FLECKED GLASSWARE — A decorating technique whereby small chips or specks of colored glassware are applied to a glass object to produce a multicolored mottled appearance. Molten glass is usually rolled over a flat surface that is covered by the chips and then heated to embed the chips or flecks upon the object. Flecked glassware originated in Roman times and was popular during the nineteenth century Art Nouveau movement. *See also MARVER.*

FLEMINGTON CUT GLASS COMPANY — An American firm founded in 1908 at Flemington, New Jersey, by Alphonse and Charles Muller. The Mullers purchased a building previously owned by H. C. Fry (Fry had purchased the Empire Cut Glass Company in 1904 and moved operations to Flemington, New Jersey). The Mullers cut blanks provided by several American firms up until the era of cut glass production ended in the early 1920s. The firm remained in business doing light cutting and engraving of glass, as well as producing lamp shades.

FLEMISH BLUE — A dark shade of cobalt blue Art Glass created and named by Steuben in the early twentieth century.

FLEUR-DE-LIS — A general French term for a floral pattern or design containing flowers, foliage, scrolling, vines, and wreaths. Fleur-de-Lis patterns can be found in nearly all styles of glass, including Art, cut, pressed, Carnival, and Depression.

FLINT GLASS — A term derived from the fact that glass experimenters in England, in the late seventeenth century, once used powdered and/or calcined flint as a substitute for silica in glass-making. Flint is a hard form of pure natural quartz and was combined with lead oxide to make fine quality crystal. Though they are different materials, flint glass and lead crystal became synonymous with fine quality crystal in both eighteenth century England and nineteenth century America. Nearly all fine crystal products made in America continued lead only and not flint.

FLIP-FLOP — A whimsical glass toy object that resembles a jug or flask with a long hollow tube attached at the mouth. The name is derived from the sound made when air is blown into the tube, causing the thin glass covering the bottom to vibrate. Flip-Flops were popular in the later nineteenth century.

FLIP GLASS — An American term for a style of tumbler that is usually around 6" to 8" in height and expands slightly at the rim. Some sport domed covers with finials. Most were made in the late eighteenth and nineteenth centuries.

FLOAT PROCESS — The modern method of producing smooth glass window panes and other flat sheet glass of uniform thickness and volume. In this process, molten glass is pulled from the hearth of the furnace atop a batch of molten tin.

FLOATS — Hollow glass balls that were once used for buoying up Fishermen's nets in water; glass-style floats have been replaced with cheaper and more durable plastic models beginning in the early-to-mid twentieth century.

FLORADINE — A late nineteenth century onyx design produced by DALZELL, GILMORE, LEIGHTON & COMPANY of Findlay, Ohio. Floradine is characterized by ruby and gold streaking (autumn leaf) with raised opalescent flowers and foliage. *See also FINDLAY ONYX.*

FLORENTIA GLASS — An art style of glass developed by FREDERICK CARDER of Steuben in the 1920s, it is characterized by an encircling pattern of powdered colored leaves that were fused to a vessel (typically a vase) after the initial annealing process.

FLORENTINE GLASSWARE — General term for glass made in Florence, Italy, dating from the fourteenth through the seventeenth centuries. Early products featured functional items like beakers and bottles. Beginning in the sixteenth century, Florence glassmakers were noted for producing science and laboratory items (test tubes, thermometers, and lenses for such things as telescopes and microscopes), as well as Murano-styled glass from Venetian immigrants.

FLORET OR FLORETTE — (1) A slice from a large cane of several colored rods arranged (usually concentrically) to form a floral pattern. Florets are most often found in paperweights. (2) Consolidated referred to a satinized or glossy finish of glass tableware produced in a wide variety of colors (white, blue, pink, green, yellow, apricot, Pigeon Blood, etc.) as "Florette Blown Ware" in the 1890s.

FLORIFORM — A tall glass vase, with narrow stem and top, made into the shape of a flower broom. The shape was first made by Tiffany, though others soon copied it. The term has also been applied to high-stemmed or high-footed compotes.

FLOWER BOWL OR POT — A large shallow concave hemispherical container used for holding or floating flowers with relatively short stems. Some glass models are made with holes in the bottom for water drainage.

A Fenton Snow Crest flower pot. *Photo by Robin Rainwater.*

FLOWER GLOBE — Refer to ROSE BOWL.

FLOWER STAND — An ornamental glass receptacle used for displaying cut flowers. Some are rectangular in shape while others are rounded. Many contain several vertical glass tube inserts to hold individual flower stems.

FLOWER WEIGHT — A paperweight in which a single flower is the basic or central design.

FLUOGRAVURE — A decorating technique developed by Muller Freres in he 1890s whereby an enameled glass object is acid-etched to produce an impressionistic effect.

F

FLUTING — Vertically cut decoration in long narrow or parallel sections such as bevels (usually wheel-cut but sometimes molded). In paperweights, they are sometimes cut between the windows on the exterior and/or in the base.

A collection of colorful fluted tumblers. *Photo by Robin Rainwater.*

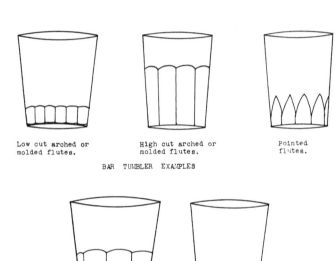

Low cut arched or molded flutes.

High cut arched or molded flutes.

Pointed flutes.

BAR TUMBLER EXAMPLES

Wide Flutes

Narrow Flutes

MORE BAR TUMBLER EXAMPLES

Fluting. *Line drawings by the author.*

FLUX — A substance such as soda, wood ash, potash, and lead oxide added to the basic ingredients in order to stabilize and lower the melting point of a batch of glass. Flux is also added to enamels prior to when they are fired on for various coloring adhesion.

FLYGSFORS — A small glass firm founded in the Varmland region of southern Sweden in 1888 by Ernst Lundgvist and August Zeitz, it began as a practical maker of window glass and tableware before expanding into cut glass and more traditional Swedish art forms in the mid-twentieth century. In 1949, Paul Kedelv was hired and he was the noted designer of the firm's "Coquille" series of sculptured glass vessels (thick opaque objects cased in clear glass). In 1959, the firm acquired the Gadderas factory as well as Maleras in 1965 (all part of the Flygsfors Group). The Gadderas factory closed soon afterward and Maleras was sold to Krona-Bruken in 1974. The original factory building was purchased by Orrefors in 1974, but closed permanently in 1980.

FOAM GLASS — A style of bubbled or foam-like glass created in 1933 by Richard Sussmuth. The formula was used initially for the production of lamp shades, but was later expanded to include ornamental bowls and vases. Note that the firm dubbed their products in this style as "Schaumglas," which translates to "Foam Glass." *See also* SCHAUMGLAS *and* SUSSMUTHGLAS.

FOGGY — Refer to SICKNESS.

FOLDED FOOT — The turned-over edge of the foot of a wine glass or similar glass object. The purpose is to give added strength to the vessel.

FOLDED RIM — A turned-over thick edge at the top of a glass vessel similar to that of a folded foot.

FONT — (1) A receptacle for holding water, usually religious in nature (i.e. holy water). (2) A font or fonts can also be a general term to describe an assortment of items competed in a similar style (i.e. writing or print type, a variety of glass lamp parts, etc.).

FOOT — The part of a glass other than the base of which it rests. A foot or feet come in a wide variety of styles; flat, folded, rounded, pedestal, conical, annulated, and square are just a few terms to describe various feet (or a single foot) present at the base of a glass object.

FOOTED WEIGHT — Refer to PIEDOUCHE.

FOOTMAKER — An assistant to a glassmaker who forms the foot of the glass in the glassblowing process.

FOREST GLASS HOUSE — Refer to WALDGLAS.

FOREST GREEN — A dark green color not as deep or rich as emerald green, first made by Anchor Hocking in the 1940s. The name was officially patented by them in 1950. The term itself referred to the color and has been applied widely to glassware made by other companies in the same or very similar color pattern. Note that "Royal Ruby" is Anchor Hocking's name for "Forest Green's" sister pattern (i.e. same style and shape, just a different color.) *See also* ROYAL RUBY.

An Anchor Hocking Forest Green vase. *Photo by Robin Rainwater.*

FORGERY — Refer to FAKE.

FORM — A mold-like heat-resistant object used to shape or create a certain piece of an object (handle, cover, foot, etc.). Many forms are used to finish off or even create the final shape of an object.

FORMING BLOCK — A heavy chunk of wood with a hollow form carved into it. A gather of glass on the end of a blowpipe can then be rotated upon the block to form a round ball with a slightly cooled outer surface.

FORMING TOOL — A specialized pair of tongs with wide flat ends used for straightening stems and other delicate shaping work. *See also* PINCERS, PUCELLAS, STEEL-JACKS, TONGS, *and* WOOD-JACKS.

FORT PITT GLASS WORKS — A corporate name filed by R. B. Curling & Sons at Pittsburgh, Pennsylvania, in 1834. The firm was purchased by Edward Dithridge, Sr. in the early 1850s. *See also R. B. CURLING & SONS and DITHRIDGE & COMPANY.*

FOSTORIA GLASS COMPANY — An American glass company founded by L. B. Martin and W. S. Brady at Fostoria, Ohio, in 1887, the firm was able to purchase some pressed glass molds from the defunct Belmont Glass Company in 1890. Fostoria moved to Moundsville, West Virginia, in 1891 and initially produced fruit jars, oil lamps, and both cut and pressed glass tableware ("American" and "Bedford" patterns). Other products included blown stemware, which was added in 1900; several Depression colored and/or etched tableware patterns ("Colony," "Fairfax," "Hermitage," "June," "Kashmir," "Royal," "Seville," "Sun Ray," "Trojan," "Verasailles," and "Vesper"); some milk/opaque glass; many colored patterns such as "Baroque," "Coin Glass" and "Jamestown"; and a wide variety of etched crystal wares/patterns (i.e. "Buttercup," "Camelia," "Century," "Chintz," "Corsage," "Heather," "Lido," "Mayflower," "Meadow Rose," "Navarre," "Romance," etc.). In 1965, Fostoria acquired the Morgantown Glassworks in West Virginia; however, this factory was shut down permanently in 1971. In 1983, Fostoria was sold to the Lancaster Colony Company, which continued producing glass at the plant until 1986. Note that the firm's most prolific output was that of the American pattern; this design was made from 1915 up until the factory closed.

A coin glass covered candy jar from the Fostoria Glass Company. *Photo by Robin Rainwater.*

Trademarks.

FOSTORIA LAMP & SHADE COMPANY — An American firm founded at Fostoria, Ohio, in 1890 by W. S. Brady, Charles Foster, and James Graham, the company produced glass lamp parts, including shades, prior to selling out to the Consolidated Lamp & Glass Company in 1894. The plant burned to the ground in 1896 and was not rebuilt by Consolidated, which moved all surviving equipment to its Coraopdis plant.

FOSTORIA GLASS NOVELTY COMPANY — A short-lived American firm founded at Fostoria, Ohio, in 1915 by J. H. Jones and R. J. Ridgeway, the company produced pressed and blown tableware prior to closing in 1916. Note, there was a separate Fostoria business with a similar name. *See also FOSTORIA NOVELTY GLASS COMPANY.*

FOSTORIA NOVELTY GLASS COMPANY — A short-lived American firm founded at Fostoria, Ohio, in 1890 by Henry and Al Crimmel, the company produced pressed and blown tableware prior to closing in 1892. Most assets were purchased by the United States Glass Company; the factory burned to the ground in 1893. Note there was a separate Fostoria firm with a similar name. *See also FOSTORIA GLASS NOVELTY COMPANY.*

FOUNDING — The making of glass by melting and fusing the ingredients together in a furnace.

FOVAL — A style of Art Glass produced by H. C. Fry Glass Company in 1926-27, it is characterized by a pearly opalescent texture trimmed in a jade green or delft blue. Some pieces may contain silver overlay.

FRACTIONAL SHOT — A small glass tumbler with capacity of less than one ounce (a fraction of an ounce; hence the name "fractional").

FRACTURE — Glass that ruptures or breaks after being formed from any number of reasons (i.e. improper fusing of materials, improper ingredients, improper temperature, rapid cooling, etc.).

FRAGMENT — A piece of a broken glass object. Fragments are generally found at archaeological excavation sites and aid in identifying and dating older glass objects. Note that since glass scraps are often used as cullet in new batches, glass fragments are far more difficult to find than pottery and metal fragments. *See also SHARD.*

FRANCES WARE — Mold blown tableware consisting of an amber color, fluted rims, and a hobnail pattern; it was produced by Hobbs, Brocunier Co. in the 1880s.

Reproduction from an 1884 Hobbs Brockunier Co. catalog.

FRANCONIAN GLASS — General term for practical glassware made in Franconia, Germany, through the sixteenth and eighteenth centuries. Items included decorated (mostly enameled) drinking vessels like beakers.

FRANKLIN FLINT GLASS COMPANY — A pressed glass manufacturer established at Philadelphia, Pennsylvania, in 1861 by English immigrant William Thynne Gillinder, Gillinger briefly joined with Edwin Bennett to form Gillinder & Bennet in 1863; however, Bennett left soon afterward. The firm first produced some blown glass lamp chimneys as well as window panes. Gillinder & Sons operated it until they joined the U.S. Glass Company in 1891. *See also GILLINDER & SONS.*

FREE-BLOWN GLASS — An ancient technique of hand-blowing glass by highly skilled craftsmen without the use of molds. However, a variety of tools are used to shape the piece on the blowpipe.

FRENCH BLUE — A transparent grayish-blue colored Art Glass created and named by Steuben in the 1920s. The color was at times contrasted with other colors such as amber feet, stems, finials, or applied threading.

FRENCH GLASSWARE — General term for glass made in France since the seventeenth century. The first artisans were Venetian immigrants who helped to produce stained glass windows and other functional items such as lighting fixtures, mirrors, and tableware. Later, France spawned the golden age of paperweights in the mid-nineteenth century (Clichy, Baccarat, St. Louis) and led the Art Nouveau/Deco periods in the late nineteenth and early twentieth centuries (Galle, Daum, Marinot, Lalique, Rousseau, and others).

FRIGGER — Refer to WHIMSEY.

FRINGE CUT — A simple miter cut in glass that consists of shallow, parallel cuts, usually of the same length (like around the base of a tumbler or decanter); or of graduated unequal lengths (such as around the top if a bowl as a border). Fringe cuts are sometimes referred to as "Blaze Cuts."

FRIT — (1) A calcine mixture of sand along with various fluxes, Frit is actually the partly fused materials of which glass is made. (2) Ground glass mixed with water and other chemicals to form glazes or enamels. *See also PATE-DE-VERRE.*

FRIZLEN CUT GLASS COMPANY —An American firm founded in 1906 at Vineland, New Jersey, by Wilber Frizlen, the company produced cut glass into the early 1920s.

FROG — A small but thick and heavy glass object, usually round or domed, it contains perforations, holes, or spikes for holding flowers in place within a vase. Frogs sometimes resemble shallow-domed paperweights.

Reproduction from an early twentieth century S. F. Myers Co. catalog.

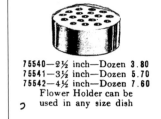

75540—2½ inch—Dozen 3.80
75541—3½ inch—Dozen 5.70
75542—4½ inch—Dozen 7.60
Flower Holder can be used in any size dish

FRONTIER CUT GLASS COMPANY — An American cut glass operation founded by John Murray in 1902 at Buffalo, New York, the firm produced cut glass up until World War I. After the war, the firm was acquired by the NATIONAL GLASS MANUFACTURING COMPANY, which continued to perform some light engraving of glassware.

Reproduction from a 1917 Frontier Cut Glass Co. patent.

FROSTED GLASS — A light opalescence or cloudy coloring of a batch of glass using tin, zinc, or an all-over acid etching as in Depression Glass. A frosted coating can also be applied on the surface of clear or crystal glass by spraying on white acid (a solution of ammonium bifluoride). Frosted glass can also be made by sandblasting the surface. Frosted glass is also referred to as "Camphor" glass and is common in a wide variety of glass. In pressed glass, many patterns contain some frosted portion (i.e. frosted block, frosted circle, frosted leaf, frosted fruits, frosted magnolia, frosted medallion, frosted stork, etc.).

Lalique frosted glass frog and angel fish. *Photo by Robin Rainwater.*

Lalique four-faced frosted glass vase.

Fruit Bowl — A large concave glass vessel, usually rounded or hemispherical in shape, that is used for holding and displaying fresh fruits (i.e. apples, bananas, grapes, oranges, etc.). Some come with underplates or stands; others may be stemmed like a large comport. *See also* Centerpiece *and* Orange Bowl.

Reproduction from an 1899 U.S. Glass Co. patent.

9½ inch Fruit Bowl, Footed, also make 10½ inch Flared Fruit Bowl.

Fruit or Nut Dish — A small flat or shallow circular container, with or without handles, used for serving small fruits, nuts, and candies.

Fruit Jar — Refer to Canning Jar.

Fry & Scott — Refer to H. C. Fry.

Fry, W. George Glass Company — Refer to the Economy Tumbler Company and the Thompson Glass Company, Ltd.

Fry, H. C. — An American glassmaker, Fry founded the Rochester Tumbler Company in 1872, the Rochester Glass Company in 1901 (renamed the H. C. Fry Glass Company in 1902); and the Beaver Valley Glass Company in 1904 — all in Rochester, Pennsylvania. Henry Clay Fry also had previously formed a partnership with William Scott in the mid-1860s (pressed tableware was made under the company name of "Fry & Scott" until closing around 1870). Fry also purchased the Empire Cut Glass Company in 1904. The glass that was produced in his later factory is sometimes referred to as "Fry Glass" and included some Art Glass styles, cut glass, as well as both practical table and ovenware. Fry closed for good in 1934 and the plant was purchased by Libbey. *See also the* Beaver Valley Glass Company, *the* Empire Glass Company, *the* Rochester Glass Company, *and the* Rochester Tumbler Company.

An H. C. Fry cut glass nappy. *Courtesy of Wheaton Village.*

Trademarks.

Fuddling Glass — A mall drinking glass developed in England around 1800 that has no foot. They are also referred to as a "Coaching Glass."

Fulgurites — Crude, brittle, slender glassy-formed tubes that are created when lightning strikes a sandy area with the right combination of glass-forming minerals.

Full Antique — A general term applied to Art Glass produced by the mouth-blown cylinder method. A cylindrical form is blown, annealed, and cooled; then scored lengthwise, separated, reheated, and folded out into a flat sheet. The final form then contains a pristine surface that may include decorative linear striations.

Full Lead Crystal — Colorless glass containing a minimum of 30% lead content.

Funeral Urn — Refer to Funeral Vase and Urn.

Funeral Vase — A round angled glass vessel with a depth that is far greater than its width and used for holding flowers. Funeral vases or urns tend to be very large — some consider any vase that exceeds 16" in height to be a funeral vase. However, many Art Glass styles were designed to be quite large and not specifically for funerals.

Funnel — A wide circular object that narrows to a thin tube used for pouring liquids into a narrow-necked receptacle. The first glass funnels were made in the 1st century A.D. by the Romans and were later popular in laboratories.

Furnace — An enclosed structure for the production and application of heat. Furnaces today are usually heated by natural gas for clean burning. In glass-making, furnaces are used for melting a batch of glass, maintaining pots of glass in a molten state, and for reheating partially formed objects at the glory hole. Originally, they were heated by wood, peat, or coal; and typically held up to twenty pots. In modern times, furnaces are usually heated by natural gas for clean burning. *See also* Continuous Furnace, Day Tank, Lehr, *and* Pot Arch or Furnace.

Furniture Caster — Refer to Caster or Castor.

Fused Art Glass — A process of placing two or more different pieces of glass together in an arranged design and then firing them together at a high enough temperature to fuse them into a single piece.

Fusion — The process of liquefying or when the melting point is reached for a batch of glass. Temperatures can range from 2,000–3,000 degrees Fahrenheit (1,100 to 1,650 degrees Celsius) depending on the ingredients used. Full led crystal generally requires a higher temperature while thinner lime-based glassware melts at a much lower temperature.

Gg

{ Gg }

Trademarks/Signatures.

GADGET — A special rod developed in the late eighteenth century to replace the pontil to avoid leaving a mark on the foot. A spring clip at the end of the gadget grips the foot of a just-finished piece of glass while the worker trims the rim and applies the finishing touches on the glass. A gadget avoids leaving a pontil mark on the foot; however, it still leaves a small pressure mark.

GADROONING — A decorative band derived from a silver form made of molded, applied, or deep cut sections of reeding, Gadrooning is sometimes referred to as "Knurling" and may be applied in horizontal, vertical, diagonal, twisted, or wavy bands.

GAFFER — A term of respect for an experienced master or head glassmaker dating back to the sixteenth century; the gaffer usually remains seated while constantly rotating a blow-pipe with a glass object at the end. Rotating allows an object to retain its shape without collapsing or thickening on one end. Gaffers generally complete the most intense and intricate detail work prior to the completion and annealing of an object. Note that the word gaffer is an Old English word related to "Grandfather."

GALL — A layer of scum that forms at the surface of a batch of glass during the heating process (it is skimmed off). Gall is also sometimes referred to as "Sandever."

GALLATIN, ALBERT — A Swiss immigrant who was responsible for establishing the first glassworks in what is considered the Midwest of America (west of Pittsburgh, Pennsylvania). Gallatin founded the New Geneva Glass Works along the Monongahela River in 1797; he went on to become a U.S. Senator and Secretary of the Treasury while his associates built another glasshouse across the river in Greensboro (c.1817). Both factories made bottles, jars, tumblers, decanters, pitchers, bowls, goblets, and other household items. Note that the firm has also been referred to as Gallatin Glass Works. *See also NEW GENEVA GLASS WORKS.*

GALLE, EMILE — A French glassmaker and pioneer in the nineteenth century Art Nouveau styled glass, Galle (1846-1904) established his own glass operation in 1867 at Nancy, France, and is noted for unique styles of art cameo glass, cut cased glass, and floral designs created in several color effects and styles. He was also one of the first to begin signing his works, which sparked a trend followed by other artisans. Galle built a much larger factory at Nancy in 1894, and the firm won a grand prize at the Paris Exhibition in 1900 for art glass. Galle passed away in 1904 and the factory closed for a few years during the First World War. It reopened in 1919 and continued to produce Art Glass until 1936. After Galle's death, items produced contained his signature and an added star.

Galle vase. *Courtesy of the Corning Museum of Glass.*

GALWAY CRYSTAL — An Irish firm established in 1967 at Galway, Ireland, it is noted most as a producer of handmade crystal stemware, tableware and novelty items. The firm was acquired by Josiah Wedgwood & Sons, Ltd. in 1974 and continues to produce glass today under the "Galway" namesake. *See also WEDGWOOD GLASS.*

GANG WHEEL — A special mitered v-shaped cutting wheel that was introduced in 1913 by the Norton Company of Worcestershire, Massachusetts, gang wheels have several parallel sharp edges with diamond tips that allow precise or fine-line cutting, as well as ease of cutting any motif with parallel lines. Note that gang wheels were also utilized by cutleries in making knife blades with serrated edges.

GARLAND — A chain formation of canes intertwined to form a continuous ribbon-like or garland effect within the interior of paperweights.

GASOLIER — A style of chandelier developed in the nineteenth century whose source of illumination consists of gas fired lights rather than the traditional candles.

GATE, SIMON — A famous artist and glass designer who joined Orrefors Glassbruk in Sweden in 1915, Simon (1883-1945) teamed up with Edward Hald to create the award winning "Graal" line of art glass. *See also GRAAL.*

GATESHEAD STAMPED GLASS WORKS — Refer to SOWERBY'S ELLISON STREET GLASS WORKS.

GATHER — A blob of molten glass attached to the end of a blowpipe, pontil, or gathering iron. The gather is then formed into an object usually by blowing or is blown into a mold. Note that a gatherer is one who might gather the molten glass from the furnace on the end of a pontil and then deliver it to a blower or presser.

GATHERING IRON — A metal rod, usually made of iron or bronze, used to remove a small blob or gather of molten glass from the pot. The rod ordinarily has one end bent at a right angle in order to aid in the application of a decorative trailing of glass upon an object. Gathering irons are also known as "Dipsticks."

GAUZE — Refer to LACE.

GAY FAD GLASSWARE — An Ohio decorating company founded by Fran Taylor in the late 1930s, the firm was noted for frosted glass objects/novelties (tumblers, stemware, pitchers, decanters, cocktail shakers, mugs, etc.) that were hand-painted or enameled with floral designs, state themes, Christmas motifs, and barware (bartenders, drinkers, can-can girls, etc.). Some pieces were trimmed in gold and silver as well. The firm was sold in 1963 and closed permanently in 1965.

GEAR SHIFT KNOB — A rounded projecting part that rests at the top of a lever and is used for selecting gears for a power transmission system in a motor vehicle. Most gear shift knobs made of glass are after-market accessories or novelty items.

GEMEL OR GIMMEL FLASK — A glass container with two inner divisions, each connected to its own neck and mouth. They were produced in England and America in the early nineteenth century and were made from two separate bottles that were then fused together. The name was derived from the Zodiac Gemini sign (meaning twins).

GEMMAUX — A French decorating technique involving fusing small pieces of various colored glass into relief patterns upon glass objects.

GENESEE CUT GLASS COMPANY — An American cut glass operation established at Rochester, New York, in 1910, the firm produced some limited cut glass tableware until closing directly after World War I.

GERMAN CUT GLASS COMPANY — An American firm established in 1903 at Jermyn, Pennsylvania; the name was changed to Laurel soon after. *See also LAUREL CUT GLASS COMPANY.*

GERMAN GLASS — General term for glassware made in Germany since the early fifteenth century. The first operations were forest glasshouses that produced practical items like windows and drinking vessels. Beginning in the later sixteenth century, Germans were noted for decorating glassware with etching and enameling, and inventing several new engraving techniques. In the eighteenth century, they were cutting lead crystal in the English/American style and, in the nineteenth, they followed the ART NOUVEAU ("Jugendstil" in German) movement. *See also BAVARIAN, BRANDENBURG, FRANCONIAN, HESSE, NUREMBERG, SAXON, and THURINGIAN.*

A 1650 German humpen or large drinking vessel. Courtesy of the Corning Museum of Glass.

A collection of modern German glass vases made in Zweisel.

GESU, AL GLASSWORKS — A Venetian firm founded on the island of Murano in 1537 by Nicolo Andrigo, it was sold to Antonio Miotti in 1542 and operated by his descendants until closing in the late eighteenth century. The company made traditional Venetian glassware, but was noted most for opaque white (milk glass) that was further enameled; aventurine glass; and glass plaques with enameled Venetian scenery.

GIBBS, KELLY & COMPANY — An American cut glass operation established at Hinesdale, Pennsylvania, in 1895 by William Gibbs, Michael Kelly (an Irish immigrant), and Frank Steinman, former employees of Mount Washington/Pairpoint. Kelly and Steinman left in 1905 to form their own firm while Gibbs continued on and changed the name to William H. Gibbs & Company. Gibbs moved to Hawley, Pennsylvania, in 1909 and opened another factory in Barryville, New York (known briefly as the Barryville Cut Glass Shop) in 1910; it was sold to the Krantz & Sell Company in 1912. Gibbs built another factory in Stroudsburg, Pennsylvania in 1911. The firm produced cut glass products until closing in 1928. *See also PEERLESS CUT GLASS COMPANY.*

Reproduction from an 1899 Gibbs, Kelly & Co. patent.

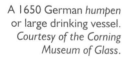

GIBBS, WILLIAM H. & COMPANY — Refer to the GIBBS, KELLY & COMPANY.

GIBERSON, DUDLEY F., JR. — A noted American Studio Glass artisan and inventor of studio glass equipment who was born in Alton, Illinois in 1942, Giberson received his Fine Arts degree from the Rhode Island School of Design and has served in a teaching capacity at the Haystack Mountain School of Crafts, the Penland School of Crafts, Massachusetts College of Art, the Rhode Island School of Design, and the Sheridan School of Art in Toronto, Canada. Giberson continues to work as both an independent glass artisan and inventor in Warner, New Hampshire.

GIBSON GLASS — An American firm established at Milton, West Virginia, by Charles Gibson in 1983. Gibson had previously worked for Bischoff, Blenko, and St. Clair prior to opening his own firm. Gibson is noted for animals, figurines, paperweights, marbles, and other novelty items produced in a variety of colors and styles.

Gibson Glass novelties. Photo by Robin Rainwater.

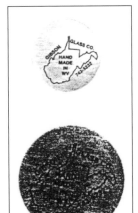

Trademark.

GILDING — An applied decorating technique with gold leaf, enamels, dust, or paints to the exterior of finished glass objects. Most gilding is permanently affixed to glass objects by heating in a small muffle kiln. *See also* AMALGAM *and* ZWISCHENGOLDGLAS.

A Baccarat gilded and frosted camel glass centerpiece.

GILL BROTHERS — An American firm founded around 1900 at Steubenville, Ohio, the company produced fruit jars, lamp chimneys, and some limited amounts of Depression Glass prior to closing in the early 1930s.

GILLILAND, JOHN L. AND COMPANY — A pressed and cut glass firm founded in 1822 by John Loftus Gilliland at Brooklyn, New York. Gilliland had previously worked for the New England Glass Company. The company produced both cut and pressed glass tableware and won first prize for lead glass at the 1851 Great International Exhibition in London (Crystal Palace). The firm, under his direction, operated the Brooklyn Flint Glass Works (factory renamed in 1843), which was eventually obtained by Amory Houghton Sr. and Jr. in 1864. The factory shut down permanently in 1868 when Houghton moved to Corning, New York. After selling his firm, Gilliland continued briefly as a cut glass operation in New York City as the South Ferry Works, the original name of the plant.

GILLINDER & SONS — (1) An American firm founded by English immigrant William T. Gillinder at Philadelphia, Pennsylvania, as the Franklin Flint Glass Works in 1861. Prior to establishing his own firm, Gillinder had once worked with George Bacchus & Sons and served as superintendent of the New England Glass Company. The name was changed to Gillinder & Sons in 1867 when his two sons, James and Frederick, joined. The company produced a wide variety of pressed (especially those with lion motifs/finials), cut glass, some milk/opaque styles, frosted glass (first to introduce frosted glass in America around 1875), and limited amounts of colored Art Glass. Their products were a big hit at America's Centennial celebration held in Philadelphia in 1876, especially pressed glass and other novelties that sported the Liberty Bell. The pressed glass department of the firm was moved to Greensburg, Pennsylvania, in 1888, and became part of the U.S. Glass Company conglomerate in 1892 as Factory G. (2) Three third-generation Gillinders opened a new plant at Port Jervis, New Jersey, called Gillinder Brothers, Inc. The Philadelphia plant closed permanently in 1930 while the small Port Jervis facility is still run by members of the Gillinder family today (Charles and Susan Gillinder). The latest venture features hand blown and pressed glass, etched, opal, colors, and some industrial and commercial glass.

Reproduction from an 1896 Gillinder & Sons advertisement.

Trademark.

G

GILLINDER BROTHERS — Refer to GILLINDER & SONS.

GIN GLASS — A drinking goblet similar to a wine glass, only slightly smaller, that is used specifically for serving gin. A wine glass has a typical capacity of four ounces while a gin glass is usually in the two to three ounce range (still larger than a cordial).

GIRANDOLE — An elaborate branched candle holder that usually contains attached cut glass prisms. *See also* MANTLE LUSTRE.

GLADDING-VITRO AGATE COMPANY — Refer to the VITRO AGATE COMPANY.

GLANCY, MICHAEL — A noted American Studio Glass artisan born in Detroit, Michigan, in 1950, Glancy received his Master of Fine Arts degree from the Rhode Island School of Design and has served in a teaching capacity at the Pilchuk Glass School; the Appalachian Center in Smithville, Tennessee; Ohio State University; and the Rhode Island School of Design. Glancy continues to work as an independent glass artisan in Rehoboth, Massachusetts.

GLASRAFFINERIE UND KRONLEUCHTERFABRIK — *Refer to* CARL HOSCH.

GLASS — (1) A hard, brittle artificial substance made by fusing silicates (sand) with an alkali (soda or potash) and sometimes with metallic oxides (lead oxide or lime to make glass insoluble). (2) A general term for a drinking vessel. *See also* DRINKING GLASS, STEMWARE, TUMBLER, *and* WINE GLASS.

GLASS BLOCK OR BRICK — An architectural building unit consisting of a hollow or solid block of translucent glass that is also ordinarily square on the face. The outer surface is usually treated to resist weathering as the blocks are often fashioned into walls, or used to fill glazed openings and/or construction partitions.

GLASSBORO GLASSWORKS — An American factory established at Glassboro, New Jersey, by Jacob Stanger in 1781; the company produced windows, bottles, and tableware into the twentieth century. The company was sold repeatedly and was eventually acquired by the Owens Bottle Company in 1918.

GLASS FIBER — A thin thread that is drawn from molten or spun glass; fibers can be drawn out in continuous filaments that can further be wound on a spool. They are often used in insulation compounds, for sound absorption, in certain fabrics, in boat hulls, and most recently in fiber optic cables. Light and electricity flow through extremely fine but flexible glass rods by internal reflection within the cables.

GLASSHOUSE — The building that contains the glass-melting furnaces and in which the actual handling and shaping of molten glass takes place. *See also* GLASSWORKS.

A glasshouse, or *glasshutte*, located in Zweisel, Germany.

GLASS LETTER & NOVELTY COMPANY — An American firm founded at Wheeling, West Virginia, in 1902 by George House and Otto Jaeger, the company produced pressed glass letters for advertising purposes (primarily on doors/storefront windows), along with vault lights. The firm closed during World War I. Note that the firm was also known as the NOVELTY GLASS LETTER COMPANY and the WHEELING GLASS LETTER & NOVELTY COMPANY.

GLASS PICTURE — A design that is ordinarily etched on flat sheets or flat pieces of glass.

GLASS SOAP — Refer to MANGANESE.

GLASS TANK — A reverberatory furnace in which glass is melted directly under the flames. *See also* "Day Tank" *and* TANK.

GLASSWARE — General term for most any object made of glass (i.e. windows, panes, plates, tableware, vessels, vases, art objects, novelties, toys, jewelry, etc).

GLASS WOOL — Spun glass in thin strands, similar to that of wool, used for insulation filters. *See also* GLASS FIBER.

GLASSWORKS — The factory or building that contains the glass-melting furnaces and in which the actual handling and shaping of molten glass takes place. *See also* GLASSHOUSES.

GLASTENBURY GLASS — A short-lived American glasshouse founded in 1812 near Hartford, Connecticut, the firm changed hands numerous times and produced some crude bottles before closing in 1824.

GLAZE — A thin, smooth material, such as enamel or paint, usually applied to glass window panes. Glaziers were artisans and/or craftsman who fitted and painted flat glass for windows beginning in Europe in the fourteenth century. Glaze can also be applied to both glass and pottery objects.

GLEASON-TIEBOUT GLASS COMPANY — Refer to the NATIONAL GLASS MANUFACTURING COMPANY.

GLOB — A small rounded mass of glass usually dropped upon a flat surface (becomes flat on the bottom, but still rounded on top) and then incorporated into leaded glass artwork. Note that globs are also called NUGGETS. *See also* GATHER.

GLOBE — (1) A sphere on which is usually depicted a terrestrial map of Earth. The first crystal globe was reportedly made for Louis XVIII of France by the St. Louis Glass Factory in 1818. Today, many companies, including Steuben, Baccarat, and Waterford, make glass globes in a wide variety of sizes. (2) A spherical paperweight that has a large rounded or globe-like cover. Globe paperweights generally have a very small flat area so that the paperweight can stand on its own; however, others are completely spherical and require a stand for displaying. Also note that some globe paperweights contain maps of the world — many of these styles were made by the Lundberg Studios of California.

GLORY HOLE — A small-sized opening in the side of the furnace used for inserting cool glass objects in order to reheat them without melting or destroying the shape (sometimes named the reheating furnace). Objects are often reheated to further fashion and/or decorate them, as well as to remove any mold imperfections. The Glory Hole is also sometimes referred to as the "Bocellas," "Bye Hole," "Spy Hole," or "Nose."

GLOVE BOX — A rectangular glass object, with or without a cover, used specifically on dressing tables or vanities for holding gloves.

Reproduction from an early 20th century Pitkin and Brooks Company catalog.

GLUE-CHIP — A frosted-like texture created on the surface of cold glass made by applying hot animal glue to it and then allowing it to dry under controlled temperature and humidity. As the glue dries and contracts, it chips the glass into the desired design.

GOB — A quantity of molten glass that is gathered at the end of a pontil or blowpipe and then either worked by the blower or dropped into a mold. A uniform weight of molten glass that is fed into an automatic pressing machine is also known as a "Blob."

GOBLET — A stemmed drinking vessel with a large bowl that comes in various sizes and shapes and rests upon a foot (the foot is usually circular). Water goblets tend to have the largest capacity when compared to other stemware used specifically for alcoholic beverages (i.e. wine glass, cordial, champagne glass, etc.).

Goblet.   Claret.   Wine.

Reproduction from an 1892 U.S. Glass Company catalog.

GOLD — A metallic coloring agent that, when dissolved in a chloride acid solution, produces cranberry or a deep ruby red color. Generally, it requires about an ounce of gold for every sixty pounds of a glass batch to produce a deep red. The metal is also used to decorate glass both externally and internally as in paperweights (i.e. gold inclusion). *See also* AQUA REGIA, RUBY RED, *and* GILDING.

A collection of gold-decorated tumblers. *Photo by Robin Rainwater.*

GOLDBERG, CARL — A noted Bohemian/Czechoslovakian-styled glass decorator, who, with sales manager Josef Kreys, established a workshop at Arnsdorf, Germany, in 1891. Goldberg gained an international reputation after displaying his wares at major exhibitions throughout Europe and America. The firm was moved to Haida (changed to Novy Bor, Czechoslovakia, after World War I). After World War II, the firm came under national control by Czechoslovakia.

GOLDEN AGATE — Refer to HOLLY AMBER.

GOLDEN FOLIAGE — A style of glass tableware produced by the Libbey Glass Company in the 1950s, it is characterized by a machine-applied wide satin band (appears frosted) that contains gold and/or silver leaves around the glass. The majority of items produced in this style included beverage sets (pitchers and tumblers), as well as other drinking vessels (tumblers and goblets, shot glasses, etc.) Some were included as free promotional items in boxes of laundry detergent.

Golden foliage patterned tumblers from Libbey, 1950s. *Photo by Robin Rainwater.*

Golden foliage patterned tumbler set from Libbey, 1950s.
Photo by Robin Rainwater.

GOLDEN & JACOBSON — Refer to the GOLDEN NOVELTY MANUFACTURING COMPANY.

GOLDEN NOVELTY MANUFACTURING COMPANY — An American firm established in 1895 as Golden & Jacobson at Chicago, Illinois, the name was changed to the Golden Novelty Manufacturing Company in 1897. Although one of the principals of the firm (Charles Golden) patented a design for a cut glass lamp in 1911, the company did not manufacture any cut glass products of their own; rather, they served as a wholesale/retain operation who represented clocks, silverware, china, and glassware made by others.

Reproduction from a 1911
C. D. Golden U.S. patent.

GOLDEN ORANGE — An opaque colored art style of glass created and named by Victor Durand Jr. The color is a moderately dull, pumpkin-colored orange that was iridized somewhat like Marigold Carnival Glass.

GOLDEN YELLOW — A brilliant opaque colored art style of glass created and named by Victor Durand Jr. The color is a brightly colored golden yellow that occasionally shades from golden yellow to golden orange (some pieces are noted to be golden orange with yellow highlights).

GOLDSTONE — Refer to AVENTURINE.

GONE WITH THE WIND LAMP — A kerosene or electric table lamp containing a glass base with a round, globe-shaped glass shade.

GOOFUS GLASS — Late nineteenth and early twentieth century pressed glass items containing designs in relief. The designs (either front or back) were then hand-painted (red and/or green were the most common colors) with a metallic gold ground. Like Carnival Glass, they were given as inexpensive prizes at carnivals and fairs; however, by 1920, its popularity ended as people discovered that the paint did not wear well after general use and repeated cleanings.

GOTHIC — A pressed glass design consisting of concentric continuous oval arches reminiscent of Gothic architecture.

GOWANS, KEN & COMPANY LTD. — A Canadian cut glass firm that operated in the late nineteenth and early twentieth century; like most Canadian cut glass firms, they purchased lead glass blanks from both American and European firms.

Gowans, Kent &
Company, Ltd.: Trademarks.

GRAAL — A technique developed in 1916 by Orrefors of Sweden, Graal is created by cutting a pattern within the core of colored glass that is encased in clear glass and then blown into its final shape (much like the reverse of cameo glass since the cut-away portion forms the design instead of the background).

GRADUATED CYLINDER — Refer to CYLINDER.

GRAL-GLAS — A German art glass firm established in 1930 at Goppingen (near Stuttgart) by Karl Seyfang (1881-1971) and Herman Fischer, though Fischer left in 1932. Early on the factory produced blanks for other cutting/decoration shops; however, the firm began decorating its own glass objects (i.e. vases, stemware, some table items, etc.) with color effects, etching, crackling, and bubbling. A new factory was built in 1947 and a second plant was added in Durnau. The company further expanded in 1959 when they purchased Glashutte Rheinkristall at Leichlingen; and again in 1978 when they purchased Josephinenhutte in Schwasbisch Gmund. The company went bankrupt in 1981, changed hands several times over the next decade, and finally closed permanently in 1992.

GRANJA, LA DE SAN ILDEFONSO — The site of the Royal Glassworks established in Spain near the Spanish Royal Palace in 1728. The firm produced mirrors, chandeliers, and ornamental objects primarily for the Royal Palace up until 1829. The factory was leased thereafter and produced practical glass wares in the Anglo-Irish styles of the day.

GRAPE — A common design applied to glass dating as far back as ancient Egyptian and Roman times. Since then, grapes, grape clusters, grapes and vines, and grape bunches, and so forth have been applied to glass in a wide variety of forms (etched, cut, engraved, mold-embossed, pressed, Art-styles, enameled, gilded, relief cut, etc.). Several pressed, cut, Depression, and Carnival patterns combine them with other designs in such pattern names as arched grape, beaded grape, beaded grape medallion, grape and cable, grape and festoon, grape band, grape bunch, paneled and late paneled grape, grape with overlapping foliage, grape with thumbprint, grape with vine, vintage, grape and gothic arches, grape and cherry, grape arbor, grape leaves, grapevine lattice, grape wreath, and magnet and grape.

Carnival glass grape patterned pitcher. *Photo by Robin Rainwater.*

Fenton Carnival grape patterns reproduced from a 1915 Butler Brothers catalog.

Floral and Grape Embossed Asst. — 2 styles, golden iridescent, 11 in. plain top tankard and 9 in. crimped top squat blown jugs, cap. ½ gal., stuck handles, SIX 9 oz. tumblers to match. 3 sets each,
C1868 — Asstd. 6 sets in bbl., 53 lbs.   **Set, 68c**
(Total $4.08)

Grapevine Embossed—Jug, ht. 11½ in., ½ gal., SIX 9 oz. tumblers, relief grape clusters and lattice embossing, golden iridescent finish.
C1871—6 sets in bbl., 70 lbs.
(Total $4.50)   Set, **75c**
C2248—2 sets in carton
(Total $1 54)   Set, **.77c**

GRAPEFRUIT BOWL — A concave glass vessel, usually circular in shape and ordinarily with a wide foot, used for serving one-half of a grapefruit. Grapefruit bowls may contain short or long stems and are usually hemispherical in shape. A Grapefruit Bowl is sometimes referred to as a "Grapefruit Dish" or "Grapefruit Glass."

Reproduction from an early 20th century Pitkin & Brooks Company catalog.

GRAVIC — A name given to Intaglio styled cut glass made by T. J. Hawkes. *See also* INTAGLIO.

GRAVY BOAT — An oblong bowl-like object with handle and spout used for pouring gravy (may or may not be accompanied by a matching platter or pedestal).

Ruby red Cape Cod patterned gravy boat; Avon commissioned it for Wheaton Industries.

GRAY & HEMINGRAY — Refer to the HEMINGRAY GLASS COMPANY.

GRAY, HEMINGRAY, & BROTHERS — Refer to the HEMINGRAY GLASS COMPANY.

GRAYSTAN OR GRAY-STAN GLASS — Glass made by Elizabeth Graydon-Stannus between 1922 and 1936. Born in Ireland in 1873, Graydon-Stannus moved to London, England, and set up a glass-making studio there in 1922. She moved to Battersea (south London) in 1925 and opened a new studio called Graydon Studios in 1926. Products made in her studio include cut and engraved crystal and colored glass similar to that of swirled Monart and Venetian styles.

GREEK KEY — A common design applied to glassware that consists of a continuous interlocking pattern of straight-edged scrolling at right angles. Greek Key can also be thought of as a maze of interlocking "e" designs. Greek Key patterns can be found on most forms of glass, including Art, cut, pressed, Depression, and Carnival.

GREEN GLASS — The natural color of ordinary alkaline or lime-based glassware, usually produced by iron present in the sand. Additional iron and chromium is added to make a clear green. Uranium was once added, too, in order to produce a vibrant, glowing green color. *See also* ANTIQUE GREEN, EMERALD GREEN, FOREST GREEN, GREEN OPAQUE, POMONA GREEN, *and* SEA FOAM GREEN.

G

GREEN OPAQUE — An opaque satinized or gloss green style of Art Glass created and named by the New England Glass Company in the late 1880s. It was made by adding copper oxide to an opal batch of glass to produce the base color. Wares were then further decorated with a mottled blue metallic stain and gold bands.

GREENAL & PILKINGTON — Refer to the PILKINGTON BROTHERS.

GREENER, HENRY — Refer to HENRY GREENER'S WEAR FLINT GLASS WORKS.

Greener, Henry: Trademark.

GREENLIGHT HOT GLASS — A contemporary glass studio founded in Oregon in 1998 by Sunshine Kesey and Matt Wallace, the firm is noted for producing glass sculptures and paperweights with water/ocean motifs.

GREENSBURG GLASS COMPANY — An American firm established at Greensburg, Pennsylvania, in 1889 by A. M. Bacon, J. S. Cockburn, James Kuhn, W. S. Kuhn, and H. C. Stewart, the company produced pressed glass barware and tableware, some in color, prior to becoming part of the National Glass Company in 1899 as factory #8. In 1900, National sold the plant to the Standard Glass Company, a bottle glass maker. In 1920, the plant was acquired by the L. E. Smith Company.

GREENTOWN AGATE — Refer to HOLLY AMBER.

GREENTOWN GLASS — A general name for pressed tableware and other glass products produced in and around the town of Greentown, Indiana, in the late nineteenth and early twentieth centuries. Firms included the INDIANA TUMBLER & GOBLET CO., the NATIONAL GLASS CO., MCKEE BROTHERS, and JACOB ROSENTHAL.

GREENTOWN GLASS WORKS — Refer to the INDIANA TUMBLER & GOBLET COMPANY.

GREGORY, MARY — Refer to MARY GREGORY.

GRENADE — In glassware, a grenade is a glass vessel with a globular body and narrow neck. At one time, they were used in attempt to put out fires (i.e. filled with water and then thrown into the flames).

GRID CUT — A series of symmetrical shallow narrow grooves cross cut into the base of a paperweight in order to form a pattern or grid.

GRILL PLATE — A large individual or serving plate with divisions (similar to relish dishes only larger).

Hocking Glass Company's Cameo Ballerina patterned Depression Glass grill plate. *Photo by Robin Rainwater.*

GRINDER — A fairly small, electrically operated device, that has a variety of uses in glass-making. Most sport a wheel and, when combined with abrasives, are used in polishing, smoothing, and finishing glass. Stained glass artisans for instance use portable grinders to smooth the edges of cut-out glass. They are also used in optics to grind lenses mostly to fit prescription glasses (spectacles).

GROTESQUE GLASS — A negative term for glass objects that are somewhat distorted, unattractive, or ludicrous in appearance. Frederick Carder of Steuben actually named one of his creations "Grotesque," a style of glass that was clear at the bottom and then shaded to various transparent colors as one moved up to the top. Note that the Italian name for grotesque is "Grotteschi."

GROUND — The background or base glass object on which decorations are applied. In paperweights, it's the surface just above the base, above which the design is set, and can be a single or combination from a huge variety of styles: basket, carpet, checker, colored, cushioned, filigree, jasper, lace, latticino, moss, mottled, muslin, pebble, rock, sand, scale, sodden snow, stardust, etc.

GUERNSEY GLASS COMPANY — An American novelty glass-making firm established at Cambridge, Ohio, in 1970 by Harold Bennett. Guernsey produced some reproduction colored pressed pattern glass along with glass novelties.

GULLASKRUF — A bottle-making facility established in Sweden's Smaland district in 1893. The firm expanded into window glass, but due to cheaper imports, it closed in 1921. In 1927, it was purchased by William Stenberg and the new operation included the production of laboratory glass, auto headlights, and press-molded tableware. In 1930, artist Hugo Gehlin (1889-1953) was hired and the firm expanded into more traditional Swedish art glass items utilizing fish shapes and other organic forms, molten thick-walled glass, color effects, geometric shapes, etc. Another noted artistic designer, Kjell Blomberg (b. 1931), joined in 1955. In 1974, the firm was sold to Krona-Bruken; and, in 1977, it was briefly leased to Orrefors until 1983. Some production resumed in 1983; however, the factory closed permanently in 1995. See also SWEDISH GLASS.

GUNDERSON GLASS WORKS, INC. — Robert Gunderson (1872-1952), along with Thomas Tripp and Isaac Babbitt, purchased the silverware and glass departments of Pairpoint in 1939 and continued production until Gunderson's death in 1952 under the new name. It was then changed to the Gunderson-Pairpoint Glass Works. Gunderson had begun work as a glass apprentice at age seven at Hadelands, Norway, and later joined up with Mount Washington/Pairpoint in 1888 as a skilled glass blower. Glass made by Gunderson is often referred to as "Gunderson's Pairpoint." See also PAIRPOINT MANUFACTURING COMPANY.

GUNDY-CLAPPERTON — A Canadian cut glass firm founded by N. F. Gundy and G. H. "Harry" Clapperton in 1906. Like most Canadian cut glass firms, they purchased lead glass blanks from both American and European businesses. The firm proceeded through many name changes when Gundy left in the early 1920s, including Clapperton's and then Clapperton & Sons. Products marked by the company first contained "GCCo" in a shamrock, and then simply a "C" in a shamrock when Gundy departed. Cut glass products made by them were also occasionally marked or labeled by distributors ("Birks" or "House of Birks" for example).

Gundy-Clapperton: Trademarks.

Hh

{ Hh }

HADELANDS GLASVERK — A Norwegian glasshouse founded at Jevnaker in 1762 under a charter by King Frederick V, the firm began producing practical items such as bottles and came under the state's control in 1814. It was sold into private ownership in 1824. In the early-to-mid-nineteenth century, the company produced lead crystal and colored tableware, bottles, flasks, jars, and fishing net floats. In the 1850s, the firm was acquired by the Berg family and they still own and operate it today. Under the direction of the Bergs, the company expanded into colorful Scandinavian art glass designs in the early twentieth century. Since its origin, the firm has been noted as Norway's largest producer of art glass forms. *See also NORWEGIAN GLASS.*

HAEMATINON or HAEMATINUM — An ancient Egyptian technique utilized in enamels and mosaics that involves producing crimson or blood-red colored glass pieces with copper (cuprous) oxide. The Romans also used this method for decorating.

HAIRPIN — A small, somewhat U-shaped object used to hold hair in place. Some were made of glass, particularly in the Victorian era. Hairpin also refers to a mid-nineteenth century pressed sandwich pattern with loops that resemble hairpins called the "Sandwich Loop."

HAIRPIN BOX — A small, square, rectangular, or circular glass container, with or a without cover, used specifically on a dressing table or vanity for holding hairpins.

HAIR RECEIVER — A circular glass object, usually with a cover, that has a large hole in the middle. It is used on tables, dressers, and vanities to hold hair that accumulates in the hair brush. Hair receivers were popular during the Victorian era.

Reproduction from an early 20th century Pitkin & Brooks Co. catalog.

HALD, EDWARD — A famous painter and glass designer who joined Orrefors Glassbruk in Sweden in 1917, Hald (1883-1975) teamed up with Simon Gate to create the award winning "Graal" line of art glass. *See also GRAAL.*

HALE, ATTERBURY & COMPANY — Refer to the ATTERBURY GLASS COMPANY.

HALEM, HENRY — A noted American Studio Glass artisan born in New York City in 1938, Halem received his Master of Fine Arts degree from George Washington University and has served in a teaching capacity at the Virginia Museum of Fine Arts, Mary Washington College of the University of Virginia, Kent State University, and the Pilchuk Glass School. Halem also works as an independent glass artisan in Kent, Ohio.

HALF LEAD CRYSTAL — Colorless glass containing a minimum of 24% lead content (lower lead content and hence, lower quality than full lead crystal).

HALF-POST METHOD — A technique of molding a glass object by which a gather (the post) is dipped a second time into the pot so as to be covered half-way up (half-post). The result is that the lower half is thicker and stronger. It was used in making such objects as Pitkin Flasks. *See also PITKIN GLASS WORKS.*

HALL & CALLAHAN — An American cut glass operation established at Meriden, Connecticut, in 1914 by John Hall and Thomas Callahan. When Hall passed on in 1917, Callahan moved operations to Hawley, Pennsylvania; working then as a division of the Monoghan Brothers. In 1918, Callahan joined the J. J. Niland Company.

HALL-IN-TYROL — Refer to AUSTRIAN GLASS.

HALTER CUT GLASS COMPANY, INC. — Refer to the HALTER, J. & COMPANY.

HALTER, J. & COMPANY — An American cut glass firm founded in 1905 in Brooklyn, New York, by Joseph Halter, the company produced cut glass products until ceasing operation in 1921. Note that the firm was also filed under the HALTER CUT GLASS COMPANY name.

HAMILTON — A pressed pattern design originating in the mid-nineteenth century, it consists of a strawberry diamond and fan design imitative of cut glass. It also exists in a pattern variant called "Hamilton with Leaf."

HAMMONTON GLASSWORKS — An American factory established at Hammonton, New Jersey, by William Coffin and Jonathan Haines in 1817, the company produced windows, bottles, and some tableware before going out of business.

HAND-BLOWN GLASS — Glass formed and shaped with a blowpipe and other hand-manipulated tools without the use of molds.

HAND-CAST GLASS — Refer to CAST GLASS and the SINGLE ROLL METHOD.

HAND COOLER — A solid ovoid or small glass object originally developed in ancient Rome for ladies to cool their hands. Later, hand coolers were also used by ladies when being wooed or for darning. Modern hand coolers are made in the form of animals and eggs and are used as paperweights and/or as simple objects of art.

HAND-PRESSED GLASS — Glass objects produced in hand-operated mechanical presses. *See also PRESSED GLASS.*

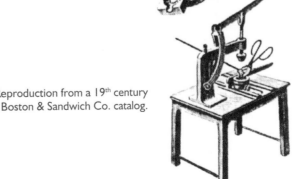

Reproduction from a 19th century Boston & Sandwich Co. catalog.

HAND VASE — A style of vase that includes a blown or mold-pressed replica of a human hand as part of the stem.

HANDEL, PHILIP J. — An American glassmaker who founded the Handel Company in Meriden, Connecticut, in 1885, Handel was noted for producing Art Nouveau acid cut-back cameo vases and Art Nouveau lamps similar to but less expensive than Tiffany Lamps. The quality of Handel's lamps was still outstanding and many were signed by numerous individual artisans working in the company. Chipped glass effects, hand decorated interiors, bent inserts, metal or leaded shades, fired-on metallic stains, gilding, cameo engraving and etchings can all be found on these famous lamps. Even the bases were quite elaborate; copper, brass, bronze, and white plated metals were utilized and decorated. Handel also produced some tableware, opal glass and a few non-glass products (wood, metal, porcelain, and pottery items). The firm closed in 1936.

Handel, Philip J.: Trademarks.

HANDKERCHIEF BOX — A rectangular glass receptacle with cover designed specifically for storing handkerchiefs.

HANDKERCHIEF VASE — A style of vase whereby the sides of the object are pulled straight up and then randomly pleated to resemble a large ruffled handkerchief. The Venetian term is "vaso fazzoletto" and sometimes they are referred to as handkerchief bowls. *See also FAZZOLETTO.*

HANDLE — General term for the part of an object that is grasped and held by the hand when used or carried. Objects usually have a space for the fingers to pass through between the handle and base object, though some are closed off. Handles are commonly found on cups, mugs, jugs, pitchers, vases, steins, measuring cups, etc. Some objects have been created with two or more handles. Bale or overhead handles are typically found on pails like ice buckets while small tab handles are also part of bowls, plates, and small dishes like olives or bon bons. *See also TAB HANDLES.*

HANDLE-SHEARS — A scissor-like tool with blades that are molded to form opposing right angles and have curved tips. They are used to close gently around a pontil or blowpipe in order to guide it into place. This is necessary when an assistant is bringing a new gather of glass to add to an already blown shape (i.e. a handle to a pitcher or vase) or when a blown shape is being transferred from the blowpipe to the pontil. Regular shears are used to shear or cut off excess glass. *See also SHEARS.*

HANNA & WALLACE — Refer to the UNION FLINT GLASS WORKS.

HARAND & GUIGNARD — Refer to ROUSSEAU.

HARCOURT — A style of lead crystal tableware developed by the French firm of Baccarat in 1842. Most are made in the form of goblets with hexagonal bases, stems, and an ovoid bowl with six facets and were presented to many Heads of State through the years. Some pieces contain elaborate gilding as well.

HARMON, JAMES — A noted American Studio Glass artisan born in Warsaw, New York, in 1952, Harmon received his Master of Fine Arts degree from Illinois State University and has served in a teaching capacity at the Pilchuk Glass School, the Penland School of Crafts, the Pratt City Arts Center in Seattle, Washington, the University of Hawaii, New York University, and the Rhode Island School of Design. Harmon continues to work as an independent glass artisan and designer in New York City.

HARMONY GLASSWORKS — An American company founded by former workmen of the OLIVE GLASSWORKS at Glassboro, New Jersey, in 1813. The firm produced glass in the South Jersey style before selling out to Thomas & Samuel Whitney in 1835. *See also OLIVE GLASSWORKS, SOUTH JERSEY GLASS, and WHITNEY GLASSWORKS.*

HARRACH OR HARRACHOV GLASSWORKS — A glasshouse founded in Northern Bohemia in 1712 (at modern day Neuwelt, Czech Republic) by the noble Harrach family (Harrochov was the name of the village under control of the family). Some place the founding as early as 1630, but written records only date back to 1712. The works began much as a forest glass operation producing practical items such as bottles and windows. They also produced a good deal of blanks that were sold to Silesian decorators. Since 1764, the firm has produced some colored ornamental and tableware including opal glass. Harrachov was acquired by noted engraver Johann Pohl (1796-1850) in 1808; under his direction, Harrach produced a good deal of high quality decorated and engraved crystal tableware in a wide variety of Bohemian styles. From 1884-1900, Bohdan Kadlec served as director; in the meantime, in 1887, it was acquired by Josef Riedel, who further expanded operations, making a good deal of colored Bohemian glassware under Kadlec's supervision. The firm survived Germany's occupation during World War II and became nationalized like all Czech firms in 1948. After becoming part of other conglomerates including Crystakex in 1972, it reverted to private ownership in 1993 and continues to operate today in the Czech Republic. *See also SILESIAN GLASS and RIEDEL FAMILY.*

HARTMANN & DIETERICHS — A Bohemian glass company founded at Schaiba, Germany, in 1881 by Arnost Hartmann and Hermann Dieterichs, the firm was moved to Haida, which later became the Czechoslovakian city of Novy Bor. Hartmann died in 1892 and Dieterichs passed on in 1905. The heirs of both families allowed two co-workers, Pavel Jakub and Adolf Strubell, to run the firm. Strubell purchased it in 1912, but did not change the firm's name. The firm produced engraved and enameled Bohemian glass until 1940.

HARTWELL & LANCASTER — A short-lived American maker of pressed glass founded at Philadelphia, Pennsylvania, in 1847, the company purchased the defunct Union Glass Company that had been established in 1825. The firm's name changed once again to Hartwell, Letchworth & Company in 1858 and produced pressed tableware into the mid-1870s.

HARTWELL, LETCHWORTH & COMPANY — Refer to HARTWELL & LANCASTER.

HASKINS GLASS COMPANY — An American pressed glass-making firm established at Martins Ferry, Ohio, in 1905 by Dr. Thomas Haskins, H. Bone, and associates. The company purchased the WEST VIRGINIA GLASS WORKS, which had previously been part of the NATIONAL GLASS COMPANY, and made some blown glass lighting fixtures along with pressed glass. A fire destroyed the factory in 1909, and Haskins closed permanently in 1912.

HASKINS-JACOBS GLASS COMPANY — A short-lived American pressed glass operation founded at Grafton, West Virginia by Dr. Thomas Haskins and Bernard Jacobs in 1903. The two had purchased a factory previously owned by the Beaumont Glass Company and named it the Cooperative Glass and Electric Company. The two split soon after as Haskins moved on to establish the Haskins Glass Company in 1905. *See also HASKINS GLASS COMPANY.*

HAT OR HAT VASE — A whimsical glass object in the shape of an upside down head covering or top hat. The space where one's head would usually rest is often used for holding flowers or other tiny objects.

HAT PIN HOLDER — A tall glass object in the shape of a cylinder that is used on tables, dressers, and vanities for storing hatpins.

Carnival Glass hat pin holders. *Courtesy of Wheaton Village.*

HATCH & CLARK — Refer to T. B. CLARK & COMPANY and HATCH & COMPANY.

HATCH & COMPANY — A short-lived cut glass operation founded by George Hatch in 1886 in Brooklyn, New York. Hatch had previously worked for the New England Glass Company, the Meriden Flint Glass Company, and in a brief partnership with noted cutter T. B. Clark (1884-1886) prior to establishing his own business. Hatch continued on his own producing cut glass tableware until 1891.

HATCHED OR HATCHING — An engraved decoration consisting of fine lines that give the effect of shading. When two sets of parallel lines cross each other at right or obtuse angles, it is referred to as "cross-hatching."

HAUGHWOUT & DAILEY — One of New York's largest china and glass retailers in the seventeenth century, the company was originally known as E. V. Haughwout & Company in the 1850s, employed noted glass cutters such as John Hoare and John S. O'Connor, and sold a good deal of imported goods (primarily from Europe).

HAWKES, T. G. & COMPANY — An American company established at Corning, New York, in 1880 by Thomas Gibbon Hawkes (1846-1913), who first worked and even lived with John Hoare before establishing his own firm. The company produced high quality cut crystal tableware as well as lead crystal blanks for others. In 1903, Hawkes and Fredrick Carder merged to form the Steuben Glass Works. Note also that in the early twentieth century, Hawkes added

a silver department (to make silver fittings and holders for glass) and two glass subsidiaries, Signet and Edenhall (cheaper glass products were made under these names). Edenhall items were generally lightly engraved and contained silver mounts while Signet products contained light engraving only. Both Edenhall and Signet were discontinued around 1917. Hawkes' products were of such quality that they graced the tables of Presidents Cleveland, Harrison, both Roosevelts, Truman, and Eisenhower, as well as many foreign heads-of-state. Noted families like the Astors, Rockefellers, Vanderbilts, Whitneys, and Duponts also purchased cut glass made by Hawkes. As the era of cut glass production ended, the Steuben name lives on today for high quality crystal products. *See also STEUBEN.*

Hawkes Cut Glass.

As the famous Hall-Mark attests the genuineness of English silverware so does this

Trade HAWKES Mark

show highest quality in cut glass.

Grand Prize—Paris.

Reproduction from a late 19th century Hawkes advertisement.

Hawkes cut glass. *Photo courtesy of the Corning Museum of Glass.*

Trademarks.

HAY & CAMPBELL — Refer to UNION FLINT GLASS WORKS.

HAY & McCULLY — Refer to UNION FLINT GLASS WORKS.

HAZEL ATLAS GLASS COMPANY — An American firm originally founded as the Hazel Glass Company in 1885, the company also founded a separate entity in 1896, the ATLAS GLASS COMPANY, to produce fruit jars. The two names were merged to create the Hazel-Atlas Glass Company in 1902 at Washington, Pennsylvania. The company produced large amounts of machine pressed crystal and colored glassware, especially during the Depression period. The firm also produced glass food containers. Factories were added throughout Ohio, Pennsylvania, and West Virginia until the company was sold in 1956. CONTINENTAL CAN then continued to produce glassware under the Hazel Ware name. Patterns/designs made by them included "Aurora," "Capri," "Cloverleaf," "Colonial Block," "Crinoline," "Florentine No. 1" or "Old Florentine" or "Poppy No. 1," "Florentine No. 2," or "Poppy No. 2," "Fruits," "Moderntone," "Moderntone Platonite," "Moroccan Amethyst," "New Century," "Newport" or "Hairpin," "Ovide," "Roxana," "Royal Lace," "Ribbon," "Sportsman Series" (also known as "Sailboat & Windmills" or "Ships & Windmills"), and "Starlight." See also HAZEL GLASS COMPANY.

Hazel Atlas Depression green glass bowl. *Photo by Robin Rainwater.*

Hazel Atlas Glass Company Trademark.

HAZEL GLASS COMPANY — An American glass-making firm established at Wellsburg, West Virginia, in 1885 by Charles Brady and C. H. Tallman, the company began as a producer of opal glass liners for Mason fruit jar caps. The firm moved to Washington, Pennsylvania, in 1886 and named their furnace "Hazel." The firm expanded into jars and bottles and was one of the first to make wide-mouthed jars with automated machinery. Hazel founded the Atlas Glass Company in 1896 at Washington, Pennsylvania, strictly for producing fruit jars. The two names were merged in 1902. See also HAZEL-ATLAS GLASS COMPANY.

HEART — A pressed or cut glass design resembling a single or series of interlocking conventionalized representations of hearts. Hearts are often combined with other decorations to produce unique patterns (i.e. heart band, heart stem, heart with thumbprint, interlocked hearts, etc.).

A pressed glass heart-patterned creamer. *Photo by Robin Rainwater.*

HEAT CHECK — Refer to CHECK.

HEAT REACTIVE — Glass that changes color as a result of localized cooling and reheating. Such color effects as Amberina, Peachblow, and many opalescent varieties are created by controlled heating and gradual cooling.

HEATON AGATE COMPANY — An American marble-making firm founded by William Heaton in 1939 at Cairo, West Virginia, the company produced glass marbles until 1971, the same year the company was sold to Clayton E. Bogard & Sons. See also BOGARD COMPANY.

HECKERT, FRITZ — A Bohemian glass enameler who founded a decoration firm at Petersdorf in 1866. The company began as a producer of mirrors and cut chandelier parts before expanding into enameled decorating. Heckert purchased blanks to decorate with from the nearby firm of Josephinenhutte before building his own hut or glasshouse in 1889. Heckert died in 1890 and the firm was carried on by his widow, Zurillie Heckerty, and son-in-law, Otto Thamm. The company was noted most for decorating large beakers called humpen, copying Medieval woodcuts and engravings in glass, and for blowing glass in wire netting. The firm was awarded both a silver and gold medal at the 1902 Turin Exposition and a gold medal at the 1904 St. Louis World's Fair. In 1905, Fritz's son Bruno gained control of the firm until the end of World War I. It was then acquired by the Von Loesch family, who in turn, merged with Josephinenhutte in 1923.

HEINZ BROTHERS — Brothers Richard, Emil, and Otto Heinz worked for both Pitkin & Brooks and the American Cut Glass Company prior to establishing the Monarch Cut Glass Company at Chicago, Illinois, in 1901 (with temporary partners Herman and Frank Kotwitz). In 1902, the Heinz Brothers bought out the Kotwitz's and changed the name. They built a new factory in 1905 at St. Charles, Illinois, and became one of the largest producers of cut glass in the Midwest. Cut glass produced by the firm was never marked by them, though some distributors, like C. H. Wheelock of Peoria, Illinois, placed their own labels on the Heinz products. The Heinz Brothers remained in business until 1927.

Reproduction from a 1905 Heinz Brothers newspaper advertisement.

HEISEY, A. H. GLASS COMPANY — An American company established at Newark, Ohio, in 1895 (though Augustus H. Heisey was producing glass as early as the 1860s). Heisey began his glass-making career with several firms including King & Son, Ripley, and then with his father-in-law, George Duncan. He was noted early on as a skilled maker of cut patterns and finely etched glass before forming his own business. His most distinguished employee was an Austrian immigrant cutter named Emil Krall (Krall's son, Emil Krall Jr., also cut glass for Heisey). When Heisey died in 1922, he was succeeded by his three sons (George Duncan, Edgar Wilson, and Thomas Clarence). Heisey produced some cut and Carnival Glass; colored art wares including a good deal of custard glass (which the firm named "Ivrena Verde"); above-average pressed crystal (many elegantly etched); colored wares during the Depression era ("Charter Oak," "Chintz," "Empress," "Ipswich," "Lodestar," "Old Colony," "Old Sandwich," "Pleat and Panel," "Quaker," "Ridgeleigh," "Rococo," "Saturn," "Tudor," "Twentieth Century," "Twist," "Victorian," "Warwick," "Yeoman," etc.); collectible crystal glass animals (introduced in 1933); and a wide variety of tableware patterns ("Cabochon," "Crystolite," "Greek Key," "New Era," "Lariat," "Minuet," "Octagon," "Orchid," "Plantation," "Provincial," "Queen Ann," "Rose," "Stanhope," "Victorian," "Waverly," etc.). The company closed in 1958 and the molds were purchased by the IMPERIAL GLASS COMPANY. When Imperial shut down in 1985, the HEISEY COLLECTORS OF AMERICA (HCA) purchased all known Heisey molds, which they have used occasionally since 1985 to reproduce Heisey glass (all new glass is marked "HCA"). Also note that HCA hires other firms to fill the molds (FENTON, BOYD, and MOSSER). *See also* GEORGE DUNCAN & SONS.

Here is the interesting No. 1405 Early American Scroll design by Heisey. Illustrated are the following items . . . Sherbet, Saucer Champagne, Goblet, Plate, 10-Ounce Soda, 8-Ounce Soda, 5-Ounce Soda. A small part only of this line.

Heisey, A. H. Glass Company: Reproduction from a 1932 Heisey advertisement.

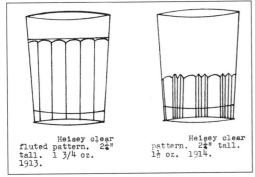

Heisey clear fluted pattern. 2¼" tall. 1 3/4 oz. 1913.

Heisey clear pattern. 2¼" tall. 1⅛ oz. 1914.

Line drawing by the author.

Trademarks.

HELENS CROWN GLASS COMPANY — Refer to the PILKINGTON BROTHERS.

HELIOS — A name given to a style of CARNIVAL GLASS made by the IMPERIAL GLASS COMPANY, Helios is characterized by a sprayed silver or gold iridescent sheen over a green glass base.

HEMINGRAY GLASS COMPANY — An American glass-making firm established at Cincinnati, Ohio, in 1848 by Samuel and Robert Hemingray, along with Ralph Gray. The firm was first known as Gray & Hemingray. The company added a second factory at Covington, Kentucky, in 1851. In 1856, Anthony Gray joined and the name of the company was changed to Gray, Hemingray & Brothers. The main offices were moved to Covington in 1861 and the Grays withdrew in 1863, with the name then becoming Hemingray Brothers & Company. When Samuel died in 1868, the name was changed to R. Hemingray & Company and then finally to the Hemingray Glass Company in 1874. The firm's primary product was that of glass insulators, many produced in an aquamarine color. In 1925, they developed a new method of pressing inner threads of insulator, which accelerated production. The firm was moved to Muncie, Indiana, in 1888 and remained in the Hemingray family until 1933 when they sold out to the Owens-Illinois Company (became plant #26 as the Hemingray division). In 1949, Owen-Illinois renamed it the Structural Division and then to the Kimble Division in 1954. The factory was closed in 1972. Owens-Illinois used the plant to make structural glass block, glass lighting panels, television face plates, and some tableware.

Hemingray insulator.
Photo by Robin Rainwater.

HENRY GREENER'S WEAR FLINT GLASS WORKS — An English pressed glass-making firm established by Henry Greener in the Newcastle/Sunderland region of Northeast England in 1827. James Angus joined in 1858 and the firm was known as Angus and Greener until Angus died in 1869 (then became Greener & Company). The firm produced pressed glass wares originally and added cut glass products later in the nineteenth century. When Greener died in 1882, the firm suffered financial difficulties and eventually was acquired by its principle creditor in 1886 (James Augustus Jobling). The firm was officially renamed in 1921 as James Jobling and Company Ltd. and art glass products were added (molds were commissioned from the famous French firm of Frankhausser). Art glass production ended during World War II. Jobling also received an exclusive franchise agreement from America's Corning to produce Pyrex ovenware in the United Kingdom. Corning actually purchased Jobling in 1973, but then sold it, along with the rights to Pyrex, to the Newll Company in 1994.

HERBECK-DEMER COMPANY — A short-lived American cut glass operation founded in 1904 at Honesdale, Pennsylvania, by Emil Herbeck and John Demer, the firm produced some limited cut and engraved glass before ceasing operations in 1911. John Demer, along with several of his brothers, went on to form a new company. *See also* DEMER BROTHERS COMPANY.

HERBERT & NEUWIRTH — Refer to the MAX HERBERT COMPANY.

HERBERT, MAX COMPANY — An American firm founded in 1910 at New York, New York, by Max Herbert, the company sold cut glass novelties by others and produced a few of their own as well. Herbert, along with Samuel Neuwirth, also established the United Cut Glass Company the same year at the same location. After World War I, operations were consolidated under the Herbert & Neuwirth Company name and cut glass production was discontinued.

HERBERT, S. CUT GLASS COMPANY — An American cut glass operation founded at New York, New York, in 1910 by Sigmund Herbert, the firm operated primarily as a wholesale company for lamps, cut glass, and other goods; nevertheless, they did cut some limited amounts of glass of their own. In 1926, the company name was changed to the Herbert Glass & Import Corporation, but operations ceased in 1927.

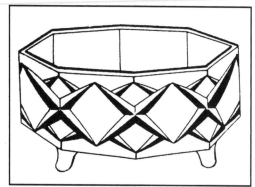

Reproduction from a 1910 Sigmund Herbert U.S. patent.

HERO GLASS WORKS — An American glass company founded at Philadelphia, Pennsylvania, in 1858, the firm produced blown glass canning/fruit jars along with pressed glass jar necks and lids for the jars. Hero closed in 1918.

HERRFELDT, J. H. & COMPANY — An American cut glass operation founded in 1908 in Brooklyn, New York, by J. Hugo Herrfeldt, the firm produced cut glass products until ceasing operations in 1923.

HERRINGBONE — A common design in pressed glass consisting of continued wide "v"-like rows. The design is often combined with others to form herringbone weave, herringbone diamonds, herringbone chains, herringbone dewdrops, etc. Note that there is a specific pressed glass pattern named "Emerald Green Herringbone." As the name implies, it was only produced in the color green and contains alternating vertical columns of plain and herringbone designs.

HESSE GLASS — A general term for glassware produced in Hesse, Germany, through the fifteenth and seventeenth centuries. Hesse was one of the earliest glasshouses established in Germany and served as an important glass center in the Middle Ages. Glass items produced were primarily in the Bohemian Style: heavy engraved designs, gilding, and enameled coats-of-arms. Most items produced consisted of simple table wares such as drinking vessels and bowls.

HIBBLER & RAUSCH — Refer to GEORGE H. HIBBLER & COMPANY.

HIBBLER, GEORGE H. & COMPANY — An American firm established at Brooklyn, New York, in 1866 by George Hibbler and Mr. Rausch. The two had previously worked for Dorflinger and purchased one of his plants. The firm was first known as HIBBLER & RAUSCH until Rausch died in 1886. The firm produced some limited cut glass, but primarily specialized in bottles and lighting glassware. Hibbler was succeeded by his son, Joseph Hibbler (name later changed to J. S. HIBBLER & COMPANY). The firm ceased operations in 1894.

HIBBLER, J. S. & COMPANY — Refer to the GEORGE H. HIBBLER & COMPANY.

HIGBEE GLASS COMPANY — An American firm established by John B. Higbee in 1907 at Bridgeville, Pennsylvania; Higbee once worked with John Bryce in 1879 before opening his own business. John died before the factory was completed in 1907 and was succeeded by his son Oliver J. Higbee; the company operated for a short period of time, but much of its pressed glass tableware and novelties are easily identified with the famous raised bee trademark. The firm declared bankruptcy in 1913, but reorganized in 1914. They remained in business until 1918; the plant was then acquired by General Electric. See also BRYCE, HIGBEE, & COMPANY.

Higbee Glass Company: Trademarks.

HIGGINS & SEITER — An American wholesale firm that operated out of New York City in the late nineteenth and early twentieth centuries (primarily represented cut glass companies and products).

HIGH RELIEF — A cut glass technique made by designing the outline on the surface and then cutting away the background. The design is then raised in relief similar to that of a cameo engraving. High relief refers to the projected portion that is at least half of the natural circumference of the object of the design. See also LOW RELIEF and MEDIUM RELIEF.

HIGHBALL GLASS — A tall narrow tumbler of at least four ounces capacity that is used for serving and drinking mixed drinks. Most highball glasses are in the 8- to 12-ounce capacity range.

HILL, JOHN — An English pioneer in making fine lead crystal tableware. Raised in glass-making in the famous city of Stourbridge, England, Hill earned an international reputation for producing high quality lead crystal tableware. Hill took fifty workers, along with a large supply of glass-making tools, and immigrated to Waterford, Ireland, in 1785. There, he joined the Penrose family to help establish the first successful Waterford glass company. Hill returned to England in 1786 to resume glass-making there. See also WATERFORD.

Hinsberger, L. Cut Glass Company — An American firm founded at New York, New York, in 1894 by Louis Hinsberger, who produced cut glass until 1913.

Hinsberger, L. Cut Glass Company: Trademark.

HISTORICAL FLASK — A style of flask produced in great numbers in America in the nineteenth century. They are mold-blown colored glass containers depicting low relief portraits of presidents and famous people, as well as national emblems and transportation items. They are sometimes referred to as PICTORIAL FLASKS. Many were later reproduced in miniature. *See also* COMMEMORATIVE GLASS *and* PICTORIAL FLASK.

Liquor flask with half brass mold; 1824-25 pressed design of Marquis de Lafayette. *Courtesy of the Corning Museum of Glass.*

HISTORICAL GLASS — Refer to COMMEMORATIVE GLASS.

HOARE, J. & COMPANY — An American firm established at Corning, New York, in 1868 when John Hoare purchased the Brooklyn Flint Glass Company. Hoare was an immigrant from Cork, Ireland, where he had worked as a cutter both in England and Ireland with his father James. He ran a business there before moving to Philadelphia, Pennsylvania, in 1848. Hoare formed many partnerships beginning in 1853 (Hoare & Burns, Gould & Hoare, Hoare and Dailey, Hoare, Burns & Dailey, etc.) before forming his own cut glass department under the Corning Flint Glass Company name (products still contained the "Hoare" trademark through 1920). Hoare died in 1896; however, his cutting shop came under control of his son James Hoare II, along with George Abbott. James then had a son, John S. Hoare, who joined the business in 1906. The surviving Hoares briefly expanded with a branch factory at Wellsboro, Pennsylvania, that opened in 1913 (they also acquired the Elmira Cut Glass Company that same year in Elmira, New York); however, it closed in 1916 as the market for cut glass waned. The Hoares' went bankrupt in 1920 and ceased operations in 1921, the same year that James Hoare II died. *See also* BROOKLYN FLINT GLASS COMPANY *and* CORNING GLASS WORKS.

Trademarks.

Cut glass dish by J. Hoare & Company. *Photo by Robin Rainwater.*

HOBBS, BARNES, & COMPANY — An American firm established at Wheeling, West Virginia, in 1845 by John L. Hobbs and James B. Barnes when the two purchased Plunkett & Miller's South Wheeling Glass Works, the company was first known as Barnes, Hobbs and Company until 1849. Both Hobbs and Barnes had previously worked for the New England Glass Company. The firm produced jars, lamps, chimneys, and pressed glass tableware. Sons of the two founders, John Henry Hobbs and James F. Barnes, joined the firm soon after in 1849. The business expanded and a new factory was built in 1854 at Martins Ferry, Ohio. The name was changed to HOBBS, BROCKUNIER, & COMPANY when Charles Brockunier (former bookkeeper of the company) joined up in 1863. The company also purchased EXCELSIOR GLASS WORKS in 1863. *See also* HOBBS, BROCKUNIER, & COMPANY.

HOBBS, BROCKUNIER, & COMPANY — An American firm established at Wheeling, West Virginia, in 1863 by John L. Hobbs, John H. Hobbs, James F. Barnes, and Charles Brockunier. John L. Hobbs formed many partnerships beginning as early as 1820 before teaming up with Charles Brockunier. The company purchased the Excelsior Glass Works in 1863 (founded in Wheeling in 1849). The firm produced many art styles of glass, cut lead crystal, and chandeliers, but were noted most for developing a cheaper lime glass formula as a substitute for lead crystal by an employee named William Leighton Sr. (Leighton was a former superintendent of the New England Glass Company). The new formula worked well in making cheaper pressed wares. The company was also noted as one of the largest producers of colored pressed glass in America in the nineteenth century. Charles W. Brockunier and William Leighton Jr. left the firm in 1887 when the partnership of Hobbs & Brockunier officially ended. John H. Hobbs briefly reorganized as the Hobbs Glass Company and remained on as a superintendent. The company became part of the United States Glass Company in 1891 as Factory H, and was later sold to Harry Northwood in 1902. *See also* HOBBS, BARNES & COMPANY.

Hobbs, Brockunier & Company: Trademarks.

Hobnail — A pressed or cut pattern in glassware resembling small raised knobs referred to as "hobs" or "prunts," the name originated in England from the large heads of hobnail fasteners. The majority of hobnail-styled objects contain a good deal of or an all-over pattern of hobs and may be combined with other designs too (i.e. Hobnail band, hobnail in diamonds, paneled hobnail, printed hobnail, pointed hobnail, flattened hobnail opal hobnail, hobnail and bars, hobnail-in-square, hobnail with fan, etc.). In paperweights, V-shaped cuts are sometimes made in the base of paperweights that resemble hobnails.

Fenton Hobnail milk glass creamer and sugar.
Photo by Robin Rainwater.

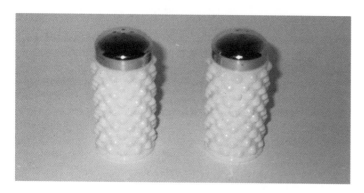

Fenton milk glass hobnail patterned salt and pepper shakers.

Hobstar — A cut glass star design with generally few points that comes in many styles and shapes, Hobstars are generally cut with six points for symmetry, though 8- and 12-point hobstars have been cut as well. The interior portions of the stars are also cut into many different geometrical patterns. Other stars, like buzz stars, may have as many as thirty-two separate points. Note that stars that are molded into pressed glass are made to resemble those of cut glass, but the edges are not nearly as sharp. *See also* BUZZ STAR, PYRAMIDAL STAR, *and* STAR-CUTTING.

Reproduction from a late nineteenth century Higgins-Seiter catalog.

Cut Glass Carafe. Fine Hob Star Cutting.
No. 9517 .... $7.50 Each

Hochheimer Glass — A tall German-style wine goblet designed specifically for drinking hochheimer (German term for white Rhine wine), the wine glasses are generally decorated in a wide variety of styles including enameling, etching, engraving, and gilding. Note that the English spelling or nickname is simply "Hock" or "Hock Glass."

Hocking Glass Company — An American factory established at Lancaster, Ohio, in 1905 by Isaac J. Collins, Lucian B. Martin, and L. Phillip Martin (Lucian's son). A year later, they merged with the OHIO FLINT GLASS COMPANY. The firm began as a hand operation, but converted fully to automation during the Depression era. The plant burned in 1924, but was rebuilt (the Lancaster Glass Company was purchased in 1923 by Hocking and glass production was completed there while the new factory was being built). The company also acquired the National Glass & Lens Company in 1925 (also located in Lancaster, Ohio) and the Turner Glass Company in 1931 (located at Terre Haute, Indiana). Hocking was one of the largest manufacturers of machine-pressed tableware and containers prior to merging with the Anchor Cap and Closure Corporation in 1937. Up until 1937, patterns produced by Hocking included "Block" or "Block Optic," "Cameo" or "Ballerina" or "Dancing Girl," "Circle," "Colonial" or "Knife & Fork," "Coronation" or "Banded Rib" or "Saxon," "Fortune," "Hobnail," "Lace Edge" or "Open Lace" or "Old Colony," "Lake Como," "Mayfair" or "Open Rose," "Miss America" or "Diamond," "Old Café," "Philbe Fire-King," "Princess," "Rings" or "Banded Rings," "Roulette" or "Many Windows," "Spiral," "Vitrock" or "Flower Rim," and "Waterford" or "Waffle." *See also* ANCHOR-HOCKING.

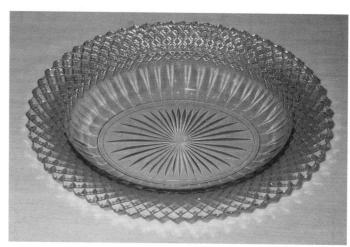

Hocking's Miss America Depression Glass patterned serving bowl.
Photo by Robin Rainwater.

Trademark.

Hodgetts, Richardson, & Company — A glasshouse established in the mid-nineteenth century near Stourbridge, England, by William J. Hodgetts and Henry G. Richardson. The firm is noted most for patenting a glass threading machine that was used to decorate patterns automatically upon glass objects.

Hoki Tika Glassworks — A New Zealand Art Glass firm established at Christchurch in 1980 by a group of former employees of the Crown Crystal Glass Company. The firm produces animal figurines, paperweights, and other novelty items. *See also* CROWN CRYSTAL GLASS *and* NEW ZEALAND GLASS.

HOLLY AMBER — A type of Art Glass that was only made in 1903 by the Indiana Tumbler and Goblet Company in Greentown, Indiana. It is a pressed design characterized by creamy opalescent to brown amber shading (also known as "Golden Agate" or "Greentown Agate") with pressed holly leaves.

A Holly Amber plate from the Indiana Tumbler & Goblet Company. *Courtesy of Wheaton Village.*

HOLLOW WEIGHT — A blown glass paperweight with a purposeful central hollow air bubble surrounded by glass that is used in creating both crown weights and to encase lamp work designs.

HOLMEGAARD — A glass firm founded in Denmark in 1825. Countess Henriette Danneskiold funded a Norwegian glassmaker, Christian Wendt, to build a glasshouse at Homegaard Marsh near Naestved at Fensmark. Early on, the company produced dark green bottles and then expanded into tableware in 1835. Glass workers were imported from Bavaria and a good deal of glass in the nineteenth and early twentieth centuries resemble that of German origin. In 1847, a second factory was added at Kastrup (on the island of Amager near Copenhagen), but this one was sold off in 1873 to fund an expansion at Holmegaard. The firm eventually merged with this new Kastrup in 1965, and then with Royal Copenhagen in 1985; which was absorbed into the Royal Scandinavia conglomerate in 1997 (included Orrefors, Kosta-Boda, & Venini). *See also BAVARIAN GLASS, BOHEMIAN GLASS, and KASTRUP & HOLMEGAARD.*

HOME BEAUTIFUL — A modern brand of tableware and gifts produced under the Mikasa Crystal, Inc. name. *See also MIKASA CRYSTAL, INC.*

HOMESTEAD GLASS WORKS — Refer to BRYCE, HIGBEE & COMPANY.

HONESDALE DECORATING COMPANY — An American factory founded by Christian Dorflinger and his sons at Honesdale, Pennsylvania, in 1901. The firm was sold to Carl Prosch, a Viennese glassmaker and decorator who had worked for Dorflinger. Under the Dorflingers and Prosch, the firm produced hand-cut quality crystal wares with some gold decoration. The business closed permanently in 1932.

Honesdale Decorating Company: Trademarks.

HONEY AMBER — Refer to AMBER.

HONEY DISH — A tiny flat or shallow dish used for serving honey.

HONEY JAR — A fairly small receptacle, somewhat cylindrical, globular, or tapered and containing a cover, used for serving honey. Some may have an opening in the lid for a matching spoon dabber.

HONEYCOMB PATTERN — A decorative pattern in the shape of interlocking hexagons that are usually molded or cut into a glass object. The pattern can be traced back to Roman times in the fourth century A.D. and has been a popular design on pressed glass wares since the eighteenth century. In paperweights, honeycomb or hexagonal canes are often used along with six-sided facets that take the form of a honeycomb.

Honeycomb Pattern: *Line drawing by the author.*

HOOD ORNAMENT — A decorative object placed in the very front center of the hood of an automobile, the first glass examples were produced in the early 1900s. However, it was French artisan Rene Lalique who produced the most impressive ornaments in the 1920s (i.e. clear or frosted horse heads, nude figures, birds, ram's heads, etc.).

HOOKED DÉCOR — Feather-like or similar designs applied to glass objects that are created by pulling glass threads with a hook-shaped tool.

HOOSIER CUT GLASS COMPANY — An American cut glass operation established in 1921 at Walkerton, Indiana, by Grant Baugher and Roy Hostetler, the firm closed in 1925.

HOPE GLASS WORKS — An American company established at Providence, Rhode Island, in 1872 by Martin L. Kern, the firm was noted primarily for creating cut glass. In 1891, Kern's son resumed the business; in 1899, it was sold to the DeGoey family (led by John R. DeGoey) who continued to operate under the "Hope" name until 1951.

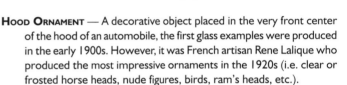

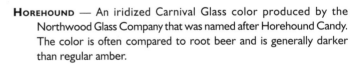

Trademark.

HOREHOUND — An iridized Carnival Glass color produced by the Northwood Glass Company that was named after Horehound Candy. The color is often compared to root beer and is generally darker than regular amber.

HORIZONTAL RIBBING — Refer to RIB OR RIBBING.

HORIZONTAL STEP — A type of prismatic cutting where objects are cut in parallel rows usually leading upward from the base.

HORN — A glass receptacle made in the shape of a horned vase, horned musical instrument, or powder horn used in hunting (hunting horn). *See also CORNUCOPIA.*

HORN-OF-PLENTY — A popular pressed glass pattern that originated in America in the mid-nineteenth century, it is characterized by a series of alternating cornucopias; some of which contain raised diamonds in the circular mouth and bull's eyes in the horn while those that alternate in between contain the opposite design.

Pressed glass Horn-of-Plenty pattern footed bowl. *Courtesy of Wheaton Village.*

HORS D'OEUVRE DISH — A small flat or shallow glass object, oblong or rectangular, that may or may not be divided; it is used specifically for serving small finger foods or snacks.

HORSERADISH JAR — A small to medium-sized covered glass receptacle used for serving horseradish.

HORSESHOE — A pressed glass design in the shape of a not-quite-full oval, usually with the ends turned up slightly to resemble a horseshoe. Horseshoe patterns have also been referred to as "Good Luck" and "Prayer Rug." Although they named it as simply their "No. 612" pattern, the Indiana Glass Company produced a Depression glass design from 1930 to 1933 that is best known by collectors as the "Horseshoe Pattern." Note that horseshoe designs have also been applied as finials and handles on certain objects.

HOSCH, CARL — A Bohemian glass company founded by Carl Hosch at Reichstadt, Germany (became the Czech city of Zakupy in 1918), in 1864. The firm began as a maker of crystal and bronze ornaments for lighting. The firm was moved to Haida (became the Czech city of Novy Bor in 1918) in 1868 and the name was changed to "Glasraffinerie und Kronleuchterfabrik – Carl Hosch." The firm expanded into traditional enameled and engraved colored Bohemian wares. Carl's two sons, Carl A. G. and Alexander, inherited the firm in 1893. Alexander died in 1916 and his son, Richard, assumed his portion of the business. Richard became the sole director when his uncle died in 1932. The firm became a nationalized Czechoslovakian firm after World War II.

HOT GLASS COMPANY — Refer to NEW ZEALAND GLASS.

HOT METAL — A term for molten glass that is ready for working, such as for blowing and pressing.

HOT PLATE — A usually thick, sturdy flat glass object used to sit under hot items in order to protect the surface beneath it.

HOT-WORKED — A general term for glass that is worked and manipulated while it is in a molten state. A variety of tools are used in hot-working, including blowing and/or gathering irons, pincers, and shears. Glass can be decorated too in its molten state (i.e. internally with bubbles or externally with applied decorations like prunts, hobs, trailings, ribbons, threads, etc.).

HOUGHTON, AMORY SR. — Houghton began his glass-making career with the Union Glass Company in the 1850s. Along with his son Amory Houghton Jr., Houghton purchased a controlling interest in the Brooklyn Flint Glass Works (run by John Gilliland) in 1864 and then moved all operations to Corning, New York, in 1868. Also note that the grandson of Amory Houghton Jr., Arthur Amory Houghton Jr., served as the president and policy director of Steuben from 1933 until 1972. Under Arthur Amory's direction, Steuben ceased producing colored glassware in favor of high quality crystal exclusively. *See also CORNING GLASS WORKS and STEUBEN.*

HOUR GLASS — An instrument for measuring time that consists of a glass vessel having two reversible vertically connected compartments in which a substance like sand, water, or mercury runs through a small neck from the upper compartment to the lower. Traditionally, it took approximately an hour for the substance to flow from one compartment to the other; then, the device could be turned over to repeat the process. Smaller hour glasses or timers are used to measure shorter periods of time (i.e. 14-28 minutes for log glasses on ships to measure sailing speed based on the amount of line played out; 15 minutes for egg timers; 1-3 minutes in certain timed games, etc.).

HOUSE OF BIRKS — A Canadian firm established as Henry Birks and Company at Montreal in 1879, the company began as a retail store for jewelry and silverware. Birks opened a jewelry factory in 1887 and added his sons name to the business in 1893 (changed the name to Henry Birks & Sons). In 1894, he employed cutters in a glass factory that operated until 1907 (sold to George Phillip & Company). The "Birks" name can be found on glass made by many firms as well as their own since they did serve primarily as a distributor and retailer.

House of Birks: Trademarks.

HUCHTHAUSEN, DAVID — A noted American Studio Glass artisan born in Wisconsin Rapids, Wisconsin, in 1951, Huchthausen received his Master of Fine Arts degree from Illinois State University and has served in a teaching capacity at the Wooden Art Museum and Tennessee Tech University. Awards he has received include the Newberry Award in 1973, a Woodson Foundation grant (1973-1974), an Elizabeth Stein Fellowship at Illinois State University (1976), a Fulbright Research Scholarship (1977-1978), and a National Endowment for the Arts Fellowship (1982). Huchthausen continues to work as an independent glass artisan in Smithville. Tennessee.

HUMIDOR — A glass jar, with a cover or case, used for holding cigars and/or tobacco. The cover or casing is necessary in order to keep the air inside properly humidified.

HUMPEN — A German-styled drinking glass resembling a very large tumbler: tall, cylindrical, and wide. Some are equipped with dome covers and projecting bases. Most are enameled and/or gilded, but may contain prunts and engravings. At times, the height could reach as high as two feet and the capacity could exceed half of a gallon. Nearly all were made from the mid-sixteenth to the mid-eighteenth century and were used for drinking beer or wine in large quantities. Note that the French made a few and referred to them as "Chope."

A late nineteenth century Bohemian Glass Humpen.
Photo by Robin Rainwater.
Item courtesy of the Corning Museum of Glass.

HUMPHREY GLASS COMPANY — Refer to the STEUBENVILLE GLASS COMPANY.

HUNEBELLE GLASS — Glass made by French artisan Andre Hunebelle in Paris, France, in the late 1920s and 1930s. Hunebelle produced art deco designs, ordinarily in geometrical patterns, in clear, frosted, and opalescent styles similar to that of Lalique. Hunebelle ceased making glass near the beginning of World War II; he became a film producer after the war.

HUNGARIAN GLASS — General term for glass made in Hungary beginning in the late fourteenth century. The first items produced were practical ones, like window panes and tableware. After the Middle Ages, Hungarian glass was made in the typical Venetian and Bohemian styles of the day. Beginning in the late twentieth century, Hungarian products consist primarily of cut and/or engraved (some case) table pieces in both crystal and color.

Reproduction from a 1993 Hungarian Glass advertisement.

HUNT & SULLIVAN — Refer to HUNT GLASS COMPANY.

HUNT GLASS COMPANY — An American firm established at Corning, New York, in 1895 by Thomas Hunt and Daniel Sullivan (originally as Hunt & Sullivan). Hunt's son Harry Hunt was also active in the operation of the company. Both Hunts were English immigrants who had worked for other firms such as Hawkes prior to establishing their own cut glass company. The company's name was changed to the Hunt Glass Company in 1907. The firm used blanks from the Corning Glass Works and pressed blanks from the Union Glass Company. The company continued to produce cut glass into the 1930s. After that, Hunt remained in business as a maker of machine-made glass products.

Reproduction from a 1911 Hunt Glass Co. patent.

Trademark.

HUNTING HORN — Refer to HORN.

HUNTINGTON GLASS COMPANY — An American pressed glass-making firm established at Huntington, West Virginia, as the Central City Glass Company in 1891. Addison Thompson and associates were the original founders of the company. The firm purchased some molds from the defunct Greensburg Glass Company and produced both blown and pressed glass tableware. In 1895, it reorganized under the Huntington name with Thomas Mears (president), Addison Thompson (general manager), and W. B. McGregor (secretary-treasurer). In 1896, the firm went bankrupt and all machinery was sold to the Royal Glass Company and moved to Marietta, Ohio, in 1898. In 1900, the Huntington plant was purchased by Anton Zihlman. *See also* HUNTINGTON TUMBLER COMPANY.

HUNTINGTON TUMBLER COMPANY — An American glass-making firm established at Huntington, West Virginia, in 1900 by Swiss immigrant, Anton Zihlman, who purchased the vacant plant previously occupied by the Huntington Glass Company with the backing of the Huntington Chamber of Commerce led by A. W. Werringer and Timothy Scanlon. When Zihlman died, the business was inherited by his sons. The firm initially produced mold-blown tumblers for the bar trade and eventually expanded into colored tableware (some etched/engraved/decorated Depression wares) and novelty items (i.e. canes and paperweights). The firm closed in 1932.

HURRICANE LAMP — A style of lamp that usually contains a glass base, a separate glass shade, and a glass chimney, some are shaped like a candlestick with wicks while others are powered by electricity. Hurricane lamps or shades debuted in the late nineteenth century and were originally used to protect a lamp's or candle's flame from being extinguished by the wind.

HUTCHINSON-STOPPERED BOTTLE — A style of glass bottle invented in 1879, its name was given to its rounded expanded lip in which a closure or stopper that consisted of a rubber disk sandwiched between two metal plates was placed within. In turn, an attached wire loop extended both above and below the stopper. The bottle was then sealed by pulling the stopped by the wire. The design lasted until the end of the nineteenth century.

HYALITH GLASS — A dark opaque black glass developed by Count Georg Von Buquoy at Silesia (Southern Bohemia) around 1817. A form of red hyalith was also produced, which consisted of a brownish-red color that is sometimes referred to as sealing-wax red. Hyalith has a smooth shiny finish and was developed specifically to resemble semi-precious stones. It was further decorated with engraving, but mostly with the application of gold enamel and/or trim. In 1835, a third bluish-gray color called "Agatine" was added to the hyalith line. *See also* BLACK GLASS *and* BUQUOY.

Mid-nineteenth century Hyalith drinking vessels.
Items courtesy of the Corning Museum of Glass.

HYDROFLUORIC ACID — A colorless corrosive acid similar to hydrochloric acid, but weaker in that it attacks silica. It is used to finish, frost, gloss, and etch glass.

Ii

{ Ii }

ICE BLOCK OR SCULPTURE — A jagged, semi-circular, semi-oval, or irregularly-shaped block of crystal that is usually carved on the reverse side to provide a mirrored three-dimensional image when viewed from the front. Ice blocks originated in Sweden with such companies as Kosta-Boda (designer Vicke Lindstrand), Maleras (designer Mats Jonasson), and Nybro.

ICE BLUE — A very light shade or tint of transparent blue-colored glass (the color of ice) usually applied as a light iridescence on Carnival Glass. Ice Blue opalescent glass contains a white opalescent edge or background applied to the ice blue (also found in iridized Carnival Glass).

ICE BUCKET OR TUB — A glass vessel shaped as a medium-sized bucket or pail, with or without a semicircular handle, used for holding ice. Larger buckets or pails are utilized for chilling bottled drinks such as wine. Those without a typical bail handle usually sport tab handles for gripping and carrying.

Ice Tub with Handle
Packs 3½ doz. to bbl.

HANDLED ICE BUCKET
Packs 3½ doz. to bbl. Weight 120 lbs.

Reproductions from a 1930 Indiana Glass Co. catalog.

ICE CREAM PLATE — A small flat glass plate, usually round in shape, used for serving a single scoop of ice cream.

ICE CREAM TRAY — A large shallow or flat glass container used for serving ice cream or ice cream related treats. Large ice cream trays were originally designed to hold several dishes (i.e. small bowls for ice cream, sundae glasses, etc.).

Reproduction from an early twentieth century Higgins-Seiter catalog.

ICE GLASS — A type of Art Glass characterized by a rough surface resembling cracked ice. *See also* CRACKLE GLASS *and* CRACKLING.

ICE GREEN — A very light shade or tint of transparent green-colored glass (the color of ice) usually applied as a light iridescence on Carnival Glass. Ice Green opalescent glass contains a white opalescent edge or background applied to the ice green (also found in iridized Carnival Glass).

ICE LIP — A rim at the top of a pitcher, it prevents ice from spilling out of the spout when tilted or poured.

ICE SCULPTURE — Refer to ICE BLOCK OR SCULPTURE.

ICICLE — 1) A style of glass produced by Boston & Sandwich Glass Company in the 1880s. It was made in a variety of colors (amber, blue, cranberry, etc.) and derives its name from its icicle-like decorations. Sharp pointed crystal protrusions hang from the rim of each object, while those with feet contain applied crystal icicle forms for each foot. 2) In modern times, icicle projections are often made by twisting or spinning clear glass into Christmas ornaments.

IDEAL CUT GLASS COMPANY — An American firm founded by Charles E. Rose in 1902 at Corning, New York, the company moved their cut glass business to Canastota, New York, in 1904. The firm was sold to W. B. Hitchcock, a wholesale jeweler living in Syracuse, New York, in 1908. The firm was moved to Syracuse in 1909 and continued in operation until 1934.

Reproduction from a 1927 Ideal Cut Glass Co. U.S. patent.

IGC LIQUIDATING CORPORATION — A subsidiary of Lenox, Inc. of New Jersey; Lenox purchased the Imperial Glass Company in 1972 and continued to produce glass under the IGC name until it was sold to Arthur Lorch in 1981. Lorch sold out to Robert Strahl in 1982 and the company closed for good in 1985. *See also* LENOX, INC.

IHMSEN, CHRISTIAN — Christian Ihmsen aided in establishing Whitehead, Ihmsen, & Phillips, an American pressed glass-making firm founded at Pittsburgh, Pennsylvania, in 1836 along with Thomas Whitehead and William Phillips. The three purchased the former Birmingham Glass Works that had been founded in 1810. The factory name was first known as the Pennsylvania Flint Glass Works until 1846. William Young and Francis Plunkett replaced Whitehead & Phillips and the name was changed to Young, Ihmsen & Plunkett until 1850. Ihmsen bought out the other two and changed the name to C. Ihmsen and then further to C. Ihmsen & Sons when his three sons (Charles, William, and Christian Jr.) joined in 1860. Charles Ihmsen had briefly worked in partnership with A. T. Ulam. In 1875, the company's name was changed one final time to the Ihmsen Glass Company. The firm produced a good deal of pressed glass prior to closing permanently in 1895. *See also* O'LEARY MULVANEY COMPANY.

IITTALA GLASSWORKS — Founded in Finland in 1881 by a Swedish glassblower, Petter Magnus Abrahamsson, the firm acquired the Karhula Glassworks in 1888 and became known for awhile as the Karhula-Iittala Glasbruk. In 1917, it merged with, and became a subsidiary of, the Ahlstrom Group and continued producing glass in the modern Swedish/Finnish tradition under the Iittala name. The company produced both practical blown glass tableware (especially tumblers) and some colored art forms. Another merger occurred in 1988 with Notsjo, and then both were acquired by Hackman. Both glassworks were placed under a separate division of the company and glass is still being produced today under the "Iittala-Nuutajarvi" name. In the meantime, Ahlstrom merged Karhula with Riihimaki in 1988 to form Ahlstrom Riihimaki Lasi Oy. The Riihimaki factory closed in 1990 and Karhula was sold to the American firm of Owens-Illinois in 1995. *See also NOTSJO GLASSWORKS.*

IMAGE 3 CRYSTAL — A Russian style of engraving developed by Fyodor Lebedev during the 1950s, it was first used for military purposes, but was later adapted to paperweights and small glass sculptures.

IMPERIAL CUT GLASS COMPANY — An American firm founded at Philadelphia, Pennsylvania, in 1896 by John White, the company produced cut glass tableware until closing in 1915.

Reproduction from an 1896 Imperial Cut Glass Co. U.S. patent.

IMPERIAL GLASS COMPANY — An American Manufacturer founded at Bellaire, Ohio, by Edward Muhleman in 1901 (actual glass production began in 1904), they were a major producer of Carnival Glass in the early twentieth century and were responsible for many reproductions of it beginning in the early 1960s (reproductions were marked "IG"). The company also produced some art styles, milk glass, and pressed glass (including colored glass during the Depression). Depression/pressed patterns attributed to Imperial include the huge "Candlewick" as well as "Beaded Block," "Cape Cod," "Crocheted Crystal," "Diamond Quilted" or "Flat Diamond," "Laced Edge" or "Katy Blue," and "Twisted Optic." The company declared bankruptcy in 1929, but was able to operate while in receivership: an order for a premium piece by the Quaker Oats Company in 1931 aided them in surviving.

Imperial acquired Central Glass Works in 1940 and purchased many molds from both Cambridge and Heisey in 1958-59. In 1972, the company was sold to Lenox, which continued producing glass under the IGC Liquidation Corporation (a division of Lenox, Incorporated) name until 1982. The firm was purchased in 1984 by the Lancaster Colony Corporation; however, glass production was not resumed. Note that all known Heisey molds owned by Imperial were purchased by the Heisey Collectors of America in 1985 for $200,000 (retired and now part of the National Heisey Glass Museum in Newark, Ohio). Also note that there were a couple of other short-lived firms that sported the Imperial name: a bottle maker located at Beaver Falls, Pennsylvania (IMPERIAL GLASS WORKS, 1904-08); its successor (IMPERIAL GLASS COMPANY, 1909); and a small blown glass operation located at Steubenville, Ohio (IMPERIAL GLASS COMPANY, 1908).

Imperial Carnival Glass Robin patterned pitcher and tumblers.
Photo by Robin Rainwater.

Reproduction from a 1910s Imperial catalog.

Trademarks.

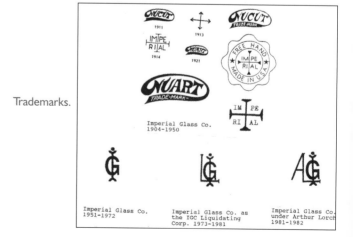

IMPROVEMENT GLASS COMPANY — Refer to the VALLEY GLASS COMPANY.

IMPURITIES — Tiny bits of unfused sand particles that show up as flaws in finished glass articles.

INCALMO — The Venetian-name technique of combining two or more distinct colors of glass by fusing two or more gathers of hot glass into a single object. The word itself refers to a calm but intense concentration required by the glassmaker in order to perform this delicate operation successfully.

INCISING — The technique of cutting or engraving designs and/or inscriptions into the surface of glass. The Italian term is "Inciso."

INCLUSIONS — Mica, metallic, or other colorful flecks, they are used in certain decorative styles of Art Glass.

INCRUSTATION — Another name for the sulphide cameo relief design within crystal or clear glass paperweights. *See also* SULPHIDE.

INDENTING — A decoration technique involving a series (usually symmetrical) of pressed-in recesses or concavities that may by vertical, horizontal, or circular. This style was first used by the ancient Romans for decorating flasks and beakers.

INDIAN GLASS — General term for glassware produced in India during the Mogul Period (1526-1857). Indians were noted for decorating glassware with engraving, gilding, and enameling floral designs in Persian styles (sometimes referred to as "Mogul" or "Mughal" glass). For modern styles of glass made in India in the twentieth century, refer to JAIN GLASS WORKS.

An 18th century East Indian (Mughal) candleholder,
blown, cut, gilded, and hukkak base.
Photo courtesy of the Corning Museum of Glass.

INDIANA GLASS COMPANY — (1) An American manufacturer founded at Dunkirk, Indiana, in 1904 by Frank Merry (original plant superintendent and first president), Henry Batsch, and others. At first, they leased the Beatty-Brady Glass Company from the National Glass Company and then purchased it outright in 1908. Early on, they were noted for many machine-pressed Depression patterns along with more recent reproductions of them. The company continues to operate today as a subsidiary of the Lancaster Colony Corporation and has produced pressed patterns in a wide variety of colors, including "Avocado" or "No. 601," "Christmas Candy," "Daisy," "Horseshoe" or "No.612," "Lorain" or "Basket," "Old English Threading," "Pineapple & Floral" or "No.618," "Pretzel," "Pyramid" or "No. 610," "Sandwich," "Tea Room," and "Vernon" or "No. 616." (2) A couple of other companies were also known as the Indiana Glass Company, including a short-lived maker of flasks that operated at Middletown, Indiana, in the 1890s and another one was founded by Henry White at Indiana, Pennsylvania, in 1892. The plant closed in 1893; the firm filed for bankruptcy soon afterward and it was purchased by Harry Northwood in 1896. *See also* TIARA.

Reproduction Carnival Glass grape patterned laced-edge candy jar.
Photo by Robin Rainwater.

Trademark.

INDIANA TUMBLER & GOBLET COMPANY — An American manufacturer founded in 1893 at Greentown, Indiana, by the Jenkins family: David C. Jenkins Jr. (president), David C. Jenkins Sr. (secretary-treasurer), Thomas Jenkins (night manager), and Lewis Jenkins Jr. (shipping foreman). David Jenkins Sr. had previously worked for McKee. The firm produced clear pressed glass tableware, barware, jelly glasses, and condiment containers; however, they were also noted for producing unique, though inexpensive and experimental colored tableware including milk/opaque forms, chocolate, caramel, and pink slag glass. Jacob Rosenthal worked for the firm and developed the chocolate glass formula, which was quite profitable to the company. Note that in 1894, the firm was also known as the Greentown Glass Works. The company became part of the National Glass Company in 1899, and the chocolate formula was acquired by National in 1902. The factory closed permanently when it burned in 1903.

INDUSTRIE VETRARIE RIUNITE (I.V.R.) MAZZEGA — A small Venetian art glass firm founded in the 1930s on the island of Murano by Romano Mazzega, who sold the business to Aureliano Toso in 1937; however, Mazzega, with his brother Gino and sister Maria, formed a new factory in 1938. The firm produced typical Venetian colored glass until closing in 1983.

INGIRD GLASS — Refer to H. G. CURT SCHLEVOGT.

INITIAL CANE — Refer to SIGNATURE.

INK BOTTLE — A small glass receptacle, usually with a stopper, used for holding ink (namely for quill pens).

Glass pen and matching ink bottle. *Photo by Robin Rainwater.*

A collection of ink bottles. *Courtesy of Wheaton Village.*

INKSTAND — A receptacle, with a base and made of various substances, used for holding ink or pens. Stands date back to the early eighteenth century and were fashioned from a variety of metals, ceramics, and glass. Some also hold small sanders, pen trays, and even a candle for melting the sealing wax.

INKWELL — A small but heavy glass container used for holding ink (originally for quill pens). Inkwells are generally shorter and squatter when compared to ink bottles. Inkwells were first created in the 1830s when ready-made ink was first sold in bottles.

Glass inkwell with cork top. *Photo by Robin Rainwater.*

A collection of inkwells. *Courtesy of Wheaton Village.*

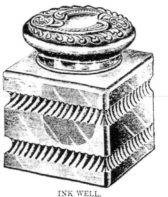

INK WELL.

No. 2683 ....$3 75
Cut Glass, Sterling Silver Chased Top.

Reproduction from an early 20th century S. F. Myers Co. catalog.

INLAY — An object embedded into the surface of another object

INNSBRUCK GLASS — Refer to AUSTRIAN GLASS and SWAROVSKI.

INSCRIPTION — Words and symbols, like names, dates, events, commemoratives, signatures, and marks, usually etched or lightly engraved on glassware. Artist signatures and/or manufacturer marks are ordinarily inscribed on the bottom of an object, but may appear elsewhere.

INSULATOR — A glass or ceramic, somewhat bell-shaped/rounded object, that is a poor conductor of electricity. Insulators were made specifically to separate or support conductors in order to prevent the undesired flow of electricity on telegraph/telephone poles since 1844. The most common are made of a bluish-green or aqua-colored glass (i.e. Hemingray models); however, rare and desirable ones have been made in cobalt blue, amber, amethyst, and other colored glass. Note that insulators are also made of porcelain/ceramic compounds (also poor conductors of electricity).

Insulators. *Photos by Robin Rainwater.*

Hemingray insulators. *Photo by author; item courtesy of Wheaton Village.*

INTAGLIO — An engraving or cutting made below the surface of glass so that the impression left from the design leaves an image in relief ("Intaglio" is the Italian name for engraving; in Germany, it is known as "Tiefschnitt"). T. J. Hawkes referred to his firm's intaglio engraved objects as "Gravic."

INTARSIA — The name given to a type of glass produced by Steuban in the 1920s, it is characterized by a core of colored glass blown between layers of clear glass and then decorated by etching into mosaic patterns.

A Steuben Intarsia vase. *Photo by Robin Rainwater. Item courtesy of the Corning Museum of Glass.*

INTERNATIONAL CUT GLASS COMPANY — A short-lived American cut glass company founded at Buffalo, New York, in 1904 by Robert Adams, Charles Caroll, John Conway, John Vallely, and M. J. Vallely. It was known originally as the International Glass Company until 1910. The firm produced cut glass products up until the start of World War I.

INTERNATIONAL GLASS COMPANY — Refer to the INTERNATIONAL CUT GLASS COMPANY.

INTERNATIONAL SILVER COMPANY — An American firm established at Meriden, Connecticut, in 1898, the company originally produced silver-related items such as silverware, dishes, and holders for cut glass products. Note that the company trademark was applied to both the silver items that they made as well as to cut glassware that was made by others. The firm continues in operation today, but ceased all related cut glass products just after World War I.

INWALD GLASSWORKS — A Bohemian/Czechoslovakian glass-making firm founded at Havlickuv Brod by Joseph Inwald in 1862, a second factory was added at Dobronin in 1876. Inwald was noted most for producing a unique style of glass called Barolac Glass. Business boomed and additional factories were built at Zlichov (1878), Siendorf (1884), Podebrady (1893), and Teplice (1905). The firm continued to produce both crystal and colored ornamental glass in traditional Bohemian styles until merging with Antonin Dul in 1945 to briefly form the Jihlava Glassworks. When all Czechoslovakian firms were nationalized after World War II (1948), it eventually became part of the Bohemia Glassworks National Corporation conglomerate in 1965. The firm regained its independence in 1993 and produces cut glass products today under the Jihlava name. *See also* BOHEMIA GLASSWORKS NATIONAL CORPORATION *and* BAROLAC GLASS.

IOWA CITY FLINT GLASS MANUFACTURING COMPANY — A short-lived American pressed glass-making firm that was founded at Iowa City, Iowa, in 1880 by W. H. Brainerd, E. Clark, R. J. Coulter, and J. Harvey Leighton. The firm produced some pressed tableware and glass marbles before ceasing operation in 1882.

IPSEN, KENT — A noted American Studio Glass artisan born in Milwaukee, Wisconsin, in 1933, Ipsen received his Master of Fine Arts degree from the University of Wisconsin and has served in a teaching capacity at Mankato State University (founded a glass-working department), the Art Institute of Chicago, and the Virginia Commonwealth University (founded another glass-working department). Awards he has received include the National Endowment of the Arts Grant (1975), First Governor's Awards for the Arts (1979), Virginia Commonwealth University Grants (1980, 1985), and Second Governor's Awards for the Arts (1985). He also served as a state representative to the American Crafts Council (1970-1972) and continues to work as an independent glass artisan in Richmond, Virginia.

IRIDESCENCE — A sparkling rainbow-colored or oily-colored finish on the exterior of glass objects produced by spraying metallic oxides on the surface of hot glass. Iridescent glass dates back to Roman times, but was most popular during the Art Nouveau (1880s-1920) and Carnival Glass eras (early 1900s-1920s). *See also* ART NOUVEAU *and* CARNIVAL GLASS.

Duran iridescent Art Glass vases. *Courtesy of Wheaton Village.*

IRIDIUM — A silvery-white hard metallic element that, when dissolved in hydrochloric acid and/or oxidized and then added to a batch of glass, aids in producing gray, black, or deep violet colors.

IRIDIZED — Glass coated with iridescence.

IRIS GLASS — (1) A style of iridescent Art Glass created by the Fostoria Glass Company around 1910 (patented in 1912). It is characterized by colored glass trailings that are formed into various patterns (i.e. leaf, spider web, and various floral designs). (2) Iris was also the name of a prolific pattern first produced by the Jeannette Glass Company from 1928-1932. The pattern consists of irises along with vertical ribbing. It was revived in the 1950s by Jeannette and remained in production into the 1970s.

Covered candy dish – reproduction from a 1950 Jeannette Glass Co. advertisement.

Iris patterned creamer and sugar set from the Jeannette Glass Company. *Photo by Robin Rainwater.*

IRISH GLASS — Glass production originated in Ireland in the late sixteenth century; however, it is the period from about 1780 to the 1830s that is known as the Golden Age of Irish Glass. As a concession in 1780, the British Parliament granted the Irish free trade without any taxes on glassware. Large glasshouses were constructed in the cities of Belfast, Cork, Dublin, Newry, Waterloo, and Waterford. For the next fifty years, Ireland's cut glass production was characterized by quality lead crystal tableware, new wheel cutting and engraving techniques, and improved methods of press-molded accessories (i.e. handles and feet on bowls, vases, and stemware). A duty was placed on Irish products in 1825 and the Irish glass industry fell into a state of decline. In the mid-twentieth century, several modern factories sprung up in Ireland beginning with Waterford in 1951. Others such as Tipperary, Cavan, Galway, Kerry, Killarney, and Tower followed.

Kerry Glass of Ireland, 40 shades of green paperweights. *Photo by Robin Rainwater.*

IRON — (1) A natural occurring metallic element in sand that imparts a murky green or brownish color in glass; other elements are used to neutralize the effect of iron. Depending on the composition of a batch, the addition of iron oxide (ferrous oxide – FeO or ferric oxide – Fe2O3) produces an olive green or pale blue color. Iron oxide and manganese oxide together in a batch aids in producing dark amber or black glass. Iron oxide and copper oxide together produced various shades of green. (2) A heavy rounded object used to press the wrinkles out of clothing: glass irons are somewhat rare, but originated in the eighteenth century in Europe (called linen smoothers, slickers, slick stones, or smoothing irons). A few were made in America as well, particularly during the Depression era.

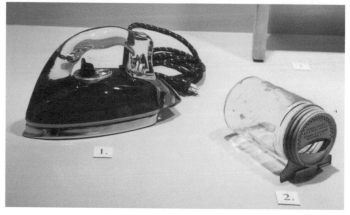

Glass iron. *Courtesy of Wheaton Village.*

IRVING CUT GLASS COMPANY, INC. — An American company established at Honesdale, Pennsylvania, in 1900 by William Hawken and five partners (Eugene Coleman, John Gogard, George Reichenbacher, George Roedine, and William Seitz). It was known early on as the Union Cut Glass Company. They purchased blanks from H. C. Fry and were noted for cutting flowers and figures. Many of their products were shipped worldwide to such places as China, Japan, South Africa, and Spain. The company closed in 1933.

Irving Cut Glass Company, Inc.: Trademark.

ISLAMIC GLASS — General term for glassware made in Egypt, Mesopotamia, Persia, Syria, parts of India, and other regions of Islamic conquest during the Islamic Period (early seventh to the early fifteenth centuries). Glass produced included practical tableware as well as some ornamental items (i.e. drinking vessels, vases, beads, etc.). Several new decorating styles originated with Islamic Glass, including advanced wheel-engraving, applied decorations, painting, enameling, and gilding. The best glass products in the world between the fall of the Roman Empire, up until the Venetian monopoly beginning in the fourteenth century, were produced in the Islamic world.

A 9th-10th century Islamic vase. *Courtesy of the Corning Museum of Glass.*

ISLE OF WIGHT GLASS — An English firm established by Michael Harris (1933-1994) at St. Lawrence on the Isle of Wight. Harris had previously founded Mdina Glass in Malta in 1969, but left in 1972 to form a new studio. Harris produced similar art glass items, many in blue/green and brown/gold internal swirled combinations (named tortoiseshell and seaward). When Harris passed away, the firm continued under his wife's control and today under the direction of their sons, Timothy and Jonathan Harris.

ISLINGTON GLASS WORKS — An English glass firm founded in very early nineteenth century in Birmingham, it was originally operated by Owen Johnson. In 1849, the company was known as Rice, Harris, and Son; and then as Islington in 1860. The firm produced some ornamental wares including paperweights before going out of business.

ITALIAN GLASS — Refer to ROMAN GLASS and VENETIAN GLASS.

IVORY — A cream- or off-white-colored opaque glass (the color of ivory). Ivory is also at times comparable to light custard-colored glass.

IVRENA VERDE — A name given to a form of custard glass made by the A. H. Heisey Glass Company. Heisey's custard was somewhat of a light yellow (a bit lighter than regular custard) and was usually further decorated by hired decorating companies (by fired-on enameling). Some of Heisey's custard glass was also produced for the souvenir trade. *See also* CUSTARD GLASS.

IVRENE — A white colored opaque Art Glass with a light pearl-like transparent iridescent coating; originally invented by FREDERICK CARDER of STEUBEN in the 1920s.

IVY BALL — A small round concave glass vessel usually with three feet (tri-footed) with a small opening in the center for holding a single ivy bloom or perhaps a for few very short-stemmed flowers. Ivy balls are almost identical to rose bowls only they tend to be a little smaller. *See also* ROSE BOWL.

IZMAILOVSKII GLASS — A Russian state-owned glasshouse established at Izmailovskii (near Moscow) in 1660, the firm produced some Venetian-style glassware for the Royal Court before ceasing operation in the early 1700s. *See also* RUSSIAN GLASS.

I

Jj

{ Jj }

JABO, INCORPORATED — An American marble-making firm founded by a group of stockholders in 1987 at Reno, Ohio, the company purchased the marble-making machinery from the defunct Bogard Company and then purchased the Vitro Agate Company soon after. The firm continues producing glass marbles today at Williamstown, West Virginia.

JACK-IN-THE-PULPIT — A style of vase made to resemble the American Woodland flower of the same name. It usually consists of a circular base, thin stem, and a large open ruffled bloom or trumpet at the top.

A Tiffany Favrile Jack-in-the-Pulpit style vase.

JACKS — Another name for pincers or tongs. See also FORMING TOOL, PINCERS, PUCELLAS, STEEL-JACKS, TONGS, and WOOD-JACKS.

JACKSON BROTHERS — Refer to BAGLEY GLASS.

JACKSON MARBLE COMPANY — An American marble-making firm founded by Carol Jackson in 1945 at Pennsboro, West Virginia. Jackson had previously worked for Champion Agate as a machine operator. Jackson operated for only a year before going out of business.

JACOBITE GLASSWARE — Late seventeenth and early eighteenth century English lead crystal glassware, usually wine glasses or goblets, that have engraved political inscriptions, portraits, and other symbols of King James II (exiled in 1698) and his descendants (James Edward Stuart, known as the "Old Pretender," and his son, Prince Charles Edward Stuart, known as the "Young Pretender" or "Bonnie Prince Charlie"). One style of Jacobite Glass contains engraved inscriptions from the Jacobite Verse that ends with the word "Amen" (also known as "Amen Glass"); another style contains the motto "Redeat" (Latin for "May He Return"). See also WILLIAMITE GLASSWARE.

A 1740-1750 English Jacobite goblet.
Photo courtesy of the Corning Museum of Glass.

JACOB'S LADDER — A pressed glass pattern that consists of vertical diamond bonds that alternate with vertical rows of horizontal steps (made to resemble a ladder). The design is also known as "Maltese."

JADE GLASS — A pale green style of colored Art Glass created by Steuben of Corning, New York, and Stevens & Williams of England. Although colors may vary (i.e. shades of blue, pink, or yellow), the body of items are made with translucent alabaster and then colored with metallic oxides. The final product resembles that of the stone jade.

JADEITE OR JADE-ITE — A pale lime-colored opaque green glass (the color of jade). Many oven products, such as Fire King, as well as tableware in America's post-Depression era, were made in this style.

JAGDGLAS — A German term for various styles of glass (Humpen, Romer, Stein, Goblet, etc.) that are decorated with hunting scenes (i.e. hunters, hounds, stags, and other game). Jagdglas translates into English as HUNTING GLASS and such objects have been popular in Germany since the sixteenth century.

J

JAIN GLASS WORKS — An Indian glass company founded at Firozabad in the north central area of India in 1928 by Shri Chhadamilal Jain, at one time, it was the largest glass producing firm in India. The company is noted for producing tableware, tumblers, globes, chimneys (for lamps), and iridized Carnival Glass. They referred to their iridized products as "Lustre" glass. The company closed permanently in 1986. Note that the firm was also known as "Jain Glass World of Firozabad, India."

Jain Glass Works: Trademark.

JAM JAR — A tiny covered glass receptacle used for serving jams and jellies. The cover usually has an opening for a spoon handle.

JAMESTOWN — The first permanent English settlement (colony) was established in North America (Virginia) in 1607. In 1608, Captain Christopher Newport brought eight Polish and Dutch glassmakers who established a glasshouse in 1609. Some crude tableware items (mostly bottles) were made and were included in the first cargo exported from the New World. The operation was a very short-lived one; however, it was not the first such operation in the New World. The Spaniards had set up a glasshouse in 1535 in Argentina, and another one in 1592 at the town of Cordoba del Tucaman in the Territory of the Rio de la Plata; both were very short-lived operations (broken glass from Europe was remelted and formed into crude objects). A second glasshouse was constructed at Jamestown in 1620 by the London Company and six Italian workers were imported to work there; the workers primarily made beads and marbles to trade with the Native American Indians. It lasted only a few short years.

JAPANESE GLASS — General term for glassware made in Japan since the mid-eighteenth century. Articles that were produced consisted mostly of engraved items in European styles. Note that some limited glass items such as beads, bottles, and urns were produced in Japan in the sixth to the eighth centuries. In the late twentieth century, many contemporary glass firms were established including Awashima (founded in 1956 by Masakichi Awashima) and Kagami (founded by Kozo Kagami).

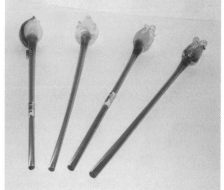

Mikasa colored glass flowers.

JAR — A fairly deep wide-mouthed container of various shapes used to hold a variety of substances (usually foods like jam, honey, mustard, fruit, etc.). Jars vary greatly in size and shape and generally do not contain handles, but do ordinarily have covers or lids. One special distinction of a jar is that along with its wide mouth, it also has almost no neck. Some that hold condiments like mustard have openings in the lid for a matching spoon.

Steuben Art Glass jar. Courtesy of Wheaton Village.

JARDINIERE — A ornamental glass stand or vase-like vessel used for holding plants or flowers.

Reproduction from a late 19th century T.G. Hawkes advertisement.

Jardiniere with Lining
A symphony in cut glass which in design and workmanship expresses in the highest degree the glass workers art.

Hawkes Cut Glass

is famous the world over for its rare perfection in quality, its individuality of pattern and its crystalline clarity.
At the best dealers. No piece without this trade-mark engraved on it is genuine. If your dealer does not sell Hawkes Cut Glass, write for address of one who does.
T. G. Hawkes & Co., Corning, N.Y.

JARVES, DEMING — An early pioneer instrumental in getting glass-making started in America. Jarves (1790-1896) founded the New England Glass Company in 1818, the Boston & Sandwich Glass Company in 1825 (both produced paperweights), the Mount Washington Glass Works in 1837 (with his son George Jarves), the Cape Cod Glass Works in 1858, and several others.

Deming Jarves, early American glass pioneer.
Photo courtesy of the Sandwich Glass Museum.

JARVES AND CORMERAIS — An American firm established in 1839 as "Labree & Jarves" at Boston, Massachusetts, by John D. Labree, George Jarves, and Henry Cormerais, the company's name was changed to Jarves and Cormerais in 1840 and operated as a maker of glass lamps and chandeliers. It was better known as the Mount Washington Glass Works. Jarves died of consumption in 1850 and Cormerais carried on the business. William L. Libbey joined the firm in 1851 as a bookkeeper while Timothy Howe was added as a clerk in 1856. Howe and Libbey assumed control of the firm in 1861. Howe died in 1866 and Libbey purchased his interest. See also MOUNT WASHINGTON GLASS WORKS and WILLIAM L. LIBBEY.

JASPER — An opaque, usually colorful, form of quartz. Glass made to imitate it is generally referred to as agate glass. In the seventeenth century, the English used jasper glass synonymously with agate glass while the French term is "Jaspe." See also AGATE GLASS.

JASPER GROUND — An extremely fine-grained ground consisting of two colors to form a speckled effect in paperweights.

JEANNETTE GLASS COMPANY — An American company established at Jeannette, Pennsylvania, in 1898 by Joseph Stoner, W. A. Huff, and others, the firm was originally known as the Jeannette Bottle Works and made hand-blown bottles. In 1927, the company switched to automated machinery in order to produce machine-pressed clear and colored glass tableware patterns (including milk/opaque styles) and kitchenware during the Depression era. They purchased McKee/Thatcher in 1961 and became the Jeannette Corporation in 1971 after acquiring china, plastic dinnerware, and candle factories. Jeannette remained in operation until 1983. Large tableware patterns attributed to Jeannette include "Adam," "Anniversary," "Buttons & Bows" or ""Holiday," "Cherry Blossom," "Cube" or "Cubist," "Dewdrop," "Doric," "Doric & Pansy," "Floragold" or "Louisa," "Floral" or "Poinsettia," "Harp," "Hex Optic" or "Honeycomb," "Homespun" or "Fine Rib," "Indiana Custard" or "Flower & Leaf Band," "Iris" or "Iris & Herringbone," "National," "Shell Pink" milk glass, "Sierra" or "Pinwheel," "Sunburst" or "Herringbone," "Sunflower," "Swirl" or "Petal Swirl," and "Windsor" or "Windsor Diamond."

Jeannette's Depression Glass Cube/Cubist pattern.
Photo by Robin Rainwater.

Trademarks.

JEANNETTE SHADE & NOVELTY COMPANY — An American glass-making firm founded at Jeannette, Pennsylvania, in 1900 as the Empire Glass Company. The name was changed in 1910 to the Jeannette Shade & Novelty Company. The firm specialized in making glass lighting items including lamp shades. It was purchased by Thomas Crock (former sales manager of the Jefferson Glass Company) in 1919. When Crock died in 1955, he was succeeded by his sons Homer and David Crock. The firm is still in operation today.

JEANNETTE TOY & NOVELTY COMPANY — An American maker of toy glass candy containers, it was founded in 1917 by George Sailer (former associate of the McKee Glass Company) at Jeannette, Pennsylvania. The firm was sold to the Turney H. Stough Company and then to J. C. Crosetti in 1946. The company continued to produce toy glass containers until closing in 1980.

JEFFERSON GLASS COMPANY — A pressed glass manufacturer established at Steubenville, Ohio, in 1900 by Harry Bastow, G. Grant Fish, George Mortimer, and J. D. Sinclair, the firm first leased the plant previously occupied by the defunct Sumner Glass Company and then purchased it in 1903. In 1907, the company moved to Follansbee, West Virginia, where a new factory was built (the Steubenville plant was then leased to the Imperial Glass Company; however, it burned in 1908). Jefferson produced pressed glass tableware, novelties, some opalescent glassware, and lighting-related glass prior to closing in the early 1930s. Note that a partnership was also established with a firm in Toronto, Canada, and glass was produced under the Jefferson Glass Company, Ltd. name in Canada (mostly lamps and lighting glassware). See also DOMINION GLASS COMPANY.

Decorated Custard covered butter dish by the Jefferson Glass Company. *Photo courtesy of Wheaton Village.*

JELLY DISH OR TRAY — A small flat or shallow dish used for serving, jelly, jam, marmalade, and other preserves.

JELLY GLASS — A small stemmed or footed vessel, with a small bowl, used for serving jelly, jam, marmalade, other preserves, and small quantities of desserts like custard pudding. Jelly glasses originated in England in the mid-eighteenth century and some were made with one or two handles.

Reproduction from an early 20th century McKee catalog.

JENAER GLASSWORKS — Refer to SCHOTT AND GEN.

JENKINS, D.C. GLASS COMPANY — Refer to the KOKOMO GLASS MANUFACTURING COMPANY.

JENNY LIND FLASK — A particular style of historical flask made in America in the 1850s, they were produced by several different companies with a low molded relief design of the famous Swedish singer, Jenny Lind.

JENNYWARE — The nickname for kitchenware glass made by the Jeannette Glass Company, mostly during America's Depression era. *See also* JEANNETTE GLASS COMPANY.

JERSEY CITY GLASS COMPANY — An American company founded in Jersey City, New Jersey, in 1824 by William Bull, George and Phineas (P.C.) Dummer, and Joseph Milnor, the firm produced cut and pressed glass tableware including lacy glass up until 1860. The company did proceed through several name changes, including George Dummer and Company and P. C. Dummer and Company. Also note that there were a couple of other firms that sported the Jersey City name: a maker of glass lamp parts (H. O'NEILL'S JERSEY CITY FLINT GLASS WORKS, 1875) and a glass jar maker (JERSEY CITY GLASS WORKS, 1867).

JERSEY ROSE — A stylized pink or yellow rose found in some paperweights, whose petals contain opalescent tips. They were first created by Ralph Barber (while working for WHITEHAM, TATUM, AND COMPANY) in the early twentieth century and then copied by others.

JEWEL — A tiny gem-shaped cut piece of faceted glass. Glass jewels are made both to simulate gem stones, as well as in some quantity for applied decorations to other objects (usually on the exterior in decorative patterns or incorporated into leaded glass artwork).

JEWEL BOX — A glass receptacle, usually rectangular, oval, or circular in shape and with or without a cover, used for storing jewelry. Jewelry boxes come in a wide variety of colors and styles; however, most made in glass vary from tiny to small (rarely larger than a few inches in diameter or length).

Reproduction from an early 20th century Pitkin & Brooks Co. catalog.

JEWEL CUT GLASS COMPANY — An American firm established at Newark, New Jersey, in 1906 by C. H. Taylor, the company had previously began as the C. H. Taylor Glass Co., but changed its name to Jewel in 1907. Jewel made most of its cut glass products up until World War I. The company patented a few patterns, but in 1928, as the market for fine cut glass declined, they stopped cutting glass and began selling greeting cards.

Trademark.

Reproduction from a 1912 Jewel Cut Glass Company U.S. patent.

JEWISH GLASS — General term for glass objects decorated or made in the form of Jewish religious symbols (i.e. Menorahs, Star-of-David decorations, hexagon-shaped bottles, etc.). These objects originated in Roman times.

JIGGER — A small tumbler or measuring glass used for serving single measures of alcoholic beverages. A standard jigger is 1-1/2 ounce. *See also* SHOT GLASS.

JIHLAVA GLASSWORKS — A Bohemian/Czechoslovakian glass-making firm founded at Antonin Dul and Dobronin in 1945 by the merger of Antonin Dul and Inwald Glassworks. The company continued to produce both crystal and colored ornamental glass in traditional Bohemian styles. When all Czechoslovakian firms were nationalized after World War II, it eventually became part of the Bohemian Glassworks National Corporation conglomerate in 1965. Jihlava regained its independence in 1993 and produces cut glass products today under the Jihlava name. *See also* ANTONIN DUL, INWALD GLASSWORKS, *and* BOHEMIAN GLASSWORKS NATIONAL CORPORATION.

JOBLING, JAMES A. — Refer to HENRY GREENER.

JOE RICE'S HOUSE OF GLASS — Refer to the SAINT CLAIR GLASS WORKS INC.

JOHANSFORS — A Swedish company founded by A. Ahrends in the Smaland region in 1889. Ahrends was a painter and initially the firm acted as a decoration company. In 1891, along with partner F. O. Israelson, a factory was built and named the Johansfors Glassworks. The firm expanded into pressed and blown glassware while specializing in the engraving and enameling of traditional Scandinavian designs. In 1972, Johansfors was acquired by the Afors Group and then absorbed by Kosta-Boda. In 1990, the factory was closed, but was purchased in 1992 by the Norwegian firm of Magnor Glassverk. *See also* SWEDISH GLASS.

JOHNSON-CARLSON CUT GLASS COMPANY — An American company founded in 1906 at Chicago, Illinois, by Swedish immigrant Oscar Johnson and John Carlson. Johnson's brother Turry, and Carlson's brother, Gustave, both joined the firm soon after. The company produced cut glass products and established two other cut glass firms as well: the Twin City Cut Glass Company at Minneapolis, Minnesota, in 1908 and the Warsaw Cut Glass Company at Warsaw, Indiana, in 1911. The Twin City branch was moved to St. Paul, Minnesota, in 1910 and closed around 1918. With the exception of the Warsaw location, the firm closed in the early 1930s. Bothers Oscar and Carl Hugo were active in the Warsaw plant and took control of it in 1933; however, cut glass production (except for some light engraving) had ended.

JOHNSON, KING & COMPANY — Refer to KING, SON & COMPANY.

JONASSON, MATS — A noted Swedish designer, born in 1945, he is the third-generation of master glass craftsman and specializes in reverse sculpting of crystal (irregularly shaped ice blocks) for the Maleras Glasbruk of Sweden. He actually joined Maleras in 1959 as an apprentice engraver, but left ten years later to join Kosta. He later returned to Maleras in 1975, but the firm, under Royal Krona's direction, went bankrupt in 1977. It was purchased by Kosta-Boda; however, they decided to close the factory in 1980. Jonasson, along with several employees and villagers, pooled their resources to purchase the company. Under Jonasson's direction, the firm is known most for reverse engraved glass ice blocks, most with images of wildlife. In 1988, Jonasson purchased a controlling interest in Maleras and currently serves as both managing director and chief engraver. The blocks he sculpts are usually carved on the reverse side to provide a mirrored three-dimensional image when viewed from the front. Jonasson has created a huge variety of wildlife designs in this method. *See also ICE BLOCK OR SCULPTURE and MALERAS GLASBRUK.*

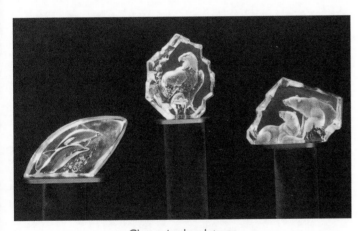

Glass animal sculptures
by Mats Jonasson for Maleras Glass.

Maleras Glassbruk factory.

Trademarks/signatures.

JONES, CAVITT & COMPANY, LTD. — Refer to CAMPBELL, JONES & COMPANY.

JONES, McDUFFEE & STRATTON COMPANY — An American firm established at Boston, Massachusetts, in 1810 by Otis Norcross, the company was arguably the largest wholesaler and retailer of crockery, china, and glassware in America in the nineteenth century.

JOSEFHUTTE — Refer to JOSEF RINDSKOPK.

JOSEFODOL GLASSWORKS — A Bohemian/Czechoslovakian glass cutting shop founded at Josefodol in 1861 by Viennese glass merchant Josef Schreiber. A complete glass factory was added in 1878 and the company began producing crystal and colored ornamental glass (especially ruby red and purple vases) in traditional Bohemian styles. When all Czechoslovakian firms were nationalized after World War II, Josefodol served as a maker of scientific and optical glass for a few years before returning to traditional glass-making. It eventually became part of the Bohemian Glassworks National Corporation conglomerate in 1965, but regained its independence in 1989. The firm specializes in cut cased colored glass today. *See also BOHEMIAN GLASSWORKS NATIONAL CORPORATION.*

JOSEPHINENHUTTE — A Bohemian glasshouse built in 1840 in Silesia by Count Schaffgotch, the firm became one of the largest producers of Bohemian glass in the nineteenth and twentieth centuries. It was also a noted producer of blanks for many other firms/decorators including Fritz Heckert. The general area in which Josephinenhutte was located became part of Czechoslovakia after World War I and acquired Heckert's firm in 1925 after a merger in 1923. The company's most famous designer was Alexander Pfohl Jr., a member of the noteworthy Pfohl family. *See also CZECHOSLOVAKIAN GLASS, FRITZ HECKERT, PFOHL FAMILY, and SILESIAN GLASS.*

JUG — A large deep glass vessel, usually with a wide mouth, pouring spout, and handle, used for storing or serving liquids.

JUGENDSTIL — The German term for the Art Nouveau movement. *See also ART OR ART NOUVEAU GLASS.*

JUICE GLASS — A short narrow glass tumbler, with or without a foot and with a capacity of 3-6 ounces, used for drinking fruit and vegetable juices in small quantities. Originally, the height of a juice glass was about twice the diameter.

JUICER — Refer to REAMER.

Kk

{ Kk }

KAGAMI GLASS WORKS — Refer to JAPANESE GLASS.

KAISERKRISTALL — Refer to LEDNICKE ROVNE GLASSWORKS.

KANAWA GLASS COMPANY — Founded in 1955 in Dunbar, West Virginia, Kanawa was noted for creating glass novelty items, pitchers, and vases (many in milk/opaque colors). The company was purchased by the Raymond Dereume Glass Company of Punxsutawney, Pennsylvania, in 1987.

KARHULA — Refer to the IITTALA GLASSWORKS.

KAROLINKA GLASSWORKS — A Czechoslovakian firm founded in 1861 in the general area of Bohemia by the Reich family, initially, it produced drinking glasses and expanded into container glass. Etching was adding too, and, by the early twentieth century, the company won several awards for its etched glass. Like all Czech firms, it became part of the state in 1948 and was merged with the firms Rosice and Kvetna. It was eventually absorbed by the conglomerate Crystalex and still serves as a glass-making factory today.

KASTRUP & HOLMEGAARDS GLASSWORKS — A Danish company established in 1825 as Holmegaards Glasvaerk on the island of Zealand, the firm began as a bottle-making operation and soon afterward produced Bohemian-styled tableware. The company expanded operations and opened a second factory in 1847 at Kastrup (near Copenhagen). Kastrup was sold in 1873 and merged with several other small glass firms in 1907. In 1965, Kastrup merged with Holmegaards to become the largest producing glass conglomerate in the Danish world today (the name was officially changed to Kastrup & Holmegaards at this time). The firm is noted for modern styles of functional tableware as well as some ornamental glass wares. The company became part of Royal Copenhagen in 1985, which was, in turn, absorbed into the Royal Scandinavia conglomerate in 1997 (includes Orrefors, Kosta-Boda, and Venini). See also HOLMEGAARDS.

KAUKALAHTI GLASSWORKS — A Finnish firm founded in 1923 at Espoo, Finland, the company produced lighting glassware and was sold to Riihimaki in 1927. See also RIIHIMAKI GLASSWORKS.

KEENE GLASS WORKS — An American company founded in Vermont in 1815, the firm was noted most for producing clear and colored figural flasks, particularly one with a Masonic design. The firm was also known as the Marlboro Street Glass Works.

KEHLMAN, ROBERT — A noted American Studio Glass artisan born in Brooklyn, New York, in 1942, Kehlman received his Master of Arts degree from the University of California, Berkley, and has served in a teaching capacity at the Pilchuk Glass School and the California College of Arts and Crafts. Awards he has received include the Massachusetts Artists Fellowship (1987), a National Endowment for the Arts Fellowship (1977).

KELCH — The German term for chalice. Refer to CHALICE.

KELLNER & MUNRO — An American cut glass operation founded by Frank Kellner and Angus Munro in 1908 at Brooklyn, New York, the firm produced cut glass items until 1918.

KELLY & STEINMAN — Refer to the PEERLESS CUT GLASS COMPANY.

KELP — A fast-growing brown seaweed whose calcined ashes are occasionally used for a source of soda in the glass-making process. Kelp was used mostly by Scandinavian countries and the United Kingdom for producing some pressed wares in the late nineteenth and early twentieth centuries.

KELVA — A style of art glass produced by the C. F. Monroe Company of Meriden, Connecticut, from 1880 to the company's closing in 1916. Kelva is characterized by a light opal glass in various colors (white, cream, custard, light rose, and pink were the most common grounds) decorated with enameled and/or gold scrolling, foliage, or floral designs. Some pieces, such as vases, wall pockets, and covered jars, were set in silver or silver-plated holders. Identical products made by Monroe were also referred to as "Nakara" and "Wave Crest."

Kelva box from C. F. Monroe. *Courtesy of Wheaton Village.*

KEMPLE, JOHN E. GLASS COMPANY — A pressed glass manufacturer established at East Palestine, Ohio, in 1945 by John E. Kemple, who had previously worked for the Fostoria Glass Company. Kemple began as a maker of pressed glass from molds that he acquired from several firms including Co-operative Flint Glass, Dithridge, Gillinder, Mannington, McKee, Phoenix, and Sinclaire. The firm procured over 1,100 molds, most from defunct glass companies that operated in the late nineteenth century. When a fire destroyed the plant in 1956, operations were moved to Kenova, West Virginia, where Kemple purchased a plant previously occupied by Gill Glass Works. The firm reproduced many McKee and Phoenix patterns, especially in milk/opaque styles that were further enameled and decorated, and made covered animal dishes and a wide variety of small glass novelty items (boxes, trays, jars, etc.) in many different colors. When John Kemple died in 1970, the firm closed and all factory equipment (including molds) was sold to the Wheaton Glass Company, which produced some limited amounts of glass. The molds are now part of the Wheaton Village & Museum.

K

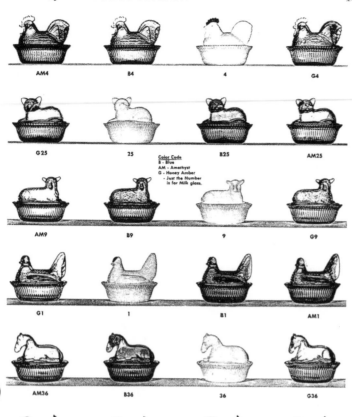

Kew Blas bowl. *Photo by Robin Rainwater.*

Reproduction from a 1960s Kemple catalog.

KEMPTON, C. H. COMPANY — Refer to the NAZEING GLASSWORKS.

KENSINGTON GLASS WORKS — An American glass firm established at Philadelphia, Pennsylvania, in 1772 by John Elliott & Company, it produced lead cut crystal tableware before ceasing operations in 1804.

KEOTA GLASS — Refer to EAGLE GLASS WORKS.

KEROSENE LAMP — A glass vessel with a wick and oil receptacle used to produce light. Kerosene lamps come in a various shapes and forms and were created specifically to burn kerosene oil. *See also* OIL LAMP.

KERR, A. H. AND COMPANY — An early twentieth century manufacturer of fruit/canning jars established at Sand Springs, Oklahoma. The mold-impressed word "Kerr" was first used as a trademark in 1915. The company moved to Los Angeles, California, in the 1940s.

KEW BLAS — A name given to a type of iridescent opaque Art Glass produced by the Union Glass Company in the 1890s. The primary color is brown with various shadings of brown and green. Kew Blas is actually an anagram from the manager of the factory's name, W. S. Blake, and was made into the early 1920s.

Trademarks.

1853

KEYSTONE CUT GLASS COMPANY — An American company established in Hawley, Pennsylvania, in 1902, Keystone was a small company that purchased their blanks from Corning Glass Works and Dorflinger. The company produced cut glass products until ceasing operations in 1918.

Keystone Cut Glass Company: Trademark.

KEYSTONE FLINT GLASS WORKS — Refer to the MACBETH-EVANS GLASS COMPANY.

KEYSTONE TUMBLER COMPANY — A short-lived pressed glass manufacturer established at Rochester, Pennsylvania, in 1897 by Charles Bentel, James Conlan, John Conway, August Heller, George, Malone, John Mould, and Charles Runyon, the company produced tumblers, jelly glasses, barware, and blown tumblers. The firm joined the National Glass Company in 1899 as the Keystone Tumbler Works. In 1907, a fire destroyed much of the plant and it was never rebuilt. Note that there was a couple of other American companies that produced lamp parts (mostly glass chimneys) and filed under the Keystone name: Keystone Glass Works (1867) and Keystone Flint Glass Manufactory (1872), both of Pittsburgh, Pennsylvania.

KICK — A small purposeful indentation in the bottom of a glass object. Although it reduces capacity a little, a kick does add some stability to an object such as a bottle or tumbler. The base of an object with a kick is sometimes referred to as a "kick base."

Wine bottle with a kick base. *Photo by Robin Rainwater.*

KIEFER BROTHERS CUT GLASS COMPANY — An American firm founded in 1908 by brothers Charles and Edward Kiefer in Brooklyn, New York, it produced cut glass products into the mid-1920s.

KILGORE & HANNA — A short-lived practical maker of blown glass tableware founded in 1830 at Steubenville, Ohio, the firm went bankrupt and the factory was acquired by Edward Stillman and Joseph Beatty, Sr. in 1845. *See also* ALEXANDER J. BEATTY & SONS.

KILN — An oven used for firing or refiring glass objects. Kilns are also used for fusing enamels onto glass objects. Kiln-forming refers to glass that is fused or shaped by heating in a kiln. Note that kilns are typically smaller than furnaces. *See also* FURNACE *and* MUFFLE KILN.

KIMBERLY COMPANY — Refer to DUFF & KIMBERLY.

KIMBLE GLASS COMPANY — An American firm established in 1931 when Colonel Evan F. Kimble purchased Victor Durand Jr.'s factory in Vineland, New Jersey, after Durand's death. The new endeavor operated for a short period and was noted for producing items in the Art Glass "Cluthra" style.

KING, ALEXANDER GLASS WORKS — Alexander King was one of the first Americans to import soda ash from England, which he furnished to several American glass companies beginning in the 1840s. King operated out of Pittsburgh, Pennsylvania, and eventually set up his own factory to produce some limited amount of pressed glass. King died in 1890 and his son, William S. King, went on to help form KING, SON AND COMPANY.

KING, SON AND COMPANY — An American company founded in 1859 as the Cascade Glass Works near Pittsburgh, Pennsylvania, the firm was renamed Johnson, King and Company in 1864 and then King, Son and Company in 1869. Principal owners included brothers Ralph and James Johnson, David C. King, King's son William F. King, and another King relation, William S. King (son of Alexander King). The Johnsons were out of the firm by 1869. Fire destroyed the plant in 1884 and temporary quarters were leased at the idle factory of the Crystal Glass Company while the main plant was being rebuilt. In 1888, the name was changed to the King Glass Company. The firm manufactured clear and colored pressed glass tableware before becoming part of the United States Glass Company in 1891 as Factory K. U.S. Glass operated the plant into the mid-1930s. *See also* ALEXANDER KING GLASS WORKS.

KINGS COUNTY GLASS WORKS — An American firm established in 1905 in Brooklyn, New York, the name was changed to the Kings County Rich Cut Glass Works in 1909. The company produced cut glass products until closing in 1923.

KING'S CROWN — A pressed glass pattern originally produced in the late 1880s by the U.S. Glass Company, it consists of a single row of circles or ovals (elongated thumbprints) with a wide band of ruby-stained glass above them. The staining comes in both a light (cranberry) and dark (ruby red) version, as well as a few other odd colors (gold, platinum, blue, green, or yellow). It was later reproduced throughout the twentieth century by other companies, such as Tiffin and Indiana, and is present in a wide variety of tableware items. Note that U.S. Glass originally referred to this design as "Ruby Thumbprint."

KINGS CROWN

Wedding Bowl and Cover 6" Diameter 10½" High

Flower Floater 12½" Diameter

Torte Plate 14" Diameter

Ash Tray 5¼" Square

Footed Cake Salver 12½" Diameter 4¾" High

Reproduction from a 1955 Tiffin Co. catalog.

KING'S LYNN GLASS, LTD. — An English crystal making company established at King's Lynn, Norfolk, in 1967 by Ronald Stennett-Willson, the company expanded into more colorful forms of tableware and ornamental art items in Scandinavian styles. The firm was purchased in 1969 by Josiah Wedgwood & Sons, Ltd.; however, the factory was closed in 1992. *See also* WEDGWOOD GLASS.

KIRKPATRICK, JOEY — A noted American Studio Glass artisan born in Des Monies, Iowa, in 1952, Kirkpatrick received her Fine Arts degree from the University of Iowa and completed graduate work in glass at Iowa State University. She has served in a teaching capacity at the Pilchuk Glass School, the University of California, and the University of Illinois. Kirkpatrick continues to work as an independent glass artisan in Seattle, Washington.

KITCHEN GLASSWARE — General term for both crystal and colored glass items used for cooking, food preparation, food storage, and other purposes in a kitchen. Kitchen-styled glassware was most prevalent during America's Depression Era and consists of such glass items as measuring cups, rolling pins, utensils (knives, spoons, forks, ladle, etc.), canisters, juicers, refrigerator dishes, egg cups, dispensers, funnels, mixing bowls, pie dishes, and reamers.

K

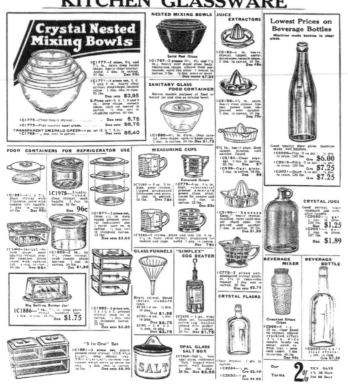

Reproduction from a 1928 Butler Brothers catalog.

KLEIN, ALAN — A noted American Studio Glass artisan born in New Haven, Connecticut, in 1947, Klein received his Masters of Fine Arts degree from the Rochester Institute of Technology and has served in a teaching capacity at the Massachusetts College of Arts, the Toledo Museum of Art, and Bowling Green State University. Awards he has received include a New York State Art Park Grant, a Massachusetts Council for the Arts and Humanities Fellowship, and a National Endowment for the Arts Artist in Residence Grant. Klein continues to work as an independent glass artisan in Jamaica Plain, Massachusetts.

KLENGLIN ET CIE — Refer to Vallerysthal Glass.

KNICKERBOCKER CUT GLASS COMPANY — A small American cut glass decorating firm established in the late 1890s, the company was purchased by Almy and Thomas in 1903; it continued to produce cut glass until 1918. *See also* ALMY AND THOMAS.

KNIFE — A table utensil with handle and blade that is used to slice or spread foods; knives made entirely of glass originated with the Venetians in the sixteenth century and were popular during America's Depression Era.

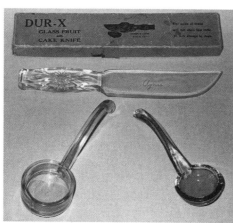

Depression Glass knife and ladles. *Photo by Robin Rainwater.*

KNIFE REST — A small thick barbell-shaped glass object used for holding knife blades off of the table while eating.

Cut Glass Knife Rest.
No. 9666—4¼ Inches............$1.25 Each

Reproduction from an early 20th century S. F. Myers Co. catalog.

Crystal knife rest. *Photo by Robin Rainwater.*

KNOP — An ornamental ball-shaped swelling on the stem of stemmed glassware such as goblets, wine glasses, and cordials. Knops come in many sizes (usually small) and shapes like balls or spheres, melons, mushrooms, acorns, and buttons.

KNOWLES AND TAYLOR — Refer to "Alexander J. Beatty and Sons."

KNOX AND MCKEE — Refer to the "Virginia Green Glass Works."

KNURLING — Refer to "Gadrooning."

KOCH AND PARSCHE — Refer to F. X. PARSCHE AND SON COMPANY and EDWARD J. KOCH AND COMPANY.

KOCH, EDWARD J. AND COMPANY — An American cut glass-making firm established by Edward Koch at Chicago, Illinois, in 1899. Koch had been a former employee of Mount Washington/Pairpoint. In 1912, the name of the company was changed to the Koch Cut Glass Company and a plant was run in Elgin, Indiana (sales and administrative offices remained in a Chicago). Koch also served as president in two other Chicago area wholesale/retain firms that represented cut glass products: KOCH AND PARSCHE (1893-1907) and the MIDLAND CUT GLASS COMPANY (1917-1926). Koch produced cut glass products until 1926. *See also* F. X. PARSCHE AND SON COMPANY.

Trademark.

Koch, Edward J. & Company:
Reproduction from a 1902 E. J. Koch U.S. patent.

KOH-I-NOOR — A trademark occasionally found on cut glass products that were registered by Richard Murr in 1926 in San Francisco, California. The name was taken from a famous diamond as part of the British Crown Jewels. Murr was a sales agent who did not produce cut glass of his own; rather, he represented products made by other cut glass firms. Murr moved to Chicago, Illinois, in 1907, and represented cut glass products into the mid-1920s.

Reproduction from a 1908 R. Murr U.S. patent.

KOHINUR CUT GLASS COMPANY — Refer to LAUREL CUT GLASS COMPANY.

KOKESH, WILLIAM J. — A glass cutter who first worked for the Washington Cut Glass Company in 1915. In 1939, Kokesh opened his own glass engraving shop in his home city at Seattle, Washington. He is noted for producing engraved glass by sandblasting into the 1960s. During Seattle's Century Exposition in 1962, Kokesh produced engraved plaques of Seattle's Space Needle.

KOKOMO GLASS MANUFACTURING COMPANY — An American pressed glass-making firm established at Kokomo, Indiana, in 1899 by David C. Jenkins Sr. (president), his son David C. Jenkins Jr. (superintendent), and grandson Addison Jenkins (secretary-treasurer, son of David C. Jenkins Jr.). The factory opened in 1901, but was destroyed by fire in 1905. It was rebuilt in 1906 and reorganized as the D. C. Jenkins Glass Company with David C. Jenkins Jr. (1854-1930) as president and his son, Addison, as secretary-treasurer. A second factory (previously owned by the Globe Bottle Works) was purchased in Arcadia, Indiana. Throughout its history, the firm produced pressed tableware, jelly glasses, goblets, condiment containers, and novelty items. The company went bankrupt in 1932 and both factories closed. In 1945, the Slick Glass Company purchased the Arcadia plant, but closed it the following year after producing a small amount of pressed glass tableware.

KOPP GLASS, INC. — Refer to the KOPP LAMP AND GLASS COMPANY.

KOPP LAMP AND GLASS COMPANY — An American firm founded at Pittsburgh, Pennsylvania, in 1900 by George Barrett, Nicholas Kopp, Edward Kitzmiller, Frank Wallace, and James Willock. Wallace and Kopp had previously worked for the Consolidated Lamp and Glass Company. The company produced pressed glass, mostly in color, and sold out to the Pittsburgh Lamp and Brass Company in 1901. Many of the original owners/officers remained as employees of the new firm, which continued to produce colored pressed glass as well as signal light lenses. When the Pittsburgh Lamp and Brass Company went out of business in 1926, the firm was acquired by brothers Albert C. and C. H. Kopp. The name was changed to Kopp Glass, Inc. and continues to operate today making lenses, filters, signals, and other industrial glass products.

KOSTA-BODA — Refer to BODA GLASSWORKS and KOSTA GLASSWORKS.

Kosta-Boda contemporary Art Glass.

KOSTA GLASSWORKS — Established in 1742 in Sweden by Anders Koskull (1677-1746) and Georg Bogislaus Stael von Holstein (1685-1763), it is one of the oldest glass makers still in operation today. Located in the Varmland region, the factory originally produced windows and bottles; it later added chandeliers and tableware. Engraving was introduced in 1752, cutting in 1828, and pressing in 1838. In 1946, it merged with Afors and the Boda Glassworks to form Kosta-Boda and is noted for decorative cut glass, tableware, and many traditional Scandinavian art styles of glass. In 1970, Kosta, Boda, Johansfors and Afors all became part of the Afors Group, making it the largest glass-producing firm in Sweden (known as "Aforsgruppen" in Swedish). The group also acquired other small Swedish glass firms too like Skruff and Sendvik; Johansfors in 1972, and even Orrefors joined in 1990. The company is also known today as the Royal Scandinavian Group. *See also AFORS GLASBRUK, BODA GLASSWORKS, and ORREFORS GLASBRUCK.*

Kosta Glassworks: Selection of crystal vases, bowls, and candlesticks by Kosta-Boda of Sweden.

K

Kosta Glassworks: Kosta factory located in Sweden.

Trademarks.

KRAKA GLASS — An art style of glass developed by Orrefors of Sweden (designer Sven Palmqvist) in the 1940s, it is characterized by an opaque shade of white, dark blue, or gold-colored glass that is networked much like a fish net between two layers of glass (similar to the Venetian style known as "Muranese Reticello"). Kraka was a Viking legend who came to her hero dressed in a fishing net.

KRALIK, WILHELM — A Bohemian glassmaker who inherited several glass firms along with his cousin Josef Taschek from their uncle Jan Meyr (son of Josef Meyr). They changed the primary name to "J. Meyr's Neffen" (The Nephews of J. Meyr) in 1854 and acquired two additional glasshouses: Ernsbrunn and Franzenthal. When Taschek died in 1862, Kralik changed the name to "Meyr's Neffe." Under Kralik's direction, the firm produced high quality engraved, enameled, and some iridescent Bohemian glass that was awarded numerous prizes at international exhibitions. Kralik is noted most for the creation of Peloton glass, which is characterized by random color streaking on an opaque base. Kralik was even knighted for his work. When Kralik died in 1877, the business was passed on to his four sons; Karl and Hugo were given the glasshouses at Adolfshutte, Idahutte, Luisenhutte, and Transmute (retained the name "Meyr's Neff") while Heinrich and Johann were given Eleonorhutte and Ernsthutte (went by the name of "Wilhelm Kralik Sohne"). The firms remained in the family until 1922 and World War II respectively. Meyr's Neff merged with Moser in 1922 while Wilhelm Kralick Sohne closed around 1939. See also ADOLFSHUTTE and PELOTON GLASS.

Kralik, Wilhelm: Trademarks.

KRANTZ AND SMITH COMPANY — In 1893, John Krantz and John Smith established a glass cutting shop on the second floor of Wyman Kimble's factory located in Honesdale, Pennsylvania. Cut glass was produced up until the factory burned in 1932.

Krantz & Smith Company: Trademark.

KRONA-BRUKEN — Refer to MALERAS GLASBRUK and SKRUF.

KRYSTAL KRAFTERS — Refer to GEORGE L. BORDEN AND COMPANY.

KUAN LIAO — A Chinese term for a variety of art-styled glass objects that were created for the Imperial Court. Some items produced included opaque colored forms, carving and cased styles, and fired-on enamel forms. *See also* CHINESE GLASS.

KULKA, WENZEL — A Bohemian glassmaker who opened a studio at Novy Bor, Czechoslovakia, in 1917; Kulka produced a variety of Bohemian-styled cut and engraved glass similar to that of Moser before closing in 1939.

KUNCKEL, JOHANN — Refer to the POTSDAM GLASS FACTORY.

KUPFER, EMIL F., INC. — A cut glass decorating firm established by Emil F. Kupfer at Brooklyn, New York, in 1912. The firm employed cutters and sold cut glass until 1929.

KUSAK CUT GLASS COMPANY — An American cut glass operation founded in 1916 at Seattle, Washington, by Bohemian immigrant Antone Kusack, who previously worked for Fostoria as well as with his brother-in-law, Edward Zelasky, at the Washington Cut Glass Company. Kusak traveled yearly to purchase blanks from his native Czechoslovakia, which he cut in his shop. His son, Antone, joined the business and operated it as a glass engraving firm into the 1960s.

KVETNA GLASSWORKS — A Czechoslovakian firm founded in 1794 as Stanier Glashutte in the general area of Bohemia. Initially, it produced basic tableware and window glass and was purchased by Josef Zahn in 1850. Under Zahn, cutting, etching, engraving, and enamelling were all added and the name was eventually changed to Zahn and Goepfert in 1894. Like all Czech firms, it became part of the state in 1948 and was merged with the firms Rosice and Karolinka. It was eventually absorbed by the conglomerate Crystalex, and still serves as a glass-making factory for tableware and stemware.

K

L1

{ L1 }

LaBastie Flint Glass Works — Refer to the Constitution Flint Glass Works.

Label — A slip of paper, marked or inscribed, affixed to an object indicating its nature, brand, and description. In glassware, labels are most often found on wine bottles and older pharmaceutical items.

LaBelle Glass Company — An American company founded at Bridgeport, Ohio, in 1972 by Andrew Baggs, E. P. Rhodes, and F. C. Winship, it operated as a maker of pressed glass tableware, barware, blown and pressed lamps, colored/opalescent art glass, and some limited engraved glassware until the factory burned in 1887. The plant was rebuilt in 1888; however, the rights to the firm were purchased by Edward Muhleman of the Muhleman Glass Works. Muhleman went out of business in 1888.

Labino, Dominick — A noted American glass artisan and inventor of the twentieth century, Labino (1910-1987) was born in Clarion County, Pennsylvania, and graduated from the Carnegie Institute of Technology. He worked for both Owens-Illinois (1934-1946) and served as vice president and research director at Johns-Manville Fiber Glass Corporation (1946-1965). Labino won numerous awards and is noted most for supplying critical technical information, along with glass, for the ground-breaking glass blowing workshops held at the Toledo Museum of Art in the early 1960s. Labino also is credited with over sixty patent inventions concerning glass and/or glass-making.

Blown vase by Dominick Labino.
Photo courtesy of the Corning Museum of Glass.

Labree and Jarves — Refer to Jarves and Cormerais.

Lace Glass — A mid-sixteenth century Venetian-styled glass characterized by transparent threaded designs layered on the sides of various glass objects. The popularity of lace-decorated glass heightened during the Victorian era with English and American makers. In paperweights, lace is a bundle of twisted colored (opaque white is the most common) canes that resemble lace. Lace is sometimes referred to as Filigree, Gauze, or Muslin. *See also* Merletto *and* Spanish Lace.

Lackawanna Cut Glass Company — An American cut glass-making firm established at Scranton, Pennsylvania, in 1903, the company produced cut glass tableware until ceasing operations in 1905.

Lackawanna Cut Glass Company: Trademark

Lacy Pressed Glass — A mid-nineteenth century American style of pressed glass characterized by an overall angular and round braided pattern that is stippled on. The tiny dots that make up lacy designs added a refractory quality that in turn lent a somewhat silvery sheen to the glass. Typical lacy patterns also include central floral designs, foliage, scrolling, acanthus leaves, peacock feathers, rosettes, and an overall Sandwich pattern. Lacy patterns are typically combined with other designs too (lacy dais, lacy dewdrop, lacy medallion, lacy spiral, etc.). *See also* Sandwich Glass.

Lacy pressed glass candlesticks.
Photo courtesy of the Sandwich Glass Museum.

Ladder — A vertical step-like design in cut glass made up of horizontal rungs that resemble those of a ladder. Ladder-like cut designs are usually combined with other cut motifs to form unique patterns.

Ladle — A handled (long or short) spoon used for dipping jam, gravy, punch, or other foods and liquids from jars or bowls. Large dipping ladles are referred to as "Trulla" in Latin. Some ladles, like those designed for dipping pickles from a barrel, have holes in the bottom for draining.

Depression Glass ladle. *Photo by Robin Rainwater.*

LAFAYETTE FLINT GLASS WORKS — An American cut glass operation established at Brooklyn, New York, in 1865, the name was changed to the East River Glass Works in 1880. The firm produced cut glass tableware and perfume bottles prior to closing in 1895.

LAKEFIELD CUT GLASS COMPANY — A Canadian cut glass firm established at Lakefield in 1915. Like most Canadian cut glass firms, they purchased lead glass blanks from both American and European firms. Lakefield closed in 1920.

LALIQUE, RENE — An early twentieth century French glassmaker who continued the trends of the nineteenth century Art Nouveau movement in glass-making, Lalique (1860-1945) became a master jeweler (opened his own jewelry business in 1885), but got his start in glass-making when he was commissioned by Coty Parfums to design fancy decorative perfume bottles for Coty's various fragrances (early 1890s in Paris). From this point, the true artist was born and Lalique's famous creations branched into glass sculpture. Figurals, nudes, vases, paperweights, inkwells, ashtrays, clock cases, jewelry boxes, picture frames, mirrors, lamps, chandeliers, and even car hood ornaments were formed into frosted crystal works of art. He experimented a little with colors, but worked primarily with crystal. Lalique ceased making jewelry by 1911 to concentrate on glass. In 1918, a second factory was added at Alsace. When Lalique passed away in 1945, the firm was passed on to his son, Marc Lalique (1900-1977), and in turn to Marc's daughter, Marie-Claude Lalique (b. 1935). Glassware with the Lalique name is still being produced today (after Rene Lalique's death, the "R" was removed from the etched signature).

Reproduction from a 1931 Lalique catalog.

Lalique vase. *Photo by Robin Rainwater.*

Trademarks and signatures.

LAMINATED GLASS — Shatterproof glass, which is produced by adding an inner layer that is sandwiched between two outer layers. John Wood of England is credited with the invention around 1905. When laminated glass breaks, it cracks; however, the shards adhere to the inner layer.

LAMONT GLASS COMPANY — Refer to the DIAMOND GLASS COMPANY.

LAMP — A glass vessel with a wick or bulb used to produce artificial light. Those with wicks usually burn an inflammable liquid such as oil or kerosene. Those with bulbs are lit by electricity. There is a huge variety of lamps including fairy lamps, hurricane lamps, table lamps, desk lamps, pole lamps, night lamps, sparking lamps, peg lamps, burners, camphenes, etc. Some, like hurricane lamps, have separate glass bases and globes.

Waterford Crystal lamps.

Waterford cut crystal lamps.

THE LAMP MAKERS OF AMERICA.

A FIRM WHICH MAKES OVER 2,000,000 LAMPS ANNUALLY.

In a recent issue of the trade journals, the Consolidated Lamp & Glass Co. freely concede that "the lamp of the future may be made by others," and express themselves content to make the lamp of the present. A visit to either their salesrooms in New York, Pittsburgh, or their gigantic manufacturing plant in Coroapolis will fully convince the visitor that they not only make the lamps of the present, but they make them in ample quantities, from the tiniest colored gem that glows through the darkness while all the household dreams, to the mammoth and stately banquet, graceful, superb, attractive and artistic, whose center draft duplex burner sheds radiance over feast and festival in courtly halls of luxury, the parlors of leisure, the residences of the cultured, and the millions of homes of the people, whose ensemble constitutes humanity.

Reproduction from a 1900 Consolidated Lamp & Glass Company press release.

LAMP SHADE — Glass coverings that shelter lights in order to reduce glare. At times, large glass bowls have been converted to lamp shades by drilling holes in their center in order to attach them above the light.

LAMPWORK — The process of forming delicate glass objects out of thin rods or canes while working at a small flame. The flame is referred to as the "lamp," hence the name "lampwork" (in the modern world, precision torches are used and this process is also known as "flamework" or "torchwork"). Along with sulphide and millefiori, lampwork is one of the three basic types of paperweight styles. Lampwork is also a common technique for producing three-dimensional sculptures that are assembled one very small piece at a time.

St. Louis lampworked paperweight. Photo by Robin Rainwater.

LANCASTER COLONY CORPORATION — An American conglomerate based in Columbus, Ohio, that consists of several companies. In 1962, the firm acquired the Lancaster Lens Company of Lancaster, Ohio, and the Tiara and Indiana Glass companies of Dunkirk, Indiana (both operate as subsidiaries today). They purchased Bischoff in 1963, and also acquired Bartlett-Collins, which is filed as a subsidiary of the Indiana Glass Company. Lancaster also owns a plastic plant in Jackson, Michigan; a glove factory in Coshocton, Ohio; and a glass tableware distributor in New York, New York. Also note that the firm purchased the Imperial Glass Company from Lenox in 1984; however, glass production was not resumed at the Imperial factory.

LANCASTER GLASS COMPANY — An American firm established in the city of Lancaster, Ohio in 1908 by Wallace Graham, Lucian Martin, Fred Von Stein, (all three had previously worked for the Hocking Glass Company), and associates including Lucian's son, L. Philip Martin. The company specialized in pressed glasswares (i.e. the Depression Glass patterns "Jubilee" and "Patrick") before selling out to the HOCKING GLASS COMPANY in 1923. Hocking used the plant exclusively in 1924 while their plant was rebuilt after a fire. Hocking continued to use the "Lancaster" name through 1937.

LANCASTER GLASS WORKS — Refer to the OHIO FLINT GLASS COMPANY.

LANCASTER LENS COMPANY — An American firm founded at Lancaster, Ohio, in 1910 by Edmund Dickey, W. E. Gunyon, Albert Steiner, and Scott Wilson, the company produced lenses and merged with the INDIANA GLASS COMPANY of Dunkirk, Indiana, in 1955. The firm then became the LANCASTER GLASS CORPORATION, and in 1962, a subsidiary of the LANCASTER COLONY CORPORATION.

LANSBURGH & BROTHERS, INC. — A trademark occasionally found on cut glass products. The firm began using a trademark for cut glass in 1922, but did not produce cut glass of their own; rather, they were a wholesale distributor of products made by other cut glass firms. Lansburgh operated out of Washington, D.C. in the 1920s.

Lansburgh & Brothers, Inc.: Trademark. **Lansburgh & Bro.**

LANSING CUT GLASS WORKS — Refer to BUSH GLASS COMPANY.

LANTERN — A portable lighting fixture, with a handle, used for carrying or hanging. Lanterns generally have a metal support frame and a central enclosed glass area that serves to protect a flame or bulb. The glassed area tends to be square, rectangular, spherical, rounded, or cylindrical; some sport a chimney as well. *See also* SIGNAL LANTERN.

Photo by Robin Rainwater.

Courtesy of Wheaton Village.

Steam railroad signal lantern. *Photo by Robin Rainwater.*

LARGE STOPPER BOTTLE — A small glass receptacle, with a narrow neck and unusually large stopper, used for holding liquid perfumes or colognes. This style of perfume bottle was mostly made in Czechoslovakia in the early-to-mid twentieth century in cut, pressed, plain crystal, and colored glass. The tops or stoppers were often as tall as the bottle and contained floral, animal, female figures, and geometric designs. At times, the bottle was made with a matching design, but could also be a different design or color. Many women kept them on trays with perhaps ten to twenty different bottles, each filled with a different perfume. *See also* COLOGNE BOTTLE and PERFUME BOTTLE.

LASER LIGHT SCULPTURING — A late twentieth century technique of sculpting the inside of crystal through the use of lasers. Computer Assisted Drafting (CAD) is used to create a three-dimensional image and each dot or point at which the laser will fire to create the design is by hand. Laser designs usually incorporate from 10,000 to as many as 100,000 of these points.

LATHE-CUTTING — A decorating/cutting technique originating in ancient Rome whereby an object is mounted and turned with a bow or handled wheel and then engraved or polished with a cutting tool fed with abrasives (also known as "Bow Lathes"). In the Renaissance era, prior to the discovery of electricity, mechanical foot-powered (pedals) devices were used to turn the objects at hand. In modern times, machine-powered lathes, wheels, or other various turning apparatus are revolved automatically by electricity.

LATTICE — A decorating style found in both mold-pressed and cut glass consisting of an overlapping framework of diagonally-crossed strips.

Line drawing by the author.

LATTICINO OR LATTICINIO — A style of decoration that originated with sixteenth century Venetian glassmakers. It is characterized by fine opaque white ("latte" is Italian for milk) glass threads embedded in clear glass objects.

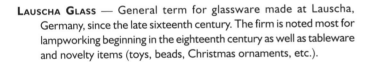

Venetian Latticino bowl.

LATTIMO — A style of opaque white glass that originated with sixteenth century Venetian glassmakers. Where latticino consists of white lines over crystal, lattimo is simply a style where the entire surface or body of an object is made in opaque white.

LAUENSTEINER — A German glass-making firm established in 1701 at Lauenstein, the company produced a good deal of English/Irish-styled lead crystal tableware before closing in 1870.

LAUREL CUT GLASS COMPANY — An American company founded in 1903 as the German Cut Glass Company in Jermyn, Pennsylvania; the name was changed to Laurel soon after. In 1906, it changed briefly to the Kohinur Cut Glass Company, but switched back to Laurel in 1907. The company produced limited cut glass and merged with the Quaker City Cut Glass Company after World War I. The two split soon after and Laurel disbanded in 1920.

Laurel Cut Glass Company: Trademark.

LAUSCHA GLASS — General term for glassware made at Lauscha, Germany, since the late sixteenth century. The firm is noted most for lampworking beginning in the eighteenth century as well as tableware and novelty items (toys, beads, Christmas ornaments, etc.).

LAVA GLASS — A style of Art Glass first invented by Louis Comfort Tiffany characterized by dark blue and gray opaque hues (the color of cooled lava) that is sometimes coated with gold or silver decorations. The lava-like coloring was produced by the addition of basalt to the glass formula. It was originally referred to as "Volcanic Glass." Others produced their own style of lava glass. Mount Washington patented an Art Glass style of the same name, but produced very little of it. Victor Durand Jr. produced a crackle style of lava glass that resembled lava spilling out from the rim of an erupting volcano (a globular portion of glass at the top that flowed down from the rim to the outside of the object).

A 1907 Tiffany lava glass vase. *Photo by Robin Rainwater. Item courtesy of the Corning Museum of Glass.*

LAVENDER — A light pastel shade of purple-colored glass produced by the addition of manganese, lavender tends to be a bit lighter than regular amethyst. See also AMETHYST and PURPLE.

LAWRENCE GLASS NOVELTY COMPANY — Refer to the "Alley Agate Company."

LAYERED GLASS — A general term for glass objects made with overlapping levels or layers of glass. See also CASED GLASS, CAMEO GLASS, LAMINATED GLASS, and RELIEF GLASS.

LAZARUS AND ROSENFIELD — An American wholesale firm that operated in New York, New York, from the late 1870s into the mid-1920s. The firm imported most of its glassware, including cut wares, from Bohemia. The company did not make any cut glass of their own.

LAZY SUSAN — A large revolving tray used for serving condiments, relishes, or other foods. Lazy Susans may be all glass or have wooden and/or metal bases with multiple glass inserts. Lazy Susans are sometimes referred to simply as "Revolving Servers."

L

LEAD — Lead, or oxides of lead, is a dull gray metallic element that, when added to a batch of glass, produces a fine colorless crystal that has resonance, brilliance, and a higher density than non-lead glass. In its highly oxidized form, it is a reddish color (red lead – Pb04), that is prized in glass-making. The discovery of true lead crystal glass-making is attributed to Englishman George Ravenscroft (around 1676). Regular lead oxide is also known as litharge (Pb0 or Pb304) and is much cheaper than higher quality forms of red lead. Lead is also combined with chromium in the creation of yellow-colored glass.

LEAD CRYSTAL — Crystal or colorless glass made with a high lead content. Most lead crystals are based on the European Standard Formula of 1865 for a typical batch: 1,200 lbs. of silex, 800 lbs. of red lead, 440 lbs. of pearl ask, 50 lbs. of niter, 10 lbs. phosphate of lime, 10 oz. white oxide or antimony, 24 oz. manganese, 32 oz. arsenic, and 20 oz. borax. *See also* HALF AND FULL LEAD CRYSTAL.

LEAD-PRESS — A Czechoslovakian type of press-molded glass made exclusively from lead crystal, first in the 1960s. Up to this point, press-molded glass was always made of the cheaper soda-lime based formula, which is usually superior at withstanding the pressure of the press-molding process.

LEDGE — Another name for a rim. The ledge or rim is a narrow area adjacent to the edge of a glass vessel. *See also* RIM.

LEDLIE AND ULAM — Refer to O'LEARY MULVANEY AND COMPANY.

LEDNICKE ROVNE GLASSWORKS — A Bohemian firm founded in 1892 at Lednic Rona (currently Lednicke Rovne in Slovakia), the factory initially produced window panes and was under the control of a glass conglomerate known as Josef Schreiber and Neffen. Soon afterward, production was expanded into pressed glass tableware marketed as Kaiserkristall and Ronacrystal. Etching, engraving, and enameling in traditional Bohemian styles were added a few short years later. In 1909, the factory was purchased by Sklarske Huty and after World War I, production expanded to include lamp shades and chimneys. During World War II, it was taken over by the Stolze Company. When the Slovak state was formed in 1942, the factory regained independence and was changed to Slovenske Sklene Huty (or simply the Slovak Glassworks). In 1948, it was nationalized under the United Glass Works (or Spojene Sklarne) and produced machine-pressed tableware. In 1992, the factory was privatized under the LR Crystal name and continues to produce machine-made tableware (some marketed under Rona Crystal) and some hand-made artistic wares.

LEER — Refer to LEHR.

LEERDAM GLASSWARE — Refer to ROYAL DUTCH GLASS WORKS.

LEGRAS AND CIE — A French firm established in the late nineteenth century by August J. F. Legras at St. Denis, France, the company was noted most for producing art-styled cameo glass with enameling (marked with "Legras" or "Mont Joye and Cie"). Around 1920, it merged with the Pantin Glassworks and continued to produce art-styled glassware (marked with "Pantin" or "De Vez" – De Vez was a pseudonym for one of the firm's art directors, De Varreux). After the merger, the firm became known as the Verreries et Cristalleries de St. Denis et de Pantin Reunies.

Legras & Cie: Trademarks.

LEHMAN, CASPAR — Lehman (1570-1622) was a German who is usually credited with being the first to use wheels to engrave glass (1590s). He also generally worked with Venetian cristallo and founded an engraver's school in the early seventeenth century.

LEHR — An annealing, or slow-cooling, oven with a moving base that travels slowly through a controlled loss of heat until glass objects are completely cooled, and hence, can be taken out at the opposite end. The rate of speed is adjustable as needed and often takes several hours. Modern lehrs are electrically heated and glass objects travel through them on conveyor belts (prior to conveyors, objects were slowly pushed through brick-lined heated tunnels). Note that lehr has also been spelled as "Leer."

LEIGHTON, WILLIAM — Leighton, one of seven sons of Thomas Leighton (Thomas was an English glassmaker who migrated to America in 1826 to become superintendent of the New England Glass company), began his glass-making career in New England. He patented a process for making silvered glass in 1855, devised a new formula for ruby red glass in 1858, and then went on to join Hobbs, Brockunier, and Company in 1864. At the new firm, he is noted most for inventing lime glass, an inexpensive substitute for lead in making colorless glass. *See also* LIME GLASS.

LEMONESCENT—The English term for Vaseline glass. *See also* VASELINE GLASS.

LENOX, INC. — In 1889, Walter Scott Lenox and Jonathan Cox founded the Ceramic Art Company at Trenton, New Jersey. Lenox left and established his own independent firm in 1906. Lenox is noted most for producing a wide variety of porcelain dishes, tableware, novelties, and collectables. Beginning in the late twentieth century, the firm expanded into glassware, creating a wide variety of collectible glass figurines, stemware, and novelty items. Lenox acquired Bryce Brothers in 1965, but shut down the plant in 1970 (a new plant was built in Mt. Pleasant, Pennsylvania). Lenox also purchased Imperial in 1972 and continued producing glass under the IGC Liquidating Corporation (as a division of Lenox) name until 1982 when he sold it to the Lancaster Colony Corporation. Based in Lawrenceville, New Jersey, Lenox is still a major producer of china and glassware today (glass is produced at the Mt. Pleasant, Pennsylvania, factory).

Lenox, Inc.: Trademark.

LENS — A curved piece of glass used to refract light rays so that they converge or diverge to form an image. Lenses are utilized most in optics for eye-glasses, microscopes, and telescopes.

LETTER-WEIGHT — A large style of paperweight with an oval or rectangular flat base. Some sport a centralized metal ringed handle or glass finial.

LEVEILLE-ROUSSEAU — Eugene Rousseau (1827-1891), a pioneer of the Art Nouveau movement in France, was noted for floral and Oriental designs created in several color effects and styles in his glass creations. He gained much fame at the Paris Art Exhibitions of 1878 and 1884. When he retired in 1885, his pupil and successor, Ernest Baptiste Leveille, continued to produce art-styled glass under the name "Leveille-Rousseau." In 1900, the firm was sold to Harand & Guignard, which continued producing Art Glass up until World War I.

LeVerre — Glass with this mark or signature (also "Le Verre Francais") was produced by French-maker Charles Schneider, who established a factory in 1908 in France. Most products were cameo engraved, exported to the United States, and marketed through Ovington's of New York City. Schneider produced art glass products at his factory until 1933.

LE VERRE FRANCAIS

LeVerre Francais

Le Verre Francais

Charder

LeVerre: Trademarks.

LEVIN, ROBERT — A noted American Studio Glass artisan born in Baltimore, Maryland, in 1948, Levin received his Master of Fine Arts degree from Southern Illinois University and has served in a teaching capacity at the Penland School of Crafts, Pilchuk Glass Center, and Ohio University. Levin also received a North Carolina Arts Council Fellowship (1980) and was chosen to create special presentation objects for the North Carolina Governor's Business Awards in the Arts & Humanities (1980). Levin continues to work as an independent glass artisan in Burnsville, North Carolina.

LEVINE, LOUIS CUT GLASS COMPANY — An American firm founded in 1910 by Louis Levine at New York, New York. Levine produced cut glass tableware and plate glass, and served as a distributor of glass products for others. The firm ceased operations in 1923.

LIBBEY & HOWE — Refer to the MOUNT WASHINGTON GLASS WORKS.

LIBBEY GLASS COMPANY — An American company originally established as the New England Glass Company in 1818; in 1878, it was purchased by William L. Libbey, who transferred the business to his son, Edward Drummond Libbey. In 1888, the firm was moved to Toledo, Ohio, and then became known as the Libbey Glass Company. During the Brilliant period of cut glass production, Libbey became the largest cut glass operation in the world. The firm also continued many of the art styles developed by New England and its most noted designer, Joseph Locke (amberina, cranberry, peachblow, Pomona, maize, etc.). Libbey also produced a good deal of pressed glass tableware and continues to operate today as one of the nation's largest producers of glass. Since 1936, the firm has been part of Owens-Illinois, which still produces glass under the "Libbey" name (Libbey Glass, Inc.). Primary plants are located in Toledo, Ohio; City of Industry, California; Shreveport, Louisiana; and two in Ontario, Canada (Lindsay and Wallaceburg). See also NEW ENGLAND GLASS COMPANY, MICHAEL J. OWENS, and OWENS-ILLINOIS, INC.

Apr. 16, 1901
(for use on pressed
[figured] blanks)

W.L. Libbey & Son

Trademarks.

Reproduction from an early 20th century Libbey advertisement.

LIBBEY-OWENS-FORD (LOF) — Refer to MICHAEL J. OWENS and OWENS-ILLINOIS, INC.

LIBBEY, L. WILLIAM — Libbey began his career in the glass industry as a bookkeeper for the Mount Washington Glass Works (known as Jarves and Cormerais at the time) in 1851. Timothy Howe joined the same firm in 1856 as a clerk, and Libbey and Howe took over the business in 1861. Libbey purchased Howe's (when Howe died) interest in 1866. The firm primarily produced glass lamps and chandeliers. Libbey purchased the New Bedford Glass Company in 1870 and changed its name to the W. L. Libbey Company. A few short years later, he purchased the New England Glass Company (1878) and transferred ownership to his son, Edward Drummond Libbey. See also LIBBEY GLASS COMPANY.

LIBERTY BELL — Glass objects that were either made in the shape of America's Liberty Bell or mold embossed with the bell (usually in relief). Most were made specifically in crystal to celebrate America's Centennial celebration held in Philadelphia, Pennsylvania, in 1876. Some contain additional molded writing such as "100 Years Ago," "1776-1876," and "Declaration of Independence."

Liberty Cut Glass Works — An American company established at Egg Harbor, New Jersey, in 1902, it began as a cut and engraved glass decorating firm that purchased lead glass blanks from European glass firms. In 1910, the name was changed to Liberty Works, and the firm began producing its own glassware. Aside from cut and engraved glass, the company expanded into pressed glass tableware, mostly in color (i.e. the Depression era "American Pioneer" and "Octagon Optic" patterns) before a fire destroyed the factory in 1932.

LIBERTY GLASS COMPANY — Refer to the BARTLETT-COLLINS GLASS COMPANY.

LIBERTY WORKS — Refer to the LIBERTY CUT GLASS WORKS.

LIBISCH, JOSEPH — A noted glass engraver born in Hungary, Libisch served as an apprentice at glass firms in Vienna and Prague. He migrated to America in 1921 and became one of Steuben's primary engravers of the twentieth century.

LID — A covering for closing the mouth of a jar, box, mug, stein, tankard, tea-caddy, or similar object, lids are usually attached to the body of an object with a metal hinge (as opposed to covers that do not contain hinges).

LIGHT BULB — A rounded clear glass object that encloses the light source of an electric lamp or lighting fixture. Light bulbs were invented by Thomas Edison in 1879, which brought on the decline of oil-burning lamps. In modern times, light bulbs come in a huge variety of shapes and sizes, with some made of colored glass.

LIGHTENING-STOPPERED BOTTLE — A style of glass bottle invented in 1875, its name was given to its rounded, expanded lip whereby a closure or stopper (usually made of porcelain) was attached to a rubber ring that was held in place by a clamp. It was a superior design for preventing leaking, as well as to keep the contents sealed; however, it proved too costly and was not used widely.

LILY OF THE VALLEY — A pressed glass pattern that contains the Lily of the Valley flower as its primary design (variations include scrolling, dots, Sandwich-like designs, cables, etc.).

LILY PAD — A name given to a decoration applied to glass objects characterized by a superimposed layer of glass. Several styles of leaves (including lily pads, hence the name), flowers, foliage, and stems were then designed on this layer.

LIME GLASS — A glass formula developed by William Leighton in the 1860s as a substitute for lead glass. Calcined limestone was substituted for lead, which made glass cheaper to produce. Lime glass also cools faster than lead glassware, but is lighter and less resonant. The chemical formula for limestone or calcium carbonate is $CaCO_3$.

LIME ICE GREEN — A light shade or tint of transparent yellowish-green colored glass (the color of ice) usually applied as an iridescence on Carnival Glass. Note that lime is slightly darker than ice green Carnival Glass. Lime green colored glassware with a white opalescent edge or background is sometimes referred to as "Lime Green Opalescent."

LINDFORS GLASBRUK — A Swedish glass-making firm established in 1876, the company produced practical items such as tableware and some colored art forms in typical Swedish styles. The firm was sold to Edward Stromberg, the former head of Orrefors, in 1933. See also STROMBERGSHYTTAN and SWEDISH GLASS.

LINDSHAMMAR GLASBRUK — A Swedish firm founded in 1905 at Vetlanda by German immigrant Robert Rentsch, a glassblower who had previously worked at Kosta, initially the firm produced cut glass tableware and some colored ornamental Swedish art glass. In 1916, the firm was sold to C. J. Petersson, who turned over management to his son, Anton Petersson (1882-1949), and automated tableware was added to the factory's output. When Anton died, the firm was purchased by Erik Hovhammar (b. 1922) and, in the 1950s, he rebuilt the factory. Products included architectural glass blocks, cut lead crystal, machine-pressed tableware, and ornamental wares. The firm is still in operation today.

LINER — A glass object made to fit snugly within another vessel in order to prevent contents, such as food, from coming into contact with the underlying vessel. The underlying vessel may be made of metal, wood, or even glass.

LION — A fancy pressed glass pattern made by Gillinder & Sons in the 1870s, tableware in this pattern usually contains a frosted lion on the base, as a finial on covers, and/or molded directly in to the pattern. Gillinder also produced a miniature five-piece table set in the Lion pattern.

LIP — A short spout or everted projection at the front top edge of a pouring vessel, such as a jug, pitcher, creamer, gravy/sauce boat, measuring cups, and some bowls. See also ICE LIP.

LIPOFSKY, MARVIN — A noted American Studio Glass artisan born in Barrington, Illinois, in 1938, Lipofsky received his Master of Fine Arts degree from the University of Wisconsin and has served in a teaching capacity at the University of Wisconsin, the University of California at Berkeley, and the California College of Arts and Crafts. Lipofsky has also been a guest lecturer at numerous overseas locations, including Japan, and has won many craft/art exhibition awards. He continues to work as an independent glass artisan in Berkeley, California.

LIPPER — A wooden tool shaped like a truncated cone, with handle, used to form lips on certain vessels.

LIPPINCOTT GLASS COMPANY — An American firm established in the early twentieth century at Alexandria, Indiana, initially, the company produced lighting-related glassware (i.e. globes, shades, and lamp chimneys); however, they converted to the production of stemware and tableware in the 1920s (decoration/colored Depression patterns include "Bird of Paradise," "Cut Commodore," "Cut Windsor," "Hammered White Gold," "Mother O' Pearl," "Petalon," "Real," "Vintage," and "Waltham"). Like many companies, they did not survive America's Depression Era.

LIQUEUR OR LIQUOR GLASS — A very small stemmed and footed glass resembling a cordial glass. Liqueur glasses generally have a capacity between one and two ounces and are designed to drink alcoholic beverages in small amounts.

LITHARGE — Lead monoxide (PbO), or red lead, used in making quality lead crystal glassware. See also LEAD and RED LEAD.

LITHYALIN — An oily free-flowing marbled or swirled enameled technique patented by Bohemian decorator Friedrich Egermann. It was produced by Egermann from 1828 to 1840, and copied by others up until about 1855. The appearance mimicked that of semi-precious swirled stones and was made mostly in red, though other color effects were created. One style of greenish-gray lithyalin was referred to as "Chamaleon-Glas" (German for chameleon glass) and was created in 1835. See also EGERMANN, FRIEDRICH.

An 1830s Lithyalin box by Friedrich Egermann. *Courtesy of the Corning Museum of Glass.*

LITTLETON, HARVEY — A professor of ceramics at the University of Wisconsin who began his university career in 1951. Littleton (b. 1922) received his Master of Fine Arts degree from the Cranbrook Academy of Art in 1951 and has taught at numerous universities while winning many awards as a glass artisan. In March 1962, he held a workshop at the Toledo Museum of Art and proved that art glass could be blown by independent artists in small studios. He established a new graduate design program at Wisconsin and is credited with spawning the new Studio Art Glass Movement in America in the late twentieth century; and hence, a good deal of independent artisans, many who make paperweights today. After retiring from university life, Littleton continued to work as an independent artist in Spruce Pine, North Carolina.

LIVERPOOL GLASS MANUFACTURING COMPANY — Refer to the EAST LIVERPOOL GLASS MANUFACTURING COMPANY, LTD.

LOBMEYR, J & L — An Austrian glass operation established in 1822 by Josef Lobmeyr (1792-1855), who first opened a retail store on Kartner Strasse in Vienna and then later built a glasshouse and gradually employed glass workers. The company specialized in cut and engraved glass tableware, but produced some Bohemian-styled ornamental wares as well. The firm was carried on by his sons, Josef Lobmeyr II (1828-1864) and Ludwig (1829-1917). Ludwig actually joined in 1860 and the firm became officially known as J & L Lobmeyr. After that it was purchased by the Rath family (August Rath was the brother-in-law of the two brothers). In 1945, it became a state-controlled glass operation by the new Czechoslovakian government, but is still managed by the Rath family today. The firm is noted for Bohemian-style glass, enameled and iridescent art glass, tableware, and crystal lighting fixtures such as chandeliers.

LOBMILLER DECORATING COMPANY — An American firm established by John and Joseph Lobmiller at Wellsburg, West Virginia, in 1893. The Lobmillers decorated glass made by others primarily by gilding and ruby flashing. In 1911, the company was purchased by the Crescent Glass Company, which continued to operate Lobmiller as a subsidiary. See also CRESCENT GLASS COMPANY.

LOCKE, JOSEPH — An English pioneer in the Art Glass field who moved to America in 1882, Locke (1846-1936) is noted for designing and creating several varieties of Art Glass, including agata, cameo styles, amberina, plated amberina, and pomona, most while working for the New England/Libbey Glass Firm. In the early 1890s, he opened his own art glass studio and continued producing art glass until his death (signed "Locke" or "Locke Art").

Trademarks.

LOETZ OR LOTZ GLASS — The original factory was founded by Johann Eisenstein in 1836 at Klostermuhle, Bohemia (Austria). In 1840, Johann Lotz (1778-1844) acquired the firm, which was continued by his widow, Susanna, and her second husband, Dr. Franz Gerstner, after Lotz's death. The two renamed it as "Johann Lotz Witwe" (The Widow of John Lotz). The majority of art glass was produced with the "Lotz" or "Loetz" namesake under his nephew's direction (Maximilian Ritter Von Spaun II, 1856-1909) beginning in the late 1870s (Von Spaun assumed control of glass production as a manager in 1979) into the early 1900s. The firm produced a huge amount of iridescent art-styled glass similar to Tiffany's favrile, along with some black and white styles. In 1889 and 1900, they won grand prizes at exhibitions in Paris, as well as numerous medals through the years. In 1900, the firm's name was given the English spelling of "Loetz" purposefully to represent the international nature of the firm. In 1908, Maximilian II turned operations over to his son, Maximilian III. The company declared bankruptcy in 1913 and the firm's creditors gained some measure of control, including renaming it "Johann Lotz Witwe G.M.B.H." Operations were suspended in 1914 because of World War I, briefly revived after the war, and then nearly ended when a fire destroyed the factory in 1930. Although they filed for bankruptcy in 1931, the factory was rebuilt, however, they went back into receivership in 1939. The factory and all support buildings were demolished in 1947.

Trademarks.

An early 20th century Loetz iridescent vase.
Photo courtesy of the Corning Museum of Glass.

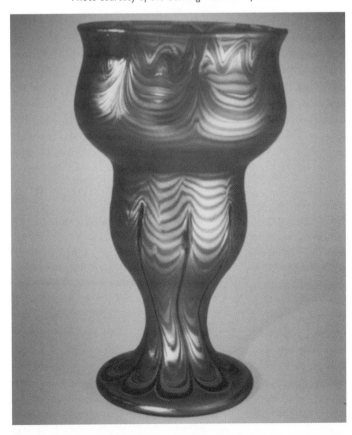

LOG CABIN — A unique set of pressed pattern-ware created by the Central Glass Company in the 1870s. Tableware in this pattern consists of pieces in the shape of rectangular log cabins complete with mold-embossed doors, windows, shingles, trim, logs along the edges, and a chimney that serves as a finial for covered dishes. Many were mounted on circular bases and stems.

LOG GLASS — Refer to HOUR GLASS.

LONACONING GLASS COMPANY — Refer to the DUGAN GLASS COMPANY.

LONG ISLAND FLINT GLASSWORKS — An American glass company established at Brooklyn, New York, in 1852. The firm produced some lead cut crystal tableware and was purchased by German immigrant and noted glass cutter Christian Dorflinger in 1860. The factory remained in operation until 1863.

LOOP — A molded decoration common in pressed glass consisting of a large oval or set of concentric ovals. In turn, there may be several adjacent or interlocking ovals to complete an all-over pattern. Loops may be further decorated with other designs within their borders and are often combined with others to form unique pattern combinations (i.e. beaded loop, loop and dart with round ornaments, loop and fan, looped cord, loop and moose eye, loop with dewdrop, loops and drops, loop and pillar, oval loop, petal and loop, scalloped or yoked loop, stippled loop, loops with stippled panels, etc.).

LOOPING — A decorating technique formed by a series of threaded arcs that usually extend above or outward from the rim of a vessel. Ordinarily, the arcs or loops are not applied to the surface of the object, but may be attached to the edge or rim.

Cranberry glass pitcher with opalescent looping. *Courtesy of Wheaton Village.*

LORNETA GLASS COMPANY — An American firm founded by Max G. Biberthaler at Point Marion, Pennsylvania, in 1944. Biberthaler had previously served as president with the New Martinsville Glass Company. The company produced blown and pressed glass (mostly milk glass) prior to closing in 1950.

LOST COAST ART GLASS — A contemporary art glass firm established in California in 2000 by Jesse Taj and Jared DeLong. DeLong had previously worked for Lundberg Studios. Taj creates art glass using the murrhine technique while DeLong concentrates on lampworking and cutting.

LOST WAX PROCESS — Refer to CIRE PERDUE.

LOTUS CUT GLASS COMPANY — Refer to LOTUS GLASS COMPANY, INC.

LOTUS GLASS COMPANY, INC. — An American decorating firm originally established as the Lotus Cut Glass Company at Barnesville, Ohio in 1911. Matthew Hanse was an early employee and acquired the company soon after. As the era of cut glass ended in America around World War I, the firm changed from cutting glass blanks (provided by others) to decorating machine-pressed and blown tableware, tumblers, stemware, and novelties (a good deal with etching, enameling – including silk screening, hand-painting, silver deposit, and/ or gold or platinum banding). Note that the company continued to decorate some of their products with limited cutting and engraving too. When Matthew passed on, his son Francis Hanse inherited the firm until he, too, passed away in 1994; the company closed down a short time afterward.

Lotus Glass Company, Inc.: Trademark.

LOTZ — Refer to "Loetz or Lotz Glass."

Iridescent glass by Johann Lotz.

LOUIE GLASS COMPANY — A small pressed glass manufacturer established at Weston, West Virginia, in 1926 by Louie Wohinc, a glassworker who had several glass interests in the Weston area. Wohinc served as manager of the Weston Glass Company, a small firm that he acquired in 1919. He also acquired the West Virginia Glass Specialty Company and the Crescent Window Glass plant in 1929. Similar products were made at the various plants, mostly machine-pressed tableware, which, during the 1920s and 1930s, included colored Depression Glass. The Weston Glass Company ended when the plant was destroyed by fire in 1932. The West Virginia Specialty Company's plant closed in 1987; however, glass is still produced under the Louis Glass Company name today in Weston. See also LUDWIG GLASS COMPANY.

LOVING CUP — A glass drinking vessel, with or without a foot, that usually contains two or three handles. Loving cups were often passed around at celebrations or even shared by more than one person during a single drinking.

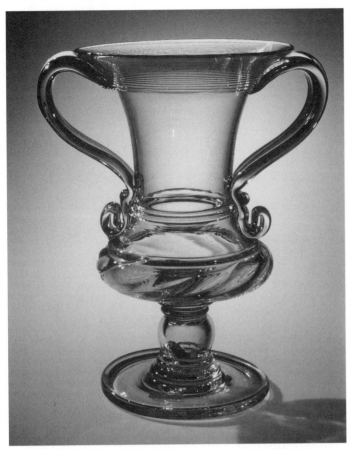

A crystal urn/loving cup by the New England Glass Co., 1837-1840. *Photo by Robin Rainwater. Item courtesy of the Corning Museum of Glass.*

LOW RELIEF — An engraving process where the background is cut away to a very low degree, like that of a coin. *See also RELIEF CUTTING, MEDIUM RELIEF, and HIGH RELIEF.*

LR CRYSTAL — Refer to LEDNICKE ROVNE GLASSWORKS.

LUDWIG GLASS COMPANY — An American glass-making firm established at Glenville, West Virginia, by Louis Wohinc in 1940, the company produced decorated and cut vases, beverage sets, and stemware before closing in 1951. Note that "Ludwig" is also spelled "Ludwik."

LUG — A small but solid attachment, like an ear or knob, that serves as a device for lifting, grasping, or holding an object. Unlike handles, lugs are generally much smaller and do not contain space for fingers to be passed through (some, like certain flasks, may have an opening for a carrying strap to be passed through).

LUM, WILLIAM H. AND SON — An American cut glass firm established in 1869 by William Lum and his son, Elmer. Lum primarily sold the products of other cut glassmakers until opening his own factory in 1885. The firm expanded into bottles and tableware until closing in 1929. Note that the firm was also known briefly as "Lum and Ogden" in the mid-1870s.

Lum, William H. & Son: Trademark.

LUM AND OGDEN — Refer to LUM, WILLIAM H. AND SON.

LUMINARC — A modern brand of crystal glass tableware produced under the Arc International glass conglomerate. *See also ARC INTERNATIONAL.*

LUMINOR — A small night light or lighting fixture made of clear or light transparent-colored glass used as a covering to hide an electric light. Frederick Carder of Steuben is credited with inventing them (most of Steuben's creations were in the shape of crystal birds such as eagles).

LUNCHEON PLATE — A flat glass object, usually round in shape and about 8" in diameter (an inch or two smaller than a dinner plate but larger than a salad plate), used for serving lunch.

LUNDBERG STUDIOS — A contemporary American Art Glass firm founded by brothers James and Steven Lundberg, along with Rebecca Lundberg, in 1972 at Davenport, California. James had studied glassblowing at San Jose State University. The firm was later joined by noted artisan Daniel Salazar. The company specializes in iridescent art forms including a wide variety of paperweights and vases. Steven eventually left to establish the Steven Lundberg Art Glass with his son Justin.

Lundberg Studios globe paperweight. *Photo by Robin Rainwater.*

LUSTER — A general term for the appearance of glass whose outer surface is finished with a high gloss or a radiant colorful finish. Bright, lustrous glass is usually created by painting the surface with acidized ,metallic oxides, and then firing them on (similar to iridescence). *See also LUSTRED.*

LUSTERLESS — A style of Art Glass created by the Mount Washington Glass Works in the early 1880s. It is an off-white colored glass produced by an all-over hydrofluoric acid bath. The final finish appears like a soft alabaster. Multicolored enameled scenes were applied to the exterior, including foliage/floral motifs, forest/village scenes, and some pond/lake themes. Primary items produced in this style were vases, bottles, tableware, paperweights, and novelty items.

LUSTRE — Lustre was also a name given to iridized glass made by the Jain Glass Works of India. *See also LUSTRED, GIRANDOLE, MANTEL LUSTRE, and JAIN GLASS WORKS.*

L

LUSTRE ART GLASS COMPANY — An American company established at Maspeth on Long Island, New York, by Conrad Vahlsing (son-in-law and former employee of Quezal) and Paul Frank in 1920, the firm produced some iridescent glassware including semi-opaque Art Glass lamp shades that served as a cheaper imitation of Tiffany's FAVRILLE (nearly identical to those made by the Quezal Art Glass Company). The firm closed in 1929. *See also* QUEZAL ART GLASS AND DECORATING COMPANY.

A blown-molded lampshade by the Lustre Art Glass Co. of New York, 1920s. *Photo courtesy of the Corning Museum of Glass.*

LUSTRED — An iridescent form or finish applied to glass by use of a brush. Brushes are used to apply metallic salt solutions to glass that has already been cooled to room temperature. The glass is then placed in a lehr to fire-on the lustrous iridescent finish. Lustred glass is also referred to as "Lustre Painting."

LUTZ GLASS — A thin clear glass striped with colored twists first created by Nicholas Lutz of the Boston & Sandwich Glass Company. Lutz worked there from 1869 to 1888 and his creations are sometimes referred to as "Striped Glass" or "Candy Stripe Glass." Lutz was born in Lorraine, France, where he also worked as a blower. He migrated to America in 1869 and joined the Boston & Sandwich Glass Company. When the firm closed in 1888, Lutz moved to Mt. Washington, and then to the Union Glass Company. Lutz is also noted for producing paperweights, marbles with goldstone stripes (referred to as "Lutz" marbles), and other Venetian-styled glassware.

LUZERNE CUT GLASS COMPANY — An American firm established in the early 1900s in West Pittson, Pennsylvania. Under the operation of O. S. Atterholt, the company produced some cut glass products before going out of business in 1929.

Luzerne Cut Glass Company: Trademark.

LYON, JAMES B. AND COMPANY — Refer to the UNION FLINT GLASS WORKS.

LYONS CUT GLASS COMPANY — An American firm founded in 1903 at Lyons, New York, by William Baltzel, James Bashford, Chester Blaine, William Burrell, George Getman, Albert Marshall, and Louis Smith, the company purchased lead crystal blanks from both American and European firms and produced cut glass until 1906.

Lyons Cut Glass Company: Trademark.

Mm

{ Mm }

MAASTRICHT — A ceramics and glass firm founded in the Netherlands in 1827 by Petrus Regout at Maastricht. Regout initially obtained crystal blanks from the Belgian firm of Val St. Lambert and operated as a cutting shop. In 1839, a glass factory was built and named Petrus Regout & Co. The firm continued to produce ceramics, cut and engraved crystal, and some pressed glass tableware. The name was changed to NV Kristal in 1899 and, in 1925, it merged with another glass company called Stella at Meerssen. The name was further changed to NV Kristalunie Maastricht, but is usually referred to as simply Maastricht or NV Crystal. After the merger, the firm still specialized in cut and engraved glass; however, more colored ornamental wares were produced from commissioned artists. In 1959, the company was incorporated into the United Glassworks, which produces container glass only at the Maastricht factory today.

MACBETH-EVANS GLASS COMPANY — An American company established in Pennsylvania and Indiana in 1899 when plants owned by George MacBeth and Thomas Evans merged. Evans started a pressed glass firm known as Reddick & Company in Pittsburgh, Pennsylvania, with James Reddick in 1869 (the plant itself was called the Crescent Glass Works). Reddick retired in 1873 and the firm became Evans, Sell & Company; and then Evans & Company in 1877. In 1881, Evans sold out and went on to establish the Crescent Glass Works of Thomas Evans & Company. In the meantime, George MacBeth, along with some others, originally purchased the Keystone Flint Glass Works in Pittsburgh in 1872 and produced pressed glass until 1880. The firm closed and MacBeth went on to lease the White House factory once occupied by Atterbury & Company under the Geo. A. MacBeth & Company name (later abandoned in 1895). MacBeth also built a new plant in Elwood, Indiana, in 1890 while Evans built one in Marion, Indiana, in 1892. MacBeth was a scientific/optical glassmaker while Evans was primarily a manufacturer of lamp chimneys. After the merger in 1899, MacBeth-Evans continued briefly as a hand operation, but switched to machine pressed patterns during the early twentieth century. In 1936, they were acquired by Corning, which continues to operate the Charleroi, Pennsylvania, plant today. The firm continued producing optics and lamp chimneys as well as many machine-pressed tableware patterns. Patterns attributed to MacBeth-Evans include "American Sweetheart," "Chinex," "Cremax," "Dogwood" or "Apple Blossom" or "Wild Rose," "Petalware," "S" or "Stippled Rose Band," and "Thistle."

Macbeth-Evans Glass Company: Trademark.

MACE, FLORA — A noted American Studio Glass artisan born in Exeter, New Hampshire, in 1949, Mace received her Master of Fine Arts Degree from the University of Illinois and has served in a teaching capacity at the Pilchuk Glass School, the Haystack Mountain School of Crafts, and at Nordisk Glass '85 in Reykjavik, Iceland. She continues to work as an independent glass artisan in Seattle, Washington.

Giant fruit by Flora Mace and Joey Kirkpatrick.

MACEDOINE — A somewhat haphazard jumble of canes or filigree twists that were once known as an end-of-day scrambled paperweight.

MAGEE-DIETERS — Refer to the McGEE-DIETERS GLASS COMPANY.

MAGNIFYING GLASS OR LENS — A convex or curved piece of glass used to refract light rays in order to enlarge an image; they are used in eye glasses (i.e. bifocals or trifocals), binoculars, microscopes, telescopes, and handheld magnifying glasses.

MAGNOR GLASSVERK — Refer to JOHANSFORS.

MAGNUM — A rather large paperweight, there is some debate in the paperweight community as to what size qualifies one as "magnum" status: some indicate that it must exceed four inches in diameter while others put it as low as exceeding 3-1/4 inches (note that most standard paperweights are made in the 2-1/2" to 3-1/4" range).

MAIZE GLASS — A style of art glass created by Joseph Locke for the New England Glass Company (and Libbey) that was patented in 1889, it is characterized by an opaque white or cream color (the color of sweet corn) with molded vertical rows of corn. Partial husks that end in wavy tips are ordinarily made of green or brown and rise from the bottom of each object. Maize was made in a good deal of functional tableware.

Libbey Maize glass bowl. *Courtesy of Wheaton Village.*

M

Libbey Maize glass muffineer and spooner.
Courtesy of Wheaton Village.

MAJESTIC CUT GLASS COMPANY — An American firm established at Elmira, New York, in 1900 by Wolf Spiegel and his son, Saul Spiegel, the company produced cut glass tableware up until World War I.

Majestic Cut Glass Company: Trademark.

M

MALERAS GLASBRUK — A Swedish firm founded in Sweden's Smaland District in 1924. Early on, the firm produced tableware as well as some art glass. Noted engraver Mats Jonasson entered the firm in 1959 as an apprentice, but left ten years later to join Kosta. In 1965, Maleras became part of Flygsfors and then part of Krona-Bruken (also known as Royal Krona) in 1974. After Jonasson returned in 1975, Krona went bankrupt two years later. It was purchased by Kosta-Boda; however, they decided to close the factory in 1980. Jonasson, along with several employees and villagers, pooled their resources to purchase to company. Under Jonasson's direction, the firm is known for its reverse engraved glass ice blocks, most with images of wildlife. In 1988, Jonasson purchased a controlling interest in Maleras and currently serves as both managing director and chief engraver. *See also* ICE BLOCK OR SCULPTURE *and* MATS JONASSON.

A Mats Jonasson ice sculpture for Maleras Glasbruck of Sweden.

MALLORYTOWN GLASS WORKS — A Canadian company founded in 1825 in Mallorytown, Ontario, the firm was Canada's first glassmaker that produced blown vessels and containers. The firm closed in 1840.

MALTESE — Refer to JACOB'S LADDER.

MALTESE CROSS — A style of design applied to Christian, Jewish, and Syrian glass bottles through the fourth and seventh centuries. One side (usually the front) contains the cross; some contain the cross raised above a relief column or altar. In the nineteenth and early twentieth centuries, Maltese Cross designs appeared in both pressed and cut glass designs.

Maltese Cross patterned pressed glass plate.
Photo by Robin Rainwater.

MAL'TSEV GLASSWORKS — A Russian glass factory founded in 1723 by Vasily Mal'tsev near Moscow, the firm first produced some practical wares before being forced to close by the State for fear of fire in 1746. Operations were moved to Gusev, and Dyat'kov expanded into enameled wares, cut crystal, and some art-styled glass (the Dyat'kov location became known as the Dyat'kov Crystal Works in 1793). After the Russian Revolution in 1917, the entire Mal'tsev operation became part of the Dyat'kov Crystal Works. Note that the English spelling of "Mal'tsev" is sometimes given as "Maltsov."

MANDARIN GLASS — Refer to PEKING GLASS.

MANDARIN YELLOW — An Art Glass form developed by Frederick Carder of Steuben in 1916, it is characterized by a translucent yellow color (like the yellow color of porcelain made during the Ming Dynasty in China). It was only made in small quantities since the formula turned out to be very fragile and easily cracked.

MANGANESE — A grayish-white hard metallic element that, when oxidized (manganese oxide) and added to a batch of glass, produces various amethyst or purple hues. When combined with cobalt and iron, it produces a dark amethyst nearly black. At high temperatures, manganese can also turn glass to pale brown, an off-yellow, and even a somewhat murky green color. Manganese dioxide (also known as pyrolusite) is added to most batches of lead crystal, serving as a de-colorizing agent to neutralize the greenish/brownish color imparted by trace amounts of iron found in most sands. The neutralizing compound is sometimes referred to as "Glass Soap" or "Glassmaker's Soap" since it is said to clean up the murky color inherent in iron/sand. *See also* BLACK AMETHYST *and* BLACK GLASS.

MANNINGTON ART GLASS COMPANY — An American firm founded at Mannington, West Virginia, in the mid-1920s, the company produced small pressed glass novelty items including cuff link boxes, match holders, plates, pen boxes, pin trays, pomade and/or powder jars, salt dips, soap dishes, stamp boxes, toothpick holders, and toy mugs. The company ceased operation in the early 1940s, and all molds were then acquired by the John E. Kemple Glass Works.

MANSON, WILLIAM — Manson joined the Caithness Glass Company in 1966 as an apprentice glassblower. He left and studied under Paul Ysart before returning to Caithness in 1974. After becoming one of the firm's leading glass blowers and paperweight makers, Manson left. He continues to make paperweights on his own.

MANTLE LUSTRE — A decorative candle-holder or vase for use above fireplaces, mantle lustres usually contain attached cut glass prisms. *See also GIRANDOLE.*

A Victorian mantle luster. *Item courtesy of the Wichita Museum.*

MAPLE CITY GLASS COMPANY — An American firm established in 1910 in Honesdale, Pennsylvania, by J. S. O'Connor, the company produced some limited cut glassware into the early 1920s before selling out to T. B. Clark.

Reproduction from a 1910 Maple City Cut Glass catalog.

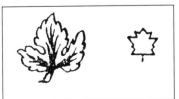

Trademarks.

MARBLE — A small glass sphere, or ball made of glass, used in playing the game "marbles." Marbles come in a variety of sizes and decorating styles. Some are a solid color (transparent or opaque) while others contain one or more colored swirls. Originally, marbles were hand-made spheres using tiny molds; however, during the late nineteenth and early twentieth centuries, a variety of marble-making machines were invented. Rare marbles may contain sulphide figures within. Marbles also have industrial uses (as an aerosol mixing can ball, ball bearings, and in the perforation of oil bearing geological strata). *See also CANDY STRIPE, CAT EYE, PURIE, and SHOOTER.*

MARBLED GLASS — Glass objects with single or multiple color swirls made to resemble natural-occurring marble limestone. Ordinarily, two or more pots of various-colored glass are melted and then combined into one pot (usually one of the colors is opaque white). The colors are then intermingled, reheated, and formed or pressed into their final shape. Marbled glass has also been called agate, calico, mosaic, onyx, and slag. In paperweights, Marbrie or Marbled designs are those that consist of looped colored bands emanating from a cane at the top of the weight and then running down the sides to the bottom.

MARBLE KING — An American marble-making company established when Berry Pink and Sellers Peltier bought out the Alley Glass Manufacturing in 1949 at St. Marys, West Virginia. The St. Marys plant burned in 1958 and operations, including the surviving machines, were moved to Paden City, West Virginia. In 1963, the firm was purchased by Duncan Peltier, Cornell Medley, and Roger Howdyshell, with Howdyshell becoming sole owner in 1983. The company still produces marbles under the Marble King name. *See also ALLEY AGATE COMPANY.*

M

Marbles by Marble King. *Courtesy of Wheaton Village.*

MARIGOLD — The most common iridized form of Carnival Glass, Marigold consists of a flashed-on iridescent orange color created by spraying on a mixture of metallic salts. The effect is produced by the addition of selenium and cadmium sulfide. *See also IRIDESCENT.*

Carnival Glass tumblers in cobalt and marigold colors. *Photo by Robin Rainwater.*

MARINOT, MAURICE — Marinot (1882-1960) was one of France's most noteworthy glass artisans of the early twentieth century. He began as a studio artist in 1911 producing functional but highly decorated items such as bowls and bottles. In 1923, he began producing monstrous abstract art sculptures in opaque glass, swirling and streaking, gold-speckled, and bubbled effects. He retired in 1937 from glass-making, but continued on as a painter. His studio was destroyed in 1944 by extensive bombing during World War II.

A 1934 Acid Etched vase by Maurice Marinot. *Courtesy of the Corning Museum of Glass.*

MARK — An inscription or imprint on glassware indicating the place it was made and/or the artist who created it. Typically, the mark is etched, engraved, or impressed on the bottom of a glass object.

MARLBORO STREET GLASS WORKS — Refer to the KEENE GLASS WORKS.

MARMALADE DISH — Refer to JELLY DISH.

MARMALADE JAR — Refer to JAM JAR.

MARQUETRY — A decorating technique in which hot glass pieces are applied to molten glass and then marvered onto the surface creating an inlaid effect. Marquetry is a common decoration in wood and was developed for glass by French artisan Emile Galle around 1897. The French term is "Marqueterie de Verre." *See also* GALLE.

MARQUIS, RICHARD — A noted American Studio Glass artisan born in Bumblebee, Arizona, in 1945, Marquis received his Master of Arts degree from the University of California, Berkeley, and has served in a teaching capacity at the University of Washington, Seattle; San Francisco State University; and the University of California (both at Berkeley and Los Angeles). He has also been a guest designer with Venini Fabrica at Venice, Italy. Marquis continues to work as an independent glass artisan in Freeland, Washington.

MARRIAGE GLASS — A glass vessel (usually a goblet or other drinking glas) made and decorated to commemorate a marriage. Most contain inscriptions with either gold/silver enameling or etching/engraving.

MARVER — A marble, metal, or stone plate/base on which blown glass is rolled upon and shaped. Marvers are also used to pick up tiny surface embellishments, such as mica or gold leaf, as a molten object is rolled over them (sometimes referred to as "Pick-up Decoration"). Marver derives from the French word for marble, "Marbre."

A blown-molded lampshade by the Lustre Art Glass Co. of New York, 1920s. *Photo courtesy of the Corning Museum of Glass.*

MARY GREGORY — Clear and colored glassware (commonly pastel pink) decorated with white enamel designs of one or more boys and/or girls playing in Victorian scenes. Mary Gregory actually worked as a decorator for the Boston and Sandwich Glass Co. from 1870-1880, but did not decorate the glass of her namesake. The original Mary Gregory was produced in Bohemia in the late nineteenth century and has been made in a wide variety of styles throughout Europe and America in the twentieth and twenty-first centuries. Note that the term "Mary Gregory" was not associated with this style of glass until the 1920s; prior to that, it was known as "Painted Cameo" or "Poor Man's Cameo."

Mary Gregory cruet and tumbler. *Photo by Robin Rainwater.*

Mary Gregory glassware. *Photo by Robin Rainwater.*

MASCOT — Refer to HOOD ORNAMENT.

MASK — A relief or three-dimensional decorative object made in the shape of a face. Those made of glass originated with ancient Egyptians. Mask also refers to a relief form that may be applied to another object such as a vase or bowl or as a stand-alone art object in the shape of a face or mask.

MASON FRUIT JAR COMPANY — An American company founded at Philadelphia, Pennsylvania, in 1885, the firm produced blown glass fruit/canning jars along with some pressed glass necks and lids for the jars. The firm closed in 1900. The name "Mason Jar" originated with this company and became a generic term for fruit/canning jars. *See also* CANNING JAR.

Mason canning jar. *Photo by Robin Rainwater.*

MASON JAR — Refer to CANNING JAR and the MASON FRUIT JAR COMPANY.

MASONIC GLASSWARE — Glass objects decorated with Masonic symbols, emblems, or inscriptions.

MASSELLO — A Venetian term for the technique in which pre-formed colored shapes are cased in clear glass.

MASSILLON GLASS TABLEWARE COMPANY — Refer to the STOEHR GLASS COMPANY.

MASTER GLASS COMPANY — An American marble-making company founded by Clinton Israel in 1941 at Bridgeport, West Virginia. Israel had previously worked for Akro Agate and had been an officer (Secretary) with the Master Marble Company. Israel acquired some materials (i.e. boxes, marble stock, formulas, etc.) from Akro Agate when that firm closed in 1951; Israel also purchased the right to use Akro Agate's trademark. The firm expanded into making pressed glass tableware and signal and automotive lenses. The company closed in 1973; Israel passed away in 1975.

Master Glass Company: Trademark.

MASTER MARBLE COMPANY — An American marble-making firm founded in 1930 at Anmoore, West Virginia, by a group of employees who had previously worked for Akro Agate (John Early, Claude Grimmett, and John Moulton). Another former Akro employee, Clinton Israel, joined them soon after. The company produced glass marbles until 1941, when its land and buildings were sold to the National Carbon Company. Clinton Israel was able to purchase the marble-making machinery and went on to establish the Master Glass Company at Bridgeport, West Virginia. *See also* MASTER GLASS COMPANY.

MATCH SAFE — A small container used to safely carry matches in one's pocket. Match safes date back to around the 1850s and were made of metal (tin, silver brass, etc.). Later examples were produced in glass and porcelain.

MATSU-NO-KE — An art style decoration created by Frederick Carder for Stevens and Williams in the 1880s. It is characterized by applied gnarled branches of ornamental pine trees that serve as a crystal or an iridized color decoration on the surface of glass objects. The base of the objects may be clear or colored as well. Note that "Matzu" in Japan is the name for pine tree. Carder also used this decorating style for Steuben in the 1920s.

MATTE — A dull finish as opposed to a gloss or luster. Smooth matte finishes are applied to glassware usually with an all-over hydrofluoric acid bath or by shallow engraving. Matte is also spelled "Mat" or "Matt."

MAUDER, BRUNE — Mauder (1877-1948) was a noted German glass artisan who began producing naturalistic art sculptures in contrast to the more abstract items created during Europe's Art Nouveau period. He is also noted for many frosted styles of glass, and taught glass-making at Zwiesel, influencing many future artisans.

MAYER FAMILY — In 1906, Michael Mayer opened a glass cutting shop at Port Jervis, New York. The shop was relocated in Brooklyn, New York, in 1910. When Mayer died, his son, Edward W. Mayer, assumed control. When Edward died in 1933, the shop was run by the Gillinder Brothers, who purchased it in 1935.

MAYONNAISE DISH — A small flat or shallow indented dish used specifically for serving mayonnaise. Mayonnaise dishes may have matching under plates and/or serving spoons/ladles.

Reproduction from a late 19th century Higgins-Seiter catalog.

No. 35P. Lorraine Mayon-aise Bowl and Plate
5 in' Each............$5.20

MAZARENE BLUE — A light purplish blue similar to the ultramarine that is typically used as a ground or overlay color in paperweights.

McCULLY AND COMPANY — Refer to the PHOENIX GLASS COMPANY and UNION FLINT GLASS WORKS.

McDONALD GLASS WORKS, INC. — A short-lived American firm that operated in McDonald, Pennsylvania, in the latter 1920s, the company produced some blown stemware, tumblers, and beverage sets. They were out of business by 1929.

McGEE-DIETERS GLASS COMPANY — An American glass decorating firm established at Brilliant, Ohio, in 1904 by N. H. and L. J. McGee, along with W. E. Dieters, the company specialized in decorating glass by gilding and ruby-flashing. The company remained in business until 1912; the decorating facility was then purchased by the Pennsylvania Glass Manufacturing Company (manufacturers of lighting glassware). Note that the firm has been misspelled in many old journals and publications and listed erroneously as Dieters and McGee, Dieters-McKee, and Magee-Dieters.

McKANNA CUT GLASS COMPANY — An American firm established at Honesdale, Pennsylvania, in 1906, the company produced cut glass products before closing in 1927.

McKanna Cut Glass Company: Trademarks.

McKEE BROTHERS — An American company founded in Pittsburgh, Pennsylvania, by three McKee brothers (James, Thomas, and Samuel McKee) in 1834; it went through many name changes early on (S. McKee and Co.; J. and F. McKee in 1850 when Frederick McKee joined; Bryce, McKee and Co. from 1850 to 1854; and McKee and Brothers in 1865). The firm was moved to Jeannette, Pennsylvania, in 1889 and briefly joined the National Glass Company in 1899 (until 1904). McKee began as a hand operation and continued producing a wide variety of pressed glass tableware, including milk glass, and a line they named "Prescut" (imitation cut glass or pressed glass that resembled cut glass) until 1951, when the company became a division of the Thatcher Glass Company. Throughout the twentieth century, the company switched to automation and expanded into industrial glass products (signal lenses, auto headlights for the Ford Motor Company, lighting glassware, etc). Thatcher purchased McKee in 1951, but sold off about three hundred of the original McKee molds to the John E. Kemple Glass Works throughout the 1950s. Thatcher converted to full automation (thus they had no use for the old molds) and continued to used the McKee name until 1961, when they were purchased by the Jeannette Glass Company. Jeannette closed in 1983.

M

LAUREL PATTERN TABLEWARE
New French Ivory Glass Dinnerware

Reproduction from a 1936 McKee advertisement.

Trademarks.

PRESCUT

MDINA GLASS — A style of Art Glass that was first produced in Malta in 1969 by Michael Harris (1933-1994). Mdina glass is characterized by two primary color schemes; turquoise with amber streaks and brownish-amber glass with yellow and green streaks. Most products made in this style are vases and novelty items (a small seahorse sculpture has been the most prolific piece made). Due to political troubles in Malta, Harris moved on to form Isle of Wight Glass while Mdina was run by Eric Dobson until 1981 and then by Joseph Said afterward.

MEAD GLASS — An English goblet invented in the seventeenth century containing a shallow bowl, stemmed foot, and inverted rim. Others were much like a tumbler with a kick base. Whatever the style, they were used for drinking mead, a fermented mixture made of honey, water, and yeast. Mead glasses were most popular during the seventeenth and eighteenth centuries in Europe.

MEASURING BOTTLE — A style of bottle whose capacity is some specified volume. Common items produced as early as the seventeenth century in Europe were specifically designed to hold such capacities as one pint (16 ounces), one quart (32 ounces), one gallon, etc. Some contain mold or enameled lines directly on the object for measuring specific amounts. Modern European designs contain metric measurements (American designs contain both English and metric).

MEASURING CUP — An open, somewhat bowl-shaped or cylindrical vessel, usually with a handle and small spout, whose capacity contains a series of graduated measurements. One cup units are the most common and contain measurements ranging from one ounce to eight ounces,

as well as fractional measurements too. Beginning in the 1960s in America, most cups contain cross-listed measurements with the metric system. Larger measuring cups have also been produced, i.e. 1-1/2 cup, 2-cup, 3-cup, 4-cup, etc. Some, particularly during the Depression era, may have more than one handle and spout.

MEASURING GLASS — An open, cylindrical vessel, usually in the shape of a tumbler, whose capacity contains a series of graduated measurements. Variations include those with pouring spouts, English and/or metric measurements, and pouring lips. Size can vary from small shot glass size tumblers to those that hold several cups. Note that a measuring glass is much like a measuring cup; the primary difference is that measuring glasses do not sport handles.

MEDALLION — A circular or oval (though shapes may vary) decoration in the form of a portrait, emblem, picture, commemorative, or inscription; most are made in low relief and bare the portraits of famous people, replica coins, historical subjects or symbols, or simple decorations as in some pressed glass patterns (beaded oval or grape medallion and medallion sunburst for instance). Medallions in the form of sulphides are a common theme in paperweights. *See also* SULPHIDE.

An early fourth century A.D. Roman Glass Medallion.
Photo courtesy of the Corning Museum of Glass.

MEDICI PAPAL GLASSWARE — A series of decorative glass objects (ewers, vases, and other dishes) created in Venice in the early sixteenth century for Pope Leo X and Pope Clement VII. Most were decorated in standard Venetian styles with enameled and/or gilded Papal coats-of-arms.

MEDICINE BOTTLE — A glass container, with a narrow neck and mouth, used for ointments, medicines, and other pharmaceutical purposes; most have a stopper, cap, or similar device to enclose the top. Many also contain various labels and/or advertising with the pharmacy/doctor's name that might be mold embossed, lightly etched/engraved, enameled, or by a simple attached paper label. See also PHARMACY GLASS.

Pharmacy glass medicine bottles. Items *courtesy of Wheaton Village.*

MEDIUM RELIEF — A cut glass technique made by designing the outline on the surface and cutting away the background. The design is then raised in relief similar to that of cameo engraving. Medium relief refers to the projected portion that is less than half of the natural circumference of the object of the design; higher than that of low relief but less than that of high relief. See also LOW RELIEF and HIGH RELIEF.

MEIER, WILLIAM GLASS COMPANY — Refer to the BEAVER VALLEY GLASS COMPANY.

MEITNER, RICHARD — A noted American Studio Glass artisan born in Philadelphia, Pennsylvania, in 1949, Meitner received his Arts degree from the University of California, Berkeley (1972) and then moved to the Netherlands to further study glass-making (at Rijksakademie v. Beeldende Kunsten, Amsterdam, 1972-1975). He remained in Amsterdam, where he is both an instructor and independent glass artisan.

MELTING POINT — The temperature at which a typical batch of glass liquefies. Temperatures can range from 1,800-3,000 degrees Fahrenheit (1,100 to 1,650 degrees Celsius) depending on the ingredients used. Full lead crystal generally requires a higher temperature (in the 2,500 to 3,000 degree range) while thinner lime-based glassware melts at a much lower temperature (in the 1,800 to 2,000 degree range).

MENU CARD HOLDER — An object designed to hold a menu with a list of food and drinks that can be ordered from it. Menu card holders are usually present on dining tables at restaurants and are mostly made of plastic since the mid-twentieth century. Fine or gourmet restaurants occasionally contain holders made of glass. Smaller holders indicating seating arrangements are referred to as place card holders. See also PLACE CARD HOLDER.

MERCER CUT GLASS COMPANY — A short-lived American cut glass operation established in 1915 at Trenton, New Jersey, by Robert and William Burrough, the company ceased operations in 1920. Note that the firm was also known as the MERCER GLASS COMPANY.

MERCER GLASS COMPANY — Refer to the MERCER CUT GLASS COMPANY.

MERCHANT'S CUT GLASS COMPANY — An American cut glass-making firm established in the early 1890s at Philadelphia, Pennsylvania. In 1896, the company moved operations to Woodbury, New Jersey. The firm produced cut glass, primarily for Wanamaker's department store located in Philadelphia, up into the World War I era. Note that the firm was also known as the MERCHANT'S CUT GLASS WORKS and was incorporated in 1906 as the MERCHANT'S CUT GLASS COMPANY, INC.

MERCURY BAND — A thin thread resembling silver, though made from the metallic element mercury, once used to decorate the rims of certain objects (i.e. paperweights and tumblers). Due to the inherent dangers of mercury, the decorative bands were replaced with silver or platinum in the early-to-mid twentieth century.

MERCURY GLASS — Glass objects characterized by two outer layers of clear glass with an inner layer of mercury or silver nitrate between them. The silver nitrate solution was usually added to the inside of an object through a hole in the base. It was first made in the 1850s and was occasionally produced during the Art Nouveau movement. It is also sometimes referred to as "Silvered Glass" because of its appearance.

MERESE — An ornamental notch, disc, knob, or collar carefully placed between the stem and bowl of stemware. Some goblets contain a pair or a series of several pairs.

MERIDEN CUT GLASS COMPANY — An American firm established in 1895 at Meriden, Connecticut, by Charles Casper, who had previously run a cut glass operation with Charles Parker beginning in 1867. Meriden operated as a cut glass subsidiary of the Meriden Silver Plate Company (organized in 1869 by Casper), which, in turn, became part of the International Silver Company. Cut glass was produced by Meriden until 1923. Note that the New York firm known as the Wilcox Silver Plate Company merged with International Silver (occasionally, the Wilcox name can be found on silver items/decorations applied to cut glass).

Trademark.

M

A Meriden cut glass bowl. *Photo by Robin Rainwater.*

MERLETTO — A Venetian term for a lacework design in glass. The style can be produced by fine threading or by using an acid etching technique. See also "Lace Glass."

MESOPOTAMIAN GLASS — General term for glassware made in the ancient Mesopotamian region (northeast of Syria and west of Persia between the Tigris and Euphrates Rivers) beginning around 2000 B.C. Objects produced included core-formed designs, beads, mosaic glass, and simple objects decorated with glass strands. It is generally believed that glass-making began in this region nearly five hundred years before Egyptian glass-making. The archaeological record indicates that glass-making continued in Mesopotamia for about 1,000 years.

METAL — A term used by chemists for a batch of glass in its molten state. *See also "Best Metal" and "Hot Metal."*

METAL CROWN SEAL — A metal (usually tin or aluminum) seal that is crimped on drinking bottles (i.e. soda or beer) to seal them. The first metal bottle caps were developed in 1891 and required a bottle opener to remove them. In the latter twentieth century, twist caps were invented to eliminate the need for a bottle opener (on most modern glass beer bottles); though some caps, mostly on glass soda bottles, still require an opener. *See also BOTTLE CAP.*

METALLIC OXIDE — A powdered or liquefied medium whereby oxidized metal elements, like cobalt, copper, iron, manganese, gold, silver, and selenium, are employed as coloring agents for glass. Metallic oxides are used in a variety of forms: added to a batch of glass to impart a specific transparent or opaque color, to make pigments for enameling, and sprayed directly on the surface of an object for an iridized effect.

MEXICAN GLASS — General term for glass made in Mexico since the early twentieth century. Early makers such as the Cristales de Mexico produced pressed glass tableware including some Carnival Glass. Modern Mexican designs include such things as applied peppers (i.e. chilies, jalapenos, etc.) and cacti on glassware and transparent color trims such as emerald green and cobalt blue. *See also CRISTALES DE MEXICO.*

MEYERS, S. F. COMPANY — A wholesale/retail jewelry company established in New York, New York, in the 1890s. Aside from jewelry, Meyers also dealt in giftware including cut glass made by others. Cut glass was represented by the firm up until the end of World War I.

MEYR, JOSEF — Refer to ADOLFSHUTTE.

MEYR'S NEFFE — Refer to WILHELM KRALIK.

MEZZA-FILIGRANA — Italian word for "Half-Filigree," Mezza-filigrana is the technique of producing filigree threads that run parallel or diagonal to each other, as well as for wider rods that are utilized in creating a diagonal striped pattern. In mezza filigrana, the threads do not completely circle or spiral the object as opposed to full filigrana. *See also FILIGRANA and FILIGREE.*

MEZZA-FORMA — Italian word for "Half-Molding," Mezza-forma is the technique of producing ribs on the lower portion of blown glass vessels by use of a mold.

MICA — Small chips or specks of colored glassware that are applied to a glass object to produce a multicolored mottled appearance. *See also FLECKED GLASSWARE and MARVER.*

MICHIGAN CUT GLASS COMPANY — An American cut glass operation founded in 1906 at Lansing, Michigan, by Herbert Flint, Thomas Kinney, T. Rogers Lyons, and John Mauer, the company produced cut glass tableware until closing in 1911.

MIDLAND CUT GLASS COMPANY — Refer to the EDWARD J. KOCH AND COMPANY.

MIKASA CRYSTAL, INC. — A crystal tableware manufacturer founded in 1948 in Secaucus, New Jersey, by George Aratani. In the early 1980s, the company expanded into other decorative accessories to compliment their crystal wares (i.e. stainless flatware, gifts, table linens, etc.). Under Mikasa, as well as its subsidiary names of Studio Nova, Home Beautiful, and Christopher Stuart, the firm's annual sales volume exceeded $500 million. In 2001, Mikasa merged with the Mountain Acquisition Corporation, a subsidiary of J. G. Durand Industries; however, Mikasa continues to operate today as a stand-alone subsidiary of Durand, which also owns Arc International, thereby making it the largest crystal tableware manufacturer in the world. *See also ARC INTERNATIONAL and J. G. DURAND INDUSTRIES.*

MILK BOTTLE — A glass container with a narrow neck and mouth designed to hold milk. Milk bottles usually do not contain handles, but do have a threaded cap or foil seal at the top. Many are mold embossed or enameled with the name of a dairy.

Courtesy of Wheaton Village.

MILK GLASS — A semi-opaque opalescent glass originally colored by a compound of arsenic or calcined bones or tin. The result is a white color resembling milk. The milk glass formulas were perfected by the Venetians in the sixteenth century. With its popularity on the rise, milk glass production spread to England in the latter eighteenth century and in America in the late nineteenth. Modern milk glass usually contains aluminum and fluorine as additives. Note that milk glass marbles are sometimes called "Milkies."

Sawtooth patterned milk glass items. *Courtesy of Wheaton Village.*

Atterbury covered milk glass cat dish. *Courtesy of Wheaton Village.*

MILK PITCHER OR JUG — A medium-sized jug or pitcher designed specifically for serving milk. Milk pitchers generally vary from about 24-48 ounces and are larger than creamers or syrup pitchers, but smaller than water pitchers.

MILL — The name for a large iron or steel wheel that, when revolved, is used to cut glass. The name was derived from millstones that were used to grind grain into flower. Glass cutting stones, no matter how large, were much smaller than the giant mills used in the grain refining process.

MILLED GLASS — A decorating technique characterized by closely spaced parallel grooves, usually around the foot or rim of an object (like the grooves around the edge of a coin).

MILLEFILI — Italian term for a thousand threads; it is used to describe a style of filigrana glass composed of many extremely fine threads.

MILLEFIORI — Italian term for a thousand flowers; this decorating style originated in ancient Roman times, but was more popularized with Venetian glassmakers beginning in the sixteenth century. In modern times, it signifies a typical nineteenth to twenty-first century European-style paperweight made with several different colored circular glass pieces that have been sliced from glass rods or canes. The pieces are arranged together in a pattern and then covered with an extremely thick outer layer of glass. Multicolored pieces are embedded in clear glass to create the "Thousand flower" design. Millefiori techniques have been applied to other objects as well (vases, bowls, perfume bottles, jewelry, etc.).

Venetian millefiori bowl.
Photo courtesy of the Corning Museum of Glass.

MILLEOCCHI — Italian term for thousand eyes; this style of glass was developed by Venetian glass artisans Fabbrica Salir and Vinicio Vianello in 1954. It is characterized by various irregular patterns of small adjacent incised circles that resemble eyes.

MILLER, CATHERINE — A noted modern American glass engraver and artist born in 1956 in West Virginia, Miller worked as an engraver for Princess House, Crystal and Glass, and Louis Glass prior to setting up her own home studio in 1995 in Buckhannon, West Virginia.

MILLERSBURG GLASS COMPANY — An American company established in Millersburg, Ohio, by John and Robert C. Fenton in 1908; they were a major producer of Carnival Glass, but the business only lasted until 1911. After filing for bankruptcy, Millersburg Glass continued to be produced under the Radium Glass Company name until 1913 when it was sold to the Jefferson Glass Company. Jefferson briefly produced lighting glassware until 1916 and then closed the plant. Millersburg glass is often referred to as "Rhodium Ware" or "Radium" because of the minor trace of radiation measurable within the glass.

Millersburg Carnival Glass 1910 courthouse souvenir and trout and fly patterned bowl. *Photos by Robin Rainwater. Courtesy of the Fenton Art Glass Museum.*

Trademark.

MILLS, GARDNER AND COMPANY — A short-lived American cut glass operation established in 1913 at St. Charles, Illinois, the company leased a plant owned by the Heinz brothers until ceasing operations in 1915.

MILLVILLE GLASS — An early glasshouse established in America in 1800 at Port Elizabeth, New Jersey. A new factory was founded in 1806 at Milville, New Jersey. The firm produced some functional glass items such as windows and limited tableware. The company changed hands several times and was eventually acquired by Whitall Brothers and Company in 1844. *See also WHITALL, TAUM AND COMPANY.*

MILSTEIN, J. H. COMPANY — Refer to the VICTORY GLASS COMPANY.

MINERAL BOTTLE — Refer to WATER BOTTLE.

MINIATURE — A tiny copy or replica of an object, glass miniatures abound and include a variety of objects such as animals, lamps, paperweights, pitchers, vases, flasks, toys, bottles, whimsies, plates, baskets, and tea sets.

MINT CONDITION — A perfect, undamaged glass object with no scratches that appears brand new. "Mint in the Box" refers to an unopened item in its original packaging.

MINT DISH — Refer to BONBON or FRUIT DISH.

MIOTTI — A noteworthy family name of Murano glassmakers who began making glass in Venice, Italy in the 1540s (founded by Antonio Miotti). Glass-making in traditional Venetian styles continued with the family until the late eighteenth century.

MIRROR — A polished or smooth surface that forms images of reflection. Lead-backed glass mirrors originated with the ancient Romans and were improved upon by Germans as early as the twelfth century. The first truly, all-glass mirrors originated with the Venetians in the early sixteenth century, after the discovery of cristallo, a clear glass formula. Beginning in the seventeenth century, glass mirrors were in great demand throughout Europe. Since then mirrors have been produced in many forms and styles (i.e. square, rectangular, those with beveled edges, large full-length designs in metal/wooden frames, small hand-held or compact forms, and those with etched or monogrammed decorations). In the seventeenth and eighteenth centuries, reverse painting of mirrors occurred in both Europe and China.

MISKEY-REYNOLDS-ROTHFUS COMPANY — A short-lived American cut glass-making firm founded at Hammonton, New Jersey, in 1906, it closed in 1912.

MISSOURI GLASS COMPANY — Refer to the ST. LOUIS GLASS WORKS.

MITER OR MITRE CUT ENGRAVING — General term for glass cut and/or engraved with a sharp groove on a V-edged wheel.

MIX — Refer to BATCH.

MIXER — The term for a worker who combines and blends a batch of glass (also called a "Founder"). Mixers may also change the pots in a furnace.

MIXING GLASS — A style of glass vessel, usually in the shape of a goblet or tumbler with a pouring lip, used for mixing ingredients together. Some have covers and come in a wide variety of shapes and forms. *See also COCKTAIL SHAKER.*

MODEL FLINT GLASS COMPANY — A short-lived American pressed glass manufacturer established at Findlay, Ohio, in 1888 by J. W. Davidson, Anderson C. Heck, J. T. Leahy, William Parsons, Andrew L. Stephenson, Elmer Stephenson, William Stephenson, Abraham L. Strasburger, and W. C. Walters. The firm was briefly known as the Novelty Flint Glass Company and became a manufacturer of pressed glass tableware. The firm moved to Albany, Indiana, in 1893 and joined the National Glass Company in 1899. The factory closed permanently in 1902. *See also FINDLAY GLASS.*

MODERNISMO — The Spanish term for the Art Nouveau movement. SEE ALSO ART OR ART NOUVEAU GLASS.

MOGUL OR MUGHAL GLASS — Refer to INDIAN GLASS.

MOIL — The unused waste glass left on the blowpipe or pontil after an object has been removed. It usually is recycled as cullet in subsequent batches of glass. It is also referred to as "Overblow."

MOLASSES CAN — A small cylindrically-shaped vessel, with or without a cover, used specifically for serving molasses. If lids are present, then they may or may not contain an opening for a matching spoon or they may be hinged like that of a syrup bottle.

MOLD — A clay, wooden, or iron form used to shape glass into various designs. In paperweights, they are used to create silhouettes, initials, geometric designs, numerals, characters, and other desired shapes. Pattern or half-molds are used before glass has totally expanded. Full or three-part molds are used to give identical or same-size shapes to glassware. Glass can be blown (mold-blown) into or pressed (by hand or machine) into a mold. A carbon paste mold is one that is used in making blown-mold glass; the lining of the mold is covered with a carbon paste, which permits rotation of the object being blown (it also eliminates mold marks). Note that the Old English spelling of mold is "mould."

Waterford glass blowing equipment.

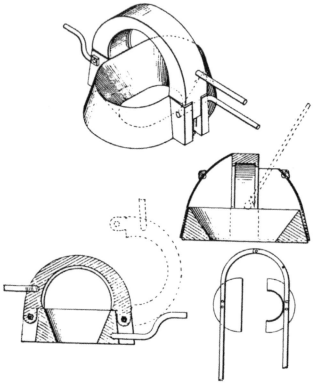

Reproduction from an 1882 John Hoare U.S. patent.

MOLDED GLASS — Blown or melted glass that is given its final shape by the use of molds. Glass may be blown directly into the mold (mold-blown) or mold-pressed; that is, pressed into a mold by a hand-operated pressing machine (nineteenth century) or automatically (automatic machine-pressed – early twentieth century and beyond).

MOLLICA, PETER — A noted American stained glass artisan born in Newton, Massachusetts, in 1941, Mollica served as an apprentice to Christy Rufo in Boston (1964-1968) and traveled throughout Europe studying stained glass window designs (especially in England and Germany with Ludwig Schaffrath). Mollica's own stained glass window designs have received numerous awards and he has served as a teacher/guest lecturer throughout the world. He continues to work as an independent glass artisan in Oakland, California.

MOLTEN GLASS — Glass in its workable or liquid state after the primary ingredients have been fused at a high temperature.

MONARCH CUT GLASS COMPANY — Richard, Emil, and Otto Heinz, along with Herman and Frank Kotwitz, established Monarch in 1901 at Chicago, Illinois. The following year, the three Heinz Brothers bought out the Kotwitz's and changed the name to "Heinz Brothers." *See also* HEINZ BROTHERS.

MONART GLASS — A style of At Glass, characterized by opaque and clear marble swirls, created by Salvador Ysart, a Spaniard who moved to the Scottish firm of Moncrieff Glassworks (founded by John Moncrieff) in 1904. Monart glass was introduced in the 1920s and the firm was continued by Ysart's successors, especially his son, Paul. Note that the name "Monart" is a combination of Moncrieff and Ysart.

MONAX — (1) A heat resistant laboratory glass produced by the Moncrieff Glassworks in the World War I era. (2) A partially opaque or nearly transparent cream-colored or off white glass first produced and named by the MacBeth-Evans Glass Company during America's Depression era.

MONAX GLASS, LTD. — Refer to MONCRIEFF GLASSWORKS."

MONCRIEFF GLASSWORKS — A glass operation founded by John Moncrieff (1836-1899) at Perth, Scotland, in 1864 (originally known as the "North British Glassworks"). Initially the firm produced containers such as bottles, lighting, and some industrial/scientific glass. The company was passed down to John Moncrieff Jr. (1874-1950) and his wife Isabelle Moncrieff (1874-1961). In 1921, the firm hired noted Spanish glass-maker Salvador Ysart and Salvador's son Paul Ysart. The Ysarts were noted most for creating a style of art glass dubbed "Monart Glass" while working for Moncrieff. The Moncrieff's lost control of the firm in 1933 and, after many ownership changes, the firm went bankrupt in 1992. The factory briefly reopened as Monax Glass, Ltd., a maker of laboratory glass; however, the new venture closed in 1996. *See also* NORTH BRITISH GLASSWORKS.

MONOCHROME — Glass or decoration made with a single color or hue. *See also* POLYCHROMMIC GLASS.

MONOGRAM — A sign or identity usually formed by the combined initials of a name. *See also* SIGNATURE *and* MARK.

MONOGRAPH GLASS COMPANY — An American firm founded at Fairmont, West Virginia, in 1903 by George DeBolt, H. L. Heintzelman, and William Moulds. Heintzelman and Moulds had previously worked for the Rochester Tumbler Company. Production of blown and pressed glass tumblers along with barware began in 1904. To expand capacity, which included an agreement with the Beech-Nut Packing Company to produce food containers, Monongah leased the old Fairmont Glass Works factory in 1912 and purchased it outright in 1916. The company remained in business until 1930 when it was acquired by the Turner Glass Company, which, in turn, became part of the Hocking Glass Company in 1931, and the original Monongah plant was closed in 1932.

MONOT — Refer to LEGRAS and PANTIN.

MONROE, C. F. COMPANY — An American company established at Meriden, Connecticut, in 1880, they were noted for some Art Glass designs particularly "Kelva," "Nakara," and "Wave Crest" (all similar in style). They also made some cut glass and novelty items before ceasing operation in 1916.

C. F. Monroe Wave Crest designed covered box. *Courtesy of Wheaton Village.*

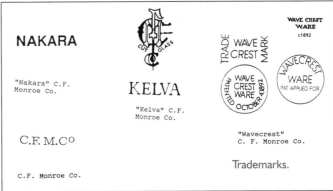

NAKARA

"Nakara" C.F. Monroe Co.

C.F.M.C°

C. F. Monroe Co.

KELVA

"Kelva" C.F. Monroe Co.

TRADE WAVE CREST MARK

WAVE CREST WARE PATENTED OCTOBER 4 1892

WAVE CREST WARE c1892

WAVECREST WARE PAT. APPLIED FOR

"Wavecrest" C. F. Monroe Co.

Trademarks.

MONROE GLASS COMPANY — An American firm established in 1903 at Monroe, Michigan, by Ralph Bowdell, George Burkhart, and H. F. Coon, the company began as a pressed glassmaker of opal jars and later expanded into some novelty glass items. The plant closed in 1913 due to a labor strike and reopened in 1915. Labor troubles persisted and the plant shut down permanently in 1916.

MONT JOYE GLASS — A style of Art Glass created by the French firm of Cristallerie de Pantin of Saint-Hilaire, Touvier, de Varreaux and Company. It is characterized by a lightly acid etched coating that provides a frosted appearance. The frosted object was then decorated or enameled, usually with floral decorations. *See also* PANTIN.

M

MOON AND STAR — A common pressed pattern characterized by a large round orb (moon) inscribed with stars. This pattern originated in the 1850s and has been widely reproduced in various colors since. Variations include alternating circles (moons without inscribed tars), frosted moons, ruby staining, colors, and independent stars.

Moon and Star pressed glass spooner. *Photo by Robin Rainwater.*

Reproduction from a late 1890s U.S. Glass Company catalog.

MOONLIGHT — A transparent light shade of blue Art Glass created and named by Steuben in the early twentieth century.

MOONSTONE — A somewhat light transparent white opalescent color or clear glass with a white opalescent edging. Moonstone is sometimes described as transparent milk glass because of its low density. The name has been applied to some Art Glass and iridized Carnival Glass styles. Also note that Anchor Hocking produced a wide variety of tableware in the 1940 that they named "Moonstone." Anchor Hocking's pieces are crystal with opalescent hobnails and edges (the design was also produced in green).

Moonstone patterned plate by Anchor Hocking. *Photo by Robin Rainwater.*

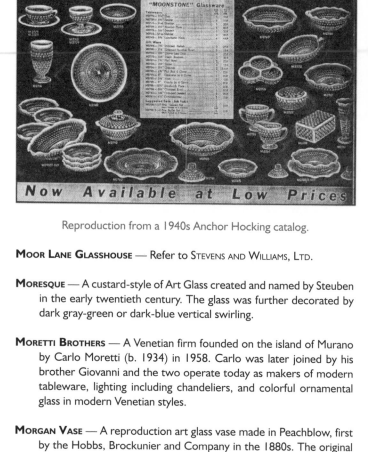

Reproduction from a 1940s Anchor Hocking catalog.

MOOR LANE GLASSHOUSE — Refer to STEVENS AND WILLIAMS, LTD.

MORESQUE — A custard-style of Art Glass created and named by Steuben in the early twentieth century. The glass was further decorated by dark gray-green or dark-blue vertical swirling.

MORETTI BROTHERS — A Venetian firm founded on the island of Murano by Carlo Moretti (b. 1934) in 1958. Carlo was later joined by his brother Giovanni and the two operate today as makers of modern tableware, lighting including chandeliers, and colorful ornamental glass in modern Venetian styles.

MORGAN VASE — A reproduction art glass vase made in Peachblow, first by the Hobbs, Brockunier and Company in the 1880s. The original Chinese porcelain vase sported a peach-bloom ceramic glaze and was produced during the Ch'ing Dynasty in the seventeenth century. The vase was once owned by Ms. Mary Morgan (hence the name "Morgan Vase"). Reproduction glass bases were made by a variety of other firms as well.

MORGANTOWN GLASS WORKS — An American company established in Morgantown, West Virginia, in the 1899, initially, the firm primarily produced pressed wares. Morgantown reorganized in 1903 and changed its name to the Economy Tumbler Company. When the company introduced colored wares in 1924, the firm's name was changed one again to the Economy Glass Company; however, products produced throughout the company's history are still referred to as MORGANTOWN GLASS. In fact, the firm reverted back to the MORGANTOWN GLASS WORKS name in 1939. It closed for good in 1972. *See also ECONOMY TUMBLER COMPANY.*

MORNING GLORY — A pressed glass pattern that contains the Morning Glory flower as its primary design (variations include scrolling, dots, Sandwich-like designs, cables, etc.).

MORTAR — A strong, thick, open-rounded vessel in which material is rubbed or pounded with a pestle; glass mortars originated in Germany in the sixteenth century.

MOSAIC — A surface of a glass object that is decorated by many small adjoining pieces of varicolored materials, such as stone or glass, to form a picture. Small square-shaped glass pieces called tesserae that are formed into mosaics originated in Venice as early as the seventh century.

MOSAIC GLASS COMPANY — A short-lived American firm founded at Fostoria, Ohio, in 1891, the company produced pressed glass molds and some limited amounts of pressed glass tableware. The plant closed in 1893 and was permanently destroyed by fire in 1895.

MOSER — Ludwig Moser was a famous Austrian glassmaker who opened the Moser Art Glass studio in 1857 at Meierhofen (near Karlsbad, Czechoslovakia). Moser (1833-1916) is noted for deeply carved and richly enameled wildlife sculptural scenery upon glass, cut colored scenery, classical cameo design, and a good deal of gilding. The firm actually began as a decorating/cutting shop, but built their own factory at Meierhofen near Karlsbad (present day Nove Dvory) in 1892. In 1900, his four sons — Rudolf (1860-1908), Gustav (1861-1959), Richard (1887-193), and Leo (1879-1974) — joined the firm and the name was changed to Ludwig Moser and Sohne. Rudolf served as director from 1901 to 1908, and then was succeeded by Leo. In 1922, Leo and Richard Moser purchased Meyr's Neffe, their largest rival in Bohemian-styled Art Glass. Leo left in 1932 and later joined St. Louis in France and then came to America in 1941.

Moser was briefly annexed by Germany during World War II and then became nationalized like all Czech firms in 1948 after the war. Glass was still produced under the Moser namesake as it is today. Note that the "Moser" or "Moser Karlsbad" signatures refer to glass actually made by the Moser family. In 1962, Moser was merged with Mstisov and eventually both were absorbed into the Crystalex conglomerate. In 1988, Moser once again became independent and began trading under the name "Sklarna Moser." Furthermore, the factory is now a share-holding company known simply as "Moser A. S."

Moser H T M	1956 - to the present
Moser	1956 - 1958
	1941 - 1945
Moser (Karlovy Vary)	1946 - to the present

Moser	1970s and 1980s
	1970s and 1980s
Moser	1992 - to the present
Moser	1991 - 1992
Moser STUDIO	1996 - to the present

Moser c1940   Moser Karlsbad c1940

Moser Karlsbad

MK

Moser Glass Works

Moser, Ludwig: Trademarks and signatures.

MOSER, KOLO L. — A glass artisan who established a glass-making studio at Karlsbad, Czechoslovakian, in the early 1900s, he was noted for working in many styles of art glass including cameo cut glass and iridescent forms.

MOSQUE LAMP — A style of glass lighting fixtures originating in Syria and the Islamic world as early as the eleventh century; they are characterized by an inverted bell-shape with an inner oil receptacle and side handles (up to six), and were used to hang from ceilings by chains in Egyptian mosques. Many are further decorated with enameling, gilding, and may contain quotes or inscriptions from the Koran.

MOSS AGATE — An Art Glass first created by Frederick Carder and John Northwood in the 1880s for the English firm of Steven and Williams, Carder continued the style for Steuben in the 1920s. Moss Agate is characterized by red, brown, and other swirled or marble-like colors cased in clear glass (made to resemble agate stones).

MOSS GROUND — A ground of closely-packed green canes that resembles moss typically found in paperweights. Some green canes are centered around a white one that may also have a pink or other colored center for further decoration (those with extra coloring are often sprinkled among the pure green ones).

MOSSER GLASS COMPANY — An American company founded by Thomas R. Mosser at Cambridge, Ohio, in 1971. Mosser had previously worked with the Cambridge Glass Company prior to establishing his own firm. The company is noted for glass miniatures, novelty items, and some reproduction glass tableware in colors including iridescent Carnival. The firm is still in operation today, and, aside from collectibles, the company also makes headlight and taillight lenses and pharmaceutical and laboratory glass products.

Mosser Glass Company: Trademark.

MOTHER-OF-PEARL — An Art style of glass produced by a double flashing of light opalescent glass layers in which air bubbles are trapped between the layers. The base of the object is usually blown in a patterned mold and may contain an inner mold-formed design such as herringbone, swirled, diamond-quilted, or feathered. Mother-of-Pearl was created in the 1850s by both American and English glass-making firms. The Mt. Washington Glass Works produced the most examples in this style. Some objects sported alternating pastel shades of pink, blue, and yellow stripes that were sometimes referred to as "Rainbow" or "Rainbow Satin Mother-of-Pearl."

Mother-of-Pearl ruffled bowl from the Mount Washington Glass Works. *Item courtesy of Wheaton Village.*

MOTTLED GLASS — Glass that has been decorated with irregular colored spots or blotches on the surface. Two or more colors are often formed in decorative patterns in mottled glass. The surface may be quite thick or heavier than regular enamels.

MOULD — Refer to MOLD.

MOUND VALLEY GLASS COMPANY — An American firm founded at Mound Valley, Kansas, in 1906 by W. Collins, George Priest, and associates. The company produced pressed glass tableware prior to closing in 1913.

MOUNT — A decorative metal base, lid, or ornamental fixture, usually of gold, bronze, or silver, that is attached to glass objects (i.e. a hinged cover on a box or stein, a fancy handle, or base).

MOUNT CITY GLASS COMPANY — Refer to the ST. LOUIS GLASS WORKS.

MOUNT VERNON GLASS COMPANY — An American Art Glass company founded in the late nineteenth century. They were noted for producing some fancy glass vases and novelty items.

MOUNT WASHINGTON GLASS COMPANY — Refer to the MOUNT WASHINGTON GLASS WORKS.

MOUNT WASHINGTON GLASS MANUFACTORY — Refer to MOUNT WASHINGTON GLASS WORKS.

MOUNT WASHINGTON GLASS WORKS — An American Art Glass manufacturer established in South Boston, Massachusetts, in 1837 by Deming Jarves for his son, George D. Jarves. Henry Cormerais joined in 1847 and the partnership was also known as Jarves and Cormerais. George Jarves passed away in 1850 and the firm was continued by Cormerais. The company was one of America's most successful early firms and was noted for high quality and innovative Art Glass styles such as Burmese Glass, Crown Milano, Mother-of-Pearl, Peach Blow, Royal Flemish, Verona, and cameo-engraved designs. William L. Libbey joined the firm as bookkeeper in 1851 while Timothy Howe joined as a clerk in 1856. Libbey and Howe purchased the firm in 1861 (briefly known as Libbey and Howe), and when Howe died in 1866, Libbey acquired his share. The name was changed in 1867 to the Mount Washington Glass Manufactory. Libbey moved the firm to New Bedford, Massachusetts, after purchasing the defunct New Bedford Glass Company in 1870. Libbey left in 1871 and sold the firm to a new stock company that named it the Mount Washington Glass Company. Aside from art and pressed glass (much of it in color), the firm also produced a good deal of cut crystal glass tableware before merging with the Pairpoint Manufacturing Company in 1894. Pairpoint continued producing many similar items until it closed in 1958. *See also* PAIRPOINT MANUFACTURING COMPANY, WILLIAM L. LIBBEY, *and* FREDERICK SHIRLEY.

Reproduction from a late 19th century Mount Washington catalog.

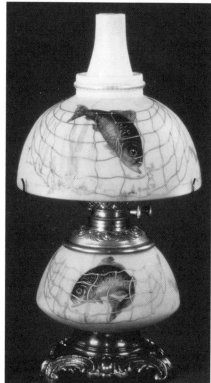

Mount Washington Burmese lamp. *Item courtesy of the Corning Museum of Glass.*

A Mount Washington cameo engraved bowl.
Item courtesy of Wheaton Village.

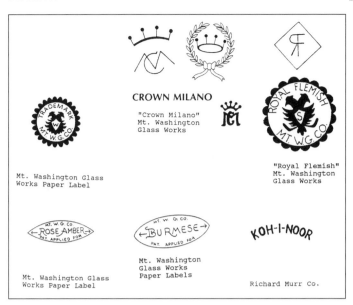

CROWN MILANO

"Crown Milano"
Mt. Washington
Glass Works

"Royal Flemish"
Mt. Washington
Glass Works

Mt. Washington Glass
Works Paper Label

ROSE AMBER
PAT. APPLIED FOR
MT. W. G. CO.

BURMESE
PAT. APPLIED FOR
MT. W. G. CO.

KOH-I-NOOR

Mt. Washington
Glass Works
Paper Labels

Mt. Washington Glass
Works Paper Label

Richard Murr Co.

Trademarks.

MOUTH — The top opening of a pouring vessel from which the contents are poured. Some may or may not have a pouring lip and may be flared or turned. They are commonly found on pitchers, jugs, bottles, carafes, jars, vases, and other vessels.

MOUTH-BLOWN — The process of blowing air through a metal tube or blowpipe in order to shape a molten glass blob attached to the front, top, or mouth end of an object as opposed to the bottom. See also *BLOWING* and *FULL ANTIQUE*.

MSTISOV GLASSWORKS — A Czechoslovakian firm originally founded as Eintrachthutte in the Bohemian area near Teplice in 1868 by S. Fischman and Sons. The company originally produced glass rods for the jewelry industry, but eventually expanded into the production of tableware. When all Czech firms were nationalized in 1948, Mstisov was eventually merged with Moser and then into the conglomerate known as Crystalex. In 1964, the Mstisov factory was razed. *See also MOSER.*

MUDDLER — Refer to *PESTLE*.

MUELLER, A. E. GLASS STAINING COMPANY — An American glass-decorating firm established in 1894 at Pittsburgh, Pennsylvania, by A. E. Mueller, the company specialized in decorating glassware through enameling, ruby staining, and some light engraving. The firm did the majority of decorating for the Cooperative Flint Glass Company located in Beaver Falls, Pennsylvania. Mueller was acquired by the National Glass Company in 1900. National moved all plant materials to a new decorating plant (the former McKee and Brothers facility) in Jeannette, Pennsylvania.

MUFFINEER — An upright glass container, usually cylindrical or angular in shape and with metal or plastic covers containing holes, used for sprinkling sugar on various foods (namely muffins). Muffineers were popular during the Victorian era. See also *SUGAR SHAKER*.

An opal muffineer from the Mount Washington Glass Works. *Item courtesy of Wheaton Village.*

MUFFLE KILN — A low temperature (900-1200 degrees Fahrenheit) oven used for refiring glass to fix or fire-on enameling. Note that a muffle can be a separate removable box, usually made of clay, that can be moved in and out of a kiln.

MUG — A cylindrical drinking vessel that usually has a flat base and single handle; larger mugs with hinged metal lids are usually referred to as "Steins" or "Tankards."

Glass mug with enameled teddy bear. *Photo by Robin Rainwater.*

Monopoly mug with attached pewter.

MUHLEMAN GLASS COMPANY — Refer to the LABELLE GLASS COMPANY.

MULHAUS, JULIUS — A Bohemian glassmaker who opened a studio at Haida, Germany, in 1867 (changed to Novy Bor, Czechoslovakian, in 1917), Mulhaus operated primarily as a decorator (enameling, gilding, and lightly engraving) of blanks provided by noteworthy firms (Harrach, Meyr's Neff, and Loetz). When he passed on in 1879, his two sons, Julius II and Erwin, carried on. The firm became a significant producer of fine Bohemian decorated glassware including some Mary Gregory-styled glass. Erwin died in 1907; the company ceased operations when Julius II died in 1945.

MULLER FRERES — A glass firm originally founded by Henri Muller at Luneville, France, in 1895, the company began as a decorating workshop under Henri's direction. He was later joined by his four brothers: Desire, Eugene, Pierre, and Victor. All had trained at Galle's factory in Nancy. The brothers specialized in acid-etched cameo engraved and other Art Glass forms up until World War I. The brothers split up at that time and worked at different factories. Eugene was killed during the war, but, in 1919, the remaining brothers purchased the Hinzelin Glass Works in Luneville and began making commercial glassware (i.e. lamps, light fittings, etc.) and some art glass. The new venture, known as the Grandes Verreries de Croismare et Verreries d'Art Muller Freres Reunies, closed permanently in 1936.

Muller Freres: Trademark.

MULVANEY, CHARLES AND COMPANY — Refer to DUBLIN GLASS.

MULVANEY AND LEDLIE — Refer to the O'LEARY MULVANEY COMPANY.

MURANESE RETICELLO — Refer to RETICULATED GLASS.

MURANO — A group of small islands that are part of Venice, Italy, glassmakers settled here in the tenth century and all Venetian glass has been produced here since 1292 (the year, for fear of fire, that glass-making was banned on mainland Venice). Today, there are over one hundred small glass-making firms present on the island. *See also* VENETIAN GLASS.

Venetian glass candy made on the island of Murano.
Photo by Robin Rainwater.

Murano Island, Venice, Italy. *Photo by Mark Pickvet*

MURR, RICHARD — Refer to KOH-I-NOOR.

MURRHINE OR MURRINA OR MURRINO — A Venetian technique where colored cane sections are embedded within hot glass before a piece is blown into its final shape. The result is a colorful mosaic design. Murrhine-like items originated in the Greek city-state of Alexandria around 200 B.C. (colored glass slices that were fused into mosaics over a mold). Note that molded mosaics were not made by Venetians. Also note that murrina or murrino ("murra") in Latin refers to an expensive stone in which vessels are made.

MUSHROOM — An accumulation of canes in a paperweight that are brought in at the bottom in a stem-like formation and then spread out to the dome to form a mushroom-like tuft. Note that the stem is often striped.

MUSLER, JAY — A noted American Studio Glass artisan who was born in Sacramento, California, in 1949, Musler attended the California College of Arts and Crafts from 1968 to 1971. Since then, he has served as an instructor/guest lecturer worldwide and has won numerous awards for his glass designs. Musler continues to work as an independent glass artisan in Berkley, California.

MUSLIN GROUND — A spiral of twisted opaque canes, usually white, that forms the base in some millefiori style paperweights. *See also* LACE.

MUSTARD DISH OR JAR — A small flat or shallow dish, with or without a cover, used specifically for serving mustard. If lids are present, then they may or may not contain an opening for a matching spoon.

Reproduction from an early 20th century S. F. Myers Company catalog.

Cut Glass Mustard, with Lid.
Height, 2¾ inches.
No. 9669 .... $1.75

MYERS, JOEL PHILLIP — A noted American Studio Glass artisan who was born in Paterson, New Jersey, in 1934, Myers received his Master of Fine Arts degree from Alfred University and also studied under Richard Kjaergaard in Copenhagen, Denmark. He served as director of design at the Blenko Glass Company from 1963 to 1970 and then moved on to head Illinois State University's Art Glass/Ceramics Department. Myers also has won numerous awards/fellowships for his work and continues to operate as an independent glass artisan in Bloomington, Illinois.

MYRA-KRISTALL — A style of Art Glass created by German artisan Karl Weidman in 1925 while employed at the Wurttembergische Metallwarenfabrik. It is characterized by iridized opalescent coloring cased over crystal.

Nn

{ Nn }

NAILSEA GLASS — A style of art glass that originated in England in the Bristol-Somerset-Nailsea region around 1788. The style was copied by others (including American factories) and was popular through much of the mid-to-late nineteenth century. It is characterized by swirls and loopings (ordinarily white) on a crystal or colored opaque base. Other color effects, such as flecking and broader ribbon and/or festoon-like banding, are also present on this style of glassware.

Nailsea looped glass. *Photo by Robin Rainwater.*

NAILSEA GLASS HOUSE — An English glass factory established at Somerset, England, in 1788 as the Nailsea Crown Glass and Bottle Manufacturers by John Robert Lucas and William Chance, the firm began as a maker of bottles, window panes, and some tableware, but was also noted for producing many unusual glass items such as rolling pins, walking canes, and some swirled glassware. See also NAILSEA GLASS.

NAKARA — A style of Art Glass produced by the C. F. Monroe Company of Meriden, Connecticut, beginning in 1880, up until the company closed in 1916, Nakara is characterized by a light opal glass in various colors (white, cream, custard, light rose, and pink were the most common) that was further decorated with enameled and/or gold scrolling, foliage, or floral designs. Some articles, such as vases, wall pockets, and covered jars, were set in silver or silver-plated holders. Identical products made by Monroe were also referred to as "Kelva" and "Wave Crest."

A Nakara letter box and wave crest cigar jar by C. F. Monroe. *Items courtesy of the Corning Museum of Glass.*

NAPKIN RING — A small circular glass band with a hole in the center used for holding rolled-up napkins.

Ruby Red Cape Cod patterned napkin rings commissioned by Avon from Wheaton Industries. *Photo by Robin Rainwater.*

NAPOLI — Art Glass objects that are completely covered with gold or gold enamels, both inside and out. The design was patented by the Mt. Washington Glass Works in the late nineteenth century. Additional decorations were occasionally applied to the gold covering.

NAPPY — An open shallow serving bowl without a rim that may contain one or two handles. Note that the English spelling is "Nappie."

Reproduction from an early 20th century McKee Brothers catalog.

NASH — A wealthy American family of English heritage that included several glass designers and manufacturers. They were noted for expensive high quality Art Glass similar to Tiffany's designs and styles during the Art Nouveau movement (English immigrant Arthur J. Nash and his sons, Douglas A. Nash and Leslie Nash, all worked for Tiffany).

Of particular note, A. Douglas Nash, helped to create the Libbey-Nash series of colorful Art Glass in the 1930s when he moved on to work for the Libbey Glass Company.

Trademark.

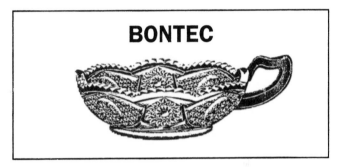

Iridescent gold and chintz style Art Glass vases by Arthur Nash. *Item courtesy of Wheaton Village.*

NASON AND MORETTI — A Venetian glass-making venture founded on the island of Murano in 1923 by two glass-making families, the Nasons and Morettis, the company remains in operation today as a producer of traditional and modern Venetian colored styles of tableware and ornamental glassware.

NATIONAL CUT GLASS COMPANY — An American cut glass operation founded at Minneapolis, Minnesota, in 1908 by Ernest Bersbach, Edward Otis, and Peter Thompson, the firm produced some cut glass tableware until ending production right after World War I.

DORIC DESIGN.

Reproduction from a 1901 National Glass Co. catalog.

NATIONAL GLASS AND LENS COMPANY — Refer to the HOCKING GLASS COMPANY.

NATIONAL GLASS COMPANY — 1) A short-lived American pressed glass manufacturer established in 1898. National was a brief conglomeration of nineteen merged companies in 1899-1900. The company declared bankruptcy in 1904 and completely broke up in 1905, as many of its members became independent firms once again. Firms that joined National included the Beatty-Brady Glass Company, the Canton Glass Company, the Central Glass Company of Summitsville, Indiana, the Crystal Glass Company, the Cumberland Glass Company, the Dalzell, Gilmore and Leighton Company, the Fairmont Glass Company, the Greensburg Glass Company, the Indiana Goblet and Tumbler Company, the Keystone Tumbler Company, McKee Brothers, the Model Flint Glass Company, the Northwood Company, the Ohio Flint Glass Company, the Riverside Glass Company, the Robinson Glass Company, the Rochester Tumbler Company, the Royal Glass Company, and the West Virginia Glass Company. National also purchased the decorating firm of A. E. Mueller in 1900. 2) Note that there was also a separate, short-lived pressed glass company of the same name established at Bellaire, Ohio, in 1877.

NATIONAL GLASS MANUFACTURING COMPANY — 1) An American pressed glass-making firm established in 1869 at Bellaire, Ohio, by John Fink, B. Scott (Fink's bother-in-law), William Morgan, and James Dalzell. In the beginning, the firm produced pressed glass blanks for decorating firms. In 1877, the firm declared bankruptcy and was purchased by three Rodefer Brothers: Albert, John, and Thornton. The name was changed to the Rodefer Brothers in 1882. Under the new owners, the product line changed to glass lamp parts, lantern globes, and jelly glasses. The factory burned in 1892, but was rebuilt. Albert died in 1898 and Thornton became the sole owner; the name was changed to the National Glass Works. When Thornton died in 1910, his son C. M. Thornton, inherited the business. In 1953, the firm merged with the Gleason-Tiebout Glass Company of Brooklyn, New York, and the name became the Rodefer-Gleason Glass Company, which still produces industrial and special order glassware. 2) Another company of the same name was established at Buffalo, New York, in the early 1920s. This firm purchased the Frontier Cut Glass Company and continued to produce some lightly engraved glassware.

NATIONAL GLASS WORKS — Refer to the NATIONAL GLASS MANUFACTURING COMPANY.

NATRON — The original name for sodium carbonate first used in making ancient Egyptian glass. In the modern world, sodium carbonate is used as a substitute for potash as the alkali or flux ingredient in a batch of glass; the resulting product is known as soda or lime glass. See also LIME GLASS, SODA, and SODA-LIME GLASS.

NAVARRE — An etched crystal pattern (Plate Etching #327) produced in the 1930s to 1985 by the Fostoria Glass Company. See also FOSTORIA GLASS COMPANY.

NAVARRE GLASS MARBLE AND SPECIALTY COMPANY — An American marble-making firm founded in 1897 at Navarre, Ohio, the company produced handmade glass marbles, but failed soon after. In 1902, the company reopened at Steubenville, Ohio, under the direction of Emile Converse; however, they failed to operate profitably. In 1904, they sold the company to Martin F. Christensen, who established a successful glass marble-making firm. See also M. F. CHRISTENSEN COMPANY.

NAVARRE, HENRI — A noted French studio glass artisan who created tinted and transparent colored art glass sculptures similar to Maurice Marinot, Navarre (b. 1885) completed the majority of his work in the 1920s and 1930s.

NAZEING GLASSWORKS — An English company founded at Broxbourne in Hertfordshire (twenty miles north of London) by Richard Kempton in 1928. Kempton (1868-1936) had previously worked for a firm founded in 1874 by his brother Charles Henry Kempton (1839-1899), the C. H. Kempton Company. The Kemptons produced practical items such as tableware. In 1932, the Nazeing factory was acquired by John Ismay who produced light bulbs and glass tubing. Ismay retired in 1938 and the firm was purchased by Malcolm Pollock-Hill. The new venture expanded into lamps, tumblers, and some colorful ornamental art glass. Today, the company is run by Stephen Pollock-Hill and the firm produces mostly industrial glassware as well as some tableware for the hotel/restaurant business.

NEAR CUT — Pressed glass patterns that are very similar to designs of hand-decorated cut glass. Near-cut was often used as an advertising ploy for cheaper pressed wares that resembled more expensive cut glass.

NECK — The narrow part of a glass vessel, such as a bottle, jug, or vase, that lies between the body and mouth. Necks do vary in length: they may be very short or quite long.

NECKLACE — An ornament composed of a string of beads, stones, or jewels and made for wearing around the neck. Necklaces composed of glass beads or paste date back at least to the fourteenth century B.C. and have been made ever since.

NEEDLE — A very small slender and pointed instrument that has an eye for a thread at one end. Needles made of glass date back to ancient Roman times; many were used as hair pins or hair ornaments.

NEEDLE ETCHING — A process of etching glass by machine; fine lines are cut by a machine through a wax coating on the glass and then hydrofluoric acid is applied to permanently etch the pattern into the glass.

NELSON GLASS COMPANY — An American firm established at Muncie, Indiana, in 1892, Nelson produced bottles and fruit jars and patented a new sealing device on their glass lids. The company had difficulty competing with other jar makers, such as Ball Brothers, and closed in 1896.

NEODYMIUM GLASS — A yellow-colored metallic element that, when oxidized (neodymium oxide or NdO3) and added to a batch of glass, produces a light but rich lavender color. Furthermore, the color appears as pale blue under fluorescent lighting. Note that many companies used other names for this style of glass: "Alexandrite" by Boyd, Heisey, Morgantown, and Moser; "Heatherbloom" by Cambridge; "Luxodin" by the Czechoslovakian firm of ZBS; "Neo-Blue" by Lotton; "Twilight" by Tiffin; and "Wisteria" by Fenton, Fostoria, and Stueben.

NERI, ANTONIO — An Italian (Florentine) glass chemist and priest who wrote an important work titled L'Arte Vetraria (The Art of Glass) in 1612. Neri wrote down many formulas for glass-making including those for producing colors. The book was widely translated and circulated throughout Europe and is said to be partly responsible for the Venetians losing their monopoly on glass-making by the early eighteenth century.

NET FLOATS — Refer to FLOATS.

NETHERLANDS GLASS — General term for glassware made in and around the Netherlands since the late sixteenth and early seventeenth centuries. The first items produced were practical items like windows, drinking vessels, and some limited tableware. During the latter seventeenth and eighteenth centuries, the Dutch were noted for heavy engraved wares in the Bohemian tradition. Modern glass is still being produced today in variety of styles. *See also "Royal Dutch Glass Works."*

NETWORK — A decorating style found in several mediums (art, mold-pressed, and cut glass) consisting of an overlapping framework of crossed strips. The strips may be horizontal and vertical (meet at right angles), diagonal like a lattice, or more free-formed intersecting parallel curves as in some art styles.

NEUE OBERLAUSITZER GLASHUTTENWERKE SCHWEIG AND COMPANY — Refer to the VEREINIGTE LAUSITZER GLASSWERKE AG.

NEVERS GLASS — General term for glass made at Nevers, France, beginning in the sixteenth century. Items were produced in typical Venetian styles (the Duke of Never had imported Italian glass artisans), but of particular note were small glass figurines of people and animals, referred to as "Nevers Figures." Most were made from about an inch to seven inches in height.

NEVILLE, ASA G. COMPANY — An American company founded at Blairsville, Pennsylvania, in 1892 by Thomas Maher, T. W. McQuaide, and Asa G. Neville, the company produced glass globes, lamps, fonts, and battery jars before closing in 1895.

NEW BEDFORD GLASS COMPANY — An American firm established in 1866 at New Bedford, Massachusetts, by a group of workers who left the Boston and Sandwich Glass Company over a labor dispute. They were led by Theodore Kern and the company produced some cut and pressed glass before going bankrupt in 1869. The company was purchased by William L. Libbey in 1870. *See also MOUNT WASHINGTON GLASS WORKS.*

NEW BREMEN GLASS MANUFACTORY — An American firm established at New Bremen, Maryland, by Johann F. Amelung in 1784, the company was one of the first glass-making operations to produce useful tableware in America, some with fancy engraved decorations. Many of their products were signed and dated (rare for that time period). Unfortunately, the enterprise was not profitable and was sold in 1795.

NEW BRIGHTON GLASS COMPANY — An American pressed glass manufacturer founded at New Brighton, Pennsylvania, by John Young and Christian Sigelen originally as the American Ferrraline Company in 1885. Under the direction of chemist Enrico Rozenzi, the firm produced an expensive black glass formula; however, sales of the product failed. The company reorganized as New Brighton in 1886 and began producing pressed tableware, mostly in a hobnail pattern. Glass production halted in 1891. In 1894, the company attempted to reorganize as the New Brighton Flint Glass Company; however, they went bankrupt and the plant was then sold off to the New Brighton Steel Company.

NEW BRUNSWICK CUT GLASS COMPANY — A short-lived American cut glass operation founded in 1916 at New Brunswick, New Jersey. The firm closed in 1919.

NEW CARNIVAL — Reproduction iridescent glass made in America since 1962, sometimes with the original Carnival Glass molds. Both the Imperial and Indiana Glass companies produced the majority of it. Imperial's reissues are marked with "IG" while Indiana's contain no new identification marks.

Indiana Glass Company's reproduction of a Carnival Glass grape patterned jar. *Photo by Robin Rainwater.*

NEW CRYSTAL GLASS COMPANY — Refer to the CRYSTAL GLASS COMPANY and the IMPERIAL GLASS COMPANY.

NEW CUMBERLAND GLASS COMPANY — A short-lived American firm established at New Cumberland, West Virginia, in 1920. Fire destroyed the factory in 1923; however, it was rebuilt. The company produced some limited amounts of colored Depression (some etched) and novelties before closing permanently in 1929.

NEW ENGLAND CRYSTAL COMPANY — An American firm established in 1990 by Philip E. Hopfe in Lincoln, Rhode Island, the company is noted for hand cut and copper wheel engraved Art forms as well as Pate de Verre styles.

NEW ENGLAND GLASS COMPANY — An American Glass company established at Cambridge, Massachusetts, by Deming Jarves, Edmund Monroe, Daniel Hastings, Amos Binney, and associates in 1818. The group had purchased the bankrupt firm of the Boston Porcelain and Glass Company. New England became one of the first highly successful American glass companies; they produced pressed, cut, engraved and a variety of Art Glass such as Agata, Amberina, Pomona, Wild Rose Peachblow, engraved ruby red or ruby flashed glass, and paperweights. New England acquired other companies as well, like the Northern Liberties Glass Facture in 1820. They also established the Union Glass Works in Philadelphia, Pennsylvania, in 1820. Jarves left in 1825 to establish another successful firm, the Boston and Sandwich Glass Company. Thomas Leighton Sr. succeeded Jarves as superintendent in 1826; and then by his son Thomas Leighton Jr. in 1849 (when the senior Leighton died). William L. Libbey became a sales manager with the firm in 1872 and acquired the company after it declared bankruptcy in 1878. Libbey changed the name and continued many of New England's noteworthy patterns and designs. *See also* LOUIS VAUPEL and LIBBEY GLASS COMPANY.

New England Glass Company: Trademarks.

NEW GENEVA GLASS WORKS — An American company established in Fayette County, Pennsylvania, by Swiss immigrant Albert Gallatin in 1797, the firm made some tableware and windows before closing in the 1820s.

NEW MARTINSVILLE GLASS COMPANY — An American company established in 1901 at New Martinsville, West Virginia, by Mark Douglass and George Matheny. New Martinsville began as an Art Glass company and later produced pressed pattern glass tableware (like the etched "Prelude" pattern and the Depression "Janice," "Moondrops," and "Radiance" patterns), some novelty items (i.e. animal figurines, decanters in the shape of faces or animals, decorated tumblers, etc.), and colored Depression Glass. In 1944, they sold out to the Viking Glass Company. Note that the firm was also known as the New Martinsville Glass Manufacturing Company.

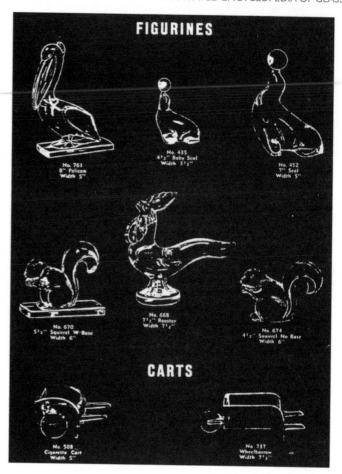

Reproduction from a 1930s New Martinsville advertisement.

NEW MARTINSVILLE GLASS MANUFACTURING COMPANY — Refer to the NEW MARTINSVILLE GLASS COMPANY.

NEW WORLD GLASS-MAKING — General term for glass made in America through the sixteenth and eighteenth centuries. Early items produced included crude tableware, windows, beads, and marbles. *See also* AMELUNG GLASS, JAMESTOWN, CASPAR WISTAR, and STEIGEL GLASS.

NEW YORK GLASS WORKS — Refer to the BLOOMINGDALE FLINT GLASS WORKS.

NEW ZEALAND GLASS — General term for glass made in New Zealand since the early twentieth century. Numerous attempts were made to make glass in New Zealand in the nineteenth century; however, all attempts failed. Nearly all glass, including some with etched/engraved New Zealand inscriptions, was imported from America up until the 1920s. At that time, the Australian Glass Manufacturers Company built a bottle plant at Penrose, Auckland, which is still in business today. The Crown Crystal Glass Company was established in 1950 and was the only New Zealand firm ever to produce blown and pressed tableware in the twentieth century (the firm closed in 1987). Beginning in 1980, the art glass studio movement spread to New Zealand with the founding of two firms: the Hot Glass Company ad the Hoki Tika Glassworks. Note that the New Zealand Society of Artists in Glass was also established in 1980. Peter Raos is one of New Zealand's leading paperweights makers and has been working with glass since 1979.

NEWARK CUT GLASS COMPANY — An American firm founded in 1906 at Newark, New Jersey, the company produced some limited cut glassware until closing in 1918.

Newark Cut Glass Company: Trademark.

NEWCASTLE GLASS — General term for glassware made in the English region of Newcastle-upon-Tyne beginning in the seventeenth century. Newcastle was an important center for window glass, tableware, and heavily engraved glassware in the seventeenth through nineteenth centuries.

NEWEL POST — A paperweight post at the end of a foot or flight of stairs used to support a handrail.

NIAGARA CUT GLASS COMPANY — An American firm founded at Buffalo, New York, in 1906 by Edward J. Eisle, and his son, Edward A. Eisle. Edward J. Eisle was an immigrant from Luxembourg and first went into business as a partner in a jewelry firm (King and Eisle). He later formed his own jewelry business as Eisle and Company, and then formed Niagara to produce cut glass products. Like most other cut glass firms, Niagara ceased cutting glass in the World War I era (the family did remain in the jewelry business though).

NICKEL — A silvery-white metallic coloring agent that, when added to a batch of lead glass, imparts a deep violet or purple color. In soda or lime glass, it produces a yellowish-brown color. Nickel was first used in the latter half of the eighteenth century as a de-colorizing agent to aid in eliminating the murky green or brownish color inherent in iron particles within sand (though manganese does a better job of this).

NICKEL PLATE GLASS COMPANY — A short-lived pressed glass manufacturer established at Fostoria, Ohio, in 1888, it was named for the Nickel Plate railroad tracks in which it was built adjacent to. Aside from pressed glass, the company also produced some bar goods in both crystal and opalescent colors. The firm joined the U.S. Glass Company in 1891 as Factory N.

NICOLAI, HENRY COMPANY — Refer to the ROTHFUS-NICOLAI COMPANY.

NIGHT LAMP — Refer to SPARKING LAMP.

NILAND CUT GLASS COMPANY — An American cut glass operation established at Deep River, Connecticut, as Thomas A. Niland and Company by English immigrant Thomas Niland in 1896. Niland had formerly formed a partnership with James D. Bergen in 1880, but sold his interest to Bergen in 1885 (Niland continued to work for Bergen until 1896). Niland then sold his interest in the new firm to his partners James and Ansel Jones in 1897 (the firm's name was then changed officially to the Niland Cut Glass Company). Thomas Niland returned to work for Bergen in 1897 while the firm bearing his namesake closed in 1902. Thomas left Bergen again in 1902 to join his brother James at the J. J. Niland Company.

NILAND, J. J. COMPANY — An American cut glass firm founded at Meriden, Connecticut, by English immigrant James J. Niland in 1902. James came to America in 1882 and had previously worked for James Bergen and his brother, noted cutter Thomas A. Niland. The company remained in business until 1959; however, heavy cutting of glass ended just after World War I.

Reproduction from an early 20th century Niland advertisement.

NIPT DIAMOND WAVES — A pattern applied to glass objects produced by compressing thick vertical threads into diamond-like shapes.

NITER OR NITRE — Potassium nitrate ($KNO3$) or Sodium Nitrate ($NaNO3$), Niter is basically a white salt that is used in a batch of glass to aid in speeding up the melting process.

NIVISION-WEISKOPF COMPANY — A short-lived American marble-making firm established at Cincinnati, Ohio, in 1921, the company produced glass marbles until ceasing operation in 1924.

NIZBOR — This famous glass-making city is in the Bohemian/Czech Republic area. See also ANTONIN RUCKL AND SONS and BOHEMIA GLASSWORKS NATIONAL CORPORATION.

NORTH BRITISH GLASSWORKS — A Scottish firm founded by John Moncrieff (1836-1899) at Perth in 1864, the company was initially set up to produce container and industrial glass (i.e. bottles, tubing, lighting, etc.). In 1905, the firm became John Moncrieff, Ltd. (also known as the MONCRIEFF GLASSWORKS) and produced heat-resistant glass for laboratories in the World War I era (sold under the trade name "Monax"). In 1921, the company hired noted Spanish glass-maker Salvador Ysart and Salvador's son Paul Ysart. The Ysarts were noted most for creating Monart Glass while working for Moncrieff. See also MONCRIEFF GLASSWORKS and MONART GLASS.

NORTH STAR GLASS COMPANY — A small Studio Art glass firm started by Mark Abilgaard at Davis, California, in 1986, Abilgaard received his Master of Fine Arts degree from the University of Hawaii in 1983 and served a fellowship at the Wheaton Village glass center in Millville, New Jersey.

NORTH WHEELING FLINT GLASS WORKS — Refer to SWEENEY, MICHAEL, THOMAS, AND R. H.

NORTHERN LIBERTIES GLASS FACTURE — An American glass firm established at Philadelphia, Pennsylvania, in 1771, it first produced some lead crystal tableware and window panes before being purchased by the New England Glass Company in 1820.

N

NORTHWOOD GLASS COMPANY — An American company established at Martins Ferry, Ohio, in 1888 by English immigrant Harry Northwood, son of John Northwood, and Harry Heeling. The firm was first known as the Northwood Glass Works and they took over the defunct plant once occupied by the Union Glass Works. Harry Northwood was born in England in 1860 and migrated to America in 1881. The firm was moved to Ellwood City, Pennsylvania, where Northwood purchased a defunct company briefly called the Indiana Glass Company. Harry's brother Carl Northwood also joined the firm. Northwood produced pressed glass tableware including a good deal of custard glass. The company became briefly part of the Dugan Glass Company in 1896 and joined National Glass in 1899. Both Harry and Carl returned to England to temporarily manage the London sales office for National. As National did not last long, the Northwoods returned to America and built a new factory in 1902 at the former Hobbs, Brockunier and Company site in Wheeling, West Virginia. The firm was noted for decorated glass with gold and opalescent edges as well as producing Carnival Glass in some quantity. Carl died in 1918 while Harry passed on in 1919. Harry Northwood's son, Harry Clarence Northwood, was active as a salesman; however, he too passed away in 1923. The plant closed in 1924 and the firm ended in bankruptcy in 1925.

Northwood Carnival Glass Grape and Cable patterned dish and poinsettia and lattice patterned bowl. *Photos by Robin Rainwater.*

Reproduction from an 1898 *China, Glass, and Pottery Review* advertisement.

Trademarks.

NORTHWOOD GLASS WORKS — Refer to the NORTHWOOD GLASS COMPANY.

NORTHWOOD, HARRY — Son of noted English glass artisan John Northwood, Harry Northwood was born in 1869 in Stourbridge, England. Harry came to America in 1881 and served as a glass etcher for Hobbs, Brockunier and Co. He founded his own company in 1887 and after several moves, remained in business until his death in 1919. *See also* NORTHWOOD GLASS COMPANY.

Northwood, John — A noted English glass artisan who specialized in making multi-colored and layered cameo glass during the Art Nouveau movement, Northwood (1836-1902) worked for several firms, established his own briefly (J. and J. Northwood with his brother Joseph in 1860), and served as a technical advisor for both Stevens and Williams and Thomas Webb and Sons. He also invented a machine to make herring-bone style decorations by automatically pulling glass threads in a molten object. His cameo-style work was continued by his son, John Northwood II, and by George and Thomas Woodall. His other sons, Harry and Carl Northwood, were also involved in glassmaking. *See also* Harry Northwood *and* Northwood Glass Company.

Norwegian Glass — General term for glassware made in Norway since the mid-eighteenth century. The first firm was the Nostetangen Glasverk (beginning 1741), which produced tableware and lighting fixtures such as chandeliers. They were soon followed by Hurdals Verk (1755) and the Hadelands Glasverk (1765), tableware and bottle makers respectively. Most glass produced was directly influenced by the English and Netherlands. In the late nineteenth/early twentieth centuries, the Hadelands factory produced some ornamental art-styled glass, including Scandinavian themes much like Swedish Glass, as well as a good deal of practical tableware. *See also* Hadelands Glasverk *and* Swedish Glass.

Nosegay — Refer to Bouquet.

Notched Prism Cut — A decorating technique in cut glass consisting of cutting the prism between the miter cuts to make a pattern that resembles a string of beads. The notching was usually completed horizontally or vertically, or could be flared out. Notched designs have been found in press-molded glass as well. Glass pieces that are notched are known as "Strigled" glass. *See also* Prism Cutting.

Notsjo Glassworks — A Finnish glass firm founded in 1793 at present day Nuutajarvi (originally Urjala), Finland, by Jacob Wilhelm de Pont and Harald Furnhjelm (1760-1809), the company began as a maker of window, bottled glass, and some tableware. In 1843, it came under the control of the Torngren family; Johan Torngren, and later his son, Adolf Torngren (1824-1895). By the middle of the nineteenth century, it became the largest glass-producing firm in Finland. Because of its location, glass produced by the firm is sometimes referred to as "Nuutajarvi Glass." In 1972, it was sold to Torsten Costiander and, aside from tableware, the firm followed the trends of the Art Nouveau movement as well as those in Scandinavia and Sweden. It eventually became part of the Wartsila Group in 1950, and then merged with littala in 1988 to form littala Nuutajarvi Oy. The company continues to produce a wide variety of tableware as well as some art glass products today. *See also* Swedish Glass.

Nourot Glass Studio — An American Art Glass studio founded by Michael Nourot and Ann Corcoran in 1974 at Santa Monica, California, it specializes in creating colorful Art Glass vases, sculptures, and other novelties.

Nova Scotia Glass Company — A short-lived Canadian cut glass firm established at Trenton in 1881, the company primarily made cut and engraved glass tableware before ceasing operation in 1892.

Novelty — A glass object made in the form of a toy, animal, boat, hatchet, souvenir, flower, etc.

Venetian glass fish novelties. *Photo by Robin Rainwater.*

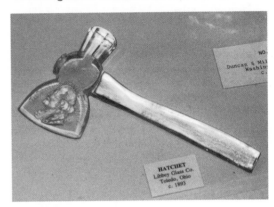

Libbey whimsical glass hatchet. *Courtesy of Wheaton Village.*

Novelty Flint Glass Company — Refer to the Model Flint Glass Company.

Novelty Glass Company — 1) A pressed glass manufacturer established at La Grange, Ohio, in 1879 by E. J. Brown, Charles Henderson, and E. C. Long, the firm was sold in 1881 and operations were moved to Brilliant, Ohio, and merged with the Brilliant Glass Works. The factory burned in 1882, but was rebuilt, and then joined the U.S. Glass Company in 1891 as Factory T. The company was moved to Fostoria, Ohio, in 1892; it burned a year later. 2) Another firm known as the Novelty Glass Company was founded at Ottawa, Illinois, in 1886 by Victor Peltier. The company operated as a maker of glass marbles until the factory burned to the ground in 1919. The company's name was then changed to the Peltier Glass Company and marble production was resumed in the early 1920s. Note that his firm was also known as the Ottawa Novelty Glass Company. 3) There were many other short-lived American glass firms that sported the Novelty Glass Company name: one was in Washington, Pennsylvania, in 1896 that made pressed glass until ceasing operation in 1908 (also known as the Perfection Bottle Company, the Perfection Manufacturing Company, and the Sterling Glass Works). Others that operated for a few short years under the Novelty namesake included one founded at East Liverpool, Ohio, in 1886; one at Findlay, Ohio, in 1888, and one at Fostoria, Ohio, in 1891. *See also* Peltier Glass Company *and* Specialty Glass Works.

Novelty Glass Letter Company — Refer to the Glass Letter and Novelty Company.

Nugget — Refer to Glob.

NUREMBERG GLASS — General term for decorated glassware produced in Nuremburg, Germany, since the sixteenth century. Decorating techniques consisted primarily of shallow wheel engraving and enameling. Most were applied to drinking vessels in the Bavarian style, including some gilding and decorated coats-of-arms. *See also "German Glass" and "Bavarian Glass."*

NURSING BOTTLE — A cylindrically-shaped glass container with a narrow neck and mouth. The mouth may be threaded in order to hold a screwed-on nipple-shaped cover used by babies while nursing. The nipple itself may be rubberized, but note that rubber was not used until the early 1900s (nineteenth century bottles contained glass tubes and corks that were later found to be unsanitary). Some nursing bottles contain embossed or enameled writing designs related to babies and measuring lines placed vertically down the side.

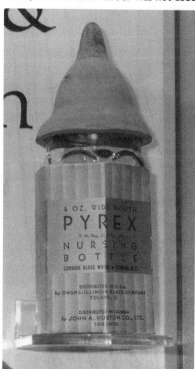

An early 1900s nursing bottle by Pyrex. *Item courtesy of the Van Andel Museum.*

NUT DISH — A small flat or shallow dish used for serving nuts.

NUTTALL AND COMPANY — Refer to the "Francis Dixon and Company" and "United Glass Bottle Manufacturers Limited."

NUUTAJARVI — Refer to the "Notsjo Glassworks."

NV KRISTAL — Refer to "Maastricht."

N

Oo

{ Oo }

OBERLAUSITZER GLASWERKE — Refer to "Vereinigte Lausitzer Glaswereke AG."

OBSIDIAN — A mineral resembling dark glass that is formed by volcanic action. Black glass is sometimes referred to as "obsidian glass," which is considered to be the first form of glass ever used by humans (arrowheads, spears, knives, and other simple tools).

An Obsidian fragment from Ancient Rome.
Photo courtesy of the Corning Museum of Glass.

O'CONNOR, JOHN S. — A small cut glass shop established by Irish immigrant John Sarsfield O'Connor at Hawley, Pennsylvania, in 1890, O'Connor had worked for several firms (i.e. Turner and Lane, Haughwout, and Dorflinger) prior to establishing his own business. O'Connor sold the Hawley factory to the Maple City Glass Company in 1900, and went on to open a new shop in Goshen, New York. He briefly opened another factory in 1902 at Port Jarvis, New York (known as the American Cut Glass Company or the American Rich Cut Glass Company); however, it closed in 1903. O'Connor remained in business until 1910.

O'Connor John S.: Trademark.

OERTEL, JOHANN — A Bohemian glass artisan who began painting glass in Haida, Germany, in 1896 (Haida later became Novy Bor, Czechoslovakia, in 1917). Oertel purchased blanks from such noted firms as Moser and Loetz and decorated them by painting, enameling, and engraving. He is particularly noted for his two-layered colored cut glass (red or blue are most prevalent) over crystal. When Oertel died in 1909, his son, Johann Jr., assumed control and decorated glass was produced under the Oertel name up until World War II.

OESTERLING AND COMPANY — Refer to the CENTRAL GLASS WORKS.

OESTERLING, HENDERSON, AND COMPANY — An American firm established at Wheeling, West Virginia, in 1863 by John Oesterling. The company was rechartered as the Central Glass Works in 1865. *See also* CENTRAL GLASS COMPANY *and* CENTRAL GLASS WORKS.

OFF-HAND GLASS — Glass objects (i.e. whimseys, art pieces, paperweights, or other novelty items) created by glassmakers from leftover or scrap glass.

OGIVAL-VENETIAN DIAMOND — A pattern applied to glass objects produced by pressing or cutting. The shape is of large or wide diamonds and is sometimes referred to as "Reticulated Diamond" or "Expanded Diamond."

O'HARA AND CRAIG — Refer to PITTSBURGH GLASS WORKS.

O'HARA FLINT GLASS WORKS — Refer to the UNION FLINT GLASS WORKS.

O'HARA GLASS COMPANY — (1) An American pressed glass-making firm originally established as the Union Flint Glass Works at Pittsburgh, Pennsylvania, in 1829, the company became part of the U.S. Glass Company conglomerate as Factory L in 1891. 2) The O'Hara Glass Company, Ltd. operated briefly as a pressed glass manufacturer in Canada in the late nineteenth century. *See also* UNION FLINT GLASS WORKS.

OHIO CUT GLASS COMPANY — An American firm established at Bowling Green, Ohio, in 1904, the company worked primarily as a cutting shop for Pitkin and Brooks; however, products were advertised and labeled with the "Ohio Cut Glass Company" name. The firm was managed by Thomas Singleton and produced cut glass until 1912. The factory burned to the ground in 1912 and was not rebuilt.

Reproduction from a 1904 Ohio Cut Glass Company patent.

NEW YORK SALESROOM, 66 West Broadway.
CHICAGO SALESROOM, Silversmiths' Building.
ST. LOUIS SALESROOM, Holland Building.

Trademark.

O

OHIO FLINT GLASS COMPANY — An American pressed glass manufacturer established at Bowling Green, Ohio, in 1891, the firm purchased the Buckeye Novelty Glass Company that had gone bankrupt. Ohio Flint produced pressed glass along with some lamps and blown glass. A second plant was completed at Dunkirk, Indiana, in 1893. The Bowling Green plant burned to the ground in 1895 and was not rebuilt. In 1899, the Dunkirk plant also burned and a new one was built at Lancaster, Ohio (sometimes referred to as LANCASTER GLASS WORKS in advertising). In 1900, the firm joined the National Glass Company conglomerate. In 1904, when National was failing, the plant was leased back to Ohio Flint, which continued to produce tableware until they went bankrupt in 1907. In 1908, Hocking acquired all of the equipment from Ohio Flint.

Reproduction from an 1897 Ohio Flint Glass Co. patent.

OHIO GLASS — Refer to ZANESVILLE GLASS.

OIL BOTTLE — A glass receptacle with a top used for serving vinegar or other salad oils. In the nineteenth century, a few odd glass oil bottles were filled with such things as motor oil, battery fluid, and other lubricating oils. *See also* CRUET.

Reproduction from a 1904 trade journal advertisement.

Reproduction from a late 19th century T.G. Hawkes advertisement.

OIL GLASS — Refer to AMBERGRIS.

OIL LAMP — A glass vessel, with a wick and oil receptacle, used to produce light, these lamps come in a wide variety of shapes and forms and were created to burn many different types of inflammable liquids (i.e. whale oil, kerosene, and many other types of oil). American inventor Aim Argand patented the first oil-burning lamp in 1784. *See also AIM ARGAND.*

Photo by Robin Rainwater.

OINTMENT JAR — A small circular or oval glass receptacle, with a cover, used for storing ointments, creams, or hair dressing. Ointment jars were popular in the Victorian era and were usually part of dresser sets.

OLD COLONY CUT GLASS CORPORATION — An American firm founded in 1914 at Providence, Rhode Island, by George Dinkel, Samuel Ginsburg, and Harry Magid, the company produced some limited amounts of cut glass tableware before going out of business in 1925.

OLD FASHIONED GLASS — A short squat tumbler used for serving and drinking mixed drinks that contain alcohol. Old Fashioned glasses usually contain a uniform diameter and vary from about 8 to 12 ounces in capacity.

OLD GOLD — A deep amber stain or amber applied to glass made to resemble gold.

O'LEARY MULVANEY AND COMPANY — An American pressed glass-making firm established at Birmingham, Pennsylvania (Southside Pittsburgh), in 1832 by William O'Leary and Patrick Mulvaney. The factory was also known as the Birmingham Flint Glass Company. O'Leary left in 1845 and James Ledlie joined; the name was changed then to "Mulvaney and Ledlie." Mulvaney left in 1850 and A. T. Ulam joined; the name was then changed to "Ledlie and Ulam." Up until 1850, the firm produced hand-pressed tableware; afterwards, under Ledlie and Ulam, operations switched exclusively to blown bottle and cut lass production. Ledlie died in 1858 and Charles Ihmsen joined; the name was then changed to Ihmsen and Ulam. Due to financial problems, the firm closed in 1860. The factory was later occupied by Adams and Company.

OLIVE DISH — A small flat or shallow glass object, oblong or rectangular, that may or may not be divided; it is used specifically for serving olives.

Reproduction from a late 19th century Higgins-Seiter catalog.

MURRAY PATTERN
Very elaborate design cut glass Olive Dish.
No. 16812. 7½-inch, price.................$4.40

OLIVE GLASSWORKS — An American glass firm established in 1781 at Glassboro, New Jersey, by the five Stanger Brothers. All had worked for Caspar Wistar and produced South Jersey styled glass. Olive eventually became part of the Owens Bottle Company. *See also CASPAR WISTAR and SOUTH JERSEY GLASS.*

OLIVE GREEN — A green color in glass similar to Army olive drab. Olive green can be found in regular transparent glass as well as some flashed-on Carnival Glass items.

OLIVE JAR — A small to medium-sized glass container with a wide mouth and cover used for serving olives.

ONION SKIN GLASS — Colored glass that is sometimes rolled in mica flecks and then enclosed within a layer of clear glass. Glass objects referred to under this name were made during the ART NOUVEAU period. Some glass playing marbles were produced in this method. *See also LAYERED GLASS.*

ONYX GLASS — A dark-colored glass with streaking of white or other colors made by mixing molten glass with various color mediums. Most forms of Onyx glass are brown or murky gray with white streaking. In the late nineteenth century, the firm of Dalzell, Gilmore, Leighton and Company is noted for producing a specific style of Onyx Glass by adding several metals in the batch; the result was a lustrous silvery color with white streaking. Onyx produced by Dalzell, Gilmore, Leighton and Company was also known as Oriental Ware. *See also FINDLAY ONYX and MARBLED GLASS.*

O

Dalzell, Gilmore & Leighton Company Onyx Art Glass creamer and sugar. *Item courtesy of Wheaton Village.*

OPAL GLASS — An opalescent opaque-like white milk glass usually produced by the addition of tin or aluminum and fluorine. Shades of opal glass vary from those that are somewhat transparent and transmit light, to those that are nearly fully opaque. White opal glass that glows with a pale bluish-tinge where the glass is thin and held next to a light is sometimes referred to as "Fiery Opal." Other examples are sometimes cased in two or more layers to produce an opal-like effect. *See also* MILK GLASS.

Opal glass vase from the Boston and Sandwich Glass Company. *Item courtesy of Wheaton Village.*

OPALESCENCE — A milky or cloudy iridescent coloring or coating of glass, an opalescent coating is usually made by adding tin or zinc and calcium phosphate; along with other metal oxides. The result is often colors that shade from a milky white at the edges to the desired pastel hue in the center. The degree of opacity often depends on the exact composition and temperatures used in the manufacturing process. Opalescent glass was first made during the Art Nouveau movement in the nineteenth century. Frederick Carder, while working for Steuben in the early twentieth century, developed a unique method of producing colored opalescent glass: he cooled hot glass objects with direct bursts of compressed air and then reheated them. *See also* IRIDESCENCE.

Hobbs Brockunier cranberry opalescent hobnail patterned pitcher and tumbler. *Item courtesy of Wheaton Village.*

OPALINE GLASS — A translucent, semi-opaque Art glass, pressed or blown, that was first developed by Baccarat in the early nineteenth century. As opposed to opalescent glass, opaline tends to be more transparent. Like opalescent glass, it also comes in a wide variety of colors such as white, blue, and green. Opaline-style paperweights were made by Clichy in the shape of flat or book-shaped paperweights with an oval medallion or millefiori design encased within.

OPAQUE GLASS — Glass that is so dark in color it does not transmit light (milk glass for example); in other words, it cannot be seen through (the opposite of transparent). Opaque white glass is produced with tin oxide and was originally made to resemble porcelain. Opaque glass is made in a wide variety of colors and is occasionally confused with porcelain at times.

Opaque glassware made in Zweisel, Germany.

OPEN HANDLES — Refer to TAB HANDLES.

OPTIC BLOWN — Glass that is sometimes further blown or expanded once it is removed from the mold. *See also* OPTIC MOLD.

OPTIC MOLD — An open mold with a patterned interior in which a parison of glass is inserted and then inflated to decorate the surface. Ribbed molds (Optic Ribbed Glass) are most popular in this style.

OPTICAL GLASS — A curved piece of glass used to refract light rays so that they converge or diverge to form an image. They are utilized most in making prisms, eye-glasses, microscopes, telescopes, and other reflective or refractive devices. *See also* "Lens."

ORANGE BOWL — A large concave glass vessel, either rounded or hemispherical in shape, used for holding and displaying fresh oranges or other fruits. Some come with matching under-plates or stands. *See also* CENTERPIECE *and* FRUIT BOWL.

ORANGE GLASS — Glass colored by the addition of selenium and cadmium sulfide. Orange flashed glass is referred to as "Marigold" in Carnival glass. Czechoslovakian makers produced a good deal of orange-colored glassware during the twentieth century.

A Czechoslovakia cut and engraved orange goblet from the 1840s Navy Bor region. *Photo courtesy of the Corning Museum of Glass.*

ORCHID — A light translucent shade of amethyst Art Glass created and named by Steuben in the early twentieth century. Steuben also created a similar line referred to as "Oriental Orchid" (orchid-hued with white vertical strips) and "Oriental Poppy" (rose-colored with vertical opalescent strips).

ORIENT AND FLUME — A glass studio established in San Jose, California, in 1972 by Douglas Boyd and David Hopper. Both had received Master's Degrees in glass from San Jose State and soon gained a reputation for reviving iridescent glass forms of the past. Both are responsible for sparking the West Coast Glass Studio Movement beginning in the 1970s. The firm continues in operation today producing vases, paperweights, and other mostly iridescent forms of glass.

ORIENTAL GLASS COMPANY — An American glass decorating firm founded at Pittsburgh, Pennsylvania, in 1889 by Emil and C.W. Mueller along with Andrew Stock. The company decorated pressed glassware for other firms by enameling, light engraving, gilding and color-staining (especially amber and ruby-staining). Oriental declared bankruptcy in 1918 and closed permanently.

ORIENTAL WARE — Refer to ONYX GLASS.

ORLOV GLASSHOUSE — A Russian glass operation established at Milyutino in the Kaluga Province in the late eighteenth century by Fyodor Grigoryevich Orlov. It was purchased by his brother Mikhail F. Orlov (1788-1842) in 1814 and the house produced some practical tableware as well as some artistic wares (mostly hand-enameled and/or painted). When Orlov passed away, the firm became the property of A. D. Zalivskaya until 1849. The company stopped producing glass until it was acquired by S. I. Mal'tsev in 1884, and then by the Russian State in 1894. *See also MAL'TSEV GLASSWORKS and RUSSIAN GLASS.*

ORMOLU — A decorative piece usually made of brass, bronze, or gold and applied to glass objects (i.e. a stand or finial in paperweights).

ORNAMENT — A relatively small Art Glass object or accessory applied to a larger object that lends grace and beauty to it. An ornament might be a free-standing or hanging glass object or perhaps a fancy finial, handle, or applied decoration to another object. *See also CHRISTMAS ORNAMENT.*

ORNAMENTAL GLASS — A general term for Art Glass objects that are generally designed for show, display, and beauty rather than for use.

ORPLID GLASS — Refer to BIMINI WERKSTATTE.

ORR, L. A. COMPANY — An American cut glass operation founded in 1908 at Rochester, Minnesota, by Latham A. Orr. The firm cut some limited amount of tableware prior to closing by the start of World War I.

ORREFORS GLASBRUCK — A Swedish glass-making firm established in 1898 at Smaaland by Johan August Samuelson, the company continues to operate today as a maker of fine crystal products and Art Glass styles. It began as a maker of practical glass items like bottles, window panes, and some tableware; however, it is noted most for contemporary Art Glass forms including cased glass, crystal stemware, traditional Swedish art-styled items, and especially exquisite engraving (the GRAAL line is of particular note). In 1913, the factory was purchased by Consul Johan Ekman. In 1917, Orrefors leased the Sandvik Glassworks, purchased it in 1918, and then appointed Edward Stromberg as its director. When Ekman passed away in 1919, the company was jointly managed by Stromberg. Domestic glass was mostly produced at the Sandvik plant while art styles continued at Orrefors, which also opened both a school for glass artisans and a museum in 1957, and then joined the Afors group in 1990. *See also ARIEL, KRAKA, and RAVENNA GLASS; SIMON GATE and EDWARD HALD; GRAAL and AFORS GLASBRUK.*

O

A collection of Orrefors candlesticks.

Orrefors crystal glass heart.
Photo by Robin Rainwater.

Orrefors glass factory in Sweden.

Trademarks.

OSIER GLASS — A style of opaque white pressed glass characterized by an overall pattern of interlaced willow branches made to resemble basketwork. It originated in the mid-nineteenth century and was produced in some quantity by the English firm of Sowerby's.

OSLER, F. AND C. GLASSHOUSE — An English glass firm established at Birmingham in 1807, the company was noted for producing large glass objects such as chandeliers and window panes, in addition to some tableware and ornamental glass.

OTTAWA NOVELTY GLASS COMPANY — Refer to the NOVELTY GLASS COMPANY.

OUTPUT COMPANY OF AMERICA — Refer to the ROSEEN BROTHERS CUT GLASS COMPANY.

OVERBLOW — Refer to MOIL.

OVERLAY — A decorating style that involves the attaching or fusing of ornaments to the body of an object. Common ornaments include flowers, leaves, foliage, fruit, and scrolling.

Austrian glass decorated overlay tumbler. *Photo by Robin Rainwater.*

OVERLAY GLASS — The technique of placing one colored glass on top or over another, with designs cut through the outermost layer only. Overlay is actually the outer layer in cased glass. In paperweights, an overlay design is one where the weight has been dipped into an opaque colored glass and then cut away in places to form windows.

Boston & Sandwich Company ruby overlay compote.

Ruby overlay glass blow. *Photo by Robin Rainwater.*
Item courtesy of the Sandwich Glass Museum.

OVERSHOT GLASS — A type of glass with a very rough or jagged finish produced by rolling molten glass objects into crushed glass. The first examples in this style were produced by the Venetians in the sixteenth century.

Boston & Sandwich Glass Company overshot pitchers.
Items courtesy of Wheaton Village.

OVINGTON BROTHERS — A large china and glass retailer that operated in Brooklyn, New York, c. 1860 into the early 1930s; though the firm sold cut glass made by others, they occasionally placed their own company trademark on the products sold.

OWANDA GLASS COMPANY — A short-lived American cut glass company founded at Honesdale, Pennsylvania, in the early 1900s, the firm operated for only a few short years and closed permanently when the factory burned to the ground in 1908.

OWENS, MICHAEL J. — A glass blower who began his career at Libbey in 1888, Owens became superintendent of glass production at Libbey and, in 1903, invented the automatic bottle blowing machine, which produced bottles quickly and efficiently at a much lower cost. He went on to form Owens-Illinois Inc. *See also OWENS-ILLINOIS, INC.*

OWENS-ILLINOIS, INC. — An American firm established at Toledo, Ohio, in 1929 when the Owens Bottle Machine Company, under the direction of Michael J. Owens, merged with the Illinois Glass Company. In 1936, it acquired the Libbey Glass Company and continues producing huge quantities of glassware under the Libbey name today. Another offshoot of the company became Libbey-Owens-Ford (operates currently in both the state of Michigan and Canada making automobile and other industrial glass products). *See also MICHAEL J. OWENS and LIBBEY GLASS COMPANY.*

O

Pp

{ Pp }

PAD-BASE — A ring at the bottom of an object that is made by applying a small gathering of glass to form a base; they are also referred to as "Base Rings."

PADDLE — A glassmaker's tool that consists of a broad flattened blade connected to a handle. Paddles are used to flatten the bases of blown objects. Also a curved wooden tool used to shape the dome of a paperweight. Paddles were sometimes referred to as "Battledores" and are also simply known as "Blocks."

PADEN CITY GLASS COMPANY — An American company established at Paden, City, West Virginia, in 1916 by David Fisher, W. J. McCoy, Charles Schupback, and associates. Fisher had previously served as president of the New Martinsville Glass Company. The firm was also known as the Paden City Glass Manufacturing Company and began as a maker of pressed crystal tableware; it added cut glass, barware, and restaurant glassware later. The company was noted most for creating many elegant colored Depression Glass patterns (some etched and lightly gilded in the firm's decorating department) including "Black Forest," "Crow's Foot," "Cupid," "Gazebo," "Nora Bird," "Orchid," "Peacock and Wild Rose," and "Peacock Reverse." When Fisher passed away in 1933, his son, Samuel, assumed control; however, business slackened and Paden City closed permanently in 1951. Paden City's molds were acquired by Canton, Fenton, and Viking. In 1962, the Paden City plant was occupied by Marble King, Inc., a maker of glass marbles.

PADEN CITY GLASS MANUFACTURING COMPANY — Refer to the PADEN CITY GLASS COMPANY.

PAINTED CAMEO — Refer to MARY GREGORY.

PAINTED DECORATION — Designs or decorations applied to glassware by colored pigments. Painted designs are either applied to glass objects that have been cooled (cold painting) or by firing on the fuse enamels. *See also* ENAMELING.

PAIRPOINT MANUFACTURING COMPANY — (1) An American company established at New Bedford, Massachusetts, in 1865, it acquired the Mt. Washington Glass Company in a merger in 1894 and continued producing glass in many of Mt. Washington's established styles under the Pairpoint name. The firm almost went bankrupt in 1900, but reorganized as the Pairpoint Corporation. In 1939, after numerous ownership changes, the glass factory was purchased by Isaac Babbitt, who renamed the plant Gunderson Glass Works, Inc. (after skilled artisan Robert Gunderson). In 1952, it became the Gunderson-Pairpoint Glassworks; and in 1957, the operation was moved to East Warehem, Massachusetts, and briefly became Pairpoint Glassworks. Robert Bryden joined the firm in 1950 as a trainee and became sales manager in 1952. During the last year of operation, glass produced by the factory was also known as "Bryden's Pairpoint" or "Pairpoint of Warehem." The business closed permanently in 1958; however, that same year Bryden leased facilities in Spain and continued to make glass until 1970 (paper labels marked "Pairpoint – Made in Spain"). 2) A new company bearing the Pairpoint name opened in 1967 at Sagamore, Massachusetts; it produces some hand-made glassware and novelty items such as small pressed wares, cup plates, and suncatchers. *See also* MOUNT WASHINGTON GLASS WORKS, GUNDERSON GLASS WORKS, *and* ROBERT BRYDEN.

Reproduction of an 1894 Pairpoint U.S. patent.

P

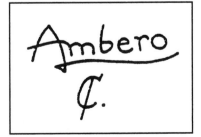

Trademarks.

PALDA, KARL — A Bohemian glass artisan who began decorating glass in Haida, Germany in 1888 (Haida later became Novy Bor, Czechoslovakian, in 1917). The firm produced decorated glass in typical Bohemian fashion by painting, enameling, and engraving up until World War II.

Reproduction from a 1935 Karl Palda catalog.

PALLET — A tool with a wide square piece of metal or wood that is attached to a handle. It is used to flatten the base of vessels such as jugs, pitchers, vases, etc. Pallets are also referred to simply as wooden paddles.

PALLME-KONIG — In the mid-eighteenth century, under Franz Josef Pallme and his son, Ignaz Pallme, the Pallmes entered the glass industry as makers of pitch in the area of Bohemia. Ignaz delved into engraving and passed his skills onto his son, Ignaz II, who became director of an engraver's guild at Steinschonau and received numerous awards for his abilities. In turn, Ignaz II had three sons who all entered the glass-making business; Ignaz III and Josef Karl (engravers) and Franz (painter). Many heirs of the three Pallme brothers became involved in the glass industry also. As a result, a large amount of Bohemian-styled decorated glass was produced under the Pallme-Konig name until all firms in Czechoslovakian became nationalized after World War II (1948).

PALM CUP — An open, somewhat bowl-shaped or hemispherical vessel used for drinking small quantities of liquids. Palm cups are generally smaller than regular cups (made to fit in the palm of one's hand), do not have handles, and may have a thicker or kick base.

PALMQVIST, SVEN — A noted mid-twentieth century Swedish glass designer, who, while working for Orrefors, developed many artistic styles of glass including Kraka and Ravenna. Palmqvist (b. 1956) is also noted for inventing a process of creating thick colorful glass bowls by centrifugal force without any further hand-finishing. See also ORREFORS, KRAKA, and RAVENNA GLASS.

PANE — A large piece of flat sheet glass used for glazing windows.

PANEL — 1) A decorative flat piece of glass like a plaque, usually rectangular in shape, used to hang on or in a suspended portion of a wall. Most glass examples are decorated in relief designs or mosaics. 2) An enclosed section on a glass object, usually rectangular or horizontal, that contains a single or series of vertically-spaced decorations. See also "Paneling."

PANEL WEIGHT — A paperweight in which clusters of canes form alternating or panel-like sections separated either by exposed sections of the paperweight's ground or by other things such as filigree twists, canes, or rods.

PANELING — A decorative pattern or series of parallel panels on a glass subject, the panels may come in a wide variety of forms and designs, such as arches, columns, simple rectangles, or flutes. Furthermore, there may be additional decorations within each panel; pressed paneled designs, particularly in the late nineteenth and early twentieth centuries, have contained such things as canes, stars, bands, buttons, cables, cherries, cosmos, daisies, dewdrops, forget-me-nots, grapes, heather, hobs (hobnail), honeycombs, ivy, oak, ovals, pleats, saw teeth, buttons, scrolling, strawberries, sunflowers, thistle, and wheat stalks.

PANTIN GLASSWORKS — A French firm established in 1851 by E. S. Monot at La Villette, Paris, the company relocated to Pantin in 1855 and proceeded through a variety of name changes, including Monot and Stumpf; Monot Pere et Fils and Stumpf; and Stumpf, Touvier, et Viole and Cie. The firm was noted as a maker of paperweights and then joined the Art Nouveau movement in the latter nineteenth century (primarily as a maker of cameo-styled cut glass). Around 1900, it was known as the Cristallerie de Pantin of Saint-Hilare, Touvier, de Varreux et Cie. Around 1920, it merged with Legras to become the Verreries de Cristtaleries de St. Denis et Pantin Reunies (products made were marked with 'De Vez,' 'Degue,' and 'Pantin').

PAPERWEIGHT — A small heavy glass object, usually with an inner design, used as a weight to hold down loose papers. Paperweights are often oval or rounded and are made of extremely thick domed glass. The three most popular inner styles consist of Millefiore floral designs, fancy Lampwork designs, and Sulphide reliefs of famous people and other figures (i.e. mostly from the animal kingdom). Paperweights were originally made in Europe in the 1840s hand have become one of the most popular of all glass collecting categories. See also MILLEFIORI, LAMPWORK, and SULPHIDE.

VERSAILLES 2102086

CHAMBORD 2102087

CHENONCEAUX 2102088

Reproduction of a 1999 Baccarat advertisement.
Courtesy of Baccarat.

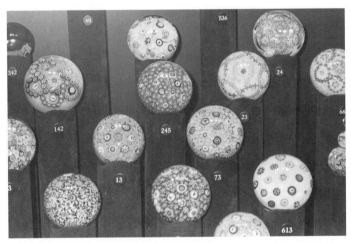

A collection of French Baccarat and St. Louis paperweights.
Photo by Robin Rainwater.

Venetian Millefiori paperweights. *Photo by Robin Rainwater.*

PARAMOUNT GLASS COMPANY — An American firm established in 1924 at Star City, West Virginia, by A. K. Gainer, the company produced blown glass stemware and tumblers, some with patterns (from molds) and iridescent finishes. The company moved to St. Mary's, West Virginia, in 1928; it closed in 1938.

PARFAIT — A tall, narrow glass, with a short stem and foot, used for serving ice cream. *See also* SUNDAE.

PARISON OR PARAISON — A blob of molten glass gathered at the end of the blowpipe, pontil, or gathering iron (same as "gather"). Note that parison is the English spelling of the French word, paraison.

PARKE AND CAMPBELL — Refer to UNION FLINT GLASS WORKS.

PARKE, CAMPBELL AND HANNA — Refer to UNION FLINT GLASS WORKS.

PARKE AND HANNA — Refer to UNION FLINT GLASS WORKS.

PARKER CUT GLASS MANUFACTORY — An English glasshouse established by Jerome Johnson and William Parker in the 1760s at London, the firm was noted most for producing cut glass chandeliers.

PARSCHE, F. X. AND SON COMPANY — An American firm founded in 1876 at Chicago, Illinois, by German immigrant Franz X. Parsche, who worked as an engraver/cutter in Bohemia, in Scotland, and for a couple of American firms prior to establishing his own business. Parsche's son, Frank C. Parsche, joined in 1890. Edward Koch also joined in 1893 as a partner (the business name then became Koch and Parsche). Koch left in 1907 and the firm officially became the F. X. Parsche and Son Company. Parsche cut glass tableware and bottles up until 1918. After 1918, the firm switched to other glass-making concerns including the production of custom lamps and glass grinding. *See also* EDWARD J. KOCH AND COMPANY.

Reproduction from a 1902 F. X. Parsche U.S. patent.

P

Trademark.

PART-SIZE MOLD — A small dip or piece mold used to impress an additional design on a glass object. Many are further expanded with additional blowing.

PASTE JEWELRY — Glass imitations of precious stones or gems made from strass. *See also* STRASS.

PASTE MOLD — Refer to MOLD.

PASTRY MOLD — A cane, usually millefiori in design, that takes the form of a pastry mold with deep and well-defined edges and flares or skirts out at its basal end.

PATE-DE-CRISTAL — A French term meaning "Paste of Crystal," it is an offshoot of pate-de-verre and was created by French artisan Joseph Gabriel Argy-Rousseau in the early twentieth century. Powdered crystal is used to form the paste and the finished product has a translucent quality rather than opaque like true pate-de-verre.

PATE-DE-VERRE — A French term meaning "Paste of Glass," it is an ancient material made from powdered glass or glass-like substances formed into a paste-like material by heating and then hardening. The resulting opaque form is carved, painted, or applied with other decorations. Similar translucent art wares made of fine quality crystal are sometimes referred to as "Pate-de-Cristal."

Daum Pate-de-Verre glass animal figurines.

PATERNOSTRI — An Italian or Venetian term for glass beads used commonly in prayer and in jewelry. Glass beads have been produced on the island of Murano as early as the eleventh century and served as an important trade commodity during the Middle Ages.

PATRIOTIC GLASS — Commemorative glass items decorated usually with mold-embossed, engraved or enameled designs that commemorate an historical event, famous person, or patriotic theme. *See also* BICENTENNIAL GLASS *and* COMMEMORATIVE GLASSWARE.

PATTERN GLASS — Glass produced by mechanically pressing it into molds. The design is cut directly in the mold and is formed into the glass object after the pressing operation. Machines have been pressing patterns designs into glass automatically using mass-production machine molds since America's Depression era.

PATTERN-MOLDED GLASS — A type of glass that is first impressed into small molds and then removed and blown to a larger size (blown-molded).

PATTI, THOMAS — A noted American Studio Glass artisan born in Pittsfield, Massachusetts, in 1943, Patti received his Master's in Industrial Design from Brooklyn, New York's Pratt Institute and has served in a teaching capacity at Berkshire Community College and as the director of the Savoy Art School in Massachusetts. Awards received include a National Endowment for the Arts Fellowship (1979), the Massachusetts Foundation of the Arts Fellowship (1981), and first prize at Germany's glass festival (Freies Glas, Glaskunst '81) in 1981. Patti continues to work as an independent glass artisan in Plainfield, Massachusetts.

PAULSKY, ROBERT CLARK — A noted American Studio Glass artisan born in Duluth, Minnesota, in 1942, Paulsky received his Master of Fine Arts degree from the Rochester Institute of Technology and has served in a teaching capacity at Hamilton College. Awards received include the Huber Grant (1971-1974), a Mellon Foundation Research Grant (1973-1975, 1978, 1982), and a fellowship to study at the Victoria and Albert Museum in London (1984). Paulsky continues to work as an independent glass artisan in Deansboro, New York.

PEACH BLOW GLASS — An American Art Glass first produced by several companies in the late nineteenth century (some attribute its origin to Hobbs, Brockunier in 1883), it was made to resemble peach-bloom Chinese porcelain under K'ang Hsi (1662-1722) and is characterized by multicolored opaque shades such as cream, white, pink, orange, red, etc. The colors were ordinarily shaded from lighter hues at the bottom to darker colors at the top. The style spread to some English firms such as Webb and Stevens and Williams. Note that it is also occasionally spelled as one word, "Peachblow." American makers have included Mount Washington; Pairpoint and Gunderson-Pairpoint; New England; New Martinsville; Hobbs, Brockunier; and Wheeling.

Peach Blow bottle in holder.
Photo by Robin Rainwater.

PEACH OPALESCENT — Peach colored glassware with a white opalescent edge or background (usually found in iridized Carnival Glass).

Dugan Peach Opalescent Carnival Glass Question Marks patterned dish. *Item courtesy of the Fenton Art Glass Museum.*

P

PEACOCK-FEATHER GLASS — A style of iridescent Art Glass created by Arthur J. Nash while working for Tiffany. This style is characterized by a variety of inlaid colored pieces around an off-centered eye. The eye is a larger and darker colored piece while the smaller pieces tail off into a feathered design. The overall design resembles that of a peacock feather. A similar art style was also created by Victor Durand Jr. Note that there is also an early twentieth century pressed glass pattern called Peacock Feather; it contains large ovals at the top with vertical bands of v-shaped feathering on the lower half (made to resemble peacock feathers). Peacock-feathered glass is also sometimes referred to as "Pulled Feather."

PEAR — 1) A common glass ornament or novelty item made in the shape of the yellowish-green fruit of its namesake. Pears are ordinarily larger at the apical end. Some are solid while others are hollowed in the center. A few inner gold-dust Venetian designs have been made into bookends (usually with a flattened base and one partially-flattened vertical side for resting flush against books). 2) Pears are also present as pressed/relief designs in pressed glass including Depression and Carnival glass. Most patterns contain a pair of the fruits and are referred to as "Baltimore Pear," "Maryland Pear," "Twin Pear," and even "Fig" (by Adams and Company) and "Gipsy" (some early Pittsburgh pressed glass-making firms).

Venetian glass pear.
Photo by Robin Rainwater.

PEARL — A small glass bead of various color, but often like that of a natural pearl, applied to the exterior of glass objects. Some are applied in quantity to form a decorative pattern while others may be applied on the tips of prunts.

PEARL OR PEARLIZED GLASS — Light custard-style Art Glass with a delicate, pastel iridescent finish made to resemble that of natural pearls. It is sometimes referred to as "Pearl Satin-Glass." See *also* MOTHER-OF-PEARL *and* VERRA DE SOIE.

PEARL ORNAMENTS — A molded glass pattern consisting of diamonds, squares, and other diagonal bandings.

PEARLINE GLASS — A late nineteenth century style of Art Glass with a color variance of pale to deep dark opaque blues.

PEASANT ART — A general term for decorating scenes of Old World peasant life from the Middle Ages to the present. These might encompass village scenes, forests, fruits, birds, and floral designs. Floral and foliage designs are particularly present in Czechoslovakian-made glass and porcelain in the twentieth century as there was a company named the "Czecho-Peasant Art Company." See *also* CZECHOSLOVAKIAN GLASS.

PEBBLED GLASS — An European colored decorating style first created in the seventeenth century, it is characterized by many small irregularly-shaped and haphazardly-placed brightly colored glass spots upon a vessel with a separate base color from that of the spots.

PEDESTAL WEIGHT — Refer to PIEDOUCHE.

PEERLESS CUT GLASS COMPANY — An American cut glass-making firm established in 1905 at Honesdale, Pennsylvania, by Michael Kelly and Frank Steinman (originally as Kelly and Steinman). Both Kelly and Steinman had previously been active in Gibbs, Kelly and Company. In 1907, they moved operations to Deposit, New York, and continued to cut glass up until the beginning of World War I. See *also* GIBBS, KELLY AND COMPANY.

Trademark. **PEERLESS**

PEG LAMP — A small oil lamp whose base is a cylindrically-pointed or tapered piece (peg) at the bottom; the peg fits into the socket of a candlestick or holder and served as an oil-burning (usually whale oil) substitute for candles. Peg lamps were popular beginning in the latter eighteenth century in both Europe and America.

PEGGING — The technique of poking a tiny hole in a molten glass object in order to trap a small quantity of air or bubble. The hole is then covered with other molten glass, which expands the bubble into a tear shape or teardrop inside the object.

PEILL AND SOHN — A German firm founded by Leopold Peill in 1903 at Duren in the Westphalia region of Germany. Initially, the factory produced tableware (especially tumblers) and some ornamental glassware. In 1946, the company merged with Putzler, which specialized in glass lighting, and the name was changed to Peill and Putzler. After the merger, the combined resources of both firms became one of Germany's largest producers of lighting, tableware, and some art glass; nevertheless, production declined steadily through the decades and the factory ceased production in 1997. Note that the Peill and Putzler trade name was purchased and some lighting fixtures are still produced under that name today.

PEISER, MARK — A noted American Studio Glass artisan born in Chicago, Illinois, in 1938, Peiser attended Purdue University, the Illinois Institute of Technology, and DePaul University. He has served in a teaching capacity at the Penland School of Crafts, the Toledo Museum of Art, Alfred University, the Pilchuk Glass Center, The School for American Craftsmen, the Rochester Institute of Technology, and the Haystack Mountain School of Crafts. Awards received include a Tiffany Foundation Grant and a National Endowment for the Arts Fellowship. Peiser continues to work as an independent glass artisan in Penland, North Carolina.

P

PEKING CAMEO — Colorful cameo engraved glass first made in China in the late seventeenth century in the city of Peking (at the Peking Imperial Palace Glassworks in 1680). It was made to resemble more expensive Chinese porcelain. The most popular medium was in the form of free-standing artistic items such as vases, animals, vegetables, and snuff bottles. It is also at times referred to as MANDARIN GLASS or PEKING GLASS.

Peking cameo engraved glass vase. *Photo by Robin Rainwater.*

PELL-MELL — Refer to SCRAMBLE.

PELOTON GLASS — A style of Art Glass first made and patented by Wilhelm Kralik in Bohemia in 1880, it is produced by rolling colored threads into colored glass directly after it was removed from the furnace. The object was then reheated to permanently fuse the threads or filaments. Because of the resulting final exterior texture, Peloton products have sometimes been referred to as "Spaghetti Glass" or "Shredded Coconut Glass."

PELTIER GLASS COMPANY — An American marble-making firm established at Ottawa, Illinois, by brothers Sellers H. and Joseph Peltier in 1920. Their father, Victor Peltier, had previously founded the Novelty Glass Company at the same site in 1886. The original factory burned in 1919 and a new one was built; at the same time, the company name was changed to Peltier. Sellers's son, Duncan Peltier, also became active in the family business. Aside from producing glass marbles, the company also made opalescent glass for Pullman Car windows, specialty glass for cathedrals, and glass gear shift knobs for automobiles. Both Sellers and Duncan were also involved in the Marble King firm. Duncan passed away in 1973, and the firm was sold in 1984. The new ownership still produces industrial marbles under the Peltier name as well as a variety of other glass products (i.e. glass gems, automotive signal and illuminating lenses, pressed glass, and candle-holders). *See also NOVELTY GLASS COMPANY and MARBLE KING.*

PEN — A pointed implement used for writing or drawing with ink or a similar fluid. Glass pens come in a variety of crystal or colored styles, and originated in Europe in the latter eighteenth century. Glass stands to hold pens date back to the mid-eighteenth century (some are called "Pen Stands" or "Pen Holders").

Glass pen. *Photo by Robin Rainwater.*

PENN GLASS WORKS — A short-lived American glass-making firm established at Pittsburgh, Pennsylvania, in 1874 by Peter Kunzler and Company. The company produced limited amounts of tumblers and lamp chimneys before closing in 1877. Note that there was another bottle-making firm established in 1859 (also Pittsburgh, Pennsylvania) that also went by the name of the Penn Glass Works.

PENNSYLVANIA ART GLASS — A small contemporary art glass firm established by Edward Nesteruk in 1980. Nesteruk studied Chemical Engineering at Penn State University and worked for chemical and glass industries for seventeen years before establishing his own business. Noted art glass designer Edward Kachurik joined on and the firm today is noted most for producing art glass sculptures and paperweights with transparent veils (created by applying precious metals to hot glass).

PENNSYLVANIA FLINT GLASS WORKS — Refer to CHRISTIAN IHMSEN and WHITEHEAD, IHMSEN AND PHILLIPS.

PENNSYLVANIA GLASS AND MANUFACTURING COMPANY — An American firm founded at Brilliant, Ohio, in 1912 by three men from Pittsburgh, Pennsylvania: M. K. Koster, R. S. Giese, and Frank Stonecipher. The company had purchased the plant previously occupied by the defunct decorating firm of McGee-Dieters. The firm specialized in making pressed glass lighting prior to closing in the early 1920s.

PEPPER BOTTLE — A small jar or bottle, with a notched cover, used specifically for serving ground black pepper with a small spoon. The spoon is ordinarily made of metal and is used to scoop out pepper in small quantities to be sprinkled over other foods. By the latter nineteenth century, they were replaced by pepper shakers.

PERCOLATOR TOP — A percolator is a type of coffee pot in which boiling water is forced up a hallow stem, filters through ground coffee, and then returns to the pot below. In the late nineteenth and midway through the twentieth centuries, glass tops or covers were common on these pots whereby the percolating action could be viewed. These tops were usually made of glass while the percolators were most often made of metal.

PERFECTION BOTTLE COMPANY — Refer to the NOVELTY GLASS COMPANY.

PERFECTION MANUFACTURING COMPANY — Refer to the NOVELTY GLASS COMPANY.

PERFUME BOTTLE — A tiny glass receptacle, with a narrow neck and stopper, used for holding liquid perfumes or colognes. Perfume bottles come in a wide variety of styles and forms, including cut, pressed, art glass designs, enameled, etched, and engraved. *See also COLOGNE BOTTLE and LARGE STOPPER BOTTLE.*

P

Egyptian glass modern perfume bottle.
Photo by Robin Rainwater.

PERFUME SPRINKLER — Refer to SPRINKLER and ATOMIZER.

PERSIAN BLUE — A somewhat light transparent blue opalescent color or clear glass with a blue opalescent edging (similar to "Moonstone," but only blue instead of white). The name has been applied to some Art glass and iridized Carnival Glass styles.

PERSIAN GLASS — General term for glassware made in Persia (modern day Iran) as early as the sixth century B.C. Most, however, was produced from the third to the nineteenth centuries. Glass produced in this region consists of blown, wheel-engraved, and relief-cut glass. During the Middle Ages, glass vessels and beads made in this area served as important trade commodities throughout Europe and the East. In the late sixteenth century and beyond, Persian styles were identical to those made at Murano (Venetian Glass) and Bohemia. *See also ISLAMIC GLASS.*

PERTHSHIRE PAPERWEIGHTS, LTD. — Established in 1968 by Stuart Drysdale in Crieff, Scotland, the firm is noted for producing high quality collectible millefiori and lampworked paperweights. Drysdale passed away in 1990; however, Perthshire continues to produce paperweights today, many in limited editions.

Perthshire paperweights.

PESTLE — A small club-shaped instrument used for pounding or grinding substances in a mortar. Most are made of porcelain, but some have been made of glass. Pestles date back to sixteenth century Germany and are sometimes referred to as "Muddlers." *See also MORTAR.*

PETRUS REGOUT AND CO. — Refer to MAASTRICHT.

PEZZATO — The Italian term for patchwork. Pezzato designed glass usually consists of various pieces of glass or separately colored sections on an object arranged in a hodgepodge or patch-worked design. The firm of Barovier and Toso is noted for producing a good deal of Venetian colored art glass in this style.

PFOHL FAMILY — In the late eighteenth century, Wenzel Pfohl, the first Pfohl family member, entered the glass business as a Bohemian cutter. He passed his skills to his son Josef, who became a noted cutter/engraver; Joseph, in turn, passed his trade onto his sons, Karel (1826-1894) and Josef Jr. Both worked at Steinschonau and were noted for wheel engraving, particularly that of horses. Josef Jr. had a son Alexander Pfohl (1866-1943), who became a noted painter of old German styles such as medallions and coats-of-arms. Alexander opened his own shop in 1888 at Haida, Germany (which later became Novy Bor, Czechoslovakia in 1917), and expanded into painting typical Bohemian scenery on glass: forest scenes, floral designs, and birds. Alexander's son Erwin (1906-1975) assumed control of the business in 1939. Erwin studied art and painting in Vienna and Paris, and became a noted artist like his father. Alexander had another son, Alexander Jr., whose reputation as an artist exceeded that of his brother. Alexander Jr. painted in water colors and, after serving in World War I, became head of design for Josephinenhutte. He joined his brother Erwin in 1939, but left in 1948 to open a school in Hadamar, Germany. Erwin stayed on as director of what became another Czechoslovakian state-run operation after World War II. *See also JOSEPHINENHUTTE.*

PHARMACY GLASS — A general term for various glass objects used in a pharmacy (i.e. bottles, jars, vials, and other dispensary containers). Many contain various labels and/or advertising with the pharmacy/doctor's name that might be mold embossed, lightly etched/engraved, enameled, or evidenced by a simple paper label.

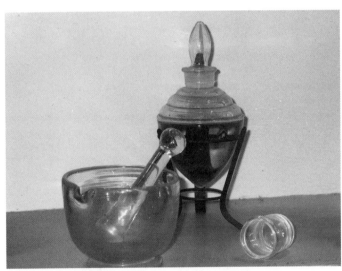

A collection of Pharmacy Glass items and bottles.
Items courtesy of Wheaton Village.

PHIAL — A small glass bottle used for ointments, medicines, and perfumes (same as "Vial"). Most have a stopper, cap, or similar device to enclose the top.

PHILADELPHIA AND KENSINGTON GLASS WORKS — A glasshouse founded in 1771 in the Kensington District of Philadelphia, Pennsylvania, the firm produced some crystal tableware. It was sold to Thomas Leiper in 1780 and, under Leiper's direction, the firm produced bottles and other containers before it was sold off to a group of investors in 1800. One of the new owners was Thomas Dyott, who eventually obtained sole ownership of the company in 1831. *See also DYOTTVILLE GLASS WORKS.*

PHILADELPHIA CUT GLASS COMPANY — A short-lived American cut glass operation established at Philadelphia, Pennsylvania in 1912, the firm produced some limited cut glass wares prior to closing at the end of World War I.

PHILLIPS AND COMPANY — 1) An American pressed glass-making business established at Pittsburgh, Pennsylvania, in 1840 by William Phillips. John Best became part of the firm in 1857 and the name was changed to Phillips, Best and Company. The firm produced pressed glass tableware. Phillips left in 1867 and the business was continued by John Best into the early 1870s. 2) There was another company located in Pittsburgh that was first known as Beck, Phillips and Company; and then became Phillips and Company in 1874. This venture produced window panes for a short time period.

PHILLIPS, BEST AND COMPANY — Refer to PHILLIPS AND COMPANY.

PHILLIPS, GEORGE AND COMPANY — A short-lived Canadian cut glass firm established at Montreal in 1907. The company ceased operations during World War I.

PHILLIPS GLASS COMPANY — Refer to the STERLING GLASS COMPANY.

PHILLIPS, JOSEPH AND COMPANY — Refer to the STERLING GLASS COMPANY.

PHILLIPSBURGH GLASS WORKS — Refer to DOYLE AND COMPANY.

PHOENIX GLASS — A term usually applied to cased milk glass also known as "Mother-of-Pearl" made specifically by the Phoenix Glassworks Company in Pittsburgh, Pennsylvania, in the late nineteenth century.

PHOENIX GLASS COMPANY — 1) An American firm founded by Englishman Thomas Caines at South Boston, Massachusetts, in 1820. Caines's son William joined in 1832, and William's brother-in-law, William Johnston, joined also. The company produced pressed and cut glass tableware before the plant closed in 1870. Note that the name was changed to Caines and Johnston in 1852 when Thomas temporarily retired, to Thomas H. Caines and Son in 1855 when Johnston died and Thomas became active again, and then to William Caines and Bro. in 1867 when William's brother Joseph joined (Thomas had died in 1865). 2) An early nineteenth century glass firm established in Bristol, England, by Wadhams, Ricketts, and Co. The company produced some limited cut and engraved glass. 3) An American company founded by William McCully at Pittsburgh, Pennsylvania, in 1832 (also known as McCully and Company). This firm produced pressed and cut tableware before closing in 1880. 4) An American company established in Monaca, Pennsylvania, in 1880 by Andrew Howard and William Miller, the factory burned in 1884 and again in 1893 (rebuilt both times). The firm later moved to Pittsburgh and was noted for producing cut glass gas and electric lighting fixtures, lamp chimneys, light bulbs, general glass items, pressed tableware,

and some figural Art Glass similar to that of Lalique. Phoenix became a division of Anchor Hocking in 1970 and was later sold to the Newell Group in 1987. Anchor Hocking still produces lighting glassware and other industrial glass at a plant named the "Phoenix Glass Plant" in Monaca, Pennsylvania. It is this fourth and final "Phoenix" company that is most familiar to glass collectors.

Pheonix Art Glass vases. *Items courtesy of Wheaton Village.*

Trademarks.

PHOSPHOROUS — A nonmetallic substance from the nitrogen family that, when combined with calcium (calcium phosphate), produces an opaque white color when added to a batch of glass. *See also CALCIUM and CALCITE GLASS.*

PHOTOCHROMIC GLASS — A tinted glass developed by Corning Glass Works in Corning, New York, in 1964. When the glass is exposed to ultraviolet radiation such as sunlight, it darkens; when the radiation is removed, the glass clears.

PICKLE CASTOR — A glass jar held within a silver or silver plated metal frame, usually with a handle and matching spoon, used for serving pickles. They were most popular during the Victorian Period.

PICKLE DISH — A flat or shallow dish, oblong or rectangular, used specifically for serving pickles. For comparison, pickle dishes are generally a little smaller than a banana boat or celery dish.

Reproduction from an 1899 U.S. Glass Company catalog.

PICKLE JAR — A glass receptacle, usually cylindrical or globular and that contains a flat-topped stopper or cover, used for serving pickles. A special type of pickle jar was made in America and Europe (during part of the Victorian Era) from around 1880 to 1920; they are characterized by a large capacity (one quart to one gallon), made with four or eight sides, had a large mouth for ease of removing pickles, were usually made in green or blue colors, and had a top that was sealed with a tin or cork cover. Pickle jars are also sometimes referred to as "Picklers."

PICKLE LADLE — Refer to LADLE.

PICK-UP DECORATION — Refer to MARVER.

PICTORIAL FLASK — A style of flask produced in great numbers in America in the nineteenth century. They are mold-blown colored glass containers that depict low relief designs of pressed patterns, floral patterns, dancers, scrolling, and violins. Those with noteworthy Americans, national emblems, and commemorative events are usually referred to as "Historical Flasks." Many were later reproduced in miniature. *See also* HISTORICAL FLASK.

PIE PLATE — A large shallow round glass dish used for baking and serving pies.

An Avon Cape Cod pattern ruby red pie plate commissioned for Wheaton Industries. *Photo by Robin Rainwater.*

PIECE MOLD — A mold that usually consists of two pieces hinged together. Glass is then pressed or blown into the mold to form a full glass object or part-sized object that will be added to become part of a larger object. The mold may contain a pattern and the molded piece may also be expanded by further blowing. *See also* MOLD.

PIEDOUCHE — A French term for a paperweight that is raised on a low, applied crystal foot. Many resemble ice cream cone-like structures with a slender stem that tapers out, topped by a rounded paperweight that is larger in diameter than the stem. They are also known as Footed Weights or Pedestal Weights.

PIGEON BLOOD — A color of glass characterized by brown highlighting over a somewhat transparent deep scarlet red (or blood red). Pieces produced in this style tend to have a glossy or shiny finish. Pigeon blood was popular during the Art Nouveau movement and this form of coloring was applied to many glass patterns.

PILGRIM GLASS COMPANY — A contemporary Art Glass company founded in 1949 by Alfred E. Knobler in Ceredo, West Virginia, Pilgrim is noted for producing paperweights, marbles, lamps, and several art forms including a wide variety of modern cameo cut glass.

Reproduction of a 1997 Pilgrim advertisement. *Courtesy of the Pilgrim Glass Company.*

Pilgrim glass vases. *Photo by Robin Rainwater.*

Trademark.

PILKINGTON BROTHERS, LTD. — A British firm established by John William Bell and Associates in 1826 as the St. Helens Crown Glass Company at St. Helens (near Liverpool). The company was renamed Greenal and Pilkington in 1829, and then changed permanently to Pilkington Brothers, Ltd. in 1849. Early on, the firm primarily produced plate glass for windows. Pilkington purchased the British Cast Plate Glass Company in1901, the Chance Brothers in 1945, and a variety of other firms as well. Today, the company is one of the largest producers in the world of both plate and industrial glass (i.e. laminated, safety, optics, pressed, and fiber glass). In addition, the firm operates in partnership with Libbey-Owens-Ford of America producing flat glass for automobiles and construction.

Pilkington Brothers, Ltd.: Trademark.

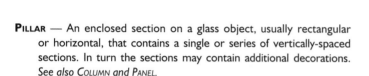

PILLAR — An enclosed section on a glass object, usually rectangular or horizontal, that contains a single or series of vertically-spaced sections. In turn the sections may contain additional decorations. *See also* COLUMN *and* PANEL.

PILLAR CUTTING — A decorative pattern of cut glass in the form of parallel vertical ribs in symmetrical pillar shapes (similar to flute cutting).

PILLAR FLUTES — A decorative design consisting of a series of adjacent curved vertical sections that are either molded or cut. The sections are usually squared off or slightly curved at the bottom while more completely curved at the top.

PILSENER GLASS — A tall narrow glass vessel with foot that is primarily used for drinking beer.

PIN TRAY — A tiny flat or shallow glass dish used for holding hairpins.

PINCERING — A decorating technique that originated with Venetian glassmakers, it is completed by applying pincers, usually to the stems of goblets. The result is a squeezed-on or impressed decoration such as threading, wings, or other protuberances.

PINCERS — A glassmaker's tool consisting of two short handles and grasping jaws. They are usually used to squeeze on various pieces of ornamentation while glass is still in its molten state (like pincering). *See also* FORMING TOOL, PUCELLAS, STEEL-JACKS, TONGS, *and* WOOD-JACKS.

PINCHBECK WEIGHT — A metallic disk usually made of a copper-zinc alloy that simulates gold or silver that has a design in bas-relief. The disc is usually covered with a magnifying lens fitted to a pewter or alabaster base. Since the motif is not entirely encased in glass, they are generally not considered true glass paperweights.

PINK GLASS — Glass colored by the addition of neodymium and selenium. Pink-colored glass was most popular during America's Depression era in the 1920s and 1930s.

PINK SLAG GLASS — A style of glass characterized by colorful pink swirling or marbleized designs. Pink slag was a popular art form of the Indiana Tumbler and Goblet Company, which produced it in the 1890s. *See also* CARAMEL SLAG *and* SLAG GLASS.

PINKWATER GLASS, INC. — A modern American art glass company founded by Kurt Swanson and Lisa Schwartz in Carmel, New York, in 1983. Both had received Masters of Fine Arts degrees in 3-D design from the Massachusetts College of Art the same year. The firm specializes in one-of-a-kind limited edition colorfully blown glass art objects.

PINNACLE — A tall thin glass object that tapers upward and serves as an ornamental fixture on a chandelier. Most are faceted, cut, or beveled to provide a faceted and refractive appearance.

PINWHEEL — A 12-point star formed in cut glass by splits that are pointed in a counter-clockwise direction. Fan motifs are usually pointed in the same direction between the points. Pinwheels were often combined with other cut designs including diamonds, notched prisms, scrolling, etc. Pinwheels are also synonymous with 12-point "Buzz Stars."

PIONEER CUT GLASS COMPANY — An American cut glass operation established at Carbondale, Pennsylvania, in 1905, the firm produced cut glass products until ceasing all operations in 1920.

PIONEER FLINT GLASS COMPANY — Refer to the BARTLETT-COLLINS GLASS COMPANY.

PIONEER GLASS COMPANY — An American glass-decorating firm established at Pittsburgh, Pennsylvania, in 1891, the company specialized in staining glass, mostly in ruby red. The company operated for only a few short years, primarily as a staining subcontractor for the U.S. Glass Company combine.

PIPE — A short tube or cylindrical-type structure, with a small bowl at one end, used for smoking tobacco; pipes are made of such materials as wood, clay, hard rubber, and even glass on occasion.

PITCHER — A wide-mouthed glass vessel, usually with a spout and handle and with or without a lip, used for pouring or serving liquids. See also DISK PITCHER, MILK PITCHER, SYRUP PITCHER, *and* WATER PITCHER.

An Avon Cape Cod pattern ruby red pitcher, commissioned for Wheaton Industries. *Photo by Robin Rainwater.*

PITKIN AND BROOKS — An American firm established as a cut glass operation and distributor of crocks and glassware at Chicago, Illinois, in 1872. The team of Edward Hand Pitkin and Jonathan William Brooks Jr. operated as a partnership until closing in 1920. Note that the company ran another cut glass plant in Valparaiso, Indiana, from 1911 to 1918.

Pitkin & Brooks: Reproduction of an early 20ᵗʰ century
Pitkin & Brooks advertisement.

Trademarks.

PITKIN GLASS WORKS — An American firm founded by Richard Pitkin, William and Elisha Pitkin, and Samuel Bishop in 1783 at East Hartford, Connecticut (adjacent to the Connecticut River), the company began as a window pane operation, but soon expanded into producing bottles and flasks. One such small mold-blown flask, known as a "Pitkin Flask," is characterized by colored glass (amber, green, blue, or amethyst), vertical or swirled ribbing, a double-thick lower half, and a flattened ovoid shape that tapers to a short cylindrical neck. Pitkin flasks were made by other firms as well. The company ceased operation in 1830. *See also HALF-POST METHOD.*

An early 19ᵗʰ century American Pitkin flask and bottles.
Photo courtesy of the Corning Museum of Glass.

PITTSBURGH BRASS COMPANY — An American firm founded in 1889 at Allegheny City, Pennsylvania (across the Allegheny River from Pittsburgh), by Cornelius Birmingham, Thomas Hipwell, Edward Kitzmiller, Joseph McNaughton Sr., and Joseph McNaughton Jr. The company began as a manufacturer of metal goods including brass lamp parts. In 1898, the name was changed to the Pittsburgh Lamp and Brass Company; reorganization occurred in 1901; and the name was changed again to the Pittsburgh Lamp, Brass and Glass Company. The firm acquired the Kopp, Lamp, and Glass Company and Dithridge and Company in 1901, and began producing pressed glass in both clear glass and color, as well as signal light lenses. The firm closed in 1926; however, the Kopp family acquired the original plant and reorganized as Kopp Glass, Inc. The Dithridge Division was in turn reorganized by Paul Zimmerman and remained in operation until 1935.

PITTSBURGH CITY GLASS WORKS — Refer to CUNNINGHAM AND COMPANY.

PITTSBURGH CUT GLASS COMPANY — An American cut glass operation founded in 1910 at Pittsburgh, Pennsylvania, by William Carey, Michael Liston, and Brenton Lydey. The firm produced cut glass tableware until ceasing operations in 1921.

PITTSBURGH FLINT GLASS WORKS — The early name for Benjamin Bakewell's first glass company established in 1808. *See also BAKEWELL, PEARS AND COMPANY.*

PITTSBURGH GLASS — High quality pressed glass made in America by several companies in and around Pittsburgh, Pennsylvania, in the late eighteenth and nineteenth centuries.

PITTSBURGH GLASS COMPANY — Refer to WHITLA GLASS COMPANY, LTD.

PITTSBURGH GLASS WORKS — An American glass firm established at Pittsburgh, Pennsylvania, in 1796 by two Revolutionary War officers, General James O'Hara and Major Isaac Craig (Craig was a deputy major under O'Hara). The two employed noted French glass artisan Peter Eichbaum, a skilled cutter and the son of John Amelung. The firm produced some lead cut crystal tableware, bottles, window glass, and pressed ware later. The company proceeded through many ownership and name changes (i.e. Craig and O'Hara or O'Hara and Craig; Eichbaum, Wendt and Company – Frederick Wendt was one of the firm's early managers; O'Hara Works; Pittsburgh Glass Company; and Pittsburgh Glass Works). The company closed after the War of 1812, but opened again later. The plant remained open off and on with a wide variety of interests until ceasing operation in 1890.

P

PITTSBURGH LAMP AND BRASS COMPANY — Refer to the PITTSBURGH BRASS COMPANY.

PITTSBURGH LAMP, BRASS AND GLASS COMPANY — Refer to the PITTSBURGH BRASS COMPANY.

PLACE CARD HOLDER — An object designed to hold a card with the name of a guest on it and then placed on a dining table indicating where he or she is to sit. Glass place card holders are made today by major crystal companies such as Baccarat and Waterford. Larger place cards are sometimes referred to as "Menu Cards," which are designed to house menus. *See also MENU CARD HOLDER.*

PLANTERS' PEANUTS GLASSWARE — Glass objects, mostly tumblers and covered jars, that have been mold-embossed or enameled with the Planters' Peanut company logo. The Planters Nut and Chocolate Company was founded in 1906 in Wilkes-Barre, Pennsylvania, while the trademark Mr. Peanut figurine was adopted in 1916, the same year the company was sold to Standard Brands, Inc., which later merged with Nabisco in 1981. Many barrel-shaped jars were produced with the peanut finial covers. Early jars were commissioned by Tiffin in the 1930s. Mr. Peanut jars can be difficult to date since many are being reproduced. For instance, older emerald green Depression style jars sell for about ten times the price of the newer darker forest or olive green jars.

Reproduction from a 1930 Tiffin Glass Company catalog.

PLAQUE — A decorative flat piece of glass or thin tablet, usually rectangular in shape, used to hang on or in a suspended portion of a wall. Most glass examples are decorated in relief designs or mosaics.

PLATE — A flat glass object, usually round in shape (occasionally square or oval), used for serving dinner, lunch, desserts, and other foods.

PLATE GLASS — Glass produced in thick sheets used for mirrors, windows, cabinets, and table tops. Plate glass is sometimes referred to as "Flat Glass" since it is often rolled or cast into flat sheets and then subjected to grinding and polishing.

PLATED AMBERINA — A style of cased art glass developed by Joseph Locke while he served as an employee of the New England Glass Company in 1866. Glass objects were created with a creamy opalescent lining and then cased with an outer layer of amberina. The pieces were difficult to make and were produced in limited quality. They are also far more valuable than regular amberina items. *See also AMBERINA.*

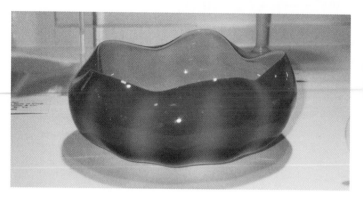

Plated Amberina bowl from the New England Glass Company. *Item courtesy of Wheaton Village.*

PLATED GLASS — Glass that is cased or covered by more than one layer; usually clear glass that is dipped or completely covered with colored glass. *See also OVERLAY and CASED GLASS.*

PLATINUM BAND — A metallic silver-colored trim applied to rims or by banding around glass objects (made of genuine platinum or a combination of mercury and platinum).

PLATONITE — A heat resistant opaque white-colored glass first produced by the Hazel-Atlas Glass Company in the 1930s. Hazel Atlas patented the name "Platonite" and continued producing tableware in this style into the 1940s.

PLATTER — A large flat glass object, usually round or oval in shape (larger than dinner plates), used for serving large amounts of foods.

Avon Cape Cod pattern ruby red platter commissioned for Wheaton Industries. *Photo by Robin Rainwater.*

Hocking Glass Company's Miss America Depression Glass patterned platter.

PLEATED — A design found most often in pressed glass that contains several ruffled or folded segments set in parallel rows.

PLUM GLASS COMPANY — An American firm founded at Plum, Pennsylvania, in 1986 by siblings John and Annie Bondich. John had previously worked at Westmoreland and purchased some of Westmoreland's molds. Other siblings joined soon after, including Zora, Helen, and George. The company is noted for producing pressed milk glass; however, early on, they did not change the Westmoreland mold mark (eventually they did replace it with a PG inside a keystone in addition to the Westmoreland mark).

PLUM JADE GLASS — A three-layered style of colored Art Glass created by Frederick Carder of Steuben in the 1920s, it was produced by casing two layers of amethyst glass around Alabaster and then acid dipped and etched more than once to provide a multi-shaded effect.

PLUNGER — A metal device or toll that presses molten glass against a mold to create the interior or primary pattern of an object (the mold ordinarily produces the pattern on the outside surface). Plungers can also be used to press glass into blank molds in order to form an initial cavity for subsequent blowing operations.

PLUNKETT AND MILLER — An American glass firm established at Wheeling in 1837, prior to West Virginia becoming a state, by Francis Plunkett and H. M. Miller. (Note that Plunkett and Miller established a second venture in the same city in the same year, East Wheeling Glass Works.) Operations were moved to South Wheeling and renamed the South Wheeling Glass Works in 1840. The firm produced some lead cut/engraved crystal and colored tableware before going bankrupt in 1841. The factory was sold in 1845 in John L. Hobbs and James B. Barnes. Francis, along with James Plunkett, went on to establish the Excelsior Glass Works in Pittsburgh, Pennsylvania, in 1859. *See also* EAST WHEELING GLASS WORKS *and* HOBBS, BARNES AND COMPANY.

POCKET-FLASK — A small glass container, with a narrow neck and mouth and a stopper or cover, used for carrying alcoholic beverages in one's pocket. Pocket-sized flasks ordinarily have a capacity of up to eight ounces.

POCKET-TUMBLER — A small oval drinking vessel, without a foot, stem, or handle, that contains a pointed or convex base and is small enough to be carried in one's pocket. Pocket Tumblers originated in Spain in the seventeenth century and were further decorated (i.e. colored threading, striping, and gilding).

POHL FAMILY — In the late eighteenth century, Franz Pohl (1764-1834) was employed at the glasshouse known as Josephinenhutte in Bohemia. Franz had three sons: Franz (1788-1856), Johann (1768-1850), and Joseph. The younger Franz managed the refinery at Harrachs while Johann managed glass operations at Harrachs from 1808-1848. Joseph moved to Steinschonau and gained a reputation for his quality engraving. Another member of the Pohl family, Karl Pohl, also operated a glass decorating shop at Haida, Germany. The firm painted and engraved glass in typical Bohemian style, but ceased operations by World War I.

POINT MARION GLASS NOVELTY COMPANY — An American firm founded at Guyaux, Pennsylvania, in 1916, the company produced pressed glass, which consisted primarily of milk glass novelty items. The firm closed in the late 1930s. Note that there was a window-producing firm established in 1911 as the Point Marion Window Glass Company, Ltd. in the same region.

POISON BOTTLE — A tiny pharmaceutical receptacle with a small neck and mouth (or two tiny holes) used for containing harmful substances. Most contain external ridges on the body so as to be easily distinguished by touch while others may have a corked hole in the bottom for filling. They also contain some form of labeling or perhaps a skull and crossbones.

POKAL — A Bohemian-styled goblet with stemmed foot and cover (the cover may or may not contain a finial) first made in the late seventeenth century. *See also* STEIN.

1740s German Pokal cut, engraved, and gilded.
Photo courtesy of the Corning Museum of Glass.

POLI, FLAVIO — A twentieth century Venetian (Murano) glass artisan noted for a variety of contemporary art-styled glass – inlaid color, bubble effects, heavy crystal cased glass in multiple contrasting colors, and elaborate chandeliers.

P

POLISH GLASS — General term for glass made in and around Poland beginning as early as the late fourteenth century. Early items produced consisted of practical items like window panes and tableware. After the Middle Ages, Polish glass was made in the typical Venetian and Bohemian styles of the day. Beginning in the latter twentieth century, contemporary Polish style consisted primarily of cut and/or heavily engraved crystal. Occasionally, some pieces are flashed in color and then further cut to provide a crystal and color combination.

Reproduction of a 1995 Polish glass advertisement.

POLISHING — The process of giving glass objects a smooth and glossy finish. Polishing with fine-grained wheels (stone, wood, cork, or metal) is completed with very light-grained abrasive powders and is usually applied to fine lead crystal that may be cut or engraved. *See also* ACID POLISHING *and* FIRE POLISHING.

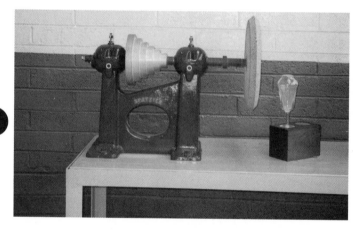

Waterford polishing wheel.

POLLARD, DONALD — A noted twentieth century American glass designer born in Bronxville, New York, in 1924, Pollard received his Fine Arts degree from the Rhode Island School of Design and served as a designer for Steuben for over thirty years (1950-1981).

POLYCHROMIC GLASS — Glass or decorations characterized by two or more colors. For single colors, refer to MONOCHROME.

POMADE BOX — A small rectangular, circular, or oval glass receptacle, with a cover, used for storing perfume, oils, or hair dressing. Pomade boxes were popular in the Victorian era and were part of dresser sets. Note that pomade ointment was originally made of apples.

POMONA GLASS — An art style of glass created by applying or dipping the object into acid to produce a mottled, frosted appearance. It was first developed by Joseph Locke at the New England Glass Company and patented in 1885. Pomona glass is usually stained in amber or rose, continuously enlarged by mold-blowing, and further decorated by fruits, floral designs, or foliage. Locke named it after the Roman goddess of fruit and trees.

POMONA GREEN — A somewhat medium, oily shade of green Art Glass created and named by Steuben in the early twentieth century. It is often contrasted with other colors like amber, Steuben's Rosa, pink, or amethyst for such things as handles, feet, finials, and other attachments.

PONTIE OR PONTY — Refer to PONTIL.

PONTIL — A solid but shorter iron (as opposed to a longer blowpipe) used to remove or break-off expanded objects from the blowing iron, which allows the top to be finished. Prior to the nineteenth century, it left a rough mark (Pontil Mark), but since then, it is usually grounded flat. Pontil is also referred to as "pontie," "ponty," "punty," and "puntee."

PONTIL MARK — Refer to PONTIL.

POOR MAN'S CAMEO — Refer to MARY GREGORY.

POPE CUT GLASS COMPANY, INC. — An American firm established at New York, New York, in 1916 by Frederick Grace and Frank Hastings, the company produced cut glass products into the mid-1920s.

Pope Cut Glass Company, Inc.: Trademark. **DIAMONKUT**

PORT GLASS — A fairly small stemmed and footed drinking vessel specifically designed for drinking port wine. Port glasses usually have a capacity of about 3-4 ounces and resemble small wine glasses. *See also* WINE GLASS.

PORTIEUX GLASSWORKS — Refer to VALLERYSTHAL GLASS.

PORTLAND GLASS COMPANY — An American firm founded in 1863 at Portland, Maine, by John B. Brown, J. S. Palmer, and associates. Enoch Eggington served as the plant superintendent. The plant was destroyed by fire in 1867, but was rebuilt the following year. It was reorganized as the Portland Glass Works in 1870. The company produced pressed crystal tableware until closing permanently in 1873.

PORTLAND GLASS WORKS — Refer to the PORTLAND GLASS COMPANY.

PORTRAIT GLASS — Any form or style of glass object that is decorated with the representation of a figure, person, bust, statue, historical subject, or other sculptured figures. Small glass medallions date as far back as Ancient Roman times and were made in low relief and bare the portraits of famous people. Since the Renaissance period, a wide variety of subjects have been enameled, engraved, etched, cut in relief, gilded, and applied in many forms on such objects as vases, goblets, drinking vessels, and within paperweights.

PORTS — Any vents or openings in a furnace through which flames or fuel enter, or form, and which exhaust gases escape.

PORZELLANFABRIK HUTSCHEN-REUTHER — Refer to THERESIENTHAL GLASS.

P

POT — A vessel made of fired clay in which a batch of glass ingredients is heated before being transferred to the furnace. Many varieties include open, closed, and smaller for colored glass, but most only last three to six weeks before breaking up. Modern pots hold 1,100 to 1,650 pounds of glass, but smaller ones are generally used for paperweight making. (Also known as "Piling Pot," "Jockey Pot," "Monkey Pot," or simply "Clay Pot").

POT ARCH OR FURNACE — A type of furnace in which one or more relatively small ceramic pots are fired before being transferred to the main furnace for melting. A pot arch or furnace generally allows for the melting of many different glass colors at once (as many as there are pots).

Waterford Twin Pot Furnace.

POTASH — Potassium oxide (K_2O) or potassium carbonate (K_2CO_3) or a type of ash that results from burning of various plant materials (ferns, brackens, trees etc.). Potash is used as a substitute for soda as an alkali source is a glass mixture.

POTSDAM GLASS FACTORY — A German glasshouse founded by Elector Friedrich Wilhelm of Brankenburg in 1679 at Potsdam near Berlin. Johann Kunckel was its first director, and he is noted for developing a process for creating ruby red glass with gold and discovering that the addition of chalk to a batch of glass eliminates crisselling. In 1736, the glass-making operation was moved to Zechlin, where it remained as a government-run operation until 1890.

POWDER BLUE — An opaque blue-colored glass made with cobalt and aluminum.

POWDER HORN — A glass receptacle, made in the shape of a powder horn, used in hunting. *See also* HORN.

POWDER JAR — A small glass receptacle, usually with a cover, used for holding various body powders. Powder jars are ordinarily part of dresser sets.

A cut glass powder jar by J. Hoare & Co., early 1900s.
Photo by Robin Rainwater.
Item courtesy of the Corning Museum of Glass.

POWDERED GLASS — A style of Art Glass produced by applying (usually by fusing) a coating of various colored powered glass particles on to the surface of an object. The particles are often arranged into some pattern form or design prior to fusing. The process was created and patented by Englishman John Davenport in 1806.

POWELL, JAMES AND SONS — Refer to the WHITEFRIARS GLASS WORKS.

POWELTON CUT GLASS COMPANY — An American firm founded in 1910 at Philadelphia, Pennsylvania, by Iredell Eachus, Raymond Fender, James Jamison, and E. Ellis Stalbird. The company produced cut glass tableware until 1918; after that, they switched to less expensive engraving. Powelton remained in business until 1953.

PREMIUM GLASS COMPANY — Refer to the BARTLETT-COLLINS COMPANY.

PRESCUT — A name given to a line of pressed glass tableware produced by the McKee Brothers in the late nineteenth and early twentieth centuries. The glass contained elaborate and/or fancy pressed patterns that were made to resemble more expensive cut glass, though the finished products were not nearly as sharp as typical cut glass. Pattern names included Aztec, Bontec, Carltec, Martec, Plutec, Plytec, Quintec, Rotec, Sextec, Toltec, Valtec, Wiltec, and Yutec. Others such as Anchor-Hocking adopted the Prescut name later. Early American Prescut was a huge line of pressed glass made and named by the Anchor Hocking Company in 1960 through the mid-1970s. *See also* MCKEE BROTHERS *and* EARLY AMERICAN PRESCUT.

Prescut: Reproduction from an early 20th century McKee Brothers catalog.

PRESERVE DISH — A small flat or shallow dish, with or without foot, used for serving jelly, jam, and other fruit preserves.

PRESERVE JAR — A glass vessel, usually rounded or somewhat cylindrically-shaped and with a cover (usually metal), used for preserving fruit-based jams and jellies. Preserve jars can also be thought of as small canning jars. See also *CANNING JAR*.

PRESENTATION GLASS — A general term for glassware decorated to commemorate a specific person, occasion, or event. See also *COMMEMORATIVE GLASS*.

PRESSED GLASS — Hot molten glass mechanically forced into molds under pressure. An important American invention in the 1820s was the hand press: Enoch Robinson, while working for the New England Glass Company, is often credited with inventing it and receiving the first U.S. patent for it in 1827. The original hand presses were also known as a "Side Lever Press" since it was manually actuated with a side lever. The mold forms the outside of the piece while the glass is then pressed inside with a plunger to form the inner shape. Pressing began in America, but quickly spread to Europe. Carnival Glass (hand-pressed) and Depression Glass (the first widely produced machine-pressed) were two of the most popular forms of pressed glass in the twentieth century. See also *PRESSING*.

Pressed glass comet patterned tableware.
Photo by Robin Rainwater.

Reproduction of a 1901 National Glass Co. catalog.

PRESSING — The process begins with molten glass poured into a mold that forms the outer surface of an object. A plunger lowered into the mass leaves a smooth center with a patterned exterior. Such things as flat plates and dishes are formed in a base mold and an upper section folds down to mold the top (like a waffle iron).

PRINTY — The English term for a circular or concave window cut into the surface of a paperweight.

PRISM — 1) A type of decorative oval or triangular dangling glass piece used in chandeliers, mantel lustres, and candelabras. 2) In optics, it is a thick piece of crystal used to refract light. 3) Prism is also used as a somewhat generic term for crystal that has been faceted or beveled. 4) In cut glass, prism cuts are parallel miter splits radiating from the rim of an object toward a large hobstar in the center.

PRISM CUTTING — General term for cut glass made with long horizontal grooves or lines that usually meet at a common point. See also *NOTCHED PRISM CUT*.

PROFILE — The shape of an object viewed from the side.

PROMOTIONAL GLASSWARE — Refer to CHARACTER GLASS.

PROOF — A term often used in Carnival Glass to describe a trial impression from a plunger and mold combination. Often in a proof, certain areas contain incomplete patterns (if noticed by glassworkers in the factory, proofs were usually pressed back into the mold to complete the pattern).

PROVIDENCE FLINT GLASS COMPANY — A short-lived American glass-making firm established at Providence, Rhode Island, in 1831 by Benjamin Dyer, William Eayres, George Holmes, and John Mackie. The company produced some pharmaceutical glass and pressed glass items including lacy salt dips prior to closing in 1835. The firm was also known as the Providence Flint Glass Works and the Providence Flint Glass Manufacturing Company.

PROVIDENCE FLINT GLASS MANUFACTURING COMPANY — Refer to the PROVIDENCE FLINT GLASS COMPANY.

PROVIDENCE FLINT GLASS WORKS — Refer to the PROVIDENCE FLINT GLASS COMPANY.

PRUNTS — A German decoration or ornamentation characterized by small glass knobs or drops attached to drinking vessels; they later became another name for hobs on hobnail patterned glass. For glasses that did not have handles, larger prunts also served as a gripping ornament to hold a vessel. See also *HOBNAIL*.

PUCELLAS — A glassmaker's tool, shaped like tongs, used for gripping or holding glass objects while being worked. They are sometimes referred to as "Jacks." See also *FORMING TOOL, PINCERS, STEEL-JACKS, TONGS, and WOOD-JACKS*.

PUFF BOX — A small square, rectangular, or circular glass container, with cover, used on dressing tables or vanities for holding powders.

Reproduction from an early 20th century Pitkin & Brooks catalog.

PUKEBERG — A Swedish glass-making firm founded in 1871 at Nybro by Jonas Bergstrand, J. E. Lindberg, and Conrad Wilhelm Nystrom (1828-1902). Initially, the factory produced press molded tableware. It was purchased by AB Arvid Bohlmarks Lampfabrik, a Stockholm-based lamp manufacturer, who began producing lamps at the factory in 1894. Production of colored art glass objects in typical Swedish styles was instituted at the plant in the 1930s. The firm went bankrupt in 1978, and, after changing hands several times, it was eventually acquired by Zero Interior AB. The new firm commissions or leases space to individual artisans who continue to produce art glass today at the factory. *See also* SWEDISH GLASS.

PULEGOSO — Italian term for bubbled glass made by randomly placed air bubbles or varying sizes inside as well as on the outer surface of glass (those that burst on the surface resemble small craters). The Italian base word is "Pulega," meaning "small bubble."

PULL TEST — A test of compatibility between two separate batches of glass to determine if they will blend well enough together to make cased glass objects. Ordinarily, a glass rod is made from equal amounts of both glass. If the rod remains fairly straight, then they are compatible; if it bends or curls, then the finished object would likely crack or shatter. The technique is also used in making multicolored glass canes or rods that, after cooling, are cut into small pieces for use in millefiori paperweights.

PULLED FEATHER GLASS — Refer to PEACOCK-FEATHER GLASS.

PULL-UP VASE — A style of vase created by John Northwood in the 1880s while working for the English firm of Stevens and Williams. Vases in this style are decorated by inserting colored (usually white) glass thread in the base and then drawing them up into the body with a pointed iron hook. Northwood eventually developed a machine to produce glass vases in this style.

PUMICE — Volcanic rock that is ground into powder and used for polishing glass objects.

PUNCH BOWL — A huge concave glass vessel, usually hemispherical in shape, used for serving beverages in large quantities. Most come in a set with long ladles and cups; they may have a stand as well.

Reproduction from an early 20th century Libbey advertisement.

PUNCH CUP OR GLASS — An open, somewhat bowl-shaped or cylindrical vessel, usually with a single handle, that is used for drinking punch as dipped from a punch bowl. Six, eight, ten, or twelve are the common number of cups that accompany a punch bowl. Those without handles are sometimes referred to as "Punch Glasses."

Flashed ruby red trim cube-patterned punch bowl and punch cups. *Photo by Robin Rainwater.*

PUNCH LADLE — A long handled utensil with a concave dipping cup at the end used for dipping out liquids from a punch bowl. Punch ladles are generally longer than all other ladles and were once referred to as "Punch Fillers" or "Toddy Lifters."

Blenko glass punch bowl cups and ladle. *Photo by Robin Rainwater.*

PUNCH STAND — A matching support base on which a punch bowl rests.

PUNTEE OR PUNTY — Refer to PONTIL.

PURIE — A single-colored transparent marble, Puries are also referred to as "Clearie" or "Clearies."

PURLED GLASS — Glass characterized by a ribbing or trailing applied around the base of the object.

PURPLE — A violet-colored glass produced by the addition of manganese. Note that purple is usually a bit darker than amethyst; this is particularly true in Carnival glass. *See also* AMETHYST *and* MANGANESE.

PURPLE OF CASSIUS — A reddish-purple colored glass (not quite ruby red) named after Andrew Cassius. The color formula was actually invented by German chemist Johann Rudolf Glauber in 1659; however, it was Cassius who first applied it to glass-making. The pigment is formed by precipitating an acidized gold solution; a similar technique that was eventually used to produce true ruby red glassware.

PURPLE SLAG GLASS — A style of glass characterized by colorful violet or purple swirling, marbleized designs. Purple slag was a popular art form of the Challinor, Taylor and Company of Tarentum, Pennsylvania, which produced it in the 1870s-1880s. Other American and English firms produced it as well. See also SLAG GLASS.

Mosser purple slag covered rooster dish. *Photo by Robin Rainwater.*

Challinor, Taylor & Company purple slag glass.
Item courtesy of Wheaton Village.

PUTZLER — A German firm founded by Oskar and Edmund Putzler in 1869 in Lower Silesia, initially, the factory produced lighting fixtures and lighting-related glassware. In 1946, the company merged with Peill and Sohn and the name was changed to Peill and Putzler. Peill and Sohn previously specialized in glass tumblers, tableware, and some art glass. After the merger, the combined resources of both firms became one of Germany's largest producers of lighting, tableware, and some art glass; nevertheless, production declined steadily through the decades and the factory ceased production in 1997. Note that the Peill and Putzler trade name was purchased and some lighting fixtures are still produced under that name today.

PYRAMIDAL STAR — A cut glass star design produced by cutting triangular prisms that radiate from a central focus. Pyramidal stars are most often found in the center of the button of hobstars. See also HOBSTAR.

PYREX — A type of heat-resistant glass created by Corning Glass in 1912 for making stronger and more durable railroad lanterns. It contains oxide of boron, which makes the glass extremely heat resistant (sometimes referred to as "Borosilicate Glass"); thus, the glass in lanterns was much stronger and less likely to break when exposed to rain and snow. Soon after, the formula was adopted to a wide variety of oven and tableware.

Canadian Pyrex

English Pyrex

French Pyrex

U.S.A. Pyrex
Corning Glass Works

Trademarks.

Pyrex Label

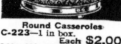

Reproduction of a 1932 Butler Brothers catalog.

PYROLUSITE — Refer to MANGANESE.

P

Qq

{ Qq }

QUAKER CITY CUT GLASS COMPANY — An American firm established at Philadelphia, Pennsylvania, in 1902 by Thomas Wolstenholme and Thomas Strittmatter, Quaker City was also known as the Cut Glass Corporation of America. Few examples of their products have been found that are easily identified. They did use paper labels with a bust of William Penn, but the gummed labels easily fell off or were removed. The most impressive and valuable piece are the vases typically made in three separate pieces that screw together. The company produced cut glass products until closing in 1927.

Trademark.

A Quaker City cut glass bowl.
Photo by Robin Rainwater.

QUARTZ — A source of silica (silicon dioxide or sand) that serves as a basic ingredient in glass-making. Quartz occurs naturally in hexagonal crystals or in crystalline masses.

QUARTZ GLASS — A style of crackled Art Glass that was rolled over various colored powders of glass and then cased in crystal, it was created by Frederick Carder of Steuben in the 1920s (designed specifically to imitate the appearance of the mineral quartz).

QUATREFOIL — A decorative motif formed by four lobes or leaves radiating outward from a common center, usually set at right angles to one another. Originally it was applied to stained glass windows in medieval Europe. In paperweights, it can be a four-lobed design used as the central element in a millefiori cane or for the exterior design in others.

QUEEN CITY CUT GLASS COMPANY — An American cut glass operation founded in 1913 at Rochester, Minnesota, by Kerry Conley, Arthur Olson, Lathan Orr, Thomas Phelps, and Charles White, the firm produced some limited amounts of cut glass tableware prior to closing during World War I.

QUEZAL ART GLASS AND DECORATING COMPANY — An American company founded at Brooklyn, New York, in 1901 by Martin Bach, Sr. (1865-1924) and Thomas Johnson (both former disgruntled Tiffany Employees). The two hired Percy Britton and William Wiedebine, two more former Tiffany employees. The firm was noted most for producing opalescent Art Glass known as "Quezal Glass" that, as one would expect, imitated Tiffany's styles. Note that the name Quezal is derived from the colorful Quetzal bird of South America. Johnson left in 1905 while Bach died in 1924. The company was briefly carried on by Bach's son, Martin Bach Jr.; however, Martin Bach Jr. went on to work for Vineland. Quezal was then sold to a group of investors led by Dr. John Ferguson. The shop operated for about a year and closed permanently in 1925.

Quezal

Quezal Art Glass & Decorating
Company: Trademark.

QUEZAL GLASS — An iridescent semi-opaque imitation of Tiffany's "Favrille" Art Glass made by the Quezal Art Glass and Decoration Company in the early twentieth century.

Quezal Glass iridescent gold luster vases.
Items courtesy of Wheaton Village.

Quezal iridescent Art Glass vases.
Items courtesy of Wheaton Village.

QUILLING — A wavy pattern applied to glass by repeated workings with pincers. It is most often done in opaque white and is a common design in Nailsea products. *See also NAILSEA GLASS.*

QUILTED — A cut or pressed style of decoration consisting of an all-over pattern of rectangles (made to resemble a patchwork quilt) or diamonds. *See also DIAMOND MOLDED and DIAMOND-QUILTED.*

Rr

{ Rr }

RADIUM — A brilliant transparent iridescence applied to Carnival Glass (mostly by Millersburg), the base color can usually be observed without holding radium iridized pieces to a light.

RADIUM GLASS COMPANY — An American company established in 1911 at Millersburg, Ohio, by Samuel Fair, John W. Fenton, C. J. Fisher, M. V. Leguillon, and Carl Schuler. Radium assumed control of the Millersburg Glass Company after it filed for bankruptcy in 1911. Radium continued to produce glass (mostly Carnival Glass) until 1913, when it was then sold to the Jefferson Glass Company. *See also MILLERSBURG GLASS COMPANY.*

RAINBOW ART GLASS COMPANY — An American firm that operated in Huntington, West Virginia, as a subsidiary of the Viking Glass Company from 1954 to 1972. *See also VIKING GLASS COMPANY.*

RAINBOW GLASS — Refer to MOTHER-OF-PEARL.

RAINDROP — A pattern in pressed glass consisting of several rows of small circles; ordinarily the circles do not touch each other. Raindrop was made as a pressed pattern in the 1880s and as a Depression pattern by the Federal Glass Company in 1929-1933. At both times, the glass was made in both clear and colored styles.

A Depression Glass Raindrops pattern from the Federal Glass Company. *Photo by Robin Rainwater.*

RAISED DESIGN — A method of cutting or dissolving (by acid) glass by designing the outline on the surface and then cutting or dissolving away the background. The design is then raised in relief similar to that of cameo engraving. Raised diamond cutting is one such method whereby a cut diamond or similar pattern (i.e. strawberry diamond, hobnails, crosscuts, etc.) is completed on one part of the object that is raised above another part that may be only lightly etched or engraved.

RAMEKIN OR RAMEQUIN — A small, somewhat cylindrical dish in which food can be baked or served. Ramekins are often used for serving some sort of cooked cheese, or cheese-preparation, and do not contain lids.

RAND AND SIMONI — Refer to the UNITED GLASS BOTTLE MANUFACTURERS LIMITED.

RANDOM SPACING SCHEME — An assortment of canes packed tightly together in a paperweight, usually in an upright position, to form an overall design.

RANGE SETS — Kitchenware glass sets developed during America's Great Depression. Items might include canisters, flour jars, sugar jars, shakers, etc.

RAOS, PETER — A noteworthy New Zealander who has been creating superb paperweights since 1979, Raos is recognized most for translating imagery from famous painters (i.e. O'Keefe and Monet) into glass paperweights. *See also NEW ZEALAND GLASS.*

RATAFIA GLASS — A small cordial-like stemmed glass used to serve the liquor ratafia in small quantities (1 to 2 ounces), Ratafia is distilled with fruit like brandy and is usually flavored with almonds.

RAVENHEAD — Glassware produced at several small factories in and around Ravenhead, England, beginning in the mid-nineteenth century. Ravenhead Glass, Ltd. was once a subsidiary of England's United Glass Bottle Manufacturer's Ltd. in 1965 due to a name change; nevertheless, the firm was eventually taken over by Owens-Illinois of America in 1987 and then by Belgium's Durobor in 1992. *See also FRANCIS DIXON AND COMPANY and UNITED GLASS BOTTLE MANUFACTURERS LIMITED.*

RAVENNA GLASS — An art style of glass developed by Orrefors of Sweden (designer Sven Palmqvist) in 1947. It is characterized by a very heavy or thick transparent colored glass that is inlaid with abstract patterns with brilliant coloring effects and then blown into its final shape. The result is an internal mosaic-like pattern.

RAVENSCROFT, GEORGE — The first commercially successful glassmaker in England who developed a high-quality durable lead crystal formula in the seventeenth century (patented in 1674; however, the first viable lead crystal formula was developed in 1676, and then perfected in 1681). Ravenscroft (1632-1683) also established a glass operation in 1673 in London and was eventually succeeded by his brother, Francis Ravenscroft, and Hawley Bishopp.

RAVENSWOOD NOVELTY WORKS — An American marble-making firm founded by Charles Turnbill in 1931 at Ravenswood, West Virginia. Ownership was passed down to his son-in-law, Paul Cox. The company produced glass marbles into the early 1950s under the "Buddy Brand" name. After halting their own production, Ravenswood continued on a short while as a wholesaler of marbles produced by other companies. The firm closed in 1955 and the marble-making machinery was acquired by both the Bogard Company and the Champion Agate Company.

RAYED BASE — A sunburst-like cut or pressed design usually applied to the bottom of glass objects. *See also STAR CUTTING.*

REACTIVE GLASS — A style of Art Glass created by Louis Comfort Tiffany in the late nineteenth century that changes color when reheated. Most contained iridescent coloring with a separate inner luster that exhibits a so-called "Under-the-Water" effect. Most were made into floral patterns. Reactive Glass has also been referred to as "Pastel Tiffany" and "Tiffany Flashed Glass."

R

READING ARTISTIC GLASS WORKS — This American company was established by French immigrant Lewis Kremp in Reading, Pennsylvania, in 1884, but closed soon after in 1886. In its two years of operation, the factory produced several styles of high quality Art Glass products.

A Reading turquoise Art Glass vase.
Item courtesy of Wheaton Village.

REAMER — A juice extractor with a ridge and pointed center that rises in a shallow dish; they are usually circular in shape and may be attached to a machine and/or a collection vessel (i.e. large bowl or pitcher). Reamers are also referred to as "Juicers" or "Juice Extractors."

CRYSTAL LEMON JUICE EXTRACTOR

Efficient twisted cone. A regular 15 center that you can sell for a dime.
1C2185—5 in. saucer, handled and lipped, extra efficient seed retainer, twisted cone, finest quality crystal.
2 doz. in case, 20 lbs.
(Total $1.74)   Doz.   **87c**

Reproduction from a 1922 Butler Brothers catalog.

RED CARNIVAL GLASS — An iridized coating produced by a gold metallic coloring agent that produces a brilliant cherry red finish. Original Red Carnival Glass is generally rare and very valuable.

RED GLASS — Refer to AQUA REGIA, CRANBERRY, GOLD, PURPLE OF CASSIUS, ROSE, RUBY RED, and SELENIUM.

RED HOUSE GLASSWORKS — An English glass-making firm established by George Ensell in 1778 at Wordsley, near Stourbridge, the company produced some tableware and art items, but was purchased by Frederick Stuart (1816-1900) in 1881 after numerous ownership changes. Stuart changed the name to Stuart and Sons in 1885. *See also STUART AND SONS, LTD.*

RED LEAD — The oxidized form of lead, somewhat reddish in color, that serves as the primary ingredient in making the highest quality lead crystal. Red Lead is also known as litharge. *See also LEAD.*

RED OPALESCENT — Red colored glassware with a white opalescent edge or background (usually found in iridized Carnival Glass).

REDDICK AND COMPANY — Refer to the MACBETH-EVANS GLASS COMPANY.

REDUCING ATMOSPHERE — A somewhat smoky condition created in a furnace to achieve certain color effects in glassware. The burning of wood and/or other such plants creates carbon monoxide or another non-oxidizing condition that affects the surface finish of glass.

REDUCTION LATHE — A style of lathe designed to cut a reduced but accurate reproduction of an original bronze image into steel. In paperweights, it is typically used in creating sulphide designs of famous people.

REEDING — A decorating technique applied with very fine threads or tiny rope-like strings of glass. The strings are usually colored and applied in a variety of patterns. It is also sometimes referred to as "ribbing."

REFINING STATE — The point in the glass-making process after a batch is melted and the tanks are opened, allowing the molten glass to give off gas.

REFLECTION — An image that is cast back, usually with the use of a glass mirror. Note that reflecting telescopes contain optical concave mirrors as opposed to those used by refracting telescopes. *See also REFRACTION.*

REFRACTION — The change of direction of a ray of light, sound, or heat by passing obliquely from one medium to another. Glass prisms are one such medium that can cause this type of refraction. Note that a refracting telescope consist of an objective glass lens and an eyepiece that not only magnify distant images, but make them appear closer than they actually are like all telescopes. *See also REFLECTION.*

REFRACTORIES — Materials used where resistance to extremely high temperatures is necessary, such as in furnace lining. Clay is a common refractory material.

REFRIGERATOR DISH — Stack-able square or rectangular covered glass containers of various sizes used for storing foods in the refrigerator.

REGOLLEAU CRISTALERIAS COMPANY — An Argentinean glass company established in the early twentieth century at Buenos Aires. They began producing practical tableware and some Carnival Glass items early on.

REHEATING — The process of softening a partly-formed object by plunging it back into the furnace (usually at the glory hole) in order to further shape or rework it.

REIJMYRE GLASSWORKS — A Swedish glass-making operation founded in 1810 by Johan Jacob Graver at Ostergotland, near Linkoping, in 1813, it was acquired by Count Mathias Alexander von Ungern-Steenberg and his son-in-law Ernst Gustav von Post. The firm began as a maker of practical items such as window panes, pharmaceutical glass, and some limited tableware. Beginning in the 1830s, it became Sweden's leading producer of pressed glass. The firm also produced some cut and engraved tableware as well. In the late nineteenth century, it came under the control of Josue Kjellgren and his son, Sten. Under the Kjellgrens, the company produced a good deal of cased and enameled art glass. In 1903, the firm joined the Association of Swedish Crystal Manufacturers (AB De Svenska Kristallglasbruken), commissioning various artisans to produce colored art glass in a variety of styles. In 1926, the company went bankrupt and then changed ownership numerous times until 1950, when Lennart Rosen, a previous manager at Kosta, acquired it. Rosen ran it as an art glass company successfully until selling it in 1975. The firm continued to change hands several times and is currently run today by Benny and Katharina Fihn.

R

RELIEF CUTTING — A difficult and expensive method of cutting glass by designing the outline on the surface and then cutting away the background. The design is then raised in relief similar to that of cameo engraving.

RELIQUARY — A glass vessel of various sizes and shapes used for storing sacred religious relics.

RELISH DISH — A small to medium-sized shallow glass serving tray with divisions, usually rectangular or oval in shape, that many contain one or two handles.

A Depression Glass Horseshoe patterned relish dish from the Indiana Glass Company. *Photo by Robin Rainwater.*

RENNINGER BLUE — A medium iridized blue color named by the Northwood Glass company for some of their Carnival glass products. The color is darker than sapphire but lighter than cobalt.

REPRODUCTION — A close imitation or exact copy of an original object made at a later time. Reproductions pose problems for collectors, particularly for originals that are rare and valuable.

REPUBLIC GLASS COMPANY — An American firm founded in 1900 at Clarksburg, West Virginia, by W. S. Brady, James Graham, Charles Runyon, and associates, the company produced pressed glass including tableware, jelly tumblers and other food containers. In 1901, Republic was purchased by the Atlas Glass and Metal Company, which in turn became part of the Hazel Atlas Glass Company. *See also HAZEL ATLAS GLASS COMPANY.*

RESONANCE — The sound that results when a glass object is struck; sometimes used as a test for crystal, though other types of glass resonate similar sounds.

RETICELLO — Refer to RETICULATED GLASS.

RETICULATED GLASS — A decorating style in the form of a web or network of glass threads, etchings, cuttings, or glass that is blown into a metal mesh frame. The style originated with Venetian glassmakers and is referred to by them as "Reticello" or "Muranese Retticello."

A 1650s Italian reticello (reticulated) glass vase. *Items courtesy of the Corning Museum of Glass.*

RETORTOLI — Italian term for a twisted filigree or spiral-like decorations in glass. Note that retortoli is synonymous with zanfirico. *See also FILIGREE, LATTICINO, or RETICULATED GLASS.*

REVERSE PAINTING — Designs that are painted on the back side of glass that appear in proper perspective when viewed from the front. It originated on glassware with Italian artists in the thirteenth century and spread to other parts of Europe (i.e. Bavarian/German artisans) and even to China in the seventeenth century. This style shows up often in mirrors and panels, as well as many contemporary Chinese decorated glass articles (i.e. vases, snuff bottles, etc.). Reverse painting is also sometimes referred to as back painting.

REVOLVING SERVER — Refer to LAZY SUSAN.

REYEN AND SCHANING — An American cut glass operation founded by Nicholas Reyen and G. Schaning in 1912 at Brooklyn, New York. The two produced cut glass products up until the end of World War I.

RIB OR RIBBING — A decorative pattern common in pressed glass. It ordinarily consists of several parallel rows of molded vertical lines and is often combined with other designs (i.e. fine ribbed, block and rib, ribbed acorn, ribbed drape, ribbed forget-me-not, ribbed grape, ribbed palm, ribbed pineapple, etc.). Although horizontal lines are sometimes referred to as "Horizontal Ribbing," they are usually referred to as "Bands" or "Banding." Broken-swirl ribbing is a mold-blown decoration that has two sets of ribs ordinarily made by redipping an object a second time in the same (or different) mold. Melon ribbing contains varying degrees of oval lines that meet at the ends (much like those of a melon fruit).

Rib or Ribbing: Reproduction from an 1860s Boston & Sandwich Glass Company catalog.

R

RIB MOLD — A pattern mold for bowls, bottles, and tumblers marked with heavy vertical lines or ribbing. *See also* REEDING.

RIBBON — A cane containing a flat twisted element that is used as a decoration in paperweights such as crowns, torsades, checquers, etc.

RIBBON GLASS — A decorating style consisting of various-sized applied colored bands. The bands can be found in a wide variety of applications — vertical, horizontal, diagonal, intertwined, curving, and spiraling — all made to resemble a ribbon. Such styles were first produced by Venetian glassmakers as early as the sixteenth century. Pressed glass dubbed "Ribbon" ordinarily includes alternating panels of clear and frosted glass though numerous variations exist (i.e. frosted ribbon, fluted ribbon, clear ribbon, etc.). *See also* LATTICINO.

RICE, JOE — Refer to the SAINT CLAIR GLASS WORKS, INC.

RICHARD — A French firm established in Lorraine, France, in the early twentieth century, the company produced cameo art glass primarily in floral and landscape designs during the 1920s.

Richard: Trademark.

RICHARDS AND HARTLEY FLINT GLASS COMPANY — An American pressed glass-making company founded at Pittsburgh, Pennsylvania, in 1865 by Robert and William Hartley, Joseph Richards, and John Wilson. Richards and Hartley had previously been associated with Bryce, Richards and Company. The firm moved to Tarentum, Pennsylvania, in 1883-84 and the name was changed to the Richards and Hartley Glass Company (after the move was complete and the old Pittsburgh factory was sold off, it was leveled to become a housing community). The company manufactured press glass tableware and a little opalescent/colored glassware before becoming part of the U.S. Glass Co. in 1891 as Factory E. U.S. Glass closed the plant in 1893; it was then purchased the following year by the Tarentum Glass Company.

RICHARDS AND HARTLEY GLASS COMPANY — Refer to the RICHARDS AND HARTLEY FLINT GLASS COMPANY.

RICHARDSON, HENRY G. AND SONS, LTD. — An English glass-making firm that succeeded W.H.B. and J. Richardson at Wordsley, England, in the latter nineteenth century. The principals were Henry Gethin Richardson and his sons Benjamin Richardson III and Arthur Richardson. The company produced many art styles of glass, especially iridescent forms of the Art Nouveau period. The firm was purchased by Thomas Webb and Sons in the 1930s.

RICHARDSON, J. AND W.H.B. — An English glass-making firm that assumed control of the Wordsley Flint Glassworks at Wordsley (near Stourbridge) in the mid-1830s. The principals were William Haden Richardson, Benjamin Richardson, and Jonathan Richardson. In 1842, they purchased the White House Glassworks from Thomas Webb. The company was a noted producer of opaque white glass that was further enameled and/or gilded. In 1857, Benjamin Richardson patented certain forms of etched and molded glassware and a machine that decorated glass by automated threading (i.e. the diamond air-trap method). Noted glass artisan John Northwood was employed with the firm at one time. The company later became Henry G. Richards and Sons, Ltd.

RICHMOND, JAMES N. — A glassmaker from Cheshire, Massachusetts, who built a glasshouse in 1850, which attracted many curiosity seekers. Richmond is credited with being the first to make plate glass in America.

RICHTER, PAUL COMPANY — An American cut glass operation founded in 1914 at Maywood, Illinois, by Paul Richter, Harry Bucholtz, and A. E. Winterroth, the firm produced cut glass into the early 1920s. The company also sold pottery and remained in business until 1940.

RIEDEL FAMILY — The family first became involved in the glass industry in the late seventeenth century under Johann Christoph Riedel, who served as a glass merchant for glassmakers in northeastern Bohemia. Johann Leopold Riedel (1726-1800) built a glasshouse in the late eighteenth century, which was carried on by his son, Anton (1762-1821), and Anton's son, Franz Anton Riedel (1786-1844). The Riedels specialized in engraved Bohemian-styled glass. Franz's nephew, industrialist Josef Riedel (1816-1894), owned several businesses including foundries, refineries, and mills before expanding into glasshouses. Josef bought his first glass hut at Polaun, Germany, in 1849, purchased another in 1858, and later bought out rival Harrachov in 1887. Josef was known to produce a good deal of colored Bohemian glassware including a bright florescent greenish/yellowish uranium glass that was named "Annagrun" (named after his wife Anna – originally Annafruen for green and Annagelb for yellow; however, it is known today as Annagrun). Josef's son, Josef Riedel Jr. (1862-1924), and his grandsons, Walter (1895-1974) and Arno (1897-1924), continued on in the business up until World War II. All glass factories in the Czecholovakian area were nationalized in 1948. Another relative, Claus Josef Riedel, designed and produced some decorative colored tableware after establishing another firm in 1956 at Kufstein, Austria; he was noted most for producing candlesticks with very thin stems. Claus's son, Georg Josef Riedel (b. 1949), currently runs the firm today. Note that the name is occasionally spelled as "Riedl." *See also* HARRACH GLASSWORKS.

RIETHOF — Refer to JOSEPH RINDSKOPF.

RIGAREE — A narrow vertical band decoration applied to glass in various colors.

RIIHIMAKI GLASSWORKS — A Finnish glass firm founded in 1910 at Riihimaki, Finland, by M. A. Kolemainen (1886-1944). The elder Kolemainen had previously served as the technical director at Karhula and his son worked there as well. The company began as a maker of windows, containers, and tableware. A bottle-making machine was added in 1919. In 1927, they purchased the Kaukalahti Glassworks at Espoo and used it to make lighting-related glassware. Beginning in 1928, the firm began producing modern art-styled abstract glass in typical Scandinavian/Finnish styles, as well as a limited amount of iridized Carnival Glass. In 1985, Riihimaki was purchased by Ahlstrom, which merged it with Karhula in 1988 to form Ahlstrom Riihimaen Laso Oy. The Riihimaki factory closed in 1990 and Karhula was sold to the American firm of Owens-Illinois.

Riihimaki Glassworks: Trademarks.

RIM — The narrow area adjacent to the edge of a glass vessel, rims are usually associated with bowls, vases, cups, and plates. Rims are sometimes decorated with applied colors or enamels or are perhaps ruffled, flared, scalloped, and designed with other similar motifs.

RIM SOUP BOWL — Refer to SOUP BOWL.

RINDSKOPF, JOSEF — A Bohemian glasshouse built by Josef Rindskopf at Kosten bei Telitz, Germany, in 1891, it was known as Josefhutte and the firm specialized in both cut/engraved glass and some typical styles of colored Bohemian glass; however, they were best known for producing iridized glass during the Art Nouveau period (some names include "Ahambra," "Diluvium," "Grenada," and "Pepita"). Josef's four sons, Albert, Edwin, Sidney, and Sherman, joined the business and purchased another glass hut at Dux. In 1900, the family name was changed to Riethof. The company nearly went out of business during World War I. In 1920, it became a public corporation and produced pressed glass. The company closed permanently in 1927.

RING — An ornamental circular band for wearing upon one's finger. Glass rings date back to ancient Mesopotamian and Egyptian times. Larger rings were also created in glass for use as bracelets and/or armlets.

RINGTREE — A glass object in the shape of a miniature tree with knobs that taper upward (the knobs are used to hold finger rings). Some are made with only one vertical finger-like column protruding from a shallow dish, which is designed to hold several rings (on the protrusion as well as in the dish encircling it).

A Depression green glass ringtree.

RIPLEY AND COMPANY — 1) An American firm established in 1865 at Pittsburgh, Pennsylvania, by Daniel Ripley Sr., Thomas and Ira Coffin, John and Jacob Strickler, and Nichokas Kunzler. In 1866, a factory was completed and named the Tremont Glass Works. The Coffin brothers left in 1867 and George Duncan Sr. joined, John Strickler died in 1868, and Kunzler left in 1869. Daniel Ripley Jr. joined on as a partner in 1871 and inherited his father's portion of the business. The company produced pressed glass items until Duncan and Ripley split in 1874. Both continued on their own (Ripley and Co. and George Duncan and Sons) until becoming part of the U.S. Glass Company in 1891 as Factory F. Daniel Ripley Jr. actually became the first president of U.S. Glass and the central office for the conglomerate was located at Ripley's factory. The plant and office were abandoned in 1937 when U.S. Glass moved their primary operations to Tiffin, Ohio. 2) In 1910, Daniel Ripley Jr., along with his son D. A. Ripley, purchased a vacant plant once owned by the Baldwin Automobile Company at Connellsville, Pennsylvania, in 1910. Glass equipment was installed and a new Ripley and Company was born. Daniel Ripley Jr. died in 1912 and was succeeded by his son D. A. In 1913, William Anderson, a long-time associate of the Ripleys, succeeded D. A. Ripley as president. The new venture produced pressed and blown glass tableware, novelties, bottles, and jars. The plant closed in 1918; however, Anderson purchased all holdings and formed the Capstan Glass Company, which sold it to the Anchor Cap and Closure Company in 1934; Anchor continued to produce glass containers at the factory.

A Ripley & Co. 1880s pressed and engraved crystal lamp. *Photo courtesy of the Corning Museum of Glass.*

RIPPLE — A surface texture in Art Glass consisting of linear, concentric, or irregular waves (ripples) that seem to flow in an undulating motion. Light ripples tend to occur naturally in some sheet-forming processes while others are imitated with an embossing roll. In pressed glass, unintentional ripple marks are sometimes caused by a mold that has been insufficiently heated.

RITCHIE — An American glass firm established at Wheeling in 1829 (prior to West Virginia becoming a state) by the Ritchie family (primarily by Scottish immigrant Craig Ritchie and his son John), Jesse Wheat, and James Thompson (the early venture was also referred to as "Ritchie and Wheat" and the "Wheeling Flint Glass Works"). In 1831, Wheat bought out Thompson, and in turn, the Ritchies bought out Wheat. Craig Ritchie, Jr. also joined the firm in 1833. The company produced some lead cut crystal and pressed tableware, as well as window panes, before ceasing operation around 1839. The firm was also known as "Ritchie and Wilson" when George Wilson joined as a partner in 1834 (together with Wilson, they had purchased the Fairview Glass Works and Wheat, Price, and Company in 1834). *See also WHEELING FLINT GLASS WORKS and WHEAT, PRICE, AND COMPANY.*

RITCHIE AND WHEAT — Refer to RITCHIE.

RITCHIE AND WILSON—Refer to RITCHIE.

RIVERSIDE GLASS COMPANY — Refer to the RIVERSIDE GLASS WORKS.

RIVERSIDE GLASS WORKS — An American glass-making company established at Wellsburg, West Virginia, in 1879 by Charles Brady, John Dornan, and J. E. Ratcliffe. Dornan had previously worked for the Buckeye Glass Company while both Brady and Ratcliffe had been employed with Hobbs, Brockunier and Company. Fire destroyed the plant in 1886, but it was rebuilt in 1887. The company produced pressed glass tableware, bottles, covered animal dishes, some opalescent glass, and kerosene lamps until they joined the National Glass Company in 1899. In 1904, National leased the plant to a stock company primarily owned by J. Edwin Hill, John Quay, and Charles Windsor. The new company name became the Riverside Glass Company and continued making pressed glass tableware until going bankrupt in 1907. The plant was acquired by the Ohio Valley Brass Company in 1911 to set up a foundry; however, they sold it off later in the year to the Crescent Glass Company. See also CRESCENT GLASS COMPANY.

ROASTER — A deep round, oblong or angled dish, with or without a cover and handles, used to bake or cook foods. Many are made of metal, porcelain, or heat resistant glass like Pyrex or Fire-King and may further contain a glass cover.

ROBINSON, ANDERSON AND COMPANY — Refer to the STOURBRIDGE FLINT GLASS WORKS.

ROBINSON AND ENSELL — An American glass factory built at Pittsburgh, Pennsylvania, in 1807 by Edward Ensell and George Robinson, the two partners went bankrupt before any glass was produced and the factory was sold to Benjamin Bakewell Sr. Ensell remained on as factory superintendent, but was not a principal owner. See also BAKEWELL, PEARS AND COMPANY.

ROBINSON GLASS COMPANY — An American pressed glass manufacturer established at Zanesville, Ohio, in 1893 by John and Edwin Robinson, the firm produced pressed glass tableware, barware, and novelties prior to joining the National Glass Company in 1899. National operated it shortly under the Robinson Glass Works name before dismantling the plant in 1900. The factory remained idle until burning to the ground in 1906.

ROBINSON GLASS WORKS — Refer to the ROBINSON GLASS COMPANY.

ROBINSON, J. AND T. — Refer to the STOURBRIDGE FLINT GLASS WORKS.

R

ROCAILLE — The French term for rockwork. Rocaille is a style of ornamental Art Glass developed by France in the late eighteenth century that is characterized by curved ornate forms in the shape of rockwork and/or pierced shellwork, flowers, foliage, and scroll work. It is also known as "Rococo."

ROCHESTER BULB CORPORATION — Refer to the ELLWOOD CITY GLASS COMPANY.

ROCHESTER DECORATING COMPANY — Refer to the ROCHESTER TUMBLER COMPANY.

ROCHESTER GLASS COMPANY — An American firm established at Rochester, Pennsylvania, in 1901 by brothers Henry C. and J. Howard Fry and Harry C. Fry (son of Henry C.). The factory was renamed the H. C. Fry Glass Company in 1902. Henry C. Fry retired in 1904 and Harry C. Fry became president. The glass that was produced by the firm is sometimes referred to as "Fry Glass" and included some Art Glass styles, pressed glass wares, automobile headlight lenses, and cut glass; as well as both practical kitchen and oven ware. The firm developed its own formula for heat-resistant oven glass in 1922, declared bankruptcy in 1925, and briefly reorganized in 1933. They ceased production in 1934 and the plant was the leased to the Libbey Glass Company. The plant was idled in 1935 and the company closed permanently.

ROCHESTER TUMBLER COMPANY — An American pressed glass manufacturer established at Rochester, Pennsylvania, in 1872 by brothers Henry C. and J. Howard Fry, and other associates who had previously worked for the O'Hara Glass Works in Pittsburgh, Pennsylvania. The firm produced a good deal of pressed glass tableware including tumblers. As a side business, the company also established the Rochester Decorating Company to further decorate their pressed wares. The firm joined the National Glass Company in 1899. The plant itself was almost completely destroyed by fire in 1901. It was rebuilt and then leased in 1904 to a new company that filed under the Rochester Tumbler Company name, led by Charles Runyon, Charles Darraugh, and John Miller. The factory closed in 1905 due to a flood. Runyon purchased the plant in 1909 and moved his Ellwood City Glass Company operations here. Runyon's firm produced pressed glass tableware up until just after World War I. In 1918, it was sold to General Electric and was then known as the Rochester Bulb Corporation, a division of General Electric. See also ELLWOOD CITY GLASS COMPANY.

ROCK CRYSTAL — A somewhat translucent pale white form of natural quartz, rock crystal is carved into decorative objects and glassmakers from early times sought to imitate it in their creations. Rock Crystal is also the name given to a prolific pattern of Depression Glass produced by the McKee Glass Company in the 1920s and 1930s. Note that the German term for rock crystal is "Bergcristal" while the French refer to it as "Cristel de Roche."

ROCK CRYSTAL GLASS COMPANY — An American firm founded in 1916 at Jersey City, New Jersey, by Abraham Gordon, John Halpin, and Joseph Hinsberger, the company produced some limited amounts of cut and pressed glass tableware up until closing permanently in 1925.

ROCK GROUND — An uneven granular paperweight ground formed with un-fused sand, mica flakes, and green glass (also known as "Sand Ground").

ROCKWARE GROUP — Refer to BAGLEY GLASS.

ROCOCO — Refer to ROCAILLE.

ROD — A very thin solid cylinder or small stick of glass; many, including those of different colors, are fused together to form a cane. Multicolored canes are then often sliced into small pieces to make floral and symmetrical designs within paperweights. See also CANE.

RODEFER BROTHERS — Refer to the NATIONAL GLASS MANUFACTURING COMPANY.

RODEFER BROTHERS NATIONAL GLASS WORKS — Refer to the NATIONAL GLASS MANUFACTURING COMPANY.

RODEFER-GLEASON GLASS COMPANY — Refer to the NATIONAL GLASS MANUFACTURING COMPANY.

RODEN BROTHERS — A Canadian cut glass firm that operated in the late nineteenth and early twentieth centuries at Toronto, the original company was established as a manufacturer of silver-plated wares around 1891. Soon after, they employed glass cutters, and, like most Canadian cut glass firms, they purchased lead glass blanks from both American and European firms.

Roden Brothers: Trademarks.

ROLLED EDGE — A curved lip or circular base on which glass objects may turn over or rotate on.

ROLLED TEXTURE — A design imprinted in a glass sheet by using an embossed forming roll. The pattern is present in the metal roll and forms the desired motif when it is rolled over the glass. Ordinarily, this produces glass that is textured on one side (the top) and smooth on the other (the bottom). *See also* DOUBLE ROLLED METHOD and SINGLE ROLL METHOD.

ROLLING PIN — A long cylindrically shaped object, with handles or knobs at each end, used for rolling out dough. Glass rolling pins were first made in England (Nailsea region) in the early nineteenth century and often were hollow. Aside from filling them with hot or cold water for ease of rolling dough, rolling pins were also used to store such staples as flour, sugar, tea, salt, etc. Many rolling pins of milk or other colored glass were also made during America's Depression era.

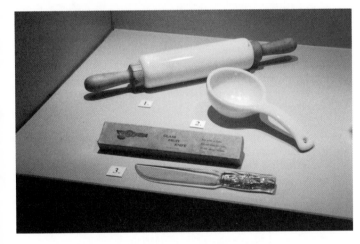

A rolling pin can be seen among other kitchen glass items, including the pickle ladle and knife rest.

ROMAN GLASS — General term for all glassware made throughout the ancient Roman Empire (i.e. Gaul, Italy, England, the Mediterranean, the Rhineland, etc.), especially with the advent of glass-blowing by the Romans in the first century B.C. until the fall of the Empire in the late fifth century. Aside from inventing blowing, the Romans produced glass medallions, cameo or relief-cut glass, molded glass, Greek-style vases, mosaics, panels, and a wide variety of drinking vessels (i.e. beakers decorated with battle and gladiator scenes).

First century A.D. Roman glass examples.
Items courtesy of the Corning Museum of Glass.

ROMER — A German-styled drinking glass consisting of a fairly large spherical bowl, wide hollow stem, and a flared foot. Some are equipped with dome covers and are often decorated in a wide variety of styles (i.e. engraved, prunts, gilded etc.). *See also* BERKEMEYER.

RONA CRYSTAL — Refer to LEDNICKE ROVNE GLASSWORKS.

RONDEL — A mouth-blown glass object that has been spun into a somewhat irregular circular shape. Pressed rondels can also be made by machine. Rondels are at times incorporated into leaded glass artworks.

ROOT BEER GLASS OR MUG — A cylindrical drinking vessel that usually has a flat base and a single handle. As the name implies, they are designed for drinking root beer and other beverages. Root beer mugs vary in capacity from as little as three ounces on up to sixteen and are usually made of clear glass. They were most popular during the late nineteenth and early twentieth centuries; however, those with the enameled A&W logo can still be found today at A&W restaurants served with A&W brand root beer or other soft drinks.

ROPE EDGE — A twirled thread-like design usually applied around the edge of glass objects. Rope edges were first applied by ancient Roman glassmakers and were made to resemble ropes as the name implies.

ROSA — A somewhat cloudy, pale shaded rose amber colored style of Art Glass created and named by Steuben in the 1920s. It was usually accentuated with Alabaster and combined with Steuben's Pomona Green color.

ROSALINE GLASS — A type of jade-colored glass that is somewhat dark pink or rose-colored; it was first made and named by Steuben in the 1920s and usually contains additional engraved designs. *See also* ROSE DU BARRY.

ROSARIA — A style of Art Glass created by Pairpoint in the early-to-mid twentieth century. It is a transparent light cranberry color found in tableware, vases, and paperweights. Some were made in a molded diamond quilted pattern while many contain applied crystal feet, finials, handles, and swirled and/or controlled bubble connectors.

R

ROSE — 1) A deep red cranberry-colored glass applied by staining or flashing (not as deep or as dark as ruby red). 2) A pressed or cut glass design that contains the rose flower bloom as its primary design (variations include scrolling, dots, Sandwich-like designs, cables, etc.).

Hocking Glass Company's Depression Glass Mayfair Open Rose patterned tumbler. *Photo by Robin Rainwater.*

ROSE AMBER — Mount Washington Glass Company's name for amberina glass. *See also* AMBERINA.

ROSE BOWL — A small round concave glass vessel usually with three feet (tri-footed) and a small opening in the center for holding a single bloom or perhaps a few very short-stemmed flowers. Rose bowls made of glass first became popular during the Victorian Era and are also known as "Flower Globes" and "Ivy Balls."

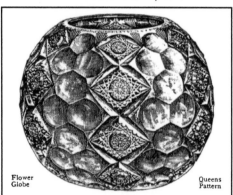

Flower Globe   Queens Pattern

Flower tints—the green of the stems, the delicate blossom tones—bring into vivid relief the distinctive beauty of

Hawkes Cut Glass

Glittering like some great jewel, in color the sought-for perfect white, in design an expression of the finest art—a piece of Hawkes Cut Glass is indisputably the welcomest gift to brides.

At the best dealers. No piece without this trade-mark engraved on it is genuine. If your dealer does not sell Hawkes Cut Glass, write for address of one who does.

T. G. Hawkes & Co., Corning, N. Y.

Reproduction from a late 19th century T.G. Hawkes advertisement.

Tipperary crystal cut glass rose bowl.

ROSE CAMEO — Refer to CAMEO.

ROSE DU BARRY — A type of jade-colored glass that is somewhat light violet-hued (similar to Steuben's Rosa). It was first made and named by Steuben in the 1920s and was primarily used as an inner liner in crystal or Alabaster glass items (mostly vases). *See also* ROSA.

ROSE POMPADOUR — A pink ground used in some Clichy paperweights (the name is derived from Sevres Porcelain).

ROSEEN AND COLLINS — Refer to the CENTRAL CUT GLASS COMPANY.

ROSEEN BROTHERS CUT GLASS COMPANY — A short-lived American cut glass-making firm established in 1904 at Chicago, Illinois, by brothers Joseph and Herman Theodore Roseen (Swedish immigrants). The firm sold out to the United States Cut Glass Company a year later. Herman Roseen went on to found the Central Cut Glass Company with Andrew Swanson in 1906. Herman Roseen was also active in a wholesale business that was located in Chicago: the Output Company of America, a firm that represented cut glass products made by others from 1918 to 1919. *See also* UNITED STATES CUT GLASS COMPANY *and* CENTRAL CUT GLASS COMPANY.

ROSENFIELD, KEN — Rosenfield earned his Master of Fine Arts degree from Southern Illinois University and then returned to his native California. He worked as Correia for five years and then worked briefly as a scientific glassblower. Rosenfield now specializes in intricately-detailed lamp-worked paperweights in floral, fruit, and vegetable designs.

ROSENTHAL PORZELLAN AG — A German firm founded at Eskersreuth in 1879 by Philipp Rosenthal (1855-1937), the company initially operated as a decorating/cutting shop and was supplied with blanks by others. In 1891, the business was moved to Seib and began producing porcelain. During World War II, Rosenthal temporarily took over the famous French glassworks, St. Louis (1942-1944). In 1950, Philipp's son, Phillip Rosenthal Jr. (b. 1916), expanded the glass-making operation to include a decorating/cutting workshop at Schwabisch Gmund in Baden-Wurttemberg. A year later it was moved to Bad Soden. The firm specialized in drinking glasses and stemware, most with a good deal of cutting and engraving. Though the Bad Soden factory closed in 1983, other factories still operate today in both Germany and the Czech Republic. In 1997, Rosenthal partnered with Waterford Wedgwood, which became a majority shareholder in Rosenthal; however, products are still produced today with the Rosenthal name.

ROSE-TEINTE — A style of Art Glass created by Baccarat of France in 1916 (reintroduced in 1940), it is characterized by gradual shading from amber to rose, similar to AMBERINA. It is also sometimes referred to as "Baccarat's Amberina."

ROSETTE — An ornament or decorating motif based on an old English daisy medallion in the shape of a circular rose or floral design, rosettes might be applied, enameled, or cut in various glass objects. The "Roman Rosette" was once a popular circular rose-like pattern, both in the latter nineteenth and early twentieth centuries. Exquisite hobstars are sometimes referred to as rosettes.

Line drawing by the author.

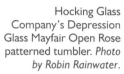

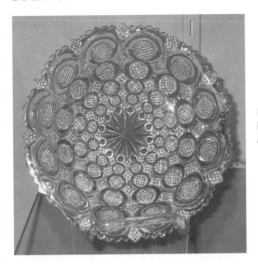

Rosette cut glass bowl. *Photo by Robin Rainwater.*

ROSICE GLASSWORKS — A Czechoslovakian firm founded in 1921 to produced modern machine-pressed tableware. Like all Czech firms, it became part of the state in 1948 and was merged with such firms as Kvetna and Karolinka. From the late 1950s through the early 1970s, the Rosice factory specialized in producing beer mugs. It was eventually absorbed by the conglomerate Crystalex and still serves as a glass-making factory today.

ROTHFUS-NICOLAI COMPANY — A short-lived American cut glass-making firm founded in 1912 by John Rothfus and Henry Nicolai at Hammonton, New Jersey. Rothfus left in 1914 to establish another firm while Nicolai continued on under the "Henry Nicolai Company" name up into the World War I era. *See also* FIGUEROA CUT GLASS COMPANY.

ROUGE FLAMBE GLASS — A style of Art Glass developed by Frederick Carder at Steuben in 1916-17, it is characterized by a color ranging from red to orange to pink (made to resemble Chinese famille rose porcelain). The glass was not iridized and, since it was quite fragile, was discontinued soon after production.

ROUGHER — The term for a worker who makes the first deep incisions in cut glass by holding an object against a large stone or iron wheel. Most cutters start as roughers and cut edges and then panels before graduating to smaller wheels (including copper) for more precision cutting.

Roundel — A circular or slightly oval plaque or plate; those made of glass are generally enameled or contain gilded decorations along with a separate border (i.e. like a framed picture).

Rousseau, Francois Eugene — A French glassmaker and pioneer in the nineteenth century Art Nouveau styled glass, Rousseau (1827-1891) is noted for floral and oriental designs created in several color effects and styles. He gained much fame at the Paris Art Exhibitions of 1878 and 1884. When he retired in 1885, his pupil and successor, Ernest Baptiste Leveille, continued to produce art-styled glass under the name "Leveille-Rousseau." In 1900, the firm was sold to Harand and Guignard, which continued producing Art Glass up until World War I.

Rousseau, Argy Gabriel Joseph — A French glass designer and artisan who set up a small art glass factory in 1921, Rousseau (1885-1953) produced a good deal of art deco styled glass in the early twentieth century that bears his impressed mark (usually on the underside of object). Rousseau was also noted for producing pate de verre opaque glass and pate de crystal (a refined type of pate de verre using powered lead crystal rather than colored glass). The factory closed in 1931; however, Rousseau continued as an independent glass artisan up until his death. Note that glass made at the factory is also known as "Argy-Rousseau" glass.

ROYAL BRIERLY CRYSTAL — In 1931, the English firm of Stevens and Williams was changed to Royal Brierly Crystal. It was initially founded by Joseph Silvers Williams-Thomas (1848-1932); when he died it was turned over to his son, Hubert Silvers Williams-Thomas (1880-1973). Hubert's son, Reginald Silvers Williams-Thomas (1914-1988), was also active as a managing director. Royal Brierly continues today primarily as a maker of cut and engraved crystal products. In 1998, it was acquired by Epsom Activities, which still produces products under the Royal Brierly namesake. *See also* STEVENS AND WILLIAMS, LTD.

ROYAL DOULTON CRYSTAL — Refer to WEBB, CORBETT, LTD.

ROYAL DUTCH GLASS WORKS — The company began when a factory was established in 1765 at Leerdam (near Rotterdam) in the Netherlands; it was a producer of lead crystal tableware and later (early twentieth century) produced some ornamental and artistic wares. Glass products produced here are sometimes referred to as "Leerdam Glass." In 1937, the company became part of the United Glassworks, which also has factories at Maastricht and Schiedam. The company continues in operation today producing mostly machine-made stemware at Leerdam and containers at Maastricht.

A 1924 Leerdam, Netherlands, tea set made by Royal Dutch Glass Works. *Items courtesy of the Corning Museum of Glass.*

Royal Flemish Glass — A style of Art Glass made by the Mount Washington Glass Works that is characterized by a raised gilded decoration over a lightly stained acid-finished surface. The style was first produced in the early 1890s and patented in 1894. It contains many ornate patterns such as waterfowl, Oriental design, and other abstract artistic scenes.

A Royal Flemish Vase by Mount Washington. *Photo by Robin Rainwater. Item courtesy of the Corning Museum of Glass.*

R

ROYAL GLASS COMPANY — An American firm founded at Marietta, Ohio, in 1897-98 by M. F. Noll (president), A. D. Follett (vice president), H. C. Chamberlain (secretary), Addison Thompson (general manager), and D. B. Torpy. The company purchased the factory machinery from the defunct Huntington Glass Company and produced pressed glass tableware. The firm joined the National Glass Company conglomerate in 1899. Fire destroyed the plant in 1903 and it was not rebuilt.

ROYAL KRONA — Refer to MALERAS GLASBRUK and SKRUF.

ROYAL RUBY — This is the older sister pattern of "Forest Green." "Royal Ruby" was first made in the late 1930s, but is usually considered as later than the Depression era. It was patented by Anchor Hocking and the pattern is named for the color, which is a little darker than standard ruby red. It is made with selenium in the batch to achieve the color, unlike the more expensive gold for true ruby red and cranberry. Note that many pieces from Depression patterns were made in this color, including "Coronation," "Old Café," "Oyster and Pearl," "Queen Mary," and "Sandwich." Also note that both Royal Ruby and Forest Green were made in great quantities of various tableware and some pieces contain a combination of crystal and ruby red.

ROYAL SCANDINAVIA GROUP — A multinational glass-making conglomerate established in 1997, members of this group include Kastrup and Holmegaard, Kosta-Boda, Orresfors, Boda-Nova, Keramik, and Venini. Glassware is still produced under the individual company names.

RUBIGOLD — A name given to a marigold-colored Carnival Glass by the Imperial Glass Company, rubigold was advertised as a dark red iridescence with tint of other colors; nevertheless, it is truly marigold only and not red CARNIVAL GLASS.

RUBINA GLASS — A style of Art Glass popular during the Art Nouveau movement, Rubina articles gradually change in color from crystal at the bottom to a cranberry or rose color at the top (also spelled as "Rubena"). Some pieces have shading that is not gradual, but contains a distinct line of color separation. Pieces are also at times accented with clear crystal (handles, lids, stoppers, feet etc.). Many cut patterns were decorated with Rubena shading. George Duncan and Sons is credited with the original introduction of this design and others soon followed.

Rubina crystal. *Items courtesy of Wheaton Village.*

RUBINA VERDE — A style of Art Glass similar to that of Rubina Glass, Rubina Verde items gradually change in color from a light yellow-green or aqua green at the bottom to a cranberry or rose color at the top (also spelled as "Rubena"). Hobbs, Brockunier, and Company is usually noted as the original maker; however, others followed soon afterward. Rubina Verde was most popular during the Art Nouveau movement.

A Rubina Verde hobnail patterned pitcher from Hobbs Brockunier. *Item courtesy of Wheaton Village.*

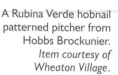

RUBY RED — A gold metallic coloring agent that produces the most powerful red color within glass. An acidized solution of gold must be held in colloidal suspension, added to a batch, and then, through carefully controlled heating, will yield the deep crimson color of its namesake. The process was perfected by Johann Kunckel, a German glassmaker at Potsdam in the late 1670s. Since the mid-twentieth century, selenium has replaced gold as the primary coloring agent in ruby red glass. *See also "Aqua Regia," "Purple of Cassius," "Gold," "Royal Ruby," and "Selenium."*

A Ruby Red Overlay bowl by the Boston & Sandwich Glass Company. *Photo by Robin Rainwater. Item courtesy of the Sandwich Glass Museum.*

RUBY STAINED — Pressed clear or crystal glass that is decorated by fusing metal (gold) oxide onto the surface. Gold oxide produces the somewhat transparent light red color or stain. Ruby stained items were popular as souvenirs in the 1880s up to America's Depression Era, with many etched or engraved with tourist places, names, dates, and fairs.

RUCKL, ANTONIN AND SONS — A Czechoslovakian glass-making business founded at Nizbor in 1903 when Antonin Ruckl purchased an existing factory in 1875. The Ruckls were glassmakers of Swiss descent who settled in Bohemia in the mid-eighteenth century. Early on, the company produced both crystal and colored cut glass products including prisms for chandeliers. Production of lead crystal began in 1926, and many colored ornamental Bohemian art glass styles were produced from the late 1920s on up. The family acquired other small firms in 1945 (in Nizbor, Skalice Ceske Lipy, and Vcelnicka). When all companies were nationalized after World War II, it eventually became part of the Bohemia Glassworks National Corporation conglomerate in 1965. The firm regained its independence in 1989, reverted to its original name in 1992, and is currently owned by Jan and Jiri Ruckl (the great-grandson of the factory's original founder).

R

RUFFLED — A decorative technique applied during the molding process that gives an object a wavy or scalloped rim. It is usually applied to the rims of bowls, plate, and vases. *See also* SCALLOPING.

RUMMER — A small stemmed glass of small capacity, like a cordial, used exclusively for serving and drinking rum. Rummers originated in England as early as the late seventeenth century and were an adaptation of the German drinking vessel "Romer."

RUSSIAN GLASS — General term for glassware made in Russia since the early eleventh century. The first operations were forest glasshouses that produced drinking vessels and some jewelry and beads. Beginning in the late seventeenth century, two known firms near Moscow, Dukhanino and Izmailovskii, produced window panes, tableware, and pharmaceutical glass. The glasshouse at Izmailovskii began in 1668 under Czar Alexis I. In the eighteenth century, several state-run glass operations produced a good deal of ornamental and art wares for the royal families (i.e. colored, etched, engraved, relief cut, gilded, etc.). In the early nineteenth century, a government decree banned the importation of any foreign glass; as a result, many glass-making companies sprang up throughout the country (most near major western cities). Most glass produced in the nineteenth century consisted of containers, mirrors, sheet glass, and tableware. Some Art wares were

also produced during Europe's Art Nouveau movement in the latter nineteenth and early twentieth centuries, mostly for the royal family. State-run factories in Russia that made glassware from 1917 to 1991 are usually referred to as Soviet Glass, which occurred as a result of the Bolshevik Revolution. *See also* SOVIET GLASS *and, for specific Russian factories,* BAKHMETIEV, IZMAILOVSKII, MAL'TSEV, ORLOV, *and* ST. PETERSBURG IMPERIAL GLASS FACTORY.

A Russian glass egg with the Romanov Royal Design. Item was made in St. Petersburg. *Photo by Robin Rainwater.*

RYON CUT GLASS COMPANY — Refer to the EYGABROAT-RYON COMPANY, INC.

R

Ss

{ Ss }

S REPEAT — A pattern in pressed glass that resembles a series of parallel S's (shaped like the letter "S"). The S's usually contain fancy scrolling at the ends and additional scrolling as well. This pattern was produced in Carnival Glass too.

SABINO, MARIUS-ERNEST — A French glassmaker noted for producing opalescent art figurines in the 1920s-1930s, Sabino products are characterized by a pearly opalescence with clear, frosted, and light blue effects. When the Art Nouveau period in France came to a final halt in the 1930s, Sabino stopped production. He resurfaced in the 1960s with his own hand-made wooden molds and a special formula for a gold satinized opalescent glass. Sabino died in 1971 and, though his family continued the sale and export of the glass, they were unable to duplicate his original formula (new pieces are a slightly different color from the originals).

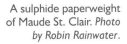

SABINO FRANCE

SABINO FRANCE

SABINO PARIS

Sabino Art Glass Co., France

Sabino, Marius-Ernest: Trademarks and signatures.

SACHET JAR — A small glass receptacle, with or without a cover, used for holding perfumed powders for scenting clothes and linens.

SACK GLASS — A stemmed goblet or wine glass used for drinking sack, an obsolete name for strong dry white wines. In the seventeenth century, the English used the term sack for most any wine imported from southern Europe (i.e. various French and Italian wines as well as the Spanish sherry). In the mid-nineteenth century, the term "sack" went out of fashion and ceased to be used for wine.

SAINT CLAIR GLASS WORKS, INC. — A small American novelty glass operation founded in 1941 at Elwood, Indiana, by the St. Clair family (John St. Clair and his five sons; John Jr., Paul, Edward, Joseph, and Robert). All of the St. Clairs had previously worked for the MacBeth-Evans Glass Company. Saint Clair began as a producer of paperweights and miniature novelty items. The factory burned in 1964, but was rebuilt. Along the way, they added some limited pressed glass tableware, lamps, and some colored art styles including custard glass to their product line. In 1971, the factory was sold, but purchased back again in 1974 by Joe St. Clair. Many molds (over fifty) were sold

to the Summit Art Glass Company in 1977; however, the company continues in operation today as a maker of blown Art Glass and is still run by members of the St. Clair family (renamed Joe Rice's House of Glass – Joe Rice is Robert St. Clair's nephew).

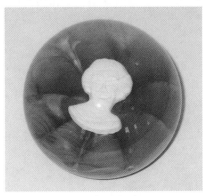

A sulphide paperweight of Maude St. Clair. *Photo by Robin Rainwater.*

SAINT CLOUD GLASSWORKS — A French glass firm founded by Philippe-Charles Lambert at St. Cloud, west of Paris, in 1783, the company's original name was Verrerie de la Reine and it was noted as one of the first French producers of English-style tableware.

SAINT GOBAIN GLASS COMPANY — A French glass firm established in 1693 at St. Gobain in Picardy. Under the patronage of Louis VIV, the state-run firm held a monopoly on plate glass production for nearly one hundred years until England's Pilkington Brothers also began producing it in 1773. St. Gobain also made mirrors and is still in the plate glass business today and operates as a subsidiary of the Ball-Foster Container Company. *See also* BALL BROTHERS GLASS MANUFACTURING COMPANY.

SAINT HILAIRE — Refer to PANTIN.

SAINT LAWRENCE GLASS COMPANY — A short-lived Canadian cut glass firm established at Montreal in 1867, the company primarily made cut glass lamp shades before ceasing operation in 1875.

SAINT LOUIS — A famous French glass-making town that was producing glass as far back as the sixteenth century (1586), in 1767, the Cristalleries de Saint Louis became a new upstart competitor of Baccarat in making tableware and other usable glass. In 1782, the firm was regarded as the first French glass company to perfect the manufacture of crystal. In the 1840s, the Compagnie des Verreries et Cristalleries de St-Louis was noted most for making paperweights, but production halted when the popularity of paperweights severely declined. The firm actually became part of Germany (located in Alsace-Lorraine in eastern France) from 1871 to 1918 as well as a brief partner with rival Baccarat. The St. Louis factory produced art wares during the Art Nouveau movement; however, in 1952, paperweights production was revived, and St. Louis continues today as a major producer of sulphide, lampwork, overlaid, and milllefiori paperweights.

Trademark.

A St. Louis lampworked swirl-ribboned paperweight. *Photo by Robin Rainwater.*

SAINT LOUIS FLINT GLASS WORKS — An American firm founded in 1842 at St. Louis, Missouri, by James B. Eads and associates, the company produced both blown and pressed glass tableware into the mid-1880s.

SAINT LOUIS GLASS MANUFACTURING COMPANY — An American firm established in 1846 at St. Louis, Missouri, by Case, Nelson, and James B. Eads, the company produced some pressed glass tableware before going bankrupt in 1858.

SAINT LOUIS GLASS WORKS — An American firm founded at St. Louis, Missouri, in 1849 by Henry Blow and John Farrell, production of glass window panes began in 1850. The firm went bankrupt in 1854 and was purchased by James and Samuel Wallace. The new venture was named the Mount City Glass Works and produced blown green glass bottles. In 1859, it was reorganized as the Missouri Glass Company and production was expanded to include glass tubing, vials, lamp shades, syrup bottles, and pressed and cut tumblers. The company remained in business until 1863, when it was sold to the St. Louis Plow Manufacturing Company.

Reproduction from a 1902 St. Louis Glass Works U.S. patent.

SAINT PAUL GLASS COMPANY — An American cut glass operation founded in 1907 at St. Paul, Minnesota, by Paul Schneider, the firm produced cut and beveled flat plate glass until closing in 1943.

SAINT PETERSBURG IMPERIAL GLASS FACTORY — The first Russian state glasshouse was established by Peter the Great or Peter I (1682-1725), Tsar of Russia, in the early eighteenth century in St. Petersburg. A few other state-owned glasshouses in towns like Jamburg, Zhabino, Moscow, and Izmailovskii were ordered closed by Peter; all were shut down permanently by the 1730s. Another state glasshouse opened in 1743 at St. Petersburg, but closed in the 1770s. Yet another state glasshouse opened 1777; it was leased to the Russian prince, Potemkin, who moved it to the city of Ozerki just outside of St. Petersburg. When Potemkin passed on in 1792, the glasshouse reverted back to the state. It then became known as the St. Petersburg Imperial Glass Factory. By the very end of the eighteenth century, the state-run glass factory and the Imperial Porcelain Factory were brought together under one directorship. Both interests created intricate items principally for the Court and Russian aristocracy. They served nearly every Russian leader of the

eighteenth century: Peter II (Czar, 1727-30), Anna Ivanovna (Czarina 1730-40), Elizabeth Petrovna (Czarina, 1741-62), and Catherine the Great (1762-96). Glass items produced consisted of crystal goblets, massive chandeliers, girandoles, samovars, huge vases, urns, ewers, and other decorative items. During much of the nineteenth century, the Imperial factory was noted for elaborately cut and engraved crystal drinking vessels, some containing hand-painting or enameling. Some articles were even cased in two or three colors while a few were cameo cut into separate layers. Many sported such elaborate designs as the imperial monogram or the heraldic eagle. The Russians also experimented with the Venetian technique of "Smalto," which literally translates to enamel; the St. Petersburg Imperial Glass Factory and the studio of M. V. Lomonosov were noted experimenters with the smalto. In the 1860s, the Russian economy worsened and the government attempted to sell the factory, but to no avail. In the 1880s, the glass factory was moved to the same site as the Imperial Porcelain Factory and the two were combined into one operation. During the Russian Revolution in 1917, the factories were viewed as an excess of the old ruling class and were shut down.

Russian table by the St. Petersburg Imperial Glassworks, 1804.
Photo courtesy of the Corning Museum of Glass.

SALAD BOWL — A medium-to-large sized concave glass serving vessel, hemispherical in shape, used for holding and serving salads (or other foods).

SALAD PLATE — A flat glass object, usually round in shape and about 7 to 7-1/2" in diameter (slightly smaller than a lunch plate), used specifically for serving salads.

SALAZAR, DAVID — Salazar first worked as an apprentice glassblower for Lundberg Studios in 1973. Salazar is credited with aiding in the invention of precision torch work utilized in paperweight-making. Salazar continues today as an independent glass artisan and his work can be found in both museums and in some publications (his work once graced the cover of *The Smithsonian*).

SALIVA — An undesired or unintentional string of air bubbles in glass created from the insufficient expulsion of air. It is usually associated with the assembly of a paperweight.

SALT AND PEPPER SHAKERS — Refer to SHAKER.

SALT CELLAR — A tiny open bowl, with or without a foot, used for sprinkling salt on food prior to the development of shakers (may or may not have a matching spoon). They are also known as "Salts" or "Salt Dip."

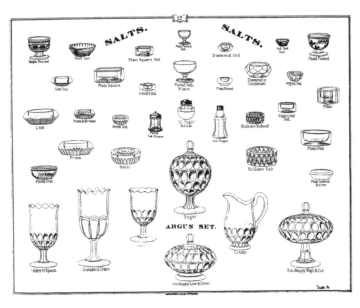

Reproduction from an 1875 King, Son & Co. catalog.

Pressed glass lacy-patterned salt cellars.
Photo courtesy of the Sandwich Glass Museum.

SALT DIP — Refer to SALT CELLAR.

SALTPETER — An oxidizing agent, such as sodium nitrate (NaNO3) or potassium nitrate (KNO3), used during the melting process of a batch of glass. In the early-to-mid nineteenth century, saltpeter was obtained from Kentucky caves and was also imported from India. In modern times, chemists are able to produce it from regular salt.

SALTS BOTTLE — A small glass bottle, with a silver or silver-plated top, used for holding smelling salts. They were most popular during the Victorian Period.

SALVE BOX — A small jar, with a cover, used on dressing tables and vanities for holding salves, ointments, or cold creams.

Reproduction from an early 20th century S.F. Myers Company catalog.

SALVER — A large platter or tray used for serving food or beverages. Most are circular in shape and have a pedestal foot. *See also* CAKE SALVER.

Reproduction from an 1899 U.S. Glass Company catalog.

SALVIATI AND COMPANY — A Venetian firm founded in Murano, Italy, in 1859 by Dr. Antonio Salviati (1816-1890), Enrico Podio, and Lorenzo Radi (1803-1874). The original workshop was set up to produce glass mosaic tiles and was called Salviati Dott. In 1866, they established a glass-making factory with the financial backing of two Englishmen, Sir Austin Henry Layard and Sir William Drake. A shop was added in London in 1868, dubbed the Venice and Murano Glass Company. The factory in Murano produced chandeliers, vessels, and mosaics. In 1877, Antonio Salviati opened his own glass factory in Murano and the name was changed to Salviati and Company. When he passed on, it was run by a relative, Amalia Salviati, and ornamental art glass was added in the latter nineteenth century. Today, the company is noted most for aiding in the revival of traditional colored Venetian glass styles like latticino and filigree. Maurizio Camerino (1859-1931), who managed the firm beginning in 1896, eventually purchased it. Camerino's sons, Mario and Renzo, joined in the 1920s and eventually assumed control of the company. Although the factory was destroyed during World War II, they managed to lease space from Barbini and Toso until purchasing a new building in 1959. The firm was sold in 1988 to the Gardini and Ferruzzzi families who had also purchased Venini. The Salviati factory was closed; however, the Salviati name was then acquired by Arc International in 1995. Arc continues to produce glass tableware under the Salviati brand name today. *See also* VENETIAN GLASS *and* ARC INTERNATIONAL.

SAMOVAR — An urn-shaped lamp that ordinarily contains a metal spigot at its base and other metal hardware (base, top, and handle). Samovars originated in Russia as both lighting fixtures and heating units for liquids like tea.

SAND — The most common form of silica used in making glass, the best sands are found along inland beds near streams of low iron content and other impurities. Prior to mixing in a batch of glass, sand is typically washed, heated to remove carbon-based particles, and screened to obtain uniformly small grains.

S

SANDBLASTING — A decorating process invented by American Benjamin Tilghman of Philadelphia, Pennsylvania, in 1870. A design drawn upon a piece of glass is coated with a protective layer and then the exposed surface that remain are sandblasted with a pressurized gun. The result is that the original design is left in somewhat of a matted relief or frosted finish.

SAND GLASS — Refer to HOUR GLASS.

SAND GROUND — Refer to ROCK GROUND.

SANDEVER — Refer to GALL.

SANDWICH GLASS — (1) An American mold-pressed style of pattern glass produced in the Eastern United States in the nineteenth century, it was a substitute for more expensive hand-cut crystal glass and is characterized by an all-over pattern of small dots that are present in the mold. The dots serve as the background for other designs such as floral patterns, foliage, scrolling, and stars. (2) Sandwich also refers to the technique of decorating glass squeezed or sandwiched between two separate layers. (3) A pattern name given to a huge set of machine pressed tableware produced by the Indiana Glass Company beginning in the Depression Era and then widely reproduced by them afterward. As is typical with original Sandwich designs, Indiana's pattern contains an all-over pattern of scrolling and flower. (4) A pressed pattern name given to a set of tableware produced by the Anchor Hocking Glass Company first produced in 1939 (made until 1964 and then again in 1977). This pattern is sometimes confused with Indiana's "Sandwich," but there are more leaves surrounding each symmetrical flower pattern in Anchor Hocking's "Sandwich" (four leaves off the main stem as opposed to Indiana's two). (5) One other prolific pressed "Sandwich" pattern was Duncan Miller's; there are more spiral curves with Duncan Miller's than either Hocking's or Indiana's. Duncan Miller's design was referred to as "Early American Sandwich" and was produced during the Depression Era. *See also* BOSTON AND SANDWICH GLASS COMPANY, CASED or PLATED GLASS, and TIARA.

Reproduction from a 1925 Indiana Glass Co. advertisement.

A Depression Glass Sandwich patterned punch bowl from the Indiana Glass Company. *Photo by Robin Rainwater.*

SANDWICH MANUFACTURING COMPANY — Refer to the BOSTON AND SANDWICH GLASS COMPANY.

SANDWICH SERVER — A large platter or serving tray with an open or closed center handle.

SAPPHIRE BLUE — The color of sapphire or sky blue, darker than ice blue but much lighter than cobalt blue.

SARDINE DISH — A small, oblong or oval, flat or shallow dish used for serving sardines.

SASSANIAN GLASS — General term for Pre-Islamic glassware made in Persia and Mesopotamia in the third through seventh centuries under Sassanian rule. Items produced included mold-blown and cut glass typical of the period. *See also* ISLAMIC GLASS and PERSIAN GLASS.

SATAVA ART GLASS STUDIO — A contemporary American Art Glass studio founded by Richard Satava at Chico, California, in 1977. Satava studied at the College of San Mateo and California State University at Chico. He specializes in producing hand-blown opaque glass vases, sculptures, and other art glass forms.

SATIN GLASS — An American Art Glass form characterized by a smooth lustrous appearance obtained by giving layers of colored glass an all-over hydrofluoric acid vapor bath.

Satin glass rose bowls. *Items courtesy of Wheaton Village.*

SAUCE BOAT — An oblong bowl-shaped vessel usually with a handle on one end and a pouring spout on the other. They are used for serving sauces or gravy and may contain a separate base, foot (feet), or cover.

SAUCE DISH — A small, usually flat or shallow dish, with or without handles and possibly footed, used for serving condiments or sauces.

SAUCER — A small flat or shallow plate usually with a circular indentation for a matching cup.

Reproduction from a late 19th century Mount Washington catalog.

Saucer, Priscilla.

No. 205, 6 inches, $4.00.

SAVOI GLASS — Free-blown studio art glass object created by Charles Savoi, who was born in Albany, New York, in 1959 and received a Masters of Fine Arts from the University of Illinois in 1993. Savoi then opened a studio in Wisconsin, where he continues to create jewel-colored and twisted forms of blown art glass including paperweights.

SAWTOOTH — Refer to SERRATED.

SAXON GLASS—General term for glassware produced in Saxony, Germany, during the Middle Ages. Most items produced were in the standard German or Bavarian style of this time period (i.e. engraving, enameling, and gilding).

SCALLOPING — A decorative technique applied during the molding process that gives an object a wavy or ruffled rim. It is usually applied to the rims of bowls, plates, and vases.

SCENIC DECORATION—Glass objects with a variety of techniques (enameled, painted, cameo cut, transferred, embossed, etc.) depicting scenes of famous cities, states, countries, buildings, and tourist attractions. *See also SOUVENIR GLASS.*

SCENT BOTTLE — Refer to COLOGNE BOTTLE or PERFUME BOTTLE.

SCHAUMGLAS — A style of bubbled or foam-like glass created in 1933 by Richard Sussmuth. The formula was used initially for the production of lamp shades, but was later expanded to include ornamental bowls and vases. Note that "Schaumglas" translates to "Foam Glass." *See also SUSSMUTHGLAS.*

SCHECK M. E. AND COMPANY — A short-lived American cut glass-making firm established in 1907 at Chicago, Illinois, by Max E. Scheck, who produced some cut glass tableware until closing in 1908.

SCHLEVOGT, H. G. CURT — Schlevogt was the son-in-law of Heinrich Hoffman, who owned a factory in Jablonec, Czechoslovakia, that produced beads, cut gems, and glass eyes for the doll industry. Schlevogt worked for Hoffman from 1928 until the early 1930s. Schlevogt then had molds produced from the Zelezny Brod Glass School and created his first glass items for the Leipzig Exhibition in 1934. The articles produced consisted of Lalique-styled vases made in a somewhat marbleized, turquoise-green color. The glass was further engraved and finished by removing the mold seams. Schlevogt named the series "Ingrid" after his daughter with his first wife (Charlotte Hoffman who died in childbirth). The molds are still being used today to produce figural-styled vases; however, later pieces do not have the extensive hand-finish work as the originals.

SCHNEIDER, GEORGE CUT GLASS COMPANY — An American cut glass operation established in 1905 in Brooklyn, New York, by George Schneider, the firm produced cut glass products up until World War I.

SCHNEIDER GLASS — A French firm founded in 1908 in Epiney-sur-Seine near Paris by brothers Ernest (1877-1937) and Charles (1881-1953) Schneider. Charles had previously worked for Daum and Galle while Ernest had worked for Daum. Schneider is best known for art glass items, but they also produced some tableware, lamps, and stained glass. They relied extensively on more modern Art Deco styles as opposed to the older Art Nouveau. The firm closed during World War I, but reopened afterward. The company went bankrupt in 1938; nevertheless, the family name was carried on. Charles Schneider's sons, Charles Jr. (b. 1916) and Robert (b. 1917), set up a small factory in Epinay-sur-Seine in 1946 and dubbed it Cristallerie Schneider. They produced some art glass candelabras and ashtrays. Charles Sr. served as one of the new venture's designers. After a gas explosion in 1957, operations were moved to Lorris, France, in 1962. Note that pieces signed by the company include "Schneider," "La Verre Francaise," and "Charder." When the Schneider brothers retired in 1981, the business closed permanently.

Schneider Glass: Trademarks.

SCHOTT AND GEN. — A German firm originally founded as the Jenaer Glassworks at Jena in Thuringia in 1884 by Otto Schott (1851-1935), Ernst Abbe, Carl Zeiss (1816-1888), and Roderich Zeiss, the company initially produced scientific and optical glass including lenses for cameras, microscopes and telescopes; incandescent lamps; and heat resistant (borosilicate) glass for laboratory items. The name was changed to Schott and Gen, in 1919. In the 1920s, the firm expanded into baby bottles and ovenware marketed under "Jenaer Glass." When Otto Schott retired in 1927, his son Dr. Erich Schott (1891-1989) took over. The product line expanded to include additional tableware, goblets, and stemware. In 1945, Erich, along with most key staff members, were deported to West Germany while the Russians occupied East Germany, where the plant was located. The glassworks was dismantled, but rebuilt in 1948. At that time, it became a state-owned enterprise producing tableware until it became part of the Kombinat VEB Carl Zeiss conglomerate. In the meantime, Schott leased an existing plant in Zweisel for the production of optical glass. A new factory was built in 1952 at Mainz and the company operated as Jenaer Glaswerk Schott and Gen., Mainz. Aside from laboratory glass and optics, the firm produced tableware, stemware, and some colored ornamental glass. In 1991, Schott was able to reacquire the plant at Jena and the combined plants today make up one of Germany's largest producers of scientific glass known as the "Schott Group."

S

SCHULZE, PAUL — A noted American Studio Glass artisan born in New York City in 1934, Schulze received his degree from New York University and has served in a teaching capacity at the Parsons School of Design, the Rhode Island School of Design, the Rochester Institute of Technology, and the Pilchuk Glass Center. Schulze is best known for serving as director of design for Steuben from 1970 to 1987 and still works as an independent glass artisan in New Suffolk, New York.

SCHUYLKILL GLASS WORKS — An American glass firm established at Philadelphia, Pennsylvania, in 1780, the company produced some blown decanters and stemware, which were wheel engraved, before closing in 1786. Note that Schuylkill employed noted French glass cutter William Peter Eichbaum, who went on to head the Pittsburgh Glass Works until 1800. Eichbaum then cut glass on his own as well as for Bakewell, Pears, and Company.

SCONCE — A glass candlestick bracket, with one or more sockets, used for holding candles.

SCOTTISH GLASSWARE — General term for glassware made in Scotland since the early seventeenth century. The first operations were forest glasshouse that produced practical items like windows, bottles, and drinking vessels. In 1615, wood was banned for glass-making in England and all the companies had to switch to coal. Beginning in the latter nineteenth century, Scottish makers produced a good deal of crystal tableware and some art forms. Beginning in the mid-to-late twentieth century, the country, particularly the Perthshire region, is noted most for collectible paperweight production. *See also* CAITHNESS, MONART, MONCRIEFF, PERTHSHIRE, STRATHEARN, *and* VASART.

SCRAMBLE OR SCRAMBLED — A jumble of canes encased in clear glass to form a paperweight, the majority is of millefiori design and may contain white or colored lace. Most were thrown together at the end of the day from whatever scrap or broken canes were left (also referred to as END-OF-DAY or PELL-MELL).

SCRATCH MARK — A thin straw-like mark on glass that usually results from light wear and movement (i.e. bumping or scraping an article against another surface). Scratch marks are also referred to as "Straw Marks." A small scratch-like fissure with rough edges ordinarily appears on the inside bottom of pressed glass (or on the outside bottom for articles that have been pressed upside down like cup plates). This mark is due to contact with the plunger during pressing and is sometimes referred to as a "Shear Line."

SCREEN PRINTING — A decorating technique involving the passage of a printing medium through a stenciled specialized fabric.

SCREW CAP — A threaded cover made to fit securely and tightly over the mouth of a vessel (i.e. jars, bottles, flasks, castors, etc.). Most tend to be made of metal; however, they are occasionally made of glass.

SCRIBED ANTIQUE — Glass that is similar to that of full antique, only it is made by the double roll method rather than by blowing. If texture striations are desired, then the glass should be blown. If textural striations are not desired, then they are scribed directly into the hot glass surface as opposed to those that are hand-applied in full antique. *See also* FULL ANTIQUE *and* DOUBLE ROLL METHOD.

SCROLL OR SCROLLING — A common design or add-on decoration to many forms of glass. Scrolling generally consists of a riband with rolled ends, but may also contain more elaborate curves, spirals, and/or ornamentation. Scrolling can be cut, mold-pressed, applied, enameled, fired-on, gilded, or applied with other metals.

SCULPTURE — General term for a piece of Art Studio glass that is shaped by an artist from a solid block of molten glass. Most sculptures are hand-worked or hand-carved without the use of any blowing or molding.

Glass sculpture from Maleras of Sweden.

SEA FOAM GREEN — A color in Art Glass that resembles the greenish-blue hue of sea foam for which it is named. Depending on the maker and/or formula, shades of sea foam green vary from lightly tinted bluish-green to aquamarine. Generally, the addition of both copper and chromium are necessary to achieve this color. Steuben named one of their colors sea foam green in the 1920s that consisted of tinted green glass with light overtones of blue.

SEA GLASS — Glass items or pieces that wash up on sea shores that have been worn down by sand.

SEALED BOTTLE — A glass object, ordinarily a bottle, that bears a monogram or design in the glass that recognizes the owner, maker, tavern name, factory, etc. Most seals are mold-embossed or hand-pressed, and circular in nature.

SEAM — A tiny, narrow line, groove, or ridge on a glass object indicating that it has been made by molding. The mold line is produced from where the arts of the mold meet. Multiple piece molds will form more than one seam (i.e. a three-piece mold will form two such seams). On some glass, the seam may be smoothed away by fire polishing.

SEATTLE CUT GLASS COMPANY — An American firm established in 1917 at Seattle, Washington, by J. L. Hutchinson, Paul Kowarsh, Joseph Prosser, and Peter Sibo, the company produced some cut glass tableware until closing in 1922.

Seattle Cut Glass Company: Trademark.

SECESSION — The Austrian term for the Art Nouveau movement. *See also* ART OR ART NOUVEAU GLASS.

SEEDS — Tiny air bubbles in glass indicating an under-heated furnace or impurities caused by flecks of dirt or dust.

SEGUSO VETRI D'ARTE — An Italian Art Glass firm established on the island of Murano in Venice in 1932 by Archimede Seguso (b. 1909), Napoleane Barovier (1881-1957), Antonio Ernesto, Olimp Ferro, and brothers Angelo and Bruno Seguso. The firm was first known as "Artistica Vetreria e Sooffiera Barovier Seguso Vetri d'Arte" until 1933 when Ferro left the firm. The company is noted most for flashed and colored blown glass, particularly in shades of amethyst. Flavio Poli (1900-1984) served as the firm's most noted designer. Archimede Seguso left in 1942 and, in 1946, formed the "Vetraria Archimede Seguso" company. In 1954, the firm won the Compasso d'Oro award for its "Valva" series of thickly layered colored glass. Both colored art glass and blown crystal are still being made today in the "Seguso" name under the direction of Archimede's sons, Gino (b. 1938) and Giampaolo (b. 1943), and Gino's son, Antonio (b. 1967).

SELENIUM — A nonmetallic element that produces a pink color in non-lead glass or an amber color in lead crystal. When combined with cadmium sulphide, it produces a red or ruby red coloring in glass. Selenium serves as a cheaper substitute for gold in the modern era for achieving red glassware. Steuben named one of their vibrant red colors "Selenium Red" in the 1920s that also utilized selenium rather than acidized gold to achieve the desired red color.

SELTZER BOTTLE — A late eighteenth and nineteenth century glass container, with a narrow neck and mouth and usually without a handle, used for drinking mineral water that supposedly had medicinal purposes. *See also PHARMACY GLASS and WATER BOTTLE.*

SEMPLE, REYNOLDS AND COMPANY — Refer to the CRESCENT FLINT GLASS WORKS.

SENECA CRYSTAL, INC. — Refer to the SENECA GLASS COMPANY.

SENECA GLASS COMPANY — An American firm established by a group of German immigrants in 1891 at Fostoria, Ohio, the company started as a maker of mold-blown tableware, barware, and stemware. In 1896, Seneca moved to Morgantown, West Virginia, added a second factory (Factory B) in Star City in 1913, and began producing etched glassware in 1920. Seneca continued to produce etched and cut crystal through the Depression and then added a number of color lines in the 1970s. In 1982, the firm was purchased by a group of Malaysian investors and the name was changed to Seneca Crystal, Inc. This new effort went bankrupt in 1983 and both the stock and equipment were sold off.

Seneca Glass Company: Trademarks.

SERRATED — A form of notching along the rims of glass objects that resembles the edge of a saw blade. It was a popular finish on cut glass and is sometimes referred to as "Sawtooth."

A cut glass bowl with serrated rim from T. G. Hawkes.
Photo by Robin Rainwater.

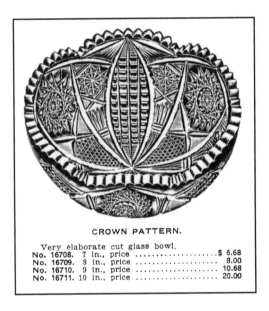

CROWN PATTERN.

Very elaborate cut glass bowl.
No. 16708. 7 in., price .... $ 6.68
No. 16709. 8 in., price 8.00
No. 16710. 9 in., price 10.68
No. 16711. 10 in., price 20.00

Cut glass bowl with serrated rim, reproduced from a
late 19th century Higgins-Seiter catalog.

SERVICE — General term for a set of glass pieces designed for a particular use. A beverage service set usually has a pitcher and matching cups/goblets; wine service includes a decanter and matching goblets; ice cream service includes a large serving bowl with small matching bowls; tea service contains a pot, cups, creamer, and sugar; and a punch service contains a large bowl and matching cups. Most service sets contain a large serving tray for which the other objects rest upon.

SERVING BOWL — A medium-to-large sized concave glass serving vessel, hemispherical in shape, used for holding and serving a wide variety of foods.

SERVITOR — A glass attendant, helper, or apprentice who aids the gaffer (glass-blower) in glass-making.

SET — General term for two or more matching (though not necessarily identical) pieces that have something in common and are intended to be used together. A set may simply be a cup and saucer while complete table sets in some matching patterns may number over one hundred pieces. *See also SERVICE and TABLE SET.*

SETTING — General term for a set of pieces for one person wile seated at a dinner table. These likely include plates (i.e. salad, dinner, dessert), cup and saucer (or goblets), a serving bowl or soup cup, and silverware. Most settings, except for the silverware, are composed of porcelain or glass.

SFUMATO — A Venetian technique that produces a smoky effect in glass by enclosing fine inner veils of color within the glass.

SHADE — Protective glass coverings that shelter lights in order to reduce glare. At times, large glass bowls are converted to lamp shades by drilling holes in their center in order to attach them above the light. Dome shades have also been used as protective coverings over mantel clocks, figurines, floral displays, collectibles, and older gas lights (gas shades). Shades were also at one time referred to as candle covers.

SHAFT — The part of a candlestick between the base at the bottom and the cup or nozzle at the top.

SHAKER — A small glass upright container, usually cylindrical or angular in shape and with a metal or plastic cover containing tiny holes, used for sprinkling salt, pepper, sugar, and others spices on foods.

Reproduction from a 1930 Indiana Glass Company catalog.

SALT AND PEPPER
Nickel Plated Top

SHAM — Fragile glass tumblers that are somewhat small and very thin.

SHANK — A drinking vessel made in three parts by attaching a stem and foot to a bowl.

SHARD — A piece or fragment of broken glass ordinarily found at a factory dump site. Shards are frequently excavated by archaeologists at old glass factory sites to aid in the attribution of products, patterns, and colors. See also FRAGMENT.

SHAVING MUG — A cylindrical glass vessel, with or without handles, that is usually larger than a drinking mug. They are used for repeated dipping and rinsing of shaving cream from a razor and were popular from the 1880s through the mid-1920s.

SHEAR LINE — Refer to SCRATCH MARK.

SHEARS — A scissor-like tool used in the glass-making process to trim objects. In pressed glass, they are used specifically for cutting hot glass from a gather on a pontil rod in order to be dipped into a pressing mold. See also HANDLE-SHEAR.

SHEET GLASS — A large piece of flat glass, usually rectangular in shape, used for window panes.

SHELL DISH — A fairly small dish produced in the shape of a seashell. Though varieties exist, most resemble scallop shells and are used to hold jewelry and other trinkets. Shell dishes date as far back as the third century A.D. with the Romans.

SHELL FLASK — A style of molded flask made in the shape of a scallop shell on both sides. Like shell dishes, shell flasks also date back to ancient Roman times.

SHELL PINK MILK GLASS — A large set of tableware produced by the Jeannette Glass Company from 1957 to 1959. The pattern was named for its satin milk-like finish that is tinged with a light pink or a pale peach-bloom color. Note that Jeannette used a variety of its molds and patterns to produce glass in this color.

SHEPHERD AND WEBB — A short-term glass-making partnership established by Englishmen John Shepherd and John Webb. They leased the White House Glassworks in the early 1830s near Stourbridge, England, and produced tableware. The firm closed in 1835 when Webb died and Shepherd retired. Webb's son, Thomas Webb I, inherited it from his father; however, Thomas went on the other ventures: Webb and Richardson and then to Thomas Webb and Sons.

SHERBET — A small footed serving dish with or without a small stem. Sherbets are used for serving desserts such as pudding, ice cream, and jell-o.

Green Depression Glass sherbet dishes.

SHERRY GLASS — A fairly small glass with foot and stem that contains a shallow angled or straight-edged bowl. As the name implies, they were produced specifically for drinking sherry (an amber-colored wine originating in Spain). Though sherry glasses contain about the same capacity of wine glasses (i.e. 4 ounces), they tend to be taller with a narrower tapering bowl.

SHIP GLASS — A drinking glass that originated in England for use on ships. Ship glasses tend to have wide thick feet and short stems in order to prevent tipping and to provide some stability at sea.

SHIP-IN-A-BOTTLE — Miniature replicas of sailing ships enclosed within glass bottles. They are made as decorative novelty items to baffle those as to how they are created. Originally, wooden hulls had masts hinged to them with strings attached; once inserted into a bottle, the strings were pulled upright to raise the masts. As a consequence, the strings became part of the rigging and were made in a variety of forms: some are lamp worked or threaded piece by piece with long tweezers. However, many makers refuse to disclose their techniques.

SHIRLEY, FREDERICK — A glass artisan employed with the Mount Washington Glass Company in the late nineteenth century. During the 1880s, Shirley received patents for several of Mt. Washington's most noteworthy art styles, such as Burmese and Crown Milano, and obtained licensing for Peach Blow. See also MOUNT WASHINGTON GLASS WORKS.

SHOE — A decorative novelty item made in the shape of a lady's slipper or shoe. See also BOOT GLASS.

SHOEPEG — Refer to HOBNAIL.

SHOOTER — (1) A large glass marble minimum of 7/8" in diameter; in the game of classic marbles, the shooter was usually the player's most prized marble and was used to shoot at his/her opponent's marbles. (2) A shooter is also another name for a shot glass. See also SHOT GLASS.

S

SHOP — Another name for a crew of glassworkers, usually up to six, who work as a team to manufacture glass.

SHOT GLASS — A small whiskey tumbler with a capacity of at least one ounce but not more than two and a height of at least 1-3/4" but strictly less than three inches. Shot glasses were originally filled with lead shot (hence the name "Shot") to support and clean quill pens. In modern times, they are used to serve a single shot or ounce of hard liquor. Shot glasses tend to taper outward at the top as opposed to toothpick holders, which tend to taper inward. *See also* JIGGERS, SHOOTERS, *and* WHISKEY TUMBLERS.

A collection of pressed and cut glass shot glasses.
Photo by Robin Rainwater.

SHOTTON CUT GLASS WORKS — An American cut glass operation founded in Brooklyn, New York, in 1904 by Thomas Shotton, the firm produced cut glass tableware into the World War I era and then switched briefly to pressed wares prior to going out of business in 1923. The firm was also known as the "Thomas Shotton Cut Glass Company" and "Thomas Shotton and Sons."

SHOULDER — The bulged section just below the neck of a glass object (usually present in vases and bottles).

SHULL-GOODWIN GLASS COMPANY — Refer to the WHEATON GLASS COMPANY.

SICKNESS — Glass that is not properly tempered or annealed and shows random cracks and flaking, eventually breaking or disintegrating. Another type of sickness in glass known as "Foggy," where the surface of clear glass becomes cloudy due to a chemical change in the glass surface. The change ordinarily results when a cleaning agent used on glass reacts with the alkali in the glass formula (in window glass, this is also known as "Weathering").

SIDE-LEVER PRESS — Refer to PRESSED GLASS.

SIDONIAN GLASS — General term for some of the earliest glassware ever produced in the world at Sidon, along the Syrian Coast, as early as fifteenth century B.C. Early glass was made identical to that of the Mesopotamians. Around the first century B.C., glass-blowing was also prevalent along the Syrian coast until the Phoenician civilization collapsed. Many glass artisans migrated to other regions such as Italy, where they continued to produce glassware. *See also* "Mesopotamian Glass."

SIEGE — A term that refers to the floor or bed of a pot furnace on which the melting pots are set upon.

SIGNAL LANTERN — A portable lighting fixture, with a handle, once used by a signal man to communicate with incoming or outgoing steam engine railroads. *See also* LANTERN.

SIGNATURE — The mark of the maker or manufacturer usually applied near the bottom or the underside of glass objects, but it may be applied elsewhere. In paperweights, the factory or individual's initials may be etched within a single millefiori cane placed in the internal design (known as a "Signature Cane" or "Initial Cane"). *See also* DATE CANE.

SIGNET CUT GLASS — Refer to T. G. HAWKES AND COMPANY.

SILESIAN GLASS — General term for glassware made in Silesia from as early as the mid-fourteenth century. The area was once part of Poland (eleventh century) until it was acquired by the Austrian Hapsburgs in 1526. As a result, the area fell under Bohemian rule and glass made here was in the traditional Bohemian styles. Silesia was further captured by Frederick II of Prussia in the late eighteenth century. The region was eventually split between Poland and the Czech Republic. *See also* BOHEMIAN GLASS *and* CZECHOSLOVAKIAN GLASS.

SILHOUETTE — A likeness of a figure or portrait that is usually cut from darker glass and then mounted on a lighter ground color. In glassware, silhouettes might appear as medallions in goblets or bottles; enameled or engraved on various objects; inserted in canes in making millefiori glass; and as the primary design in paperweights. In addition to people, animal subjects have also been made as silhouettes. *See also* SULPHIDE.

SILICA — An essential ingredient in making glass. The most common form is sand, which is impure silica. Sand is usually taken from the seashore or along inland beds near water. The Venetians historically used ground white pebbles from rivers. Powdered flints were once used, too, as silica. Chemically, silicon dioxide is SiO_2. *See also* FLINT GLASS.

SILVART — Refer to the DEIDRICK GLASS COMPANY.

SILVER — A metallic agent with an almost white lustrous sheen used in coloring and decorating glassware. When added to a batch in small quantities (silver oxide or chloride), silver enhances lead in crystal-making; when added as a silver-sulphide compound, a deep yellow color is produced for staining. Like gold leaf, silver leaf serves as an applied decoration on the exterior of glass objects. Silver is also applied for scrolling, rims, and floral work. Also note that Silver nitrate is used for the backs of mirrors.

SILVER CITY CUT GLASS COMPANY — An American company founded in 1905 at Meriden, Connecticut, by A. Abercunos, Percy Phoenix, and Joseph Schick, the firm produced cut glass along with silver holders and silver decorations. The firm was purchased by Carl Schultz in 1920 around the same time that cut glass production ended. The company remained in business as the "Silver City Glass Company."

SILVER CITY GLASS COMPANY — Refer to the SILVER CITY CUT GLASS COMPANY.

SILVER DEPOSIT OR OVERLAY — Glass objects that are decorated by applying silver (usually Sterling silver) directly to glass by a chemical method so that a cutout design of silver metal appears against a clear or colored glass background.

SILVERED GLASS — Refer to MERCURY GLASS.

SILVER-ELECTROPLATE — A style of Art Glass characterized by an electro-deposit of silver upon the outer surface.

SILVER THREAD — A decorating technique first developed by Sinclaire in cut glass floral engravings. Silver thread is a fine line cutting that fills in the background of a piece in order to provide a higher degree of brilliance.

S

SILVER VEILING — This process involves melting silver within glass and then drawing the silver to the surface by reheating where the design is further developed. It is a delicate process whereby the finished design is encased in crystal to form more of an abstract paperweight, one that is usually larger and more upright than traditional paperweights. Both Michael O'Keefe and Ed Nesteruk have been known to create paperweights utilizing this technique.

SILVERIA GLASS — The technique of rolling an extremely thin layer of silver over glass and then blowing it. The process shatters the silver into glittery decorative flecks. This style of Art Glass was first produced by the English firm of Stevens and Williams around 1900.

SILVERINA — A type of Art Glass created by Frederick Carder at Steuben in he 1920s. It was made by casing particles or flakes of silver and mica within a crystal glass object. The particles were also combined with trapped air bubbles to produce varying effects.

Sinclaire, H. P. and Company — An American firm established in Corning, New York, in 1904 by H. P. Sinclaire, who used blanks from Dorflinger for cutting and engraving crystal products. A few rare Sinclaire items were also cut in colored glass (i.e. amber, blue, green, and ruby red). The company closed permanently in 1929.

Cut glass pitcher and tumblers by H. P. Sinclaire, c. 1916. *Photo by Robin Rainwater.*

Trademark.

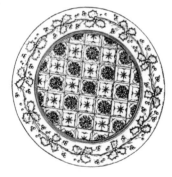 

Reproductions from a 1909 and 1911 Sinclaire U.S. patents.

SINGLE ROLL METHOD — Sheet glass that is produced by pouring molten glass on a metal table and then rolling it flat with a single metal roll. This method is also referred to as "Hand Cast" glass.

SIPPO VALLEY GLASS COMPANY — Refer to the STOEHR GLASS COMPANY.

SISTER PATTERN — A line of tableware usually identical in size and shape, but differing in color. Anchor-Hocking's Forest Green (dark green pieces) and Royal Ruby (dark ruby red) are an example of sister patterns, as is Hazel Ware's Capri (light blue pieces) and Moroccan Amethyst (dark amethyst colored pieces).

SITE — A Venetian glass mirror made of cristallo beginning in the sixteenth century. *See also* CRISTALLO.

SITULA — A small bucket-shaped vessel, with handle, originally used to hold holy water. Situlas were made in ancient Roman and Byzantine times.

SKINNER GLASS COMPANY — An American cut glass operation established at Philadelphia, Pennsylvania, in 1895 by William Skinner and his son, Thomas, English immigrants. The Skinners had previously worked for both Dorflinger and Pairpoint prior to establishing their own business. The Skinners cut glass and moved operations to Hammonton, New Jersey, in 1901. They ceased cutting glass around 1920 and switched to producing stemware for the next decade. In the 1930s, the firm produced mirrors and ashtrays before getting out of the glass business in favor of plastics. Note that the company was also known as "William Skinner and Son."

SKITTLE — A small fire-clay pot used for melting a specialized small batch of colored glass or enamel.

SKRUF — A Swedish firm established in 1897 in the southern Varmland region by Robert Celander, who had previously served as manager of Johansfors. The company made practical household glass before going bankrupt in 1908. The firm reorganized in 1909 and continued to produce glass until 1946, when the factory burned to the ground. It was rebuilt in 1948, and Skruf expanded into colored art styles in the 1950s that were produced in traditional Swedish styles. In 1974, Skruf, along with Gullaskruf, Bjorkschult, Aseda, and Maleras, became part of Royal Krona (also known as Krona-Bruken AB). Royal Krona went bankrupt in 1977 and Skruf was taken over by Kosta-Boda, which closed the factory in 1980. However, it was purchased the following year by the community of Lessebo and, since then, Skruf has been run as a cooperative producing traditional Swedish art styles of glass. *See also* SWEDISH GLASS.

SLAG GLASS — A type of glass made with various scrap metals including lead that was first produced in England in the mid-nineteenth century. Slag is characterized by colorful swirling or marbleized designs and is sometimes referred to as "Marbled Glass." *See also* MARBLED GLASS, PINK SLAG, PURPLE SLAG, *and* CARAMEL SLAG.

A Challinor, Taylor & Company purple slag glass creamer. *Item courtesy of Wheaton Village.*

SLANE AND BURRELL — Refer to the AMERICAN FLINT GLASS WORKS.

SLICK GLASS COMPANY — Refer to the KOKOMO GLASS MANUFACTURING COMPANY.

SLIPPER — Refer to SHOE.

SLOVAK GLASSWORKS — Refer to the LEDNICKE ROVNE GLASSWORKS.

SLOVENSKE SKLENE HUTY — Refer to the LEDNICKE ROVNE GLASSWORKS.

SLUMPING — A technique of forming glass by heating it until gravity forces it to conform to the shape of the form or mold from which it rests upon. When glass reaches an extreme temperature, it is said to soften and then sag or slump into or over a mold. Slumped glass is sometimes referred to as "Bent Glass."

SMALT — A deep-blue pigment (though not quite as deep as cobalt blue) created by fusing together zaffer, potassium carbonate, and silica. The ingredients are mixed into a powder and added to a batch of glass.

SMALTO — The Italian word for enamel, "Smalto in Pan" is the phrase used to describe a piece of opaque colored glass formed into a thin slab. The individual pieces or slabs were then formed into mosaics for mirror frames, tables, consoles, jewelry, and decorating glassware. The Russians used them to inlay floors.

SMITH BROTHERS — Harry A. and Alfred E. Smith worked in the Art Glass decorating department of Mt. Washington beginning in 1871. They opened their own shop in 1874 in New Bedford, Massachusetts, and produced cut, engraved, and other Art Glass products until 1899. Both were sons of English immigrant glass artisan, William Smith, a decorator who immigrated to America in 1851 and worked for the Boston and Sandwich Glass Company. The elder Smith trained both of his sons in decorating.

Smith Brothers: Trademarks

A Smith Brothers' opal box. *Item courtesy of Wheaton Village.*

SMITH-BRUDEWOLD GLASS COMPANY — An American firm founded at Hammondville, Pennsylvania, in 1891 by C.N.L. Brudewold and William L. Smith, the company produced lamps, lamp shades, novelties, vases, and tumblers that were blown, cut, and pressed. The company declared bankruptcy in 1893 and the factory was purchased later that year by Bryce Brothers.

SMITH, L. E. COMPANY — An American company established by Lewis E. Smith and Thomas Wible in 1907 at Jeannette, Pennsylvania. Smith leased a decorating plant previously owned by McKee (leased from the National Glass Company) and began as a decorating firm. Operations were moved to Mt. Pleasant, Pennsylvania, when they purchased a factory previously owned and operated by the Anchor Glass Company. The company produced its own glassware here. Smith left in 1911 and the factory burned in 1913; however, it was rebuilt. To expand, they acquired the Greensburg Glass Company in 1920. The new plant was located in Greensburg, Pennsylvania, which they operated as plant #2. Though Smith left, the firm continued to produce glass under the same company name including many unique novelty items (i.e. fish bowls, food containers, toy glass candy containers, percolator tops, barbershop mugs, egg separators, premium items given away at movie theaters, electrical glass, etc.); non-glare auto headlamp glass for the Ford Motor Company; and colored glass during the Depression era (like the "Mt. Pleasant," "Double Shield," and "Romanesque" patterns). In 1975, the firm was acquired by Owens-Illinois, Inc., which continues to operate the plant as a subsidiary (mostly as a manufacturer of glass containers, crystal including punch bowl sets, and some colored glassware).

SMOKE — A smoky or light to medium gray charcoal color. Smoke-colored glassware is most often found in iridized Carnival Glass examples.

SNAKE — (1) An ornamental decoration in the form of a curving or tapering snake that is often found applied to candlesticks, candelabra, covered jars, and mantle lustres. Snake-like decorations originated in England, but quickly spread to America. (2) Glass objects that have intertwined curving threads as a decoration are sometimes referred to as "Snake Glass," "Snake-Threaded Glass," or glass decorated with a "Snake Trailing." The German term for serpentine decorated patterns that date as far back as the second century is "Schlangenfadenglas."

SNAP OR SNAP ROD — A glass-maker's tool, which consists of a long metal bar with moveable jaws on one end. The jaws open to grasp a hot glass article in order to move it around prior to annealing. Widespread uses of snap rods began in the 1850s; prior to this, the pontil remained connected to the article for moving. Snap rods are also called "Snap Clamps."

SNAP CLAMP — Refer to SNAP OR SNAP ROD.

SNEATH GLASS COMPANY — Refer to the TIFFIN GLASS COMPANY.

SNOWFLAKE GLASS — A style of Art Glass produced in China in the mid-eighteenth century, it is characterized by bubbles and white inclusion that resemble snowflakes.

SNUFF BOTTLE — A small to medium-sized phial, originating in China, used for holding dried and scented plant materials like tobacco (snuff). They are similar to scent bottles only most sport a wider mouth and are fitted with tiny dipping spoons attached to the cover.

Collection of Chinese snuff bottles.
Photo by Robin Rainwater.

SOCK DARNER — Refer to DARNER.

SODA — Sodium carbonate (once known as "Natron") that is used at times as a substitute for potash as the alkali or flux ingredient in a batch of glass. Alkali and soda are both used to lower the fusion point of sand/silica in the glass-making process. Note that it is also called bicarbonate of soda or sodium bicarbonate (Na_2CO_3 or $NaHCO_3$). *See also LIME GLASS, NATRON, and SODA-LIME GLASS.*

SODA BOTTLE — Refer to WATER BOTTLE.

SODA-LIME GLASS — General term for glass that serves as a cheaper substitute for lead crystal. In this process, sand (silica), soda (sodium oxide or sodium carbonate), and lime (calcium oxide or calcium carbonate) are all utilized in the formula. Today, inexpensive types of glass such as containers, window panes, bottles, jugs, tumblers, and other forms of tableware are made with soda-lime based formulas. *See also LIME GLASS, NATRON, and SODA.*

SOHO AND VESTA GLASS WORKS — Refer to JOHN WALSH.

SOMMERSO — The Venetian technique of encasing small particles or larger colored glass shapes within a thick glass of an opposing color. The result is a somewhat heavy, sculptured effect that is sometimes referred to as colored underlay glass.

SOUP BOWL — A concave glass vessel, hemispherical in shape, used for holding and serving soup. Soup bowls are designed for individuals (as opposed to larger serving bowls like salad bowls) and generally have a capacity of 8 to 16 ounces and a diameter of 4 to 8 inches. Note that a Rim Soup Bowl contains an additional narrow area or rim adjacent to the top edge of the base bowl.

SOUTH BOSTON FLINT GLASS WORKS — Originally, the Boston Crown Glass Company built a glasshouse at Boston, Massachusetts, in 1787. A second plant was built in the south part of Boston. The firm produced some crude tableware and window panes, but shut down during the War of 1812. After the war, the South Boston plant was leased by glassmaker Thomas Caines and Charles Kupfer, with Kupfer serving as superintendent. Caines left in 1820 to open his own firm, the Phoenix Glass Works. In 1827, the South Boston plant was leased to A. A. Jones and David Jackson. The two operated the company as the South Boston Flint Glass Works until closing permanently in 1829.

SOUTH BOSTON WORKS — Refer to the AMERICAN FLINT GLASS WORKS.

SOUTH FERRY WORKS — Refer to the JOHN L. GILLILAND AND COMPANY.

SOUTH JERSEY GLASS — A unique style of tableware first made in America by Caspar Wistar in the southern New Jersey area in the eighteenth century. Items in this style tend to be wide, bulbous-formed and contain a superimposed winding thickness the bottom. The majority of South Jersey Glass was colored (transparent aquamarine and opaque white) and further decorated (i.e. applied lily pads and swan finials). It was fairly crude, but bold and copied by others. The style spread to European glassmakers and was being produced into the mid-nineteenth century.

SOUTH NETHERLANDS GLASS — General term for glass produced in the southern part of the Netherlands (modern-day Belgium) since the sixteenth century. The first glass produced in cities such as Antwerp and Leige were made by Venetian immigrants. English styles of tableware were produced later as well. *See also BELGIAN GLASS.*

SOUTH WHEELING GLASS WORKS — Refer to PLUNKETT AND MILLER.

SOUTHWICK, D. AND COMPANY — Refer to the WHEELING GLASS WORKS.

SOUVENIR GLASS — Glass objects decorated in a variety of techniques (enameled, painted, transferred, embossed, etc.) depicting cities, states, countries, advertising, and tourist attractions. Souvenir paperweights often depict pictures or writing that have been encased in glass. *See also COMMEMORATIVE GLASSWARE and WORLD'S FAIR.*

Reproduction from a 1902 W. E. Cummings Co. advertisement.

Reproduction from a 1910 Butler Brothers catalog.

SOVIET GLASS — General term for glass made in Russia from the Socialist Revolution of 1917 up until the Union of Soviet Socialist Republics (U.S.S.R.) broke up in 1991. Glass-making during this era is usually divided into two periods. The first era lasted into the early 1950s and was characterized by a few primary glassworks that produced essential items such as bottles, drinking glasses, jars, lamps, and some tableware (the former Mal'tsev factory, Gus and Dyat'kovo Works, Chudovo Glassworks, and the Nikol'skoye-Bakhmetiev glasshouse). In the later 1930s and 1940s, some artistic glass was produced consisting of sculptures, fountains, lamps, stained glass windows, mosaic, and some limited colored glass. The second period began in the 1950s and 1960s and was characterized by a turn away from extravagant ornamental-style opaque glass. Artists concentrated on crystal and sulphide glass, sometimes produced in large artistic forms. A return to the cutting and engraving of both crystal and colored glass was also part of this movement (i.e. cameo relief decorations, carved plant ornaments, sandblast-style engraving, blown objects in the form of animals, enameled Russian people and scenery, etc). *See also RUSSIAN GLASS.*

SOWERBY'S ELLISON STREET GLASS WORKS — An English firm established on East Street in the city of Gateshead-on-Tyne in England in 1763 (originally called the New Stourbridge Glass Works). John Sowerby (1808-1879) purchased it in 1846 and renamed it "Gateshead Stamped Glass Works." The company was reputedly the first British firm that was devoted exclusively to making pressed glass, both clear and colored. A new factory was built in 1852 and the name was changed to Sowerby's Ellison Street Works. By 1882, the company employed over 1,000 workers and was arguably the largest pressed glass factory operating in the world at that time. The name was changed again by John's son, John George Sowerby, to "Sowerby and Company." After John George's death, the name was changed again by his son-in-law to Sowerby's Ellison Glassworks, Ltd. During the 1920s, Sowerby was also England's largest producer of Carnival glass and opaque/milk glass. In 1957, Sowerby's was taken over by Suntex Safety Glass Industries, Ltd., which continued to market products under the "Tyneside Glassware" name. The firm continued making pressed glass tableware and novelties until closing in 1972.

Sowerby's Ellison Street Glass Works: Trademark.

SPACED MILLEFIORI OR SCHEMES — A paperweight with scattered millefiori canes that are spaced symmetrically to create a design scheme.

SPALL — A shallow rounded flake on a glass object that is usually applied near the rim of a piece.

SPANGLED GLASS — A style of art glass created by William Leighton Jr. while working for Hobbs, Brockunier and Company in 1883. It is characterized by an inner layer of crystal embedded with mica that is encased by an outer layer of tinted glass. The most popular medium in the style produced by the firm was glass baskets with fancy decorated handles and rims, though other objects like vases were also made.

SPANISH GLASS — General term for glass produced in Spain from the sixteenth century to the present. The primary glass centers consist of modern day Barcelona, Cadalso, Seville, Granada, and the Royal Factory at La Granja De San Ildefonso. Spanish products consisted of stained glass windows, mirrors, lighting fixtures, vases, jugs, and drinking vessels. Earlier pieces were engraved and enameled while those in the nineteenth century featured many of the art styles that originated in Europe during the Art Nouveau periods.

SPANISH LACE — A style of Victorian Era glass characterized by a white lace (threaded designs that resemble lace). It was produced in the 1880s by both English and American firms and usually contained a colored glass base (i.e. blue, yellow, cranberry, or plain crystal), which was then decorated with applied white lace. *See also LACE.*

SPANISH YELLOW — Refer to AMBERGRIS.

SPARKING LAMP — A name for an oil lamp given in the nineteenth century to light a room when a young suitor came "A-Sparkin-in" or "A-Courtin"; supposedly, when the oil burned out, it was time for the young man to leave. Sparking lamps, or Night Lamps, were generally made in two styles: low squat-like designs and those that appeared like wine-glasses (actually referred to as "Wine-Glass Lamps" since they resembled the shape of wine glasses). *See also LAMP.*

SPATTER GLASS — An opaque white or colored glass produced in both England and America in the late nineteenth century. The exterior is sometimes mottled with large spots or splotches of colored glass. Spatter Glass is also sometimes referred to as "End-of-Day" glass since whatever colored pieces of glass were left at the end of a working day were thrown together in its creation.

SPATTER PAPERWEIGHT — An early twentieth century Bohemian paperweight that has two or more colors haphazardly strewn about the internal ground area. Many are usually signed or etched in script with a German name.

SPECIALTY GLASS COMPANY — An American pressed glass manufacturer established at East Liverpool, Ohio, in 1888 briefly as the Novelty Glass Company (for two weeks only until changing the name to Specialty). The firm purchased the defunct factory of the former East Liverpool Glass Company. Specialty was founded by George Irwin and Frank Kubler and, under their direction, produced both blown and pressed glass, goblets, tableware, and glass designed for drugstores/pharmacies. The firm moved to East Jeannette, Pennsylvania, in 1889 when a new factory was completed. The plant was destroyed by both flood and fire in 1898 and was never rebuilt. Note that there was another short-lived bottle-maker who produced glass bottles under the Specialty Glass Company name separate from the Ohio company (Tarentum, Pennsylvania, 1901).

Reproduction from an 1898 Specialty Glass Co. advertisement.

SPENCER CUT GLASS COMPANY — A short-lived American cut glass operation founded in 1910 by Arthur Spencer at Newark, New York. Spencer had previously managed the cut glass department of the Arcadia Cut Glass Company prior to founding his own business. The firm closed in 1912.

SPIDER WEBBING — A style of Art Glass created by Victor Durand Jr. consisting of an overall pattern of fine glass trailings that resemble a spider's web. *See also DURAND and VINELAND FLINT GLASS MANUFACTURING COMPANY.*

SPILL HOLDER — A cylindrically-shaped short-stemmed vase, with a heavy bucket-shaped bowl, used for holding spills. A spill is a wooden splinter, a small roll, or twist of paper that is used for lighting fires (i.e. pipes, candles, lamps, etc.). Note that the two words are sometimes combined to form one word: "Spillholder."

SPINDLE — A rounded or cylindrical stick used in the hand-spinning of yarn. Spindles usually taper toward each end and are twirled on one's leg as it is drawn from a bunch of raw wool or flax held upon the distaff. Spindles made of glass were popular in Spain in the eighteenth and nineteenth centuries.

SPIRAL — A whirling mass of somewhat concentric or parallel curves that usually make-up an all-over curving pattern on a glass object. Most spiral designs tend to curve or spiral inward around a common center as opposed to swirled designs that emanate outward from the center.

Spiral-patterned Depression glass plate. *Photo by Robin Rainwater.*

SPIRAL LATTICINO — A convex or funnel-shaped ground in paperweights formed by threads of latticino.

SPIRITS GLASS — A general term for a tumbler or stemmed glass that was specifically made to drink hard liquor (or spirits) in small quantities.

SPITTOON — A fancy glass vessel or receptacle used for containing saliva (or spit, hence the name "Spittoon"). Spittoons are sometimes referred to as cuspidors and are usually wide-mouthed or funnel-mouthed, and may or may not have covers. *See also CUSPIDOR.*

SPLAYED BASE — A style of base or bottom of a glass object that flares outward. They are also referred to as "Spreading Bases."

SPLIT — A deep miter cut that often separates (or "split") elements of a pattern in cut glass. Note that cured miter splits were first introduced by John O'Connor while working for Dorflinger in 1886.

SPOJENE SKLARNE — Refer to the LEDNICKE ROVNE GLASSWORKS.

SPOKE — A paperweight made to resemble a spoked wheel. Both Saint Louis and New England were noted for making paperweights in this style motif.

SPON LANE GLASSWORKS — An English firm established in 1824 at Birmingham by Robert Lucas Chance, the company was primarily a producer of flat and pane glass throughout the nineteenth century.

SPOON — An eating or cooking implement consisting of a small shallow bowl with handle. The first glass spoons were made in ancient Roman times and were also popular with Venetian glassmakers beginning in the sixteenth century. In modern times, glass spoons come in many lengths (i.e. small for eating to large for serving) and colors. They are used for measuring and are also often part of a matching serving set in such things as honey jars, mayonnaise jars, mustard jars, and relish dishes.

SPOON DISH — A flat or shallow glass object, rectangular or oval in shape, used for holding dessert spoons horizontally.

SPOONER OR SPOON HOLDER — A tall cylindrically-shaped short-stemmed glass vessel, with or without handles, used for holding dessert spoons vertically. Spooners often resemble short-stemmed goblets, and/or vases, and were popular in pressed glass table sets of the nineteenth and early twentieth centuries.

Pressed glass oval patterned spoon holder. *Item courtesy of the Sandwich Glass Museum.*

Cut Glass Double Handle Spoon Holder. Fine Cutting. Height, 4½ inches. No. 9366..............$7.00 Each

Cut Glass Spoon Holder. Height, 4 inches. No. 9367..............$4.50 Each

Reproduction from an early 20th century S. F. Myers Company catalog.

SPOT MOLD — A type of mold utilized in the paperweight-making process or for other fairly small but solid glass objects. Spot molds ordinarily have spike-like projections inside that serve to create small cavities within glass. After casing, air bubbles are then trapped and formed into various patterns.

SPOUT — A tubular protuberance through which the contents of the vessel are poured. Spouts are most often found on pitchers, jugs, bottles, measuring cups, bowls, etc.

SPRAYED-ON IRIDESCENCE — The process of adding iridescence to glass by spraying a warm object with metallic salt particles and then fusing them by heating. *See also IRIDESCENCE.*

SPRINKLER — A glass vessel with a somewhat rounded body and narrow spout (of varying lengths) used to dispense perfumes in drops or very small quantities. Some resemble vases with long or curved spouts while others sport handles. They are sometimes referred to as "Perfume Sprinklers." Modern perfume dispensers are also called "Atomizers." *See also ATOMIZER.*

SPUN GLASS — Glass threading that was originally spun by hand upon a revolving wheel. Glass fibers are automatically spun by machine today and are utilized to make animals, Christmas ornaments, and other novelty items.

SPY HOLE — Refer to GLORY HOLE.

STAGE BROTHERS CUT GLASS COMPANY — Refer to the STAGE-KASHINS GLASS COMPANY.

STAGE-KASHINS GLASS COMPANY — An American cut glass operation established at Lawrenceville, Pennsylvania, in 1911 by brothers Everett and Leigh Stage (originally named the Stage Brothers Cut Glass Company). In 1914, Everett Stage bought out his brother and formed a partnership with Herman Kashins, a salesman in the company; the name of the firm then became the Stage-Kashins Glass Company. The company produced cut glass products until closing in the early 1920s.

STAINED GLASS — (1) Originally, stained glass windows were made by colored glass pieces that were first cut, fitted into channeled lead strips, and then set into an iron framework. The first stained glass windows date back to eleventh century Europe. The French term for this method is "Dalles de Verre." (2) Beginning in the sixteenth century, stained glass windows were for the most part imitation colored glass created by painting clear glass with metallic stains or transparent paints. In modern times, they are produced by either method. During the Art Nouveau movement, Louis Comfort Tiffany was noted for creating lamps utilizing the original, more expensive method.

STAINING — The process of applying colored pigments or transparent paints to annealed clear glass. The resulting color only coats the surface of the object rather than penetrating the glass itself. Stains that are applied by heating were once referred to as "Burning."

STANDARD — An American term for the stem of a glass.

STANDARD CUT GLASS COMPANY — (1) An American firm established at New York, New York, in 1893 by Harry Broden, the company produced cut glass tableware up until World War I. (2) Another American cut glass operation of the same name (also known as the Standard Engraving and Cut Glass Company) was founded in 1911 at Minneapolis, Minnesota, by Charles Merriell, Arthur Olson, and D. D. Rider. It also produced cut glass up until World War I.

Reproduced from a 1912 Standard Cut Glass Co. U.S. patent.

Trademark.

STANDARD ENGRAVING AND CUT GLASS COMPANY — Refer to the STANDARD CUT GLASS COMPANY.

STANDARD GLASS MANUFACTURING COMPANY — An American company established at Lancaster, Ohio, in 1924, Standard served mostly as a decorating company for cutting and etching. The firm was purchased in the early 1930s by the Hocking Glass Company, which eventually became part of the Anchor Hocking Corporation (Anchor and Hocking merged in 1937).

STANDARD GLASS WORKS — Refer to CHALLINOR, TAYLOR AND COMPANY, LTD.

STANDING BOWL — A large serving bowl that rests upon a wide hollow spreading foot.

STANGENGLAS — The German term for pole glass: a tall, narrow, cylindrically shaped drinking vessel, in the shape of a pole, with a pedestal or kick base. Most were made in the fifteenth to seventeenth century, but a few date as far back as the fifth and sixth centuries.

A 19th century German blown and England Stangenglas. *Photo courtesy of the Corning Museum of Glass.*

S

STANGER BROTHERS — Refer to the OLIVE GLASS WORKS.

STANIER GLASHUTTE — Refer to KVETNA GLASSWORKS.

STANKARD, PAUL — Born in Attleboro, Massachusetts, in 1943, Stankard began his career as a scientific glassblower. He worked as manager of Rohm and Haas' scientific glass-blowing, next for McAllister Scientific in Nashua, New Hampshire, and then moved on to Philco Ford as a maker of electron-optical glass. In 1969, he began making paperweights and sold his first two in 1971. Sine then, he has become one of the leading artisans ever to create lamp worked paperweights; many of his works contain exquisite and miniature detail of plants, foliage, and insects set in traditional circles as well as in sculptured blocks of crystal. Stankard continues to produce paperweights as an independent artist in Mantua, New Jersey.

STAR CUTTING — A cut glass design that comes in many styles and shapes, they are ordinarily made by continuing radiant miter cuts around a focus point. Some are shaped as five-point pentagrams while others have less or more points (i.e. for symmetry, many come in factors of four or six points: 6, 8, 12, 16, 24, and 32). Pressed stars are often found on the bottom of objects like vases and pitchers and are sometimes referred to as a "Rayed Base." Stars that are molded into pressed glass are made to resemble those of a cut glass, but the edges are not nearly as sharp. *See also* HOBSTAR, BUZZ STAR, and PYRAMIDAL STAR.

STAR-CUTS — A design cut in paperweights, usually along the base, that consists of five or more points to form a star. At times, small stars may be cut along the exterior sides between windows or other designs.

STAR HOLLY — A milk glass design created by the Imperial Glass Company in the early 1900s. Made to duplicate pressed English Wedgwood Glass, it was characterized by intertwined Holly leaves raised in relief with background color mattes of blue, green, or coral.

STARDUST GROUND — A ground of condensely arranged colored canes (usually white) featuring tiny star-shaped dots.

STATT BROTHERS — An American cut glass operation established by three Statt brothers (Fred, James, and John) in 1905 at Philadelphia, Pennsylvania, the firm produced cut glass tableware until closing in 1920. Fred Statt also operated a glass-engraving firm from 1900 to 1936 as the "Fred Statt Company."

STATT, FRED COMPANY — Refer to the STATT BROTHERS.

STAVE — A flat, narrow strip of glass used in the decoration of paperweights. The strips are usually opaque colors that may be twirled or twisted into various designs within the paperweight (i.e. ribbons, baskets, geometrical designs, flowers, etc.).

STEEL-JACK — A tool used in glass-making resembling a large pair of tongs tipped with steel. They are used for spreading the open mouth of a goblet or for pinching a bubble of glass inward to form a narrow neck or the lip of a pitcher. Older jacks are similar, only they were once tipped with wood and were known as "Wood-Jacks." *See also* FORMING TOOL, PINCERS, PUCELLAS, TONGS, and WOOD-JACKS.

STEIMER GLASS COMPANY — Refer to the "Valley Glass Company." (Note that T. C. Steimer, one of the founders of the Valley Glass Company, has erroneously been spelled as "Steiner" or the "Steiner Glass Company.")

STEIN — A cylindrical or square drinking vessel, with a single handle, that is ordinarily larger than a mug (originally they had a capacity of 1 pint). They originated in Bohemia as early as the late sixteenth century and may be equipped with a hinged lid (the lid and handles are typically made of metal like pewter). They are used for serving beer.

STEM — The cylindrical support connecting the foot and bowl of glass vessels (goblets, wine glasses, comports, etc.). Stems come in a wide variety of styles and designs, including air-twist, faceted, figural, filament, hollow, and knopped.

STEMWARE — A general term for a drinking vessel that is raised on a slender pedestal or stemmed base (wine, goblet, claret, champagne, cordial, etc.).

Reproduction from an early 20th century Bryce Brothers catalog.

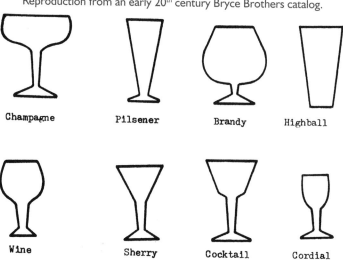

Champagne   Pilsener   Brandy   Highball

Wine   Sherry   Cocktail   Cordial

Line drawing of the basic stemware styles by the author.

STENCILING — A glass decorating technique created by sprinkling a colored glass powder through a template or stencil (usually thin wax, plastic, or even paper that is perforated with lettering and/or a design). A thin sheet of glass is then placed on top of the design and heated until fused.

STEP CUTTING — Glass decorated in the form of continuous horizontal angular parallel cuts.

STERLING CUT GLASS COMPANY — Refer to the STERLING GLASS COMPANY.

STERLING GLASS COMPANY — An American firm established in 1904 at Cincinnati, Ohio, by Joseph Phillips and Joseph Landenwitsch, the company was known by several names including Joseph Phillips and Company, the Phillips Glass Company, and the Sterling Cut Glass Company. The company was noted most for cut glass production and closed for good in 1950.

Sterling Glass Company: Trademark.

STERLING GLASS WORKS — Refer to the NOVELTY GLASS COMPANY.

STERLING SILVER — A metal alloy that is 92.5% silver (925 parts per 1,000), and 7.5% copper (75 parts per thousand). Copper adds strength as with most alloys. Sterling silver is used in the glass decorating process as a deposit or overlay similar to gilding. *See also* SILVER DEPOSIT OR OVERLAY.

STEUBEN GLASS COMPANY — An American company founded at Corning, New York, in 1903 by Frederick Carder (1863-1963), Thomas G. Hawkes, and Mr. and Mrs. Willis Reed. They were a leader in colored Art Glass styles and production early on and were purchased by Corning Glass Works in 1918. In 1933, due to financial concerns, the firm was reorganized under the direction of Arthur Amory Houghton, who ceased all production of colored glass in favor of a new high grade of crystal created by the firm's production manager (Robert J. Leavy) a year earlier. Steuben continues to produce some of the finest quality crystal in the world today. Noted artisans in the latter twentieth and early twenty-first century that worked, designed, or been commissioned by Steuben have included Doug Anderson, Lloyd Atkins, Donald Pollard, Paul Schulze, and Howard Ben Tre. *See also* FREDERICK CARDER, AMORY HOUGHTON, CORNING GLASS WORKS, LLOYD ATKINS, DONALD POLLARD, *and* PAUL SCHULZE.

Steuben art glass goblets, 1920s.
Photo courtesy of the Corning Museum of Glass.

Steuben
Glass Works

Steuben
Glass Works

"Cire Perdue"
Steuben Glass
Works

Steuben Aurene

Trademarks.

STEUBENVILLE FLINT GLASS WORKS — Refer to ALEXANDER J. BEATTY AND SONS.

STEUBENVILLE GLASS COMPANY — An American firm founded at Steubenville, Ohio, in 1884 by William J. Fox, Steubenville produced some blown glass wares until Fox died in 1893. The company was then acquired by Alexander Humphrey and named the Humphrey Glass Works, which not only continued the blown glass operation, but also added pressed barware. Humphrey sold out in 1897 to Robert Englehardt, William Garrett, and S. G. Robinson. The company then became the Steubenville Glass Company, but after going bankrupt in 1898, it was sold to the Steubenville Marble Company (also known as American Marble Company). This new entity closed soon afterward as well.

STEUBENVILLE MARBLE COMPANY — Refer to STEUBENVILLE GLASS COMPANY.

STEVEN LUNDBERG ART GLASS — Refer to LUNDBERG STUDIOS.

S

Steuben crystal hand coolers. *Photo by Robin Rainwater.*

STEVENS AND WILLIAM, LTD. — In 1819, the Moor Lane Glasshouse near Stourbridge, England, was leased by Joseph Silvers (1779-1854), whose two son-in-laws, William Stevens and Samuel Cox Williams, joined later as glass artisans. The name was changed to Stevens and Williams in 1847. The two had produced a wide variety of Art Glass products and designs beginning in the late 1830s at the Brierly Hill Glassworks in Stourbridge. A new factory was built in 1870 and the firm was noted for inventing the style "Dolce Relievo," a cheaper method of making cameo glass, as well as Moss agate, Verre de Soie, Rose du Barry, and Mat-Su-No-Ke. Famous glass artisans Frederick Carder and John Northwood, who joined the company in 1880 and 1882 respectively, were instrumental in patenting new styles of art glass and glass-making inventions. In 1931, the name of the company was changed to Royal Brierly Crystal and was run by Samuel's son, Joseph Silvers William-Thomas (1848-1932); when he died, it was turned over to his grandson, Reginald Silvers Williams-Thomas (1914-1988), who was also active as a managing director. Royal Brierly continues today as a maker of cut and engraved crystal products. In 1998, it was acquired by Epsom Activities, which still produces products under the Royal Brierly namesake.

Stevens & Williams, Ltd.: Trademark.

STIEGEL GLASS — A style of eighteenth century glass made in both Europe and America, the name originated with Baron Henry William Stiegel, who founded a glass factory at Elizabeth, New Jersey, in 1763. Stiegel founded two additional glasshouses in Manheim, Pennsylvania (1765 and 1769). Stiegel Glass primarily consists of some limited colors, but was mostly made of crystal. Stiegel produced some window panes and practical tableware items (i.e. barware, bottles, and flasks) that may or may not contain enameled decorations. Stiegel's operation lasted only into the early 1780s; however, he is credited with training an estimated 130 men in glass-making who went on to establish or work in other glass operations throughout Ohio and Pennsylvania.

STILE LIBERTY — The Italian term for the Art Nouveau movement. *See also* ART OR ART NOUVEAU GLASS.

STIPPLING — A decorating technique consisting of shallow dots or short lines produced by striking a diamond or steel point against a glass object. Image highlights are produced by the dots while the untouched finished glass leaves a shadowy background. Mold-pressed stippling can be found in pressed glass and is often combined with other designs (i.e. stippled band, stippled chain, stippled cherry, stippled clover, stippled daisy, stippled dart and balls, stippled double loop, stippled fleur-de-lis, stippled forget-me-not, stippled fuchsia, stippled grape and festoon, stippled leaf and flower, stippled medallion, stippled pal, stippled peppers, stippled sandbar, stippled star, stippled star flower, stippled strawberry, stippled violet, stippled woodflower, and loop with stippled panels).

STIRRING ROD — Refer to SWIZZLE STICK.

STOEHR GLASS COMPANY — An American firm founded at Massillon, Ohio, in 1880 by Lorenz Stoehr Sr. and his sons, Daniel and Lorenz Jr., the company produced some pressed glass tableware. The factory was destroyed by fire in 1881, but rebuilt the following year. It was renamed first to the Stoehr, Keech and Company in 1882, when W. H. Keech joined as the firm's secretary, and then later in the year to Massillon Glass Tableware Company. The firm continued to produce pressed tableware until being sold to the Sippo Valley Glass Company in 1883 (Lorenz Stoehr Sr. remained on as president while Lorenz Jr. became the secretary-treasurer). The company went bankrupt in 1885 and all of its equipment was purchased by the Canton Glass Company of Canton, Ohio.

STOEHR, KEECH AND COMPANY — Refer to the STOEHR GLASS COMPANY.

STOKE HOLE — A term that describes the opening or hole in the lower side of a glass-melting furnace through which the fuel is fed. Prior to the widespread use of natural gas beginning in the latter nineteenth century, common fuels included both wood and coal. Stoke holes are also called "Tease Holes." Those workers who actually fed the fuel were known as "Stokers" or "Teasers."

STOLZE COMPANY — Refer to the LEDNICKE ROVNE GLASSWORKS.

STOLZLE GLASINDUSTRIE — An Austrian company founded by Carl Stolzle in 1843, the firm's major factories are located at Koflach and Nagelberg. Stolzle is noted for producing a good deal of industrial and household glass products along with a limited amount of art and/or ornamental glass.

STONE — A small impurity or speck of foreign matter in a batch of glassware. If not removed, it will result in a flaw within the glass object produced, which, in turn, may cause the item to be rejected and scraped. Also note that the Austrian firm of Swarovski refers to stones as the base material for cutting crystal miniatures.

STOPKA — A Russian-styled tall cylindrical beaker that tapers toward the bottom; most sport a flared mouth and thin rounded foot. Stopkas originated in Russia as early as the eleventh century.

STOPPER — A matching piece that fits into and closes the mouth of a glass vessel. They are made in many shapes and styles (i.e. ball, faceted, triangular, cylindrical, with a possible finial, etc.) and are ordinarily found on perfume or cologne bottles, decanters, cruets, and other similar items. Glass beer and soda bottles generally contain sealed metal caps. Also note that marbles were once used in the late nineteenth and early twentieth centuries as stoppers in the neck of bottles. *See also* BOTTLE CAP, MEAL CROWN SEAL, *and* BOTTLE MARBLES.

Cranberry cruet with faceted ball stopper.
Item courtesy of Wheaton Village.

STOUGH, TURNEY H. COMPANY — An American maker of toy glass candy containers founded in 1910 by Turney H. Stough at Jeannette, Pennsylvania, the firm purchased the Jeannette Toy and Novelty Company (another maker of toy containers), but later sold out to J. C. Crosetti in 1946. Crosetti continued to produce toy glass containers until closing in 1980.

STOURBRIDGE FLINT GLASS WORKS — An American firm established at Pittsburgh, Pennsylvania, in 1823 by English immigrant John Robinson Sr. (born in the famous glass-making town of Stourbridge, England). A separate facility was opened in 1825 as a decorating department (etching, engraving, and cutting). The name was changed to J. and T. Robinson in 1830 when Robinson's sons, John Jr. and Thomas, joined the company. When John Sr. died in 1836, the firm became Robinson, Anderson and Company with Alexander Anderson joining (former partner of Benjamin Bakewell). The company produced some pressed wares, cut/engraved/etched glass, and a little opalescent glass before closing in 1845. In 1851, the factory site was occupied by Adams, Macklin and Company.

STOURBRIDGE GLASS — Glassware made as far back as the sixteenth century in or near Stourbridge, Worcestershire, England. Many later English factories sprung up in this area including Webb, Stevens and Williams, and Stuart and Sons. The first products produced were practical items such as windows and bottles. Once Englishman George Ravenscroft discovered the secret of lead crystal making in the latter seventeenth century, crystal tableware flowed from the Stourbridge area. Many of the above-named firms also served as leaders during the Art Nouveau Movement in England.

STOUT AND CRAWFORD — A short-lived American glass decorating firm established in 1920 at Mt. Pleasant, Pennsylvania, by two glass cutters previously employed by Bryce Brothers, A. H. Stout and John Love Crawford; Crawford's brother, William James Crawford, and nephew, William E. Crawford, were also active in the company. Stout and Crawford decorated glass by cutting, etching, and applying gold bands and gold decorations prior to closing in 1934.

STOUVENAL, JOSEPH COMPANY — An American firm founded by Joseph Stouvenal at New York, New York, in 1840, the company's name was changed to Joseph Stouvenal and Brothers when Francis and Nicholas Stouvenal joined in 1843. Stouvenal produced blown, cut, and pressed glass tableware before closing in the early 1870s.

STRASS — A high quality refractive form of lead crystal used for making artificial gemstones. In its clear form, it is used to make imitation diamonds; when colored, it can be used to simulate most precious stones. Like gems, it is intricately cut with small facets. The name is derived from Georges-Fredric Strass (1701-73), an Englishman who moved to Paris in 1724. While in France, he perfected many techniques of making artificial gems from glass.

STRATHEARN GLASS, LTD. — A Scottish paperweight-making business founded in 1963. The whiskey distilling firm, William Teacher and Sons, founded this new venture after purchasing a major interest in Vasart Glass, Ltd. Operations were moved from the city of Perth to Crieff in 1964. In 1980, Strathearn was sold to Stuart Crystal. *See also STUART AND SONS, LTD.*

STRAUS AND SONS — An American company established by German immigrant Lazarus Straus in 1865 at New York, New York. Straus, with his wife (Sara Straus) and two sons (Isidor and Nathan Straus), came to America (originally to the state of Georgia) in 1852. They moved to New York and opened a retail shop selling china and glass products. In 1888, they hired glass cutters and began selling cut glass under the "L. Straus and Sons" name. As the demand for cut glass declined, the company returned to the retail market and ceased cutting glass in the World War I era.

Reproduction from an 1894 Straus U.S. patent.

Trademark.

STRAW MARK — Refer to SCRATCH MARK.

STRAWBERRY DIAMOND CUTTING — This is one of the most popular patterns in cut glass. As a variation of raised diamond cutting, an uncut space is left between the diagonal grooves so that a flat area results instead of pointed diamonds. The flat areas are then cross-hatched to form a group of low relief diamonds that is sometimes confused with hobnail. Grooved fans were also a popular addition above the strawberry diamond region to produce the strawberry and diamond with fan cut design. In paperweights, strawberry-diamond cuts are some times cut on the base at right angles to form a fine grid.

Jug, Straw-Dia-Fan.
No. 450—3 pints, $14.00.

Reproduction from a late 19th century Mount Washington catalog.

STREAKY GLASS — Refer to CATHEDRAL GLASS.

STRETCH GLASS — A type of iridescent or Carnival-like glass made with an onion-skin surface effect, the finished product appears to have been 'stretched' into shape because of the rib-like effect. It was primarily made in America during the Carnival glass era (early 1900s-1920s).

STRIATED GLASS — Glass decorated by a series of parallel lines (straight or curved) or cord-like markings. The design is actually caused by varying the temperature directly in the furnace.

STRINGLED GLASS — Refer to NOTCHED PRISM CUT.

STRIKING — The process of reheating glass after it has been cooled to finish or color the surface.

STRINGING — Refer to TRAILING.

STRIPED GLASS — An American Art Glass style from the late nineteenth century characterized by wavy bands of contrasting colors.

S

STROMBERGSHYTTAN — A Swedish glass-making company established in 1933 when Edward Stromberg (1872-1946) purchased the Lidfors Glasbruk (originally founded in 1876). Stromberg had previously served as manager of Kosta, Eda, and Orrefors. The firm's noted designer was his wife Gerda Stromberg (1879-1960), who served as chief designer from 1933 to 1955. Note that their son, Eric Stromberg, purchased the company in 1945 and continued to employ his mother. When Eric passed away, his widow Asta Stromberg continued to run the firm. Throughout its history, the company produced art glass items in typical Swedish styles. A major fire destroyed most of the factory in 1973 and the company was sold to Orrefors in 1975. The factory closed permanently in 1979. *See also SWEDISH GLASS, LINDFORS GLASBRUK, and ORREFORS.*

STUART AND SONS, LTD. — The Red House Glass Works at Wordsley near Stourbridge, England, was established by George Ensell in 1776. It was taken over by Richard Bradley in 1787. After changing hands several more times, it was eventually acquired by Fredrick Stuart (1816-1900) in 1881. The name was changed in 1885 to Stuart and Sons as five of Frederick's seven sons were active in the firm. The company produced a good deal of colored glass and chandeliers prior to World War II. After the war, the firm concentrated on crystal only, though occasionally colored glass was made as well. Stuart acquired Strathearn Glass in 1980 in Crieff, Scotland; however, the location serves as a factory outlet and visitor center today. Stuart was run by descendants of Frederick Stuart until 1995; at that time, it was sold to Waterford Wedgwood PLC; nevertheless, glass is still made under the Stuart Crystal namesake.

STUART, CHRISTOPHER — A modern brand of tableware and gifts produced under the Mikasa Crystal, Inc. name. *See also MIKASA CRYSTAL, INC.*

STUART CRYSTAL — Refer to STUART AND SONS, LTD.

STUDIO GLASS — Art Glass that is generally fashioned or created in a small working place as opposed to a large factory. *See also ART GLASS STUDIO MOVEMENT, CONTEMPORARY GLASS, and WEST COAST GLASS STUDIO MOVEMENT.*

STUDIO NOVA — A modern brand of tableware produced under the Mikasa Crystal, Inc. name. *See also MIKASA CRYSTAL, INC.*

STUMPF — Refer to PANTIN.

STYLIZED — A decorative technique representing an abstract or nonconforming pattern from that of nature (i.e. stylized leaves may be larger, broader, raised in relief, or colored differently).

STYLIZED FLOWER — A flower design formed in a paperweight similar to that of a natural flower, but not necessarily of a known species. Depending on the artisan, stylized flowers may appear singly or in bouquets and as flat designs or uprights.

SUFFOLK GLASS WORKS — An American company founded at South Boston, Massachusetts, in the early 1850s by Joshua Jenkins. G. S. Laselle joined in 1862 while Jenkins was replaced by S. B. Lowland in 1880. The firm produced kerosene lamps and some pressed tableware before declaring bankruptcy in 1884. In 1885, the plant was sold to the Boston Antique Glass Company, which made colored glass window panes. The factory was destroyed by fire in 1900.

SUGAR AND LEMON TRAY — A two-tiered object used for serving lemons and sugar. Cut lemons are placed on the bottom level while sugar held in a bowl makes up the top level.

SUGAR BASIN — A pressed or cut glass short-stemmed and footed container, much like a small open compote, used for serving granulated sugar. The term originated in England in the mid-nineteenth century and lasted into the early twentieth (the predecessor of the more simplistic "sugar" or "sugar dish"). It was usually paired with a creamer during tea service and may have one or two handles, though most do not.

SUGAR DISH OR BOWL — A small glass cup-like vessel, that may or may not have handles, used for serving sugar (often paired with a creamer for serving tea). Most sugar dishes contain a matching cover while creamers do not. Both sugars and creamers may be footed as well.

A Fenton Emerald Crest sugar and creamer set.
Photo by Robin Rainwater.

Sugar & Creamer Sets
Sugar and creamer 3½ in., pressed.
5OR-3670—2 doz sets in carton,
24 lbs.............**Doz sets 80c**

Reproduction from a 1930 Butler Brothers catalog.

SUGAR DUSTER — Refer to SUGAR SHAKER.

SUGAR SHAKER — A small glass upright container, usually cylindrical or angular in shape and with metal or plastic covers containing holes, used for sprinkling sugar on various foods (larger in size than typical salt and peppers shakers). Sugar shakers were originally referred to as sugar dusters or sugar sifters when they first appeared in the 1870s-1880s.

Reproduction from an early 20th century S.F. Myers Co. catalog.

Cut Glass Sugar Sifter. Quadruple Silver Plated Top.
Height, 5¾ inches.
No. 936S.............**$5.50 Each**

SUGAR SIFTER — Refer to SUGAR SHAKER.

SULFIDE — Refer to SULPHIDE.

SULFUR — A somewhat yellow crystalline nonmetallic substance that, when combined with various metals, produces opaque colors in glass (i.e. mostly white, cream, ivory, custard, yellow, and similar off-white and yellow tones). Note that it is also spelled as "Sulphur."

S

SULPHIDE — A ceramic or salt-based relief incrusted within a clear glass paperweight, usually a portrait of an historical figure (though other mediums such as plant and wildlife are represented as well). It is also known as a "Cameo Incrustation" and is spelled as "sulfide" occasionally. Along with lampwork and millefiori, sulphide is one of the three basic types of paperweight styles.

Pressed glass sunburst and diamond pattern.
Photo by Robin Rainwater.

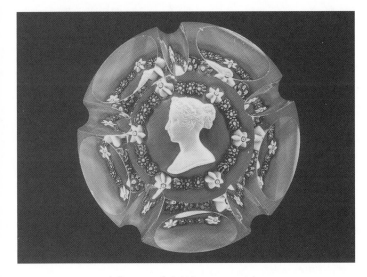

A Baccarat Sulphide paperweight.
Photo courtesy of the Corning Museum of Glass.

A Baccarat Sulphide paperweight of George Washington.
Photo by Robin Rainwater.

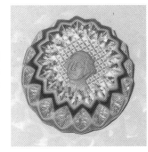

SULPHUR — Refer to SULFUR.

SUMAVA GLASSWORKS — Refer to CESKY KRISTAL.

SUMMIT ART GLASS COMPANY — An American firm founded at Akron, Ohio, in 1972 by Russell and Joanne Vogelsang, the company specializes in colored reproduction glass (including milk glass) made from molds purchased from both the St. Clair Glass Company and Tiffin Glass Company (new products made by them contain their own trademark). In 1984, the plant was moved to Rootstown, Ohio, where the firm also produces unique contemporary art glass and novelty items today.

SUNBURST PATTERN — A popular nineteenth and early twentieth century pattern applied to some cut glass, but mostly pressed glass that consists of a rectangular or oval that in turn contains a multi-rayed sun within. The rayed sun comes in many different styles; nevertheless, all are generally lumped under the "sunburst" name. Like many pressed patterns, sunburst was combined with other styles (i.e. divided block with sunburst diamond and sunburst, buttressed sunburst, flattened diamond and sunburst, medallion sunburst, sharp sunburst and file, squared sunburst, whirled sunburst in circle, sunburst and star, sunburst rosette sunburst in square, waffle sunburst, waffle diamond sunburst, bull's eye sunburst, etc.).

SUNDAE — A glass vessel, with a short stem and foot, used for serving ice cream. *See also* PARFAIT.

LOW FOOTED SUNDAE
Packs 16 doz. to bbl. Weight 140 lbs.
Packs 6 doz. to ctn. Weight 50 lbs.

TALL FOOTED SUNDAE
Packs 12 doz. to bbl. Weight 130 lbs.
Packs 3 doz. to ctn. Weight 50 lbs.

Reproduction from a 1930 Indiana Glass Co. catalog.

SUNSET-GLOW GLASS — The name for an early (eighteenth century) style of European milk or opalescent white colored glass.

SUNTEX SAFETY GLASS INDUSTRIES, LTD. — Refer to SOWERBY'S ELLISON STREET GLASS WORKS.

SUNSHINE CUT GLASS COMPANY — An American cut glass operation established at Cleveland, Ohio, in 1915, the firm produced some limited amounts of cut glass and novelty items prior to closing in the latter 1920s.

SUPERIMPOSED DECORATION — A glass decoration separate from the object that it is applied to.

SUSQUEHANNA CUT GLASS COMPANY — An American cut glass operation established in 1910 at Columbia, Pennsylvania, by Harry Glasser and Albert Roye, the firm produced cut glass tableware in the World War I era and then switched to other glass products such as lighting. The name of the firm was changed to the Susquehanna Glass Company when cut glass production was ended.

SUSQUEHANNA GLASS COMPANY — Refer to the SUSQUEHANNA CUT GLASS COMPANY.

S

SUSSMUTHGLAS — A Silesian (modern day Czech Republic) firm established as Werkstatten Richard Sussmuth Glaskunst in 1924 by noted glass engraver Richard Sussmuth (1900-1974) at Penzig. Sussmuth served as a decorator and concentrated mostly on engraving (abstract, geometric, and figurative designs including leaping deer, birds in flight, female figures, etc.). The firm also produced many blown and plain crystal wares. In 1933, Sussmuth developed its own formula for bubbled glass that was dubbed "shambles," which translates to foam glass. In 1945, the workshop was destroyed and Sussmuth relocated operations to Immenhausen near Kassel, West Germany. It was renamed Sussmuthglas and, aside from table and art wares, the firm produced lighting and decorative windows. Sussmuth left in 1970 and the company was run as a cooperative by workers (renamed Glashutte Sussmuth GmbH). It was changed once again in 1989 to KG SUSSMUTH GLASSMANUFAKTUR GMBH AND COMPANY before closing permanently in 1996.

SWANKY SWIG — Small decorated (usually by machine-applied enamels or transfers) collectible glass tumblers that were filled with Kraft® cheese spread. Once the cheese spread was emptied, the container could then be washed and used as a juice tumbler. They first debuted in the 1930s, discontinued briefly during World War II (paints were needed for the war effort), and then revived after the war up until 1975.

Swanky Swig:
Line drawing by the author.

SWAROVSKI SILVER CRYSTAL — Swarovski was established in Wattens, Austria, by Daniel Swarovski I in 1895. The original purpose of the business was to set up a factory to produce tiny crystal stones used for jewelry. With few rival glassmakers in Austria, the firm expanded into optics, chandelier parts, grinding and abrasive tools, and glass reflecting elements for road and rail safety and scientific instruments. In 1976, the company sparked an entire new field in glass novelty collectibles by making jewel-quality faceted Silver Crystal (full lead crystal) figurines. In 1979, the company established the Swarovski Collector's Society (SCS). Swarovski products are for the most part miniature crystal animals and novelties with applied color accents (i.e. eyes, ears, noses, tails, fins, whiskers, snouts, legs, feet, horns, tusks, beaks, hats, leaves, vines, wheels, windows, roofs, propellers, and finials).

Swarovski Silver Crystal miniatures. *Photo by Robin Rainwater.*

Swarovski factory located in Wattens, Austria.

Trademarks.

SWEATING — Refer to *CRIZZLING*.

Swedish Glass — General term for glassware made in Sweden since the late sixteenth century. The first firms were established by Venetian and Bohemian glassmakers who made items in their own native styles. Beginning in the later nineteenth and early twentieth centuries, traditional Swedish companies such as Kosta, Boda, and Orrefors were responsible for creating a new style of art glass designs that are distinctly Swedish. These include such items as "Graal" engraving by Orrefors; other art styles such as Ariel, Kraka, and Ravenna Glass; ice sculptures (particularly those by Matts Jonasson who works for Maleras), avant-garde colored art sculptures; and etched and engraved glassware featuring traditional Swedish cultural items (i.e. the North Star or northern constellations, floral and leaf designs of local plants, village scenes, and most anything native to the region). *See also* AFORS, ARIEL, KRAKA, LINDFORS GLASBRUK, RAVENNA, BODA, FLYGSFORS, GRAAL, KOSTA, ORREFORS, PUKEBERG, SKRUFF, *and* STROMBERGSHYTTAN.

A collection of Art Glass vases by Nybro of Sweden.

Seal sculpture by Nybro of Sweden. *Photo by Robin Rainwater.*

A pink and white swirl pitcher. *Item courtesy of the Van Andel Museum.*

Nybro Trademark.

SWIZZLE STICK — A thin glass rod with an enlarged end that is used to stir liquids (swizzle originally was a sweetened alcoholic beverage made with rum). They originated in ancient Roman times and are also known as "stirring rods" or "toddy sticks."

SWEENEY, MICHAEL, THOMAS, & R. H. — An American glass firm established at the north end of Wheeling in 1831 (prior to West Virginia becoming a state) by the three Sweeney Brothers. The factory was built in 1835; and hence, when glass production begun. Sweeney produced a good deal of lead cut crystal tableware and pressed wares (reportedly the largest glass producer in the Wheeling area prior to America's Civil War). Robert H. Sweeney passed away in 1845. Thomas Sweeney, along with his son, Andrew J. Sweeney, quit in 1863. Throughout the company's history, it proceeded through a wide variety of name changes (M. & R.H. Sweeney, 1835-45; M. & T. Sweeney, 1845-48; Sweeney & Bell, 1848-51; T. Sweeney & Son, 1852-63; Sweeney, Bell & Co., 1863-67; Sweeney, McCluney & Co., 1867-68; and Bell & Company, 1875-76—the year that Michael Sweeney died). Other than the name Sweeney, it was also known as the North Wheeling Flint Glass Works when Michael Sweeney formed one of his many partnerships. The Wheeling plant closed in 1867; the following year (1868), operations were moved to Martins Ferry, Ohio (note that the Martins Ferry plant went by the name of the Excelsior Glass Works too). The last Sweeney-related glass business closed during the financial panic of 1873. The firm was officially bankrupt in 1874; however, Joseph Bell briefly operated as Bell & Company from 1875-1876. In 1877, it was sold off to the Buckeye Glass Company.

SWEETMEAT DISH OR COMPOTE — An open, somewhat small bowl-shaped or cylindrical vessel, usually with handle, that is used for drinking tea. Teacups generally do not exceed eight ounces in capacity (four-ounce cups are the most common) and ordinarily contain a matching saucer. A small flat or shallow, tray or bowl-like glass object that is used for serving sweetmeats, hors d'oeuvres, nuts, candies, dried fruits, and so on. Most are stemmed like compotes and contain a circular base or foot.

SWIRL — A paperweight with two or three opaque colored rods that radiate in a pinwheel fashion from a central millefiori cane or group of canes. Swirl was first popularized by Clichy in the 1840s and was one of their most classic styles.

Glass swizzle sticks. *Photo by Robin Rainwater.*

SYRIAN GLASS — General term for glassware produced in the region of Syria, beginning at Sidon, along the Syrian Coast as early as the fifteenth century B.C. Early glass was made identical to that of the Mesopotamians and around the first century B.C., glass-blowing was also prevalent along the Syrian coast until the Phoenician civilization collapsed. They Syrian period of glassmaking ended around 1402 in the Islamic world. See ISLAMIC GLASS, MESOPOTAMIAN GLASS, and SIDONIAN GLASS.

SYRUP PITCHER — A small wide-mouthed vessel; with spout, handle, and hinged metal lid; that is used for pouring syrup. Syrup pitchers are generally small, varying from about eight to sixteen ounces in capacity; though a few larger ones have been produced. Syrup pitchers are also called syrup jugs, and are used for dispensing other, usually thick substances like molasses or honey.

S

Tt

{ Tt }

TAB HANDLES — An open, somewhat small bowl-shaped or cylindrical vessel, usually with handle, that is used for drinking tea. Teacups generally do not exceed eight ounces in capacity (four-ounce cups are the most common) and ordinarily contain a matching saucer. Small protrusions usually attached or connected to the rims of bowls and plates allowing one to grasp the object. Tab handles may be closed (solid glass) or open (holes within the handles). Bon Bon dishes and nappies typically have a single tab handle.

TABLE CHANDELIER — An open, somewhat small bowl-shaped or cylindrical vessel, usually with handle, that is used for drinking tea. Teacups generally do not exceed eight ounces in capacity (four-ounce cups are the most common) and ordinarily contain a matching saucer. A small chandelier used as a free-standing object as opposed to one that is hung from a ceiling (see CHANDELIER).

TABLE FACET — A flat circular cut at the very top of a paperweight; it is also known as a top window.

TABLE SET — An open, somewhat small bowl-shaped or cylindrical vessel, usually with handle, that is used for drinking tea. Teacups generally do not exceed eight ounces in capacity (four-ounce cups are the most common) and ordinarily contain a matching saucer. Originally in nineteenth century pressed glass, a table set consisted of a matching spooner, sugar, creamer, and butter dish (all made in the same pattern). Some of the early sets did not have a butter dish. By the time of America's Depression era (1920s and 1930s), table sets expanded into matching pieces that have numbered over one hundred pieces in some patterns (i.e. various bottles, bowls, butter dishes, cake plates, candle sticks, candy jars, cheese dishes, cocktail shakers, compotes, cookie jars, creamer and sugar, cruets, cups and saucers, decanters and goblets, ice buckets or tubs, jam jars, pitchers, plates, platters, relish dishes, salt and pepper shakers, sandwich servers, sherbet glasses, stemware, trays, tumblers, vases, and so on). Note that a single "table setting" ordinarily consists of a plate, tumbler or goblet, cup and saucer, and silverware. See also SET.

TACSHEK, JOSEF — Refer to KRALICK, WILHELM.

TANK — A large holding vessel constructed in a furnace for melting a batch of glass. Tanks replaced pots in large glass factories in the latter nineteenth century.

TANKARD — A large drinking vessel, somewhat straight-edged, with a single handle that may or may not contain a hinged lid (as in steins, the lid and handle may be made of metal).

TARENTUM GLASS COMPANY — An American pressed glass manufacturer established at Tarentum, Pennsylvania in 1893 by Henry Morgan Brackenridge, John Hemphill, and James Wilson. In 1894, the newly formed company purchased the old Richards & Hartley Flint Glass Company plant from U.S. Glass and began producing pressed glass tableware (some in colors including custard), a small amount of cut glass, lamps, and other lighting glassware. The firm closed in 1918 when a fire destroyed the plant. The American Bridge Company bought the land and built a new factory in 1923 to produce lighting glassware. Owens-Illinois bought the factory in 1930 but closed the facility in 1931.

Tarentum Glass Company: Reproduction from a 1901 *China Glass & Pottery Review* advertisement.

Reproduction from a 1906 Tarentum Glass Co. U.S. patent.

TASSEL — A decorative add-on that consists of a dangling ornament made by parallel cords or threads of even length that are fastened at one end. Tassels are common on pressed glass and are often combined with other decorations to form patterns: cord and tassel, shell and tassel, shell and tassel round, shell and tassel square, teardrop and tassel, etc.

TAVERN WARE — A style of art glass tableware created by Pairpoint in the 1920s and 1930s. It is either crystal or a light transparent gray color, and contains numerous bubbles in the interior as well as on the exterior. Most contain multicolored enameled or fired-on transfers that include such things as fruits, animals, ships, and so forth. The glass was also sometimes referred to as "tourist ware."

TAYLOR BROTHERS — An American firm established in 1902 at Philadelphia, Pennsylvania by Albert Taylor and Lafayette Taylor. They operated as a cut glass company until 1915.

Taylor Brothers: Trademark.

TAZZA — An unusually wide dessert cup or serving plate, with or without handles, mounted on a stemmed foot.

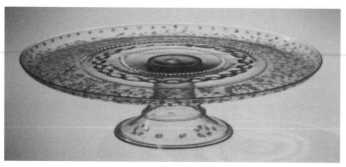

An early 17ᵗʰ century Venetian engraved Tazza.
Photo courtesy of the Corning Museum of Glass.

TEA CADDY — A large wide-mouthed glass canister with cover that is used for storing tea bags or loose tea.

TEA PLATE — A flat glass object usually round in shape like a saucer (most tea plates are around six inches in diameter) that is either used as an under-dish for tea-cups, or for serving small quantities of food. Like saucers, some have a circular indentation for a matching cup. Those used for serving foods have also been referred to as small cake plates, bread and butter plates, dessert plates, fruit plates, and so forth.

TEA SERVICE — A set of vessels used for serving tea. Most include a teapot, tea caddy, creamer, sugar, milk jug, cups & saucers, and a large matching undertray.

TEACUP — An open, somewhat small bowl-shaped or cylindrical vessel, usually with handle, that is used for drinking tea. Teacups generally do not exceed eight ounces in capacity (four-ounce cups are the most common) and ordinarily contain a matching saucer.

TEAL — A bluish green colored glass (a little darker with a stronger blue coloring than ultramarine).

TEAPOT — A vessel with handle, spout, and lid that is used for serving tea. Glass tea pots are typically found in miniature children's tea sets; nevertheless, full-size pots have occasionally been made of glass.

A 1984 Richard Marquis glass teapot. *Item courtesy of Wheaton Village.*

TEAR OR TEARDROP — A bubble of air trapped in glass that is sometimes purposefully created for decorative effect.

TEKTITES — Small, rounded bodies of glass that form as a result of the impact of fiery meteorites upon sand on both the Earth and moon. Tektites have been found in Eastern Europe, Indonesia, Vietnam, Australia, America, and other places. Yellowish lumps of tektites are occasionally found in the dunes of the Sahara Desert.

TEMPERING — A technique that increases the strength of glass by heating it slightly below the softening point and then suddenly cooling it with a blast of cold air.

TEMPLATE — In paperweight making, a small cast iron disc on which the motif is carefully arranged prior to being picked up.

TENDRILS — These slender, coiling stem-like glass trailings resemble those by which a plant attaches itself to a support.

TESSERAE — Small square-shaped glass objects used to form mosaics. They originated in Venice as early as the seventh century and were cut from long sticks or straight-edged (thin rectangular prisms) canes of glass. *See also* MOSAIC.

TESSUTO — The Italian term for fabric. In glassware, tessuto is a spiral filigree design produced by various colored canes in a lace or fabric-like effect. *See also* FILIGREE, LATTICINO, *and* RETICULATED GLASS.

TEST-TUBE — A hallow cylinder of thin glass with the top end open and the bottom end closed. Test-tubes are widely used in scientific experiments (biology, chemistry, physics, etc.).

THALLIUM — A grayish-colored metallic element that, when added to a batch of glass in its oxidized form, generally increases the color effects of other oxidized metals.

THAMES STREET GLASS HOUSE — Refer to the VITRIX HOT GLASS STUDIO.

THATCHER BROTHERS — An American firm established by English immigrants George and Richard Thatcher in 1891 at New Bedford, Massachusetts. George had worked as a cutter/engraver in England and came to America in 1873. Prior to establishing his own business, George cut glass for Boston and Sandwich, Mount Washington, and Smith Brothers. In 1886, he purchased Smith Brothers' cutting department. In 1891, he sent for his brother Richard, who had been employed at Corning as a cutter. The two then established their own company and produced cut glass products until going out of business during the Panic of 1907.

Thatcher Brothers: Trademark.

THATCHER GLASS COMPANY
— An American firm established at Jeannette, Pennsylvania, when they purchased McKee in 1951. Thatcher did sell some of the original McKee molds to Kemple; however, they also continued to use the remaining McKee molds and the McKee name until 1961 when they were, in turn, purchased by the Jeannette Glass Company. *See also* MCKEE BROTHERS *and* JEANNETTE GLASS COMPANY.

THERESIENTHAL GLASS — A Bavarian glass firm founded at Zweisel (eastern Germany) in 1836 by brothers, Franz and Wilhelm Steigerwald (1804-1869), originally as Krystallglasfabrik Theresienthal, the company was named for Queen Therese, the wife of Ludwig I. Early on, Theresienthal supplied tableware and ornamental glass for several royal courts including those in Bavaria, Russia, and France. The Steigerwald brothers left in 1844 and the company went bankrupt. Baron Michael von Poschinger (1834-1901) acquired the company in 1862 and the firm employed workers who produced glass in traditional colored Bavarian and Venetian styles. Michael's sons, Benedikt von Poschinger (1892-1951) and Egon von Poschinger (1894-1977), joined the firm, which continued to produce colored art glass and followed some of the iridescent trends of the Art Nouveau movement. In 1963, Max Gangkofner (b. 1922) acquired a half-share in the firm and, in 1973, he purchased the remaining shares. In 1975, Gangkofner partnered with Porzellanfabrik Hutschen-Reuther of

Selb, which eventually took over Theresienthal in 1982; the name was then changed to Theresienthal Krystall-und Porzellanmanufaktur. One final ownership change occurred in 1997 when the company was purchased by Ralph Wenzel. The firm is known today as Theresienthaler Kristallglasmanufaktur GmbH and continues to make colored glassware in traditional Bohemian/Venetian styles.

THERMOMETER — An instrument for measuring temperature that consists of a long glass tube with a small bulb of glass at the bottom; within it is a numbered scale and a liquid (i.e. mercury or colored alcohol) that rises and falls due to changes in temperature. Thermometers were invented in 1731; the collectible ones usually contain some form of advertising.

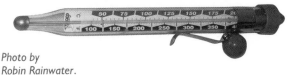

Photo by Robin Rainwater.

THILL AND COMPANY — Refer to the EMPIRE STATE FLINT GLASS COMPANY.

THILL, F. SONS AND COMPANY — Refer to the EMPIRE STATE FLINT GLASS COMPANY.

THISTLE — A pressed glass pattern that contains the thistle plant as its primary design. Variations include scrolling, dots, panels, and bees (bees were made by the Higbee Glass Company). Note that thistle designs have been found in both art and cut/engraved glass and in many Scottish-designed glassware (thistle is Scotland's national flower/plant).

THOMPSON GLASS COMPANY, LTD. — (1) A short-lived American pressed glass manufacturer established at Uniontown, Pennsylvania, in 1888 by A. C. Waggoner and Charles Zimmer. Production of pressed glass tableware and novelty items began in 1889; however, the firm went bankrupt in 1890, and the factory closed in 1891. The business was rechartered as a corporation in 1892 as the Thompson Glass Company. Production resumed; however, the plant was destroyed by fire in 1893. The factory was rebuilt in 1894, but once again, it shut down in 1895 as the company ceased all operations and went into receivership. In 1900, the factory was acquired by George W. Fry, who established the George W. Fry Glass Company, a short-lived cut glass operation. In 1901, the plant was leased by the National Glass Company and was renamed the Rochester Tumbler Works #2. National withdrew from the plant in 1903. In the meantime, Fry moved the equipment to his newly formed company in Morgantown, West Virginia. (2) Note that there was another short-lived bottle-making company that operated under the Thompson Glass Company name in the 1890s in Gas City, Indiana. *See also* ECONCOMY TUMBLER COMPANY.

THOUSAND EYE — A pressed or cut glass pattern in glassware that is very similar but slightly different from hobnail patterns. In Thousand Eye, there is an all-over pattern of slightly raised rows of circles. The circles are not raised as much nor protrude outward to the same degree as the prunts in hobnail styles.

THREAD CIRCUIT OR THREADING — A decorative pattern applied with rope-like strings or twists of glass by hand or machine. The strings or threads are often colored and applied in concentric circles or other symmetrical patterns. Threaded designs appear on mold-pressed patterns too.

Thread Circuit or Threading: A Boston & Sandwich Glass Company threaded pitcher. *Photo courtesy of the Sandwich Glass Museum.*

THREE-FACE — A late nineteenth century style of glass that contains three adjacent full-face profiles (may or may not be frosted), usually set in the base or stem of such objects. A set of pressed tableware was made in the 1870s by the firm of George Duncan and Sons in this design. It has also been reproduced by others such as Viking and, in the 1990s, as a New York Metropolitan Museum of Art commission (new pieces are marked "MMA").

This reproduction of a three-faced jar was commissioned by the New York Metropolitan Museum of Art. *Photo by Robin Rainwater.*

T

THUMBPRINT — A decorative style usually made by pressing in the form of oval-shaped shallow depressions arranged in rows. Several variations of the basic thumbprint pattern exist (i.e. almond thumbprint, diamond thumbprint, grape with thumbprint, heart with thumbprint, Lincoln band thumbprint, Orion thumbprint, teardrop and thumbprint, ruby thumbprint, and the waffle and thumbprint). Most thumbprint designs are found on matching sets of pressed glass tableware. "Argus" and "Ashburton" were early names used for thumbprint-like designs. In paperweights, thumbprint refers to an oval, elongated concave window.

A Pressed glass thumbprint-patterned covered compote. *Photo by Robin Rainwater.*

Line drawing by the author.

THURINGIAN GLASS — General term for practical glassware made in and around the region of Thuringia, Germany, as early as the late twelfth century. *See also BAVARIAN GLASS and GERMAN GLASS.*

TIARA — Glassware made specifically for in-home parties sponsored by Tiara Exclusive's of Dunkirk, Indiana. Beginning in the late 1960s up until 1998, Tiara contracted with several glass firms including Fenton, Dalzell Viking, and L. E. Smith; however, they are noted most for offering Indiana's reproduction "Sandwich" pattern glass in a wide variety of crystal and colored tableware including their famous tiara blue or teal blue colors (i.e. ashtrays, bowls, candle holders, canisters, cups, trays, pitchers, goblets, plates, and vases). Tiara also offered other reproduction Depression glassware (Indiana's Avocado pattern and Federals' Madrid pattern). The offices of Tiara were located adjacent to the Indiana Glass Company in Dunkirk and both firms operated as subsidiaries of the Lancaster Colony Corporation. *See also SANDWICH GLASS.*

A Tiara wine set made in Indiana Glass Company's Sandwich pattern. *Photo by Robin Rainwater.*

TID-BIT TRAY — A tiered dish with a pole connecting two or more levels. The pole usually runs through the center, with the sizes of the levels gradually decreasing as they go up. The dishes are usually serving plates and/or bowls.

A Fenton Silver Crest two-tiered tid-bit tray. *Photo by Robin Rainwater.*

TIFFANY, LOUIS COMFORT — The most celebrated and renowned leader of the Art Nouveau style of glass in America in the nineteenth century, Tiffany (1848-1933) established a glass factory in Long Island, New York, in 1885 and was noted for several famous worldwide art designs including favrile, lava, reactive glass, stained glass lamps and windows, as well as a host of other items. Note that modern crystal products sold by the Tiffany jewelry/department stores are made in Europe (those with the etched "TIFFANY" name are made by Tipperary Crystal of Ireland). *See also CYPRIOTE, FAVRILE, LAVA GLASS, and STAINED GLASS.*

A collection of Tiffany Art Glass vases.
Photo courtesy of the Corning Museum of Glass.

T

Reproduction from an SGCA Auction catalog.

Trademarks and signatures.

Louis C. Tiffany

Furnaces Inc. Favrile

TIFFIN CUT GLASS COMPANY — An American cut glass operation established in 1910 at Tiffin, Ohio, by H. H. Close, F. X. Close, and F. W. Lehnert, the firm produced some limited cut glass tableware until closing in 1915.

TIFFIN GLASS COMPANY — (1) An American company first established as the A. J. Beatty and Sons Company in 1862 at Tiffin, Ohio. It became part of the United States Glass Company in 1892 as Factory R and began operating as a distinct subsidiary in 1916. Employees purchased the plant in 1963. After a few additional ownership changes (Continental Can, 1966; Interpace, 1969), the company closed for good in 1980. Many molds were acquired by the Summit Art Glass Company. Tiffin was noted for good quality table, bar, stem, and decorative glass wares including a line of black glassware in the 1920s referred to as "Black Satin" and a variety of colored, crystal, and/or etched tableware patterns (i.e. "Cadena," "Cherokee Rose," "Classic," "Flanders," "Fuschia," and "June Night"). (2) Another Tiffin Glass Company was founded at Tiffin, Ohio, in 1888 by a group of investors and glass men (Samuel Beck, Theodore Creighton, W. G. Eiger, J. F. Fumm, John C. Insley, C. G. Magee, Joseph P. Myers, C. H. Phillips, and S. B. Sneath). The firm struggled to operate profitably and closed in 1891. It was purchased by Sneath and was briefly known as the Sneath Glass Company. In 1894, the plant was destroyed by fire and not rebuilt. They did produce some limited amounts of pressed wares, fruit jars, food containers, lanterns, oil lamps, and other novelties. *See also ALEXANDER J. BEATTY AND SONS.*

Tiffin Glass Company: Trademarks.

TIMERS — Refer to HOUR GLASS.

TIN OXIDE — Tin is a faintly bluish-white, low-melting crystalline metallic element that, when oxidized and acidized, is mixed in a batch of glass to produce milk and other forms of opaque white glass. Tin is also combined with copper in making copper red or deep crimson colored glass, as well as turquoise blue-colored glass. *See also COPPER.*

TINT — A very light transparent color in glass that is usually unintended due to impurities in the soil; purposeful tinting is created by adding a wide variety of oxidized metals and/or chemical compounds to impart various lighted or darker shades of a transparent color.

TIPPERARY CRYSTAL — An Irish firm that was established in 1988 in the city of Carrick-on-Suir in County Tipperary. The company was founded by a group of craftsmen who had previously worked at Waterford. Tipperary specializes in high quality hand-made crystal lighting (lamps and chandeliers), tableware, stemware, vases, and other novelty items (i.e. clocks, paperweights, and a variety of figurines). Also note that Tipperary makes a good deal of crystal products that are sold by the American-based Tiffany and Company department stores: Tipperary actually etches in the "TIFFANY" trademark on their wares made exclusively for Tiffany.

Tipperary cut crystal bowls.

The Tipperary Crystal factory at Carrick-on-Suir, Ireland.

Trademarks.   *Tipperary*
              Tiffany

TITANIUM — A light but strong silvery-gray colored metal that, when oxidized, is mixed in a batch of glass to produce various hues of yellow-brown or yellow-red.

TOBACCO JAR — A large canister-like glass container with a cover used for storing tobacco. *See also* HUMIDOR.

Reproduced from an early twenteith century Higgins-Seiter catalog.

TODDY JAR OR GLASS — A tall, wide mouthed glass receptacle, without a stem, used for serving hot toddies (alcoholic beverages consisting of liquor, water, sugar, and spices).

TODDY STICK — Refer to SWIZZLE STICK.

TOILET-WATER BOTTLE — A glass receptacle, with a narrow neck and stopper, used on dressing tables and vanities for holding water (larger than a cologne bottle). *See also* WATER BOTTLE.

TONGS — A metal tool consisting of two pieces joined at one end by a pivot or hinge, the device can be opened or closed to grasp and hold glass items while they are being worked, cooled, or even shaped. The Italian term "Borsella Puntata" refers to a special pair of tongs that have a pattern designed in the jaws (the pattern is impressed directly on a glass object when it is grasped). *See also* FORMING TOOL, PINCERS, PUCELLAS, STEEL-JACKS, *and* WOOD-JACKS.

TONIC BOTTLE — A late eighteenth and nineteenth century glass container, with a narrow neck and mouth and usually without a handle, used for drinking tonics that supposedly had medicinal purposes. *See also* "Pharmacy Glass" *and* "Water Bottle."

TOOLING — Softened or molten glass shaped by various glass-makers' tools while it is being rotated on a blow-pipe or pontil.

TOOTHBRUSH BOTTLE — A tall, narrow, and cylindrical shaped glass container with cap used for storing a single toothbrush.

TOOTHPICK HOLDER — A small glass or ceramic receptacle of small capacity designed to hold toothpicks; usually cut or patterned to taper inward at the top.

Cut Glass Toothpick Holder. Illustration ¾ Size. No. 9672...........$0.60 Each Cut Glass Toothpick Holder. Illustration ¾ Size. No. 9673...........$0.68 Each Tooth Pick Holder. Engraved and Mitre Cutting. Height, 2 inches. No. 9674...........$0.54 Each Cut Glass Toothpick Holder. Height, 2¾ inches. No. 9675...........$0.50

Reproduced from an early twentieth century S. F. Myers Company catalog.

TOOTHPOWDER JAR — A small glass receptacle with cover used for holding toothpowder.

TOP WINDOW — Refer to TABLE FACET.

TOPAZ — A mineral of aluminum silicate used as a coloring agent to produce a bright yellow color within glass.

TORCH — A small gas burner or torch used to reheat hardened crystal or colored rods for precision lampwork designs in paperweights. Fine detailed work with miniature blowtorches is known as both Lampwork and Torchwork. *See also* LAMPWORK.

TORCH-WORKING — A combination of welding, painting, and sculpting molten glass into modern art objects. The term was invented by American glass artisan Steven Lundberg of Lundberg Studios.

TORSADE OR TWIST — An opaque glass thread wound loosely around a filigree or fine-banded core, usually found in the base of a mushroom-style paperweight.

TORTOISE-SHELL GLASS — A style of Art Glass originating during the Art Nouveau Period in the late nineteenth century, it is characterized by a brown mottled appearance that is enclosed between two layers of glass with a glossy finish. The mottled portion tends to be sectioned off to resemble that of the back of a tortoise.

TOSO, AURELIANO — A Venetian firm founded in 1910 at Murano, Italy, by Aureliano Toso (1884-1979), the company is noted for a revival of filigree techniques, along with the innovative use of canes and aventurine that is scattered or forms a patch framework within glass. Dino Martens, who trained as a painter, was the company's artistic director from 1938 to 1965. Much of the firm's work resembles abstract paintings made with glass threads. In 1968, Aureliano's son, Gianfranco Toso, joined the company and then became the director after his father's death. The firm specializes mostly in lighting glassware today and operates under the name "Aureliano Toso S.P.A." For glass artisans Artemio and Decio Toso, see also BAROVIER.

An 1881 Gianni Toso Venetian Glass lampworked chess set. *Photo courtesy of the Corning Museum of Glass.*

Toso, Fratelli — A Venetian firm founded at Murano, Italy, in 1854 by six Toso brothers: Angelo (1823-1892), Carlo (1831-1881), Ferdinand (1830-1921), Giovanni (1826-1888), Gregorio (1835-1897), and Liberato (1937-1890). Liberato's son, Ermanno (1903-1973), joined in 1924 and served as artistic director. Ermanno's sons, Giusto (b. 1939) and Renato (b. 1940), took over the firm in the late 1950s. The company produced a wide variety of colored art wares in typical Venetian styles as well as blown glass chandeliers. In 1979, the firm was divided into two separate companies: Fratelli Toso and Fratelli Toso International. Production ceased for Fratelli Toso in 1980 and the International half went bankrupt in 1982. In 1987, Arnoldo Toso purchased the factory and operates today mostly as a maker of crystal and lighting-related glassware.

Tourist Glass — Refer to Souvenir and Scenic Glass.

Touvier — Refer to Pantin.

Toy Mug — A miniature glass vessel in the shape of a mug with a handle that typically has a capacity of 1 to 1-1/2 ounces.

Line drawing by the author.

Toy Whiskey Taster — A small glass tumbler first made in America around 1840 for the tasting, sampling, or consuming of whiskey in tiny amounts.

Trailing — The process of pulling out a thread of glass and applying it to the surface of a glass object in spiral or other string-like designs. Trailing is similar to threading and is also sometimes referred to as "Stringing."

Transfers — A complete design printed on a paper backing that is removed from the backing, applied to the glassware, and then fired on in a special enameling lehr. Note that transfer engraving is completed by applying a polychrome picture on the back of flat glass.

Translucent — Glass that transmits or diffuses light so that objects lying beyond cannot be seen clearly through it.

Transparent — Glass that transmits light without appreciable scattering so that objects lying beyond are clearly visible.

Tray — A flat glass object, usually oval or rectangular, used for holding or serving various items (i.e. sandwiches, ice cream, tea sets, water/beverage sets, etc.).

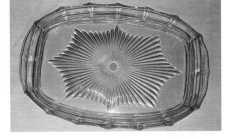

Depression Glass dresser tray. *Photo by Robin Rainwater.*

Tre, Howard Ben — A noted American Studio Glass artisan born in Brooklyn, New York, in 1949, Tre received his Masters of Fine Arts degree from the Rhode Island School of Design in 1980 and was awarded a Rakow Commission by the Corning Museum of Glass in 1987. Tre lives in Providence, Rhode Island, and works full-time as an independent glass artist.

Trefoil — A three-leaf style typical of classic Baccarat paperweight designs, Trefoil also refers to paperweights styles that contain a garland design with three loops.

Trellis — A cut, pressed, or molded decorative pattern that resembles a frame of latticework (note that a typical trellis is used as a screen to support climbing plants).

Trembleuse — A French term for a unique cup and saucer combination: the saucer is raised with a vertical projecting ring and cavity (some over two inches in depth) for which the matching cups rests partially within. Cups tend to be less than eight ounces (smaller than a coffee or tea cup) and were used to hold tea, bouillon, and even desserts such as chocolate.

Tremont Glass Works — Refer to Ripley and Company.

Tricolore — French paperweights made with red, white, and blue; popular during the nineteenth century (originally the color of the Revolutionary French flag created in 1789).

Trinkley, Karla — A noted American Studio Glass artisan born in Yardley, Pennsylvania, in 1956, Trinkley received her Master of Fine Arts degree from the Rhode Island School of Design and has served in a teaching capacity at the New York Experimental Glass Workshop (1982), the Tyler School of Art (1982, 1984), and the Rochester Institute of Technology (1986). Awards received include the Pennsylvania Council of the Arts Fellowship (1984), the Asahi Shimbun (Hokkaido Museum of Modern art in Sapporo, Japan, 1985), and a National Endowment for the Arts Grant (1986). Trinkley continues to work as an independent glass artisan in Boyertown, Pennsylvania.

Trivet — A tri-footed glass plate used under a hot dish to protect the surface beneath it (like a tabletop). Trivets are generally made of other materials such as cast iron, wood, and ceramics.

Trumpet Vase — A style of vase where the neck flares out to the mouth much like the shape of the musical instrument from which its name derives.

Tube — A thin hollow elongated stick of glass. Tubes differ from rods and canes, which are solid.

Tulip — A pressed glass pattern containing the Tulip flower as its primary design (variations include scrolling, dots, Sandwich-like designs, cables, etc.). Tulip motifs are found in cut/engraved glass as well.

Tumble-Up — An inverted glass set for a dresser or night-stand that ordinarily includes a water bottle and other items such as a tray and tumblers. The water bottle usually contains a matching tumbler that rests upside down on the top of the bottle (the tumbler doubles as a cover for the bottle).

T

TUMBLER — A drinking vessel, ordinarily without a foot, stem, or handle, that contains a pointed or convex base. Tumblers are generally of uniform diameter or taper outward slightly as they rise from bottom to top. They also come in a wide variety of sizes, from small, one-ounce whiskey tumblers to water tumblers that exceed twenty ounces.

Hocking Glass Company Depression Glass tumblers in Mayfair Open Rose and Colonial Knife and Fork patterns.
Photo by Robin Rainwater.

Cut Glass Tumbler.
Buzz Star Cutting.
Height, 3⅞ Inches.
No. 9467...............$1.25 Each

Cut Glass Tumbler.
Hob Star and Mitre Cutting.
Height, 3⅞ Inches.
No. 9468..............$2.25 Each

Reproduction from an early 20th century
S. F. Myers Company catalog.

TUNKAHANNOCK GLASS COMPANY — An American cut glass operation established at Tunkahannock, Pennsylvania, in 1894, the firm produced cut glass products until closing permanently in 1906.

TUREEN — A large round or oval covered serving bowl used for serving soup. Some have an accompanying stand. Most were made in porcelain, but glass examples have also been produced.

TURNER AND LANE — An American cut glass business established at New York, New York, in 1841 by William Turner and M. H. Lane, the firm produced some of their own cut glass, as well as importing some from Europe. The company closed in 1860.

TURN-OVER RIM — A style of edge or rim of an object (usually bowls or vases) that is curved outward and downward. *See also FOLDED RIM.*

TUTHILL CUT GLASS COMPANY — An American firm established in 1900 at Middletown, New York, by brothers Charles G. and James F. Tuthill and James' wife Susan Tuthill, the company was noted for cut glass and some intaglio engraving before it shut down in 1923.

Reproduction from a 1911 Tuthill advertisement.

Trademarks.

TWIN CITY CUT GLASS COMPANY — Refer to the JOHNSON-CARLSON CUT GLASS COMPANY.

TWISTS — Refer to AIR TWIST.

TYNESIDE GLASSWARE — Refer to SOWERBY'S ELLISON STREET GLASS WORKS.

TYRIAN GLASS — A style of Art Glass created by Frederick Carder while working for Steuben in the 1910s, it is characterized by a blending or gradual shading of a pale blue-green color to purple. Some were iridized and gilded with leaves and/or trailings.

TYRONE CRYSTAL — An Irish company established in 1970 at Tyrone, Ireland, the firm is noted most as a producer of hand-made crystal stemware, tableware, and novelty items. It is still in operation today.

Uu

{ Uu }

ULTRAMARINE — A bluish-green aqua color produced by the mineral lazulite or from a mixture of kaolin, soda ash, sulfur, and charcoal.

UNDERCUTTING — A technique of decorating glass in relief by cutting away part of the glass between the body of the object and its decoration.

UNGER BROTHERS — An American company established in 1901 at Newark, New Jersey; they began as a silver manufacturer of household items and added cut glass products shortly afterwards. They later switched to cheaper pressed blanks before closing permanently in 1918.

Unger Brothers: Trademarks.

UNGUENTARIUM — A fairly small vessel used for holding toiletry liquids such as scents, perfumes, oils, and medicines. Unguentariums were popular in ancient Greek and Roman times and resemble small bud vases or candlesticks.

UNION CUT GLASS COMPANY — Refer to the IRVING CUT GLASS COMPANY, INC.

UNION FLINT GLASS WORKS — An American pressed glass-making firm established at Pittsburgh, Pennsylvania, in 1829 by Captain John Hay and William McCully (also known as Hay and McCully). The two split in 1832; McCully formed McCully and Company while Hay partnered with Henry Campbell to form Union Glass Works (also known as Hay and Campbell). A flood destroyed the Union plant in 1832 and, in 1834, Hay sold out to John E. Parke, at which time the company became known as "Parke and Campbell." In 1837, Thomas Hanna joined, making the company's name "Parke, Campbell and Hanna"; after Campbell left in 1839, the name became "Parke and Hanna." Parke left in 1848 and was replaced by William Wallace; the firm's name became "Hanna and Wallace." James Lyon purchased Hanna's share in 1849 and the firm became Wallace, Lyon and Company. In 1851, Lyon bought out Wallace and the company's name became James B. Lyon and Company while the name of the plant itself was listed as the O'Hara Flint Glass Works. Lyon achieved a reputation as a fine maker of flint or lead pressed glass and won first prize for his products at the Paris Exposition in 1867. Another name change occurred in 1875, with the firm becoming the O'Hara Glass Company. James Lyon remained as president with John Lyon as secretary and Joseph Anderson the superintendent. Since as early as 1830, the firm has been best known as the Union Flint Glass Works. The company joined the U.S. Glass Company combine in 1891 as Factory L. U.S. Glass sold the plant in 1893 to Park Brothers and Company, a steel firm. See also PHOENIX GLASS COMPANY.

UNION GLASS COMPANY — (1) An American company established in 1854 at Somerville, Massachusetts, by Francis and Amory Houghton, it briefly operated as a cut glass operation and declared bankruptcy in 1860. Union reorganized in 1864 with Charles Chaffin (president), Amory Houghton (treasurer), and John Gregory (general manager). The firm produced some cut glass, but switched mostly to pressed glass. Houghton sold his interest soon after to Julian de Cordova, whose initials are sometimes found on the liners of certain objects, and went on with his sons to operate other firms. Meanwhile, Union remained in business until 1924, at which time the factory closed permanently; it was razed in 1935. Also note that David Walsh, a former employee of the New England Glass Company, ran a glass-cutting shop at Union beginning in 1885 up until Union closed. (2) There were a few other short-lived firms that bore the Union Glass Company name in America (i.e. in Kensington, Pennsylvania, 1826; a window pane maker at Cleveland, Ohio, 1851; and a jar and bottle producing plant at Lazearville, West Virginia, 1902). See also BROOKLYN FLINT GLASS WORKS, CORNING GLASS WORKS, HARTWELL AND LANCASTER, UNION FLINT GLASS WORKS, UNION GLASS WORKS, and UNION STOPPER COMPANY.

A Union Glass Co. crystal lamp, 1830s.
Photo courtesy of the Corning Museum of Glass.

U

UNION GLASS WORKS — (1) An American glass firm established at Philadelphia, Pennsylvania, in 1820 by the New England Glass Company, it primarily operated as a subsidiary of New England until 1874 and produced mostly cut lead crystal products and lead crystal blanks used by other firms for cutting. (2) Another Union Glass Works operated briefly at Wheeling (prior to West Virginia becoming a state) in 1849 up to America's Civil War. It had been established by R. Knowles and Company and produced bottles and figural flasks. (3) Several other short-lived American glass firms bore the Union Glass Works name: a bottle maker in New London, Connecticut (1859); other bottlemakers in Wheeling, West Virginia (1838 and 1858); a blown glass producer at Etna, Pennsylvania (1831); a window pane maker at Pittsburgh, Pennsylvania (1866); and another pressed glass-making firm at Huntington, West Virginia (1891).

UNION STOPPER COMPANY — An American firm founded at Morgantown, West Virginia, in 1905, the company produced pressed glass tableware, barware, novelties, and glass stoppers for use in non-refillable whiskey bottles before closing in 1916.

UNIONTOWN GLASS COMPANY — Refer to the WARREN GLASS WORKS.

UNITED CUT GLASS COMPANY — Refer to the MAX HERBERT COMPANY.

UNITED GLASS — Refer to UNITED GLASS BOTTLE MANUFACTURERS LIMITED.

UNITED GLASS BOTTLE (UGB) MANUFACTURERS LIMITED — A conglomerate formed in Ravenhead, England, in 1913 when six local glass manufacturers merged (Alexander, Brefflit, Candlish, Nuttall, Shaw, and Moore and Nettleford). By pooling their resources, they were able to purchase expensive automatic bottle-making machinery from Owens-Illinois of America. UGB branched out into tableware in 1931 with further purchases of large production machinery. Note that glassware produced at the various plants is sometimes referred to as "Ravenhead Glass." In 1963, the name of the company was shortened to United Glass, Ltd., which became Ravenhead Glass Ltd. in 1965. In 1987, the entire company was taken over by Owens-Illinois of America and became part of Libbey St. Clair, a Canadian branch of Libbey. In 1990, Libbey sold it to Rand and Simoni, which, in turn, went out of business in 1992. The Belgian firm of Durobor then purchased it and continues to produce tableware (mostly stemware and tumblers) today at the factory.

UNITED GLASS WORKS — Refer to LEDNICKE ROVNE GLASSWORKS, MAASTRICHT, and ROYAL DUTCH GLASS WORKS.

UNITED STATES CUT GLASS COMPANY — An American company founded in 1905 at Chicago, Illinois, when they purchased the Roseen Cut Glass Company. Herman Kotwitz ran the firm beginning in 1912 and then purchased it in 1914 with his brother Frank Kotwitz and brother-in-law Harry Baumann. *See also* WESTERN CUT GLASS COMPANY.

UNITED STATES GLASS COMPANY — An American glass conglomerate established in 1891 when eighteen separate companies from the Glass Belt (Ohio, Pennsylvania, West Virginia, etc.) merged: Adams and Company (Factory A), A. J. Beatty and Sons (Factories R and S), Bellaire Goblet Company (Factory M), Bryce Brothers (Factory B), Central Glass Company (Factory O), Columbia Glass Company (Factory J), Challinor, Taylor and Company (Factory C), Doyle and Company (Factory P), George Duncan and Sons (Factory D), Gillinder and Sons (Factory G), Hobbs Glass Company (Factory H), King Glass Company (Factory K), Nickel Plate Glass Company (Factory N), Novelty Glass Company (Factory T), O'Hara Glass Company (Factory L), Richards and Hartley (Factory E), and Ripley and Company (Factory F). The company also built new factories at Gas City, Indiana, (Factory U) and at Glassport, Pennsylvania, (new Factory O). A huge variety of pressed tableware patterns were attributed to this conglomerate. Through the years, some factories shut down while others broke off; however, U.S. Glass stayed in business until 1973. *See also* FALMOUTH GLASS COMPANY (*as well as the individually named firms above*). *See image on page 265.*

United States Glass
Company: Trademarks

UPRIGHT BOUQUET — A three-dimensional grouping of canes and stylized lampwork flowers set on a bed of leaves in a paperweight.

URANIUM GLASS — A brilliant fluorescent yellowish-green glass produced by the addition of uranium oxide. Due to the nature of the metallic element uranium, uranium glass is mildly radioactive (but not harmful) and glows brightly under a black light. It was first made in the 1830s in Germany. Small amounts of uranium oxide have also been used to produce Vaseline glass as well as opalescent forms of orange and brown. Due to most government restrictions on radioactive elements, uranium is rarely used in the glass-making process today; however, some companies are still able to use extremely low grades of it. *See also* ANNAGRUN.

URN — An ornamental glass vase that usually has two fairly small handles near the top or neck of the vessel. Urns may or may not have a pedestal base, and may sport covers as well. Funeral or Cinerary urns are vessels used to hold the ashes of cremated human remains (originated in ancient Roman times). Urns also refer to closed glass vessels with spigots that are used for serving liquids. *See also* AMPHORA.

English cameo engraved glass urns from Thomas Webb & Sons. *Photo by Robin Rainwater. Items courtesy of the Corning Museum of Glass.*

UTILITY GLASS COMPANY — Refer to the DUGAN GLASS COMPANY.

U

UNITED STATES GLASS CO., PITTSBURG, PA., U. S. A.

15052 or Illinois Pattern.

PERFECT IMITATION OF CUT GLASS.

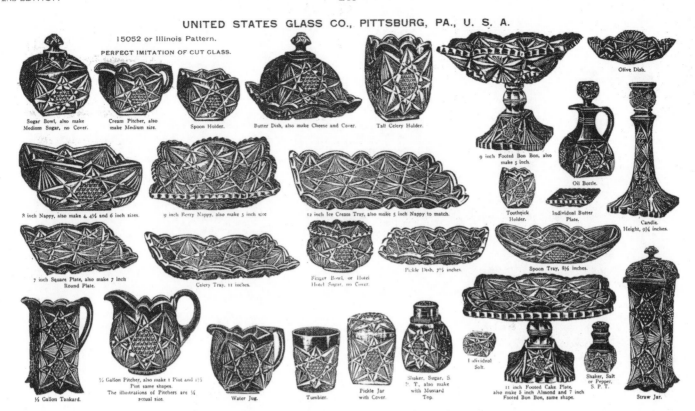

Sugar Bowl, also make Medium Sugar, no Cover.

Cream Pitcher, also make Medium size.

Spoon Holder.

Butter Dish, also make Cheese and Cover.

Tall Celery Holder.

Olive Dish.

9 inch Footed Bon Bon, also make 5 inch.

Oil Bottle.

Candle. Height, 9¼ inches.

8 inch Nappy, also make 4, 4½ and 6 inch sizes.

9 inch Berry Nappy, also make 5 inch size.

12 inch Ice Cream Tray, also make 5 inch Nappy to match.

Toothpick Holder.

Individual Butter Plate.

7 inch Square Plate, also make 7 inch Round Plate.

Celery Tray, 11 inches.

Finger Bowl, or Hotel Hotel Sugar, no Cover.

Pickle Dish, 7½ inches.

Spoon Tray, 8½ inches.

½ Gallon Tankard.

½ Gallon Pitcher, also make 1 Pint and 1½ Pint same shapes. The illustrations of Pitchers are ¾ actual size.

Water Jug.

Tumbler.

Pickle Jar with Cover.

Shaker, Sugar, S. P. T., also make with Mustard Top.

Individual Salt.

11 inch Footed Cake Plate, also make 5 inch Almond and 7 inch Footed Bon Bon, same shape.

Shaker, Salt or Pepper, S. P. T.

Straw Jar.

Reproduction from an 1899 U.S. Glass Company catalog.
See United States Glass Company on page 264

See United States Glass Company on page 264

U

Vv

{ Vv }

VAL BERGEN CUT GLASS OPERATION — An American cut glass operation established in 1907 at Columbia, Pennsylvania, by Valentine Bergen, the firm produced cut glass tableware in the early 1920s.

VAL ST. LAMBERT CRISTALLERIES — A Belgium factory established in 1822 by chemist Francois Kremlin (1784-1855) and Auguste Lelievre (1796-1879) at Seraing-sur-Meuse near Leige; in 1836, they merged with several other Belgian glassworks (i.e. Societe Anonyme des Manufacturers de Glaces, Verres A. Vitre, and Cristaux et Gobleteries). The company began as a crystal maker of tableware in English styles, but followed the Art Glass trends during the Art Nouveau Period in the latter nineteenth century. The company also produced a good deal of pressed glass, paperweights, and even some scientific glassware. Val St. Lambert is still in operation today and is noted most for crystal and colored Art Glass styles. In 1904, the firm's majority shareholder was a cooperative known as the Societe Generale de Belgique; in 1971, the Societe sold its shares to the Belgian government. In 1972, a plant was acquired in Montreal, Canada, and a subsidiary known as Val St. Lambert Canada Ltee was formed. Today, the firm is owned by a group called Region Wallone.

Trademarks.

A collection of Val St. Lambert vases.

The Val St. Lambert factory located in Seraing, Belgium.

VALLERYSTHAL GLASS — A glass producing region located in Lorraine, France, established in the early eighteenth century; in 1833, the Baron of Klinglin assumed control of a glasshouse at Plaine-de-Walsch. Five years later, it was sold to Val de Vallery. Another company, the Vallerysthal Glassworks, was founded in 1836; in 1854, it became Klenglin et Cie, which produced a good deal of art and tableware products. In 1870, Germany annexed the Alsace-Lorraine region. In 1872, Vallerysthal merged with the Portieux Glassworks, another company that had produced a good deal of Art Glass. Production nearly halted or, at the very least, was sporadic during World War II; however, the factory survived and remained in operation until 1977. In 1986, a new company named the Cristallerie de Vallerysthal opened on the original site. This firm is in operation today producing novelty glass items and some glass tableware/art items from original molds.

Vallerystahl Glass: Trademarks.

VALLEY CUT GLASS — An American firm established by Oma Oral Brown at Paden City, West Virginia, in 1942. Brown had previously worked as a cutter/engraver for the Paden City Glass Company. Brown served primarily as a decorator; cutting, etching and monogramming glassware. He also trained men returning from World War II under the veteran's job training program. Due to failing eyesight, Brown closed his glass operation in 1955 and went on to tune pianos.

VALLEY GLASS COMPANY — An American pressed glass-making firm established at Buckhannon, West Virginia, in 1903 by former governor of Pennsylvania, John K. Tener, along with Davis McCloskey, T. C. Steimer, and J. T. Ballentine. Pressed glass tableware production and some limited cut glass began in 1904. The company remained in operation until a fire destroyed the plant in 1922, though it didn't officially dissolve until 1924. Note that the firm was also known by many different names: Buckhannon Cut Glass Company (1904), Improvement Glass Company (1904), Steimer Glass Company (1904), and Belgrade Glass Company (1910). Also note that there was another company briefly known as Valley Glass Company located at Beaver Falls, Pennsylvania. *See also* WHITLA GLASS COMPANY, LTD.

V

VAN DUERZEN, JAMES — A noted American Studio Glass artisan born in De Pere, Wisconsin, in 1952, Van Deurzen received his Master of Fine Arts degree from the University of Wisconsin and has served in a teaching capacity at the Pilchuk Glass Center and Wheaton Village in Millville, New Jersey. He won a prize at The Glass Gallery Capital Glass Invitational held in Washington, D.C. in 1984, and continues to work as an independent glass artisan in Mazomanie, Wisconsin.

VAN HEUSEN, CHARLES — An occasional signature found in cut glass products, Van Heusen did not cut nor decorate glass; rather, he served primarily as a sales agent for Libbey and other cut glassmakers. Van Heusen was in business at Albany, New York, from 1893 to 1943.

Van Heusen, Charles: Trademark.

VAN HOUTEN, ERSKINE J. S. — An American cut glass company founded by Erskine J. S. Van Houten in 1886 in Brooklyn, New York, the firm was also known as the Williamsburgh Flint Glass Company and produced cut glass into the early 1920s (note that the "Van Houten, Cut Glass, New York" trademark was used from 1896-1919).

Van Houten, Erskine J. S.: Trademark.

VANADIUM — A grayish-colored metallic element that, when oxidized, is mixed in a batch of glass to produce various hues of yellow and green. Due to its rarity (and thus expensiveness), vanadium is used in very limited quantities in glass production.

VANDERMARK, BRACE AND HALL CUTTING SHOP — A short-lived American cut glass operation founded in Elmira, New York, in 1918 by George Vandermark, Adelbert Brace, and Harry Hall. The firm closed in 1921.

VARIANT — A glass item that differs slightly from the original form or standard version of a particular item or pattern.

VASA DIATRETA — A style of glass vessel created by ancient Romans consisting of a network or open pattern of glass attached to an undercoated vessel by small glass struts.

VASA MURRHINA ART GLASS COMPANY — An American business established in 1884 at Sandwich, Massachusetts, the firm produced a style of Art Glass known as "Vasa Murrhina Glass" from their company name. It is characterized by an inner layer of colored glass that has powered metals (silver, gold, copper, or nickel) or mica (colored glass chips) added for decoration. Clear glass is then flashed over the mica to add a protective outer layer. The company only operated for a few short years, but the technique was copied by other American and English Art Glass makers.

A Vasa Murrhina Art Glass tumbler and pitcher.

VASART GLASS, LTD. — A Scottish glass firm founded in 1948 at Perth by the father and brothers of Spanish immigrant Paul Ysart, the company produced paperweights in the Venetian millefiori style. In 1960, the firm was reorganized by Stuart Drysdale, who went on to form Perthshire Paperweights and then purchased by the whiskey distilling firm William Teacher and Sons in 1963. Operations were renamed Strathearn Glass, Ltd., and moved to Crieff. In 1980, the factory was taken over by Stuart and renamed "Stuart Strathearn Ltd." Today, it serves mostly as a sales, distribution, and visitor center for Stuart. See also YSART FAMILY, MONART, MONCRIEFF, PERTHSHIRE, STRATHEARN, and STUART AND SONS, LTD.

VASE — A round or angled glass vessel, usually with a depth greater than its width, used for holding and displaying flowers. Vases come in a wide variety of styles from miniatures of only a few inches in height to those several feet tall. Typical vases vary from about four or five inches to about eighteen inches in height; nevertheless, some unusual art styles exceed those dimensions. Some vases may be footed, stemmed, contain circular bases, have one or more handles, and may even have covers. See also EWER and URN.

A Steuben Art Glass vase.
Photo by Robin Rainwater.

Reproduction from an early twentieth century McKee Brothers catalog.

V

VASELINE GLASS — Glass made with a small amount of uranium oxide (usually 1% or 2%) that imparts a light greenish-yellow color (a greasy appearance like Vaseline). Vaseline glass usually glows under black light. Vaseline-like glass was first made by the Romans; however, it was not used in glass production in any quantity until the mid-nineteenth century. The term "Vaseline" was not used until about 1937. Note that the English usually refer to Vaseline glass as "Lemonescent" while it has also been called canary, yellow, uranium, topaz, magic, Canaria, Chameleon, Anna Yellow, Annagrun, and Lenora Green. *See also* URANIUM GLASS.

VASELINE OPALESCENT — Vaseline colored glassware with a white opalescent edge or background usually found in iridized Carnival Glass.

A Vaseline opalescent punch set.
Item courtesy of the Golden Pioneer Museum.

VAUPEL, LOUIS F. — A noted glass designer/engraver and German immigrant who migrated to America in 1850; as a boy, Vaupel (1824-1903) worked in his family's glass business at Breitenstein, Germany, where he learned blowing and engraving. In 1853, he was hired by the New England Glass Company and eventually became the company's most noteworthy engraver. He is recognized for creating elaborately engraved vessels in both crystal and colored Bohemian styles; especially ruby red or ruby flashed examples.

VEGETABLE DISH — A serving dish that is usually circular or oval in shape, has a cover and wide rim, and may or may not have handles. Those originating in the early nineteenth century contained detachable handles.

VENEER — An outer layer of colored glass added to the surface of clear glass. Veneers were popular in making marbles inexpensively over true solid colored ones. The process in marbles was introduced by Rodger Howdyshell of Marble King. *See also* MARBLE KING.

VENETIAN BALL — A fairly small spherical glass globe made up of a collection of fragments from various colored canes that have been compressed within a crystal glass bubble. Venetian balls, as the name implies, originated in Venice around 1840. They are similar to millefiori paperweights, only they are completely round and do not have a base with which to stand upon.

VENETIAN GLASS — Clear and colored glassware produced in Venice, Italy, and the surrounding area (mostly on the small island of Murano) from the eleventh century to the present. Early items produced included important trade commodities such as beads, panes, mirrors, and tableware. Beginning in the fifteenth century, the Venetians created a good deal of colored artistic glassware and held a virtual monopoly on glass production until the latter seventeenth century. Notable Venetian inventions include clear "Cristallo" glass; the perfection of many colored glass styles especially blue, green, purple, and milk glass; and many decorating techniques. These consist of filigrana or filigree (glass-threading), millefiori (popular in paperweight production), mosaics, ice glass (resembles cracked ice), latticino (imbedded white threads crossed like lattice), advanced enameling, gilding, gold and silver leafing, and diamond-point engraving. In the sixteenth century, many Venetians emigrated to other European countries to set up glasshouses, spreading much in the way of glass-making knowledge and Venetian styles of producing glassware. Much of the first artistic styled glass made in Europe in the sixteenth and seventeenth centuries was known as "Facon de Venise," which is French for "Style of Venice." As the rest of Europe and America caught up and surpassed the Venetians in the eighteenth and nineteenth centuries, there was a brief lull and decline of Venetian-made glass. A revival occurred in the mid-nineteenth century; since then, an entire host of new Venetian glass artisans and small companies continue to produce a wide variety of colored art glass forms on the island of Murano. *See also* MURANO and CRISTALLO.

Venetian Art Glass Vase.
Photo by Robin Rainwater.
Item courtesy of the Corning Museum of Glass.

A Venetian latticino and ribbon designed paperweight.
Photo by Robin Rainwater.

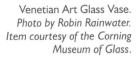

VENICE AND MURANO GLASS COMPANY — Refer to SALVIATI AND COMPANY.

VENINI AND COMPANY — A Venetian firm founded in 1921 on the island of Murano by Paolo Venini (1895-1959), Andrea Rioda, and Giacomo Cappellin (1887-1968), the company is noted for a revival of Venetian filigree techniques and the innovative use of canes and murrhine. Early on, the firm hired the most creative and talented artisans that they could find including painters. In 1925, Francesco Zecchin (1878-1947) and sculptor Napoleone Martinuzzi (1892-1977) joined on as Cappellin left to form his own firm. Venini is responsible for pioneering an incredible number of new styles or ornamental glass including "vaso fazzoletto," the classic handkerchief-styled vase developed in 1949; "vetro bollicine," whereby tiny air bubbles are captured and controlled just beneath the surface and then arranged in a decorative effect; "vetro composto," where a thin flashing of colored glass is cased in a decorative pattern over a contrasting colored object; "vetro corroso," a style of crackled ice glass created with hydrofluoric acid; "vetro groviglio," where a mass of copper wire is embedded in glass; "vetro inciso," a technique of covering an entire surface with wavy incisions or grooves; "vetro membrano," internally partitioned glassware; "vetro occhi," a style of mosaic art glass (glass with eyes); "vetro pennelato," whereby an all-over design of irregular swirling colored streaks are fused into clear-glass; "vetro pezzato," glass squares that are fused together to create a mosaic effect; "vetro pizzo," irregularly-shaped pieces of opaque glass formed into lacy designs; "vetro sommerso," cased glass with an ornamental colored under layer, and "vetro tessuto," glass decorated by narrow vertical opaque white strips. Paolo Venini died in 1959, with control of the firm taken over by Ludivico Diaz de Santillana. In 1985, Venini was acquired by the Gardini and Ferruzzi families and is still arguably the most recognizable name in modern Venetian glass-making today. In 1997, Venini became part of the Royal Scandinavia Group with glass still being made under the "Venini" namesake today.

Trademarks and signatures.

A 1972 glass sculpture by Venini.
Photo courtesy of the Corning Museum of Glass.

VEREINIGTE LAUSITZER GLASWERKE (VLG) AG — In 1899, a German company known as Neue Oberlausitzer Glashuttenwerke Schweig and Company, which made scientific glassware and light bulbs, merged with several other firms in the Oberlausitzer region of Eastern Germany. The glass operations were all purchased by AEG (an electrical company) in 1905. In 1909, the name was officially changed to Vereinigte Lausitzer Glaswerke. The headquarters were located in Weißwasser, but there were other factories in Furstenberg (for the production of lighting), Kamenz (pressed glass), and Tschernitz (pharmaceutical glass). The firm expanded into cut and engraved glass and added an art division in 1919 known as Abteilung Kunstglas. Art products included some acid-etched cameo vases; however, production of art glass ended in 1929. In the early 1930s, the company was the largest producer of household glass in Germany; nevertheless, most of the equipment was confiscated by Russia after World War II. Production of cut and engraved glassware resumed on a lesser scale in 1947 and soon after the firm was merged into a collective of nineteen East German factories called Vereinigung Volkseigener Betriebe Ostglas (VEB). The name of the collective was changed again soon after to Oberlausitzer Glaswerke (OLG) while the original VLG factory was also referred to as VEB Lausitzer Glass. The cooperative still exists today producing some engraved, machine-pressed, and industrial glassware.

VEREINIGUNG VOLKSEIGENER BETRIEBE OSTGLAS — Refer to VEREINIGTE LAUSITZER GLASWERKE AG.

VERLYS GLASS — Verlys was established in 1932 as an Art Glass branch of the French Holoplane Company in France. The Heisey Glass Company of Newark, Ohio, obtained the rights and formulas for Verlys and produced similar, but somewhat cheaper, products from 1935-1951. French-made pieces have a molded signature while the American-made pieces have a diamond etched signature with satinized frosting and/or etching (similar in style to Lalique).

A "Verlys 15" engraved oval crystal platter.

V

Reproduction from a 1962 Verlys advertisement.

Trademark.

VERMICULAR — A decorating style consisting of worm-like trailings or enamels that curve around an object.

VERONA GLASS — A style of Art Glass created by the Mount Washington Glass Works in the latter nineteenth century. It is characterized by clear glass decorated by covering it with a waxed-on design and then spraying the object with acid to fuse the design under the wax (the original wax is removed).

VERRE-DE-SOIE — An Art Glass first produced by Steuben in the early twentieth century, it is characterized by a smooth translucent pearly-iridescent white or pale green finish that is further decorated with trailings, prunts, and engravings. The name translates to "Glass of Silk."

VERTICAL DRAW METHOD — The technique of pulling molten glass through a slit in a refractory block that is floating on the glass surface. The annealing lehr must be positioned directly over the draw chamber. Glass produced in this method tends to be very clean and clear since its surface had remained untouched in the forming process (as opposed to standard rolled glass).

VERZELINI GLASS — Venetian-styled glass produced by Jacopo Verzelini beginning in the 1570s while working for England's Crutched Friars Glasshouse. Verzelini (1522-1616) originally worked as a glass artisan in Antwerp and was brought to England (along with six other skilled workers in Venetian glass-making) in 1571 by Jean Carre (manager of Crutched Friars). Verzelini is responsible for teaching the English much in the way of glass-making as well as diamond-point engraving.

VESICA — A Cut glass technique in which a pointed oval is cut into an object. Many objects sport rows of such cut ovals and may include other decorations as well.

VETTER CUT GLASS MANUFACTURING COMPANY — An American cut glass operation founded in 1916 by Theodore Vetter at Cleveland, Ohio. Vetter worked concurrently with the Sunshine Cut Glass Company. He produced cut glass into the early 1920s, but switched to pressed wares when the market ended for fine cut glass (mirrors and window panes). Vetter sold his firm in 1954 to Milton Gross.

VETRARIA ARCHIMEDE SEGUSO — A Venetian firm established at Murano, Italy, in 1946 by Archimede Seguso, who had previously aided in the founding of the Seguso Vetri d'Arte company, Seguso produced colored art glass in Venetian styles. However, he is noted most for his merletto technique: producing a wide variety of art objects with fine lacework or netted colored patterns. See also SEGUSO VETRI D'ARTE.

VETRERIA VISTOSI — A Venetian glass-making company founded by Guglielmo Vistosi (1901-1952) in 1945, originally for the production of glass lighting fixtures. Noted architect Alessandro Pianon (1931-1984) joined in 1956 along with Vistosi's son, Luciano. The firm then produced art glass in typical colorful Venetian styles.

VETRO — The Italian term for "Glass."

VETRO A RETICELLO — The Italian term for networked glass, it is characterized by applied colored threads (most often opaque white) worked into various designs (i.e. latticino, thread circuits, filigrana, etc.).

VETRO A RETORTI — The Italian term for twisted glass, it is characterized by twisted threads of glass embedded in other objects as a decoration.

VETRO DI TRINA — The Italian term for lacy glass, it is characterized by blown glass made with thin threads of white or sometimes colored canes (more precise term for certain types of filigrana glass).

VIAL — A small glass bottle used for ointments, medicines, and perfumes (same as "Phial"). Most have a stopper, cap, or similar device to enclose the vial.

VICTORIAN GLASS OR ERA — English-made or influenced glass from about the 1820s through the 1940s characterized by colors, opalescence, opaqueness, Art glass, and unusual designs and shapes. It is named for Queen Victoria (1837–1901). The entire Victorian Era encompasses colored Art Glass during this time period in England, as well as in other parts of Europe and America.

V

VICTORY GLASS COMPANY — An American firm founded at Jeannette, Pennsylvania, in 1919 by James Bugher, James Edge, W. O. Linhart, and M. H. Miller. Production began in 1920, and the name was changed to Victory Glass, Inc. in 1923. The company produced glass novelties including candy-filled glass toy containers and wide-mouthed food containers. Victory was purchased by J. H. Millstein, a former employee of the firm, in 1955. The plant was destroyed by fire in 1962, but was rebuilt. Millstein was succeeded by his son, Jack; the firm changed its product line in the 1980s to blown and pressed glass lighting fixtures. The company continues to produce glass today under the Victory name.

VICTORY GLASS, INC. — Refer to the VALLEY GLASS COMPANY.

VIKING GLASS COMPANY — An American company established at New Martinsville, West Virginia, in 1944 as a result of the purchase of the New Martinsville Glass Company, Viking continued using some of New Martinville's original molds to produce glass tableware and novelty items. The firm was noted for producing many ruby red novelties. Viking also had a subsidiary named "The Rainbow Art Glass Company" from 1954 to 1972. In 1987, Viking was purchased by Kenneth Dalzell (former president of Fostoria) to become Dalzell-Viking. The company closed in 1998. *See also* RAINBOW ART GLASS COMPANY.

Viking glass owl.
Photo by Robin Rainwater.

Trademarks.

VINEGAR BOTTLE — A glass receptacle with a top used for serving vinegar or other salad oils. *See also* CRUET *and* OIL BOTTLE.

VINELAND FLINT GLASS MANUFACTURING COMPANY — An American firm established by Victor Durand Sr. and Victor Durand Jr. in 1897 at Vineland, New Jersey. Victor Durand Jr. was noted most for producing Art Glass of his namesake and purchased his father's share of the firm in 1899. The Durand family had worked for several generations in the famous glass town of Baccarat, France, and began producing Art Glass in America in 1912. The Vineland factory burned down in 1904, but was rebuilt. When Victor Durand Jr. (1870-1931) passed away, the firm merged with the Kimble Glass Company. *See also* DURAND ART GLASS COMPANY.

VINES ART GLASS — A small art glass and paperweight-making firm established by Roger and Genevieve Vines in 1982. Roger Vines earned a Masters in Art from the University of Washington and taught glassblowing at Lower Columbia College from his own small studio that he established in 1968. His wife Genevieve is a painter who aids in design. Together, the Vines are noted for producing contemporary art studio glass and paperweights.

VIOLIN FLASK — A style of flask or bottle that was made in the shape of a violin; they originated in America in the mid-nineteenth century and were usually mold-blown in a wide variety of sizes and colors.

VIRGINIA GREEN GLASS WORKS — An American firm established at Wheeling (prior to West Virginia becoming a state) in 1829 when Charles Knox and Redick McKee purchased a factory at auction previously owned and established by George Carruthers, Peter Yarnell and Thomas McGriffen in 1824. The company was also known as Knox and McKee, and primarily produced window panes and bottles. In 1830, Knox and McKee leased the plant to Ensell and Plunkett of Pittsburgh, which operated it until 1833. Knox and McKee then sold half the interest to Jesse Wheat and John Price, who, in turn, changed the name to Fairview Glass Works. In 1834, John and Craig Ritchie, along with George Wilson, purchased Fairview and operated it until the Panic of 1836. The factory remained in operation by many other upstart interests before being torn down in 1849. *See also* FAIRVIEW GLASS WORKS *and* RITCHIE.

VISCOSITY — The state of molten glass when it is still pliable so that it can be worked and shaped into its intended form.

VISTOSI — An Italian/Venetian firm founded on the island of Murano in 1945 by Guigliemo Vistosi (1901-1952). When Guigliemo passed away in 1952, his brother Oreste Vistosi (1917-1982) assumed control. Oreste's sons, Gino (b. 1925) and Luciano (b. 1931), also eventually joined the company. Initially, the factory produced lighting glassware, but in the mid-1950s they expanded into colored art glass including traditional Venetian styles and carved/blown block sculptures of clear and colored glass (many made in the shape of birds). When Gino passed away in 1980, the factory was run solely by Luciano, who, in turn, sold it to Maurizio Albarelli in 1985. Albarelli had also acquired Seguso Vetri d'Arte and now produced lighting-related glassware exclusively.

VITRIFICATION — The actual process of transforming the basic ingredients (i.e. silicates or sand, and an alkali like soda or potash) into glass by heat and fusion.

V

VITRIX HOT GLASS STUDIO — An American studio art glass company founded in 1979 by brothers Thomas and Matthew Buechner in Corning, New York. The Buechners have gained a world-wide reputation for the design of their fine blown colored art glass. In 1983, Matthew and his wife Barbara founded their own firm in Newport, Rhode Island (Thames Street Glass House). Thomas then sold Vitrix to Thomas Kelly, a previous employee of the Buechners, in 1985.

VITRO AGATE COMPANY — An American marble-making firm founded in 1932 at Parkersburg, West Virginia, by Lawrence Alley, Henri Fisher, and Press Lindsey, though Alley, who went on to form his own company, was bought out early on by Fisher and Lindsey bought out Alley. Soon after, Fisher bought out Lindsey. In 1969, the company was purchased by the Gladding Corporation and the name was briefly changed to the Gladding-Vitro Company. In 1982, Gladding was purchased by the Paris Manufacturing Company of South Paris, Maine. Paris changed the name of their marble-making subsidiary back to Vitro Agate. In 1987, it was sold to the Viking Rope Company. After numerous more ownership changes, the company was eventually purchased by Jabo, Incorporated. Vitro Agate still produces glass marbles as a subsidiary of Jabo today. *See also* ALLEY AGATE COMPANY *and* JABO, INCORPORATED.

VONECHE GLASSWORKS — A Belgian glass operation established near Namur in the Ardennes region in 1778 as the Cristallerie de Voneche, under a charter granted by Empress Marie Therese. The firm was purchased by Aime-Gabriel D'Artigues in 1802. The company operated successfully until the French Revolution occurred in 1789-1790. It nearly shut down permanently until D'Artigues saved it. D'Artigues hired Francois Kemlin and Auguste Lelievre and operated it successfully until the French sovereignty officially ended in 1815. There was simply no market for fancy art-style glassware, at least not until another thirty years or so. Kemlin and Lelievre went on to form Belgium's most noteworthy glass company of all time, Val St. Lambert, while D'Artigues merged the Voneche operation with his newly acquired Baccarat Glass Factory in 1816.

VOTIVE GLASS — Glassware decorated by a variety of methods (in modern time, mostly by light etching or enameling with inscriptions and vows, a small prayer, poem, or verse).

VRBNO GLASSWORKS — A Czechoslovakian firm founded in 1862 in Moravia by Rudolf Richter, initially, it produced basic pressed tableware and bottles. By the early twentieth century, the firm was producing cut and enameled colored art glass in traditional Bohemian styles. Like all Czech firms, it became part of the state in 1948 and merged with such firms as Kvetna and Karolinka. It was eventually absorbed by the conglomerate Crystalex, and still serves as a glass-making factory for tableware and stemware today.

V

Ww

{ Ww }

WAFER DISH — A small flat or shallow dish, usually square or rectangular in shape, used for serving crackers or wafers.

WAFFLE — A pressed glass design that resembles an all-over design of interlocking squares or rectangles. The paneled cube design can be found in other categories of glass such as America's Carnival and Depression glass patterns and cut glass. In pressed glass, it is often combined with other designs to produce unique combinations like waffle and thumbprint, waffle with fan, waffle and bar, waffle block, and waffle with points.

WAFFLE CUT — A series of wide grid-like perpendicular cuts made in the base of paperweights.

WAISTED — A vessel (usually a vase) that has a smaller diameter in the middle than at the top and bottom; the sides then form a continuous inward curve or waist as they approach the center.

WALDGLAS — The German term for "Forest Glass." Forest Glass Houses or Huts (called "Waldglashutten") sprung up throughout Germany during the Middle Ages. The glass was made prior to modern purification techniques and usually came out as a murky green or brown color. Most items made were crude table items such as bowls and drinking vessels.

WALKING STICK — Refer to CANE.

WALLACE, LYON AND COMPANY — Refer to the UNION FLINT GLASS WORKS.

WALL-POCKET — A specialized vase, made to be attached to or hang from a wall, used specifically for holding flowers or small plants. Wall-pockets are also referred to as "Wall Vases" and are generally made of glass or porcelain.

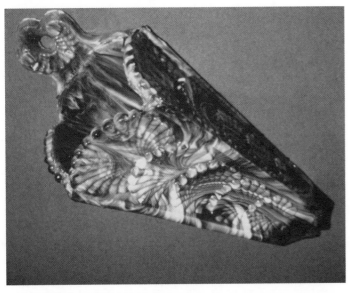

A late nineteenth century pressed glass wall vase from Sowerby's of England. *Photo courtesy of the Corning Museum of Glass.*

WALSH, DAVID — Refer to the UNION GLASS COMPANY.

WALSH, WALSH JOHN — In 1851, John Walsh Walsh (1804-1864) purchased the Soho and Vesta Glass Works in Birmingham, England. The firm remained in the family and was run by Walsh's son-in-law, Thomas Ferdinand Walker, in the 1880s. The company produced cut, engraved, and machine-etched glassware and then expanded into colored ornamental wares, mostly bowls and vases, during the Art Nouveau movement. Colored tableware was made in abundance in both Art and Victorian styles up until World War II. After the war, production was changed exclusively to scientific and industrial-related glass. In 1951, the firm was taken over by the Edinburgh and Leith Flint Glass Company (Edinburgh Crystal today). See also "Edinburgh Crystal Glass Company."

WALTER, A. — A French glass artisan who first made pate-de-verre styled glass for Daum Glassworks at Nancy, France, from 1908 to 1914 (signed "Daum, Nancy" with a cross), Walter founded his own company in 1919. His creations bear the signature of "A. Walter Nancy."

WARNER CUT GLASS COMPANY — Refer to the FINDLAY CUT GLASS COMPANY.

WARREN GLASS WORKS — An American glass-making firm established at Cumberland, Maryland, in 1880, the company moved to Uniontown, Pennsylvania, in 1888 and continued producing both blown and pressed glass tableware until closing in 1891. The factory was purchased in 1893 and became the Uniontown Glass Company, a maker of milk glass jars and bottles. Uniontown closed in 1894. In 1898, a reorganizing effort under the Uniontown Flint Glass Works name was attempted, but failed without any resumed production at the plant.

WARSAW CUT GLASS COMPANY — Refer to the JOHNSON-CARLSON CUT GLASS COMPANY.

WASHINGTON CUT GLASS COMPANY — An American cut glass operation founded in 1914 at Seattle, Washington, by Bohemian immigrants Antone Kusak and Edward Zelasky. Both had previously worked for Fostoria, though Zelasky had moved to Seattle two years later where he ran a small cutting shop. In 1916, the partnership ended when Kusak left; however, both men continued to operate as glass cutters until heavy cut glass went out of style in the early 1920s (Zelasky continued to work under the Washington Cut Glass Company name). Edward Zelasky Jr. was also trained by his father and continued to operate an engraving shop for glassware into the early 1960s.

WATCH BOX — A small rectangular or circular glass vessel, with or without a cover, used for storing a single wrist watch.

WATER BOTTLE — A glass container, with a narrow neck and mouth and usually without a handle, used for drinking water or other liquids. Water bottles are sometimes referred to as "Mineral Bottles," "Seltzer Bottles," or "Soda Bottles."

WATER GLASS — (1) A glass-like substance produced by the addition of excess soda (sometimes by accident in the regular glass-making process). When partially dissolved in water, the thick syrupy mixture can be used as a sealant (i.e. fire-proofing, coating eggs, etc.). (2) A drinking vessel, ordinarily without a foot, stem, or handle and containing a pointed or convex base, designed for drinking water. Water tumblers tend to be a bit larger (usually exceed eight ounces in capacity) than most tumblers. They may have a handle; however, those that are stemmed and footed are ordinarily referred to as "Water Goblets."

W

WATER GOBLET — A drinking vessel, with a large bowl, stem, and foot, specifically designed for drinking water. Water goblets tend to have the largest capacity when compared to other stemware used for alcoholic beverages (i.e. wine glasses, cordials, champagne glasses, etc.).

WATER PITCHER OR JUG — A fairly large jug or pitcher designed specifically for serving water and other liquids (i.e. lemonade, iced tea, etc.). Water pitchers generally exceed forty-eight ounces in capacity and are larger than milk pitchers.

WATER SET — A tableware set consisting of a large pitcher and matching tumblers or goblets (usually six).

Reproduction from an early twentieth century
Pitkin & Brooks catalog.

WATERFORD — The first Waterford glass company was established in Waterford, Ireland, in 1783 by George and William Penrose (uncle and nephew) and then sold to the Gatchell family in 1799 (operated by John Gatchell until 1823). The Penroses hired Stourbridge English glassmaker John Hill in 1785, along with other workmen from Worcestershire. Hill earned an international reputation for making fine glassware, but was disliked by William Penrose's wife; as a result, Hill returned to England in 1786. However, Hill was able to teach Jonathan Gatchell the fine points of producing lead crystal tableware and the first hand-made crystal produced by Waterford contained a bluish-tint and heavy cutting. When Jonathan Gatchell passed on in 1823, his relatives managed the factory until it closed in 1851. A new Waterford factory was built in 1951 and, since then, Waterford has become the world's largest manufacturer of hand-made crystal. Today, they operate as Waterford Wedgwood PLC after merging with Wedgwood in 1986. Waterford Wedgwood also acquired Stuart Crystal in 1995, as well as a majority interest in Rosenthal in 1998 with factories in both Germany and the Czech Republic. *See also STUART AND SONS, LTD. and ROSENTHAL PORZELLAN AG.*

A Waterford glass hedgehog.

The Waterford Glass factory located in Waterford, Ireland.

Trademarks.

WAVE CREST — A style of Art Glass produced by the C. F. Monroe Company of Meriden, Connecticut, beginning in 1880, up until the company closed in 1916, Wave Crest is characterized by a light opal glass in various colors (white, cream, custard, light rose, and pink were the most common) that was further decorated with enameled and/or gold scrolling, foliage, or floral designs. Some pieces, such as vases, wall pockets, and covered jars, were set in silver or silver-plated holders. Identical products made by Monroe were also referred to as "Kelva" and "Nakara."

A C. F. Monroe Wave Crest boxes.
Items courtesy of Wheaton Village.

WAYNE CUT GLASS COMPANY — An American cut glass operation established at Honesdale, Pennsylvania, in 1905, the firm opened another plant in 1910 at Towanda, Pennsylvania, and continued to produce cut glass products into the early 1920s.

WEALDEN GLASS — General term for English glassware made near the wooded area of Chiddingfold and the Weald of Kent by French immigrants beginning as early as the thirteenth century and up to the early seventeenth century. Most of the glass produced was murky green and included mold-blown practical items such as bottles and bowls.

WEAR FLINT GLASS WORKS — Refer to HENRY GREENER.

WEAR MARKS — Tiny, barely visible scratches on the base, foot, or rim, which indicates normal wear and tear through years of use. Glass with wear marks is usually not considered mint glassware, but it holds much more value than damaged glass.

WEATHERING — The harmful effects of age, moisture, and chemical action that all lead to the decomposition of glass. *See also* SICKNESS.

WEBB AND RICHARDSON — An English firm established in 1829 when Thomas Webb I, in partnership with William Haden Richardson and Benjamin Richardson I, purchased the Wordsley Flint Glassworks in Wordsley, near Stourbridge, England. The company produced lead crystal wares until the partnership was dissolved in 1936. The firm was then succeeded by W.H.B and J. Richardson.

WEBB CORBETT, LTD. — An English firm established in 1897 when W.H.B. and J. Richardson sold part of their glass-making operation (including the White House Glassworks) to George Corbett and Thomas Webb III (son of Thomas Webb II and grandson of Thomas Webb I). They also purchased the Tutbury Glass Works near Burton-on-Trent in 1906. After a fire in 1913, operations were moved to Coalbournhill, England, near Stourbridge. The company produced rock crystal, intaglio engraved glass, and other colored art styles and crystal wares. The company did not officially become known as Webb, Corbett, Ltd. until 1953 (originally it was Thomas Webb and Corbett, Ltd.). In 1969, the company became part of the Royal Doulton Group. In 1980, Royal Doulton named their glass operation Royal Doulton Crystal by Webb Corbett, the same year they closed the Tutbury plant. In 1986, the Webb Corbett name was discontinued; glass products are marketed today under the Royal Doulton Crystal name.

WEBB, JOSEPH GLASS WORKS — Refer to the COUDERSPORT TILE AND ORNAMENTAL GLASS COMPANY.

WEBB PATENT TILE COMPANY — Refer to the COUDERSPORT TILE AND ORNAMENTAL GLASS COMPANY.

WEBB, THOMAS AND SONS — Established in 1837 in Stourbridge, England, by Thomas Webb I (1804-1869), the company has been in continuous operation ever since and is known today as "Webb's Crystal Glass Co., Ltd.," a division of Crown House Ltd. Webb had originally set up a partnership with the Wordsley Flint Glassworks in 1929 with Benjamin and William Haden Richardson. Webb inherited the White House Glass Works in 1833 and left the partnership in 1836 to concentrate on his own firm. In 1859, it became Thomas Webb and Sons when Webb's sons, Thomas Wilkes Webb II (1836-1891) and Charles Webb, joined. When the elder Webb died in 1869, another of his sons, Walter Wilkes Webb (d. 1919), also joined the company. Webb produced cut glass tableware and chandeliers, but is noted most for being one of England's leaders during the nineteenth century Art Nouveau movement. The firm produced several popular Art Glass styles, including Cameo Engraving, Peach Blow, Alexandrite, and Burmese. Famous designers who worked for the firm included John Northwood and the Woodall brothers, George (1850-1925) and Thomas (1849-1926). In 1919, Webb merged with the Edinburgh and Leith Flint Glass Company to form Webb's Crystal Glass Company, Ltd. *See also* WEBB'S CRYSTAL GLASS, COMPANY, LTD.

A Webb Art Glass cameo engraved vase. *Photo by Robin Rainwater. Item courtesy of the Corning Museum of Glass.*

THOMAS WEBB & SONS / GEM CAMEO   Trademarks.

THOS. WEBB & SONS, LTD.

THOMAS WEBB ENGLAND   THOS WEBB ENGLAND

WEBB'S CRYSTAL GLASS, COMPANY, LTD. — A new English firm established in 1919 when Thomas Webb and Sons acquired the Dennis Glassworks at Amblecote, near Stourbridge, England. Webb also purchased the Edinburgh Leith Flint Glass Company in 1920 and the Wordsley Flint Glassworks in the 1930s. The business continues today as a major English producer of lead crystal and some limited wares as a subsidiary of Crown House Ltd. Crown had purchased Webb in 1964 and merged it with Dema, another subsidiary of Crown, in 1971.

WEBSTER AND BRIGGMAN — An American cut glass operation established at Naugatuck, Connecticut, in 1910 by Wallace Webster and George Briggman, the two moved operations to Meriden, Connecticut, in 1917 and produced cut glass tableware and ornamental wares until closing in 1923.

WEDDING CUP OR BOWL — A specialized standing cup or bowl made specifically to celebrate a wedding. Most sport a fairly tall foot and may be decorated with the portraits of the newly married couple.

WEDGWOOD GLASS — Crystal and cut glass made by two subsidiaries of Josiah Wedgwood and Sons, Ltd. The firm acquired King's Lynn Glass, Ltd. at Norfolk, England, in 1969 and Galway Crystal at Galway, Ireland, in 1974. In 1982, Wedgwood acquired a 50% share in Dartington Crystal, but sold it off in 1986 when they merged with Waterford. Aside from crystal products, the company also produced some colored glassware including paperweights. In 1988, Wedgwood Crystal was sold to Caithness, who operated it as Caithness Crystal from 1988-1992. The King's Lynn factory was closed in 1992. Today, Wedgwood concentrates more on porcelain while Waterford continues as the world's largest maker of hand-made crystal; nevertheless, glass is still produced under the Galway name as a subsidiary of Wedgwood. *See also* WATERFORD.

WEIGHT — The simplified or abbreviated term for a paperweight.

WEINBERG, STEVEN — A noted American Studio Glass artisan born in New York City in 1954, Weinberg received his Master of Fine Arts degree from the Rhode Island School of Design and won numerous awards, including the Young Americans Award from the America Craft Council (1978), National Endowment for the Arts Fellowships (1978, 1984), and third prize as the Hokkaido Museum of Modern Art (World Glass Now Exhibition, Sapporo, Japan, 1986). Weinberg continues to work as an independent glass artisan in Pawtucket, Rhode Island.

W

WELLINGTON GLASS COMPANY — Refer to the CUMBERLAND GLASS COMPANY.

WELT — A small strip of glass usually turned under at the foot to provide added strength and reduce the possibility of chipping, welts are most often present on stemware to make them more durable. Note that some are turned or folded over rather than under. *See also* FOLDED FOOT.

WELZ, FRANZ — A Bohemian who first owned and operated a coal mine near Teplitz, Germany, in the late nineteenth century, Welz expanded into glass and built a glass hut that was one of the first to use brown coal as its primary fuel source. Welz produced cut, engraved, and decorated glass in typical Bohemian styles up until the firm closed around 1920.

WEST BROTHERS COMPANY — An American firm founded at Grapeville, Pennsylvania, in 1906 by Charles and George West. The Wests were also instrumental in the founding of the Westmoreland Specialty Company and served as officers there concurrently while running their own small operation. West Brothers (also known as the West Specialty Company) produced glass candy containers until 1930; the plant was then purchased by the Jeannette Glass Company.

WEST COAST GLASS STUDIO MOVEMENT — This movement began in the early 1970s, about a decade after professor Harvey Littleton of the University of Wisconsin held a workshop in Toledo, Ohio, illustrating that art glass could easily be blown by independent artists in small studios. Many such studios sprang up in the Western United States including Chihuly, Cuneo Furnaces, Orient and Flume, Correia, Lundberg Studios, Nourot, and Satava.

WEST LOTHIAN GLASSWORKS — A Scottish glass firm established at Bathgate by Donald Fraser in 1866, the company produced practical table items before closing in 1887. Note that Fraser died in 1869 and the factory was purchased by Wilson and Sons. In the 1870s, it was acquired by James Couper and Sons and the name was briefly changed to the "Bathgate Glass Company."

WEST SPECIALTY COMPANY — Refer to the WEST BROTHERS COMPANY.

WEST VIRGINIA GLASS COMPANY — Refer to the ELSON GLASS COMPANY.

WEST VIRGINIA GLASS SPECIALTY COMPANY — Refer to the LOUIE GLASS COMPANY.

WESTERN CUT GLASS COMPANY — An American company founded in 1914 at Chicago, Illinois, when they purchased the United States Cut Glass Company, brothers Herman and Frank Kotwitz, along with their brother-in-law, Harry Baumann, were the principal owners of the firm. The Kotwitzs had previously been active in several glass-making firms. Western produced cut glass products until closing permanently in 1918. *See also* HEINZ BROTHERS, MONARCH CUT GLASS COMPANY, *and* UNITED STATES CUT GLASS COMPANY.

WESTMORELAND GLASS COMPANY — An American company established at Grapeville, Pennsylvania, in 1889 as a subsidiary of the Westmoreland Specialty Company (originally located at East Liverpool, Ohio) by brothers Charles and George West, along with George Irwin. The glass plant was sold to the West Brothers when Irwin withdrew in 1890. The Wests had also received financial backing from Ira Brainard, who bought half the business in 1920 when George West left; Brainard's family bought it out entirely in 1937. Meanwhile, the name was changed in 1923 to the Westmoreland Glass Company. Early on, the company made glass food and candy containers, but expanded into cut and pressed tableware by 1900. The firm was noted most for its production of milk glass in several styles, pressed glass, some slag glass, English Hobnail patterned glassware, and other colored wares. Note that milk glass accounted for about 90% of Westmoreland's total production. Other noted patterns produced by the firm include "Beaded Edge," "Della Robbia," and "Panel Grape." Westmoreland remained in the Brainard family until 1981 and then was sold to David Grossman Designs, Inc. The company closed permanently in 1985.

Reproduction from a 1926 Westmoreland advertisement.

Trademarks.

A Westmoreland two-handled opalescent cherry patterned candy jar. *Photo by Robin Rainwater.*

WESTMORELAND SPECIALTY COMPANY — Refer to the WESTMORELAND GLASS COMPANY.

WESTON GLASS COMPANY — Refer to the LOUIE GLASS COMPANY.

WHALE-OIL LAMP — A glass vessel with a wick and oil receptacle used to produce light. As the name implies, oil obtained from whale blubber was originally used as the fuel source. Most whale-oil lamps were fairly tall with a pedestal base, sported a tin and cork burner, and a tin cap at the top through which the wick passed out of. Glass shades were then used to protect the flame emanating from the burner. These lamps were most popular beginning in the early eighteenth century up until the late nineteenth century.

WHEAT, PRICE AND COMPANY — An American glass firm established at Wheeling in 1832 (prior to West Virginia becoming a state) by Jesse Wheat, John Price, Charles Knox, and Redick McKee. Wheat had previously partnered with the Ritchie family. The company produced some lead cut crystal and pressed tableware before selling their short-lived company to the Ritchie family in 1834. *See also RITCHIES.*

WHEATON GLASS COMPANY — An American firm founded at Millville, New Jersey, in 1888 by Dr. Theodore Carson Wheaton. Since Wheaton was a medical doctor, early on the firm specialized in producing blown pharmaceutical and scientific/laboratory glassware. Also in 1888, Wheaton bought out a short-lived (barely a year in operation) glass company known as the Shull-Goodwin Glass Company and the company expanded into pressed glass tableware production. In 1906, Wheaton's son, Frank Hayes Wheaton, joined the firm and he, in turn, was succeeded by his son, Frank H. Wheaton Jr. The firm continues in operation today as Wheaton Industries and runs more than forty plants. In modern times, Wheaton is noted for producing glass containers for cosmetics; scientific glassware; the abundant ruby red "Cape Cod" pressed glass patterned tableware set that was commissioned by Avon; reproducing some pressed glass from old molds (known as "Wheatoncraft" or "Wheatonware"); and for establishing a museum and working glass exhibit known as Wheaton Village, which contains the largest collection of American-made glass and hundreds of old glass molds once owned by a wide variety of firms, most acquired from the defunct John E. Kemple Glass Works. *See also AVON COLLECTIBLES.*

An Avon Cape Cod pattern ruby red relish dish made by the Wheaton Glass Company. *Photo by Robin Rainwater.*

WHEATON INDUSTRIES — Refer to the WHEATON GLASS COMPANY.

WHEEL-CARVED OR WHEEL-ENGRAVED GLASS — Cameo-engraved glass abraded or carved with the use of rotating stone or copper wheels. *See also COPPER WHEEL ENGRAVING, DIAMOND POINT ENGRAVING, and WHEELS.*

WHEELING FLINT GLASS WORKS — An American glass firm established at Wheeling in 1829 (prior to West Virginia becoming a state) by the Ritchie family (primarily Scottish immigrant Craig Ritchie and his son John), Jesse Wheat, and James Thomason (the early firm was also referred to as "Ritchie and Wheat"). The name was changed in 1835 to Wheeling Flint Glass Works when the company bought out Wheat, Price and Company and moved operations to another location within the city of Wheeling. The company produced lead cut crystal, pressed tableware, and window panes before ceasing operation around 1839. *See also RITCHIE.*

WHEELING GLASS — General term for glass made in the city of Wheeling, Virginia, in the nineteenth century (before West Virginia became a state) up until 1939 when the Central Glass Company closed. Wheeling, along with Pittsburgh, was a major hub of pressed glass production in America throughout the nineteenth and early twentieth centuries. *See also AMERICAN FLINT GLASS WORKS, ANDERSON AND COMPANY, CENTRAL GLASS WORKS, EAST WHEELING GLASS WORKS, HOBBS, BROCKUNIER AND COMPANY, PLUNKETT AND MILLER, RITCHIE, SWEENEY, MICHAEL, THOMAS, AND R. H., VIRGINIA GREEN GLASS WORKS, WHEELING FLINT GLASS WORKS, and WHEELING GLASS WORKS.*

W

WHEELING GLASS LETTER AND NOVELTY COMPANY — Refer to the GLASS LETTER AND NOVELTY COMPANY.

WHEELING GLASS WORKS — An American pressed glass-making firm established by Edward, William, and Franklin Anderson and Alfred Evans at Wheeling (prior to West Virginia becoming a state) in 1845, the company was first known as "Evans and Anderson." In 1847, a new factory was built (the firm had leased a factory previously occupied by the defunct East Wheeling Glass Works). When Evans left in 1849, the name was changed to "Anderson and Company." David Southwick joined in 1850 and the name was changed again to the "American Flint Glass Works" (also known as "D. Southwick and Company"). The company went bankrupt in 1852 and reverted back to its creditors, Hobbs, Barnes, and Company.

WHEELOCK, C. E. AND COMPANY — A trademark occasionally found on cut glass products. Note that Wheelock did not produce cut glass; rather, they were a distributor of products made by other cut glass firms like the Heinz Brothers. Wheelock was located in Peoria, Illinois, and operated in the late nineteenth and twentieth centuries. Cut glass with their company trademark was used from 1915 into the early 1920s.

Wheelock, C. E.: Trademark.

WHEELS — Various cutting wheels are used to cut, etch, and engrave glass that are developed from lapidary equipment. Large stone wheels are used for deep cuts and smaller various-sized copper wheels are used for finer engraving. For precise engraving, carborundum, as well as diamond-point tools, is utilized in modern times. See also COPPER WHEEL ENGRAVING and DIAMOND POINT ENGRAVING.

Reproduction from a late nineteenth century T. G. Hawkes catalog.

WHIMSEY — A small unique decorative glass object made to display a particular glassmaker's skill (sometimes called a "Frigger" by the English). Most were made at the end of a workman's day with whatever molten glass was left in the pot. Whimsies encompass such items as vases, bells, hats, canes, darners, button hooks, sticks, pipes, balls, rolling pins, stemmed flowers, and other novelties.

Whimsical glass candy canes. Photo by Robin Rainwater.

WHISKEY BOTTLE — A glass container with a narrow neck and mouth designed to hold whiskey. Bottles designed solely for the storage and transportation of hard liquor originated in England in the mid-seventeenth century. Early American bottles, somewhat generic in shape, were first blown in the eighteenth century. Bininger Bottles (1820s-1880s) were the first in America designed specifically for whiskey. After the 1860s, American distillers favored the somewhat cylindrical "fifth" design (designed to hold 1/5 of a gallon) and pint-sized flasks. Whiskey bottles come in various forms, colors, and may contain paper labels or even mold-embossed writing. Amber and clear bottles are the most common; however, some were made in amethyst, cobalt blue, and green. Whiskey bottles usually do not contain handles; however, whiskey jugs do. See also BLACK BOTTLE and WHISKEY JUG.

WHISKEY JUG — A large deep glass vessel or decanter, with a small mouth and usually a small handle, used for storing, serving, and even drinking whiskey. It may also come with a cover or stopper.

Reproduction from a late nineteenth century Higgins-Seiter catalog.

No. 15E. Clifton Whiskey Jug. Lot Each $9.00

WHISKEY SAMPLE GLASS — Small whiskey tumblers or cordials, with a capacity of up to four ounces, made specifically for sampling whiskey or other distilled spirits. Sample glasses were produced in the late nineteenth century on up to Prohibition (1919). Most contained advertising of a distiller or brand of whiskey and are also referred to as "Pre-Prohibition Advertising Glasses."

Pre-Prohibition whiskey sample glasses.
Photo by Robin Rainwater.

WHISKEY TOT — A tiny cone-shaped decanter used for serving a single measure (dram or ounce) of whiskey. Tots contain a glass body with a hinged silver lid. They originated in England in the early twentieth century by John Grinsell and Sons, Ltd.

W

WHISKEY TUMBLER — A small shot glass sized drinking vessel, usually without a foot, stem, or handle and containing a pointed or convex base, used for drinking distilled spirits in small amounts. *See also* SHOT GLASS.

Pressed glass whiskey tumblers. *Photo by Robin Rainwater.*

WHITALL BROTHERS AND COMPANY — Refer to WHITALL, TATUM AND COMPANY.

WHITALL, TATUM AND COMPANY — An American firm founded in 1806 at Milville, New Jersey, the company began as a maker of window panes, but switched to producing blown glass bottles in 1833. The Whitall brothers purchased it in 1844 and, in 1849, it was known as Whitall Brothers and Company. It was changed to Whitall, Tatum and Company in 1857 (sometimes listed as Whitall-Tatum). Under Whitall and Tatum, the firm produced a good deal of paperweights as well as apothecary and perfume bottles, fruit/canning jars, and insulators. It eventually became a subsidiary of the Armstrong Cork Company.

WHITE, DAVID — A noted American Studio Glass artisan born in Ridley Park, Pennsylvania, in 1954, White received his Science degree and completed some graduate work at Illinois State University. He has served in a teaching capacity at Tennessee Tech's Appalachian Center for Crafts and works as an exhibition preparatory at the Memphis Brooks Museum of Art. White continues to work as an independent glass artisan in Memphis, Tennessee.

WHITE FLINT GLASSHOUSE — An English glass firm established at Bristol in the early eighteenth century, the company was noted for producing opaque white glass that was decorated with gilding and enameling. *See also "Bristol Glass."*

WHITE HOUSE GLASSWORKS — (1) An English firm established at Wordsley near Stourbridge in 1825, White House was leased to the brief partnership of John Shepherd and John Webb, who operated it until 1835 (Webb died and Shepherd retired). It was then inherited and operated by Thomas Webb I. (2) An American firm briefly known as the White House Glass Works. *See also THOMAS WEBB AND SONS, WHITE HOUSE WORKS, and ATTERBURY AND COMPANY.*

WHITE HOUSE WORKS — An American pressed glass-making firm established at Pittsburgh, Pennsylvania, by Hale, Atterbury, and Company in 1859, the company was also known as the White House Glass Works and was purchased outright by James S. and Thomas B. Atterbury in 1865. *See also ATTERBURY GLASS COMPANY.*

WHITE MILLS GLASSWORKS — An American glass factory founded at Honesdale near White Mills, Pennsylvania, in the 1840s by German immigrant Christian Dorflinger, the factory remained open until 1921. *See also DORFLINGER GLASS WORKS.*

WHITEFRIARS GLASS WORKS — An English firm established in London in the 1670s at the Whitefriars Carmelite Monastery, the company produced practical glass items. It was purchased by James Powell (1744-1840) in 1834 and ran as James Powell and Sons, an early pioneer for the English in the latter nineteenth century Art Nouveau movement for colored glass, paperweights, cut crystal, etc. The company moved to Wealdstone, Middlesex, England, in 1923, and was renamed Whitefriars Glass, Ltd. in 1962. Whitefriars was reorganized as a producer of collectible paperweights, especially those in the Venetian millefiori style, and some colored art glass. The firm went bankrupt in 1980; in 1981, the Whitefriars name was purchased by Caithness, which has issued an annual "Whitefriars" collection of paperweights ever since. *See also CAITHNESS GLASS, LTD.*

WHITEHEAD, IHMSEN AND PHILLIPS — An American pressed glass-making firm founded at Pittsburgh, Pennsylvania, in 1838 by Thomas White Whitehead, Christian Ihmsen, and William Phillips; the three purchased the former Birmingham Glass Works that had been founded in 1810. The factory name was listed as the Pennsylvania Flint Glass Works until 1846. William Young and Francis Plunkett replaced Whitehead and Phillips and the name of the business was changed to Young, Ihmsen and Plunkett until 1850. Ihmsen bought out the other two and changed the name to C. Ihmsen and then to C. Ihmsen and Sons when his three sons (Charles, William, and Christian Jr.) joined in 1860. In 1875, the firm's name was changed again, this time to the Ihmsen Glass Company. The company produced a good deal of pressed glass prior to closing permanently in 1895.

WHITEHEAD, IHMSEN AND PLUNKETT — Refer to WHITEHEAD, IHMSEN AND PHILLIPS.

WHITLA GLASS COMPANY, LTD. — An American company founded at Beaver Falls, Pennsylvania, in 1887 by James Stone and John Whitla, the firm produced some pressed glass tableware before closing in 1890. Whitla reorganized in 1890 as the Valley Glass Company with James Stone as director, and then again as the Pittsburgh Glass Company in 1891. The factory was destroyed by fire in 1892 and was not rebuilt.

WHITNEY GLASS — A late eighteenth century (Early American) style of glass consisting of bottles and flasks. The Whitney family delved into many glass-making opportunities, with brothers Thomas and Samuel Whitney purchasing the Harmony Glassworks at Glassboro, New Jersey, in 1835. The name was changed to Whitney Glassworks and the firm produced bottles and tableware in the South Jersey style. The company later became part of the Owens Bottle Company. *See also HARMONY GLASSWORKS, OLIVE GLASSWORKS, and SOUTH JERSEY GLASS.*

WHORL OR WHORL ROD — An open-ended spiral cane, usually millefiori in design, often used as the center of a cluster of star rods in paperweight making.

WIEDMAN, KARL — A noted German glass artisan who, while working at the Wurttembergische Metallwarenfabrik (W.M.F.) near Goppingen, Germany, created a style of Art Glass known as "Myra-Kristall." It is characterized by an iridized opalescent coloring cased over or combined with crystal. Wiedman also studied at Daum Freres at Nancy, France, in 1947-48 before returning to W.M.F.

W

Wig Stand — A stemmed and footed stand, containing a globe-shaped object at the top, designed specifically to support wigs. Note that a Wig Stand Vase contains a globe-shaped cover that fits onto the mouth of the vase; it too, is designed to hold wigs.

Wightman, Thomas and Company — An American firm founded at Pittsburgh, Pennsylvania, in 1873 by Irish immigrant Thomas Wightman, who briefly opened a bottle plant in 1873; however, it was shut down until 1879. Wightman resumed bottle production and added additional buildings in 1880, at which time he expanded into the production of window panes and fruit jars. Thomas Wightman's son, Samuel Wightman, inherited the business when his father passed on and ran it until closing it in 1921.

Wilcox Silver Plate Company — Refer to the "Meriden Cut Glass Company."

Wild Flower — A pressed or cut glass design containing a wide variety of floral-like styles (scrolling, dots, panels, Sandwich-like designs, and cables).

Wild Rose — A style of Art Glass patented by Libbey in 1886, it was created by designer Joseph Locke while working for the New England Glass Company, which Libbey eventually purchased. It is characterized by a gradual shading from a creamy, somewhat light peach color to rose pink. Note that it is similar to Mount Washington's Peach Blow (Mount Washington sued Libbey for patent infringement, which forced Libbey to simply change the name).

Wilhelm Kralik Sohne — Refer to Wilhelm Kralik.

William Skinner and Son — Refer to the Skinner Glass Company.

Williamite Glassware — Late seventeenth and early eighteenth century English lead crystal glassware, usually wine glasses or goblets, that have engraved political inscriptions, portraits, and other symbols of King William III, the hereditary prince of Orange who assumed the English throne in 1689. His rivals and political opponents were Jacobites. See also Jacobite Glassware.

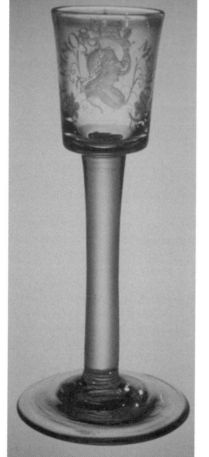

A 1740s English Williamite cordial, blown and engraved. *Photo courtesy of the Corning Museum of Glass.*

Williams, Richard, and Company — An Irish glass-making firm established at Dublin in 1764, the company produced lead crystal ware in the English-Irish styles of the day and remained in operation until 1817. See also Dublin Glass.

Williamsburgh Flint Glass Company — Refer to Erskine J. S. Van Houten.

Williamsburgh Flint Glass Works — An American pressed glass-making firm founded by Berger and Walker at Long Island, New York, in 1845. After the company was purchased by John and Nicholas Dannehoffer in 1879, the name was changed to Dannehoffer and Brothers. The firm produced blown and pressed glass tableware up until World War I.

Wilson and Sons — Refer to the West Lothian Glassworks.

Window — (1) An opening in the wall of a building for the admission of light and air that is closed by casements or panes of transparent material. The transparent material is ordinarily glass, and the window itself can be opened and closed, though some are permanently sealed. (2) In a paperweight, windows are covered openings ground into the overlay to better view the motif within. There is usually a top of window along with symmetric side windows (four or six are the most common). Some paperweights are decorated with multiple windows throughout the entire overlay. See also Pane and Sheet Glass.

A Venetian Millefiori paperweight showing multiple "windows." *Photo by Robin Rainwater.*

Windsor Glass Company — A short-lived American firm founded at Pittsburgh, Pennsylvania, in 1886 by M. Bacon, R. B. Brown, and associates. The company produced some pressed glass tableware before fire destroyed the factory in 1887. It was rebuilt and production resumed later in the same year; however, the plant closed again in 1890.

Wine Bottle — A glass container with a narrow neck and mouth, which may or may not have a handle, specifically used for storing and serving wine. Wine bottles usually come in all shapes and sizes and are ordinarily made of dark glass, though white wines tend to be stored in clear bottles.

Photo by Robin Rainwater.

W

Reproduction from an early twentieth century McKee Brothers catalog.

WINE BUCKET — A large rounded object used for chilling and holding wine bottles. Ice is usually stored in the bottom and possibly along the sides for chilling purposes. As with all glass buckets, champagne buckets may or may not have a handle and typically taper slightly outward at the top. *See also BUCKET and CHAMPAGNE BUCKET.*

WINE GLASS — A tall glass with a foot, stem, and round deep bowl. As a unit of measure for serving size, four ounces is the most prevalent. *See also CHAMPAGNE GLASS, CORDIAL GLASS, CLARET GLASS, and GOBLET.*

Reproduction from a late nineteenth century Higgins-Seiter catalog.

Cut Glass Wine Glass.
Fine Cutting.
Height About 3 Inches.
No. 9538..............$1.75 Each

WINE SET — A decanter with several matching wine glasses (four or six glasses are the most common in a set). Also note that a wine set may or may not include a matching tray. *See also "Service."*

WINFISKY, JONATHAN — Born in Danvers, Massachusetts, in 1955, Winfisky received his Fine Arts Degree from the University of Massachusetts at Amherst in 1978. He specializes in creating freeblown vibrantly colored Art Glass sculptures and forms (i.e. vases).

WINGED GLASS — Glass objects that have curving threads formed into loops, ropes, and other wing-like designs. Winged motifs originated with the Venetians as early as the sixteenth century and were most often applied to the stems of goblets. *See also "Snake Glass."*

WISTAR, CASPAR — An early American glass designer and manufacturer who established a glass works in Allowaystown, New Jersey, in 1739 (near Wistarberg, Salem County, in southern New Jersey). Wistar (1696-1752) came to America from the Netherlands and is often considered the first glassmaker to achieve some measure of success here. He imported skilled Dutch workers and produced window panes, lamp chimneys, jugs, and bottles. However, Wistar is most noted for the especially unique, wide, bulbous-formed style of glass objects that were dubbed "South Jersey Glass." South Jersey items were also characterized by a superimposed winding thickness on the bottom and the style was widely copied by others. When Wistar passed on in 1752, his son, Richard, ran the firm until it closed permanently in 1780. *See also SOUTH JERSEY GLASS.*

WITCH BALL — A spherical glass globe, usually three to seven inches in diameter, that dates from early eighteenth century England. They were used for fortune-telling and as good luck charms for warding off evil and other superstitious means. Witch balls were produced in various colors and decorated both internally and externally. Some sported small holes at the top for which a string could be passed through for hanging. Some even had a small neck and opening at the top and were called "Witch Bottles."

WOODALL, GEORGE AND THOMAS — Two noted glass engraving brothers who apprenticed under John Northwood until 1874, both George (1850-1925) and Thomas (1849-1926) then worked with Thomas Webb and Sons to create some of the best English engraved cameo Art Glass products during the Art Nouveau movement in the late nineteenth and early twentieth centuries. Many Webb creations include a signed "T and G Woodall" mark. The brothers retired in 1911.

A Woodall cameo engraved plaque for Thomas Webb & Sons.
Item courtesy of the Corning Museum of Glass.

WOOD-JACK — An older tool used in glass-making that resembles a large pair of tongs tipped with wood; they are used for spreading the open mouth of a goblet or for pinching a bubble of glass inward to form a narrow neck or the lip of a pitcher. Modern jacks are similar; they are tipped with steel and known as "Steel-Jacks." *See also FORMING TOOL, PINCERS, PUCELLAS, STEEL-JACKS, and TONGS.*

W

WORDSLEY FLINT GLASSWORKS — An English company established in 1720 by Mr. Bradley at Wordsley near Stourbridge, the firm began as a practical maker of lead crystal tableware and other functional items. Wordsley was succeeded by Bradley and Ensell and then by the Wainwright Brothers until it closed in 1825. In 1829, it was purchased and operated by Thomas Webb I in partnership with William Haden Richardson and Benjamin Richardson I (operated as Webb and Richardson). The partnership was dissolved in 1836 and the firm then became known as W.H.B. and J. Richardson.

WORLD'S FAIR — Souvenirs made specifically to commemorate a fair or exhibition. Glass is a popular medium for such events and may consist of paperweights, tumblers, shot glasses, toy mugs, sculptures resembling noteworthy or unique buildings, and small plates. The first such fair was the Great Exhibition in London in 1851. Others included America's Centennial in Philadelphia, 1876; Chicago's World's Fair/Columbian Exposition, 1893; the Pan-American in Buffalo, 1901; the St. Louis World's Fair, 1904; the Panama-Pacific in San Francisco, 1915; Philadelphia's Sesquicentennial, 1926; Chicago's Century of Progress, 1933; Cleveland's Great Lakes, 1936; San Francisco's Golden Gate International, 1939; New York's World of Tomorrow, 1939; Seattle's World's Fair, 1962; New York's World Fair, 1964; Montreal, Canada's Expo, 1967; New Orleans' World Fair, 1984; Tsukuba, Japan's World's Fair, 1985; Vancouver, Canada's World's Fair, 1986; Brisbane, Australia's World's Fair, 1988; Seville, Spain's World's Fair, 1992; and Genoa, Italy's World's Fair, 1992. See also COMMEMORATIVE GLASSWARE and SOUVENIR GLASS.

From the 1893 World's Fair, a Libbey Peach Blow two-handled cup. *Item courtesy of Wheaton Village.*

WRIGHT, L. G. — Lawrence Gale "Si" Wright (1904-1969) worked as a sale representative for the New Martinsville Glass Company. Beginning in 1936-37, Wright began purchasing glass molds from defunct glass companies and amassed over 1,000 of them in his lifetime. The L. G. Wright Glass Company was officially established in 1938 at New Martinsville, West Virginia. As with most of his career, Wright served as a jobber/distributor rather than an actual maker of glass. He contracted with other companies such as Fenton, Gibson, Imperial, Morgantown, Mosser, New Martinsville, Paden City, Summit, Viking, and Westmoreland, to press glass into his molds that contained his own trademark. Wright usually changed the design slightly, as well as his trademark in the molds he had purchased, to help distinguish reproduced products from originals. Wright also had many new molds made from area machine shops as early as 1937. Wright's products consisted of pressed tableware, lamps, vases, rose bowls, covered animal dishes, animal figurines, and other novelty items. When Wright passed on in 1969, the business was carried on by his wife, Verna Mae Wright. Ms. Wright passed away in 1990 and left the company in her will to her cousin, Dorothy Stephan, and Dorothy's daughter, Phyllis Stephan Buettner. The company closed in 1999 and all of the molds were auctioned off to other companies.

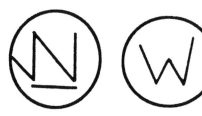

Wright, L. G.: Trademarks.

WRIGHT RICH CUT GLASS — A cut glass operation established in 1904 at Anderson, Indiana, by English immigrant Thomas Wright, his son George Wright, and his son-in-law S. Hunter Richey, it produced glass until 1915.

Wright Rich Cut Glass: Trademark.

WRYTHING ORNAMENTATION — A decoration consisting of swirled ribbing or fluting.

WURTTEMBERGISCHE METALLWARENFABRIK OR W.M.F. — A German steel company founded in 1853 at Gieslingen near Stuttgart originally as Metallwarenfabrik Straub and Schweitzer, the name was changed to W.M.F. in 1880 and the firm expanded into glassware by opening a glassworks near Goppingen in 1883 primarily for creating their own glass inserts to go in their metal products. The original plant was destroyed in World War I; however, it was rebuilt and opened in 1922. The company expanded into other areas of glass and is noted most for creating their own unique styles of iridescent Art Glass. The firm ended its production of glassware in 1984; nevertheless, inexpensive machine-made glass is still being produced with the W.M.F. namesake today at a plant in Singapore. See also KARL WIEDMAN and MYRA-KRISTALL.

W

Xx
Yy
Zz

{ Xx Yy Zz }

X-Cut Vesica — Pointed cut ovals divided into sections by curved miter splits in cut glass, the separated parts or sections are then further cut into different patterns.

Yellow Glass — Chromate of lead and silver act as the primary coloring agents in producing a deep yellow color within glass; also note that antimony and/or silver nitrate added to lead will provide an opaque form of yellow while uranium produces various glowing shades of greenish-yellow or yellowish-green colors. *See also Canary Yellow, Topaz, Uranium Glass, and Vaseline Glass.*

Young, Haines and Dyer — Refer to the Boston Silver Glass Company.

Young, Ihmsen and Plunkett — Refer to Whitehead, Ihmsen and Phillips.

Ysart Family — A noted glass-making family of Spanish descent led by Salvador Ysart (1878-1955). His son Paul Ysart (1904-1991) was born in Barcelona, but left Spain early on with his family (with his glass-blowing father too). Paul first worked as a young apprentice for the French firm of St. Louis and then further migrated to Scotland in 1915. In Scotland, he first worked for the Leith Flint Glass Company and then moved on to Moncrieff Glassworks in 1921. With his father, they produced a style of Art Glass known as "Monart Glass." In 1948, his father and brothers, Antoine (1911-1942), Augustine (1906-1956), and Vincent (1909-1971), left to form the Ysart Brothers Glassworks, which later became Vasart Glass, Ltd. Paul, however, remained with Moncrieff and continued to produce Monart Glass and paperweights. From 1961 to 1971, Paul moved on to Caithness and became one of the company's leading paperweight designers and creators. In 1971, he established Paul Ysart, Ltd., making paperweights until his retirement. *See also Caithness Glass Ltd., Moncrieff Glassworks, Monart Glass, and Vasart Glass, Ltd.*

Zahn and Goepfert — Refer to Kvetna Glassworks.

Zahn Glassworks — A Czechoslovakian firm founded in 1895 by Johann Zahn at Novy Bor, the company initially produced cut lead crystal products and, like all Czech firms, became part of the state in 1948. It was eventually absorbed by the conglomerate Crystalex and still serves as a glass decorating shop for Crystalex (i.e. cutting, engraving, etching, sandblasting, enameling, painting, and gilding).

Zanesville Glass — The general term for glassware produced by several firms in and around the town of Zanesville, Ohio, in the early to mid-nineteenth century. The first reported glass-making company was the Zanesville Manufacturing Company (also known as the Zanesville Glass Works) established in 1815; it closed in 1838, but reopened from 1842 to 1851. Items produced included crystal and colored tableware, as well as historical flasks and bottles. Zanesville Glass of this period is sometimes referred to as "Early Ohio Glass," or just "Ohio Glass," and encompasses early-to-mid nineteenth century glass products made in Mantua, Kent, Ravenna, and other Ohio towns.

Zanfirico — Italian term for twisted filigree or spiral-like decorations in glass that are twisted in one direction. Note that zanfirico is synonymous with retortoli. *See also Filigree, Latticino, and Reticulated Glass.*

Zeleznobrodske Sklo — When the Czechoslovakian glass industry was nationalized in 1948 after World War II, Zeleznobrodske Sklo was one such collective consisting of nine small glassworks in and around the town of Zelezny Brod in northern Czechslovakian. Harrachov was actually part of the collective until it was transferred to Borske Sklo in 1957. The new collective produced a good deal of glass that was cut, engraved, sandblasted, enameled, and blown into unique art figurines including people and animals. A school devoted to glass-making was also established as part of the collective. In the late 1980s and early 1990s, most of the small firms split off again regaining their independence. In 1993, what was left of Zelezobrodske became a joint-stock company, which produces glass beads for the jewelry industry today as well as some ornamental glassware.

Zero Interior AB — Refer to Pukeberg.

Zierglas — The German term for ornamental glassware, Zierglas is basically Art Glass objects designed for show, display, and beauty rather than for any practical use.

Zinc — A light bluish-white colored metallic element that, when oxidized, is mixed in a batch of glass to produce a translucent white color.

Zipper — A cut or pressed glass pattern consisting of several vertical rows or short, double-dashed or split-cut designs that resembles zippers. Pressed zipper designs are sometimes combined with other patterns (i.e. zipper borders, zippered block, zipped diamond, zippered swirl, zippered swirl and diamond, zipper slash, etc.).

Zwischengoldglas — An eighteenth century Bohemian or German glass decoration style characterized by gilding and inlaid gold decoration within another straight-sided layer of glass. In German, Zwischengoldglas translates to "Gold between glass." *See also Double Wall Glass.*

A nineteenth century Venetian blown Zwischengoldglas plaque.
Photo courtesy of the Corning Museum of Glass.

Zynsky, Mary Ann "Toots" — A noted American Studio Glass artisan born in Boston, Massachusetts, in 1951, Zynsky received her Fine Arts degree from the Rhode Island School of Design and has served in a teaching capacity at the Pilchuk Glass Center, the New York Experimental Glass Workshop, the Haystack Mountain School of Crafts, and the Parson School of Design. Awards she has received include the New York State Council on the Arts Artists in Residence Grant (1981-1982), the National Endowment for the Arts Fellowship (1982), a Stichting Klankschap Foundation Grant (Amsterdam, The Netherlands, 1984), and a Visual Arts Fellowship from the National Endowment for the Arts (1986). Zynsky continues to work as an independent glass artisan in Amsterdam.

X

Z

Bibliography

Angus-Butterworth. *British Table and Ornamental Glass*. New York, New York: Arco Publishing Co., Inc., 1956.

Annual Bulletins. New York, New York: Paperweight Collectors' Association, 1955-Present.

Arwas, Victor. *Art Nouveau to Art Deco*. New York, New York: Rizzoli International Publications, Inc., 1977.

Baccarat, Inc. *A History of Baccarat Modern Paperweights*. New York, New York: Baccarat, 1977.

Barber, Edwin A. *American Glassware*. Philadelphia, Pennsylvania: Press of Patterson & White Co., 1900.

Barbour, Harriot Buxton. *Sandwich: The Town That Glass Built*. Boston, Massachusetts: Houghton Mifflin Co., 1948.

Barlow, Raymond E. and Joan E. Kaiser. *A Guide to Sandwich Glass*. Windham, New Hampshire: Barlow-Kaiser Publishing Co., Inc., 1987.

Barret, Richard Carter. *A Collectors Handbook of American Art Glass*. Manchester, Vermont: Forward's Color Productions, 1971.

Battersby, Martin. *Art Nouveau: The Colour Library of Art*. Middlesex, England: The Hamlyn Publishing Group Ltd. 1969.

Beard, Geoffrey. *International Modern Glass*. New York, New York: Charles Scribner's Sons, 1976.

Bedford, John. *Paperweights*. New York, New York: Walker and Company, 1968.

Bergstrom, Evangeline H. *Old Glass Paperweights*. Chicago, Illinois: Crown Publishers, 1947.

Bishop, Barbara and Martha Hassell. *Your Obdt. Servt., Deming Jarves*. Sandwich, Massachusetts: The Sandwich Historical Society, 1984.

Bossaglia, Rossana. *Art Nouveau*. New York, New York: Crescent Books, 1971.

Boston & Sandwich Glass Co. Boston, Massachusetts: Lee Publications. 1968.

Bridgeman, Harriet and Elizabeth Drury. *The Encyclopedia of Victoriana*. New York, New York: Macmillan Co., 1975.

Carved and Decorated European Glass. Rutland, Vermont: Charles E. Tuttle Co., Inc., 1970.

Catalogues of Paperweight Sales. Sotheby's of London and New York: 1950s–Present.

Charleston, R. J. *English Glass*. London, England: George Allen and Unwin, 1984.

Cloak, Evelyn Campbell. *Glass Paperweights of the Bergstrom Art Center*. New York, New York: Crown Publishers, Inc., 1969; Bonanza Books, 1976.

Contemporary Art Glass. New York, New York: Crown Publishers, 1975.

Cousins, Mark. *20th Century Glass*. Secaucus, New Jersey: Chartwell Books, 1989.

Curtis, Jean-Louis. *Baccarat*. London, England: Thames and Hudson, Ltd., 1992.

Daniel, Dorothy. *Cut and Engraved Glass 1771–1905*. New York, New York: M. Barrows & Co., 1950.

Davis, Derek C. and Keith Middlemas. *Colored Glass*. New York, New York: Clarkson N. Potter, Inc., 1967.

Diamond, Freda. *The Story of Glass*. New York, New York: Harcourt, Brace, and World, Inc., 1953.

Drepperd, Carl W. *ABC's of Old Glass*. New York, New York: Doubleday & Company, 1968.

Ebbott, Rex. *British Glass of the 17th and 18th Centuries*. London, England: Oxford University Press, 1972.

Elville, E. M. *Paperweights and Other Glass Curiosities*. London, England: Country Life Ltd., 1954; Spring Books, 1967.

Fauster, Carl U. *Libbey Glass Since 1818*. Toledo, Ohio: Len Beach Press, 1979.

Feller, John Quentin. *Dorflinger: America's Finest Glass, 1852–1921*. Marietta, Ohio: Antique Publications, 1988.

Fleming, Monika, and Peter Pommerencke. *Paperweights of the World*. Atglen, Pennsylvania: Schiffer Publishing, Ltd., 2000.

Frantz, Susanne K. *Contemporary Glass: A World Survey from The Corning Museum of Glass*. New York, New York: Henry N. Abrams, Inc., 1989.

Garage Sale and Flea Market Annual. Paducah, Kentucky: Collector Books, Inc., Annual Guide, 1991–2006.

Glass Paperweights of the Bergstrom-Mahler Museum. Richmond, Virginia: United States Historical Society Press, 1989.

Grover, Ray and Lee. *Art Glass Nouveau*. Rutland, Vermont: Charles E. Tuttle Co., 1967.

Carved and Decorated European Art Glass. Rutland, Vermont: Charles E. Tuttle Co., 1967.

Haslam, Malcolm. *Marks and Monograms of the Modern Movement, 1875–1930*. New York, New York: Charles Scribner's Sons, 1977.

Hastin, Bud. *Avon Collectibles Price Guide*. Kansas City, Missouri: Published by author, 1991.

Heacock, William. *The Encyclopedia of Victorian Colored Pattern Glass (Books 1–9)*. Marietta, Ohio: Antique Publications, Inc., 1974–1988.

Heacock, William and Fred Bickenhauser. *The Encyclopedia of Victorian Colored Pattern Glass (Book 5)*. Marietta, Ohio: Antique Publications, Inc., 1974–1988.

Heirmans, Marc. *Murano Glass 1945–1970*. Antwerp, Germany: Gallery Novecento, 1989.

Hollister, Paul and Dwight Lanmon. *Paperweights*. Corning, New York: The Corning Museum of Glass, 1978.

Hollister, Paul Jr. *The Encyclopedia of Glass Paperweights*. New York, New York: Clarkson N. Potter, Inc., 1969.

Glass Paperweights, An Old Art Revived. Angus, Scotland: William Culross & Sons Ltd., 1975.

Hughes, G. Bernard. *English Glass for the Collector 1660–1860*. New York, New York: Macmillan Co., 1968.

Husfloen, Kyle, editor. *American & European Decorative & Art Glass*. Dubuque, Iowa: Antique Trader Books, 1994.

Antiques & Collectibles. Dubuque, Iowa: Antique Trader Books, 1985–1998.

Huxford, Sharon and Bob, editors. *Flea Market Trader*. Paducah, Kentucky: Collector Books, Annual Edition 1993–2006.

Imbert, Roger and Yolande Amic. *Les Presse-Papiers Francais de Cristal*. Paris, France: Art et Industrie, 1948.

Ingold, Gerard. *The Art of the Paperweight-Saint Louis*. Santa Cruz, California: Paperweight Press, 1981.

Jarves, Deming. *Reminiscences of Glassmaking*. Boston, Massachusetts: Eastburn's Press, 1854.

Jokelson, Paul. *Paperweight Pamphlets*. New York, New York: Privately Published by the Author, 1955-1968.

Jokelson, Paul. *Sulphides: The Art of Cameo Incrustation*. New York, New York: Thomas Nelson & Sons, 1968.

Jokelson, Paul, and Dena K. Tarshis. *Cameo Incrustation: The Great Sulphide Show*. Santa Cruz, California: Paperweight Press, 1988.

Jokelson, Paul, and Dena K. Tarshis. *Baccarat: Paperweights and Related Glass 1820-1860*. Santa Cruz, California: Paperweight Press, 1990.

Jokelson, Paul, and Gerard Ingold. *Paperweights of the 19th and 20th Centuries*. Phoenix, Arizona: Papier Presse, 1989.

Klein Dan and Ward Lloyd. *The History of Glass*. New York, New York: Crescent Books, 1989.

Kovacek, Michael. *Paperweights*. Vienna, Austria: Glasgalerie Kovacek, 1987.

Kovel, Ralph and Terry. *The Complete Antiques Price List*. New York, New York: Crown Publishers, Inc., 1973–2006.

The Kovels' Antique and Collectible Price List. New York, New York: Crown Publishers, Inc., 1990–2006.

Krantz, Susan. *Contemporary Glass*. New York, New York: Harry N. Abrams, Inc., 1989.

Kulles, George N. *Identifying Antique Paperweights-Lampwork*. Santa Cruz, California: Paperwegiht Press, 1985.

Kulles, George N. *Identifying Antique Paperweights-Millefiori*. Santa Cruz, California: Paperwegiht Press, 1985.

Lee, Ruth Webb. *Nineteenth-Century Art Glass*. New York, New York: M. Barrows and Co., 1952.

Sandwich Glass. New York, New York: Ferris Printing Co., 1947.

Mackay, James. *Glass Paperweights*. New York, New York: Facts on File, Inc., 1973.

Manheim, Frank. *A Garland of Weights*. New York, New York: Farrar, Straus and Giroux, 1967.

Manley, Cyril. *Decorative Victorian Glass*. New York, New York: Von Nostrand Reinhold Co., 1981.

Mannoni, Edith. *Classic French Paperweights*. Santa Cruz, California: Paperweight Press, 1984.

Mariacher, G. *Three Centuries of Venetian Glass*. Corning, New York: Corning Museum of Glass (translation), 1957.

Marshall, Jo. *Glass Source Book*. London, England: Quarto Publishing Co., 1990.

McCawley, Patricia K. *Antique Glass Paperweights from France*. London, England: Spink and Son Ltd., 1968.

Glass Paperweights. London, England: Charles Letts Books, Ltd., 1982.

McKearin, George and Helen. *American Glass*. New York, New York: Crown Publishers, Inc., 1968.

Nineteenth-Century Art Glass. New York, New York: Crown Publishers, Inc., 1966.

Melvin, Jean S. *American Glass Paperweights and Their Makers*. New York, New York: Thomas Nelson Publishers, 1970.

Metcalfe, Anne. *Paperweights of the 19th and 20th Centuries*. London, England: Octopus Publishing Group, 2000.

Miller's International Antiques Price Guide. London, England: Reed International Books, Ltd., 1996.

Mish, C. Frederick, editor in chief. *Websters Ninth New Collegiate Dictionary*. Springfield, Massachusetts: Merriam Webster, Inc., Publishers, 1983.

Moore, N. Hudson. *Old Glass European and American*. New York, New York: Tudor Publishing Co., 1924.

Newman, Harold. *An Illustrated Dictionary of Glass*. London, England: Thames and Hudson Ltd., 1977.

Oliver, Elizabeth. *American Antique Glass*. New York, New York: Golden Press, 1977.

Papert, Emma. *The Illustrated Guide to American Glass*. New York, New York: Hawthorn Books, Inc., 1972.

Penwell, Ellen Schaller. *The Morton D. Barker Paperweight Collection*. Springfield, Illinois: Illinois State Museum, 1985.

Phillips, Phoebe, editor. *The Encyclopedia of Glass*. New York, New York: Crown Publishers, Inc., 1981.

Pickvet, Mark. *The Instant Expert Guide to Collecting Glassware*. Brooklyn, New York: Alliance Publishers, Inc., 1996.

Official Price Guide to Glassware. New York, New York: House of Collectibles, 1995–1998.

Polak, Ada. *Glass, Its Tradition and Its Makers*. New York, New York: G. P. Putnam's Sons, 1975.

Pullin, Anne Geffken. *Signatures, Trademarks and Trade Names*. Radnor, Pennsylvania: Wallace-Homestead Book Co., 1986.

Revi, Albert Christian. *American Art Nouveau Glass*. New York, New York: Thomas Nelson and Sons, 1968.

Nineteenth-Century Glass. New York, New York: Galahad Books, Inc., 1967.

Rinker, Harry. *Warman's Americana and Collectibles*. Elkins Park, Pennsylvania: Warman Publishing Co., 1986.

Rossi, Sara. *A Collector's Guide to Paperweights*. Secaucus, New Jersey: Wellfleet Books, 1990.

Schmutzler, Robert. *Art Nouveau*. London, England: Thames & Hudson Ltd., 1978.

Schroeder's Antiques Price Guide. Paducah, Kentucky: Collector Books, Inc., 1993.

Schroy, Ellen. *Warman's Glass*. Radnor, Pennsylvania: Wallace-Homestead Book Co., 1992.

Selman, Lawrence H. *The Art of the Paperweight*. Santa Cruz, California: Paperweight Press, 1988.

Smith, Francis Edgar. *American Glass Paperweights*. Wollaston, Massachusetts: The Antique Press, 1939.

Stankard, Paul. *Flora in Glass*. London, England: Spink & Son Ltd., 1981.

Turner, Ian, Alison J. Clarke and Frank Andrews. *Ysart Glass*. London, England: Volo Edition, 1990.

U.S. Patent Records

Various Catalogs of Paperweight Sales. Christie's of London, 1950s – Present.

Wakefield, Hugh. *19th-Century British Glass*. New York, New York: Thomas Yoseloff Publishing, 1961.

Way, W. H. L. *Glass Paperweights*. London, England: Connoisseur, vol. lviii, 1920.

Wilson, Kenneth M. *New England Glass and Glassmaking*. New York, New York: Thomas Crowell Co., 1972.

Zerwick, Chloe. *A Short History of Glass*. New York, New York: Harry N. Abrams, Inc., Publishers, 1990.